Adapting Early Childhood Curricula for Children with Disabilities and Special Needs

Tenth Edition

Ruth E. Cook
Professor Emerita
Santa Clara University

M. Diane Klein
Professor Emerita
California State University–Los Angeles

Deborah Chen
Professor Emerita
California State University–Northridge

 Pearson

Director and Publisher: Kevin M. Davis
Content Producer: Janelle Rogers
Media Producer: Lauren Carlson
Portfolio Management Assistant: Maria Feliberty
Executive Field Marketing Manager: Krista Clark
Executive Product Marketing Manager: Christopher Barry
Manufacturing Buyer: Carol Melville
Full-Service Project Management: Thistle Hill Publishing Services, LLC
Cover Designer: Alisha Webber
Cover Image: Arman Zhenikeyev/Shutterstock
Composition: Pearson CSC
Text Font: Palatino LT Pro 9.5/13

Library of Congress Control Number: 2018959626
Library of Congress Cataloging-in-Publication Data is available upon request.

22 2022

ISBN 10:   0-13-520445-3
ISBN 13: 978-0-13-520445-0

Brief Contents

Contents

Foreword

For over three decades, *Adapting Early Childhood Curricula for Children with Disabilities and Special Needs* has educated the next generation of teachers not only here in California, but also throughout the nation. It provides a foundation for professionals seeking a career working with children with disabilities whether in general education, inclusive, or special education classrooms. When I reach into my bag and take out this book during a coaching session, I am not surprised, as I've heard it often, when teachers say, "I love that book." They frequently explain that their edition is older, highlighted throughout, and dog-eared. We laugh and then turn to a page that reminds us of a specific practice that could help support a child in need. This text and I have a long and productive history, as I have utilized it throughout my professional career as a student, inclusion trainer, and professor.

When I was a student, this text was the foundation for many of my classes while securing my early childhood special education credentials, completing an internship, and obtaining a special education master's degree. The text went everywhere with me, living as it did in the trunk of my car because I never knew when I was going to need it. I would refer to the book often in my special education classroom to remind me about the characteristics of disabilities and how to implement task analysis and make adaptations to my curriculum. I would pull it out to find evidence in support of my college reports and to discuss concepts and collaboration techniques with coworkers, colleagues, and fellow college students. After I left the classroom as a student, the text did not just sit on my shelf. It came with me and found a new home in my office.

As an inclusion training specialist and coach, I used this text as a resource for evidence-based practices that were incorporated into trainings for general and special education teachers. From the concepts of this foundational book, support materials were created to accompany trainings for teachers, coaches, and families. Now as a professor, I use this text along with the helpful online supports and the Instructor's Manual to guide the next generation of early childhood special educators. I know that college students will receive comprehensive information from this text to support both children and families, as every edition is up-to-date with the latest legislation and trends as well as evidence-based practice.

This one example of a career path shows the exponential influence that *Adapting Early Childhood Curricula for Children with Disabilities and Special Needs* has had—moving beyond serving the small number of students and families in a special education classroom to teaching college students who are using this text to make a difference in the lives of ALL their children and families.

Laurie Nielsen Dotson, M.A.
Adjunct Faculty
Mission College
Santa Clara, California

Preface

This book is written with you, the student of either early childhood or special education, in mind. Whether you are studying to become a teacher of young children with disabilities or are an early interventionist with a related background who wishes to develop greater versatility in your chosen field, we have designed this to be an easy-to-read, interesting, and comprehensive resource for you. It provides extensive use of examples, dialogues, practical illustrations, and vignettes, and a focus on the best practices in the field.

When this text was originally published, intervention with young children with disabilities was in its formative years. Since that time the field has expanded, and this book has successfully grown with it. Young children with disabilities are now enrolled in a variety of settings and are served by professionals and paraprofessionals with diverse backgrounds. Our objective now, as it was in the first nine editions, is to present a text that will play a major role in the development of all who serve young children. The focus is on the skills necessary to assist infants, young children, and their families to meet their special challenges and develop to their fullest potential.

Distinguishing Features

This book has four main strengths that make it a compelling self-teaching resource:

1. It emphasizes the importance of understanding the natures of all young children and how they learn. Adapting curricula and intervention approaches for children with disabilities works effectively only when professionals build on a strong foundation of understanding what is common to all young children. On the basis of this necessary foundation, students can consider strategies for meeting the developmental and educational needs of infants and young children who have disabilities or who experienced circumstances and conditions that potentially interfere with optimal growth and adjustment.

2. The approach taken in this text stresses the absolute necessity of understanding young children within the context of the family. Every family is unique and complex, reflecting the many influences of history, culture or ethnicity, economics, and family dynamics. Early interventionists must focus not on the detailed analysis of these many factors, but on ways of supporting families that will maximize their day-to-day fulfillment as caregivers of their young children. As explained in the text, your job, in part, is to help parents develop a sense of competence in their own abilities to nurture their children regardless of family circumstances. Appreciation of families' roles in the development of children and respect for families' concerns and priorities are critical to effective curriculum design and program development.

3. A significant portion of the text is organized according to traditional developmental domains: social-emotional, motor, communication, and cognitive skills. As an early childhood special education professional, you will seek to develop these growth areas in the children entrusted to you. Thus, you must develop a thorough understanding of each of these complex domains.

4. Finally, you must ultimately understand that all the growth areas and individual and family background factors must be synthesized into a view of the whole child. As in any other form of synergy, the whole child is much greater than the sum of his or her parts. This holistic view relates directly to the book's emphasis on activity-based and play-based approaches to intervention. You will learn how to integrate goals and objectives for all domains into developmentally appropriate and motivating activities in inclusive, community-based settings. You will also learn how to work collaboratively with others in inclusive community-based settings in an itinerant consultation role. Throughout, best practices are explained for home, center, or classroom application.

The four points just mentioned suggest the framework and approach that have consistently made this book appealing to readers of nine previous editions. They have been time tested and consistently found to be helpful.

New in This Edition

- Throughout the text, short video examples are available in the enhanced Pearson eText to further explain key concepts.

- Issues related to collaborating with families of diverse cultural and linguistic backgrounds, teaching dual-language learners, and the influence of poverty are embedded in many chapters.

- Evidence-based practices were updated based on the most current research available.

- Activities to encourage reflection and application of topics and strategies are provided at the end of each chapter.

- The glossary has been updated with relevant terms and definitions for new topics covered in the chapters.

- The appendix includes a new graphic illustrating the roles and responsibilities of special education staff in relation to general education staff within inclusive settings.

Organization

The text opens with a presentation of our philosophy for working with children who have disabilities. It explores human likenesses and value differences and discusses our belief in the importance of providing services in the most normalized settings possible. Chapter 1 highlights the historical contributions of the fields of early childhood education and special education. Important features and implications of Public Laws 94-142, 99-457, 101-336, 101-476, 102-119, 105-17, 108-446, 110-134, and 110-335 are summarized. Attention is given to the continual collaboration between professional groups involved in early childhood special education, especially the Division for Early Childhood (DEC) and National Association for Education of Young Children (NAEYC). Evolving trends in the field and alternative approaches to service delivery including the unique challenges involved in supporting inclusion are discussed. Key findings from research on preschool inclusion and the necessity of using person first language are highlighted. Finally, the challenges presented by those who are dual-language learners and the increasing number of children living in poverty receive consideration.

Chapter 2 explores the process involved in the adjustment required to successfully parent a child with disabilities. It presents techniques to involve families in a collaborative partnership with the variety of professionals with whom they must interface. In developing a family-focused approach, students are encouraged to view families from a systems perspective. Special attention is given to the various methods of parent involvement that can accommodate cultural diversity, language differences, and unique family situations. The complexities involved in developing a truly collaborative relationship with parents are examined in greater detail in this edition. Additional suggestions on how to successfully involve fathers have also been included.

Within Chapter 3, the importance of becoming a skilled observer of children is stressed as students are encouraged to link curriculum to assessment and the monitoring of progress. The components of individualized family service plans (IFSPs) and individualized education programs (IEPs) are discussed in detail, while techniques for writing goals and objectives are illustrated. New to this edition are suggestions on how to make outcome statements on IFSPs more functional. Readers are also introduced to Robert McWilliam's unique approach to truly understanding the needs of families.

Strategies for collaborative programming and transition planning are outlined. Chapter 4 focuses on curriculum development within a framework of generic instructional strategies and introduces the principles of the Universal Design for Learning. Communicative interactions, facilitation of play, the development of appropriate schedules, and optimal environmental arrangement contribute to the success of early intervention. Chapter 5 focuses on considerations and strategies for teaching young children with specific disabilities, including those with low incidence and multiple disabilities, autism, and fetal alcohol spectrum disorders. The chapter also now includes a series of questions to promote collaboration with support specialists such as speech and language pathologists. Additional topics include assistive technology, functional vision assessments, and learning media assessments.

Chapter 6 begins by describing the stages of psychosocial development as a precursor to understanding how to facilitate social skills through the medium of play. Considerable attention is given to helping children who experience particular emotional and behavioral challenges resulting from adverse childhood experiences. The use of positive behavioral supports is discussed in detail.

After describing the sequence of typical development of gross and fine motor skills, Chapter 7 examines atypical motor development, the assessment of motor skills, and techniques for collaborating with physical and occupational therapists. Practical intervention strategies are offered, including handling and positioning guidelines, as well as techniques for facilitating self-care skills and encouraging healthy diets. The role of movement education and music in the development of motor skills is considered.

Chapters 8 and 9 focus on the development of communication, literacy, and cognitive skills. The importance of caregiver–child interactions and the role of play in optimal development are recognized throughout. Special attention is devoted to specific strategies for enhancing communication skills in children with severe disabilities, autism, visual impairments, and hearing impairments. Consideration is given to young dual-language learners. The section devoted to understanding the social and linguistic factors related to children's emergent literacy skills and strategies for encouraging these skills is a valuable resource. Facilitation of phonological and phonemic awareness along with a brief synthesis of premath skills is included in this section.

The final chapter provides an overview of models, strategies, and challenges for providing inclusion support to young children with disabilities who are included in community-based early childhood settings. Consideration is now also given to transitional kindergarten, which is new to some communities. This chapter goes into depth on how to facilitate the collaboration and problem solving so necessary to the shared decision making necessary to success in early childhood special education. Productive teaming with the many specialists and paraprofessionals is essential to effective facilitation of the development of young children with disabilities.

As in previous editions, the appendices include a wealth of practical information, such as developmental guidelines, curricular adaptations for children with specific needs, modifications, and checklists to assist facilitation of inclusion. A sequence of steps for milieu approaches is included. New to this edition is an example of the roles and responsibilities of special education staff as related to general education staff in inclusive educational settings. Finally, the appendix includes a list of competencies that we hope each and every reader will develop as a result of studying this text.

Acknowledgments

We present this book with gratitude to the hundreds of children and parents who have been our teachers. From them we have learned to value and nurture the uniqueness of each child regardless of background, skills, or abilities. We believe we have found a way to meet children's unique needs in whatever setting they appear. It has been our purpose to convey the essence of this process to anyone interested in working with young children.

We wish to sincerely thank the many colleagues and friends who assisted and supported us throughout the many years since the original edition of this book. We are especially grateful for the conscientious efforts of those who so kindly read and commented on the prospectus and rough drafts of the present edition. Special gratitude goes to the following reviewers for their time, attention, and feedback: Sarah Hamsher, Malone University; Kai Kaiser, Saddleback College; Ellen Lynch, University of Cincinnati; Megan Purcell, Purdue University; Sandra C. Nichols, University of Alabama; and Allison Turner, Johns Hopkins University.

There are many people who enrich and enhance one's personal as well as professional life along the way. As indicated in the dedication that appeared in a previous edition of this text, we want to again acknowledge the support of Dr. Annette Tessier, who was a coauthor of six of the previous editions, and continues to inspire and enliven us. We will be forever grateful to her.

We also want to express our very sincere admiration and thanks to Dr. Marci Hanson, who graciously wrote the forewords to previous editions of this text. Given Dr. Hanson's recent retirement, we turned to a current user of the text to share insight into why she finds this text so useful in a variety of settings. Thank you, Laurie Nielsen Dotson, for sharing your thoughtful comments. It is gratifying to know that, after many years, our text continues to inspire and promote best practices.

Deep appreciation is extended to the parents, children, and outstanding staff of Centro de Niños y Padres, at California State University at Los Angeles, the California State University, Northridge Child and Families Studies Center, and the CHIME Early Education Program for their effective implementation of evidence-based practices that support the learning of all young children. Appreciation also goes to Sandra Hovancik and Barbara Porter for their skills as graphic artists.

Over the years, the personal support of those with whom we live and work has been invaluable. Very special thanks go to Erin Klein, Christopher Cook, and Kimberly Cook Bodemar (and, of course, our grandchildren), without whom our understandings of child growth and development would have been superficial, at best. Sincere gratitude goes to Curtis Cook, whose patience, tolerance, and editorial skills helped make this project possible.

The editors and staff at Pearson Education have worked hard to keep us on target. Particular praise and gratitude go to our editor, Kevin Davis, and our content producer, Janelle Rogers, for their attention and prompt responses have been invaluable throughout the acquisition and development of this manuscript.

Adapting Early Childhood Curricula for Children with Disabilities and Special Needs

Tenth Edition

Chapter 1
Educating Young Children with Disabilities

The Challenge

⌄ Learning Outcomes

After studying this chapter, you should be able to:

1.1 Recognize that a child who has a disability is a child first; the developmental delay or disability is secondary.

1.2 Summarize the historical and philosophical influences on the evolving field of early childhood special education.

1.3 Give examples of the enabling impact of public pressure and legislation.

1.4 Explain the foundational principles and recommended practices for quality early childhood special education.

1.5 Describe the unique challenges of providing services in inclusive settings.

Viewing the Child with Disabilities as a Child First

The culture in the United States places very high value and status on intelligence, beauty, and physical skill. Winning a beauty contest, being drafted as a quarterback for the NFL, achieving high SAT scores, and admission to Harvard are examples of our culture's notions of exceptional and highly valued achievements. The initial response to the birth of a baby who is at risk or compromised in some way is to hope and pray for the infant's survival. After this initial shock, there may be concerns about the baby's development. Parents who have had these experiences can often recall every detail for the rest of their lives.

As babies become toddlers and pre-schoolers, families often begin to face the possibilities that their child may not be "normal." They may worry that he or she may not be attractive, smart, or athletic. The diagnosis of a child with a "disability" can be an ongoing traumatic event for many families.

The U.S. provides some of the finest early intervention, special education, and rehabilitation services in the world. If you are reading this text, you have chosen one of the most important, challenging and rewarding fields of study. It is easy for professionals in special education to become intently focused on the details of the disability and the wide array of possible interventions. However, it is critical that families and practitioners in early childhood special education never lose sight of the fact that this infant or toddler **is a child first**—a unique and fascinating developing person for whom "disability" is but one feature of his or her identity. Ironically, the "disability" characteristics will contribute to the uniqueness and strengths of that child.

The disability features and the specific strategies you will learn in this text, and throughout your career, are important and valuable. However, they must not overshadow the importance of the unique characteristics and strengths of each child, and his or her relationships with family and caregivers. In support of creating and maintaining

Exhibit 1.1

How to Use Person-First Terminology When Communicating About Children with Disabilities

Respectful Language Sounds Like . . .	Instead of . . .
He has muscular dystrophy	He is afflicted with muscular dystrophy
She has cerebral palsy	She suffers from cerebral palsy
He uses a wheelchair	He is restricted to a wheelchair
She has a developmental delay	She's developmentally delayed
Students in special education	Special ed students
A child who is blind	A blind child
Students with disabilities	Disabled students
Parent of a child with disabilities	Parents of a disabled child

a respectful and positive view of each child, we begin by thinking about the importance of what language we use when we refer to children with disabilities.

Person-First Language

A disability is merely one of many natural human characteristics (Snow, 2013). Language that places the child before the disability is called **person-first language**. It acknowledges that the child is a child first with many characteristics, only one of which is a disability. For example, a child has a physical disability rather than is a "crippled" child. Another example would be to say "a child with Down syndrome" instead of "a Down syndrome child" or, worse yet, "a Down's child." This change in language acknowledges that the disability is what the child *has*, **not** *who the child is*. Nevertheless, an exception is that members of the Deaf culture may prefer the term "Deaf child" (Holcomb, 2013). Similarly, people with visual impairments prefer "a child who is blind" rather than "a child with blindness." In addition, Snow (2013) makes a case against using the term "special needs" because it evokes feelings of pity and attitudinal obstacles to true inclusion. She suggests that people should not be called names that they do not use about themselves.

Consider how outdated and disrespectful labels may negatively impact a child's view of him- or herself, the family's feelings, expectations of children and adults who interact with the child, and views of the general community. A medical diagnosis or eligibility label serves to qualify children for special education services. However, it should not be used to stigmatize a child. Therefore, we must choose language that models equity, acceptance, and respect when referring to children with disabilities. In 1990, the federal government, recognizing that language can negatively influence perception, adopted person-first language when the Education of All Handicapped Act (EHA) was reauthorized and renamed the Individuals with Disabilities Education Act (IDEA). Changing to more respectful language is a process that can take time to retrain the way we speak. See Exhibit 1.1 for more ways to use person-first terminology.

Enhanced eText Application Exercise 1.1: In this exercise, you can apply what you have learned about the view that a child who has a disability is a child first, and explain the rationale behind the use of person-first terminology.

Inclusion of Young Children with Disabilities in Community-Based Settings

For over three decades, a fundamental shift in what is considered to be the most beneficial way to provide services to young children with disabilities and their families has been taking place. Intervention services have changed from a deficit-focused, child-centered, and professional-directed model to a strengths-based, family-centered, and relationship-based approach (Raver & Childress, 2015). This shift was initiated in 1986 with the passage of Public Law (PL) 99-457, which authorized educational services to preschoolers (3–5 years) and early intervention services to infants and toddlers (birth to 36 months). To the maximum extent effective, **early intervention services** should be provided in "natural environments"; that is, settings in which the child and family would engage if the child did not have a delay or disabilities, such as their homes, child care, and community settings. Similarly, preschoolers with disabilities should be included in "the least restrictive environments," such as typical early childhood settings, child care, Head Start programs, and public and private preschools.

With the encouragement of this legal mandate and professional "recommended practices," it was hoped that young children would receive a portion, if not all, of their early intervention in inclusive environments. However, realizing that children and their families continue to face significant barriers to accessing inclusive high-quality early childhood programs and that too many preschoolers with disabilities are only offered the option of receiving special education services in settings separate from their peers without disabilities, the U.S. Department of Health and Human Services and the U.S. Department of Education issued a joint policy statement in 2015 urging reflection on the work that needs to be done to fully implement equal opportunity for all Americans.

The intent of this text is to provide information and strategies that early childhood and special educators can use to support children's development, active participation in natural settings, and the establishment of collaborative, supportive partnerships with families and colleagues. It is hoped that through quality personnel preparation, a greater number of children will be served in inclusive environments.

The commitment to inclusive intervention and education for infants and young children is well established in federal law. Part C of the *Individuals with Disabilities Education Act of 1997* states: (1) "To the maximum extent appropriate, early intervention services are provided in natural environments; and (2) the provision of early intervention services occurs in a setting other than a natural environment only when early intervention cannot be achieved satisfactorily for the infant or toddler in a natural environment" (Sec. 635 [a] [16]). Part B addresses the needs of preschoolers by requiring that "to the maximum extent appropriate, children with disabilities are educated with children who are not disabled." This part also goes on to state in Section 612 that preschoolers are not to be removed from the regular educational environment unless "education in regular classes with the use of supplementary aids and services cannot be achieved satisfactorily." This law and the differences between Part B and Part C will become clearer later in this chapter.

The most recent reauthorization of this law, the **Individuals with Disabilities Education Improvement Act (IDEIA)** of 2004, continues to support the mandate that encourages services for infants and toddlers in **natural environments**, and it requires school districts to educate children in the **least restrictive environment (LRE)**. Some specifics of these educational shifts are noted in Exhibit 1.2.

Exhibit 1.2

Trends in Early Childhood Special Education

- Community-based inclusive settings
- Relationship-focused interventions
- Routines-based or embedded interventions
- Family-centered approaches
- Interdisciplinary collaboration
- Culturally responsive programs
- Coordinated, comprehensive services
- Response to Intervention (RTI) approaches
- Standards- and evidence-based practices
- Increased use of assistive technology
- Greater focus on school readiness
- Involvement of inclusion support specialists

Philosophy of This Text

This text emphasizes that the goal of early intervention is to optimize each child's learning potential and daily well-being as well as to increase opportunities for the child to actively participate in the community. We believe this is best accomplished by facilitating the child's underlying developmental processes by encouraging the child's active and dynamic interactions with the world around him or her, particularly the social world. Perhaps the term that best reflects this orientation is **transactional**. It is through the child's active and successful transactions with the social environment that optimal growth and development can best be achieved.

To achieve this end, practitioners in early childhood special education must first have a thorough understanding of how children learn. Programs for infants and young children with disabilities must be based on developmentally appropriate practices that are effective for *all* children. In addition, systematic planning to meet the individualized needs of each child is critical to the success of early childhood programs that include children with special challenges and disabilities. This cannot be accomplished without establishing mutually respectful partnerships between practitioners and families. Successful assessment and intervention require a thorough understanding of the child within the context of the family system and a respect for the diverse linguistic and cultural backgrounds and lifestyles of families.

The importance of collaboration among families, professionals, and community agencies is acknowledged throughout the text. Understanding the roles of various disciplines and specialists and the importance of assisting families in accessing community agencies and resources are also critical elements in the success of early childhood special education services.

Many tools and strategies are available to assist the early childhood special educator. This text describes the basic developmental domains of human learning and the principles of how children learn as well as specific teaching strategies. It also demonstrates applications of these principles and strategies to meet the needs of a wide range of children within inclusive environments. It is our belief that it is incumbent on all early childhood professionals to maximize our efforts to help all children acquire an authentic sense of **belonging** (Swinton, 2012). Appendix F reveals the competencies that must be developed to be an effective early childhood professional.

Early Childhood Special Education: An Evolving Field

Whereas the 1980s opened with concern for the rights of individuals with disabilities, the 1990s recognized the rights and needs of the *families* of children with disabilities. The 2000s recognize the value of serving young children with disabilities in what has become known as their natural environment. Children with disabilities are no longer viewed in isolation. It is recognized that *all* children should have the opportunity to be served in environments where they would naturally function if they did not have a disability.

Early intervention services gained new momentum as the nation recognized its responsibility to provide services from the moment of birth. However, the field of early childhood special education is still evolving. Its historical roots are derived not only from typical early childhood education, compensatory education, and school-aged special education but also from allied fields such as medicine, psychology, human development, nursing, and sociology. A few of the major historical forces shaping the expanding field of early childhood special education are outlined in this section.

Pioneering Influences and History of Early Childhood Special Education

Jean-Marc Itard undertook one of the first documented efforts to provide intervention services to a child with severe developmental disabilities. In 1800, a child approximately 12 years old was found living in the forest near Aveyron, France. The boy, named Victor, was thought to have been raised by animals and was described as "an incurable idiot." Itard refused to accept the idea that Victor's condition was incurable and irreversible. Itard believed in what later became known as an "interactionist viewpoint" (Bijou, 1977). That is, Victor's learning potential could be enhanced through intervention that changed the stimulation in his environment. Therefore, Itard undertook to humanize Victor through a series of carefully planned lessons stimulating the senses.

Itard's feelings of optimism, frustration, anger, hope, and despair were published in a 1962 edition of *The Wild Boy of Aveyron*. Teachers today who work with children who have complex and severe disabilities may easily recognize these feelings. Although Itard did not achieve the success he visualized, his efforts had a significant impact on the future of special education. Itard was one of the first to demonstrate and record an attempt to understand empathically the needs of a child with disabilities. It is Itard's student Edouard Sequin who could be considered a pioneer in the area of special education and a proponent of early intervention. This is evident in his statement, "If the idiot cannot be reached by the first lessons of infancy, by what mysterious process will years open for him the golden doors of intelligence?" (quoted in Talbot, 1964, p. 62).

Casa dei Bambini

About a century later, another physician in Italy, Maria Montessori, created a nursery school, Casa dei Bambini, that revolutionized the notion of early education. Because of her training, early interests, and the nature of the school she was asked to develop, Montessori stressed cleanliness, order, and housekeeping skills as well as reading, writing, and arithmetic. Aspects of both the discovery approach to learning and programmed instruction can be found in the techniques developed by Montessori. She suggested that teachers observe the natural, spontaneous behavior of children and then arrange learning experiences to encourage their development (Lillard, 2017).

Like Itard, Montessori believed in developing the child's natural curiosity through systematic training of the senses. Both proceeded with optimism and determination to train those whom some might believe to be beyond hope. Today, Montessori's "sensorial" materials are advocated for use with children with disabilities because they are manipulable, three-dimensional, and concrete. Advocates cite the emphasis on task analysis, sequencing, and individualization evident in the Montessori approach as worthy for use with children who have limited abilities as well as those who are gifted.

Piaget's Theory of Cognitive Development

Until his death in 1980 at the age of 84, Jean Piaget continued to influence our understanding of cognitive development. Piaget proposed an inborn tendency toward adaptation that, in its encounter with the environment, results in categories of knowledge that are remarkably similar among all human beings. Piaget's concept of child development and his stages of cognitive development are considered again in Chapter 9. His prolific writings and those of his followers continue to remind us of the need to be aware of the unfolding internal mental capacities of children.

According to Piaget, the purpose of education is to provide opportunities that allow a child to combine experiences into coherent systems (schemes) that constitute the child's knowledge (Mooney, 2013). Therefore, each child's capacity to learn is thought to be derived from experiences. Piaget's concept of the child as an active learner stimulated by inborn curiosity has prompted the development of preschool programs designed to allow the child to become an active initiator of learning experiences. From a developmental point of view, a child's strengths, rather than deficits, receive emphasis. Most notable of the Piagetian-based programs is the Perry Preschool Project developed in the late 1950s in Ypsilanti, Michigan. An extension known as the High/Scope First Chance Preschool served as a model program for those desiring to integrate preschoolers with disabilities into programs with their typical peers (Hohmann & Weikart, 2002).

Recognition of the Role of Early Experiences

Even though Sequin recognized the critical importance of early intervention, it was the work of Skeels and Dye that drew attention to the impact of early relationships. One of the earliest attempts to demonstrate the close relationship among nurturing, environmental stimulation, and mental growth processes developed from the Iowa growth studies in the late 1930s. Skeels and Dye (1939) transferred 12 children under 3 years of age from an orphanage to an institution for individuals with intellectual disabilities. In the institution, the children were cared for with great affection by adolescent girls who were considered to have intellectual disabilities. A comparison group of children remained in the orphanage, where they received no specialized attention. Follow-up testing demonstrated that the intelligence scores of those placed in the stimulating environment increased, whereas those of the children who remained in the orphanage decreased (Skeels, 1942). Twenty-one years later, Skeels (1966) found dramatic differences between those who had been placed in the enriching environment and those who had not. The 12 children in the experimental group were found to be self-supporting. Of the comparison group, four had been institutionalized and one had died. Educationally speaking, four of those who had been in the enriching environment completed college, and the others had a median high school education. In contrast, the median education for the comparison group was only at the third-grade level.

Kirk (1958) also conducted experiments on the influence of early experiences on the development of young children with intellectual disabilities. In his textbook, Kirk's suggestion that an inadequate cultural environment might be a cause of intellectual disabilities helped to convince politicians of the need for compensatory educational programs for young children. Perhaps more convincing was the conclusion reached by Bloom (1964), who claimed that about "50% of the [intellectual] development takes place between conception and age 4, and about 30% between ages 4 and 8, and 20% between ages 8 and 17" (p. 88).

Bloom's argument was built on J. McVicker Hunt's popular book *Intelligence and Experience* (1961), which argued eloquently against the notion of fixed intelligence. Attempting to lay to rest the heredity-versus-environment controversy, Hunt supported well his contention that heredity sets the limits, whereas environment determines the extent to which the limits will be achieved. And so, under the belief that children's intelligence develops early and rapidly and that enrichment early in life can have profound influences on the child's development, federal funding for Project Head Start was provided in 1965.

Project Head Start: A Breakthrough

The primary purpose in passing the Economic Opportunity Act of 1964 was to break the cycle of poverty by providing educational and social opportunities for children from low-income families. The result was the implementation of Head Start during the summer of 1965 with approximately 550,000 children in 2,500 child development centers. Parent involvement both within the Head Start classroom and on policy committees set a precedent. This has, no doubt, influenced legislators to require parent involvement in current decisions involving children with disabilities.

The Head Start program had a significant impact on the development of early childhood special education. It was the first major public exposure to the importance of early educational experiences. Legislation enacted in 1972 required Head Start programs to include children with disabilities to the extent of at least 10% of their enrollment. Including children with disabilities in classrooms with typical children has become a major activity of Head Start. In fact, even as early as 1985, Head Start enrollment of preschoolers with disabilities exceeded 60,000.

Head Start (through its local agencies and grantees) is the largest provider of early childhood services in the United States. A total of 837,657 preschoolers were enrolled in Head Start in 2015–2016, of which 104,740 (12.5%) have disabilities (Office of Head Start, n.d.a). The addition of Early Head Start in 1994 definitely has increased efforts to promote positive prenatal outcomes for pregnant women, enhance the development of very young children (birth to 3 years), and promote healthy family functioning. A total of 190,898 children, birth to 3 years, were enrolled in Early Head Start in 2015–2016, of which 23,907 (12.5%) have a developmental delay or disability (Office of Head Start, n.d.b).

Doubts

After the extreme optimism that accompanied the establishment of Head Start, it came as a shock to those who worked daily with the children and their parents that the program failed to produce long-term gains. The Westinghouse Report of 1969 cited data suggesting that measured gains made by Head Starters faded rapidly. By the end of the first grade, there often were no significant differences between the overall academic performance of children who had attended Head Start programs and those from the same kinds of homes who had not. Doubting the validity of this investigation, influential people fought for a stay of execution (Gotts, 1973). Among them was Edward Zigler, a member of the original planning committee that conceptualized Head Start and later director of the Office of Child Development. Zigler (1978) retorted, "I ask my colleagues in the research community to forgo the temptation of delivering definitive pronouncements concerning the fade-out issue and await instead the collection and analyses of more data" (p. 73).

Although the most recent impact study of 3- to 4-year-olds in Head Start revealed minimal long-term effects on children's cognitive and social emotional development at the third-grade level (Puma et al., 2012), other studies have reported the positive effects of being in Head Start. At the end of the Head Start program, children demonstrated gains in language, literacy, and math skills, and well as increased social skills and impulse control (Aikens, Klein, Tarullo, & West, 2013). In kindergarten, compared to children who did not attend preschool, Head Start children demonstrated higher cognitive and social-emotional skills and fewer attention or behavioral difficulties (Zhai, Brooks-Gunn, & Waldfogel, 2011). As adults, Head Start graduates have been found to have an increased likelihood to graduate from high school, attend college, and receive a degree, license, or certification (Bauer & Schanzenbach, 2016). In addition, they are less likely to be unemployed or in poor health (Deming, 2009).

Impact of Early Education

Indeed, Zigler was to be rewarded for his faith. It was not long until great attention was given to the work of Lazar and Darlington (1982) and the Consortium on Developmental Continuity. These researchers conducted longitudinal investigations into the persistence of the effects of early education programs throughout the United States. The evidence from the projects clearly indicated there were long-lasting positive effects from programs of early education. Tracing children who had been involved in preschool programs into their teens or early 20s, Lazar found that children with some form of early education were far less likely to require special education or to be held back a grade.

A powerful case for federal support of early education programs is strengthened by well-designed longitudinal studies of the effects of the Perry Preschool Project (Schweinhart et al., 2005), the Abecedarian Child Care Study (Campbell et al., 2014), and the Chicago Longitudinal Study (Reynolds, Temple, Ou, Arteaga, & White, 2011). Studies of these high-quality early childhood programs have found positive long-term effects on the participants' lives, evidenced by increased employment and decreased criminal activities during adulthood (Schweinhart, 2016).

Recently, another report by Cannon and colleagues (2017) on the valuations of 115 early childhood programs has provided additional evidence of the effectiveness of these programs. Although a few programs included evaluations for the past 50 years, most programs had evaluation data of cohorts of participants from the 1990s and 2000s. Most of these programs found positive economic effects and developmental outcomes. Children demonstrated improvement in one or more areas of development. The most frequent positive outcomes were in behavior and emotional skills, cognitive development, and health.

Exhibit 1.3

Effects of Early Education

Children who have participated in early education programs:

1. Are less likely to be assigned to special education classes or to be held back a grade.
2. Have more positive attitudes toward high school and are more likely to graduate.
3. Are less likely to be arrested as youth and young adults.
4. Are less likely to experience teen pregnancy.
5. Are more likely to secure gainful employment after leaving school.

Exhibit 1.3 lists some of the gains attributed to the early education of children who are primarily at risk and disadvantaged. Although children in these programs did not have disabilities, they were considered to be at risk. More recently, Barnett and Frede (2010) discussed a meta-analysis of findings from 123 studies conducted since 1960. The findings were clear: Experience in preschool education does positively affect learning and development. Long-term findings include increased high school graduation rates, increased earnings, decreased crime and delinquency, and better mental health. Even though there has been a debate surrounding the impact of preschool education, national and international studies continue to reinforce the call for universal preschool for all by finding that "all children benefit substantially, but disadvantaged children gain more, making preschool an excellent means of increasing overall achievement while narrowing our troubling gaps" (p. 29).

Early Education for Children with Disabilities

In interpreting the findings of research, it is important to keep in mind the diversity with which this field deals. Here, we use the term *early intervention* broadly to refer to providing services to infants and young children who have disabilities or are at risk for disabilities. When policymakers ask, "What are the benefits of early intervention?," the response will inevitably be, "It depends." This is not because researchers lack agreement or because of the limitations of research methods, but because of the great diversity among children and families and the circumstances in which they live. There is no one best intervention for everyone all of the time. There is not even one best intervention for a very narrowly defined group such as infants with Down syndrome and their families. Infants with Down syndrome differ so much from one another that any specific intervention for a group of these infants probably would not be very successful. Research does provide some pieces of this complex, highly individualized puzzle, indicating that early intervention can yield important benefits. Because of the complexities involved in documenting the positive effects of early intervention, professionals in the field do not yet know enough to put together the complete picture.

Nevertheless, a longitudinal study resulting in the now-famous volume *From Neurons to Neighborhoods*, edited by Shonkoff and Phillips (2000), sheds a spotlight on the very early years and critical influence of quality early education. The following conclusion is worthy of considerable reflection:

> Model early childhood programs that deliver carefully designed interventions with well-defined objectives and that include well-designed evaluations have been shown to influence the developmental trajectories of children whose life course is threatened by socioeconomic disadvantage, family disruption, and diagnosed disabilities. Programs that combine child-focused educational activities with explicit attention to parent-child interaction patterns and relationship building appear to have the greatest impacts. In contrast, services that are based on generic family support, often without a clear delineation of intervention strategies matched directly to measurable objectives, and that are funded by more modest budgets, appear to be less effective. (p. 11)

There is also evidence of long-term effects, as demonstrated in the 18-year follow-up study conducted by McCormick and colleagues (2006). This well-designed follow-up study found that adolescents who had received early education were more likely to have higher achievement scores in math and reading and fewer risky behaviors such as drug use and antisocial behavior. As studies begin to follow early education "graduates" for a longer period of time, we may even find more impressive long-term outcomes such as higher educational achievement and impressive occupational status and eventual income.

Changing Policies: The Impact of Public Pressure and Legislation

Concerned citizens and active parent and professional associations have played a vital role in changing public policy toward children with disabilities, as discussed in this section.

Development of Professional Groups

It has been said that Alexander Graham Bell, inventor of the telephone and a strong advocate of oral education of the Deaf, should be given credit for organizing professional advocates of special education. He petitioned the National Education Association (NEA) to establish a division to be concerned about the needs of people with disabilities. In 1897, the NEA established such a division and named it the Department of Education of the Deaf, Blind, and the Feeble-Minded. As attitudes toward and knowledge of this population changed, this name was later changed to the Department of Special Education.

The formation of the international Council for Exceptional Children (CEC) in 1922 provided the impetus for what some believe to be the most influential advocacy group continuing to provide national leadership on behalf of children with disabilities. The 1930 White House Conference on Child Health and Protection was a milestone in marking the first time that special education had received national recognition. In 1973, the Division for Early Childhood (DEC) of the CEC was established. As of 2017, more than 27,000 members turned to the CEC as a continuing source of professional development and advocacy for children with disabilities.

The Power of Private Citizens

Several factors came together after World War II to give rise to the development of strong parent organizations in the late 1940s. Professional knowledge was expanding, Americans felt responsible for aiding their wounded, and prominent people such as Pearl Buck, Roy Rogers and Dale Evans, and the Kennedy family were visibly calling for better education of individuals with disabilities. Parents no longer felt it necessary to hide their children with disabilities. Pressure groups such as the United Cerebral Palsy Association, the National Association for Retarded Citizens, and the American Foundation for the Blind began to demand alternatives other than institutionalization for the education of their children with disabilities.

Professional groups joined parent groups in capitalizing on the historic Supreme Court decision in *Brown v. Board of Education* (1954). Although primarily a racial integration initiative, the Court ruled that state laws that permitted segregated public schools were in violation of the Fourteenth Amendment's "equal protection under the law" clause. Realizing that decisions applicable to one minority group must be applicable to another, pressure groups sought to secure legislation that would create significant educational changes on behalf of children with disabilities. However, little actually occurred until after the publication of an article by Dunn (1968) that provided a blueprint for changes recognizing the rights of students with disabilities.

The First Chance Program

In 1968, Congress recognized the need for seed money to develop model programs to spur the development of services for children with disabilities from birth through age 8. Legislation in the form of PL 90-538 was enacted to establish the Handicapped Children's Early Education Program (HCEEP), better known as the First Chance program. These projects were required to include parents in their activities, run in-service training, evaluate the progress of both the children and the program, coordinate activities with public schools, and disseminate information on the project to professionals and the public. In 1980, the total number of funded projects was 177, with 111 including infants in their population (Swan, 1981). These projects served two basic purposes: (1) to provide models of exemplary services that could be replicated for young children with disabilities, and (2) to disseminate information to encourage this replication. The HCEEP funds were highly effective. Hebbeler, Smith, and Black (1991) reported that 80% of demonstration projects continued operation beyond the federal funding period. After 10 years, 140 outreach projects resulted in 1,991 reported replications that served nearly 108,000 children and families.

Civil Rights Legislation

Section 504 of the Rehabilitation Act of 1973. This enactment was the first public law designed to protect children and adults against discrimination resulting from a disability. Unlike education law, this civil rights legislation uses a functional rather than categorical model to determine if a disability exists. In addition, it has no age restrictions. Any program receiving federal funds must provide equal opportunities for all individuals who have a physical or mental disability that substantially limits one or more life functions. Therefore, schools are expected to make *reasonable accommodations* for students to be able to participate in educational programs experienced by other students.

Public Law 94-142: The Education for All Handicapped Children Act of 1975

In 1975, with the passage of PL 94-142 (EHA), the right to a **free appropriate public education (FAPE)** was mandated for all children of school age. This law was limited in that it did not require states to offer services to young children with disabilities, but it did provide financial incentives for states to provide services to children with disabilities as young as 3 years of age.

Purpose. The purpose of PL 94-142 is to ensure "that all handicapped children have available to them . . . a free, appropriate public education which includes special education and related services designed to meet their unique needs, to insure that the rights of handicapped children and their parents or guardians are protected, to assist States and localities to provide for the education of all handicapped children and to assess and insure the effectiveness of efforts to educate handicapped children" (Sec. 601 [c]). In addition, the National Center for Clinical Infant Programs was founded in 1977 to recognize and promote the health and development of very young children and their families.

Free Appropriate Public Education (FAPE). The law requires that a qualified school representative, teacher, the parents or guardian, and, whenever possible, the child join together in the development of an **individualized education program (IEP)**. This written statement must include (1) a statement of the child's present level of academic functioning; (2) a declaration of annual goals complete with appropriate short-term instructional objectives; (3) a description of specific educational services to be provided to the child and the degree to which the child will participate in regular educational programs; (4) the proposed date for initiation and estimation of the required length of services; and (5) annual evaluation procedures specifying objective criteria designed to determine whether the short-term instructional objectives have been met (Sec. 602, 19).

Procedural Safeguards. The law requires that children with disabilities be served in the least restrictive environment (LRE) appropriate to their educational needs. Children can be placed in separate classes or schools only when their disabilities are so severe that regular school placement is considered inappropriate. The act also requires nondiscriminatory testing and the use of multiple criteria in the determination of placement

(Sec. 612, 5, C). This requirement implies the need for all teachers to become skilled in the education of children who exhibit a variety of educational needs. PL 94-142 provided for the right of parents or guardians to examine all records, obtain independent evaluation, and require written notification in their native language when there are plans to change a child's educational program. The intent is to ensure that the child's rights are legally protected. Parents or guardians are entitled to a hearing before termination, exclusion, or classification of a student into a special program.

Public Law 99-457: The Education of the Handicapped Act Amendments of 1986

Some believe PL 99-457 is the law that legitimized the field of early childhood special education (Bricker, 1988). At the very least, it created a national agenda that has federal, state, and local planners collaborating with parents in unprecedented efforts to develop new and expanded services for infants and young children who have disabilities or are at risk and their families. Part B of the law required all states to extend all of the provisions of PL 94-142 to children 3 to 5 years old by the 1990–1991 school year. States that did not comply were to lose federal monies they had been receiving for other preschool services.

Part H.   Part H of PL 99-457 established a discretionary program for states to facilitate the design and implementation of comprehensive systems of early intervention services for infants and toddlers with developmental delays or disabilities. As defined by the law, early intervention services "are designed to meet a handicapped infant's or toddler's developmental needs in any one or more of the following areas: physical development; cognitive development; language and speech development; psychosocial development; or self-help skills" (Sec. 672).

Part H defined the eligible population as all children from birth through age 2 (up to the third birthday) who have developmental delays, have conditions that typically result in delay, or are at risk for significant developmental delay. States have had to make independent decisions about the definition of developmental delay and "at risk" as well as the criteria used to make these determinations. Therefore, the populations of children eligible for services vary from state to state. To design "a statewide, comprehensive, coordinated, multidisciplinary, interagency program of early intervention services for all handicapped infants and their families" (Sec. 671), each governor appointed a lead agency and established an interagency coordinating council. States continue to struggle through the conceptual morass and face the political challenges that determined the nature of early intervention services in 2000 and beyond. Major features of Part H of PL 99-457 are listed in Exhibit 1.4.

Public Law 101-336: The Americans with Disabilities Act of 1990

The **Americans with Disabilities Act (ADA)** is the most significant federal law ensuring the full civil rights of individuals with disabilities. Whereas the laws described previously focused primarily on education and related services, this law is particularly important because it is broad-reaching in guaranteeing equal opportunity in employment, public accommodation, transportation, state and local government services, and telecommunications. Of particular significance is the fact that child-care centers and family child-care homes are included in the law's definition of public accommodations. According to the ADA, child-care centers must make reasonable modifications in their policies and procedures to accommodate children and adults with disabilities. This may mean that centers that do not normally accept children who are not yet toilet trained may have to make accommodations to do so if a disability is an obstacle to the

Exhibit 1.4

Major Features of PL 99-457

- Establishes state-level interagency councils on early intervention.

- Requires an individualized family service plan (IFSP), which identifies the services necessary to address the needs of the infant and enhance the family's capacity to facilitate the child's development.

- Provides case management services to families.

- Maintains a public awareness program that includes a comprehensive child-find system and a central early intervention resource directory.

- Establishes a single line of responsibility for general supervision and monitoring of services.

- Requires the development of a multidisciplinary, coordinated interagency model of service delivery.

- Establishes procedural safeguards.

- Acknowledges the family to be the central focus of service.

- Provides for smooth transitions as a family moves from one service or system to another.

- Facilitates development of a comprehensive system of personnel development.

---

toilet training. A center must also provide auxiliary aids and services when they are necessary to ensure communication with children or parents with hearing, vision, or speech disabilities. Physical access to the center is also required. Although this law creates many questions to clarify its full impact, the intent, nevertheless, is clear. Society is expected to move toward full inclusion of individuals with disabilities in all aspects of daily living. The ADA was amended in 2008 as the **Americans with Disabilities Act Amendments Act (ADAAA)**. This act sought to clarify that the term *disability* is to be interpreted broadly.

Public Law 101-476: The Education of the Handicapped Act Amendments of 1990

PL 101-476, an amendment to PL 99-457, changed the title of the EHA to the **Individuals with Disabilities Education Act (IDEA)**. By dropping the phrase "handicapped children" and replacing it with "individuals with disabilities," Congress intended that children with disabilities be recognized as children first and, if necessary, as children with disabilities second. Throughout the law, all phrases putting the term *handicapped* before *children* or *youth* were rewritten or deleted. This law became known for its "person-first" language. It also reauthorized and expanded the discretionary programs and mandated transition services and the inclusion of assistive technology services.

Public Law 102-119: The Individuals with Disabilities Education Act Amendments of 1991

IDEA was amended again in 1991 in the form of PL 102-119. Two sections of the amended IDEA contributed to the expansion and improvement of the mandate for services to infants, toddlers, and preschoolers with disabilities and their families. The first is Part H, initially included in the 1986 amendments as discussed earlier. Recall that it created a new discretionary program designed to provide the incentive to states to develop and implement a statewide system of comprehensive, coordinated, multi-disciplinary, interagency services for all children from *birth to age 3* with disabilities and their families. The second section of direct interest is Part B, Section 619, also included in the 1986 amendments, which extended the mandate to full provision of a free and appropriate public education to *3- to 5-year-olds* and increased funding through the Preschool Grant Program. IDEA places special emphasis on the provision of services designed to facilitate a smooth transition from services required through Part H to services provided through Part B.

Public Law 105-17: The Individuals with Disabilities Education Act Amendments of 1997

Amendments were made to IDEA again in 1997 that became effective in 1998. These amendments repealed the old Part H and reauthorized the early intervention program under a revised Part C. The new Part C allows states greater flexibility to serve at-risk infants and toddlers. It also requires individualized family service plans (IFSPs) to contain statements about the natural environments in which early intervention services will be provided. The IFSP must include a statement of justification when services are not provided in the natural environment.

States were also encouraged to employ appropriately trained paraprofessionals to help provide early intervention services. Part B now requires that school districts must participate in transition planning when children move from early intervention into preschool special education services. It also allows states to use the term *developmental delay* for children aged 3 to 9 instead of more detrimental labels such as *mental retardation*. In addition, Part B funds can be used for special education and related services as required on IEPs even if children without disabilities benefit from these services.

Public Law 108-446: The Individuals with Disabilities Education Improvement Act of 2004

Improvements were again made to IDEA in 2004. Of particular importance to early education is the requirement that services to young children be developed from "scientifically based research." To that end, the authors of this text continue to include and emphasize strategies and techniques substantiated by empirical research as best practices. This reauthorization of IDEA also allows states to continue early intervention services from age 3 until a child enters kindergarten. Parents and providers are therefore given the flexibility to determine when a child is ready developmentally to move from Part C (formerly referred to as Part H services) to Part B services. The arbitrary age of 3 no longer dictates that move. Under IDEIA 2004, short-term objectives are only required for the small percentage of children (less than 10% of those with disabilities) with the most significant disabilities. However, parents may request the IEP team to identify short-term objectives as steps toward making progress on annual goals. Other improvements are discussed at appropriate points in this text. Exhibit 1.5 is offered to assist in clarifying the differences between Part C and Part B services, while the most significant legislation is summarized in Exhibit 1.6.

Video Example from

You Tube

Enhanced eText
Video Example 1.1
Celebrating the 40th Anniversary of IDEA
https://www.youtube.com/watch?v=Oj4b9d4XAdY
This open-captioned video outlines the mandates and key accomplishments of IDEA.

Enhanced eText Application Exercise 1.2: In this exercise, you can apply what you have learned about IDEA and identify how the passage of the Education for All Handicapped Children Act (EHA) passed in 1975 and subsequent amendments to this legislation impacted the education of young children with disabilities.

Video Example from

You Tube

Exhibit 1.5

Comparison of Part C and Part B of IDEA

	Part C	**Part B**
Lead Agency	**Designated by State**	**State Department of Education**
Ages Served	Ages: birth to 3 years of age	Ages: 3–21
Services	Early intervention services for the child as well as services for the *family*, such as counseling to enhance their ability to meet the needs of their child. Services are to be provided in the child's *natural environment* such as the home and community locations to the maximum extent possible. Services are developed in collaboration with the family to be respectful of their unique culture, customs, and daily routines.	Specially designed instruction to meet the unique needs of the child along with any related services, such as physical occupational therapy, to allow the child to participate in the general education curriculum to the maximum extent possible. Services are to be delivered with children who are not disabled in the *least restrictive environment* possible.
Family Involvement	Participate on all teams making decisions about services for the child. Recipient of services designed to improve the family's ability to meet the needs of their child.	Encouraged to participate on all teams making decisions about services for the child.
Individualized Plans	Individualized Family Service Plan (IFSP)	Individualized Education Program (IEP)

Exhibit 1.6

Significant Legislation Influencing Infants and Young Children with Disabilities

1968	Public Law 90-538 Handicapped Children's Early Education Assistance Act	Significant to the education of preschool children with disabilities; established experimental early education programs through the Handicapped Children's Early Education Program (HCEEP).
1972	Public Law 92-424 Economic Opportunity Act Amendments	Established a preschool mandate requiring that not less than 10% of the total number of Head Start placements be reserved for children with disabilities.
1974	Public Law 93-380 Education Amendments, Buckley Amendment, Title V	Preceded PL 94-142 and established a total federal commitment to the education of children with disabilities; concerns included education within the least restrictive environment, nondiscriminatory testing, and privacy rights.
1975	Public Law 94-142 Education for All Handicapped Children Act	Revised and expanded PL 93-380; provided a free and appropriate public education with related services to all children with disabilities between ages 3 and 21.
1983	Public Law 98-199 Education of the Handicapped Act Amendments of 1983	Provided financial incentives for states to extend service levels down to birth.
1986	Public Law 99-457 Education of the Handicapped Act Amendments of 1986	Extended PL 94-142 to include 3- to 5-year-olds; added a grant program to assist states in establishing a comprehensive system of early intervention services for infants and toddlers with disabilities and their families.
1990	Public Law 101-336 Americans with Disabilities Act (ADA)	Ensures full civil rights for all individuals with disabilities, including reasonable accommodations in preschools and child-care centers.

(continued)

1990	Public Law 101-476 Individuals with Disabilities Education Act (IDEA)	Reauthorization of PL 94-142 to reflect a change in philosophy away from labeling children as "handicapped children" to referring to them as individuals first, with "disabilities" following as a secondary description.
1991	Public Law 102-119 Individuals with Disabilities Education Act of 1991	Reauthorization of PL 101-476 ensuring comprehensive early intervention services to young children and their families.
1997	Public Law 105-17 Individuals with Disabilities Education Act of 1997	Reauthorization of PL 102-119 authorized comprehensive services for infants and toddlers under Part C and for preschoolers under Part B; LRE for infants and toddlers defined as "natural environment."
2004	Public Law 108-446 Individuals with Disabilities Education Improvement Act of 2004	Reauthorization of PL 105-17 continuing preschool services under Part B and early intervention services for infants and toddlers under Part C with allowance to continue early intervention services until kindergarten. Assumes preschool services will be provided in inclusive early education classroom unless evidence and rationale for placement in a special education classroom are clearly documented in the IEP.
2007	Public Law 110-134 Reauthorization of the Head Start Act	Further aligned Head Start with IDEA to ensure that children with disabilities have an individualized education program (IEP) or individualized family service plan (IFSP) as defined by IDEA regulations.
2008	Public Law 110-335 The Americans with Disabilities Act Amendments Act (ADAAA) of 2008	To restore the intent of Public Law 101-336 Americans with Disabilities Act. Broadens the definition of disability and expands the categories of major life activities.

Note: For reliable and useful information related to special education law and policy, the reader is referred to the Wrightslaw website: www.wrightslaw.com. The website is an easily accessible, accurate source of information and materials, including articles, cases, forms, and other practical resources for families, teachers, lawyers, and advocates.

Foundational Principles of Early Childhood Special Education

After reviewing the major public policy changes influencing the field of early childhood special education, it is important to note the trends that continue to evolve as policy is being implemented. Major philosophical changes are discussed next.

Relationship-Focused Models of Early Intervention

The mechanism that maintains child change over time has become obvious. The parent or caregiver is the factor that assists the child in maintaining the advantage stimulated by early intervention. Findings provide support for assumptions underlying a **relationship-focused intervention model**. Research shows that when family-centered intervention provides emotional and informational support, positive outcomes for children and families are increased (Barfoot, Meredith, Ziviani, & Whittingham, 2015; Mahoney & Perales, 2005). Even though a great deal of additional research is needed to explore how specific interventions can influence caregiver–child relationships, research results suggest a cumulative transactional model of development (Sameroff, 2009).

If the mechanism that facilitates and maintains the impact of early intervention services is the caregiver, intervention programs need to focus on the caregiving environment as much as on the infant or child. Changes in the child may enhance parental attitudes as well as improve the interactional nature of the parent–child relationship. Conversely, changes in parent responses can reinforce and build desired responses in the child. Thus, a mutually reinforcing cycle of parent–child interactions will help to maintain the impact of early intervention services. As Meisels stated as early as 1985, "The primary intervention target should not be the child, but the child within the context of the family" (p. 8).

This recommendation was underscored more recently in a policy statement on family engagement issued by the U.S. Department of Health and Human Services and the Department of Education in 2016:

> The lives and experiences of young children are intertwined with those of their families. Families are children's first and most important teachers, advocates, and nurturers. Strong family engagement in early childhood systems and programs is central—not supplemental—to promoting children's healthy development, learning and wellness. Effective family engagement practices are a marker of quality early childhood programming. (p. 18)

Therefore, throughout this text, the importance of family–professional collaboration is emphasized, especially in Chapter 2.

Family-Centered Services

The original framers of PL 99-457 recognized the family as the constant in the life of the child as evidenced in their mandate for a family-centered approach to implementation of the law. Rather than the traditional focus on the child, a **family-centered approach** views the child's development within the context of the family system. Increasingly, it is recognized that effective service delivery is guided by a thorough understanding of family systems—including family stresses, factors influencing family functioning, and the family's ability to cope with the challenges of raising a child who has a disability. Professionals are being urged to reexamine traditional agency roles and practices as they promote the collaborative, family-directed partnerships essential to success in planning processes such as assessment, prioritizing goals, and designing and implementing intervention plans.

Community-Based Inclusive Settings

One of the basic premises of IDEA is the inclusion of young children with disabilities in the least restrictive environment. Indeed, Part C states that early intervention services for children from birth to age 3 are to be provided in "natural environments, including the home, and community settings in which children without disabilities participate" (PL 105-17, 1997). Each child's individual plan must state the degree to which the child will receive services in "natural environments." Natural environments include not only the child's home but also neighborhood play groups, child development centers, Head Start programs, and any other setting designed for children without disabilities.

The practice of fully including children with disabilities in programs and settings designed primarily for children without disabilities received a boost through the 1990 passage of the ADA. The challenge of providing services sufficient to enable all young children to function as optimally as possible within normal environments appears to be the challenge of the new millennium. At the very least, early childhood special educators are being asked to move outside the walls of a self-contained classroom and to become integrated into early education programs within the community.

Video Example from

Enhanced eText
Video Example 1.2
Christopher's Story
https://www.youtube.com/
watch?v=LEty6-c0cfQ
This video shows how a young child with multiple disabilities can be included in his home community.

Interdisciplinary Collaboration

In addition to the mandate of delivering coordinated multiagency services, the field of early childhood special education is confronted with the need to avoid the difficulties inherent in a strict categorical response to the needs of young children and their families. Part C mandates service coordination designed to provide the critical mechanism for coordinating among complex and diverse human services personnel. Deliberate service coordination reduces duplication of intake procedures, assessment of child and family needs, and direct service delivery.

This focus on interagency and interdisciplinary collaboration facilitates the learning of skills necessary to work in teams comprising various disciplines, sometimes from several agencies. As discussed further in Chapter 3, the **transdisciplinary team approach** allows the child and family to benefit from the expertise of several disciplines without necessarily having to be handled by, or meet face to face with, myriad professionals. Professionals from various disciplines work together cooperatively to educate one another so that any one professional can provide a broader range of essential services. For example, a teacher or caregiver may, on the advice of a speech-language pathologist, redirect an informal playground activity to facilitate language development. (See Chapter 3 and the Glossary for definitions of *interdisciplinary* and *transdisciplinary*.)

Culturally Responsive Practices

The United States is a land of immigrants with a rich diversity of ethnicities, cultures, languages, and lifestyles. The families of young children with disabilities naturally reflect the diversity of families in the general population. Increasingly, definitions of the family conceptualize it as any unit that defines itself as a family. A family includes any persons who are related by blood or marriage as well as those who have made a commitment to share their lives (Hanson & Lynch, 2013). Family characteristics continue to become more diverse and include the complexity of the family's social-economic and educational backgrounds. In the United States, more than 1 out of 4 children (5,975,717) under 6 years of age lives below the federal poverty level, and 1 in 18 (1,266,605) experiences homelessness (Administration for Children and Families, 2017).

Given the great diversity found among families, moving from a child-oriented view to a child and family service orientation creates a continuing challenge for change. Viewing the family as the primary mediator of child development necessitates a reconsideration of service goals. Part C recognizes this need by requiring parents to be the primary decision makers when outcomes or goals are targeted in the service plan. A culturally pluralistic, sensitive orientation is essential to service-delivery mechanisms that can respond to constantly changing family characteristics.

Across the country, children bring various experiences, abilities, talents, and challenges. Between 2004 and 2013, the number of U.S. children living in households where a language other than English was spoken increased from 20 million to 23 million children. That represents an increase from 28 to 32% (Child Trends, 2014). Early childhood special education services must respect and respond to not only a variety of languages, but also the beliefs, values, and child-rearing practices of families of diverse backgrounds that are likely to differ from those of mainstream U.S. culture. Furthermore, program staff should seek ways to extend their competence in working with families of diverse backgrounds and provide materials that address the families' cultures, values, and languages.

Coordinated Comprehensive Services

Collaboration between parents and professionals and among agency professionals is essential to the provision of coordinated comprehensive services as required by the law. Definite challenges are created by significant shifts in role emphasis as professionals develop partnerships not only with families but also with an increasing array of community service providers. The literature increasingly discusses the shift away from one-on-one infant/toddler training to a paradigm reflecting the ecological view of the child and family embedded within the larger community (Noonan & McCormick, 2014).

To meet the demands of this paradigm shift, personnel training programs have moved away from curricula that follow traditional disciplinary boundaries toward curricula that foster multiagency and multidisciplinary collaboration. Such programs enable professionals from several disciplines to work together with families through a variety of approaches, integrating the best of the consultant, transdisciplinary, and multidisciplinary models with the recommended practices from special and "regular" early childhood education.

Evidence-Based Practices

Over time, the focus on educational standards and outcomes has resulted in federal policies that increasingly emphasize evidence-based practices in early childhood special education. The most easily recognized policy is the No Child Left Behind Act of 2001 (NCLB; PL 107-110), which advanced the position that educational practices should be derived from "scientifically based" research (Buysse & Wesley, 2006). Despite the frequent use of the term **evidence-based practice (EBP)** in early childhood special education, the field of special education has struggled to agree on how to identify evidence-based practices. However, there has been considerable progress in identifying standards that EBPs must meet, including research design, quantity, and quality. Cook and Odom (2013) state: "[F]or a practice to be considered evidence-based it must be supported by multiple, high-quality, experimental or quasi-experimental studies demonstrating that the practice has a meaningful impact on consumer (e.g., student) outcomes" (p. 136).

Routines-Based and Embedded Interventions

The terms **activity-based intervention, embedded intervention, routines-based intervention**, and **natural learning opportunities** refer to everyday activities in which the child's interventions can be embedded or infused. *Embedded learning opportunities (ELOs)* result from "the intentional incorporation of specific learning objectives into play and routine classroom activities" (Allen & Cowdery, 2015). Moreover, teachers as well as family members are more likely to work on skills that can be elicited naturally during daily activities rather than having to remember to allocate a particular time to "work" on a special activity with a young child (Johnson, Rahn, & Bricker, 2015).

Standards-Based Curriculum

All 56 states and territories have developed curriculum standards for 3- to 5-year-olds, and most have standards for children from birth to 3 years old. The number of items included in the list of standards differs from state to state, and the standards are given various titles. California developed and adopted the *Infant/Toddler Learning and Development Foundations* and the *Preschool Learning Foundations.* In Colorado, they are called *Early Learning and Development Guidelines*, whereas Connecticut has the *Connecticut Preschool Assessment Framework.* Although it is not important to remember the title given to the list of standards, it is critical to remember that they are considered to be the expectations for the learning and development of young children. That is, they articulate the specific knowledge or skills that children should acquire and demonstrate through performance.

Some time ago, the National Association for the Education of Young Children (NAEYC) and the National Association of Early Childhood Specialists in the State Departments of Education (NAECS/SDE) adopted four essential features for success in creating high-quality early education programs. A summary of these is given in Exhibit 1.7.

Child Outcomes

Related to the current emphases on evidence-based practices and standards-based curriculum, early childhood special education focuses on positive outcomes for children and families. As early as 2007, the Office of Special Education Programs of the U.S. Department of Education required states providing IDEA Part C and Part B services to report outcome data on the percentage of infants and toddlers with IFSPs and

Video Example from

Enhanced eText
Video Example 1.3
Routine at Home Playing Peek-a-Boo
https://www.youtube.com/watch?v=zUfQbUNFnmg
In this video, the mother encourages her infant's communication, motor, play, social, and cognitive skills during bath and dressing routines.

Exhibit 1.7
Realizing the Conditions for Success

1. Programs should adhere to standards and expectations that are developmentally appropriate, address all areas of development, and be flexible enough to embed culturally and individually relevant experiences that create success for all children.
2. Programs should embrace standards that have been developed by experts, involve all stakeholders including parents, and are kept current by interactive review of evidence-based practices.
3. Programs should include standards-related assessment strategies that are technically, developmentally, ethically, and culturally valid while they yield information useful to educators and parents.
4. Programs should create opportunities for professional development, coaching, and mentoring that also recognize the positive impact of partnering with families.

preschoolers with IEPs who demonstrate (1) positive social relationships; (2) acquisition and use of knowledge and skills, including thinking, reasoning, problem solving, and early literacy and math skills; and (3) use of appropriate behaviors to meet their needs, including eating, dressing, self-care, and following rules related to health and safety. Family outcomes under Part C services are identified in Chapter 2.

NECTAC (2013) reported that in 2011–2012, children served under IDEA demonstrated greater-than-expected developmental progress, with 80–81% of the children studied showing greater-than-expected growth and 53–66% exiting from their programs having met age expectations. However, data collection continues to be a complex process that regularly requires improvement. Even so, the data available indicate reason for optimism.

Response to Intervention (RTI) or Tiered Instruction

The reauthorization of IDEA in the Individuals with Disabilities Education Improvement Act (IDEIA, 2004) introduced the provision of "early intervening services" for K–12 students in an effort to reduce or eliminate the possible later need for special education services. Professionals in the fields of early childhood education and early childhood special education have considered ways in which "early intervening" concepts might be applied to pre-K populations. Commonly used early intervening frameworks provide multi-tiered, gradually increasing individualized supports, such as **Response to Intervention (RTI)** and Multi-tiered Systems of Support (MTSS) (NECTAC, 2012). Additionally, an example of an early childhood framework is the Pyramid Model, which addresses social and behavioral needs (Fox & Hemmeter, 2011). The core of RTI is tiered instruction or intervention.

In 2013, the Division for Early Childhood (DEC), National Association for the Education of Young Children (NAEYC), and National Head Start Association (NHSA) produced a joint paper designed to provide guidance in understanding the implications of RTI for use in early childhood programs. This joint paper emphasized the following positive features of RTI: By providing differentiated support developed through a data-based decision-making process to all young children, RTI offers a means of providing high-quality teaching and responsive caregiving.

Tiered instructional approaches in early childhood are often based on RTI that typically consist of three tiers of instruction. Tier 1 is the well-designed, evidence-based core instructional program that meets the needs of a majority of children. Tier 2 is designed for children who fall below the expected levels of achievement and require supplemental intervention such as small-group instruction and more frequent progress monitoring. Tier 3 is designed for children who need more intensive support, such as smaller groups or individual instruction, and more frequent progress monitoring than children in Tier 2. In some RTI models, Tier 3 is considered special education services; other models view special education services as provided in Tier 4, whereas still other RTI models view special education services not as a separate tier but as integrated into Tiers 2 and 3. Key to this approach are universal screening and progress monitoring—that is, the gathering of information about a child's skills and needs, the implementation of evidence-based interventions to meet these needs, and continual monitoring of the child's progress.

Although RTI was not specifically mentioned in IDEIA 2004, the practice of RTI is in keeping with the spirit of the law and is intended to be initiated within general education programs and implemented collaboratively with special education. The hope was that future special education services might not be necessary if students who show evidence of needing additional instruction or intervention receive the support required to be successful early in their general education setting. Although provision of RTI may be primarily focused on K–12 programs, the joint paper (DEC, NAEYC, & NHSA, 2013) noted that the RTI principles just discussed encompass principles that are at the core of recommended practices in early childhood, such as assessment, intentional teaching, differentiated instruction, and ongoing progress monitoring (Copple & Bredekamp, 2009).

At the date of publication of this text, actual implementation of RTI programs, in both K–12 education and pre-K education, has yet to be fully realized, and there is variation across programs. A unique challenge faced at the preschool level is the absence of universal preschool programs and practices in the United States. Also, as pointed out in the DEC, NAEYC, and NHSA (2013) joint statement, there are several challenges in early childhood education that are not characteristic of K–12 education. Examples include involvement of a variety of different agencies, diverse settings, variable preparation of personnel, limited resources, and the much broader scope of developmental needs expected to be addressed.

Video Example from

Enhanced eText
Video Example 1.4
Tiered Instruction Framework
https://www.youtube.com/
watch?v=0xrdW45web0
The tiered instructional framework
is explained in this video.

Pre-K Response to Intervention

Given the success of RTI with K–12 students and given that RTI practices are generally consistent with recommended practices in early childhood education, several districts are adapting the RTI approach for pre-K children. Coleman, Roth, and West (2009) discuss attempts at a downward extension of RTI. They suggest that the following early childhood practices are natural facilitators of pre-K RTI (p. 7):

- emphasis on quality early childhood education;
- implementation of a tiered approach to meeting the needs of children;
- focus on standards-based curriculum and evidence-based practices;
- utilization of intentional instructional strategies such as embedded instruction; and
- increasing use of progress monitoring and data-driven instruction.

Research appears favorable in regard to a fairly recent practice named **Recognition & Response (R&R)** with origins in RTI (Buysee & Peisner-Feinberg, 2010). Key components of this model include:

Recognition = Universal screening and progress monitoring

Response = Curriculum, intentional teaching, and targeted interventions

The success of this model is partially dependent on the development of opportunities for collaborative problem solving to support instructional decision making. R&R is a framework for linking assessment to instruction, and thus may also be a promising approach for instruction of second-language learners. Further studies are needed to confirm this approach as an evidence-based practice. Our field will be anxious to learn of the results.

Universal Design for Learning (UDL)

The origins of Universal Design (UD) are in the field of architecture. The premise of **Universal Design for Learning (UDL)** understands that more than just the learning environment can be designed in such a way that all children are more likely to learn (Center for Applied Special Technology, 2014). When curbs were cut to accommodate wheelchairs, it was quickly apparent that others, such as adults with strollers and bicyclists, also benefited. UDL applies this concept to the education of children of varying disabilities, linguistic diversities, and varied learning styles. Gargiulo and Metcalf (2010) define UDL as follows: "Curriculum and instruction that includes alternatives to make it accessible and appropriate for individuals with different backgrounds, learning preferences, abilities, and disabilities in widely varied learning contexts" (p. 450). *Universal* implies the need for multiple means of representation, expression, and engagement to meet diverse needs within the classroom. This means offering learners various ways of acquiring information (through books being read during circle time, information presented on a screen, hands-on materials, etc.). It includes providing multiple means for learners to express themselves (e.g., artwork, singing, verbal expression, actions). Finally, it also means building on children's natural interests, backgrounds, and learning styles (Stockall, Dennis, & Miller, 2012). UDL is further discussed in Chapter 4.

Enhanced eText Application Exercise 1.3: In this exercise, you can apply what you have learned in this chapter to explain the key foundational principles for high quality early childhood education services.

Building on Recommended Practices

Two major professional groups that address early education and intervention services have issued definitive statements of **recommended practices**. NAEYC (2009) describes a **developmentally appropriate practice (DAP)** as an "approach" in which teachers "meet young children where they are" developmentally. DAP includes three core considerations:

1. *Thorough knowledge of what is typical at each age and stage of child development.* Our thorough knowledge of child development will help us select appropriate experiences to facilitate learning and development.

2. *Knowing what is characteristic of each individual child's interests, abilities, and developmental progress.* By thoroughly understanding each child, we can individualize our caring and instruction.

3. *Knowing what is culturally appropriate.* With understanding of the values and expectations of each child's family and community, we can provide meaningful and respectful learning experiences for all children and families.

These position statements on DAP and other practices are frequently updated and available on the NAEYC website (http://www.naeyc.org; from the home page, click on the "Position Statements" link).

Although the NAEYC's developmentally appropriate practices serve as the primary context in which to develop curriculum, age appropriateness and individualization are essential to the understanding of effective practices within early childhood special education. As Noonan and McCormick (2006) state,

Infants and young children with severe disabilities, however, will not always be ready to learn the same activities as their age peers with mild or no disabilities. To support the integration of infants and young children with and without disabilities, however, curricular activities should be age appropriate, even when the activities do not correspond to readiness levels. The activities should serve as a context for instruction. Specific objectives, or the way in which children with disabilities participate in activities, are individualized to address unique needs. (p. 85)

It is useful to consider some key recommendations that emerged from the NAEYC framework related to curriculum (see Exhibit 1.8). The NAEYC also offered essential noncurricular recommendations that focus on adult–child interactions, family involvement, and evaluation (see Exhibit 1.9).

Collaboration Between Early Childhood Education and Early Childhood Special Education Professionals

A second major professional group, the Division for Early Childhood (DEC) of the Council for Exceptional Children, issues its own recommended practices for the field of early childhood special education (DEC, 2014). Although there is substantial overlap between the developmentally appropriate practices from the NAEYC and the recommended practices from the DEC, certain differences exist.

Exhibit 1.8

NAEYC Curriculum Recommendations

- Curriculum development is responsive to families' goals and priorities as well as the individual needs of children.
- Educational goals are incorporated into all daily activities. Objectives are not taught in isolation but are integrated into meaningful activities and events.
- To the maximum extent possible, educational experiences are derived from research-based practices.
- Curriculum planning and intervention are based on specific observations of each child made by parents and the intervention team in natural contexts.
- Learning is an *interactive* process. Children's interactions with adults, peers, and the physical environment are all important.
- Learning activities and materials must be concrete and *relevant* to children's lives. Teachers should make use of real-life objects and activities (e.g., make a trip to the fire station, not just read a story about fire engines).
- Programs must be able to meet a wide range of interests and abilities. Teachers are expected to *individualize* instructional programs.
- Teachers must increase the difficulty and challenge of activities gradually and skillfully.
- Teachers must be able to facilitate the *engagement* of each child by offering choices, making suggestions, asking questions, and describing events in ways that are meaningful and interesting to the child.
- Children should be given opportunities for *self-initiation*, *self-direction*, and *repeated practice*.
- Teachers must accept and appreciate cultural differences in children and families and avoid ethnic and gender stereotypes.
- Programs must provide a balance between rest and activity and should include outdoor activities each day.
- Outdoor activities should be *planned*, not simply be opportunities to release pent-up energy.
- Programs must create careful *transitions* from one activity to the next. Children should not be rushed, and schedules should be flexible enough to take advantage of impromptu experiences.

Exhibit 1.9

NAEYC Noncurricular Recommendations

Adult–Child Interaction

- Adults should respond quickly and directly to children's needs and attempts to communicate. Whenever possible, adults should be at eye level with children.

- Children must be provided with a variety of opportunities to communicate. Interaction is best facilitated on a one-to-one basis or in groups of two to three children. Large-group instruction is less effective in facilitating communication.

- Professionals must be alert to signs of stress and provide sensitive, appropriate assistance to children.

- Adults must facilitate the development of self-esteem by being respectful and accepting of children, regardless of the children's behavior.

- Adults must use disciplinary techniques that enhance the development of self-control. These include setting clear, consistent limits; redirecting inappropriate behavior; valuing mistakes; listening to children's concerns and frustrations; helping children solve conflicts; and patiently reminding children of rules as needed.

- Adults must be responsible for all children at all times. Health and safety issues must be addressed constantly.

- Adults must plan for gradually increasing children's independence.

Family Involvement

- Families have the right and the responsibility to share in decision making regarding their children's care and education. Families are considered to be equals in a partnership and their vision guides program planning. Professionals must maintain frequent contact, and families should be encouraged to participate.

- Professionals must regularly share information and resources with parents, including information regarding stages of child development. They must also obtain and respect caregivers' views of individual children's behavior and development.

Evaluation

- Child evaluations should not rely on a single instrument.

- Evaluations should identify children with disabilities and provide information that will lead to meaningful early interventions.

- Evaluations must be culturally appropriate.

The NAEYC guidelines for DAP were generated by early childhood education (ECE) professionals who were dismayed at the growing emphasis on academic performance and structure in preschool and kindergarten classrooms. Thus, the major focus of the original guidelines was on expectations and learning environments that were appropriate for the developmental levels of typical young children. There was also a negative reaction to strongly teacher-directed approaches and to the teaching and tracking of specific skills. The NAEYC practices valued the *process* rather than the *products* of learning. Ironically, due to concern for the so-called U.S. achievement gap, there is once again a significant trend toward emphasis on academics and school readiness within early childhood education. The focus is on ensuring that young children enter kindergarten "ready to learn" (Duncan & Murnane, 2011). This focus can sometimes be at odds with the principles of developmentally appropriate practice, particularly for young children with developmental delays and disabilities.

Early childhood special education (ECSE) professionals, in contrast, have been strongly influenced by the values and tenets of special education and PL 94-142.

Exhibit 1.10

Comparison of Selected NAEYC and DEC Key Recommended Practices

Early Childhood Special Education Recommended Practices

1. A stronger emphasis on collaboration with families and other professionals
2. Greater emphasis on supporting the specific needs of individual children
3. Greater emphasis on the birth-to-3 age range
4. Viewing teacher-centered versus child-centered approaches not as a dichotomy but as a continuum; understanding that child-centered approaches do not exclude the use of teacher-directed strategies in certain situations
5. Greater emphasis on transition planning
6. Integration of developmentally appropriate practices with individually appropriate practices to address a child's specific learning needs

Early Childhood Developmentally Appropriate Practices

1. Training in natural environments, particularly within the context of play
2. Importance of child-initiated activities
3. De-emphasis on standardized assessment; integration of assessment and curriculum
4. Importance of active child engagement throughout the day in naturally occurring routines and activities
5. Emphasis on social interaction
6. The importance of cultural sensitivity and competence

The DEC-recommended practices emphasize the identification of specific expected outcomes, the accountability of professionals for ensuring steady progress toward these outcomes, the importance of direct instruction, and the necessity of a strong commitment to individualized instruction. The field of ECSE also places strong emphasis on parent–professional collaboration and family empowerment, transition planning and training for the next environment, interdisciplinary and interagency collaboration, appropriate assessment, and use of technology. The DEC also regularly updates its position statements, which are available on the DEC website (http://www.dec-sped.org; from the "Publications" tab on the home page, select "Position Statements and Papers").

Historically, the contrast in the developmentally appropriate approach characteristic of ECE versus the disability-specific approach characteristic of ECSE has created extensive discussion. Luckily, these differences in approach currently do not interfere with collaboration between these two disciplines. Joint position papers resulting from the collaborative efforts of these very influential groups, such as the one released back in 2009, have received considerable attention. In an effort to assist personnel preparation programs in creating more effective training, Chandler and colleagues (2012) compared the personnel preparation standards issued by the DEC and NAEYC. Collectively, these practices are summarized in Exhibit 1.10.

The Importance of Ongoing Pursuit of Evidence-Based Practices

Students of ECSE must realize that, as is the case with any progressive field, early childhood special education is constantly evolving. The ideas and notions that make up today's best or recommended practices may be very different from those that evolve a decade from now. Early intervention professionals must have a thirst for discovering and understanding evidence-based knowledge and a genuine desire to better understand and implement best practices in meeting the needs of young children with disabilities.

Practitioners must be responsible for maintaining an important two-way dialogue with researchers in their field. They must help identify important research questions, insist on the use of research methods that are appropriate to answer those questions, and then apply the findings of that research by incorporating evidence-based techniques into their daily instructional routines whenever possible. Current examples of robust ongoing research and application of evidence-based practices are those in the areas of autism spectrum disorders (National Autism Center, 2010) and early literacy learning for young children (Trivette, Dunst, & Hamby, 2010a, b).

Service Delivery

Unlike K–12 education, in ECSE there are many ways in which services are delivered. For example, in early intervention, service delivery may target the caregiver or may directly intervene with the child. PL 99-457 and subsequent reauthorizations and amendments clearly intend for the family to be the primary focal point and context within which the infant or toddler is viewed. However, even within this family-centered framework, some interventionists and specialized therapists may focus solely on intervention for the infant or child with relatively less concern for the role of the family in the child's development. With preschool-age children, therapists may prefer to pull the child from the classroom and provide direct intervention to the child, rather than incorporating teachers and peers.

Services for Infants and Toddlers

The primary emphasis of this text is on providing educational and developmental services for *preschool*-age children with disabilities. However, as mentioned earlier in this chapter, an equally important component of the field of early childhood special education is providing services for **infants and toddlers** with developmental delays or disabilities (i.e., age birth to age 3, who have disabilities or who are at risk for disabilities) *and* their families. These services must be carefully delineated in a legal document referred to as the **Individualized Family Service Plan (IFSP)**. As noted earlier, Part C of IDEA states that early intervention services are to be provided in *natural environments*, including the child's home and a variety of community settings. To provide the most appropriate option for each child and family, communities develop what is sometimes referred to as a "menu of services." For infants who have severe and/or complex disabilities, **home-based services** are often considered to be the "least restrictive" because they take place in the most natural or typical environment for infants. Home-based services may also be offered in the home of a relative or child-care provider.

Home-based programs are tailored to the individual needs of the child and family, as determined through assessment of each family's priorities and resources. Such assessment is sensitive to the functional demands of the child's environment. Home visitors include a wide variety of professionals from various community agencies. For young infants, early intervention services may be provided by a public health nurse who focuses on health-care issues. A nutritionist may work with a family when their child has unique nutritional needs. Or, the visits may focus on sensory processing and integration, or motor activities modeled by an infant educator or provided by an occupational or physical therapist. Perhaps the most important early intervention is the facilitation of quality caregiver–child interactions and the influence of parental mental health on these interactions (Cook & Sparks, 2008).

High-quality and effective home-based services should reflect recommended and evidence-based practices such as facilitating parent–child interactions (Dunst, Gorman, &

Hamby, 2010; Chen & Klein, 2008), using routine-based interventions and natural learning opportunities that occur in everyday activity settings or natural environments, using modeling and coaching to assist caregivers to implement interventions with their infants (Rush & Shelden, 2011; Chen, Klein, & Haney, 2007), and establishing supportive relationships with families. In-home service delivery for infants with disabilities is a complex, multifaceted phenomenon, which includes a variety of strategies and approaches to caregiver–child interactions, demonstration of disability-specific skills, and infant and caregiver mental health. As the scope of this text does not allow a thorough examination of research and practice related to in-home service delivery, the reader is referred to specific texts on this topic, such as McWilliam (2010) and Cook and Sparks (2008).

Some toddlers attend center-based early intervention programs. These are specialized group settings to which families bring their children. Such programs provide important access to parent-to-parent support. They may also provide important "one-stop-shopping" access to a variety of service providers within the same setting. Center-based programs can provide more frequent interdisciplinary contact than in-home programs. Some service-delivery models combine home- and center-based services. For example, children may be enrolled in a center three days per week and receive a monthly home visit. There continues to be ongoing discussion about whether such settings can be considered "natural environments." The case might be made that if children without disabilities are also welcomed in the center, *and* a family member attends the center with the child, it meets the requirements of a "natural environment."

Public and private *child-care* settings may also be considered natural environments. In these settings, infants and toddlers may receive specialized itinerant services, or one-to-one support. Some children may experience dual enrollment by attending an agency-sponsored segregated center-based program for children with disabilities for part of the day and participating in a typical child-care setting for the remainder of the day. As PL 101-336 (ADA) increases in influence, a greater number of infants and toddlers will be served in typical child-care settings.

Special Considerations for Infant and Toddler Group Care. Any group-care programs for children from birth to 3 years of age must be designed to create and sustain *intimacy*. Exhibit 1.11 summarizes six key components of group care for infants and toddlers offered by Lally, Torres, and Phelps (2010) that remain relevant.

Exhibit 1.11

Key Components of Group Care for Young Children

1. **Group size:** The adult-to-child ratio in programs serving young children under age 3 should be no greater than 1:3 for infants to 18 months in a group of 6–9 and 1:4 for toddlers to 3 years of age in a group of 12. However, the issue of group size is not simply the need to maintain a low adult-to-child ratio. Total group size is at least as important as this ratio. As group size increases, so does the level of stimulation. This creates a stressful environment for both infants and staff. A noisy, chaotic environment makes it difficult for staff to be sensitive and responsive to child cues and decreases the opportunity for quiet, intimate interactions.

2. **Physical environment:** Arrangement of the physical environment can either facilitate or interfere with flexible, individualized, responsive care and relationships between children and adults. For example, easy and frequent access to food and to outdoor space allows greater individualization. Furniture that is comfortable for adults, such as rocking chairs and couches, encourages holding and reading to

(continued)

infants. Reduction of off-limits items and areas minimizes discipline problems and negative adult–child interactions. Small, safe, well-defined areas for certain types of play help control overstimulation and help young children focus.

3. **Assignment of primary caregiver:** An extremely important factor in center-based care for young children is the assignment of a primary caregiver to each child. This facilitates the development of trust and intimacy. This does not mean that the child interacts *exclusively* with one adult; rather, on most days, there will be a familiar and "special" person on whom the child can rely. The assignment of a primary caregiver also increases the likelihood that at least one staff person knows each child well. A knowledge of temperament, communication cues, likes, dislikes, and fears can be shared with other staff members. This, in turn, increases the opportunity for responsive and appropriate interactions with the infant.

4. **Continuity of care:** Primary caregiving facilitates special relationships. Changing caregivers every 6 to 9 months can have a negative effect on infants and young children. Changing the caregiver (or teacher in an early intervention program) is also difficult for the child's parents, as it requires the reestablishment of trust and communication patterns.

5. **Cultural and familial continuity:** Ideally, programs should employ staff whose cultural backgrounds match those of the families they serve. Children and parents are sensitive to significant mismatches in the child-rearing values and practices of family and staff.

6. **Meeting the needs of individuals in a group:** Flexible scheduling allows individual infants to sleep, eat, and play when they need to do so. Responsiveness to an infant's biological rhythms may require a caregiver to monitor a sleeping infant, watch one who is engaged in play, and actively interact with another. This flexibility accommodates children with disabilities.

It is imperative that individuals working with young children from cultures different than their own carefully examine the roots of their own biases and values. They must also be knowledgeable about the values and attitudes of the cultural groups in their community and work to avoid being judgmental when significant differences do exist.

Services for Preschoolers

The emphasis of this text is on preschool-age children. Special education services for preschoolers begin at age 3 years and extend to kindergarten entry. They are delineated in Part B of IDEA and are governed by the same requirements and provisions as K–12 education—that is, a free and appropriate education provided in the least restrictive environment (LRE). The "least restrictive environment" must be understood as a *continuum*. The LRE continuum refers to a range of possible placements. The *least* restrictive environment is the one that can meet the child's educational needs, *and*, in cases where the general education classroom is deemed "not appropriate" by the IEP team, is as similar as is reasonable to a typical general education classroom for same-age peers. For example, Sandra is a preschool-age child with severe and complex developmental and health needs. The IEP team determined that Sandra's health and medical needs cannot be met in a typical early childhood setting (such as Head Start, or community early education center). Even though one member of the IEP team feels she should receive home schooling because of her health needs, the team may determine that this would be too restrictive. In this case, the least restrictive environment for Sandra might be a special education preschool class where staff members are available to address her health needs. Another child, Wen Li, has low vision and mild cerebral palsy. With itinerant supports from a vision specialist and a physical therapist, the IEP team determines that he can be well supported in the inclusive community-based early childhood education center in his neighborhood.

Educating Young Children with Disabilities in Inclusive Settings

As mentioned earlier, IDEA requires that services for children with disabilities be provided in the *least restrictive environment*. This provision starts with the assumption that children will be served in settings with their same-age peers. For infants and toddlers, these settings are referred to as "natural environments." For preschoolers, these settings are typical early childhood settings, such as Head Start classrooms or early childhood education centers. If, due to the child's disabling condition, his or her learning and social needs cannot be met in the typical ECE classroom, then a setting as similar to that as possible must be identified. An example of such a program might be a reverse integration classroom in which same-age peers attend the special education classroom for a portion of the day, and ECE and ECSE teachers collaborate as co-teachers.

Settings in the early years should be optimized to include children with disabilities for several reasons. First, most early education programs expect children to mature at varying rates during these years of enhanced growth and development. Differences in skills are expected and accommodated within the curriculum. The range of so-called normalcy in early education is much broader than that usually found in elementary school classrooms.

Unlike teachers of older children, early childhood educators tend to focus on the *process* more than the *product* of learning. They are busy setting up centers to allow for exploration and problem solving, rather than grading spelling papers or preparing the next day's language test. In addition, the methods and materials usually found in early education centers are conducive to the development of all young children. Exploration, manipulation, expression, sharing, and active involvement provide easy opportunities for educators to structure and reinforce meaningful interaction between children with disabilities and those without. However, with the current emphasis on school readiness and standards-based education, this tradition may be changing, as noted in the previous discussion on standards-based practices.

All who have worked with young children are readily aware of their natural abilities to accept and even appreciate individual differences. Children respond to one another without making judgments and comparisons. Spontaneous friendships abound with little in the way of ongoing expectations. When differences are observed, questions reflect a natural curiosity. If such questions are answered in genuine, thoughtful ways, children tend to accommodate and accept those who are perceived to be different. Early childhood is the ideal time to help all young children fully acquire a sense of belonging.

Unique Challenges Involved in Supporting Early Childhood Inclusion

Despite these favorable conditions for successful inclusion, there are also several challenges to successful inclusion in early childhood settings. Common examples of these challenges include lack of availability of quality child care, low pay for child-care staff, and differences in administrative structure and educational philosophies among early childhood programs.

It is also important to acknowledge that simply placing children with disabilities in educational settings with nondisabled children does not, automatically, accomplish the goals of inclusion. Although much has been written about **inclusion support** strategies in K–12 education, less attention has been given to inclusion support in early childhood settings. As Richardson-Gibbs and Klein (2014) point out, several challenges are unique to early childhood inclusion. Some of these are as follows:

1. In the K–12 inclusive classroom, the general education teacher is credentialed at the same level as the special educator who provides support to the children with

disabilities. There is generally "parity" in terms of training background, level of academic degree, credential/license status, and pay. This is very often not the case in early childhood settings. The lack of support as a society for quality child care results in inadequate resources and low staff salaries, particularly in urban communities. This can result in little motivation for advanced training in early childhood education, thus creating a "parity gap" between the training and salary levels of ECE and ECSE teachers. This difference can lead to significant challenges for the inclusion support specialist. It requires understanding and perspective-taking skills to bring about successful collaboration and effective team building.

2. The level of experience and understanding of disabilities among ECE teachers (i.e., non–special education teachers) and staff are highly varied. The inclusion support specialist must be able to explain the nature of a child's disability and learning style and to demonstrate specific strategies appropriate for that child. Thus, early childhood support specialists must have a certain level of disability-specific expertise.

3. Often the ECSE support specialist must take on the unfamiliar role of providing services on someone else's turf. The support specialist must manage his or her own role and avoid being intrusive while at the same time establishing a collaborative relationship. However, the ECE teacher may be uncomfortable with his or her own relative lack of knowledge and experience with disabilities. The ECE teacher may also be unaccustomed to having someone observing in the classroom. Thus, the ECE teacher may be understandably defensive or wary and experience additional stress in an already stressful job. The challenges posed to the development of a truly collaborative relationship in such situations can be significant.

4. Finally, even when the ECE staff is highly trained, there are sometimes significant philosophical differences between ECSE and ECE staff. Klein, Chen, and Haney (2000) found that this was perceived to be one of the major barriers to successful inclusion. These differences in philosophy and beliefs might include such issues as the following:

   - The *purpose* of early childhood education—for example, opportunities for socialization versus training in specific developmental skills or school readiness.
   - Beliefs about inclusion—for example, all children should be included regardless of severity or complexity of disability versus only certain children can be successfully included.
   - Strict adherence to a particular early childhood curriculum versus more flexible, adapted implementation of the curriculum.
   - The kinds of teaching and interaction strategies used—for example, very child-directed and unstructured approaches versus a combination of more structured, teacher-directed interventions.
   - Organization of daily activities—for example, fairly unstructured, flexible daily schedules versus predictable daily routines.

Key Findings from Research on Preschool Inclusion

Research on the benefits of inclusion for young children show that individualized, evidence-based strategies for children with disabilities are successful. In summarizing the scientific basis supporting inclusion in early childhood programs, the U.S. Department of Health and Human Services and U.S. Department of Education cited the following benefits in 2015:

1. Children with disabilities, even those with significant disabilities, can make significant developmental and learning progress in inclusive settings.

2. Some studies have shown that children with more significant disabilities have made more progress than children with similar disabilities in segregated settings.

3. Children with disabilities tend to have levels of engagement similar to peers who are typically developing.

4. High-quality inclusion that begins early and continues into kindergarten is likely to have the best outcomes.

5. Additional benefits of inclusion include fewer absences, stronger social-emotional skills, and eventually higher likelihood of employment.

6. Studies including children who develop typically also show positive development and demonstrate greater compassion and empathy as well as a better understanding of diversity.

The Role of the Early Childhood Special Educator

Inclusion does not supplant the mandate for individualized planning and services as needed by each child. Systematic intervention efforts guided by the teacher are necessary to promote successful inclusion. For children with disabilities to meet their developmental and educational goals, someone must be available to structure the environment, adapt the materials, determine the child's most profitable mode of learning, and select appropriate teaching strategies to encourage specific behaviors.

To fulfill such a multifaceted role, ECSE teachers must develop competencies characteristic of both the early childhood educator and the special educator. Fortunately, the skills needed include the same skills that are necessary to work with *all* young children. However, successful inclusion of children with disabilities requires additional skills and expertise.

The Case for Specific Training Related to Inclusion Support

A study by Dinnebeil, McInerney, Roth, and Ramaswamy (2001) offered support for the need for specific training in inclusion support. Dinnebeil et al. surveyed ECSE professionals serving in itinerant support roles for children in community-based settings and found that the primary strategy being used by these consultants was a direct instruction approach in which they simply carried out the teaching strategies they were accustomed to using in their segregated settings. They concluded that there is a significant need for training in collaborative consultation skills (see also Klein and Harris [2004]). Fortunately, over a decade later, we find the field of ECSE—including university teacher training programs—much more attuned to the importance of this skill set.

Exhibit 1.12 presents some examples of the kinds of support an inclusion specialist might need to be prepared to provide for a child placed in a community-based early childhood setting.

Exhibit 1.12

Examples of Inclusion Support Activities

- Providing in-service training and information to staff members regarding the characteristics of the child's specific disability (e.g., autism, Down syndrome, or multiple sensory disabilities) and other topics related to the child's learning needs
- Modeling or demonstration of specific intervention and teaching strategies
- Conducting ongoing observation and assessment of the child within the setting

(continued)

- Providing ongoing discussion and written feedback to teachers regarding all areas of a child's development and performance (e.g., preferences and interests, level of engagement, and participation or development across the developmental domains, such as language, self-help, social-emotional, etc.)
- Communicating regularly with families about the child's adjustment and progress
- Planning occasional individual work with the child as necessary to encourage achievement of specific goals (e.g., participation in group activities, appropriate communication with peers, or behavior management)
- Modeling of peer training and interaction techniques
- Creating or obtaining adapted equipment and other resources for the child's use in the classroom (e.g., photographs for communication or various types of adaptive equipment and technology to assist self-help and communication)
- Collaborative participation in team meetings, including regular staff meetings and IEP or IFSP meetings, to provide problem-solving and conflict resolution guidance as needed, and team leadership and coordination

For our discussion, we use the term *inclusion support specialist* to refer to an early childhood special educator who provides support for one or more children with disabilities within an inclusive early childhood setting. The inclusion support specialist role may differ from that of the discipline-specific therapist (e.g., occupational therapist, physical therapist, or speech-language pathologist) or the disability-specific specialist (e.g., teacher certified in visual impairment or the Deaf and hard-of-hearing areas) who provides specific direct services or consultative services related to a particular special need. *In this text, the role of the inclusion support specialist is to support the optimal participation of the child in the inclusive setting through collaboration and coordination with other service providers and team members.*

It is clear from examining the list in Exhibit 1.12 that the effective delivery of these services will depend not only on a wide range of knowledge and skills related to best practices in early intervention and ECSE, but also on skills in the area of collaboration, consultation, teaming, adult learning styles, and strategies specifically targeted to the child's participation in the early childhood environment. To provide optimal support, an individual should have knowledge and skills across the following broad competency areas:

- Typical child development and developmentally appropriate practice in ECE
- Disability-specific characteristics and best practices in early intervention and ECSE
- Specific strategies and methods that support inclusion of children with disabilities and interactions with typical peers
- Collaborative consultation and team building (discussed in Chapter 10)

The goal of this text is to provide not only information related to the characteristics and learning needs of children with disabilities but also the specific guidance necessary to address these needs in inclusive settings. The knowledge and recommendations included within this text reflect a long history of research, policy, and practice that are derived from the two fields of early childhood education and special education. For more detailed discussion of models and strategies for successful preschool inclusion, see Richardson-Gibbs and Klein (2014).

Enhanced eText Application Exercise 1.4: In this exercise, you can apply what you have learned in this chapter to identify the challenges and benefits of providing services in inclusive settings for young children (birth–5 years) with disabilities.

Summary

This chapter offers perspectives on the evolving field of early childhood special education, historically and theoretically, and provides an introduction to recommended practices. Over the past 100 years, the approach to children with disabilities has shifted from "hide and forget" to "identify and help." Jean-Marc Itard, Maria Montessori, and Jean Piaget were a few of the most notable pioneers in this field. Their contributions paved the way for the development of curricular adaptations to accommodate young children with disabilities in a variety of settings. More recently, significant federal legislation in the United States continued to support the evolution and solidify the future of the field of early childhood special education.

PL 94-142 mandated that appropriate public education be made available to all children with disabilities as early as possible. One significant provision of this law was that each child should have a written IEP. Children with disabilities also are to be served in the least restrictive environment that meets their needs. The law mandates inclusion in a regular classroom unless the child's disabilities are too severe. In effect, the thrust is to fit the schooling to the child rather than fit the child to the school. This goal is pursued through informed selection of intervention strategies, with preparation of the interventionist as the critical foundation.

PL 99-457 initiated legitimization of the field of early childhood special education. Federal, state, and local planners are collaborating with parents in unprecedented efforts to develop new and expanded services for infants and young children who have disabilities or are at risk and their families. Part H provides incentives for states to provide comprehensive, coordinated, family-focused interagency programs for children from birth through age 2. Unique to this law and the following amendments are the requirements for collaborative service coordination designed to implement IFSPs.

While PL 94-142 and PL 99-457 may have been the catalysts for the development of quality early childhood special education, attention must also be given to PL 101-336 and later amendments creating the Individuals with Disabilities Education Act (IDEA) that dropped the word "handicapped." IDEA and its amendments have added requirements that have significantly contributed to the quality of services for young children with disabilities.

Strategies for including children with disabilities in general early education settings have several theoretical origins. Current approaches to early childhood special education continue to combine influences from both early education and special education fields, especially in advocating for evidence-based practices. The child development and early education literature emphasizes the importance of child-directed methods that are developmentally appropriate and use play and social interaction as primary vehicles for teaching and learning. Special education legislation has mandated a focus on family involvement and education within integrated, community-based settings. The evolving delivery systems offer a variety of opportunities to meet the unique needs of each child and his or her family.

Reflect and Apply

1. Explain the rationale behind the use of person-first terminology. Practice using person-first terminology and work toward becoming self-aware of tendencies to slip into old habits of usage.

2. In many ways, Montessori's approach to early education is and was aligned with inclusive approaches today. Explore the elements of her philosophy and be prepared to discuss their current relevance.

3. Reflect on the evolution of education law for children with disabilities. Articulate how particular laws have helped to facilitate inclusion.

4. Research one or more of the principles considered to be the foundation of early childhood special education. Give specifics in stating how these principles could become operational in an early childhood classroom.

5. Outline and be prepared to discuss the differences in special education service delivery for infants and toddlers (0–3 years of age) and preschoolers (3–5 years of age).

Chapter 2
In Partnership with Families

Jaren Wicklund/Fotolia

⌄ Learning Outcomes

After studying this chapter, you should be able to:

2.1 Offer effective emotional support to families.

2.2 Realize that families are dynamic social systems.

2.3 Recognize the individual reactions and concerns of parents, siblings, and extended family members.

2.4 Explain how to facilitate a variety of options for family engagement.

2.5 Respect the richness of cultural diversity among families.

2.6 Identify and employ effective strategies for working with special family circumstances.

The essential role and impact of parents and other family members on the development of young children are well established and should not be underestimated. The significance of this role is even more evident when a child has learning challenges and disabilities. Establishing an effective family–professional partnership is a guiding principle of early childhood special education. This requires that practitioners understand and respect the critical role and inevitable impact family members and other caregivers have on the child's development and the success of the intervention process. Evidence of the family's influence on child development can be found in research with children with and without disabilities. For example, the Center on the Developing Child at Harvard University (2017) has emphasized the critical importance of positive caregiving relationships and responsive interactions on the healthy brain development of young children. Haven, Manangan, Sparrow, and Wilson (2014) reported that the parent's ability to follow the child's lead by responding to signals and interests such as physical closeness and turn taking is positively related to the social skill development of young children with autism. Tambyraja, Schmitt, Fraquharson, and Justice (2016) found that parents' home literacy practices positively influence reading skills in young children with language impairments.

As the tenth edition of this book is published, the importance of the ability to establish parent–professional partnerships has increased. Research, recommended practices, and experience continue to validate the field's commitment to supporting parents as they deal both with their own emotions and the day-to-day raising of their child. Young children spend the vast majority of their lives with their parents and families and, in comparison, a minuscule amount of time with practitioners. It is imperative that practitioners in early childhood special education value the significant role of parents and families and build collaborative partnerships with them to promote positive outcomes for children. There is good reason why studies continue to offer evidence that when schools and families work in partnership, children tend to be successful in school and afterward (Berns, 2016).

Collaboration with parents or other caregivers is also essential to the development of *families' awareness* of the importance of *their* role in facilitating, guiding, and supporting their child's development. Family–professional collaboration involves "practices that build relationships between families and professionals who work together to achieve mutually agreed upon outcomes and goals that promote family competencies and support the development of the child" (Division for Early Childhood [DEC], 2014, p. 10). Thus, a collaborative partnership with parents and caregivers is a significant requirement for the implementation of effective intervention practices. As in all relationships, the development and maintenance of the family–professional partnership require time, motivation, and effort.

(It should be noted that in this text, the terms *parents, families,* and *caregivers* refer to individuals who have primary caregiving responsibilities for, and consistent interactions with, a young child. We recognize that *parents* refers to adults who have legal parental responsibilities. *Families* refers to parents, siblings, relatives, and any one else who is considered to be *family.* The term *caregivers* includes anyone who may be providing care of the child under consideration.)

Over a decade ago, Fialka (2001) developed a metaphor that expresses the critical role a collaborative partnership plays in fostering the development of young children with disabilities. She discusses five distinct features that illustrate the complexities involved in this "dance of partnership." These include the fact that the need to collaborate extensively with a child's teachers is not a *choice* for parents, whereas professionals usually make the choice to work with children and parents. Second, parents are expected to work more intimately with professionals than is usually true of the caregivers of children without disabilities. In order for true collaboration to result, professionals must listen more intently and focus on the needs of the whole family, not just those of the child. In addition, parents are expected to "dance" with many professionals when consideration is given to all that might be involved with any one child. Even though parents may know their child better than anyone else, it is often the professionals who take the lead in the "dance." Finally, differing priorities make one think of the players wearing different headphones as they "dance" along.

More recently, Fialka, Feldman, and Mikus (2012) expanded on the parent–professional "dance" metaphor to describe three phases that parents and professionals experience in developing a partnership and five steps that promote such a relationship. At the beginning, "Phase 1: Colliding and Campaigning," each partner explains his or her own perspective about the child to persuade the other. This is solo dancing rather than a dance of partnership. At each phase, each partner must practice these steps: stop, look, listen, share, and take care to understand the other's goals and perspectives in order to move toward a collaborative partnership. In "Phase 2: Cooperating and Compromising," partners listen, developing trust and open cooperation, and there is "less stepping on toes" (p. 20). Many relationships may remain at this phase with commitment, problem solving, and some level of consensus. It takes time to develop "Phase 3: Creative Partnering and Collaboration," in which partners tend to share a common view and expectations for the child. "Power and decision-making tend to be balanced" (Failka et al., 2012, p. 27).

With time, understanding, and true collaboration, parents do become their child's best allies in interpreting his or her needs. The parent perspective that appears at the end of the chapter illustrates how time and professional concern helped enable one parent to develop the coping skills needed to face the day-to-day realities of parenting a young child with a disability. Although written several years ago, involved professionals unfortunately will attest to its continuing relevance.

Lisa Jerugim's personal perspective on raising a child with developmental challenges (see page 75) clearly illustrates that all children do affect, and are affected by, their families. When children with disabilities originally began to receive early intervention services, parents were expected to be passive bystanders watching their children "receive" therapy or infant stimulation. In 1975, PL 94-142 formalized parents' participation in the educational planning process of school-age children. Parents were encouraged to become involved, but the nature of the involvement was not clearly delineated. Parents of young children with disabilities often were trained to carry out therapeutic or instructional activities with their children. Although many found their role as "teachers" to be fulfilling, others became frustrated with these teaching expectations. Their lives were too demanding to cope with even one more expectation.

PL 105-17 of 1997 strengthened the recognition of families as integral partners in the early intervention process. The recognition of the family as the legitimate focus of early intervention services was spelled out in the formal requirements of family assessment, family outcomes, and family services within the regulations of PL 105-17. Currently, PL 108-446, the Individuals with Disabilities Education Improvement Act of 2004, further supports the critical role that families play in their child's development by requiring that families receive written notification of their rights and responsibilities annually, rather than just on the initiation of services.

Moving from a child-centered approach in early education to a family-centered approach over several decades has evolved, in concert, with an expanding diversity within our culture. Not only is there cultural and linguistic diversity, but there is greater diversity within the structure of families. Children may be raised by a single parent, two parents, grandparents, or extended family members. Parents may be foster, biological, or adoptive. They may be straight, gay, or lesbian. Our challenge as practitioners is to develop early childhood programs that demonstrate an appreciation of the family's composition and respect the diversity within the families that we seek to support.

The family is recognized as the essential component of the caregiving environment that influences and is influenced by the child over time, resulting in different outcomes for both the child and the family. To understand the reciprocal nature of the relationship between young children with disabilities and their families, the family is viewed as a system with interacting subsystems. No family member is thought to function in isolation from other family members. Therefore, after reviewing some of the needs and emotions that appear to be characteristic of families with disabilities, we explore family dynamics from a **family systems perspective** (Turnbull and Turnbull, 2014).

Emotional Supports for Families with Children Who Have Disabilities

Most new parents start out with little or no preparation to meet the unique, ongoing challenges of caring for a newborn. Even experienced parents must readjust their style of living whenever another child is added to the family. The birth of any child brings adjustments within family systems. According to the 2016 annual report of the Center on Birth Defects and Developmental Disabilities out of the Centers for Disease Control and Prevention, 1 out of 6 children in the United States has a developmental delay or disability (National Center on Birth Defects and Developmental Disabilities [NCBDDD], 2016). Parents of very young children with disabilities must deal not only with the usual adjustments of parenthood but also with additional stresses and concerns for which they likely will be unprepared. Each change in their child's condition brings about new questions, concerns, and challenges. Today, parents can obtain help and emotional support in many ways. For example, some parents may join support groups composed of other parents of children with disabilities. Participants offer support and encouragement to one another and exchange information about useful resources. Some agencies offer individual support through mentors who are experienced parents of children with disabilities. Part C of PL 108-446 mandates that psychological and service coordination services be provided to families of children from birth to 36 months who have developmental delays or are at risk for such delays. When emotionally supportive services are provided while children are very young, adjustments within family systems may be made more readily. However, it must be remembered that the emotional needs of families may be constantly changing, and the emotional and physical demands that accompany the advent of a child with disabilities should never be underestimated. The following description of basic family needs and possible emotional responses is offered to facilitate understanding of individual family reactions.

The Need for Professionals to Respect Families

The family-centered approach requires professionals to respect that parents are essential to a child's healthy development and learning. Early childhood special educators must learn about families, individualize practices and services according to family circumstances, and promote family confidence and competence in raising their child (Trivette & Keilty, 2017). First, parents should be recognized as responsible and caring people who love and want the best for their children. They need to be viewed as individuals capable of effective parenting, and they want to know they are seen in that way. Second, parents should receive the best and most up-to-date information possible that is relevant to their child's diagnosis and circumstances. They want to have confidence in those who profess to know how to help their child. Third, they want and urgently need guidance in what to do in the immediate *now*. Although they want positive opinions about what the future holds, they need to receive useful suggestions immediately. Parents of children with disabilities need encouragement from professionals to remain optimistic about their child's future (Harry, 2010).

Many of the emotional reactions attributed to families may be heightened by the failure of professionals to implement a family-centered approach that respects the family and considers the concerns of individual families that request help. There is no doubt that early education professionals, for the most part, have jumped wholeheartedly into practices designed to address the concerns of not only the child with disabilities but also other family members. However, although early educators may respond to parental concerns, they should realize that some parents may have experienced inadequate and insensitive treatment by other professionals. In these situations, early intervention becomes "early interference" when services dominate and disrupt the family's life (Snow, 2013). We cannot deny that there are professionals who may fail to recognize a disabling condition, convey negative attitudes, withhold important information, or ignore parents' concerns. This realization will help practitioners sustain the patience and develop the empathy necessary to work effectively and sensitively with parents who may be anxious, angry, or troubled.

The Need for Emotional Support

Parents of children with disabilities usually experience a higher level of stress than parents of children without disabilities (Peer & Hillman, 2014). Addressing the emotional needs of parents and other caregivers is essential to promoting a family–professional partnership. The parents' ability to cope effectively with stress will influence how responsive they can be to their child's needs. Parental responsiveness has, indeed, been shown to have a positive influence on child development and well-being (Cook & Sparks, 2008). Brotherson and colleagues (2010) summarize the emotional feelings of families as follows: "(a) a sense of hope in the child's progress, (b) a sense of urgency to provide timely early intervention and prevent or ameliorate the child's disabilities, and (c) a feeling of stress arising from multiple or complex challenges experienced by families" (p. 38).

Different Emotional Responses.   In the following excerpt, a father discusses his perception of how fathers and mothers differ in their responses to distress:

> Stereotypically fathers—and men in general—tend to be characterized as unemotional or angry. While this may be true of some fathers, it's certainly not true of all. The fact is, mothers and fathers respond to distress in different ways. Fathers are typically more task-oriented while mothers are typically more relationship-oriented. Fathers tend to process emotions internally, while mothers tend to process emotions by expressing them directly. For example, if my wife is distressed, she'll immediately seek someone to talk to about how she's feeling. If I'm distressed, I need time to understand how I'm feeling; I might take a walk or hit golf balls. (Auer & Blumberg, 2006, pp. 77–78)

Parental Reactions: Dealing with Grief and Other Feeling States

Numerous writers, both parents and professionals, have described various phases of adjustment in parents' adaptation to their child and his or her disabling condition. The grieving process related to death and dying described by Elizabeth Kübler-Ross (1969) has been used to understand the possible emotional reactions of some parents to the perceived "loss" of the perfect child. It should be noted that more recent literature emphasizes that the possible states of feeling experienced by parents of children with disabilities should *not* be viewed as a linear process of time-limited stages (Brown, 2013). A recent survey of parents' reactions to receiving the diagnosis that their infant has Down syndrome (Nelson Goff et al., 2013) found that although most parents reported initial reactions of shock, fear, anger, and grief, a few reported experiencing relief or the sense that their child was a blessing. In general, parents reported that they gradually experienced more positive feelings during the process of adjustment. Table 2.1 is a summary of the emotional reactions that may be experienced by families with children who have disabilities.

It is important to remember, however, that parental reactions are individual and unique. Some parents and professionals take issue with the whole concept of stages or phases of emotional adjustment (Turnbull et al., 2014). Also note that much of the literature about grieving comes from the work of European-American professionals who are describing their cultural peers. *Understanding the impact of disabilities on the great diversity of families within our country is a continuing challenge to professionals because the process of adaptation is not yet fully understood.* Hanson and Lynch (2013) provide important considerations of how different cultures view disabilities.

Early childhood special educators should be aware that individual family members may experience many feelings at one time, in various sequences, and at different times. Even when parents have adapted to their child's disability, a life event happens that may elicit some of their earlier feelings. For example, just realizing that their child may not be able to go out into the neighborhood with siblings can bring back feelings of sadness and loss. Given that the processes by which parents adapt to their reactions and the challenges before them are not yet understood, it is the professional's responsibility to be prepared to *listen* without judgment while providing accurate information and promoting access to available resources. It is also possible that professionals should be prepared to be accepting of parents who may feel that their emotional reactions are no one else's business. The following summary of feeling states is intended to increase the professional's sensitivity to the emotions that parents may experience and to promote compassion and understanding of each family's circumstances. (Professionals must never use these terms to label a parent's feelings.)

Shock, Disbelief, and Denial

Parents and professionals alike describe the initial reaction of many parents as one of shock and disbelief on learning of a child's disability or disfigurement. This shock and possible disbelief may be accompanied by feelings of shame, guilt, and unworthiness. As the reality of the child's condition is slowly assimilated, parents may try to deny the existing problems. Often, first attempts to find out what is wrong are really attempts to find someone who will say that nothing is wrong. For this reason, some search for answers by going to different specialists to seek opinions. Some parents do this, however, because each professional recommends that they seek additional opinions. Diagnosis of problems in young children is far from an exact science. Rather, it is a piecing together of diverse observations, bits of information, and confusing evidence.

Table 2.1 Possible Parental Reactions

Family Reactions	Feeling States	Possible Service Provider Reactions	What You Can Do
• Shame, guilt, unworthiness, overcompensation • Disbelief • "He's just like his father" • "Don't worry; he'll grow out of it" • Shopping for a diagnosis • Research mode (seeks all information/shuts down from communicating with others)	Shock, disbelief, and denial	• Frustration and concern that parent isn't moving fast enough or doing enough for the child • Anger or resentment • If you were the one to approach the parent initially, fear or uncertainty that maybe you made a mistake • Discomfort	• Listen with compassion. • Employ active listening. • Work together on behalf of the child. • Have patience. • Provide resources, if appropriate (e.g., referral for parent-to-parent support or for assessment). • Understand and honor different cultural views.
• Anger can be transferred to provider or other caregivers • Verbal abuse is common • Blaming others • Resenting others who have healthy children or children without disabilities	Anger and resentment	• Feeling hurt that parent is taking it out on you • Concern that family may display anger around child, which could be damaging to child • "Get over it" attitude • Easy to be provoked by parent because the parent is looking for a "fight"	• Do not take parent reactions personally. • Build parent confidence through successful interactions with their child. • Support and model positive parent–child interactions, and offer suggestions for what works. • Convey understanding, compassion, and caring.
• Delays acceptance of the inevitable • Working with determination (or vengeance/vehemence) • Let's make a deal: "If I do this . . . ," then this will happen • Can lead to depression when things don't go well	Bargaining	• In an effort to help the parent, it is easy to get hooked into the parent's state or stage • You can't "fix" the child—make him or her better or progress faster—which can lead to your frustration	• Show family "empathic understanding"—accept their feelings. • Help parents understand that their feelings are normal and that it's OK. • Communicate with honesty: "It must be very frustrating for you."
• Feeling of "What's the use?" or "Why bother?" • Helplessness and hopelessness • Mourning the loss of the "perfect" or healthy child	Depression and discouragement	• Potential to do too much for the child and family • Comments such as "When I hold her like this, she sits up better" can lead to the parent feeling like a failure ("She doesn't do that at home") • Setting up unrealistic expectations: "He'll be walking any time now." • Guilt that you can't "fix it"	• Help parent break down tasks into small activities. • Help parent identify the child's strengths—not focus on his or her needs. • Assure success of activities or interventions. • Help parents feel confident in their parenting skills. • Provide referrals for professional counseling or other support services.
• Realization that something can be done • Adjustment in lifestyle • Adaptation to the child's needs • Willingness to do practical things	Adaptation and adjustment	• Relief • Fear of the unknown, that you may not be able to meet the child's needs	• Encourage comfort from other parents; link families to support systems. • Encourage patience. • Model positive interaction techniques. • Praise parents when child shows progress. • Maintain open, regular communication with family. • Partner with other service providers; invite them to visit your program. • Encourage family to request your presence at special education meetings; get copies of information.

Source: Adapted from Cook, Klein, and Chen (2016).

The Positive Role of Denial. Some time ago, Gallagher, Fialka, Rhodes, and Arceneaux (2002) urged the rethinking of the role of denial by reminding us that "people need time to find their own personal way through unexpected news. Sometimes parents 'put the pause button on' to attempt to slow down the speed of change" (p. 14). What may be viewed as denial might serve to protect the family when they are not yet able to deal with a difficult problem and provides time for them to integrate complicated information and complex feelings.

Early Childhood Special Educators Can Help. Parents need help to understand that their feelings and initial reactions are appropriate and natural. Professionals need to listen with compassion and patience. Pushing parents to "face the child's limitations" is a harsh professionally driven approach that disrespects families and will only create defensiveness and inhibit the development of a trusting parent–professional relationship. Professionals must learn to allow family members to experience their reactions and emotions. In time, parents will most likely have the emotional strength to adjust to the reality of their situation. Professionals must be nonjudgmental, active listeners while providing easy-to-understand information and appropriate referral sources.

Anger and Resentment

Once parents are able to face the reality of their child's difficulties, they may experience feelings of anger, resentment, rage, or envy. They may be angry at the medical systems, therapists, teachers, or schools if they have received unhelpful recommendations or have been disappointed by unrealistic medical or educational interventions. Their children may have endured unsuccessful or stressful procedures. They may even direct their anger at the very professionals who are trying to help the most. Suspicions about a professional's motives may explode in angry accusations. In these circumstances, practitioners need to demonstrate true professionalism by showing understanding, compassion, and genuine caring. They should recognize that parents have a right to be angry and should not take these feelings personally. According to Fialka (2016), professionals should not be intimidated by or personalize a parent's anger; rather, they should listen, acknowledge, and accept the parent's strong feelings.

Build Parent Confidence.   Over time, angry feelings will usually fade with positive and successful experiences with the child. This is not the time to try to make changes with either the children or their parents. Rather, the parents need to get constant reminders that they do indeed make a difference to the quality of life for their children. They must discover and rediscover that they have resources within themselves that they did not know were there. They must be provided with supports that match their individual concerns and challenges.

Bargaining

Some parents may try to resolve their anger and resentment by going through what Kübler-Ross (1969) in her classic resource described as a process of bargaining. It resembles an attempt to postpone complete intellectual and emotional acceptance of the inevitable. During this time, parents and other family members may work with great diligence and determination. It is as if they are saying, "If I do everything you tell me to do, then surely this problem will go away." If progress is not as rapid or as great as they expect, bargaining is sometimes followed by the gray-black world of depression.

Empathy Is Essential.   To be helpful, practitioners must display empathic understanding by accurately perceiving, accepting, and actively trying to understand the natural feelings of the parents. **Empathy** is defined in the *Collins English Dictionary* as "the ability to share another person's feelings and emotions as if they were your own." Helping parents realize that their feelings and emotional states are natural can convey an attitude of interest and caring. A simple statement reflecting active listening, such as "It must be very frustrating and tiring to have to take your child to so many medical appointments," will acknowledge and validate the parent's feelings. Validation of feelings is a powerful strategy that conveys to parents that their feelings are genuine, respected, and understandable (Failka, 2016). Although only family members in the situation can have true understanding, genuine empathic responses by service providers can go a long way in supporting parents during these difficult times.

Depression and Discouragement

"What's the use?" and "Why bother?" can become the reactions of some parents to all suggestions. An oppressive weight of hopelessness can add new dimensions to the existing problems. It is common for parents to feel totally powerless. Because they feel helpless, parents may be more likely to ask for assistance. From experience, Santelli, Poyadue, and Young (2001) point out that because these feelings are terrifying, "it is hard to believe that depression is a normal and necessary part of the grieving and adjustment process. Acknowledging and working through the sadness that accompanies personal loss is an important part of the adjustment process" (p. 7).

Provide Meaningful Help.   Encourage parents to identify what's working well. Discuss the child's strengths. Recognize that a parent's overwhelming feelings of helplessness may result in difficulty managing everyday tasks and keeping appointments, lack of sleep, or appearing unkempt or tired. In these circumstances, professionals could ask whether any family members can assist with child care if the parent is interested in respite services, encourage parents to break down tasks into smaller activities, encourage parents to ask family and friends to help out, and identify possible ways for parents to take care of themselves. Service providers can reassure parents that there may be times when they need to take a break and recharge their personal resources. Professionals will want to listen for opportunities to have this discussion without giving advice. An empathic service provider can invite discussion about referrals for counseling support if the parent is open to this suggestion. Often, the simplest way is to listen carefully to the cry of "What's the use?" and then suggest the parent may find help in many ways. An informal parent support group may help some parents find comfort from one another. Many might benefit from an opportunity to look through a carefully developed file of local resources, including churches, synagogues, mental health agencies, and parenting groups.

Adaptation and Adjustment

As time passes and families have come to experience support and positive ways to make adaptations to accommodate the needs of their child as well as the family as a whole, the intense emotional feelings tend to give way to more positive emotions. Parents typically develop an increasing willingness to do practical, useful things—they have a willingness to learn and to apply new knowledge to meet day-to-day demands. Hopefully, they come to realize that each human being is unique, special, and worthy of love and affection. Even after considering the intensity of feelings that parents might navigate, it is important to realize that there is increasing recognition and growing research showing that a significant number of parents actually report numerous benefits and positive outcomes for their families associated with raising a child with disabilities. Research is also indicating that family reactions to the challenges of raising a child with disabilities may be heavily influenced by one's cultural background. For example, in a study examining the positive impact of a child with an intellectual disability, Blacher and colleagues (2013) found that Latino mothers had higher scores on the positive impact of having a child with intellectual disabilities than did Anglo mothers.

Stages of Adaptation.   Given that not all parents have reported being adversely affected by raising a child with disabilities, professionals are increasingly assuming a more positive approach to understanding the cycle of adaptation. This is also evident in the Part C legal requirement that services address the "concerns and priorities" of the family, rather than the child's "needs." Ray and colleagues (2009) describe a more positive alternative to the "grief" view of adjustment. It includes the following four levels:

1. **The ostrich phase.** The disability is not denied. Instead, the family has not fully realized its impact. For example, a child may be hyperactive just because he is a boy.

2. **Special designation.** Recognizing that their child may be facing unique challenges, parents seek help.

3. **Normalization.** Some parents may try to minimize the realization that their child might be different by asking for more time engaged in general education or fewer services.

4. **Self-actualization.** Parents accept that their child may be different, but that is OK.

Nevertheless, it is important to respect and not judge or label a parent's feelings. What is important is not understanding what stage of adjustment the family might be experiencing, but just knowing and accepting the uniqueness of each family's reactions as they work through their feelings differently and at various paces.

A Father's Perspective

Over time, parents adjust to having a child with a disability in the family. They adapt to learning skillful ways to alter the negative effects of the condition. Some parents report positive outcomes such as increased family cohesiveness and personal growth (Collings, 2008). Consider how a father might react when having a child with a disability: His view of himself as a father is influenced by roles and traditions. He may think of himself, consciously or unconsciously, as a "provider," "hunter-gatherer," and the "strong one," more than as "child rearer." These roles are traditional and were developed to help raise typical children without disabilities. Different traditions and roles are needed to successfully father a child with a disability in today's world.

Given today's stressful environment, family roles continue to change with more and more mothers working outside of the home. Therefore, it is even more important for early educators to reach out to engage with fathers as well as mothers. McClure (2017) offered the following tips to facilitate the involvement of fathers: (1) Enhance communication by learning both parent's names, directing all communication to both parents, inviting mothers and fathers to participate in all events, and reaching out personally to any who rarely or never visit to let them know how important their involvement is. (2) Offer activities for both parents, as dads tend to prefer activities with their wives and families. (3) Schedule activities after work hours. Parents who work can be asked to help with tasks that can be done at home, such as preparing objects for art lessons. (4) Encourage in-class participation by building on the interests or talents of family members. Perhaps they play an instrument or would like to read a favorite book to the children. (5) Tell each family member how much you appreciate their involvement, and not just on Father's Day.

Based on a review of the research on fathers of individuals with intellectual disabilities, Davys, Mitchell, and Martin (2017) offer additional suggestions: (1) provide information to help fathers understand their child's disability and specific ways to support the child's development, (2) give opportunities for fathers to share their experiences with other men, and (3) recognize the significance of father–child interactions and find ways to promote this relationship.

Auer and Blumberg (2006) offer this advice: "Fathers need to see what their children can do. When fathers understand the strengths and challenges of their child . . . , they're less likely to overprotect or set unrealistic expectations. Knowing their child's strengths can also alleviate some of the emotional strain caused by the worry that peers may not accept the child" (p. 86). When fathers participate in class, they may see their child doing something they did not know he or she could do.

Transitions

Parents often report that they re-experience some of the feeling states described earlier in this chapter. This is especially likely to occur at certain milestones, such as a child's birthday, or times when change or a transition is required, such as when children move from the intimacy of home-based services to classroom services in a public school. An especially vulnerable time is when children transition from school to the world

of work. Given that so many parents find this transition difficult, we can assume that periods of heightened emotional responses will reappear throughout life. Some parents conceal their feelings of heightened emotion from professionals; others do not. Nevertheless, a supportive atmosphere that offers help and encourages adaptations can make a significant difference. Parents are comforted when they know someone understands their need to cry, yell, or scream. Rather than viewing the family's reactions and feelings on a continuum of denial to acceptance, service providers should listen carefully to the family's concerns and identify opportunities to offer relevant suggestions and appropriate supports.

> **Enhanced eText** Application Exercise 2.1: In this exercise, you can apply what you have learned about the purpose of the feeling state of denial for a parent whose child has been diagnosed as having a disability.

The Family as a System

From a family systems perspective, the reciprocal nature of the relationship between young children with disabilities and their families becomes clearer. No family member is seen to function in isolation from other family members. Any intervention with one family member is found to affect other members and interactions in the family (Hanson & Lynch, 2013). The needs of the child and of the parents or siblings are viewed within the context of the entire family as it functions within the larger societal/ecological system. Every family system is composed of relational or interactive subsystems. Turnbull et al. (2014) describe four such subsystems: the **marital subsystem** (parent–parent), **parental subsystem** (parent–child), **sibling subsystem** (child–child), and **extended family subsystem** (family–extended family). Of course, the actual makeup of families differs greatly. For example, single-parent families may have no marital subsystem. However, a single-parent family may have more than one person exercising a parental role if extended family members are actively involved.

How a family member functions in one role in a subsystem is not predictive of how he or she will behave in another subsystem. Parents behave differently when interacting with one another than they do when interacting with their children. Whole families behave differently toward one another at home than they do when visiting with their neighbors. The advent of a child with disabilities has implications for all four subsystems. The disabilities of the child may impose additional stress on the marital relationship, whereas the extended family subsystem may be hardly affected. There may be no sibling subsystem if fear of giving birth to another child with a disability curtails future pregnancies. Alternatively, older siblings may be brought into the parental role to help alleviate the stress placed on either the marital or parental subsystem. Anything that happens in one subsystem has effects on all the others.

The manner in which a child with disabilities affects family members cannot be predicted or assumed because families differ along many dimensions. **Family structure** has changed dramatically in the past two decades. More and more children are living in single-parent or blended families. A growing number of grandparents have been thrust, once again, into the role of primary parents. Family membership or structure is also changing in terms of gender makeup. Increasingly, same-sex couples are creating families that include children. Professionals can better understand and appreciate family dynamics by fostering an awareness of the changing dynamics within family systems today. Professionals who look at each family in relation to its own interactional system and the manner in which these interactions fulfill the tasks of daily life will find it easier to provide services to meet the total needs of the family. As identified by Turnbull et al. (2014) in their discussion of the family system:

1. Every family is unique in composition, characteristics, culture, and lifestyle.

2. The family is an interactional system with some boundaries that may be rigid, while others are more flexible.

3. All families fulfill a variety of functions that maintain the system and support its members' growth and development.

4. All families experience various changes and transitions that create stress that each member may experience to different degrees.

Interventions planned from a family systems perspective also carefully consider the four major family components: family resources, family interactions, family functions, and the family life cycle. **Family resources** include the characteristics and strengths each family member brings to the family as they interact to meet the needs of the family. *The nature of each individual's personality, values and beliefs, health status, motivation, and desires as well as cultural background will determine the nature of the interaction or relationships developed. The effectiveness of early intervention may depend on the existence of productive interactions between the resources of professionals and the resources of families.*

Family interactions are the processes that families use to accomplish the duties or functions of the family system. Families meet their needs through such processes as sharing affection, planning together, resolving conflicts, teaching new skills, and accomplishing daily tasks. **Family functions** are the outputs of the interactional system. Turnbull et al. (2014) identify eight categories of family functions essential to meeting the needs of family members: affection, self-esteem, spirituality, daily care, economics, socialization, recreation, and education.

By working with families to understand how and when family members interact with one another while accomplishing the work or functions of the family, families can be encouraged to promote their child's learning needs during daily activities. For example, while bathing their young child, they can label body parts to encourage self-identity, body image, and vocabulary development and use gentle touch to convey affection and guidance.

Family life cycle refers to the developmental and nondevelopmental changes that alter the family's structure and needs over time. Issues evolving at each stage in the family life cycle have an impact on every member of the family. Table 2.2 lists an array of possible issues encountered when the child with disabilities is in the early childhood life-cycle stage. Of course, it is not enough to support families during the early years. They must be guided to develop coping strategies that will help them avoid the burnout that can result from lifelong challenges.

Table 2.2 Possible Issues Encountered During the Early Childhood Years

Life-Cycle Stage	Parents	Siblings
Early Childhood, Ages 0–5	Obtaining an accurate diagnosis Informing siblings and relatives Locating services Seeking to find meaning in the exceptionality Clarifying a personal ideology to guide decision making Addressing issues of stigma Identifying positive contributions of exceptionality	Less parental time and energy for sibling needs Feelings of jealousy over less attention Fears associated with misunderstandings of exceptionality

Source: Ann P. Turnbull, Patricia A. Barber, Shirley K. Behr, and Georgia M. Kerns. Family systems perspectives on early childhood special education in *Early Intervention for Infants and Children with Handicaps.* Paul H. Brookes Publishing Company, 1988, pp. 179–198.

As stated by Johnson and Kastner (2005), "A family's requirement for community supports depends not only on the characteristics of the child, but also on the structural, functional and external characteristics of the family" (p. 507). What professionals need to remember is that it is not only important to provide support, but the way in which support is provided determines whether or not there are positive results. "Family-systems intervention practices help put in place those resources and supports that ensure parents have the time and energy to interact with their children in ways that provide them development-enhancing experiences and opportunities promoting learning and development" (Trivette, Dunst, & Hamby, 2010b, p. 15).

Extended Family and Sibling Needs and Reactions

As predicted from family systems theory, extended family and siblings also have needs and reactions. Grandparents grieve deeply, too. Theirs is often a double hurt because they not only experience pain for their grandchild but they also grieve for their own children. Seeing a loved son or daughter try to cope with long-term problems is disheartening. One grandfather arrived at a diagnostic clinic with a blank check. "Just tell me what it costs," he said. "I'll find the money somehow."

Denial, blame, and anger may run rampant among grandparents. They may say, "It's because she smoked while she was pregnant," or "His family never was any good," or "If only they hadn't. . . . " In such cases, there is no doubt to whom the angry grandparents are referring.

In one of the few studies recognizing the increase in care by adult relatives other than parents, Gallagher, Kresak, and Rhodes (2010) highlight the unique needs of grandparents. These include needs for information, respite, and techniques for dealing with behaviors and/or language difficulties that are related to disabilities. These authors recommend that issues of behavior be discussed with grandparents and that extra effort be put forth to link grandparents with community resources such as summer camps that will provide respite. Grandparent caregivers often need legal information so they can understand their rights as caregivers. Services will be more effective if professionals also understand the grandparents' legal status and the biological parents' role in the child's life. All those who spend much time caring for a child with disabilities will find it helpful to be included in conferences and teaching demonstrations. Often, involved grandparents feel left out and deeply confused about what they should do. Professionals must be sensitive to this and, with the parents' approval, include these extended family members whenever possible. Turnbull and colleagues (2014, p. 41) offer the following suggestions on providing needed information and resources to assist extended family members:

- Provide information that will help parents understand the needs and reactions of grandparents.
- Encourage the development of grandparent support groups.
- Assist in matching grandparents with other grandparents who can provide support to each other.
- Encourage grandparents' participation in individualized education program (IEP) or individualized family service plan (IFSP) conferences and other school events.
- Provide library materials, communication, or Internet resources to grandparents.

Siblings

When viewing families from a systems perspective, it is readily apparent that attention must also be paid to the changing needs of siblings without disabilities. For example, young children may need to be reassured that they cannot catch their sibling's disability. School-age children need information to answer their own questions and those posed by peers about their sibling's disability. Teenagers and young adults need additional information about their sibling's future and the role they will play in that future. Bringing siblings "into the loop" through inclusion in meetings as valued members of the team benefits all members of the family.

Parents and professionals can help siblings talk about their feelings and promote positive relationships among siblings. An effective way is to provide siblings with opportunities to support the learning and participation of their brother or sister with disabilities. Even a very young child can learn to be an effective role model, particularly when there is a positive sibling relationship. Given the immense variability in family members' responses to disability, it is imperative that parents and professionals be sensitive in their expectations and requests of siblings. Parent reporters indicate that siblings of children with disabilities are more likely than siblings of typically developing children to have problems related to interpersonal relationships, school functioning, use of leisure time, behavior at home, and feeling unhappy or afraid (Goudie, Havercamp, Jamieson, & Sahr, 2013). Even so, research tends to support the notion that having a sibling with a disability is generally a positive experience (Turnbull et al., 2014).

In reviewing the literature examining the relationship between siblings with and without disabilities, Moore, Howard, and McLaughlin (2002) noted the following possible characteristic reactions:

1. Young children frequently believe that they have caused their sibling's problem and may try to compensate by being particularly well behaved. However, feelings of jealousy and envy may arise when their needs are neglected by parents who are striving to cope. Others may act out in response to feelings of isolation should their parents be preoccupied with the needs of their disabled sibling.

2. School-age children may be expected to look after their disabled sibling if they attend the same school. They might also experience social stigmatization when their disabled sibling starts public school. The resulting frustration can be in conflict with their desire to defend their sibling. Nondisabled siblings who are younger may even worry about surpassing their older sibling with disabilities.

3. Although adolescents may have a better understanding of their sibling's disability, they nevertheless often continue to encounter the stigma and embarrassment of having a sibling with disabilities. There may also be uncertainty regarding the potential for genetic inheritance of the disability.

Even though these are a few of the more characteristic reactions, it must be remembered that variations within family systems and the uniqueness of individual development create a multitude of potential responses. The Sibling Leadership Network (2013a) provides key findings of studies on siblings under 18 years of age compared to siblings of children without disabilities: (1) Young siblings of children with disabilities are more likely to have a positive self-image and exhibit more empathy and understanding toward people with disabilities. (2) Findings about negative experiences are mixed, with some studies finding an increase in behavioral problems, anxiety, and depression among siblings of children with disabilities, while other studies find no difference. (3) Childhood relationships between siblings tend to be close and positive. There are mixed findings regarding conflicts between siblings. Some studies report more fights, while others find no difference in sibling conflicts. (4) Siblings of children with disabilities have more caregiving responsibilities than siblings of children without disabilities. Some studies indicate that increased caregiving relates to a better understanding of others, while other studies find that increased caregiving leads to more anxiety and less time spent with friends. (5) Many IFSP or transition plans of older children do not include their siblings.

The Sibling Leadership Network (2013b) also highlights findings from studies of adult siblings (18 years and older) indicating that (1) these siblings also have positive relationships with their sibling with a disability, (2) these experiences are likely to influence their life choices (marriage and career decisions), (3) sisters tend to report having closer relationships with their siblings with a disability compared to brothers, and (4) about 60% of these adult siblings anticipate being primary caregivers and tend to be those with close relationships. Siblings should be included in transition meetings and plans and in planning for the future. Therefore, it is essential to address lifespan issues given that siblings play varying roles and face a variety of issues at different phases in life and, perhaps especially, during transition points (Heller & Kaiser, 2017).

One should never assume that parents are unaware of the impact of a sibling with a disability on brothers and sisters. Professionals need to listen carefully and take the time to learn about the concerns of the whole family—not just the child with disabilities and his or her parents. For instance, when parents have concerns about how to respond to another child's question about his or her sibling with a disability, practitioners can listen and encourage parents to think about and practice how they might respond. Based on her experience responding to questions and comments from her daughter about her brother's disability, Failka (2016) outlines the following: "(1) Answer questions directly; (2) show no strong emotions; (3) pause, wait, give time to hear her thought; and (4) remember that her questions are not burdened by the same reality as yours" (p. 44).

To foster positive relationships between children with disabilities and their siblings, the Pacer Center (2013) offered these tips to parents, gleaned from sibling interviews: (1) Provide open communication to encourage discussion of siblings' questions and concerns; (2) talk about their brother or sister's disability and how it affects the child so siblings have information, can teach others, and become advocates; (3) have realistic expectations for all your children and let siblings know they are not expected to be "super kids"; (4) learn about the world of siblings through readings and resources; (5) engage in activities for the whole family as well as plan individual time with each sibling; (6) find ways for all your children to be involved in community activities; (7) recognize that siblings have a right to their own lives, particularly as they get older; (8) celebrate all your children's accomplishments; and (9) find opportunities for siblings to meet other brothers and sisters of children with disabilities.

Regardless of the age or relationship of extended family members, the practitioner must be tactful, open, and honest. The parents' feelings and attitudes must always be given careful consideration and top priority. Everyone in the family interacts in some way with everyone else. Insofar as the practitioner can influence these interactions in positive ways, the children will gain. Having faith that one can be a positive help to a child with disabilities buoys young siblings and mature grandparents. Specific tasks at which success is guaranteed are the place to begin. Then everyone benefits.

Parents as Team Members

Professionals have become more aware that parents or other caregivers play an important role in not only providing an emotional support system for the developing child but also as contributing team members in educating their child at home and in school. However, some parents of young children with disabilities believe that often too much emphasis is placed on the parent as teacher. To avoid creating additional stress, professionals will want to try not to overwhelm parents who are becoming involved in their child's education.

In helping families understand the learning and development needs of a child with a disability, professionals who evaluate children's skills and developmental levels are expected to communicate the results of their testing to parents meaningfully. If family members are to become contributing team members who are **empowered,** they first need to understand what the professionals are talking about. This means that information must not be given in professional jargon. Professionals can translate test results and implications into layperson's language. For example, telling parents that their child may have a "visual perceptual problem" is meaningless to many of them. But parents can grasp their child's problem readily when the practitioner describes tasks using the eyes and hands at the same time, such as utilizing a spoon for eating, putting together puzzles, playing with blocks, or placing toys in a toy box.

Options for Family Engagement

Just as children with disabilities and children without disabilities are more alike than different, so are the parents of both groups more alike than different. They have needs, frustrations, hopes, fears, and dreams similar to those of any other parent, although they also have feelings that may be unique to parents of children with disabilities. Even so, educators cannot expect to use the same method of working with all families, just as they cannot expect to resort to the same method of working with all children.

As professionals have increased their awareness of how families function and the impact of the family on the outcome of intervention services, a philosophy of intervention has emerged known as **family-centered practice**. This philosophy moves intervention efforts from an agency-oriented or professionally directed approach to a family-oriented or family-centered approach.

According to the Division for Early Childhood's Recommended Practices, family-centered practices "treat families with dignity and respect; are individualized, flexible, and responsive to each family's unique characteristics; provide family members complete and unbiased information to make informed decisions; and involve family members in acting on choices to strengthen child, parent, and family functioning (2014, p. 10). Hanson and Lynch (2013) offer the following characteristics of family-centered practice: It (1) recognizes parents or primary caregivers as experts on their child; (2) acknowledges the family as the ultimate decision maker for their child and themselves; (3) views the family as the constant in the child's life and the service providers and systems as transitory; (4) respects and works to support family priorities, their goals for service, and the extent to which they choose to be involved; (5) values trusting, collaborative relationships between parents and professionals; and (6) works to ensure culturally competent services.

In an effort to become more family-centered, early childhood educators must recognize the impact of a **family's quality of life** on the success of early intervention and inclusion (Purcell, Turnbull, & Jackson, 2006). To that end, the Beach Center on Disability (2014) has developed a Family Quality of Life Survey that identifies five quality-of-life domains: physical-material well-being, disability-related support, family interaction, parenting, and emotional well-being. This chapter emphasizes a family-centered approach and discusses a number of activities that will, it is hoped, enhance the quality of life of participating families.

As the tenets just listed suggest, the development and implementation of family-centered services require a change in roles and relationships. Intervention practitioners are guided by family–professional collaboration, with families as the primary decision makers. Professionals are no longer considered to be "the experts." Instead, parents and professionals are expected to create relationships built on respect and appreciation for what each can contribute to the development and implementation of effective intervention practices.

The IFSP outcomes and IEP goals and objectives are derived from each family's concerns and priorities. Family members are encouraged to choose how and when they wish to be involved. To the greatest possible extent, professionals are encouraged to provide opportunities for family involvement that will fit into the family's daily living routines.

It is extremely important to remember that families should clearly feel that participation is, indeed, an *option*. Professionals are expected to help families understand the continuum of services and opportunities from which they may make choices. Procedures for helping families identify their resources and needs, as well as appropriate participation options, are discussed in Chapter 3.

A Continuum

Even though PL 108-446 sets the stage for family-centered practice, in reality family engagement falls along a continuum. Some families may elect not to be involved, whereas others will seek the fullest possible involvement. It is hoped that families will be open to active participation in decision making, program implementation, and advocacy activities. Family needs, values, and lifestyles, as well as program characteristics, are likely to determine the level of family engagement. It is the intent of the IFSP to clearly delineate the level of both family and professional involvement. *It is important for professionals to avoid implying that the degree of parent engagement is synonymous with parent concern. Parent engagement is certainly not a measure of parent concern about their child.*

Individual needs and capabilities must be balanced with the goals of parent engagement. Some parents have a greater need and capacity for information delivered through lectures, panel discussions, and films. Other parents may most desire and need one-to-one conversations with a professional when privacy is ensured and they can feel comfortably accepted. Whatever strategies early childhood educators use to encourage family engagement, success will most likely depend on the ability of the professionals to develop a sense of trust (Smith, Gartin, Murdick, & Hilton, 2006).

Much of this chapter focuses on the primary considerations to be thought through carefully in making each type of engagement effective. After all, parents are involved in their child's development and learning in various ways. The focus here is on whether or not parents are actually engaged with their child's early learning experiences and are working in collaboration with those outside the family who are responsible for their child's growth and development.

What Fathers Say About Their Involvement

Turbiville and Marquis (2001) surveyed 318 fathers of young children from six states. Of the respondents, 28% of the fathers had children with disabilities. They found that the fathers of most children preferred activities in which both the husband and wife could be involved. In fact, activities that were offered only to men resulted in the least participation by fathers. Consistent with earlier literature, fathers preferred activities that involved both men and women learning how to take action to help their child progress and how to solve problems. The degree of father engagement seemed to depend on their being specifically invited at convenient times to activities that are perceived to have learning value. They did not care if the activities were all planned by women and if extras such as refreshments or child care were offered. Fathers appreciated being asked personally to participate (Guthrie, 2000). Research suggests generally more positive outcomes for children with involved fathers (Charlesworth, 2017; Bronte-Tinkew, Carrano, Horowitz, & Kimukawa, 2008). Therefore, it is recommended that professionals seek to understand the conditions under which the fathers they serve would most likely become involved.

Supporting and Partnering with Parents

A major premise of this text revolves around the fact that families are considered the primary context for and facilitators of their children's learning. This premise is not only supported by the advocates of early childhood education, but it is also incorporated into legislation such as the examples noted earlier. Each supportive law contributes toward making parents' involvement in their children's education a national priority.

Souto-Manning (2010) highlights two common barriers to family involvement: time constraints and differing cultural expectations. Today's fast-paced society obviously creates competing demands for time, energy, and resources. Teachers are often concerned with bothering overworked parents who are already coping with the stress resulting from responsibilities related to their child's disability. Of course, scheduling conflicts have long been recognized as a barrier to collaboration.

Often, educators and families have different cultural expectations about the role of parents in their child's educational development. In some cultures, visiting a classroom is considered to be a sign of criticism. In other cases, parents' own negative experiences with schools may have led them to consider schools unresponsive. Parents may have feelings of inadequacy and feel generally reluctant to engage, especially if they have been contacted only when a problem has developed. As noted earlier, the key to effective parental involvement may be the development of a trusting relationship between the staff and parents. Critical to the establishment of a trusting relationship is the assurance that **confidentiality** will be maintained. Parents need the security of knowing that information about their child or their family will not be discussed with other individuals without their written permission. This means that they or their child will not be identified by name at any time or anywhere, including the lunchroom or on the playground, without their knowledge and permission.

A strong parent–professional partnership can be built only through the creation of a classroom climate that is open and accepting. The first few times parents come to the center or classroom will be difficult for them and for their children. Some parents will feel compelled to direct and correct their own children. They may be deeply distressed by every small infraction of the rules. Tears and tantrums are the outward signs of the distress of the children. Nervousness and apologizing for the child's "misbehavior" may be the parents' reaction. With careful planning, the center or classroom staff can prevent or at least minimize most of these problems.

Given the increasing diversity within our classrooms, it is critical that the physical environment also be welcoming and reflect the backgrounds of the children. That is, bulletin board displays, photos, and artwork represent the language, cultural, and family diversity of the children. Children's literature and stories should represent different family compositions, ethnic diversity, and a variety of activities in which families engage. If possible, a bulletin board or book display might feature pictures of every family, including those of staff members.

Maintaining Ongoing Contact with Families. Unlike teachers in general education preschool classrooms, teachers of young children with disabilities must find a way to stay in ongoing contact with families. Logs that go back and forth between homes and classrooms, phone calls, e-mails, and texts facilitate ongoing contact. Other important parent involvement strategies are discussed within this chapter. Most of all, it is essential to develop periodic and ongoing contact with all parents. Teachers should begin with a welcoming telephone call, e-mail, text, or letter long before any problems develop. It is much easier to discuss problems when trust has already been established. Once trust is established, it can only be maintained through ongoing contact.

Through family–professional collaboration and family-centered practices, early childhood special educators should implement family-capacity building practices. These "include the participatory opportunities and experiences afforded to families to strengthen existing parenting knowledge and skills and promote the development

Video Example from YouTube

Enhanced eText
Video Example 2.2
Description of Family–Professional Partnership Framework
https://www.youtube.com/watch?v=Zs4r3P2kgA0
This video presents Dr. Ann Turnbull discussing a framework for developing the family–professional partnership. She refers to the Center to Mobilize Early Childhood Knowledge's CONNECT Module 3 on communication and Module 4 on family–professional partnerships. The links are as follows:
http://community.fpg.unc.edu/connect-modules/learners/module-3
http://community.fpg.unc.edu/connect-modules/learners/module-4

of new parenting abilities that enhance parenting self-efficacy beliefs and practices" (DEC, 2014, p. 10).

First Step: Parents Meet Other Parents.   Before parents begin to observe or participate, they can benefit by meeting with experienced parents. Parents from previous years, whether or not their children are currently enrolled, can be called on to help. If these experienced parents assist with planning and presenting the program, it will be much more believable and useful to the new parents. The opportunity to talk with other parents who have been through the program is the best preparation for new families.

Centers should plan the orientation program *with* parents, not *for* them. Parents themselves can plan the agenda, choosing the items to be discussed and points to be emphasized. Both the nature of the community and the characteristics of the children will influence what needs to be done.

An invitation from the parents who are planning the meeting or from their children is more effective than an invitation from the center. For example, one parent group sent handwritten notes to each new parent a week in advance. A follow-up phone call, including an offer to pick up the new parents, resulted in nearly 100% attendance. Today, digital options facilitate communication, such as through a listserv.

Although traditionally, mothers have been the parents who come to school, fathers can be especially helpful. Having one father call another about an upcoming meeting helps make it seem less strange. Other family members should be included whenever practical.

Evening meetings are usually more convenient for parents. Parents who work at night, however, can be encouraged to come to the center during the day. When properly welcomed, parents have even been known to take a vacation day to attend.

Parents as Observers.   Experienced early childhood educators already realize that involving parents in daily classroom or center activities can be useful in a variety of ways. Teachers are able to model preferred techniques of teaching specific skills and effective approaches to behavior management. Many parents will then be able to translate some of what they have observed into more useful interactions in the home environment. While there may be many benefits that can result from involvement, it is important to remember that it may be nearly impossible for some family members to visit or participate, especially when both parents work full-time.

Teachers should consider flexible and creative ways of teaching parents about ways to promote their child's learning and development. For example, consider (1) sharing videos of the child's activities with parents to demonstrate his or her skills; (2) creating a website to demonstrate specific strategies through short handouts in the children's home languages, video examples, links to other resources, and online discussion options; and (3) conducting a needs assessment to identify topics that are most important to parents (e.g., discipline or early literacy) and schedule these events at times when they can participate.

Parents with specific skills or talents such as in music or art will feel valued about the contributions they can make to the center. Parents who accompany classes on field trips to familiar places such as the grocery store can observe and, ideally, generalize ways of using everyday activities to teach their child. Finally, many parents will feel that their child is more like other children than different from them. As they observe progress over time, they will feel encouraged and more hopeful.

All parents will feel unsure at first, even if they hide their feelings well. They will wonder what their children will do and will expect the worst. Often, their children will oblige. Program staff must strive to make parents feel comfortable and welcome, giving their children specific activities to keep them from seeking attention in undesirable ways.

Interacting with Their Own Child.   If possible, teachers should encourage parents to greet their own child and allow the child to show them around. These social skills must be taught to many children. Initial awkwardness can yield quickly to confidence and security if the program staff sets the stage and does a bit of managing. Cues such as "Show Dad where we keep our big blocks; I'll bet he can build a tall tower" or "Show Mother where we keep the easel and the markers—I wonder if she knows how well you can draw?" may be effective. Naturalness, friendliness, and a comfortable feeling for all should be the goal.

If the parents indicate they would enjoy it, encourage them to play a game with their own child and one or two others. A demonstration by a staff member starts the game, but then the professional should be busy with others to allow the parent the opportunity to develop his or her own style. The intent is to set the stage for parents and children to have a good time and feel at ease.

Keeping the Visit Short.   The time schedule should be understood by everyone before the visit begins. Parents should be encouraged to vary the time of day they visit to create a more complete understanding of their child's involvement in the program.

Providing Observation Guidelines.   Staff can help parents become astute observers by telling them what to look for. A short list of focus points might be helpful. For example, a teacher may wish a parent of Darren, a child with a hearing loss, to observe his reaction to sound in the classroom. She could prepare the following short list:

1. What does Darren do when someone calls his name?
2. Does Darren act differently when I stand directly in front of him and speak to him than when he cannot see my face?
3. Does Darren respond to noises made behind him or anywhere out of sight?

Such a list of focus points makes it easier to discuss the observations with everyone, focusing on the child's behavior rather than more subjective aspects of the child, such as personality. A teacher could prepare the following list to help the parent of Asha, a child who is hyperactive, understand his or her concerns:

1. What was the first thing Asha did? What was the second?
2. Approximately how long did Asha stay with each activity?
3. Which activity held Asha's attention the longest?

Exhibit 2.1 shows a sample of a parent observation form that helps focus the parent's attention.

Follow-Up.   Whenever possible, every parent observation or participation experience should be followed by a brief discussion with the lead teacher either in person or

Exhibit 2.1

Parent Observation Report

Date: _____

Who was involved in this experience?

What happened first?

Then what did the child do?

What did you do, or what did another adult caregiver do?

What were the results?

Do you think you or the other adult caregiver might have done something differently?
   Why or why not?

over the telephone. This provides an opportunity for parents to have their questions answered, and teachers can explain any unique behavior and point out positive attributes of the child.

Parents as Participants. In some programs, parents are encouraged to participate as aides. Parents may be willing to assist the professional in individual center or classroom activities. Such experiences provide excellent opportunities for the professional to model desired strategies for working with young children.

It is often helpful to ask parents to play a game or direct a small-group activity. Children love repetition. If they have experienced the activity before, it will be easier for the parent to facilitate their involvement. The activity should be one that is useful for the parent's own child. The following suggestions are meant to help ensure that parents experience pleasure when participating:

1. Plan activities so that both parents and children can be successful.
2. Choose an activity that can be demonstrated easily. Provide a brief written description of the objective and procedures of the activity.
3. Keep the group small (two or three children).
4. Explain the purpose of the activity. Be specific.
5. Emphasize that learning should be fun even if it is also hard work.
6. Do not emphasize "winning." Children just like to play. Winning and losing are artificial concepts that interfere with learning.
7. Select a game or activity parents can use at home. Most commercial games or lessons can be duplicated with items found in most homes. Whenever possible, choose an activity that will benefit the child and interest his or her parent.
8. Explain specifically how to manage children's errors and misbehaviors. Demonstrate and talk about various techniques. A mistake or "failure" is merely a clue to try another way.

Conferences with Parents

Individual conferences with parents can and should be one of the most effective methods of engagement. Inherent in this approach is flexibility. Either the parent or professional can request the conference. It can be held at the center or at home at any convenient time as long as parents feel the comfort of privacy and confidentiality. The content varies with the needs of the parents, the child, and the professional. The professional can individualize the specific suggestions made and level of language used. With conferences, parents who cannot read or understand written comments do not miss important information about their child.

Critical to the value of conferences is the fact that this is the time for professionals to not only establish trust if still needed, but to truly listen in order to obtain critical information and advice from those who really know their children the best. To avoid stepping on one another's toes while "dancing," the following skills must be developed:

1. The ability to be culturally responsive and develop rapport with all family members
2. The ability to obtain information without appearing to be intrusive
3. The ability to understand family concerns and what information they desire
4. The ability to provide the desired information in easily understood everyday language
5. The ability to problem-solve collaboratively
6. The ability to summarize, help identify new objectives, and make appropriate recommendations

By being aware of the need to develop competence in these important behaviors, professionals who are new to the field can focus on developing habits conducive to a successful partnership.

Preparing for the Conference.   The objectives for conferences should be planned with situational needs in mind. For some, the objectives will be general, such as merely becoming acquainted and helping to assure the parents that their child is well cared for and progressing. Another conference may be requested by the parent or professional because of a specific concern. For example, a teacher may need to know whether Asha is as inattentive and active at home as she is in the classroom. If the teacher understands Asha's parents' attitudes and reactions, she or he may be able to work with Asha's family in developing consistency between school and home. Of course, objectives have to be flexible enough to accommodate families' concerns as well.

The professional should be prepared to provide parents with adequate information. Samples of the child's work, anecdotal records, video recordings, logs, and assessment data should be readily available. Special care must be taken to discuss this information in lay terms. At all times, professionals must ensure that all information exchanged will be held in confidence.

When conferences are initiated by professionals, personal invitations should be extended by telephone, through letters, or via e-mail. A duplicated note is not very personal and does not motivate attendance. Whenever possible, parents should be given a choice of date and time. A quiet, uninterrupted setting must be prepared with comfortable adult-size chairs. The professional should not be seated behind a desk because this puts a distance between him or her and the parent, who may already be tense. Offering a beverage can make the parent feel more relaxed. Babysitting services may need to be arranged because the presence of children distracts the conversation and destroys the confidentiality necessary. Paraprofessionals can help out by taking the child and siblings to another area.

Beginning the Conference.   Often, the initial few minutes of a conference are the most uncomfortable and perhaps the most critical in building the necessary rapport. Initial impressions can create defensiveness that gets in the way of objective thinking and the creation of a productive relationship. Greetings, a handshake, and thanking the parent for coming help the parent see that the professional appreciates his or her effort to become involved. To make the parent feel at ease, it is helpful to begin with nonemotional topics, although these must be brief because the parent is usually eager to get to the purpose of the meeting.

A time limit for the conference should be made clear so the parent will not feel rejected when it is necessary to close the conversation. A statement such as the following can establish the time limit of a conference and clarify the purpose of the meeting: "I am so happy, Ms. Jones, that you are able to share the next 15 minutes with me today. I have so much to tell you about Jamie's progress, and I want to hear how you feel."

If the parent has initiated the conference, the professional might say, "I am so glad, Ms. Dickson, that you felt free to request this conference. I will be free until 4 o'clock and am eager to know where you would like to begin." If the parent hesitates, the professional should try not to become tense. If the silence or apparent reluctance of the parent to speak seems to go on too long, the professional should then make a facilitating comment, such as "It is sometimes hard to express what we are thinking or feeling." All the while, the professional should try to show by body language that he or she cares, is ready to listen, and is not pushy.

Conducting the Conference.   Once the purpose of the conference is clarified, the parent should be encouraged to talk if he or she has said very little. The professional can make a facilitating comment such as "I thought you might share some of your observations and concerns about Jessica so that we can plan a way to work together to help her progress." The professional should then listen very carefully to whatever the parent says. Parents usually express their primary concerns at this time. The professional is also given a glimpse of the sophistication level of the parent and can gear his or her language to that level.

Listening Carefully.   Listening carefully is critical in the development of productive relationships with parents. Hanson and Lynch (2013) state, "Active listening is foundational to the ability to understand others. Good communication cannot occur without the ability to understand the other person's point of view or perspective" (p. 242). Listening is a difficult skill that takes effort to master. However, it is well known that the most effective means of establishing rapport is to show interest in others through attentive listening, which not only encourages parents to express themselves but also demonstrates the professional's acceptance and concern. The following six attending skills continue to be basic to effective listening: door-opening statements, clarifying responses, restatements or paraphrasing, reflection, silence, and summarization.

Minimal encouragers to talk are expressions and nonverbal cues that let the speaker know you want to hear more of what he or she has to say. These are often referred to as *door openers.* Typical of these are such comments as "uh-huh," "yes," "that's interesting," and "hmmm." These can be useful in getting parents to continue talking, but they should not be overused or used stereotypically. The professional should be certain not to interrupt the parent with these or other comments. Leaning somewhat forward is usually a sign of listening and trying to focus on what is being said.

Clarifying responses help the listener to understand the parent or family member when, for some reason, one is unable to follow what has been said. Responses such as "I'm not sure I understand exactly what you mean. Could you say that again?" elicit clarification. Such responses encourage the speaker to elaborate and demonstrate the professional's interest and concern. They can also be used when the professional isn't sure the information he or she has offered has been clearly understood. For example, one might ask, "What is your understanding of what you have been told?"

Paraphrasing occurs when the professional attempts to restate to the parent in revised form what he or she has just said. This demonstrates that what the speaker said has been heard and gives the speaker the chance to clarify any misunderstanding the professional may have. Often, parents are more able to absorb and understand their own thoughts and motivations when they are restated by another person. This process can also help secure agreement between what is being said and what is perceived. A professional might say, "If I understand correctly, you are afraid other children will not play with Sarah because she cannot talk clearly."

Reflection involves comments that let the parent know the professional has heard and understood what the parent is saying. It helps to focus the parent's comments by recognizing a specific comment. It is a cue to parents to elaborate on that specific idea, concept, or question. If the reflection also includes the *feeling* that is perceived, then the professional will be demonstrating **active listening**. Consider the following example of a partial reflection and a reflection involving the feeling necessary for active listening:

> Parent: I had thought that when he began physical therapy, his walking would improve.

> Teacher: Would improve? Oh, you sound pretty frustrated about his progress.

Exhibit 2.2, which depicts a home conference, illustrates the skills involved in effective communication.

Active or reflective listening allows the listener to show sensitivity to the feelings and emotions being expressed as well as the content. It legitimizes the speaker's feelings and communicates that the emotions being expressed are acceptable. Active listening enables the listener to (1) respond to the speaker's affect by accurately and sensitively perceiving the speaker's apparent and underlying feelings, and (2) express

Exhibit 2.2

Dialogue: A Conference Between Parent and Teacher

SCENE: Matt is a 4-year-old who has been described by his mother as "never still" and by his father as "all boy." In the past week, the mother reports that several of her favorite plants have crashed to the floor as Matt walked by. "He never does anything mean or on purpose," she said. Rather, he bumps into things and is surprised when adults complain or he breaks things. It is time for Ms. McLynn's first home visit. Matt's mother, Ms. G., greets her at the door.

Ms. G.: Hello. Matt has been so excited about your coming, and when he heard you knock, he hid under the bed!

Ms. McL.: Good to be here, Ms. G. At school Matt is so helpful. I can always count on Matt to see what needs doing and to do it. He seems to sense the other children's needs, as well as mine.

Ms. G.: But he is so rough. And always breaking something. My neighbors say he is hyperactive.

Ms. McL.: What does that mean to them?

Ms. G.: Oh, you know, never still. He just can't seem to be quiet for a minute.

Ms. McL.: But he has been very quiet since I've been here.

Ms. G.: He's still hiding under the bed. Oh, he can be quiet when he wants to be.

Ms. McL.: So you feel he really does have control of how active he is?

Ms. G.: Yes, I guess so. But just tell him to sit still and he bounces all over the place.

Ms. McL.: You feel he is too active.

MS. G.: Yes. And he won't listen when I tell him to sit still. That burns me up.

Ms. McL.: His constant moving annoys you.

Ms. G.: You bet it does. What can I do to make him behave? I've tried spanking, but he forgets right away.

Ms. McL.: From watching at school and with what you told me, I'd like to suggest that we both try something. Let's catch him being quiet and gentle.

Ms. G.: When? How?

Ms. McL.: At school I'll keep a special paper on my desk. Every time he is quiet or gentle, I'll say something like, "Matt, I like the way you helped Missy with her coat. You were so gentle," or "Matt, you are doing a good job with that puzzle. You are so quiet that I can hear the birds singing outside." Then, I'll make a quick note—for example, 9:03—Quiet and gentle. Helped Missy with coat. 9:10—Worked puzzle. Quiet 3 minutes.

Ms. G.: Well, it can't hurt.

Ms. McL.: I'll call you in 2 days to see how it's working.

And 2 days later when Ms. McLynn called, she was not surprised that Ms. G. could report more quiet and gentle times than noisy ones. So could Ms. McLynn.

understanding of those feelings in words that are attuned to the other person's experience at the moment (Turnbull & Turnbull, 2006). The listener can be effective only if she or he is willing and able to devote the time necessary to allow the speaker to fully express him- or herself. Considering the emotional needs of parents of children with disabilities, it is well worth the effort to invest the energy necessary to become an active listener.

Silence can serve to facilitate listening. It allows the listener to concentrate on listening and observing nonverbal signals rather than talking. It may communicate a willingness to listen. Skillful use of silent periods can stimulate conversation and contribute to an effective listening environment.

Questioning. Skillful use of questions serves two primary purposes: to obtain specifically needed information or clarification, and to direct the parent's conversation when it runs astray. Questions such as "Can you tell me exactly what Lakeisha did that bothered you so much?" help focus the conversation and provide additional information. Such an open-ended question, which cannot be answered with a "yes" or a "no," encourages a reluctant parent. In contrast, a closed question, which can be answered with a "yes" or a "no," helps narrow the focus of a disorganized parent. Because professionals need to avoid interrogation, they should practice becoming skilled in using productive questions.

Recognizing and Accepting Parents' Concerns. This chapter has emphasized the importance of a warm, caring attitude that conveys understanding. Of course, this attitude and the skills to convey it are essential for an effective parent conference. Professionals must expect parents to be reluctant at first. They must be given time to learn that the professional cares. Reflective listening is one way to let parents know that their concerns have been heard and understood. Another is being prepared and honest. If parents ask a question and the professional does not know the answer, he or she should say so. The early childhood special educator is not a medical doctor or a psychotherapist and must not pretend otherwise by giving misleading information. He or she can and should be prepared to make appropriate referrals. A digital file or notebook listing names and telephone numbers of local agencies can be helpful. It is important not to be biased in referrals or to endorse anyone in particular. It is a good idea to obtain a list from the local special education regional office, school psychologist, social worker, nurse, or principal.

Describing Children's Progress. The professional should be organized and positive in describing children's progress, giving specific examples of a child's skills or behavior whenever possible. The professional should encourage parents to discuss individual points of progress and to ask questions and should not overwhelm them with information or use jargon. Evasiveness or "fortune telling" is to be avoided. The professional can discuss only what the child will be doing in the center, what the child has accomplished, and what might be expected in the immediate next step. He or she cannot predict how the child will be functioning next year or the year after.

Summarizing. At periodic intervals, the professional should offer summarizing statements that respond to both perceived content and affect. This allows family members to, once again, verify the accuracy of the professional's perceptions. A summarizing comment might be as follows: "Can we say, then, that you are feeling very uncomfortable with Shane's placement in the early intervention program because you don't understand just what he will get out of being here every day?" In addition to summarizing content and affect, the family should be asked if they have additional concerns. Reticent families may be more able to share emotionally laden concerns because of the rapport built in the earlier stages of the conference. Of course, the professional must have the time to listen if, indeed, additional concerns are solicited.

Closing the Conference. The professional has the primary responsibility for ending the conference in conformity with the time limit. Comments such as "Given the few minutes we have left, could you explain . . . ?" or "It is about time to call it a day; do you have any additional questions?" are gentle reminders that the conference must come to an end. Arranging for future contacts ("Let's see, our next regularly scheduled meeting is . . . ") and thanking parents for their time helps to bring a conversation to a close. By standing, it is easy to demonstrate that time is up. Finally, while switching back to social conversation, the professional can lead the way to the door.

After the Conference.   Professionals need to allow enough time between conferences to record what has occurred during the conference. This record retains vital information, documents the visit, and helps create continuity between meetings. Although occasional notes may be taken during the conference, extensive note taking is unwise because it interferes with listening and often makes parents uncomfortable. Parents should be apprised of any notes that are taken and the purpose they will serve. Only information that can directly be used to assist the child is worth recording.

To promote the parent–teacher partnership, early childhood educators should reflect on what happened in the conference to identify whether they acknowledged, facilitated, and drew on the parents' knowledge about the child and skill in addressing the child's learning needs. In an analysis of conversations during conferences and post-conference interviews, Cheatham and Ostrosky (2011) found that early childhood teachers provided advice, encouraged parents' child rearing skills, and facilitated positive parent–teacher relationships. However, they tended not to recognize the parents' expertise or ask about effective strategies that the parents use with their child. These researchers suggest recording the conversation (with the parent's permission) so that after the conference the teacher may analyze the quality and content of his or her conversation.

Parent Support Through Family Resource Centers

Professionals and parents involved in the planning phases of early intervention services are finding that parents' needs assessment survey results show a strong desire for increased emotional support and counseling. One of the most economical and effective ways to provide needed support is through the development of parent support groups. One example of an effective group is Parents Helping Parents, Inc., described in Exhibit 2.3. This program provides parent-run support groups for families with a variety of needs; it also has become a well-established model parent resource center. Not

---

Exhibit 2.3

Parents Helping Parents, Inc.

In 1976, two mothers of children with Down syndrome cofounded Parents Helping Parents (PHP). With help from local agencies, PHP became incorporated and a United Way agency. Financial support is realized through individual donations, grant receipts from local foundations and corporations, memberships, and various fundraising projects. Until 1985, it was an all-volunteer agency.

PHP philosophy: The most important thing a child with disabilities needs is well-informed, emotionally balanced, caring, accepting, and assertive parents. Parents Helping Parents gives to kids with disabilities what they need most—special parents.

PHP purpose: To help children with disabilities receive the care, services, education, love, hope, and acceptance they need to enable them to become all they can be, through direct services to their parents.

PHP desire: To collaborate with professionals committed enough to the benefits of peer support that they call and make the referrals. Their devastated clients should not be left to follow through on a suggestion and/or brochure placed in their unsure hands.

Like many parent support groups, PHP started because:

1. Other parents had much vital information about available resources as well as about the disability being confronted.
2. Peer counseling, with its immediate credibility and empathy, was paramount to working through the grief/loss process and on to recovery.
3. Many professionals lacked adequate knowledge about community resources and also lacked sensitivity to the financial, social, and emotional problems faced by entire families.

(continued)

4. There was no easy way for new parents to meet experienced parents. Such meetings were too important to be left to chance.

Services include visiting parents, family guidance sessions, newsletters, telephone counseling, information packets, gifts to newborns with developmental delays, workshops for parents on the individualized education program process, peer counseling, a speaker's bureau, symposiums, sibling fun days, and workshops for medical professionals on better ways of helping families cope with raising a child who has a disability.

Parents Helping Parents distributes manuals to assist other groups in the development of similar programs throughout the world. Family groups include any kind of physical, mental, emotional, or learning disability due to birth defects, illnesses, accidents, and developmental delays. Divisions include parents of near drownings, preemies and intensive care nursery support parents, an information and support network for individuals with learning disabilities, and help for those who have experienced neonatal death.

Interested individuals may contact Parents Helping Parents, http://www.php.com.

only should early educators become familiar with whatever groups may be available in their areas, but they should also be prepared to assist in the development of such groups if none are available.

Engaging Families Through Internet-Based Communication

Although we know that the various types of parent involvement discussed earlier are beneficial to children, we also know that it is very difficult to reach all families. Given that cell phones have become commonplace for most families, educators can use Internet-based communication methods such as e-mail, text, and digital media to help increase their communication with families. These new forms of communication can foster additional two-way communication opportunities that have not always been available. Some of the possibilities described by Mitchell, Foulger, and Wetzel (2009) include:

(a) Send individual e-mails to share positive information about a child's activities and accomplishments.

(b) Send photos of children engaged in activities or post photos of children's work.

(c) Through a website or an e-mail, suggest in-home activities appropriate for parent involvement.

(d) Create a center or class website, which can include a calendar of events, volunteer options, and other information.

(e) Moderate a family support discussion forum encouraging families to support one another.

Of course, time and training would have to be available to provide these opportunities. It is very important to remember not to use e-mail when sensitive, private, or personal information about students, yourself, or other staff members is involved. Handling difficult situations or emotions should be done personally via the telephone, if not in person. Remember that e-mails can easily be misunderstood and are basically public information. Never send e-mails when you are in a state of heightened emotion.

Enhanced eText Application Exercise 2.2: In this exercise, you can apply what you have learned in this chapter to create options to engage families in their children's preschool programs and to build a collaborative family-teacher relationship.

Partnering with Culturally Diverse Families

Maria Diaz, the early interventionist from Centro de Niños, is knocking on the door of the Ramirez family to do her weekly home visit with Elena, a 30-month-old girl with severe cerebral palsy. The family of seven (including a grandmother) came to the United States from Mexico to obtain help for Elena. They are currently living in a converted garage in a neighborhood known for gang activity, drugs, and high unemployment. As Maria waits for the door to open, she thinks of the risks in this area as well as the extensive number of concerns of this family. At this home visit, Maria will help set up a corner chair for Elena to use so that she can sit on the floor and play with the other children. She will also listen to Mrs. Ramirez as she expresses disappointment at Elena's progress and the desire to seek the services of a *curandera* (folk healer) rather than return to the hospital clinic. Mr. Ramirez is in agreement, but he is even more concerned about finding work.

Besides working with Elena at home and school, what is Maria's responsibility to this family? How do the culture, values, language, and resources of the Ramirez family enter into the interactions between the family and Maria, other early intervention team members at Centro de Niños, and community agencies?

The rich diversity of today's population challenges traditional patterns of communications between professionals and families. This diversity demands communication patterns sensitive to all parents. Professionals are challenged to become personally aware and use culturally responsive interaction practices. Thus, the challenge for professionals working with young children, whether in early intervention for high-risk infants or in a child-care center designed for the children of migrant workers, is to be responsive to individual family cultural and language differences. All families assume the role of socializing children to become part of the larger community. Examination and understanding of the differences between the so-called mainstream values of communities and specific families within these communities are a critical part of the ecological approach to intervention (Hanson & Lynch, 2013). The role of early childhood educators must include acknowledging different cultural perspectives and learning how to work effectively within the boundaries that are comfortable for the family while increasing the family's understanding of and improving their ability to work within the larger mainstream culture.

Cultural Models and Child-Rearing Practices

Insights into how parents view children and their upbringing are critical in developing working relationships with families. Beliefs about issues such as adult–child interactions, feeding, toileting, sleeping, and discipline will emerge as the practitioner gathers information about the child and family. Some families' beliefs and practices may even conflict with those of the practitioner. For example, "Cultures may differ radically in terms of daily life practices, such as food selection and preparation. In fact, a practice such as eating bananas may be encouraged in one culture and absolutely forbidden in another" (Lynch & Hanson, 2011a, p. 485).

In fact, having inappropriate cultural expectations for a child and/or his or her family could create more problems than the child's actual disability. **Cultural models** offer a useful way to think about child-rearing behavior. A cultural model is a shared understanding that people have of their universe and of their behavior in that universe. Cultural models help people turn their beliefs into practice. "One critical benefit of a family-centered approach is it begins to establish a continuity of care between home and program, maximizing the chance for cultural consistency and the implementation of culturally responsive education (Iruka, Durden, & Kennel, 2015, p. 14).

Video Example from

You Tube

Enhanced eText
Video Example 2.3
Starting a Relationship
https://www.youtube.com/watch?v=JBlzviQDN5k
This video of a bilingual early interventionist and a Spanish-speaking mother illustrates the importance of the first home visit in building a relationship with a family.

This understanding will make it possible for intervention practices to be family-centered and aligned with parental goals. Because attitudes toward child rearing vary in many ways and can create conflict between professionals and parents, a generalized respect for the diversity of child-rearing beliefs and practices is critical. Next are examples of some of these variations.

Values of Independence and Autonomy Versus Interdependence and Obedience. Certain Western industrialized societies, especially the United States, value the characteristics of independence and assertiveness. Most other cultures emphasize the family values of interdependence, obedience, harmony, and respect. These differences result in very different child-rearing attitudes and practices. For example, in the United States, the young child's abilities to initiate verbally, to use language to make requests, and to carry on a conversation with adults are seen as important and positive skills. They are often included in the goals and objectives identified for young children with disabilities. In many other cultures, however, such behavior in children is viewed as inappropriate. American middle-class children are often viewed by other cultures as disrespectful, aggressive, and overindulged. Children should be "seen and not heard." They should not initiate interactions with adults and should not assert their preferences and desires. Consider the conflict that may result for a family with such values when the early childhood teacher indicates they should be helping their child initiate requests. In this situation, it is important for the professional to explore the family's degree of comfort with such a goal and to communicate why this goal might be important for success in the mainstream culture.

Another related area of difference is often referred to as "individualistic" versus "collectivist" views of personal development and behavior. Being an individual is highly esteemed in mainstream U.S. culture. Phrases like "rugged individualist" and "pursuit of individual freedom" are considered positive and basic to the "American way." Many cultures, particularly Asian cultures, are influenced by Confucian values (Chan & Chen, 2011) and revere harmony, proper behavior, and maintenance of social order (e.g., conformity and hierarchical lines of authority). Family and community members must follow their proper roles. The extent to which a child or adult carries out his or her expected role is a measure of success and family pride.

Discipline Approaches. A national parent survey conducted by *Zero to Three* (2016) revealed that discipline is most challenging for parents in raising young children, both in figuring out the most effective way to discipline and managing the child's misbehavior. Decades ago, in her classic work, Baumrind (1971) conceptualized four parenting styles as authoritative, authoritarian, permissive, and rejecting-neglecting. *Authoritative* parents are responsive, demanding, and provide clear expectations for their children in a nonintrusive manner. They use supportive rather than punitive discipline. *Authoritarian* parents are demanding and directive, but not responsive. They expect their directions to be obeyed. *Permissive* parents are nontraditional, lenient, and avoid confrontation. They are more responsive than demanding. *Rejecting-neglecting* parents are nondemanding, unresponsive, and disengaged from their child-rearing responsibilities.

Discipline varies widely across cultures and is often an area of cultural mismatch between families and early childhood professionals. In the United States, the greatest difference may be between the *authoritative* and *authoritarian* parenting styles. The most *authoritative* approach to discipline is less likely to use corporal punishment and the rules are less fixed. Children are given the opportunity to offer their side of the story and sometimes may even participate in the selection of a specific punishment. In contrast, *authoritarian* families place great emphasis on obedience and respect. For them, the mark of a good parent is one who punishes children for disrespectful behavior or for not conforming to their expected roles.

European-Americans are usually viewed as having an *authoritative* style. African-American parents are often viewed as having an *authoritarian* style, while Latinos are seen as having permissive parenting styles. When the authoritarian style is understood through a historical and social context of discrimination and a balance for family well-being, then the focus on obedience can be viewed as a way to ensure the children's safety (Iruka et al., 2015). In addition, although the use of authoritarian discipline may result in less positive outcomes for European-American children, a more authoritarian style may be necessary for African-American children to survive and thrive, especially when living in dangerous neighborhoods (Keyes, Smyke, Middleton, & Black, 2015). Within the more permissive Latino cultures, parents tend to be very warm, nurturing, and indulgent with young children (Zuniga, 2011). No matter what, it is important to realize that economic and cultural differences make it difficult to generalize about the most effective parenting styles given the complexity when one considers all that impacts parenting in current times.

Variation can also be seen in the age at which discipline becomes appropriate. For example, in some Asian cultures, there is an abrupt shift in child-rearing practices as the child approaches school age. Although parents may be very nurturing and indulgent in the early years, the older preschooler is expected to begin to conform to adult expectations. Traditional Asian parents may use name-calling, teasing, criticism, scolding, and shaming to remind the child that his or her inappropriate behaviors reflect on the family. Sometimes physical punishment is used (Chan & Chen, 2011).

Attitudes Toward Disability.   Each culture has a different view of disability and belief about the cause (Hanson, 2011). Only when practitioners in early childhood special education understand and build on each family's cultural interpretations of disability is it possible to create respectful partnerships with parents. The degree and nature of parent involvement in early intervention services are related to their beliefs about the nature of the disability and its causation. Religion frequently plays a part in how families view a child's disability. A child's disability may be seen as God's punishment for some earlier wrongdoing of the parent. Thus, in some cases, the child's condition serves as a visible pronouncement of the parent's guilt. In other cultures, because the disability is seen as God's will, there may be a reluctance to intervene. Parents may be torn between the early intervention program's pressure for them to take an active role in facilitating the child's development versus their belief that trying to change or "fix" the child is questioning God's authority.

The Influence of Racism.   Unfortunately, racism is a very real phenomenon in American society. Whereas racism and prejudice are experienced to some extent by all minority groups in the United States, the racism experienced by African-American families is profound. Racism can have a major impact on child-rearing practices. African-American parents must prepare their children to survive and thrive against great odds. Recent data from the U.S. Department of Education's Office of Civil Rights (2016) reveal that African-American children make up 19% of preschool enrollment, but 47% of preschoolers receiving suspensions. In contrast, European-American children make up 41% of preschool enrollment and 28% of preschoolers receiving suspensions.

African-American children may inadvertently learn that life will not be fair. White middle-class professionals often view such attitudes as paranoid and may believe that parents are setting their children up to feel oppressed. Parents must struggle to help their children reconcile three different influences in their lives: the racism experienced by being a minority culture, the heritage and traditions passed down from their African ancestors, and the values and behaviors dictated by U.S. mainstream culture.

Family Structure.   Another area of cultural difference often encountered by early childhood professionals is family structure and composition. The heterosexual middle-class ideal (although certainly no longer the norm) is the "nuclear family," which consists of two parents and their children living in relative isolation from other family members. Today, two-parent, heterosexual family structures are becoming much less the norm in the United States. Single-parent households, especially those headed by divorced or never-married women, are increasingly common. Parents may identify themselves as lesbian, gay, bisexual, or transgender (LGBT). A recent review of the research literature on lesbian and gay parents in early childhood settings (Averett, Hegde, & Smith, 2017) emphasizes the need for preschools to create a welcoming and inclusive environment for LGBT families. Specific practices include using inclusive language; displaying representative posters, books, and media; providing safety from bullying and relevant intervention; implementing anti-discrimination school policies; and anti-bias training for all staff.

Also, many families now include numerous extended family members: grandparents, great-grandparents, and sometimes aunts, uncles, cousins, and the spouses of grown children and their children. Such large family units, often living in relatively small quarters, seem chaotic and confusing to professionals who have grown up in nuclear families. They may be concerned about overstimulation of the young child or inconsistent, unpredictable child-rearing practices. Often, however, extended family households provide important support for the family. Parents of diverse cultural backgrounds may be uncomfortable leaving their children with strangers or may not be able to afford child care. Extended family members provide trusted, culturally compatible care for children as well as important opportunities for child interaction and nurturance.

Parents' Roles.   There are cultural differences in how parents see their roles in terms of their children's development. Middle-class parents clearly view themselves as teachers of their children. They teach their children concepts and vocabulary and help them learn to solve problems. Other parents also see themselves as teachers of their children, but what they teach are morality and proper behavior, including self-help skills. For other families, there is a strong focus on not spoiling children. This often entails not being overly responsive or indulgent. For some, the goal is to teach children—especially boys—to "be tough" and able to defend themselves. Still other families may believe that all skills simply evolve as part of a normal developmental course and view their roles as teachers or interveners as minimal.

Caregiver–Child Communication.   Another area of great cultural variation that has major implications for early intervention is parent–child communication. In middle-class U.S. society, *talking* is highly valued. By the standards of other cultures, Americans are excessive talkers. This talking carries over into their interactions with young children. Parents typically respond *verbally* even to very young infants long before they have any intentional communication. It is not unusual for a parent to respond to an infant's burp or sigh as though the infant has just said something profound! Parents also value early development of language skills and verbal assertiveness in young children. Very young children are expected to be able to label, explain, and initiate and maintain a conversation. Parents also believe they can play an important role in helping children learn these skills.

This kind of verbal interaction is unusual in many cultures. In some cultures, very young children are not consistently responded to until they can talk intelligibly. As mentioned earlier, in cultures where respect and obedience are emphasized, it may not be considered appropriate for young children to initiate; thus, being responsive to young children's communications would not be a high priority.

Common strategies suggested by early intervention professionals to facilitate children's development of communication skills include asking parents to consistently label objects, follow their child's lead, and expand on the child's utterance. For some parents, such interactions will be unnatural. It will require learning a skill that is not only new but also may be contrary to the practices of their culture. In such cases, the professional must explain to the parents that although these interactions might be unfamiliar, they can prove beneficial to the language development of their child with disabilities.

Medical Practices.   Differing views on medical practices may be a significant source of family and professional conflict. Families from a wide range of subcultures may hold onto traditional health practices. Faith healers, herbs, massage, animal rites, and other rituals are often part of treatments that lead to misunderstandings. For example, some Vietnamese parents have been reported for child abuse when using the technique of "coining" to treat conditions such as colds, sore throats, and headaches. The process involves applying a medicated salve and then stroking the affected area with a hot coin. The superficial red marks raise suspicions of abuse. Such judgments often grow out of the assumption that these families are not concerned about or caring for their children. We must remember not to judge parents as uncaring when they simply care differently for their children.

Language Differences

Perhaps the most obvious difference among subcultures is communication, both verbal and nonverbal. The inability to communicate directly with families in their primary language creates a great deal of frustration for both parents and professionals. It is often the source of misunderstanding and an inadequate transmission of information. The need for translation in both spoken and written communication is critical in any early intervention program serving other than English-speaking families. Exhibit 2.4 offers some suggestions for working through an interpreter. It is equally imperative that materials such as reports, newsletters, and home programs be prepared in parents' languages.

Exhibit 2.4

Communicating Through an Interpreter

For the Service Provider

Before the meeting or visit:

1. Identify a qualified interpreter. If possible, avoid using young family members as interpreters for their families.
2. Plan with the interpreter. Identify the purpose and goal of the meeting, topics to be discussed including relevant terms and questions, forms or reports that will be presented, and who will be involved.
3. Discuss the importance of confidentiality and clarify expectations for the interpreter's role.
4. Encourage the interpreter to stop you during the meeting if something needs clarification or the family appears to be confused.
5. Schedule sufficient time for the meeting.

During the meeting or interaction:

1. Introduce yourself and the interpreter to the family and explain confidentiality and the interpretation process.
2. Sit next to the interpreter and look at as well as address your comments and questions directly to family members.
3. Use words that are easy to translate and understand. Speak clearly, naturally, and somewhat slowly (but not loudly). Limit questions and comments to a few sentences.
4. Pause and allow the interpreter to translate what you have said.
5. Listen carefully to the family's responses.
6. Be aware of your nonverbal communication. Use positive facial expressions and tone of voice. Avoid body language or gestures that may be misunderstood.

(continued)

7. Observe the parents' facial expressions and body language and try to determine the parents' reactions to the discussion.

8. When appropriate, reinforce verbal information with written materials in the family's language, visual aids, or behavioral modeling.

9. Do not engage in side conversations or whispering with other English-speaking staff, particularly while the interpreter is translating.

10. Do not assume that family members who are present do not understand English.

11. Be patient and prepared for the additional time required for the interpretation process.

After the meeting or visit:

1. With the interpreter, review the content and process of the meeting or visit.

   - What seemed to work well?
   - Were there any difficulties in translating the conversation?
   - How well did family members seem to understand the information shared?
   - Were there any concerns or issues that were not addressed?

2. Acknowledge the interpreter for his or her services and offer constructive feedback if needed.

3. Check on the interpreter's availability for future meetings with this family if you plan to work with the same interpreter again.

For the Interpreter

1. Attend relevant professional development workshops to enhance skills as an interpreter for the program.

2. Obtain resource materials related to early childhood special education services, disability, medical conditions, education, and other relevant concepts and terminology.

3. Learn about the cultural backgrounds, beliefs, and values of the families for whom you will serve as an interpreter.

4. Collaborate with the service provider to plan for and debrief after meetings.

5. Ask clarifying questions if the meaning of anything said by the service provider or family members is unclear.

6. If word-for-word translation is not possible, use your own words, confirming changes with the service provider and family members.

7. Listen carefully to the service provider and family members.

8. Make notes, if needed for your translation, and explain why you need to do so.

9. Be aware of everyone's nonverbal communication, including your own.

10. Remember to maintain ethical practice and respect confidentiality.

One way to break through the language barrier and enhance the family's involvement in a child's program is to facilitate support and encouragement from other parents. One such program is Fiesta Educativa, founded in 1978 to educate and assist Latino families in the Los Angeles area to obtain services for their children. It provides parent support groups and training programs and holds annual conferences in much the same manner as Parents Helping Parents, illustrated in Exhibit 2.3. This form of peer counseling and peer support assists other parents in understanding "the system" and community resources while offering much-needed emotional support.

As Maria Diaz discovered in her home visits with the Ramirez family, the effectiveness of her work is clearly tied not only to understanding the unique values of the family but also to her own cultural biases and values. Although Maria speaks Spanish fluently, her upbringing in an upper-middle-class family in Spain has little relation to the experiences of the Ramirez family. Conversations have raised a number of

Exhibit 2.5

Suggestions for Collaborating with Families of Diverse Cultural and Linguistic Backgrounds

1. Make every effort to recruit and retain diverse staff members who reflect the cultures and languages of the children and families being served.

2. Provide and participate in professional development opportunities related to developing cross-cultural competencies and learning about differences in values and beliefs, including child-rearing practices, views of disability, and attitudes toward treatment, medical practices, and education.

3. Invite families to share their cultures, beliefs, traditions, and artifacts. Draw on community members to provide information on relevant cultural beliefs and practices.

4. Keep in mind that cultures vary in what is known as time orientation. These differences can lead to misunderstandings. For example, those with a strict time orientation may strive to stick to an agenda, while those with a looser orientation more easily stray from the topic. Those with a strict orientation are likely to arrive promptly, while others may often be late.

5. Establish a relationship with relevant community resources (e.g., churches, community mediators, and media) for families.

6. Train bilingual staff to be qualified interpreters for interactions with non-English-speaking families.

7. Translate written materials into the preferred home languages of families. Be sensitive to required literacy levels and provide visuals when possible.

8. Include bilingual strategies, materials, and activities in children's educational programs.

9. Assume that some family members may not speak up when they disagree; watch for signs of disagreement.

10. Learn key words and phrases (e.g., greetings, routine requests, and common questions) in home languages to support interactions with family members.

11. Provide wait time and silence to let family members respond to questions or share ideas.

12. Monitor personal stereotypes and overgeneralizations and avoid them. Be aware that there are more differences within a group than between groups. Be open to learning about and appreciating each family.

differences in the way they view issues such as health, child rearing, and education. Maria feels that in recognizing their differences, she has begun to work within the boundaries that are comfortable to the family while sharing with them information about the ways of the larger culture.

In her ongoing experiences with the Ramirez family and other parents in the intervention program, Maria and the rest of the early intervention team must continually use caution in making prejudgments based on attitudes toward and stereotypes of certain subcultures. The effectiveness of programs will depend on the development of ethnic competence and behavioral changes by the service providers. First, professionals must recognize and clarify their own values and assumptions. Second, they must gather and analyze ethnographic information regarding the cultural community they serve. Third, they must determine the degree to which the family has adopted society's values. Finally, they must examine each family's orientation to specific child-rearing issues. Exhibit 2.5 offers some suggestions for working with culturally diverse families.

Parents' Expectations of the Preschool Curricula

Teachers and administrations should gather information about a family's expectations of a preschool program and provide information on the program's philosophy and curricula. Parents view their child's education as critical for future success, and some are likely to value development of academic skills over play and socialization skills (Parmar, Harkness, & Super, 2008). Furthermore, parents are not usually familiar with the concept of developmentally appropriate practice that guides many preschool programs in the United States and may become concerned about the focus on play and what they perceive to be a lack of academics. Play promotes and integrates many abilities, including children's self-regulation, symbolic thought, memory, language, and social skills (Copple & Bredekamp, 2009). Teachers should explain their program philosophy, listen carefully to parent goals, and collaborate to create ways to embed learning opportunities that promote emergent literacy and numeracy skills within the child's daily routine and play activities (e.g., singing songs about letters and numbers, counting the steps from one area to another, and writing grocery lists or menus in the grocery store and restaurant play areas). Additional suggestions may be found in Exhibit 2.5.

Finally, it is important to remember the wise words from a well-recognized text directed to counselors that states: "The journey to cultural competence requires an emotional awakening in the area of one's knowledge, beliefs, attitudes and behaviors related to race, culture, ethnicity, gender and other diverse groups" (Sue & Sue, 2016, p. 1). It is beyond the scope of this text to adequately address the issues involved in this awakening.

Working with Special Family Populations

In addition to the challenges encountered in working with all parents, many professionals who work with young children discover that they are working with parents who have unique needs themselves. The nature of the circumstances or disabilities of these parents varies widely. Although overt behaviors may appear to be similar, concerns can be very different. It is unwise and dangerous to generalize; each parent is an individual with unique needs. In some way, each one can be assisted.

Immigrant Families

Even beyond the important cultural considerations previously discussed, it is important to realize that immigrant families may present additional concerns that are not readily apparent. For example, Bang (2009) offered the following suggestions to help educators provide the understanding and support that can facilitate the involvement of these families in their children's school life:

1. Consider that newly arrived, culturally and linguistically diverse families may not understand the U.S. and its expectations and practices. Not understanding common school activities such as back-to-school nights and fund-raising events can cause embarrassment.

2. The role of communication, as already discussed, is complex. Families of some cultures are just not comfortable raising concerns in person. Therefore, suggestion boxes or anonymous surveys, in various languages, might yield some interesting results.

3. As gender roles are influenced by culture, it is important to sensitively explain the importance of both parents' participation in school-related events. Whenever possible, schedule events when working parents are available to attend.

4. Assist interested families in finding programs where it is convenient for them to learn conversational English. If local programs only stress academic English, the groups related to the school such as parent teacher organizations (PTOs) might offer programs that teach practical school-related English.

5. Teachers can encourage meetings that explain the school system in various languages. For example, many immigrants do not understand grading systems, special education including IEPs and IFSPs, classroom behavioral expectations, and so on.

Parents with Developmental Disabilities

Children of parents with developmental disabilities are often enrolled in early intervention programs because they are considered at risk rather than because they have a diagnosed disability. Although all the suggestions already made for developing partnerships with parents are appropriate for working with parents with developmental disabilities, there are two specific goals to keep in mind: helping the parents become the most effective parents possible while also carefully monitoring the children's progress. To achieve these goals, the following guidelines may be useful:

1. *Establish priorities.* To help parents with developmental disabilities develop effective parenting skills, professionals must work with these parents in choosing their priorities carefully. The first priority may be to determine whether parents would benefit from assistance in managing the basic needs of daily living. Many parents with developmental disabilities are in the lowest socioeconomic bracket. Both resources and skill in budgeting may be limited. The early interventionist may be called on to help parents plan budgets and to connect with available community resources. Assistance may also be needed in such daily living skills as selection and storage of food, in developing daily routines for both themselves and their children, and in securing transportation and attending to medical needs.

2. *Coordinate help.* As soon as possible, discover which other agencies are extending help to these families. If there are several, the development of a collaborative intervention plan with frequent communication among all those involved is essential.

3. *Make frequent, brief contacts.* Telephone calls are better than notes, and 10 minutes with the parent in the home can pay quick dividends.

4. *Avoid lengthy explanations.* Be brief. Be explicit. Show parents what to do and how to do it. They are usually willing to try if they understand what is wanted.

5. *Require little or no reading.* Send only one request or direction in notes if they can read. A list of things to do will probably be ignored.

6. *Model appropriate parent–child interaction.* Because parent–child interaction may be limited, the early interventionist may need to model responsiveness to children's cues. Teaching parents simple "baby play" games such as peek-a-boo will help these parents become more involved with their children.

7. *Help parents interpret their child's behavior.* Parents with developmental disabilities may misinterpret their children's behavior and see them as "bad children" who need to be punished.

8. *Involve parents with developmental disabilities.* Whenever possible, include these parents in center observations, volunteer activities, conferences, and meetings. Answer their questions in short sentences with simple language. Supervise their activities closely. Remember, they are with their child far more than is the professional. If interaction skills and behavior management are improved, both parent and child will benefit.

Teen Parents

Although infants of teenage mothers are definitely considered to have characteristics that place them at risk, little is found in the literature about the needs of young teen parents of children with disabilities. Among the risk factors are low birth weight, neurodevelopmental delays, and difficult temperament (Wells & Thompson, 2004). These at-risk factors are further complicated by environmental factors such as low level of maternal education, social isolation, single parenthood, and low socioeconomic status. The developmental level of the teenager who, in many ways, is still a child herself must be considered. All teen parents appear to need emotional support and specific instruction in "parenting" while they are being helped to set and reach toward some realistic goals for themselves. Providing this emotional support in a way that enhances the teen parent's self-esteem is often a significant challenge because early interventionists may represent authority figures at a time when teens tend to turn toward peers as their primary source of self-esteem and goal setting.

Teen parents who have suffered from poor parenting will benefit from the same careful approaches to providing information and modeling "parenting best practices" discussed earlier. In addition, teen parents need to be linked to education, child-care services, social groups, and agencies that provide a wide range of support so they can develop the life and vocational skills necessary to be able to provide a stable environment. Even if teen mothers are in public school programs designed for them, the curricular agenda usually is based on techniques for raising children without disabilities. These programs may not be prepared to focus on assisting mothers in developing a loving and responsive relationship with a child with disabilities.

Cook and Sparks (2008) offer practical suggestions for an early interventionist to consider:

1. Assume a developmental approach to collaboration (16-year-olds are still 16-year-olds). They are likely to think concretely and live in the present.

2. Even though the teenage parents may be encouraged to perceive themselves as the primary nurturing relationship in their child's life, interventions must take into account the fact that extended family members may have assumed the primary caregiving role.

3. Teenage parents will need assistance in understanding what their child is capable of developmentally, and they will also need coaching in understanding their child's signals for attention. These may have to be pointed out directly.

4. Interventionists will need to be patient and ready to praise young parents who actively seek to become attached to their child. These parents may have had little acknowledgment and praise while growing up.

Foster Caregivers

The foster child, in addition to possibly having developmental disabilities, often has overwhelming social-emotional needs. Caregivers and early interventionists must be concerned about such issues as attachment, diminished use of adults for comfort, passivity, inappropriate emotional responses, impulsivity, and fearfulness in their efforts to provide developmentally appropriate support to the young child. Because of the complexities associated with a child's removal from his or her natural parents, a team approach to placement, care, and reunification (when possible) is critical.

When working with foster families, early interventionists must encourage participation in home and center activities. The intervention needs of the child with a developmental disability are developed with foster parent input as well as with that of the biological parent (as appropriate). In addition, the foster parents are encouraged to be a part of parent groups to take advantage of ongoing emotional support, training, and educational opportunities.

Families That Have Experienced Divorce

It is inevitable that educators will be working with children who are being raised by a parent or parents who have experienced or are experiencing divorce. The literature is contradictory regarding whether or not the percentage of divorce is higher among families of children with disabilities. It apparently depends on which disability is under consideration. However, when parents separate, no matter the cause, all who are involved will experience considerable stress and must go through a period of adjustment that usually takes 1 to 2 years. Whatever the situation, there are actions that educators can take to make divorce easier on children and their parents. The following section will discuss some of the necessary understandings and actions that educators can take to help minimize stress and support children and families through their transition (Leon & Spengler, 2005).

1. Each parent continues as a decision maker unless a court action has removed that right. Therefore, each parent is entitled to participate in meetings and must be sent notice of these meetings. However, if only one parent obtains legal custody, then only that parent has the right to participate in special education decisions. Schools may request to see the divorce decree. The parent without legal custody should no longer be part of special education.

2. If parents who both have legal custody cannot agree, educators should use informal meetings to try to resolve the conflict. If an agreement is not reached quickly, then administrators can assist parents to learn of alternative resolution processes available within their state.

3. If both parents are involved in any part of the child's life, then both parents should be invited to all school activities and have access to health and school records unless there is legal documentation prohibiting access.

4. Avoid offensive terms such as "broken home" or "real parent." Don't assume that all family members have the same last name.

5. Offer opportunities for divorced parents to have separate conferences. Share information (positive as well as challenges) with both parents.

6. Choose curriculum materials and activities that portray different types of family structure positively. If you are making gifts for parents, encourage children to make items for all significant adults in their lives.

Understanding the Impact of Poverty

Using data from the 2016 Census, the U.S. Department of Agriculture's Economic Research Service (2017) reported that 33% of African-Americans, 31.8% of American Indian and Alaskan Natives, 25.9 % of Hispanics, and 14.6 % of Whites live in poverty in rural areas. Moreover, 46% of families in poverty have single female head of households, and 26.8% of children under age 5 years live in poverty. These poverty rates in rural areas are approximately between 5–10% less in urban areas.

Given these alarming statistics, practitioners quickly realize that many children with disabilities and their families struggle with problems more challenging than disability alone. Children with disabilities are more likely than other children to live in poverty, live in single-parent families, or have parents who are in poor health or unemployed (Aron & Loprest, 2007). The stressors associated with poverty certainly affect children as well as adults. While interviewing 90 families served by home-visiting programs, Allen (2007) found that in addition to the needs expressed in previous studies, parents also discussed the challenges they faced in meeting their families' material needs. Likewise, Parish, Rose, and Andrews (2010) found from an extensive survey of American families that, across all income levels, families of children with disabilities are more challenged by food, housing, and health issues than families without children with disabilities. Results from their survey of 28,141 families indicate that state and federal policies are not nearly extensive enough. In addition, the services that are available seem to be unconnected, with medical, educational, and financial needs addressed separately. This very fact makes it mandatory that professionals in early intervention and early childhood special education not only understand the impact of poverty on family functioning but also become knowledgeable about community resources and how to link families to them.

In an effort to address the impact of poverty on family dynamics, Park, Turnbull, and Turnbull (2002) discuss the following six areas of concern:

Health

- Did poor nutrition during pregnancy result in low birth weight and related birth defects?
- Can the family afford a nutritionally adequate diet?
- Are there related health problems such as weight loss, fatigue, headaches, irritability, inability to concentrate, and frequent colds?
- Does the family have adequate resources to secure adequate health care?

Productivity (Participating in and contributing to useful and enjoyable daily activity)

- Can the family afford adequate child care?
- Can the family afford stimulating books and toys?
- Can the family afford intellectually stimulating experiences such as visits to the zoo?

Leisure and Recreation

- Can the family afford opportunities to play, exercise, or socialize?
- Does the family have transportation and time to visit parks and other affordable places of recreation?
- Have high-risk and unhealthy habits such as smoking and drinking taken up unstructured time?
- Is the family aware of appropriate recreational and social opportunities?

Physical Environment

- Does the family live in a safe and comfortable home?
- Does the family live in an unsafe and disruptive neighborhood?

Emotional Well-Being

- Do family members suffer from stress-related life events such as unemployment, eviction, or inability to pay bills?
- Do family members seem to be suffering from lack of self-esteem due to the impacts of poverty?

Family Interaction

- Does economic stress appear to result in an increased number of family conflicts and irritability?
- Are older children expected to provide extensive child care?

Practitioners such as service coordinators, home visitors, social workers, and early childhood educators can only be effective if they are able to recommend community resources, given that there seems to be little coordination of services among the top three federal programs for children with disabilities: special education, Medicaid, and Supplemental Security Income (Aron & Loprest, 2007).

"Quality of parenting has been identified as a key factor in enabling young children to cope adaptively with adverse environmental circumstances" (Lieberman & Osofsky, 2009, p. 54). The long-term beneficial effects of focusing on the needs of both the mother and child are increasingly being documented (Olds, Sadler, & Klitzman, 2007). As long as poverty exists, the need for coordinating services that focus on social, emotional, and behavioral well-being as well as the provision of everyday quality of life is essential. Early childhood special educators must become advocates for the children and families they serve by becoming knowledgeable about local resources outside their classroom and within their community.

Homelessness

Services for homeless children and families are mandated and protected by law. The McKinney-Vento Homeless Assistance Act of 1987 (PL 100-77) was amended and reauthorized by the No Child Left Behind Act of 2001 and, again, reinforced by IDEA (2004). Homeless children and youth are defined as "individuals who lack a fixed, regular, and adequate nighttime residence." Both Parts B and C of IDEA require that all children who meet this definition be found and served. Public school districts are required to designate a liaison whose responsibility it is to reach out to homeless families.

Homeless children experience much of the same trauma that accompanies poverty, such as inadequate nutrition and poor physical health. However, they usually have additional issues related to learning and development given that they often experience constant educational disruption. Such children are four times more likely to show delayed development and twice as likely to have learning disabilities as non-homeless children (National Center on Family Homelessness, 2010).

It will require patience and flexibility along with a focus on the family's strengths to work collaboratively with parents who are experiencing homelessness. Besides their own significant problems related to poverty as already discussed, parents may feel guilty or embarrassed about not being able to meet their children's basic needs. Parents will need assistance with transportation if they are expected to attend meetings. Services should be expedited, and every effort should be made to keep children in the same program despite their mobility. Open communication about the family's living situation should be maintained if possible. As with other parents, consent to request information from other agencies and providers must be obtained.

Enhanced eText Application Exercise 2.3: In this exercise, you can apply what you have learned in this chapter by identifying how poverty might influence a preschooler's development and what teachers can do to help alleviate potential negative impacts.

A Personal Perspective on Raising a Child with Developmental Challenges

Lora Jerugim

My daughter Elisa is 5 years old. She is a developmentally delayed child whose delays range from mild to borderline and are of unknown etiology. I do not have any research findings to present. I have no statistics for you. But what I can share with you is something that I know a lot about—what it *feels* like to raise a child with developmental problems.

(continued)

When Elisa was born, I was ecstatic. I had two sons, and I had dreamed about having a daughter. I had fantasies about who she would be and what we would share. Of course she would be completely articulate by the age of 2, and someday I would teach her to play the piano. And when she grew older we would recommend books to each other to read. I had images of our whole family sitting at a table assembling a thousand-piece puzzle together. So much for the fantasy.

Elisa's birth was 5 to 6 weeks premature, but it was normal and no one suspected that there was anything wrong with her. So I took home what I thought was a perfectly normal baby. Elisa always seemed alert and responsive, but by the time she was 6 months old and was not able to roll over, I sensed that something was wrong. Like so many parents, I was encouraged to believe that Elisa would catch up. I only wish that pediatricians could be as attuned to the signs of delay as parents are so that we would not lose so much precious time in getting help for our children. By the time Elisa was a year old, she couldn't sit up and was severely hypotonic. It was clear at that point that she was not developing normally. We were finally referred to a developmental specialist. What was once like a dream come true had turned into a living nightmare. My first reaction was one of complete shock and disbelief. I would wake up in the morning and wonder if it was all just a bad dream. Certainly disabled children are born every day, but it couldn't be happening to me . . . not my child. I felt a sense of panic and helplessness as I waited for almost 2 months for the test results to come back. And when I learned that the results were negative, I felt relieved and yet confused. Elisa had no diagnosis and consequently no clear prognosis. I was told that she might have a brain dysfunction, but having a label to hold onto didn't seem to help much. We don't know what caused this dysfunction, and although I feel somehow responsible, I have nowhere to place my diffused sense of guilt. In a way I feel lucky that I do not know precisely what happened, because if I did, I would probably run that moment over in my mind for the rest of my life wishing that I'd done something differently.

There are times when I feel such rage that this has happened to my child and to our whole family. I am angry with a world that is intolerant of people who are different—a society that is so focused on achievement that we often forget to look into a person's soul. I feel jealous and lonely as I listen to friends discuss whether their children are highly gifted or just gifted while I'm praying that someday my daughter will be capable of leading an independent life. I feel so much pain as I watch Elisa at preschool struggling to do things that younger children do with ease. I am exhausted because a special child requires twice the work to get half the distance. But most of all I live in fear of the unknown because I don't know what limitations my daughter's disability will impose on her, and I do not know how the world will respond to her being different.

Having a young child whose development is delayed but whose disability is not visible poses a number of special problems. These children seem to be caught somewhere between the normal world and the world of disabilities. Normal toddler programs are not quite appropriate, and yet early intervention programs in the area are populated with children whose disabilities are more severe and/or visible. When Elisa entered her first intervention program at 20 months, I was traumatized. I wept on and off for weeks. I had never had any exposure to children with disabilities and being in their presence was a painful reminder of life's incomprehensible injustices. I also realized that I wasn't just visiting the class. I was there because my daughter had disabilities and this was her school! But it was this same environment that fostered my denial of Elisa's problems. After all, Elisa looked so "normal" compared to most of the other children.

I also decided to place my daughter in a normal preschool part time where she was the only child with disabilities, and although my daughter, who is very competent socially, adjusted fairly well, I felt lonely, isolated, depressed, and at times embarrassed. During my daughter's first few weeks there, when I stayed with her to ease her separation, I had to leave the room on a few occasions when I began to cry. Being around all those normal 3-year-olds was a constant reminder of how verbal and adept little children are and how far behind Elisa was in her development.

Furthermore, when my sons were in preschool, I became acquainted with the other parents primarily through my children playing after school with other children or being invited to birthday parties. Elisa is rarely invited to birthday parties, and she has been invited to play at another child's house twice in 2 years. I have made some attempts to invite children over, but I not only have to find an appropriate playmate, I also must determine if the parent is the type who would be receptive to having their child play with a child who is "slow."

There were times in the past when my feeling of isolation became so pervasive that I found myself wishing that somebody I knew, whether family or friend, would give birth to a child with disabilities just so that someone close to me would truly understand what I was experiencing and that I would no longer feel so alone. Then, of course, just the idea that I could entertain such a terrible thought made me feel the most unbearable guilt. For several years I felt as though I was riding a roller coaster in the dark. I could never see when the dips were coming, and when they did, I would be dropped into a depression that could last for weeks. Sometimes a stranger's question would be enough to do it, like the woman who asked me how old my daughter was and proceeded to ask me why she couldn't talk. If Elisa had been in a wheelchair, that woman would never have dared to ask me that question.

Parents of children with delays must endure many types of stress. We live with financial stress, and we worry about governmental budget cuts and changes in the laws that provide services. We are responsible for selecting schools and therapies, but when our children are receiving such a variety of services, how are we supposed to determine what's working and what's not? Often we do not know from one year to the next where our children will go to school because we can't predict what their needs will be in a year, and we don't know what programs will be available. Even a class that is appropriate now may not be appropriate 6 months from now just because the population of children in the class may change so radically. We find ourselves battling with school districts and forever fighting against society's prejudicial attitudes toward the disabled. I've often wished that I could hire a full-time advocate to deal with all these external stresses so that I could just focus my energies on raising my daughter.

There are constant family stresses as well, since one child requires more help and attention than the others. Resentments build up. I find myself doing a perennial balancing act with my husband and children trying to make sure that everyone gets their fair share of me. All this is aggravated by the fact that when you have a delayed preschooler, what you really have on your hands is a child who seems to be stuck in the terrible twos. I'm sure any of you who have raised children will remember the nightmare of the terrible twos and how grateful you were that it only lasted a year. Try to imagine the shape our nerves are in after we've endured the terrible twos for 2 or 3 years and with no end in sight. Elisa is destructive without intent and is forever testing us. She frequently spills her drinks, and the other day she tried to pour herself a bowl of cereal and poured cereal all over the floor. I sometimes wonder if she'll ever be fully toilet trained or if she will ever sleep through the night.

Testing is another source of stress for parents of delayed youngsters. Elisa's behavior and skills vary from day to day and often from one part of the day to another, so she is difficult to assess. Her most organized time of the day is usually the evening, and evaluations are generally done in the morning. Furthermore, her fine motor and language problems make assessment even more difficult. In one testing situation, she was asked to stack 1-inch cubes and was then scored in two areas: fine motor and cognitive. Her poor fine motor development prevented her from stacking more than a few blocks, so I asked the woman who was administering the test if she would try it again while steadying the tower for Elisa. Elisa then stacked all 10 blocks, and her cognitive score on that item jumped by 18 months! Sometimes Elisa can show where a puzzle piece should go but can't maneuver it into place. I often feel that the standard tests used are designed for normal children and, consequently, are inadequate for children whose disabilities interfere with their performance. They certainly fail to pick up the qualitative changes that our children's abilities undergo over time. Professionals also need to be aware that the whole concept of testing triggers a special response in well-educated parents, because for us, perhaps on a subconscious level, poor performance is equated with failure.

Yes, one of my areas of greatest frustration, anger, and despair has been the area of diagnosis. How much more difficult it is to accept your child's disability when you don't know what it is. I have received so many conflicting opinions about

who Elisa is that I've stopped listening. I just don't care anymore about having a label for her because the only appropriate label for my daughter is the one I gave her at birth: ELISA. One physician told me that I'd thoroughly confused Elisa's diagnosis by all the work I'd done with her. I remember thinking at the time that you can't teach a child anything they're not capable of learning. A psychologist labeled her mentally retarded, and 2 weeks later, I was told that according to test results from a research project, Elisa did *not* appear to be mentally retarded. I had another doctor tell me that Elisa would grow up and be able to feed herself and dress herself, while yet another doctor told me that we should have expectations of normalcy for Elisa and that she in turn would have those expectations for herself. He said that by working with children with disabilities for 30 years he knew by observing Elisa that she was not mentally retarded. Looking at the child seemed more important to him in his assessment than simply looking at test scores. He also told me that she would grow up and be able to lead a normal life, that she would not be a Phi Beta Kappa, but that where she would fall in between no expert could ascertain. The level she would attain would depend on many variables that could not be measured, and that the most important of them would be her own motivation to succeed.

This particular doctor deserves special mention because he is not only a skilled physician, he is a humanist as well. He still sees Elisa regularly, and I feel that the way he has related to us over the years could well serve as an example to everyone in the helping professions. He has treated us with sensitivity and respect and has valued our input, recognizing that we, as Elisa's parents, probably know her better than anyone else in the world. He has been honest with us and has freely admitted that he doesn't have all the answers. He has always looked at Elisa as a human being and not simply as a composite of her problems. He has made us aware of her strengths, and he has acknowledged our efforts in providing Elisa with the help that she needs. He always questions us about our whole family and reminds us of the importance of keeping our lives in balance. But the most important lesson to be learned from this man is that you must not take parents' hope away. Hope is what keeps us going, even if it's only the hope that things will be a little better than they are today. Without hope, we would stop fighting for our children and working so hard to provide the services they need. I believe that parents and professionals share the same goals for our disabled children. We want them to grow up to be independent, productive, and self-actualized human beings, so we must be sure that we are working together toward these goals, rather than in opposition.

A friend of mine shared a quote with me that says, "Thank you, God, for reminding me that thorns have roses," and with that thought in mind, I want to share with you the joy and growth I've experienced in raising Elisa, and not just the pain and frustration.

Elisa has taught me more about love and patience than anyone I have ever known, and she has drastically altered my

(continued)

perception of what matters in life. And as I have watched her development and lived with the uncertainty of not knowing when or even *if* she will acquire certain skills, I have come to appreciate my sons' normal growth in a way that I never could before. She has shown me that a "spoken word" and a simple "step" are among life's greatest gifts and that the miracle of normal development must never be taken for granted.

I have come to accept that my daughter will not be quite like everybody else when she grows up, but then who of us is? We are all unique individuals, and we should appreciate our differences rather than scorn them. We all have our strengths and weaknesses, and how many of us, even without disabilities, ever realize our full human potential?

I have struggled to redefine the meaning of joy in my life, and I have learned to live with sorrow and to move beyond it. I have discovered that life is very precious and that none of us has any guarantee of what the future will hold. Parenting Elisa has been a challenge for me, and I have found strength within myself that I didn't know existed.

Source: Courtesy of Lora Jerugim.

I've also become aware of the importance of seeing myself as a human being separate from mother and wife and of nurturing my own growth. And as I nourish myself, I find that I have just that much more to give. Elisa's education is in good hands, and I no longer want to be her teacher. I just want to be her mother and to teach her the things that I know about: appreciating life and being a caring human being. At the same time, she is teaching me because Elisa has no prejudices and doesn't let her head get in the way of establishing human relationships. Instead, she seems to have a direct line to people's hearts.

I can honestly say that I love and accept my imperfectly perfect daughter for exactly who she is rather than for who she might have been. I hope that sharing my experiences will in some way help the professional community to be more sensitive to the needs of parents of delayed children and that we will be better able to work together to serve these children.

Summary

Properly trained professionals will recognize and actively work toward involving families in a partnership of responsibility for their child's development. One of the first steps in bridging a link between parents and professionals is for the professional to recognize the emotional needs of families with children with disabilities. Parents often react to the realization that their child has a disabling condition in stages similar to the emotional adjustment encountered with the loss of a loved one. The alert and informed professional can help parents work through each stage, from initial feelings of shock, disbelief, and denial through anger and resentment, bargaining to make it go away, depression and discouragement, and on to acceptance. Understanding the family as a system is essential to true parent–professional collaboration.

Children and members of the extended family can be included in the process of emotional and educational adjustments. Siblings can be valuable allies because children typically accept a child who has disabilities. Especially in early sessions with family members, it is important to avoid jargon and technical concepts. Test results should be explained in terms of common behaviors.

Guidelines are provided for working with parents within the center under a variety of purposes. With planning, it is possible to create a developmental approach for bringing parents into contact with other parents of children with disabilities, orienting them to observation and eventual participation within the center. Parent education groups and parent–teacher conferences can be viewed as requiring special teacher skills, rather than simply as opportunities for parents to meet.

Special consideration was given to working with culturally diverse families. Understanding cultural practices and language differences is essential to successful early intervention.

Finally, professionals were reminded that some parents of children with disabilities may have disabilities themselves. These include parents who themselves have disabilities, are teen parents, or are foster parents. The special challenges of living with divorce, in poverty, or being homeless are also discussed. Throughout the chapter, sufficient details have been provided to encourage professionals to pick and choose the type and extent of engagement most appropriate for the children and parents in their programs, and for themselves.

Reflect and Apply

1. Considering the variety of emotional reactions that families may have when a child enrolls in your classroom, discuss what you would do or say to not only offer emotional support, but also to learn while being helpful.

2. Given the guidelines discussed in the chapter for establishing an effective partnership with families, outline specifically how you would go about developing trust and demonstrating respect. Be careful to consider both normal everyday stresses as well as those that may be specific to the individual family's situation.

3. Thinking about the academic year, outline a variety of options for family engagement that would honor cultural and linguistic backgrounds while facilitating family involvement. Select one option and be specific about the steps that you would go through in planning such an event, and identify any special considerations that you would keep in mind.

4. Reflect on the impact of poverty on family dynamics and child development. Describe how specific impacts could influence a child's behavior and response to curriculum. Be specific in describing what an early educator could do to help alleviate potential impacts on developmental progress.

5. It is thought that denial can actually be a positive emotional reaction. Explain how this statement can be justified.

Chapter 3
Developing Individualized Intervention Plans and Programs and Monitoring Progress

Joni Hofmann/Fotolia

Learning Outcomes

After studying this chapter, you should be able to:

3.1 Describe individualized family service plan (IFSP) and individualized education program (IEP) processes as well as how to develop the documents.

3.2 Recognize that essential to the planning processes is effective collaboration among service providers and families who are considered to be the primary decision makers.

3.3 Understand that family concerns should be directly reflected in functional IFSP outcomes and IEP goals and objectives.

3.4 Explain how to carefully observe children so that progress monitoring is effectively linked to curriculum.

3.5 Discuss approaches that will minimize family stress through careful planning of transition steps to the next educational environment.

The Individualized Family Service Plan (IFSP) Process for Infants, Toddlers, and Their Families

The *individualized family service plan (IFSP)* is the written document specified in the Individuals with Disabilities Education Act (IDEA) to guide the implementation of early intervention services for children from *birth to age 3* and their families. It is to be developed through **collaborative interchanges** between families and the professionals involved in assessment and service delivery. (Although states are allowed to use IFSPs for preschoolers with disabilities until their sixth birthday, only a few states have selected this option [Gargiulo & Kilgo, 2014]. The majority use the IEP process for children ages 3 to 5 years that will be discussed later in this chapter.)

The role of the IFSP is to identify and organize formal and informal resources to facilitate families' goals for their children and themselves. "It is not a product so much as a *process* and context for establishing and maintaining a productive and supportive professional-family relationship. There is continuous gathering, sharing, exchanging, and expanding of information as the family makes decisions about which early intervention services they want and need for their child and themselves" (Noonan & McCormick, 2006, pp. 56–57).

As noted, the written document, in and of itself, is not considered to be as significant as the *process* involved in the development of the written product. Service providers are expected to form partnerships with families built on trust and respect that are designed to be a viable part of each child's program throughout the critical first few years of the child's life. The IFSP process is intended to support the natural caregiving role of families. In keeping with the family systems dynamics outlined in Chapter 2, young children with disabilities can be understood only within the context of their families. In this way, the IFSP is viewed differently from the individualized education program (IEP), discussed later in this chapter. The IFSP process is *family centered*, whereas the IEP tends to be child centered. The IFSP approach takes into account the fact that infants and toddlers are uniquely dependent on their families for physical and emotional sustenance.

It is essential that family members are full participants in the IFSP process, including the meeting. Some IFSP meetings are conducted during home visits. Wherever the location, professionals should consider how to welcome and draw on family knowledge of the child and the family's concerns and priorities in the development of the IFSP. This may be accomplished through a respectful, conversational approach. However, it may be particularly challenging when the family and the team do not share a mutually understood language. It is most disrespectful and anxiety-provoking for a family when team members sit together and talk among themselves, while parents sit on the opposite side of the table feeling left out.

The IFSP Process

The process for developing the IFSP consists of the gathering, sharing, and exchange of information between families and staff to enable families to make informed choices about the early intervention services they want for their children and themselves.

Families may move through the dynamic process differently according to their concerns, desires, and choices. However, several key activities are expected to occur. These include the following:

1. ***First contacts and screening for eligibility.*** When a child is referred for early intervention services, an evaluation is conducted to determine the child's eligibility for services. Criteria for eligibility must be consistent with each state's definition of developmental disability. Assessment plans are developed with the family to determine the child's status in each of five developmental areas: physical development, including vision, hearing, and health; cognitive development; communication development; social or emotional development; and adaptive development.

2. ***Assessment of the family's resources, concerns, and priorities and the child's strengths and needs.*** Child and family assessment involves interviews with caregivers designed to elicit family-directed expression of family resources, concerns, and priorities. Families are also encouraged to identify the supports and services necessary to enhance the family's capacity to meet the developmental needs of their child.

3. ***Development of a service plan document.*** A meeting must be held within 45 days of referral to develop the initial IFSP document. The meeting must be held in a setting and at a time convenient for families. It is required to be conducted in the native language of the family. An ongoing service coordinator is also designated at this meeting.

4. ***Implementation and monitoring.*** Services for an eligible child and family are expected to be implemented as soon as possible after the IFSP meeting. The service coordinator is responsible for coordinating, facilitating, and monitoring the timely delivery of early intervention services. A review of the IFSP must be completed every 6 months or more frequently if deemed appropriate. In addition, a full evaluation of the IFSP is to be conducted annually.

Participants in Initial and Annual IFSP Meetings

Participants in the initial and annual IFSP meetings usually include the following:

1. The parent or parents of the child
2. Other family members as desired by the family
3. An advocate or person outside the family, if the parent requests that the person participate
4. The service coordinator who has been working with the family since the initial referral or who has been designated by the public agency to be responsible for the implementation of the IFSP

5. A person or persons directly involved in the assessment process
6. As appropriate, persons who will be providing services to the child or the family

If any of these persons are unable to participate, arrangements are to be made to include their involvement through other means, such as arranging their participation through a telephone or video conference call; employing the services of a knowledgeable, authorized substitute representative; or making available pertinent records.

Identifying Family Concerns, Priorities, and Resources

Although Public Law (PL) 99-457 originally required identification of family strengths and needs as related to enhancement and development of the child, professionals are increasingly wary of the use of the term *needs*, which implies that families may need to be fixed. The term *concerns* is used in an effort to encourage the view that families are competent and able to make choices based on their concerns and priorities. It is not that families are just "needy." It is *not* appropriate for early childhood special educators to decide what areas of family life should be assessed to determine family strengths and concerns. Therefore, the law specifically states that there must be "a *family-directed* assessment of the resources, priorities, and concerns of the family" (PL 108-446, Sec. 636).

When general difficulties in family functioning are suspected, it may be appropriate to use active listening strategies (see Chapter 2) while exploring with the family the possibility of referring them to appropriate professionals for counseling or other forms of assistance. Only families can decide for themselves which aspects of their functioning are relevant to their ability to help their child-rearing philosophy and abilities. Professionals need to understand the concerns and priorities of the family from the family's point of view and then identify the concerns and priorities from the provider's point of view. Through collaboration, concerns are then prioritized before resources can be identified.

Florene Poyadue, former executive director of Parents Helping Parents (see Chapter 2), has referred to **concerns, priorities,** and **resources** as the lifeline of families who have children with disabilities. Once concerns are prioritized, the responsibility of both the professional community and families is the identification of viable resources. It is important that professionals assist families in identifying and building on their own resources and strengths while at the same time helping them link up with appropriate community resources. It must be remembered that only resources that are easily accessible to families are useful.

Considerable discussion has been generated among professionals and families about the least intrusive way to help families identify their concerns, priorities, and resources. It is clearly acknowledged that professionals need training and experience in a more **family-centered approach to assessment** to balance their needs for specific information to determine eligibility and programming against families' priorities and concerns. As communities worked through implementation of Part C, they had to be creative in designing data-collection methods that maintain the integrity of each family as *primary decision makers*. This means that whenever there is doubt about a family's concerns or a child's intervention needs, the opinions of the family are to be sought first. Whether families complete interview forms or provide information through descriptive stories about their children, they must be given a choice in the assessment procedures used. Essential to the success of the whole collaborative process is a relationship between families and professionals built on trust and respect.

Hanson and Lynch (2013) listed four basic qualities educators must develop to effectively collaborate with families: (1) possessing knowledge and skills related to children with disabilities, (2) working within the context of the family and community, (3) being positive and open-minded, and (4) following through on promises. They further stated, "Professionals who are perceived to be dishonest with families, do not share information fully, do not respect family roles and responsibilities, display negative attitudes toward families or their job, and are not well trained for their jobs are not able to form collaborative partnerships" (p. 215).

The IFSP Document

In written form, the IFSP must contain the elements that follow below. Unique to the IFSP is a statement of "the measurable results or outcomes expected to be achieved for the infant or toddler *and* the family, including pre-literacy and language skills, as developmentally appropriate for the child" (Sec. 636). These **IFSP outcome statements** are intended to reflect changes family members want to see for their child *or* themselves. Each outcome must be stated in terms of what is to occur (process) and what is expected as a result of these actions (product). An example format is shown in Figure 3.1, but formats differ from state to state and within states. A telephone call to health, education, and social service agencies should direct interested individuals to the right sources to obtain copies of the format used locally. Whatever formats are chosen, the following content is required (Sec. 636):

1. A statement of the child's present levels of physical development (including vision, hearing, and health status), cognitive development, communication development, social or emotional development, and adaptive development based on objective criteria.

2. A statement of the family's resources, priorities, and concerns related to enhancing the development of the child.

3. A statement of measurable results or outcomes expected to be achieved for the child and family, and the criteria, procedures, and timelines used to determine the degree to which progress toward achieving the outcomes is being made and whether modifications or revisions of the outcomes or services are necessary. Outcomes must include preliteracy and language skills, as developmentally appropriate.

4. A statement of the specific early intervention services based on peer-reviewed research to the extent practical. Services listed should be necessary to meet the unique needs of the child and the family, including the frequency, intensity, and method of delivering services. Services that are not being paid for through Part C can be included as long as it is very clear how these services will be obtained.

5. A statement of the natural environments in which early intervention services shall appropriately be provided, including a justification of the extent, if any, to which the services will not be provided in a natural environment.

6. Projected dates for initiation of the services and the anticipated length, duration, and frequency of the services.

7. The name of the service coordinator who will be responsible for the implementation of the IFSP and coordination with other agencies and persons.

8. Steps to be taken or services to be implemented to support the transition of the child, on reaching age 3, to the next program of services recognized to be appropriate.

9. The contents of the IFSP shall be fully explained, and informed written consent from the parents or guardian shall be obtained prior to provision of the early intervention services described in the plan. The case of Cathy, given in Figure 3.1, illustrates one format that encompasses the requirements.

Developing Outcome Statements

The IFSP team is expected to develop outcome statements that will guide the choice of services to be delivered. These statements should have a direct connection to the concerns and priorities expressed by the family. These statements will document the changes

Figure 3.1 Example of an IFSP

INDIVIDUALIZED FAMILY SERVICE PLAN (IFSP) for Children Birth to Three Years   SANTA CLARA COUNTY

Child's name: _Cathy Rae Wright_   Birth Date: _9/14/16_   Age: _24_ months   Sex: _F_

Parent(s)/Guardian(s): _Martha and Gary Wright_   Address: _1414 Coolidge Drive Cupertino_   Zip: _95014_

Home phone: _408 398-2461_ Work phone: _408 554-2490_ Primary language of the home: _English_   Other languages _____

Date of this IFSP _9/14/18_ Projected periodic review _3/15/19_ Projected annual review _9/14/19_ Tentative IFSP exit _9/15/19_
(at 6 months or before)

Service Coordinator Name	Agency	Phone	Date Appointed	Date Ended
Sandy Drohman	_Regional Center_	_408-461-2192_	_9/1/18_	_/ /_
			_/ /_	_/ /_

Family's strengths and preferred resources   (With the family, identify the family strengths and the resources they might find helpful in addressing family concerns and priorities.) Mr. and Mrs. Wright are well educated and constantly seek additional information about Cathy's condition. They are eager to help Cathy in any way possible. Mrs. Wright's family is very supportive. They provide child care for Cathy's older brother.

Because of Cathy's tendency to be medically fragile, Mr. and Mrs. Wright prefer a home-based early intervention program. They appreciate receiving written materials to help them understand how to work with Cathy. Mrs. Wright wants to be home when the home visitor comes so she can learn from her.

Family's concerns and priorities   (With the family, identify major areas of concern for the child with special needs and the family as a whole.) Mr. and Mrs. Wright are very concerned about Cathy's delays in walking, using her fingers to pick up things, and in talking with other children. They also worry about her small size. Cathy is their second child and was born at 24 weeks' gestation. Mr. and Mrs. Wright would like to have more information on the issues of prematurity and they would like to find an appropriate support group for themselves.

Page _1_ of _6_ total IFSP

(Continued)

Figure 3.1 Example of an IFSP *(Continued)*

INDIVIDUALIZED FAMILY SERVICE PLAN (IFSP) for Children Birth to Three Years SANTA CLARA COUNTY

Child's name: _Cathy Rae Wright_ Chronological Age: _24_ months

CHILD'S STRENGTHS AND PRESENT LEVELS OF DEVELOPMENT

With the family, identify what the child can do and what the child is learning to do. Include family and professional observations in each of the following areas:

PHYSICAL *Based on parent report and HELP Strands

Health _Cathy is said by her parents to be healthy but is very petite. Her parents are working with a nutritionist to_
help Cathy gain weight.

Vision _Cathy has had corrective surgery for strabismus._

Hearing _She has had numerous ear infections and currently has tubes in her ears._

Gross Motor (large movement) _Cathy stands on tiptoes, runs on toes, makes sharp turns around corners when running,_
walks upstairs with one hand held.

Fine Motor (small movement) _Cathy grasps crayon adaptively and points with index finger; imitates horizontal_
strokes; builds 6-block tower; turns pages one at a time; has trouble picking up small objects.

COGNITIVE (responsiveness to environments, problem-solving) _Cathy finds hidden object; attempts and succeeds in activating_
mechanical toy; demonstrates use of objects appropriate for age.

COMMUNICATION (language and speech)

RECEPTIVE (understanding) _Cathy points to body parts when asked; obeys two-part commands._

EXPRESSIVE (making sounds, talking) _Cathy names 8 pictures, interacts with peers using only gestures;_
attempts to sing songs with words.

SOCIAL/EMOTIONAL (how relates to others) _Cathy expresses affection; is beginning to obey and respect simple rules;_
tends to be physically aggressive.

ADAPTIVE/SELF-HELP (sleeping, eating, dressing, toileting, etc.) _Cathy can put on socks and shoes; verbalizes need to use_
the toilet, but is not potty trained; feeds self.

DIAGNOSIS (if known)

Page _2_ of _6_ total IFSP

Figure 3.1 Example of an IFSP (*Continued*)

INDIVIDUALIZED FAMILY SERVICE PLAN (IFSP) for Children Birth to Three Years   SANTA CLARA COUNTY

Child's name: _____ Cathy Rae Wright _____

IFSP OUTCOMES

With the family, identify the goals they would like to work on in the next six months.
These should be directly related to the family's priorities and concerns as stated on page one.

OUTCOME: *Cathy will increase her attempts to vocally communicate in order to make her needs known and to positively interact with others.*

	Service Type (Individual = I Group = G) Location	Frequency of sessions Length of each session	Start Date	End Date (anticipated)	Responsible Agency/ Group Including payment arrangements (if any)
Strategy or activity to achieve the outcome (Who will do what and when will they do it?) AIM Infant Educator will model for Mr. and Mrs. Wright techniques to solicit Cathy's vocalization efforts. **Criteria** (How will we know if we are making progress?) Increased vocalization will be observed by parents and infant educator.	I – Home-based infant program	1 hour each week	9/17/18	9/1/19	AIM (funded by SARC) Family
Strategy or activity to achieve the outcome (Who will do what and when will they do it?) Mrs. Wright will take Cathy to play with neighborhood children and will invite children to her home. She will encourage play and vocalization. **Criteria** (How will we know if we are making progress?) Mrs. Wright will observe and note extent of interaction.	G – Home and in the neighborhood	once each week for at least 30 minutes	9/26/18	ongoing	Mrs. Wright
Strategy or activity to achieve the outcome (Who will do what and when will they do it?) Cathy will be assessed by a speech pathologist by 10/10/18 and followed on an as-needed basis. **Criteria** (How will we know if we are making progress?) A follow-up report will be submitted.	I – Regional Center Speech and Language Clinic	1 hour play-based assessment	9/26/18	as needed	Sandy Drohman will make arrangements (funded by SARC)

Page __3__ of __6__ total IFSP

(Continued)

Figure 3.1 Example of an IFSP (*Continued*)

INDIVIDUALIZED FAMILY SERVICE PLAN (IFSP) for Children Birth to Three Years   SANTA CLARA COUNTY

Child's name: _____Cathy Rae Wright_____

IFSP OUTCOMES

With the family, identify the goals they would like to work on in the next six months.
These should be directly related to the family's priorities and concerns as stated on page one.

OUTCOME: _Cathy will increase her weight in order to maintain health and continue a developmentally appropriate growth pattern._

Service Type (Individual = I Group = G) Location	Frequency of sessions Length of each session	Start Date	End Date (anticipated)	Responsible Agency/ Group Including payment arrangements (if any)
Kaiser Hospital Clinic	30 min. each month	ongoing	as needed	Mrs. Breez (Kaiser funded)

Strategy or activity to achieve the outcome
(Who will do what and when will they do it?)
Mr. and Mrs. Wright will continue to work with Mrs. Breez to improve Cathy's nutrition intake.

Criteria (How will we know if we are making progress?)

Strategy or activity to achieve the outcome
(Who will do what and when will they do it?)

Criteria (How will we know if we are making progress?)

Strategy or activity to achieve the outcome
(Who will do what and when will they do it?)

Criteria (How will we know if we are making progress?)

Figure 3.1 Example of an IFSP *(Continued)*

| INDIVIDUALIZED FAMILY SERVICE PLAN (IFSP) for Children Birth to Three Years | | | | SANTA CLARA COUNTY | |

Child's name: _____ *Cathy Rae Wright* _____

IFSP OUTCOMES

With the family, identify the goals they would like to work on in the next six months. These should be directly related to the family's priorities and concerns as stated on page one.

OUTCOME: *Mr. and Mrs. Wright will join Parents Helping Parents in order to receive peer parent support and learn more about Cathy's condition.*

	Service Type (Individual = I Group = G) Location	Frequency of sessions Length of each session	Start Date	End Date (anticipated)	Responsible Agency/ Group Including payment arrangements (if any)
Strategy or activity to achieve the outcome (who will do what and when will they do it?) *Sandy Drohman will provide all referral information to Mr. and Mrs. Wright and will accompany them to their first meeting if they desire.*	*G – Parents Helping Parents*	*(up to parent's discretion)*			*Sandy Drohman*
					Mr. and Mrs. Wright
Criteria (How will we know if we are making progress?) *Mr. and Mrs. Wright will find satisfaction in increased support and knowledge.*					*Parents Helping Parents*
Strategy or activity to achieve the outcome (who will do what and when will they do it?) *AIM Infant Educator will assist Mr. and Mrs. Wright in obtaining additional information about Cathy's condition.*	*I – Home*	*ongoing*	*9/26/18*	*9/1/19*	*AIM Infant Educator*
Criteria (How will we know if we are making progress?) *Mr. and Mrs. Wright will express satisfaction over the assistance received in becoming more informed.*					
Strategy or activity to achieve the outcome (who will do what and when will they do it?)					
Criteria (How will we know if we are making progress?)					

Page _5_ of _6_ total IFSP

(Continued)

Figure 3.1 Example of an IFSP *(Continued)*

INDIVIDUALIZED FAMILY SERVICE PLAN (IFSP) for Children Birth to Three Years   SANTA CLARA COUNTY

Child's name: _____ Cathy Rae Wright _____

TRANSITION PLAN — This child's transition at _____ 36 _____ months will be accomplished by completing the following steps:

1. At 30 months, Mrs. Wright will meet with the district program specialist to review placement options.

2. Mrs. Wright will visit the sites with Sandy Drohman.

3. Mrs. Wright will state her preference and will sign enrollment forms.

4. Mrs. Wright will attend the orientation with Cathy.

STATEMENT OF ELIGIBILITY — The IFSP team determines that assessment results demonstrate that the family and child are eligible for services under Part C of the *Individuals with Disabilities Education Act* — ☒ Yes or ☐ No. Percentage of time child is in natural environment _____ N.A. _____ %.

FAMILY — I (We) had the opportunity to participate in the development of this IFSP. It represents my (our) concerns, priorities, and outcomes for my (our) child and family. I (We) ☒ do ☐ do not give permission for this plan to be implemented. I (We) understand that this IFSP plan is in effect through _____ 11/15/12 _____ .

_____ Date   _____ Mrs. Martha Wright _____   9/15/19
                          Parent(s)/Legal Guardian(s) Signature(s)   Date

OTHER IFSP PARTICIPANTS — The following individuals/agencies participated in the development of the IFSP either by attending the meeting or giving input by telephone or in writing and agree to carry out the plan as it applies to their role in the provision of entitled early intervention services.

Name, Title & Phone		Agency	Gave input by telephone or writing (Person receiving input initial here)	Date
Mr. and Mrs. Gary Wright		Parents		9/15/19
Sandy Drohman	408-461-2192	Regional Center		9/15/19
Julie Maze	408-460-6190	Public Health Nursing		9/15/19
Margaret Breez	408-642-8314	Kaiser Nutritionist	JD	9/15/19
Rosalie Martinez	408-648-2941	AIM Infant Program		9/15/19

Notes for consideration at next review: _____ Consider relationship between Cathy and her older brother, John.

Page _____ 6 _____ of _____ 6 _____ total IFSP

families hope to see for their children or themselves as these changes relate to the developmental needs of their child. Outcome statements are to be jargon-free, meaningful for the family and the child, and stated in the language of the family whenever possible. They should refer to practical activities that fit into a family's daily life and represent skills that enhance the child's ability to participate in daily routines. Based on family concerns, priorities and resources, there are two categories of IFSP outcomes, family-focused and child-focused. As described by Shelden and Rush (2014), family-focused outcomes relate to (a) obtaining supports and resources for the family, (b) promoting the child's participation in routines, and (c) parenting responsibilities. Child-focused outcomes address the child's participation and learning in a routine or activity.

"Functional outcomes are practical, meaningful, and necessary to the family" (Gatmaitan & Brown, 2016, p. 19). Given differences in children's development and family lifestyle, concerns, and priorities, practitioners should be aware that what may be functional outcomes for one child and family may not be functional for another child and family.

An effective approach to collaborating with families in choosing the most relevant and timely outcome statements is the *routine-based interview* (RBI) originating from the work of McWilliam (2012) and explained by McWilliam himself in Video Example 3.1. In it, he clearly explains the reasons why RBI is so highly recommended. These include a focus on functionality by identifying real family needs; an understanding of the context (family routines) within which the family needs originate, making it easy to identify when and where changes need to be made; and clearly identifying services from which the child and family will benefit. RBI is an evidence-based interviewing technique that is a manageable form of family assessment that provides the essential information needed to develop outcomes resulting in services that can really make a difference in the lives of families and children.

Moreover, outcomes that focus on a child's participation in family routines are highly likely to promote integrated interventions by (a) targeting areas of development across domains rather than discrete skill areas, (b) involving families and other caregivers, (c) working across routines and settings, and (d) involving team members and relevant agencies (Gatmaitan & Brown, 2016). In addition, intervention that takes place within daily family routines usually does not require extra materials or setup time.

Phrasing the outcome statements as "in order to" and identifying the context for the behavior make it easy to understand the functional purpose of the action to be encouraged. For example, parents who are eager for their child to learn to walk may not be satisfied with an outcome statement that is written as "Josh will pull to stand" unless an addition is made so that it reads "Josh will pull to stand and cruise along the sofa *in order to* begin walking." This formula allows the result (product: walking) of the process (pull to stand) to be readily understood and identifies the daily routine in which the child will be motivated to practice the skill (McWilliam, 2010). That is, action A will be encouraged to realize outcome B. Activities or strategies should then flow directly from the outcome statements. In Josh's case, for example, advice from a physical therapist should be sought to determine the most appropriate strategies to encourage Josh to pull to stand and cruise along the sofa to obtain a desired toy.

Figure 3.1 illustrates three outcome statements chosen by Mr. and Mrs. Wright for their daughter Cathy. Others could have been included, but Cathy's parents decided that these three were of the highest priority at the time of the initial IFSP.

It is important to realize that the IFSP does not take the place of a **program plan.** The IFSP identifies *services* and desired *outcomes*. It does not identify a complete list of specific objectives, strategies, and activities to be used in bringing about the outcomes. Although not required by law, all service providers should prepare a written plan of specific long- and short-term objectives (including teaching steps and strategies) for reaching each outcome. (See pages 108–110 for detailed information related to writing instructional objectives.)

Video Example from

You Tube

Enhanced eText
Video Example 3.1
McWilliam on RBI and Early Intervention
https://www.youtube.com/watch?v=yhcUotSkYAY
In this video, Robert McWilliam explains why he highly recommends routine-based interviews.

Service Coordination

PL 99-457 and PL 108-446 mandate that a **service coordinator** be designated to ensure the full development of the IFSP for *birth to 3-year-olds* and their families. The law intends that professional assistance be provided to support optimal family functioning. Thus, service coordination is considered to be an integral part of the IFSP process.

Part C rules and regulations state that service coordination consists primarily of activities designed to assist and enable an eligible child and the child's family to receive the rights, procedural safeguards, and services that are authorized to be provided through each state's early intervention program. Service coordinators assume responsibility for the following:

- Coordination of the full IFSP process for each eligible child
- Informing families of the availability of advocacy services
- Inclusion of parents as full multidisciplinary team members
- Inclusion of all professionals who should be involved with the family
- If appropriate, acquiring an interpreter
- Scheduling and facilitating assessments and IFSP meetings
- Encouraging exchange of ideas and recommendations
- Encouraging creative, integrated, and coordinated intervention options
- Facilitating problem solving and conflict resolution
- Serving as the single point of contact in helping parents obtain appropriate services
- Facilitating the development of a transition plan to preschool services, when appropriate
- Filing a copy of the IFSP transition plan documents in the child's record

Service coordination is to be an active, ongoing process that involves helping parents to gain access to services identified in their child's IFSP, coordinating these services, and facilitating timely delivery of appropriate services throughout the duration of the child's eligibility. In some areas of the United States, early childhood special educators who work with birth to 3-year-olds may be expected to become service coordinators. Those who have not had training in family systems theory, in understanding the requirements of federal and state legislation, and in local service-delivery systems must seek this training before accepting such a responsibility.

Although specific service-coordination activities are listed, it is understood that these activities are fluid, interrelated, and always individually determined in collaboration with families. Activities that are helpful to one family may be irrelevant or undesired by another. Even activities that are appropriate for a family today may not be suitable for that family tomorrow. Effectiveness of service coordination will depend on the competencies of the service coordinator, including his or her ability to involve families in helping get their own needs met.

Who Can Become Service Coordinators?

Although the law does mandate the involvement of someone responsible for service coordination, it allows flexibility in the choice of service coordinator and in the model of service coordination implemented. It is the intent of the law that the person best qualified to meet the needs of the family and the child should become the family's service coordinator. Optimally, the service coordinator is selected on the basis of the desires of the family and can be from any agency. Service coordinators will change as the needs and appropriate services for the family change. Parents do have the right to reject service coordination entirely.

Models of Service Coordination

In reviewing the breadth and depth of service-coordination practices, Dunst and Bruder (2006) examined the three prevalent models of service coordination: dedicated and independent, dedicated but not independent, and blended. The **dedicated and independent model** refers to a model where "the role of the service coordinator is dedicated to service coordination only, and the agency providing service coordination is independent from service provision" (Bruder, 2005, p. 34).

In the **dedicated, but not independent model,** the service coordinator provides only service coordination. However, he or she works for the same agency or program providing early intervention services. Finally, in the **blended model,** the service coordinator provides both service coordination and early intervention services. Generally, states and territories use a combination of models.

Dunst and Bruder (2006) endeavored to find out if different service-coordination models were found to be associated with different service-coordination practices. They found that when the service coordination is done by a coordinator who is independent from a program that delivers early intervention services, there is significantly less contact with program participants than when the service coordinator is from an agency that offers early intervention services. The fact that independent but dedicated models are less efficient is explained by the need for independent coordinators to facilitate collaboration and integrate activities among more agencies than is true of the blended models. Given the fact that families often get relatively little time and attention from their service coordinators for a variety of reasons, it is up to the professionals who work with children daily to become well informed about local resources and participate in the networking discussed here.

Promoting Essential Interagency Collaboration

Educational programs that serve young children with disabilities can provide all the services that children and families require only through collaboration with other programs and agencies. **Community networking** describes the efforts involved in coordinating services among agencies. It can reduce fragmentation, avoid duplication, and help families gain easy access to needed services. States and counties differ in how interagency collaboration is achieved. Also, the lead agency responsible for overseeing services for children birth to 3 years of age is highly variable from state to state.

As discussed previously, families of children with disabilities under the age of 3 years are assigned a service coordinator whose responsibility is to facilitate interagency collaboration on behalf of families' needs. Older children or children whose disabilities are not severe enough to be deemed eligible for service coordination will look elsewhere for assistance in navigating the service-delivery maze. The most appropriate professionals to be of assistance are the early intervention specialists and early education teachers with whom families are in daily contact.

Therefore, to develop efficient and effective interagency collaboration, programs must involve a variety of networking activities. Networking activities vary because of differences in resources or community needs and geographic and cultural factors. Early education specialists need to *develop a clear understanding of the needs of each child and family and a thorough knowledge of the available resources.* A personal evaluation of programs and personnel fosters a useful match between needs and services. Attention should be paid to the quality, breadth, and cost of services. Families will need help in complying with referral procedures and support during waiting periods. Ideally, networking efforts will result in formal or informal interagency agreements that extend services to meet the disabilities of children and their families.

Figure 3.2 Example of an IEP

Note: Figure 3.2 is a downloadable Model IEP form available at http://www.Wrightslaw.com. Components and requirements of the IEP with their corresponding federal law references are presented there.

Part B | INDIVIDUALIZED EDUCATION PROGRAM

The Individualized Education Program (IEP) is a written document that is developed for each eligible child with a disability. The Part B regulations specify, at 34 CFR §§300.320-300.328, the procedures that school districts must follow to develop, review, and revise the IEP for each child. The document below sets out the IEP content that those regulations require.

A statement of the child's present levels of academic achievement and functional performance including:

- How the child's disability affects the child's involvement and progress in the general education curriculum (i.e., the same curriculum as for nondisabled children) **or** for preschool children, as appropriate, how the disability affects the child's participation in appropriate activities. [34 CFR §300.320(a)(1)]

A statement of measurable annual goals, including academic and functional goals designed to:

- Meet the child's needs that result from the child's disability to enable the child to be involved in and make progress in the general education curriculum. [34 CFR §300.320(a)(2)(i)(A)]

- Meet each of the child's other educational needs that result from the child's disability. [34 CFR §300.320(a)(2)(i)(B)]

For children with disabilities who take alternate assessments aligned to alternate achievement standards (in addition to the annual goals), a description of benchmarks or short-term objectives. [34 CFR §300.320(a)(2)(ii)]

Collaboration also includes involvement in activities that create awareness of the early education program and its contribution to the process of networking. Open houses, personal contacts, media coverage, brochures, presentations at meetings, and participation on community advisory councils develop public awareness. Even though networking activities will change with time, they remain essential to the delivery of a successful early intervention program.

Note: Federal special education law requires and carefully describes two separate processes and documents for planning educational and developmental programs. As previously discussed, for infants and toddlers, the document is referred to as the *individualized family service plan* (IFSP) and is described in IDEA Part C. For pre-school-age children—as well as students in K–12—the document is referred to as the *individualized education program* (IEP). The IEP and the process for developing it are discussed in the next section. Figure 3.2 shows an example of an individualized education program.

Figure 3.2 Example of an IEP (*Continued*)

Part B INDIVIDUALIZED E   2

A description of:

- How the child's progress toward meeting the annual goals will be measured.
  [34 CFR §300.320(a)(3)(i)]

- When periodic reports on the progress the child is making toward meeting the
  annual goals will be provided, such as through the use of quarterly or other
  periodic reports, concurrent with the issuance of report cards.
  [34 CFR §300.320(a)(3)(ii)]

A statement of the <u>special education and related services</u> and <u>supplementary aids</u> and
<u>services,</u> based on peer-reviewed research to the extent practicable, to be provided to
the child, or on behalf of the child, and <u>a statement of the program modifications or
supports</u> for school personnel that will be provided to enable the child:

- To advance appropriately toward attaining the annual goals.
  [34 CFR §300.320(a)(4)(i)]

- To be involved in and make progress in the general education curriculum and to
  participate in extracurricular and other nonacademic activities.
  [34 CFR §300.320(a)(4)(ii)]

- To be educated and participate with other children with disabilities and
  nondisabled children in extracurricular and other nonacademic activities.
  [34 CFR §300.320(a)(4)(iii)]

An explanation of the extent, if any, to which the child will not participate with
nondisabled children in the regular classroom and in extracurricular and other
nonacademic activities. [34 CFR §300.320(a)(5)]

(Continued)

Developing Individualized Education Programs (IEPs) for Preschoolers

Federal guidelines require children who may be eligible for special education services
to be seen for assessment and diagnostic study by members of a multidisciplinary team
before services can begin. The law does not specify the professionals to be included
in the assessment phase of the IEP process. However, it is expected that choice of the
members for a specific team will be determined by the characteristics and suspected
disabling conditions of a particular child. For example, in all cases of suspected speech
and/or language delays, the child should be seen by a speech-language pathologist
(SLP). This SLP should also be present at the subsequent formal multidisciplinary

---

Figure 3.2 Example of an IEP *(Continued)*

| Part B | INDIVIDUALIZED EDUCATION PROGRAM | 3 |

A statement of any individual appropriate accommodations that are necessary to measure the academic achievement and functional performance of the child on State and districtwide assessments. [34 CFR §300.320(a)(6)(i)]

If the IEP Team determines that the child must take an alternate assessment instead of a particular regular State or districtwide assessment of student achievement, a statement of why:

- The child cannot participate in the regular assessment.
  [34 CFR §300.320(a)(6)(ii)(A)]

- The particular alternate assessment selected is appropriate for the child.
  [34 CFR §300.320(a)(6)(ii)(B)]

The projected date for the beginning of the services and modifications and the anticipated frequency, location, and duration of <u>special education and related services</u> and <u>supplementary aids and services</u> and <u>modifications and supports</u>.
[34 CFR §300.320(a)(7)]

Service, Aid or Modification	Frequency	Location	Beginning Date	Duration

meeting, at which time the IEP is developed. In some cases, team members may participate through conference calls.

People expected to attend the meeting where the IEP document is developed include the following (PL 108-446, Sec. 614):

1. One or both of the child's parents

2. At least one general education teacher if the child is participating in a general education program

3. At least one special education teacher or, where appropriate, at least one special education provider of such child

4. Any member of the school staff, other than the child's teacher, who is "qualified to provide, or supervise the provision of, specially designed instruction to meet the unique needs of children with disabilities; is knowledgeable about the general education curriculum; and is knowledgeable about the availability of resources of the local education agency"

5. An individual who can interpret the instructional implications of evaluation results

6. An administrator who has the authority to make commitments on behalf of the school district

Figure 3.2 Example of an IEP (*Continued*)

| Part B | INDIVIDUALIZED EDUCATION PROGRAM | 4 |

TRANSITION SERVICES

Beginning not later than the first IEP to be in effect <u>when the child turns 16, or younger if determined appropriate by the IEP Team</u>, and updated annually thereafter, the IEP must include:

- Appropriate measurable postsecondary goals based upon age-appropriate transition assessments related to training, education, employment, and where appropriate, independent living skills. [34 CFR §300.320(b)(1)]

- The transition services (including courses of study) needed to assist the child in reaching those goals. [34 CFR §300.320(b)(2)]

Transition Services (Including Courses of Study)

RIGHTS THAT TRANSFER AT AGE OF MAJORITY

- Beginning not later than one year before the child reaches the age of majority under State law, the IEP must include a statement that the child has been informed of the child's rights under Part B of the IDEA, if any, that will, consistent with 34 CFR §300.520, transfer to the child on reaching the age of majority. [34 CFR §300.320(c)]

7. If a child has received early intervention services under Part C, the parent has the right to request that the Part C coordinator or representative be invited to the initial IEP meeting

8. Other individuals whose expertise may be desired by the parent or school

The IEP Team Meeting Process and Required Contents of the IEP

The IEP is a written plan that must contain the following elements:

1. *Present levels of performance.* A statement of the child's present strengths and levels of academic achievement and functional performance, including how the disability affects involvement and progress in the general education curriculum

2. *Disability.* Identification of the child's disability and how it may interfere with the child's learning

3. *Measurable annual goals and short-term objectives (or benchmarks).* A statement of measurable annual goals based on the child's strengths and levels of performance. The goals must include academic (readiness) and functional goals. Short-term objectives for meeting the annual goals are required if the child has significant cognitive delays.

4. A statement of the specific special education and related services and supplementary aids to be provided to the child and a statement of the program modifications, and supports for school personnel, that will be provided

5. An explanation of the extent, if any, that the child will *not* participate with nondisabled children in the regular class

6. The projected dates for initiation of services and the anticipated frequency, location, and duration of services

7. The appropriate objective criteria and evaluation procedures to measure progress toward the annual goals

8. Specific plans for provision of smooth transition into kindergarten

9. Explanation of how families will be involved and the type and frequency of communication regarding the child's progress. Progress must be reported at least four times a year.

Although the precise written format may differ from area to area, the required content must be included. The IEP must promote the child's learning and development. A recent decision by the U.S. Supreme Court clarified that "a school must offer an IEP that is reasonably calculated to enable a child to make progress appropriate in light of the child's circumstances" (U.S. Department of Education, 2017).

The IEP team, including the parents as valid members, considers "the strengths of the child, the concerns of the parents for enhancing the education of their child and the results of the initial evaluation or most recent evaluation of the child; and the academic, developmental, and functional needs of the child" (PL 108-446, Sec. 614). Priorities are chosen. Measurable IEP annual goals, including benchmarks or short-term objectives, are specified. How progress toward these **IEP annual goals and objectives** will be measured is determined. The goals must include academic and functional goals and are expected to enable the child to be involved and make progress in the general education curriculum. The team, with critical input from the family, determines what supplemental supports, aids, and services will be received; where the services will be offered; and when the services will begin. These will be written on the program plan.

Related Service-Provider Preparation. Whenever possible, the related service providers (speech-language pathologists, occupational therapists, etc.) who evaluate young children ask to see reports of observations made by others, including teachers and parents. Often, a screening test is used as a preliminary step to in-depth evaluations when children are initially being evaluated.

Each service provider will choose assessment procedures judged to be relevant to the suspected problems. During the diagnosis, it may become apparent that additional tests are needed. If one specialist obtains information that suggests additional specialists need to be included in the multidisciplinary diagnostic team, it is his or her responsibility to request the necessary additional diagnosis. The chairperson of the meeting in

Endrew F. v. Douglas County School District Supreme Court Ruling: May 2017

This ruling strongly rejected the idea that minimal progress from year to year is sufficient. In fact, Chief Justice Roberts said, " . . . a student offered an educational program providing 'merely more than de minimus' progress from year to year can hardly be said to have been offered an education at all." Instead, he went on to say, "The IDEA demands more. It requires an educational program reasonably calculated to enable a child to make progress appropriate in light of the child's circumstances. The goals may differ, but every child should have the chance to meet challenging objectives."

This landmark case clearly paves the way for an increase in expectations for children with disabilities by requiring that each child's individual strengths and weaknesses be considered when writing an IEP. Meaningful progress through 'appropriately ambitious' objectives is expected. Some small benefit will not be considered to be enough. For implications of this ruling, visit http://journals.sagepub.com/doi/pdf/10.1177/0040059917721116 (Yell & Bateman, 2017).

Source: Yell, M. L. & Bateman, D. F. (2017). Endrew F. v. Douglas County School District. *Teaching Exceptional Children, 50*(1), 7–18.

which the IEP is developed often is the person referred to in the law as the representative of the local educational agency. This person may be responsible for collecting all assessment information and ensuring that no important aspect of the diagnostic process is overlooked. Professionals involved must be prepared to relate test results, their level of confidence in the child's performance, and recommendations for placement and services to the chairperson. *They should make every possible effort to translate their findings into information directly useful to program and activity planning.*

When participating in the interdisciplinary staffing, professionals should be prepared to speak in a language that parents understand. They must remember that parents, as well as professionals, are to be included as active, vital members of the team. As Diliberto and Brewer (2012) point out, "The key to successful IEP development is open communication" (p. 31). Avoiding the use of jargon is essential.

Parents' Preparation. Parents are expected to organize any information they have received from previous examiners. They have the responsibility of honestly and accurately sharing information about their child's behavior and perceived strengths and concerns. Parents serve as the child's advocate.

Professionals can be very helpful in assisting parents to prepare the information they wish to share as well as in developing a list of questions to be asked of members of the IEP team. Parents should be given any assistance they need to fully understand the program and services being proposed. In some cases, interpreters or multilingual specialists have to be included in the multidisciplinary team. It is especially important for professionals to understand exactly which intervention goals are important to each child's parents. A questionnaire or interview asking parents to identify those skills they would *most* like to see their child accomplish in the coming year and behaviors that would reduce stress in the family, increase independence, and so on, is an effective way to ensure parents' *active participation* in selecting and prioritizing goals for their children (Patti, 2016). Parents' goals should take highest priority on the list of objectives to be achieved. For example, the parent may think the child's becoming independent in feeding is more important than making eye contact with the staff. Although professionals tend to feel they know what is most important for the child to learn and achieve, the needs and desires of the parents should take precedence whenever realistically possible. Initial understanding and genuine acceptance by parents of services to be offered can save many hours of discussion or even the necessity of changes later on.

Sending families a rough draft of goals and objectives for them to review and react to before the IEP meeting is another way to solicit active parent participation in setting priorities. This approach may also help to relieve parental anxiety. It is also very important for family members to have an understanding of what to expect at the IEP meeting. By understanding the order of events, who will be present, procedures required by law, and their own rights and responsibilities, the anxiety level of parents can be significantly decreased.

Given the advances in digital technology, most school districts have adopted an electronic IEP management system. However, teachers and administrators should consider how to make the use of this system effective for the inclusion of team members and families. More and Hart (2013) have the following suggestions:

1. Learn about and practice using the system through training and mentoring so that they are confident in using it during the IEP meeting.

2. If the teacher is the facilitator of the meeting, someone else should be responsible for word processing.

3. Use a projector so that everyone at the meeting can see the objectives and other information on the IEP form.

4. Create a personalized goal bank that meets the child's learning needs. Many electronic goal banks reflect the learning standards of the school district and may not be appropriate for preschoolers with disabilities.

5. Make sure that the IEP objectives are tailored for the individual child's learning needs.

6. Report any difficulties with the IEP electronic program to the school administrator so that he or she can determine how to resolve them.

7. Involve parents by obtaining their input and preparing them for the IEP meeting. For example, send home drafts of the IEP document and reports in advance of the meeting as permitted by the school's policy.

8. Set aside the computer if it seems to inhibit conversation with parents. Make notes on a paper copy of the form and enter the information electronically later.

Cautions to Consider When Promoting Family Participation. As Turnbull, Turnbull, Erwin, Soodak, and Shogren (2011) pointed out, "Since the 1980s, the research literature has been fairly consistent in acknowledging that IFSP/IEP conferences often fail to honor partnership practices" (p. 214). These authors emphasize the fact that IEP conferences usually do not allow enough time to plan appropriately, parents tend to have limited roles in meetings, conferences may be terminated at a set time even if the process is not complete, computer-generated IEPs are often developed before the IEP meeting, and parents often view the professionals as the primary decision makers. There is no doubt that when IEP goals are developed from a goal bank of Web-based software for online IEPs, and there is inadequate time for discussion, a family-centered approach to early education is not being practiced. Yes, attending an IEP meeting can be a very formal and uncomfortable experience for many parents, particularly if professionals primarily focus on their child's disability labels and deficits. It is necessary that school staff allocate sufficient time for meetings, desist from completing forms before parent input is obtained, and send drafts of IEP goals and objectives home for parents to review and change in advance of the meeting (Cheatham, Hart, Malian, & McDonald, 2012).

To effectively engage parents in the IEP process, Fialka and Fialka-Feldman (2017) suggest creating a conversation by asking questions to find out about the family's values and hopes. For example, "What are your dreams for your child? What do you worry about? What keeps you up at night? What supports have worked well in the past? What are your child's gifts?" (p. 48). These authors also suggest creating an "IEP One-Pager" that organizes information into five categories: (a) things the child can do independently, (b) things the child is beginning to do, (c) things the child can do with support, (d) key classroom accommodations, and (e) areas of instructional focus for the upcoming months. With photos and artifacts, the "IEP One-Pager" will create a snapshot of the child in the classroom that may be shared at the IEP meeting and, hopefully, will elicit family and team comments.

For families of diverse cultural and linguistic backgrounds, the IEP meeting can be even more unfamiliar, overwhelming, and anxiety-provoking. Lo (2012) provided specific considerations for supporting family comfort and participation in the IEP meeting:

1. **Before the meeting,** (a) notify the family about (i) the IEP process, timeline, parent rights, and importance of parent participation, (ii) relevant community resources, (iii) parent-to parent opportunities, (iv) options of dates and times for the meeting, people who will be attending, and the length of the meeting; (b) draft an agenda and invite parents to add items; and (c) be certain that documents are in the family's primary language and written for their educational level.

2. **The day of the meeting:** (a) meet with the interpreter ahead of the meeting to provide a glossary of terms and definitions of acronyms and discuss interpretation procedures (see Chapter 2), (b) identify who will meet and greet the parents when they arrive at the school to show them to the meeting room, (c) ask team members to introduce themselves and describe their roles, (d) use open-ended questions to determine if parents understand discussions, (e) note parents' nonverbal and verbal communication, and (f) encourage their questions and feedback.

3. **After the meeting:** (a) provide a brief written summary of the meeting and invite parents to meet, call, text, or e-mail if they have questions; (b) let parents know what will happen after the meeting, when they will receive a copy of the IEP, and their rights if they disagree with the IEP; (c) have the IEP translated and sent to the parents as soon as possible.

Considering Darren

The following narrative describes the background and proceedings of one child's multidisciplinary conference leading to the development of an IEP.

Background Information

Darren's parents are worried. Twice they have been asked to withdraw him from childcare centers. Now the private preschool that he has been attending has called them in for a conference. Both parents work, and they want the best possible placement for Darren. Several friends have told them that they know he would not be accepted in the public school kindergarten next year. He rarely talks, and when he does, it is very difficult to understand him. He is also stubborn. Many times when his parents tell him to do something, he acts as if he does not hear them unless they yell at him. They are worried that he might be placed in a special classroom.

October 21, 2018. Darren has now been enrolled in a private preschool for 8 weeks. His teacher, Ms. McLynn, and the site administrator, Ms. Johnson, are eager to discuss their observations with Darren's parents, the Dicksons.

Ms. JOHNSON: Thank you for coming. We are enjoying Darren and hope he is enjoying us. We have observed Darren in a variety of situations and would like to discuss our observations with you.

MRS. DICKSON: We are so pleased that Darren is coming to your program. We are grateful for the help you have given Darren and are eager to hear about how he is doing.

Ms. JOHNSON: Well, as you know, it is sometimes difficult for us to understand what Darren is saying, and it seems that often he doesn't understand us. When we try to tell him to do something, he just seems so confused. We can get him to pay attention by standing in front of him and talking directly to him. He also seems to have trouble with the names of things like colors and body parts.

MRS. DICKSON: We have also noticed some of the things you are talking about. His pediatrician examined him, as you suggested, and he said he is fine. He told us that many children don't learn to speak clearly until they are in school.

MR. DICKSON: Our friends the Joneses have a little girl who the psychologist said is very slow. She doesn't talk clearly either, and they put her in a special class. We really don't want Darren in a class with children who have problems or can't learn. Darren isn't dumb.

Ms. MCLYNN: I agree with you, Mr. Dickson. Darren isn't dumb. But something is wrong. He misunderstands us most of the time, and we can't understand him. He doesn't know the names of lots of things the others know.

Ms. JOHNSON: We feel that we aren't helping Darren enough. He needs special kinds of help that we aren't trained to provide. We are hoping that you will agree to have specialists test Darren to help us find the best ways to work with him.

MR. DICKSON: I'm not sure. Are you sure that Darren needs all of this help? We can understand him.

Ms. JOHNSON: Yes, I believe you can understand Darren, and he is obviously bright in many ways. He does the most difficult puzzles easily and builds wonderful towns with blocks. We would just like to find out what is causing Darren's communication problems and how we should be working with him.

MR. DICKSON: OK. Whom do we call?

Ms. JOHNSON: I'm sure your local school district will be able to provide the appropriate assessments for Darren. We will help you find out whom to contact.

As Mr. and Mrs. Dickson left the preschool, they still felt somewhat frightened. Mrs. Dickson remembered that one preschool teacher had said her son had a "dull expression" and another said that he seemed "bewildered." But when they spoke to friends and relatives, they all reassured them that Darren was just a late bloomer. In spite of their fears, the parents did call their local public school office and made an appointment for a diagnostic interview. They had to sign papers to release information from the preschool and to confirm that they agreed to the testing.

January 15, 2019. Once the assessments are completed, Darren's parents, Mr. and Mrs. Dickson, are informed regarding the IEP process and a date is set for the IEP team members to convene. Members of the team include Darren's teacher, Ms. McLynn from the private preschool, his parents, a school psychologist, a nurse, a social worker, a speech-language pathologist, and a special education administrator. The administrator has reviewed the background information and provided written materials regarding parents' rights to Darren's parents.

MR. DICKSON: I am eager to hear what the psychologist has to say, first.

Present Levels of Performance and Identified Strengths and Needs

PSYCHOLOGIST: Darren worked very hard and seemed to want to try everything. Because Darren appeared to understand little speech and language, and I had a hard time understanding him, I gave him two kinds of tests. Well, really three. First, I tried a vocabulary test. For that test, I showed pictures and named them. All Darren had to do was point to the picture that I named. Each page has four pictures, and only one is correct. On that test, Darren responded by naming or pointing to a few pictures correctly. He often seemed confused. He couldn't identify as many pictures as most children his age. Then I attempted to use a test that requires Darren to listen to me and answer questions and point to things, too. Again, he was unable to do most of the items that other 4-year-olds can do. So, next I used a nonverbal performance test. On this test, Darren had to listen to only a few directions and did not have to talk to me. He did have to watch me carefully and then imitate some of the things I did. And here he was more successful. He seemed to enjoy these activities. His confused expression disappeared, and he looked more interested. Darren was able to match the colors very well. He could do difficult puzzles, complete copying designs, and put pattern pieces together. When he finished, he grinned at me and seemed to want to do more.

Ms. MCLYNN: That's the way he is at school, too. He can color and draw better than most of the other children. He is quick to learn how to make things.

SPEECH-LANGUAGE PATHOLOGIST: My tests indicate that Darren says most of the vowels correctly, although the short vowels, as in p*i*n, p*a*n, p*e*n, and p*u*n, aren't distinct. He can imitate the voiced consonants, for example, /b/, /d/, /g/, /m/, and /n/, and he uses them in some words, but he often omits them on the ends of words. He says ba*w* for ba*ll* and d*aw* for d*og*, for example. When he tries to make sentences, he leaves off /s/, /t/, and /z/ at the ends of words, so he cannot "signal" past tense, as in hopp*ed* and look*ed*. He doesn't use plurals, as in car*s* and truck*s*. When I asked him to listen to me, say a sentence, and point to the picture that showed what I had said, he was really confused. One picture page has a little boy looking into a mirror, seeing himself, and another picture where he is looking at a shelf. Darren had no idea what I wanted him to do. When I said, "He sees himself," he pointed to both pictures. Also, I recorded more than 50 things that he said while we played with some cars and trucks and a toy garage. He really enjoyed that. When I analyzed what he said, I found that he is using three- and four-word sentences, although the words are not clear. He tried to ask me for things, too.

NURSE: Darren responded very quickly and accurately to my vision screening test. I showed him just once what I wanted him to do. He was all business, paid close attention, and quickly demonstrated that he has good eyesight. But the hearing testing was another story! He wiggled and giggled. He said he heard the tones when the audiometer was off. At 25 decibels, the loudness level used for hearing screening, he heard 500 and 1,000 hertz in one ear, but he did not respond to the same loudness at higher frequencies. In the other ear, he did not answer correctly at all at 25 decibels. So, I referred him to our speech and hearing center for a complete hearing evaluation with more sophisticated equipment. The audiologist, a specialist in evaluating hearing and recommending needed remediation, reported that Darren exhibited a mild to moderate high-frequency sensorineural hearing loss in both ears.

SPEECH-LANGUAGE PATHOLOGIST: Darren has problems hearing the difference between the high-frequency sounds such as consonants "s", "sh", "f'", and "h".

MR. DICKSON: But if he can't hear, how come he can hear us when he wants to? He can be sitting in front of the TV and just pay no attention when I tell him something. But if I get angry, he jumps right away.

SPEECH-LANGUAGE PATHOLOGIST: When you get angry, you probably speak louder, and your tone of voice changes.

MR. DICKSON: You bet it does.

SPEECH-LANGUAGE PATHOLOGIST: He can hear those changes because the vowels are in the lower frequencies, and he hears them almost as you and I do. He can hear the change in your tone of voice for the same reason. What he cannot hear is the consonants. All those years he must have been hearing things with the most important parts missing. For instance, with the reported hearing loss, he hears "Come to supper" as "um oo u er."

MRS. DICKSON: Why, that is exactly what he says when he tells someone it is time to eat!

SPEECH-LANGUAGE PATHOLOGIST: So, you see, he has been saying what he has been hearing.

MR. DICKSON: So what do we do now?

Supports Darren Will Need to Be Successful in His Present Preschool Setting

Ms. MCLYNN: Is there someone who can help us to teach him what he needs to know? We really want to help Darren.

SPEECH-LANGUAGE PATHOLOGIST: The first thing we must do is have the audiologist evaluate Darren for hearing aids. Then I can work with him regularly.

I can explain and demonstrate many special activities to help him to learn in spite of his hearing loss. He can learn to use his hearing better.

MR. DICKSON: I'm ashamed for all of the times I've punished him for not listening. But he always heard his brother's motorcycle when he was half a block away. And he was always the first to run outside to look for jet planes. He loves the stereo and sings right along with the tunes. You are telling me he can hear all that but not hear the speech sounds like /p/ and /t/?

SPEECH-LANGUAGE PATHOLOGIST: Right. And I can teach him how to make those sounds and to recognize them when he sees them on people's lips, even if his hearing doesn't improve. Of course, we will expect that it will.

Ms. MCLYNN: We've noticed he seems to respond better to male voices than to female voices. Should he be placed in a classroom with a male teacher?

SPEECH-LANGUAGE PATHOLOGIST: Not necessarily. But it will be helpful if you speak more slowly and in shorter sentences. Be close to Darren and be sure that you have his attention before you tell him something. Avoid having sources of bright light such as a window behind you when you talk to him. He will need to see your face, lips, and mouth. Even though he is not dependent on lip reading, he will be taught to use visual as well as auditory clues. If the light is in his eyes, it is harder to see your facial expressions and lip movements.

Ms. MCLYNN: What should we do when we don't understand Darren?

SPEECH-LANGUAGE PATHOLOGIST: Use all the situational cues available. Sometimes ask him to tell you again. If you still don't understand, ask him to show you. Encourage him to use gestures. When you do understand, let your face show your pleasure. Then say what Darren was trying to say. Look expectant. Be pleased if he repeats your model but don't insist. Make no corrections of his articulation at this time. You are striving to motivate him to talk more and to keep trying. It's also important that you help Darren understand his own hearing loss, and that sometimes he will not understand what someone says to him. It will be important for you to help Darren feel comfortable letting the speaker know when he does not understand something. For example, Darren could learn to use comments like, "Please say that again?" or "I didn't hear you." Many children who have hearing loss will try to pretend they have heard the speaker or may simply not respond when they do not understand.

MRS. DICKINSON: I don't know anything about hearing aids. I'm not sure I can help him use it. And what about Mrs. McLynn? Will someone help her or does this mean Darren will have to transfer to a special education class?

MR. DICKINSON: I hope that's not the case! He loves his teacher and classmates.

Placement Decision: Inclusive Preschool Setting, with Supplementary Supports and Services

SPEECH-LANGUAGE PATHOLOGIST: I see no reason why Darren cannot continue to participate in Mrs. McLynn's classroom. Once Darren is fitted with the hearing aid recommended by the audiologist, I will contact our teacher with Deaf and hard-of-hearing certification. He will work with both Darren and Mrs. McLynn, as well as with me. This will ensure that we're all on board with correct hearing aid volume settings, how to check the batteries, and the proper way to insert the aid. It'll be a team effort. We will monitor how Darren is using his hearing aids. Also, the teacher will wear a microphone so that her speech will be transmitted directly to his hearing aids. This is called an FM (frequency modulated) system that will really help Darren understand the teacher's directions and comments during large-group activities. Would you like us to try to coordinate our visits to your program? At the beginning we would want to come at least once every other week, and then maybe less frequently, depending on how Darren is doing. We can stay in close contact via e-mail, if that works for you. The audiologist who tested Darren will also be glad to carefully walk you through all aspects of using and taking care of the hearing aids.

MR. DICKSON: Could you copy me on those e-mails? We would like to be able to follow up on your suggestions at home.

SPEECH-LANGUAGE PATHOLOGIST: Of course! That's a great idea.

After the discussion, which was lengthy, Darren's parents agreed that it was an excellent plan. They were grateful for the care with which everyone had evaluated Darren. They felt that the specific suggestions met his needs very well. Ms. McLynn was confident that with the supports described she and her staff could meet Darren's needs in the classroom. All members of the team agreed to meet again the following week to complete the IEP by writing specific goals and objectives and benchmark dates by which each objective should be met.

Purposes and Limitations of the IEP

The *annual goals* included in the IEP describe what a child with disabilities can be expected to accomplish within a specified period. Usually, the allotted time is one school year. However, the scheduled period may be as little as a few weeks or months. Parents can work with their school personnel to update and change IEPs when necessary through written amendments without convening the entire IEP team.

There must be a direct relationship between the child's present level of educational performance and the goals and services to be provided. However, the IEP is *not* intended to be detailed enough to be used as a complete instructional plan. The written goals are expected to state skills that are most needed based on assessment of a child's level of achievement. Meaningful and measurable goals should be based on what is learned from a complete and individualized assessment (Yell, Katsiyannis, Parks Ennis, Losinski, & Christle, 2016). They are designed to target particular developmental lags or to teach specific skills. The intent is to focus attention and teaching effort on critical areas of need to enable the child to access the general education curriculum and, to the maximum extent appropriate, participate with same-age peers.

The IEP is intended to serve as a basis for the development of a detailed, individualized instructional program that encompasses the complete curriculum. For example, although Darren's IEP focuses on his goals and objectives in speech and language, his complete instructional program would include social development, gross and fine motor skills, cognitive development, and academic readiness activities related to reading and math. In all these areas, Darren would be expected to participate and learn. Adaptations to meet his needs would be made in the process of instruction. If helpful, assistive technology devices and services would be offered through the IEP. Exhibit 3.1 offers some tips to assist in preparing for IEP meetings. Remember: The IEP is a documented plan; the IEP meeting is a collaborative *process*.

Accommodations and/or Modifications

In order for special education services to be individualized for each child, IEPs must include the specific types of supports that are required for each child to be successful. The Center for Parent Information and Resources (2017) discusses two common types of support. One type of support is an **accommodation**. It is a change that helps the child overcome or work around a disability by changing how instruction is presented to the child. The instructional content is not changed. The changes are typically physical or environmental, such as the following: visual or auditory cues are added, lighting is

Video Example from

You Tube

Enhanced eText
Video Example 3.2
Transition from Early Intervention to Preschool: Model IEP
https://www.youtube.com/watch?v=MWnbHPMg2EA
This video illustrates the IEP meeting and process for a child who is transitioning from early intervention and is eligible for special education services in preschool.

Exhibit 3.1

Preparing for the IEP: Meeting Tips for Early Childhood Special Education Teachers

Do your homework:

- Review the child's progress and achievement of previous goals.
- Organize assessment data and other evidence of the child's performance.
- Identify challenges and concerns.
- Communicate with team members regarding their assessment findings and recommendations; share your own observations and recommendations regarding the child. Keep in mind that in your role as the early childhood special education teacher, you will often be the team member who is most familiar with both the child and the family.

Meet with the family before the IEP meeting:

- Determine the family's concerns and priorities for their child.
- Help the family articulate their goals and requests in terms of the child's strengths and needs.
- Help them obtain copies of assessment reports.
- If the family has questions about reports, try to facilitate contact with team members before the IEP meeting, if possible.
- When the family's preference is placement in an inclusive setting, discuss specific supports needed to ensure successful inclusion (see Chapter 5).

Explain the IEP process to the family, including the following information:

- Each service provider on the team will present:
  - Present levels of performance
  - Comparison with past goals
  - Achievements
  - Child strengths and needs
  - Recommendations regarding new goals and least restrictive environment
  - Services and supports required to meet goals
- Although each team member can bring possible goals to the IEP meeting, they do not become formal IEP goals until the team (including the parents) agrees.
- If recommendations are made for placement in a special classroom rather than a typical early childhood setting, a detailed rationale must be provided.
- Parents have the right to invite a friend or advocate to attend the meeting with them.
- Prepare parents to express their concerns and desires or disagreements during the IEP meeting and to request clarification from team members if something is unclear.
- Parents have the right to request a reconsideration of the IEP at any time.

provided, the child is moved closer to the teacher, the group is made smaller. Maybe a peer buddy is provided. An accommodation for Darren would be the provision of a hearing aid, which would ensure that instruction is fully accessible to him. Provision of visual supports and sign language during a storybook early literacy lesson is yet another example of an accommodation.

Another type of support is a **modification**, which is a change in what is being taught, or a change in what is expected from the child such as how he or she may demonstrate learning. Requiring a young child to point to an object in a picture that has been named rather than asking the child to verbally identify the picture is a modification, as there is a difference in what is expected from the child. Modifications change the instructional content and expectations of the child, such as simplifying the task or modifying the child's level of participation. A change may also be made in the amount of personal support that is provided to the child. In reality, many children require both accommodations and modifications to support their learning and development. In such cases, both types of support would be described in the IEP.

The IEP Document

IEPs are very important *legal* documents meant to ensure the provision of appropriate, effective educational services for children who have disabilities. As a result, IEPs are typically very detailed and lengthy electronic documents. In the interest of brevity, Figure 3.3 presents brief descriptions of some of the IEP components. It should be remembered that formats and local requirements vary.

Considerations Beyond the IEP

Whether the child is placed in an inclusive early childhood setting or in a special education preschool classroom, early childhood special education teachers have the primary responsibility for ongoing monitoring of the IEP, even in inclusive programs where the IEP is often implemented by the early childhood education (ECE) teacher and/or a variety of support providers. The early childhood special education (ECSE) teacher of record is expected to monitor each child's progress. If at any time the ECSE teacher or the child's parents feel the plan is no longer appropriate, they can request a meeting to review the IEP and, if needed, create an **addendum**.

General Early Childhood Educator. At the initial preschool IEP, someone with expertise in ECE curriculum must participate in discussions related to access to early childhood curriculum, placement, and classroom staffing and support. When children with disabilities attend regular classes, even part time, the general education teacher must be

---

Figure 3.3 Differences Between the IFSP and the IEP

Individualized Family Service Plan (IFSP)	Individual Educational Program (IEP)
Target Population Intended for children and their families from birth through age 2.	*Target Population* Intended for children and youth from age 3 to 21.
Focus A plan focused on providing early intervention services to meet the unique needs of the child *and* the family in the child's *natural environment*, which usually means the child's home.	*Focus* A program focused on providing services that support the child/youth within the least restrictive environment possible within the school system. The child/youth is to be educated beside his or her peers without disabilities.
Services Involves many agencies in providing services that are coordinated by a service coordinator.	*Services* Services are primarily provided and coordinated by local school districts. Specialized services may be integrated within the school day via contracts with outside agencies.
Development of the Plan Occurs during an initial meeting with the family to understand their concerns, priorities, and resources. Information is offered and desired outcomes are written to address the needs of the child and family. The child's development in all areas is considered in decisions made.	*Development of the Program* Developed by the IEP team after considering the strengths of the child; results of the initial and most recent evaluation. Annual academic and functional goals are designed to meet the child's needs, which result from the child's disability in an effort to enable the child to make progress in the general education curriculum. Accommodations and modifications are designed as appropriate.
Review of the Program Reviewed with the family at least every six months.	*Review of the Program* Reviewed whenever desired periodically, but not less than annually.

considered part of the IEP team and should have copies of the IEPs. A special education teacher will generally serve as the "case carrier" and will work in close collaboration with the preschool ECE teacher.

Ongoing Model of Inclusion Support. Because Darren will be fully included in a general education preschool classroom, part of the determination of "supplementary aids and services" will be to carefully describe the details of the "model" of inclusion support service delivery. Consultations should include a mutual sharing of concerns and information, as well as suggestions for behavior management, materials, and teaching strategies. The IEP should include clear statements of recommended services to ensure that Darren can be successful in the inclusive placement. This includes frequency of consultations and/or direct services to be provided by the speech-language pathologist and the teacher with Deaf and hard-of-hearing certification, recommended accommodations such as preferential seating, and possible modifications of the physical environment to reduce ambient noise levels in the classroom.

Interpreters of the law recognize that special education teachers have the primary responsibility for implementation of the IEP. These teachers are expected to monitor each child's progress. If at any time they feel the plan is no longer appropriate, they are expected to request another meeting to review the IEP. Parents may also request a review of the individual program.

Enhanced eText Application Exercise 3.1 In this exercise, you can apply what you have learned in this chapter about the processes for developing the IFSP and the IEP and the differences between these documents.

Writing Program Objectives

The obvious reason for writing goals and objectives that serve as benchmarks is to develop educational plans that will be individualized and measurable. The following are characteristics of well-written behavioral objectives:

1. What is to be taught is described precisely. Any adult who reads the objective knows what to do and the conditions under which it is to be done. For example, "During recess, when bikes are available and Darren indicates his interest (e.g., by looking, pointing, vocalizing), teacher models the signs for 'want bike please' and provides specific physical assistance only as needed."

2. What the child will be able to do when the objective has been achieved is defined and described, and a *benchmark* may be included, such as "By the end of the current school year, Darren will independently initiate and sign a request to ride the bike."

3. How well or how often the child must perform (the *criterion*) is clearly identified (e.g., during recess on 3 out of 5 consecutive days), because if the behavior or skill, the performance expected, and the criterion for success are clearly stated, then accountability is facilitated.

Basics of Writing Behavioral Objectives

It is difficult to select the most efficient route to a destination unless you know what your destination is. **Behavioral objectives** (or performance or instructional objectives) require that the teacher state the destination precisely. "Fuzzy" terms are appropriate in goals; however, they are not allowed in behavioral objectives. For example, a correctly written *goal* might read, "To teach the colors red, yellow, and blue." But the *objective* related to the goal must contain the following three components:

1. What the *teacher* will *provide, restrict, or do.*
2. What the *learner* will be able to do or say when the objective has been achieved.
3. *How well* or *how often* the learner must perform in this manner to convince the teacher that the task has been learned (e.g., within what time frame, or with what accuracy, this performance must occur).

An example of a correctly written objective related to the goal "To recognize the colors red, yellow, and blue" might be "When the teacher points to any one of 15 different items (5 of each color red, yellow, and blue) and asks 'What color is this?,' the children will answer within 10 seconds, stating the color correctly on 80% of the trials."

Exhibit 3.2 illustrates terms useful in writing goals and objectives. Also, Heitin, referenced by Wrightslaw (2014), recommends the following **SMART** guidelines as a mnemonic for writing IEP goals:

Specific

Measurable

Action words

Realistic

Time-limited

The standard that must be achieved to accomplish this objective is 80% of the trials. This standard is referred to as the **criterion**. Eight of 10 correct performances is usually described as "proficiency" on the task. Ten of 10 is defined as "mastery level." (The level required must vary with the needs of individual children. Most cannot be expected to reach 100%—for example, for some skills, 75% may be appropriate.)

How well the learner must perform the skill may be measured by frequency (4 out of 5 times), accuracy (80% accuracy), duration (10 minutes), and/or distance (10 feet).

Exhibit 3.2

Appropriate Verbs for Writing Goals and Behavioral Objectives

1. Goals

Although less specific verbs such as those listed here may be appropriate for writing goals, they are *not* appropriate for writing behavioral objectives.

To decrease	To discover	To improve	To practice
To develop	To demonstrate	To increase	To understand

2. Behavioral Objectives

The verbs suggested in this category are examples of those used for writing behavioral objectives and can be used to describe observable behaviors:

To answer	To follow	To name	To recall
To color	To hold (as directed)	To pick up	To say
To copy	To imitate	To place together	To sort
To cut	To list	To point to	To use
To draw	To look at	To respond	

Furthermore, the period of time that the behavior or skill may be measured should be identified by the number of days (over 4 consecutive days), number of weeks (over 3 weeks), or number of occasions (during three consecutive occasions or circle times). The criteria selected for evaluating a child's skill on an objective **must be measurable.** For example, "Amy will attend to a story with 90% accuracy" is NOT a measurable objective because the terms "attend" and "90% accuracy" cannot be measured. A measurable objective would be: *During the 10-minute story time, Amy will spontaneously answer the teacher questions correctly 4 out of 5 times.* The teacher can measure or document the number of times that Amy answers questions she is asked during the storybook reading session.

The 2004 amendments to IDEA eliminated the IEP requirement to include short-term objectives or benchmarks related to achieving the annual goal except for students who take alternative assessments. However, states have the discretion to continue using short-term objectives because of their value in monitoring student progress.

The following is an example of a short-term objective and goal related to a social skill:

Annual Goal. To increase social interaction with peers.

Short-Term Objective or Benchmark. By December, during turn-taking activities, Alisa will spontaneously (without prompts) ask a peer for a turn 4 out of 5 times over 3 consecutive days, as evaluated through the teacher charting the targeted behavior every 4 weeks. By spring break, Alisa will ask at least two different peers for a turn.

Considerations for Culturally Responsive Objectives.   Given the increasing cultural and linguistic diversity of children and families in the United States, Barrio and colleagues (2017) propose that IEP teams use the following types of questions in developing IEP goals.

How does the goal:

1. Maintain the child and family's cultural competence, and did they have a voice in the IEP process? For example, uses both English and the home language, and involves the child's interests and family's cultural values and practices.

2. Build on the child's past experiences and current knowledge? For example, develops vocabulary in English and the home language based on the child's interests and experiences.

3. Consider the child and family's frame of reference? For example, uses the family's home language, priorities, and interests.

4. Take advantage of the child's learning style, and intellectual, social, and physical abilities and skills? For example, identifies how the child demonstrates application of skills.

Becoming a Skilled Observer

Informal observations help provide a more comprehensive view of the child than the observations obtained solely with the aid of structured inventories, checklists, rating scales, and tests. The focus of the observation is limited only by the imagination and time of the observer. It is important to observe a variety of situations at various times of the day. The focus should be more general when teachers are assessing the overall development of a child.

When teachers are trying to determine whether a child has accomplished a particular objective, they narrow their observation to a very specific behavior under specified conditions. Most teachers refer to a written objective to guide their observation. For example, if the IEP requires the child to learn to button a coat, the observer watches specifically to see whether the child can button a coat, under what conditions, and with what degree of skill.

Observing How Children Perform a Task

The primary purpose of most teacher observation is to determine the strengths and weaknesses in children's learning repertoires to develop instructional goals and strategies. The teacher should not be overly concerned with diagnostic labels. The teacher must instead be concerned with exactly what children can (and cannot) do and how they do it. In closely analyzing task performances, the teacher observes children's processes or styles of performance in addition to determining whether children can perform specific tasks.

For example, when asked to describe what is happening in a picture, does a child respond impulsively? Or, does he or she give a more deliberate or reflective response, taking time to note details while carefully scanning the picture? When copying a figure, does the child seem to study the picture and plan? Or, does he or she start drawing with only a brief reference to the drawing presented?

When English Is the Child's Second Language

In the United States, the numbers of dual-language learners (DLLs) attending early childhood programs continues to increase. The term "dual-language learner" recognizes that a young child is learning two or more languages at the same time and emphasizes the positive aspects of being bilingual (Rendon, Harijusola-Webb, & Gatmaitan, 2014). Unfortunately, too many DLLs may be misidentified as having developmental delays because observers do not have sufficient experience with culturally and linguistically diverse children. Furthermore, most immigrant parents are likely to be unfamiliar with the school system in the United States or how to advocate for their children. Some of the parents may be undocumented and fearful of negative repercussions if they question any recommendations by school staff. About 21% of immigrant children grow up in poverty, with about 26% of parents not having completed a high school education (Espinoza & Gutiérrez-Clellen, 2013). It will be particularly challenging for parents who are not literate in English to learn about the school system and special education services, and assert their legal rights.

Professionals have long been challenged with the dilemma of how to facilitate nonbiased assessment that does not penalize children from diverse backgrounds for the uniqueness of their background or experience. The tendency is to measure only skills and abilities valued by the dominant culture. Careful observation must include information about the child's development, the sociocultural context and values of his or her family, and comparison of the child's development to the developmental patterns of other children from a similar background. For example, observation of self-help skills must take into account the fact that some families do not promote self-feeding as early in life as the dominant culture does. The unique linguistic, social, and cultural characteristics of each young dual-language learner should be considered in selecting culturally and linguistically appropriate assessment procedures and materials as well as when interpreting results (Espinosa & Gutiérrez-Clellen, 2013).

The child should be observed in a variety of activities and settings, including participating in natural environments during routines; playing in comfortable, familiar settings; and interacting with family members and care providers. As the *DEC Recommended Practices* indicate, practitioners should "use assessment strategies that are appropriate for the child's age and level of development and accommodate the child's sensory, physical, communication, cultural, linguistic, social and emotional characteristics" (Division for Early Childhood [DEC], 2014, p. 7). Given its importance, the techniques associated with culturally fair assessment are outlined in Exhibit 3.3.

Exhibit 3.3
Ensuring Culturally Fair Assessment

1. Use multiple assessment techniques within natural settings and developmentally appropriate activities involving the parents or other caregivers as significant partners in the process.
2. Examine test items to be certain they are not biased against children or families of a certain cultural or linguistic background.
3. Examine test manuals to determine whether the group to which the child is being compared is culturally compatible.
4. Give directions in the child's home language.
5. Use an interdisciplinary or transdisciplinary process so more than one professional, along with the parents, can contribute to hypotheses developed from the observations.

Realizing Environmental Influences on Child Performance

Various researchers continue to discuss the importance of focusing on the interaction of the child with the environment rather than focusing on either the child or the environment independently. Finding very young children difficult to test, Salvia and Ysseldyke (2007) state,

> Infants between 6 and 18 months are distressed by unfamiliar adults. Although they may have better responses to strangers when held by their caregivers, they may still refuse to respond to an unfamiliar adult. Infants and preschoolers may be very active, inattentive, and distractible; they frequently perform inconsistently in strange situations. Because the language of these children is, by definition, undeveloped, they may not completely understand even simple questions and oral requests. Thus, traditional assessment formats in which students respond to examiner questions can be problematic. Not surprisingly, many toddlers and preschoolers are described as untestable. (p. 500)

The influence of situational factors again suggests that the teacher must thoroughly understand and be ready to vary the conditions of observation to get the most comprehensive view of a child's learning strengths and weaknesses.

Recognizing the Interrelationship of Skills

Finally, observers must be aware of and attuned to the interrelationship of skills. Children who are concentrating on the development of a motor skill may or may not exhibit what might be considered to be normal verbal or social interaction with other children during that period. In contrast, children who are skilled in the motor activity may exhibit greater verbal fluency because of their confidence in their motor skills and lack of verbal inhibition.

Young children do not develop skills in isolation. The most obvious example of the interdependence of skill development is noted by psycholinguists in their study of language development. Chapter 8 elaborates on the importance of realizing that the potential for language development is present during every waking moment, assuming the child does not have severe impairments and is in a relatively stimulating environment. The teacher then must be aware of the child's total performance even when focusing on a single aspect of behavior.

In summary, observation is a complex, critical skill that can be developed only through systematic practice. The importance of becoming skilled in objective, systematic observation is obvious. Therefore, it is imperative that teachers strive to incorporate the following six abilities into their observational repertoire:

1. In-depth understanding of what is considered to be the normal behavior range of developmentally appropriate behavior

2. Skill in recognizing risk factors or high-risk signals

3. Ability to follow the guidelines for making responsible and reliable observations

4. Ability to choose types of observational techniques appropriate to the purpose of the observation

5. Awareness of the influence of performance styles, motivational factors, environmental variables, and extraneous behaviors on the judgments to be made about children's strengths and weaknesses

6. Continuous practice of professionalism through respect for confidentiality, restraint from labeling, and attempts to counteract any tendencies toward making stereotyped assumptions about children

Guidelines for Successful Observation

Observation is the skill of careful and deliberate listening to, and watching of, children's behaviors. Children can be observed alone or in a group, at any time of the day, and under a variety of circumstances. While observing, the teacher notes aspects of the child's behaviors. Specific behaviors to be observed are determined by the purpose of the observation. Observers differ considerably in the process of recording information. Teachers often just make mental notes of what they see or hear, but the use of an organized record-keeping form results in more systematic recording procedures. If the purpose of the observation is to assess the child's progress in an individualized program, systematic recording is essential to ensure objective, comprehensive data. The following guidelines help prepare teachers to become systematic, objective observers.

1. *Focus on observing exactly what the child does.* Record special detailed observations of precisely what the child *does* and *says*. Use action verbs. Note the date, time, setting, what preceded the child's action or reaction, and what followed the behavior. *Do not* record inferences or opinions. Write down what is actually seen or heard.

2. *Record the observational details as soon after the observation as possible.* With practice, teachers develop the ability to participate and observe simultaneously by making mental notes. However, it is important to plan schedules so that recording of details can be done as quickly as possible. Details are important and easily forgotten.

3. *Observe in a variety of settings and at different times during the child's day.* Changes in time and setting often provide clues about children's interests. For example, children who are not comfortable on the playground may seek the solitude they never seek when in the classroom. Or, they may become bullies on the playground, whereas they are self-controlled within the classroom. Children may be overly active when playing with other children but not so when playing alone. There may be a certain time of day, perhaps just before lunch, when some children are especially irritable. Identifying these times and circumstances makes it possible to plan needed changes that create a smoothly run day. Watching for patterns often leads to an explanation of the child's behavior.

4. *Be realistic in scheduling observations.* When the purpose of the observation is to determine the developmental level at which a child is functioning, it is critical to be able to observe and make notes as often and in as many situations as necessary to get a complete record of the developmental areas under concern. Observations that are

haphazard or incomplete jeopardize the correctness of any resulting hypotheses. Be realistic when planning observation time. Be certain there is a chance the observation will actually occur. On some days, the only available observation time might be free-choice time.

5. ***Begin by focusing on one child at a time.*** Focusing on one child at a time and using checklists or rating scales will help develop observational skills without running the risk of missing or forgetting information.

6. ***Avoid being obvious.*** Avoid calling attention to the child being observed or the fact that the observation is taking place. Interact as naturally as possible. Be seated in a place normal for the teacher to be during the activity that is being observed. For example, when observing playground activities, teachers stand in a spot providing optimal visibility. Stand or sit in the usual position when observing any activity.

7. ***At all times, ensure confidentiality.*** Notes must *never* be left around; a system of coding names should be developed to ensure privacy. *Never* discuss observations in front of other children or parents of other children. Read and become familiar with the Family Educational Rights and Privacy Act of 1974 (PL 93-380) because it is important to be aware of the parents' rights to read the records created. Never send or give data collected from observation or test scores to outside agencies or individuals without written parental permission.

8. ***Choose a workable recording system.*** Teachers often need to experiment with file cards, notebooks, three-ring binders, and digital options such as software on tablets to determine exactly what process is most convenient for them. Of course, the system used depends on the purpose and method of the observation. Well-organized, easy-to-review notes will facilitate the detection of patterns of behavior that may be vital to a real understanding of the child.

9. ***Share your observational reports with parents as appropriate.*** Objective evidence of child progress is always welcome.

The Portfolio and Its Use with Young Children

Teachers have always gathered together samples of students' work and assembled them into folders to display to parents at evening open-house gatherings. This process has become known as **portfolio assessment** and is receiving attention as a form of authentic assessment. Mindes (2011) characterizes a portfolio as one type of performance-based assessment.

Marotz and Allen (2016) described the assessment portfolio as "another effective method for tracking children's developmental progress" (p. 18). A portfolio portrays the child's efforts in one or more areas. Materials that represent a child's learning and performance in all developmental areas can be gathered and assembled in an easily accessible portfolio.

For a young child, a portfolio might include records of various forms of systematic observation, video or audio recordings, photographs, and samples of a child's productive efforts, such as drawings. In short, a portfolio (contained in a folder, box, expanding file, etc.) includes the visual evidence of the types of observations described in this chapter.

Decisions about what items to place in a portfolio depend on the purpose of the portfolio. Noonan and McCormick (2014) suggested that each item should be labeled with the date, the child's name, and a note stating why it is an important entry. Whenever possible, children should be involved in choosing the items to be included. All items should be dated and can be arranged according to curriculum area or category of development.

As an assessment technique, portfolios can be used to document an individual child's progress over time and can be compared with a standard of performance that is consistent with the curriculum and appropriate developmental expectations. Portfolios are obviously a worthwhile tool for facilitating rich communication with parents. The types of observation techniques that follow provide valuable information to be included in portfolios.

Types of Observation Samples

Teachers should observe children in a variety of situations with as many purposes as they have objectives for the children. The particular technique chosen should relate directly to the purpose established. The following list describes some of the more common types of observation. As the list progresses, the techniques become more standardized (formal), requiring greater systematic planning and structure from the observer.

1. *Photographs.* Photographs provide a quick, easy method of obtaining children's reactions to various lessons. They provide an automatic record of involvement. Pictures can be taken at planned intervals to demonstrate sequential development. A dual purpose is served when the snapshots are used to stimulate language development (see Chapter 8). Using photographs in bulletin board displays offers repeated chances to encourage the development of self-esteem. With the advent of digital cameras and smartphones, children can receive instant feedback and parents can view the images from home. Teachers must implement their program's procedures regarding parental consent for obtaining photographs and video recordings of children.

2. *Electronic recordings.* With the advancement of instructional technology, more and more classrooms commonly use electronic recording techniques. Teachers have the advantage of participating directly in the activities and can later review the children's responses to their unique teaching styles. However, care must be taken to prevent the presence of recording equipment from distorting the observation. Children thoroughly enjoy observing and listening to themselves. Again, such techniques provide ideal opportunities for language stimulation and allow the teacher to collect language samples. Videos have long been used to provide evidence of development in areas such as motor coordination and social interaction and are easy to obtain and share given current smartphone and tablet technology.

3. *Collection of children's work.* Although early childhood education is usually process oriented rather than product oriented, there are opportunities to collect children's work. Collecting samples of such things as a child's paintings, tracings, cuttings, and attempts to print his or her name allows the teacher to analyze progress and to make this obvious to parents.

4. *Activity lists.* Programs that provide activity centers with some degree of free-choice time may post lists of children's names to be dated or checked off at each center area. By listing each child's name and the length of participation, the child's interests and level of involvement can be determined. The teacher will need to decide whether choices should be limited or children should be encouraged to broaden their participation.

5. *Anecdotal records, diaries, and logs.* Teachers record specific details of their observation, including exact behavior; precisely what precedes the behavior; and any reactions to the behavior, time, setting, and individuals involved. Care is taken to avoid making judgments, choosing isolated events, or overgeneralizing from atypical incidents. Systematic and regular recording allows the teacher to study patterns of behavior.

6. *Passports.* The passport (Shea & Bauer, 2003) is an ordinary spiral notebook that the child carries daily to and from home and the intervention program. All

adults who work with the child are encouraged to make observational notations in the passport. Records are required to be brief, positive, honest, and consistent. The objective of the passport is to promote positive parent–teacher communication and cooperation.

7. *Time sampling and event recording.* In time sampling, the observer selects specific behaviors that are readily observable and occur often. A few behaviors are chosen, and their occurrence is recorded on a prepared recording sheet during regularly scheduled, short observation periods. Unlike time sampling, event recording is not restricted to specific preplanned time intervals. A targeted behavior, such as temper tantrums, is recorded on occurrence. This method is often used with infrequently occurring behaviors.

8. *Checklists and rating scales.* Checklists and rating scales help specify exactly what the observer should be observing. The use of such instruments makes it possible to vary the observer and still maintain consistency in the behavior that is observed. Illustrations of checklists and developmental scales are included throughout this text and in most texts in the field of early childhood special education. However, teachers are encouraged to design their own to ensure that the behavior observed is related to the goals and objectives of their program.

Recording Children's Progress

Record keeping in early childhood programs is not typically detailed with regard to specific learning objectives or training procedures. Nor is it individualized for each child. However, when children with disabilities are included in the class, certain information must be recorded, kept up to date, and made available to parents and other members of the child's educational team. In other words, progress must be monitored on an ongoing basis. Record keeping must be designed to facilitate constant fine tuning and adjustment of programs and procedures. Doing this in the simplest manner possible is very important. Unwieldy systems are either time-consuming or simply not used. The goal of designing a record-keeping system is that it be simple, efficient, and functional.

Data-collection and record-keeping systems must be designed to fit the child's specific learning needs and the instructional context. Particularly challenging training objectives often require very specific and careful data collection. This is especially true if the child's progress is slow or inconsistent. In such cases, it may simply be impossible to determine whether progress is being made without painstaking data-collection efforts. For example, a plan for toilet training a child with multiple disabilities or reducing the destructive tantrums of a child with a severe behavior disorder would require very careful and frequent data collection of the type shown in Figure 3.4. The form in Figure 3.4 was developed to try to determine Jon's urination pattern and help him learn to urinate in the toilet. During the first part of the week, he is checked every half hour to see if he is wet or dry. In addition, he is placed on the potty when he vocalizes because his mother reports that recently at home he has begun to signal when he is wet by vocalizing. Gradually, Jon's urination pattern emerges. He is often wet around 8:30 a.m. and again around 11:00 a.m. If he is dry at these times, he is placed on the potty and praised if he urinates there. His vocalizations continue to be recorded to determine whether he is actually using vocalization as a signal that he is wet or that he needs to go to the bathroom.

Use of carefully planned physical prompts and hand-over-hand assistance to help a child who is blind learn to eat with a spoon might require keeping records of how much assistance was required on each bite during a meal, as shown in Figure 3.5.

Figure 3.4 Progress chart: Toilet training

PROGRESS DATA

NAME: ___Jon_____   DATE: _Dec. 10–14_____

OBJECTIVE: _Jon will urinate when placed on potty_____

KEY: D = dry   W = wet   V = vocalized
        P = placed on potty
        + = urinated in potty   − did not urinate in potty

Time	MONDAY	TUESDAY	WEDNESDAY	THURSDAY	FRIDAY
8:00 A.M.	D	D	D	D	D
8:30 A.M.	W	W	P–	VP+	P+
9:00 A.M.	D	D	W	D	D
9:30 A.M.	D	D	D	D	D
10:00 A.M.	D	VP–	D	D	D
10:30 A.M.	VP–	D	D	VW	VP+
11:00 A.M.	W	W	VP+	D	D
11:30 A.M.	D	W	D	D	D

At the beginning of each meal, seven trials are recorded to determine the level of assistance required. Examining the data sheet, we see that early in the week, Sharon required total physical prompts (total assistance) on all seven trials. Although her performance is somewhat inconsistent, we see that by Thursday, Sharon appears to need less total assistance and increases the number of independent bites. Video Example 3.3 identifies the many changes or transitions that a family of a child with disabilities may encounter.

Figure 3.5 Progress chart: Self-feeding

PROGRESS SUMMARY

NAME: Sharon   **WEEK:** Nov. 9–13

OBJECTIVE: Eat with spoon independently at lunch

KEY: + = bring spoon to mouth independently
         ⊕ = support at elbow
         A = total assistance required

Trials	MONDAY	TUESDAY	WEDNESDAY	THURSDAY	FRIDAY
1.	A	A	⊕	A	
2.	A	A	A	A	
3.	A	⊕	A	⊕	
4.	A	⊕	⊕	+	
5.	A	A	+	+	
6.	A	A	A	⊕	
7.	A	A	A	⊕	

For keeping track of progress made across all IEP goals (or outcomes for IFSPs), weekly or biweekly anecdotal record keeping may be more useful. One simple strategy is to make a single page for each child, listing the IEP objectives in each domain along one side of the form and leaving ample space to write comments next to each objective. Several copies of this sheet are made for each child and placed in the child's folder. Each week, one of the sheets is used to summarize progress and problems for each objective. This provides a running anecdotal narrative of progress across all objectives. It also ensures that each objective is reviewed by the teacher and assistants weekly. Data sheets for specific problem behaviors as described earlier can be attached to these narratives.

Simple and efficient performance checklists for each child can also be created to ensure ongoing progress monitoring. The goal is for the classroom team to create ongoing progress-monitoring tools and strategies that are easily accessed and used.

The important point about record keeping is that *it must be done*. No matter how competent the early childhood professional, it will not be possible to carefully monitor the child's progress and the effectiveness of intervention procedures without such records.

Enhanced eText Application Exercise 3.2 In this exercise, you can apply what you have learned in this chapter about conducting observations and progress monitoring.

Linking Assessment to Curriculum

During the past decade, early childhood special educators have become aware of the critical need to link assessment processes to the curriculum that is implemented. The *AEPS Curriculum for Birth to Three Years* and *AEPS Curriculum for Three to Six Years* (Bricker, 2006) are a frequently used system that builds on the opportunity of making direct use of information obtained during assessment in developing individualized outcomes, goals, and objectives. Individual needs can be better met when all aspects of the intervention process, including assessment, goals and objectives, intervention, and evaluation, are interrelated. Pretti-Frontczak and Bricker (2000) state, "Thus, higher quality IEP goals and objectives that are developed from a comprehensive assessment process, and directly linked to intervention and evaluation, are likely to contribute to the individualization of services and improved outcomes for young children" (p. 92). The authors of this text, like their colleagues, believe *there must be a direct link between what is learned during assessment and the activities planned for children.*

Facilitating Program Transitions

Transitions mean change, and change normally means increased stress for children and families. Because IDEA makes a major distinction between services required for infants and toddlers (birth to age 3) and preschoolers (3- to 5-year-olds), transitions from early intervention to preschool, and from preschool to kindergarten, will occur. Fortunately, Part C does recognize the need to assist families and to ensure continuity of services. It requires that plans for transition be spelled out in IFSPs and that service coordinators assist families during these vulnerable periods of change. Interagency coordination and written agreements clarifying local transition procedures have been developed throughout the country. There is also very dramatic change as children and families move from preschool services to those provided by the public schools for school-aged children. Exhibit 3.4 notes some of the unique issues and challenges related to transition.

Exhibit 3.4

Transition from Early Intervention (Part C) to Preschool Special Education (Part B): Unique Issues and Challenges

- The transition from early intervention to preschool services often occurs at a time when families are still dealing with significant emotional issues, such as ongoing anxiety, clarification of diagnosis, difficulty obtaining services and dealing with bureaucracy, and impact on family members.

(continued)

- In some cases, this transition occurs just as families are beginning to develop important trusting relationships and partnerships with early intervention service providers. The transition may be experienced by the primary caregiver (usually the mother) as a loss.
- Part B preschool services are frequently much less family centered and less interdisciplinary. Families may perceive that they are losing services.
- A "transition plan" at 2 years, 6 months is federally mandated and crucial for a successful transition.
- During the 6-month period before the child's third birthday, the child is evaluated and the IEP document drafted. During this time, the early intervention program staff and the receiving educational program staff—who will be responsible for implementing the IEP—must work collaboratively with each other and with the family.

Enhanced eText

Video Example 3.3
Foundations of Transition
https://www.youtube.com/
watch?v=CUHkAENZiRc
This video discusses transitions that young children experience from early intervention to preschool programs, child care, and kindergarten.

Although stress may be unavoidable, it can be lessened through careful planning that should begin as early as possible. Service coordinators and other interested professionals should be certain that transition plans are made and implemented only in the context of a partnership with the child's family. Transitions are normal life events that require well-planned steps to cope effectively with the changes required. Parents who are taking a newborn home from the neonatal intensive care unit or are realizing they are leaving behind the comfort of the infant program may feel very anxious. Professionals, through the development of well-articulated transition plans, can help parents turn these anxious moments into opportunities for growth.

Steps in Transition to Center-Based or Public School Services

DEC Recommended Practices (DEC, 2014) offers guidance to service coordinators and others involved in assisting families through what can be a difficult transition when children move from early intervention to preschool services at the age of 3. The following suggestions to service coordinators and other early intervention professionals acknowledge these guidelines and requirements as outlined in PL 108-446:

1. Plan ahead to allow adequate time for planning and preparation. Planning should begin when a child is 2 years, 6 months old and must be completed by the time he or she is 2 years, 9 months of age.

2. In their preferred language, families must be given information outlining the steps in the transition process, their role, and the role of other individuals who will be involved.

3. Placement options should be discussed with family members, and they should be assisted in realizing opportunities to visit potential programs and to talk with the service providers and families who may be familiar with the programs under consideration.

4. Steps should be developed to prepare the toddler for changes in service delivery, including steps to help the toddler be successful in the new placement.

5. Service coordinators or other service providers should be knowledgeable of service options, tasks, timelines, roles, responsibilities, and related procedures as designated on interagency agreements.

6. Receiving programs should be prepared to facilitate and support the child who will be entering their program. Reciprocal follow-up between sending and receiving programs should be encouraged.

In addition, a national study on the transition process from early intervention to preschool and from preschool to kindergarten has identified practices that programs can implement to support families and children as they change programs (Rous, Myers, & Stricklin, 2007). These include the following:

1. Family participation in meetings—for example, IFSP meetings, IEP meetings, and transition conferences

2. Sharing information with families by introducing staff of the receiving school at IEP meetings

3. Offering workshops designed to familiarize families with the IEP and relevant terminology (e.g., *PLOP* stands for "present level of performance," and *PLAAP* means "present level of academic achievement and functional performance")

4. Allowing family and child visits to programs, staff visits between sending and receiving programs, and home visits by the receiving program

5. Providing an orientation meeting for families before beginning the new program

6. Providing families with transition packets or handbooks, community resources, and support groups regarding transitions

7. Creating specific strategies for the child, such as visiting the new classroom or looking at pictures of the school bus

The Role of the Early Childhood Special Educator in Facilitating Transitions

Early intervention specialists are in a unique position to help families and children make the move from programs for infants and toddlers to programs for preschool-age children. Families that are coping with their children's disabilities in a demanding environment can be especially stressed in times of transition. They have many questions and are faced with the unknown. Teachers and other early intervention personnel can encourage parents to visit and become familiar with possible new settings for their child. They can directly prepare children and families by first understanding the environmental expectations of the placement possibilities. Whenever possible, children can be exposed to new routines and requirements ahead of time. Exiting teachers can work directly with receiving teachers in person, via telephone, and through reports to smooth the way and provide reassurance and support to parents. Putting parents in direct touch with other parents who already have children in the new environment can be invaluable. These same concerns and strategies should be used when children move from preschool programs into public elementary school programs and beyond.

Enhanced eText
Video Example 3.4
Highlights of a Classroom Visit
https://www.youtube.com/watch?v=J00givT2jK0
This video highlights the visit of a parent and child to a new program and shows how the teacher might prepare the child for entry into the class.

The focus of this chapter was the process of developing individualized intervention plans and programs. Families were seen as central to these planning processes and to the success of their implementation. Chapter 4 addresses effective intervention strategies for realizing the outcomes, goals, and objectives detailed in the individual plans. Attention is given to describing generic instructional strategies while recognizing the importance of play as a primary context for learning.

Enhanced eText Application Exercise 3.3: In this exercise, you can apply what you have learned about transitions from one program to another and identify what you can do to support the child and family during these transitions.

Summary

We have moved away from categorical descriptions of children with disabilities toward an analysis of the specific instructional needs of the child. Typically, a multistage process is involved that consists of (1) initial identification of children with problems, perhaps involving observational comparisons against a developmental checklist and screening for medically related problems; (2) diagnosis resulting from practitioners of relevant disciplines developing an individualized family service plan (IFSP) or an individualized education program (IEP); (3) teacher observation and determination of daily instructional activities; and (4) continuous monitoring of children's progress for the purpose of updating each child's program and periodically reviewing the success of the overall program.

Before intervention strategies can begin, either an IFSP or an IEP must be developed. In developing either document, it is essential to remember that the process itself is much more important than the documents. Families must be the primary decision makers in determining how they wish to be involved and what outcomes or goals and objectives should be included. Both processes require assessment by a team of professionals from relevant disciplines and involvement in determining services and strategies. This team considers the child's current development level in determining eligibility for services. The IFSP requires a 6-month review and the IEP requires an annual review.

Even though IFSPs and IEPs are similar in intent, currently there are some important differences. First, the IFSP is family centered, whereas the IEP is child centered. Rather than functional outcome statements, the IEP includes goals and objectives. To date, only the IFSP process provides for service coordination and definite steps to smooth the stress of transitions. Readers may wish to watch closely to see if the IEP process becomes more like the IFSP process as families become accustomed to a family-centered approach to service planning. After all, there is "a primary common theme, regardless of the student's age. It is that both documents and the processes they launch involve partnerships between families, students and professionals" (Turnbull et al., 2011, p. 214).

Monitoring and accurately recording children's progress through astute observation are critical to ensuring that intervention practices are continuously effective and periodic reviews of individualized family service plans and programs are accurate.

Reflect and Apply

1. Reflect on the specific similarities and differences between the IFSP and IEP processes and documents. Given that an early childhood special education will be expected to participate in either one or both processes, list the steps that should be taken to ensure that families fully understand the processes. Consider how you would help families understand the differences between the processes when they face their child's transition at age 3.

2. Observe Video Example 3.1 featuring Robert McWilliam's description of a *routine-based interview*. Write out a script that could guide you through such an interview with a family member.

3. Outline and be prepared to discuss the steps that would be involved in planning for an initial IEP meeting. Consider such elements as: who you would involve in the collaborative effort, what data you should have available, what questions you will ask, and what evidence is needed to support your opinions and suggestions.

4. Draft a statement to be placed in the IFSP document that refers to "natural environments" and another to be placed in an IEP that refers to the "least restrictive environment."

5. Clearly explain how you would go about conducting observation and other informal assessment on multiple occasions and in a variety of settings, as appropriate. Then give a specific example of how you would directly move from something you learned during the assessment to a change you would make in the curriculum. That is, how would you ensure a direct link between what you learned and the activities you would plan?

Chapter 4
Designing Instructional Programs

Dragon Images/Shutterstock

Learning Outcomes

After studying this chapter, you should be able to:

4.1 Understand why a developmentally appropriate early childhood curriculum should be informed by meaningful assessments, reflect evidence-based practices, and provide a clear plan for programming that is functionally and ecologically relevant.

4.2 Demonstrate how an activity-based or routines-based approach at home and preschool will provide opportunities for children to work on several objectives simultaneously when embedded within pleasurable and motivating activities.

4.3 Summarize why children's play provides the best context for learning in early education programs.

4.4 Create a positive, predictable environment through the use of routine and repetition that is essential to maximize children's learning and adjustment.

4.5 Explain how Universal Design for Learning (UDL) creates specific steps toward the inclusion of young children with disabilities.

This chapter describes practical, general instructional strategies that can provide the methodological foundation for early education and intervention for all children (typically, developing children as well as children with disabilities). It builds on some of the concepts discussed earlier. Chapter 5 will go beyond these general instructional strategies and techniques to focus in detail on those strategies that can be used with young children who have specific disabilities requiring intensive supports. The overall approach presented in these two chapters makes it possible to include children with a variety of disabilities or developmental delays in a wide range of early education programs.

Curriculum

Definition

It is well known that a good curriculum is more than just activities and well-intentioned lesson plans. It is more than selection of a published curriculum such as those discussed later in this chapter. Instead, it is "a framework for developing a coherent set of learning experiences that enables children to reach the identified goals" (Copple & Bredekamp, 2009, p. 42). Practitioners must make decisions about what will be taught and how it will be taught. Gestwicki (2017) suggests that all effective curricula include the following components:

- Children are active and totally engaged.
- Goals are clearly defined, related to desired outcomes for children, and agreed upon by all.
- Curriculum is derived from evidence-based practices.
- Content is learned through investigation, play, and appropriate developmental teaching.

- Curriculum builds on prior learning.
- Curriculum is comprehensive.
- Any technology used should be built on developmental foundations and should expand access to content rather than replace creative play. (pp. 71–72)

Selection and development of a specific curriculum will depend on program philosophy, theoretical approach, teaching style, and beliefs about how children learn. To be effective with young children with disabilities, the curriculum should promote engagement and learning, monitor progress with sound data collection to ensure quality individualization, and provide learning opportunities within daily routines both at home and in preschool.

Choosing a Curriculum

Many types of curricula have been developed for infants and young children both with and without disabilities. Curricula are based on various theoretical assumptions and have been designed in a comprehensive way that may include criterion-referenced assessments, detailed step-by-step behavioral objectives, and suggested activities and materials. Some are commercially available as packaged programs containing a variety of media and materials. Others require extensive training before implementation, reflect broader values and applications of assumptions about how children learn, or, perhaps, focus more specifically on certain curricular content areas, such as literacy or social skills.

Examples of widely used curricula include the following: The *Creative Curriculum* includes two developmentally appropriate curricula. One is for infants and toddlers (Dodge, Rudick, Berke, Heroman, Burts, & Bickart, 2015). It focuses on development of a sense of self and becoming competent, caring learners. The other is designed for preschool children ages 3 to 5 (Dodge, Berke, Bickart, Colker, & Heroman, 2016). This preschool curriculum promotes social and emotional development plus early learning in the core areas of literacy, math, science, and social studies. The *HighScope Preschool* curriculum (Epstein & Hohmann, 2012) reflects an approach that focuses on key developmental indicators of approaches to learning: (a) initiative, (b) planning, (c) engagement, (d) problem solving, (e) use of resources, and (f) reflection. A characteristic feature of the HighScope curriculum is the process of *Plan-Do-Review* to strengthen initiative and self-reliance. Grounded in Piagetian constructivist principles, its emphasis is directed more toward readiness to learn than to direct instruction of specific academic objectives. The teacher is regarded as a participating and very observant partner in activities rather than as a manager (Gestwicki, 2017).

Some approaches derive their curricula from project work based on children's interests. For example, the *Reggio Emilia approach,* developed after World War II in the Italian village of Reggio Emilia, has a strong focus on relationships, collaboration, and documentation. The curriculum is developed through flexible planning and project work based on children's interests (McNally & Slutsky, 2017). Based on the principles of the Reggio Emilia approach, the *Emergent Curriculum* involves investigations in learning environments that are driven by relationships and reflect values and creativity (Biermeir, 2015).

The *Project Approach* (Katz, Chard, & Logan, 2014; Helm, 2015) embeds individual early childhood learning goals into activities involving a deep investigation of a specific topic that is meaningful to the children. Harte (2010) and Alfonso (2017) described the successful use of this curriculum approach with children in inclusive, early childhood classrooms. Finally, Sandall and Schwartz (2012) offer a well-regarded curriculum, *Building Blocks,* that includes teaching strategies such as curriculum modification, embedded learning opportunities, and child-focused instruction for use with preschoolers with disabilities.

In some cases, statewide assessments are aligned with or draw upon national standards for early childhood education or early childhood special education, such as those of the National Association for Education of Young Children (NAEYC), the Division for Early Childhood (DEC), and Council for Exceptional Children (CEC). With the growth of preschool education in the United States, commercial curriculum publishers such as McGraw-Hill have developed pre-K curricula targeting typically developing children to ensure "kindergarten readiness." In *inclusive* preschool classrooms, individualized adaptations of pre-K curricula for children with disabilities will be important.

As children with disabilities are increasingly included in a variety of community-based or school-based early education settings, the early childhood *special* educator seldom has decision-making input into the curriculum selection process in those programs. Thus, it is critical that the well trained early childhood special educator be able to work collaboratively with the early childhood education (ECE) teacher to find ways in which any curriculum can be appropriately adapted and augmented to meet the individual needs of children who have specific challenges.

In those situations in which the early childhood special education (ECSE) practitioner does have responsibility for curriculum selection, the following are important considerations. First, practitioners must clearly understand the abilities and learning needs of the children they are serving. They must identify their own as well as parents' educational goals for these children. Then they must examine the strengths, experiences, and learning styles of children as well as their own instructional styles. A clear conceptualization of both the desired program outcomes and the most effective intervention strategies should be generated before a curriculum is selected. Particularly challenging are those packaged curricula that include preselected materials. These may need substantial modifications and adaptations to meet the unique needs of particular children. It is essential to make and use these changes. In considering whether a curriculum will be helpful for a specific group of children, teachers, administrators, and the program team might consider the following questions:

1. What is the evidence that this curriculum produces desired outcomes?

2. Has this curriculum been used effectively by programs such as ours?

3. What developmental outcomes does the curriculum address, and are these our areas of concern?

4. How will the curriculum fit into the program's current philosophy and practices?

5. What is the cost, and what training is needed for effective implementation of the curriculum?

Considering Children with Disabilities

The use of natural learning opportunities and daily routines has been identified as an effective instructional practice for promoting the development of young children with disabilities and for increasing their families' confidence and competence in child rearing. Daily routines provide convenience for teachers and families to help a child work on a skill, and multiple opportunities for a child to develop, practice, and generalize a skill. A recommendation of the Division for Early Childhood (DEC)(2014) is that "practitioners embed instruction within and across routines, activities, and environments to provide contextually relevant learning opportunities" (p. 11).

Squires and Bricker (2006) emphasized the importance of "activity-based instruction" in which the curriculum is built around engaging and meaningful *activities*. Children's specific learning and developmental objectives are met within these motivating activities during daily routines. More recently, Bricker joined colleagues in extending an activity-based approach to curriculum suitable for children younger than 3 years of age (Johnson, Rahn, & Bricker, 2015).

For infants and young children with disabilities, there are several well-established curricula that attempt to link curriculum with assessment results, as discussed in Chapter 3. These include the *Hawaii Early Learning Profile (HELP) 3–6 Curriculum Guide* (Teaford, Wheat, & Baker, 2010) for preschoolers; the *HELP Strands 0–3* (Warshaw, 2013) for curriculum-based assessment up to 48 months; the *Assessment, Evaluation and Programming System for Infants and Children (AEPS)* (Bricker, 2006); the *Carolina Curriculum* (Johnson-Martin, Attermeier, & Hacker, 2004); and others.

Particularly for young children with significant and complex disabilities, these curricula are invaluable. They break skills into small, easily observable steps across each developmental domain. Equally important, these curricula suggest specific developmentally appropriate classroom activities, as well as in-home activities and guidelines for parents. For preschoolers with complex needs who attend inclusive, center-based programs, these specially designed curricula can be used to augment the classroom goals and strategies, or they can be used as guides for home-based service delivery.

There is no one theoretical approach or curriculum that has been found to be "the best" for children with disabilities. Programs that adapt curricula to meet the learning needs of children with a wide range of differences in skills, learning styles, backgrounds, and potential require deliberate integration of facets from both early childhood education and special education. Children's special unique learning needs must be considered in relation to cultural, environmental, educational, and developmental expectations. It is incumbent on the early childhood special educator to combine the best features of curricula in the fields of both early childhood education and early childhood special education.

Philosophy of This Text

In practice, many programs for young children with disabilities combine elements of different curriculum models. The philosophy of this text is based on the following assumptions:

1. Curricula should be derived from **evidence-based practices (EBP)** as well described by Buysee, Wesley, Snyder, and Winton (2006): "A decision-making process that integrates the best available research evidence with family and professional wisdom and values" (p. 3). This definition recognizes that informed curricula decisions should build on a variety of sources of knowledge.

2. The content of the curriculum must include goals that are meaningful and relevant to each child within the context of his or her home and community. That is, they must be functional and **ecologically relevant.** Goals should be selected on the basis of their functional utility for the child in his or her immediate or next environment. In addition, curriculum content will also include the development of children's underlying cognitive and psychological and social-emotional processes, which enable them eventually to engage in self-directed learning and establish positive human relationships.

3. As much as possible, intervention strategies should be embedded in activities that target specific skills within the context of **daily routines** and **activities** (Jennings, Hanline, & Woods, 2012). Using functional behavior to enhance skills will promote generalization through the natural use of these skills. Educators must be prepared to provide direct instruction whenever needed and learning opportunities for generalization.

4. The design of appropriate long-term goals and specific short-term objectives or benchmarks will consider information related to the stages and processes of typical development. In addition, principles and techniques from the field of applied

behavior analysis (such as task analysis, stimulus control, contingent reinforcement, and programming for generalization) will be used as tools when necessary within the activity-based intervention.

5. Teaching strategies used to reach targeted goals should reflect a strong **social-transactional approach,** rooted in the quality of the social interactions and responsive communications between children and significant adults (e.g., teachers and caregivers) as well as between children and their peers.

General Instructional Strategies

A wide body of research and theoretical work in fields such as developmental and experimental psychology, child development, neuropsychology, and education has generated an extensive knowledge base from which we can develop a catalog of principles and strategies for early intervention. These strategies and principles are general in that they apply not just to young children with disabilities but to all children. They are based on several key principles that describe how children learn. According to Odom (2016), early childhood special education teachers usually develop an individual professional theory of practice. This is a "technical eclectic" (p. 22) approach derived from different theoretical foundations to develop measurable goals for children and individualized intervention practices to address selected goals. Students wishing to develop expertise in the field of early childhood special education cannot hope to do so without understanding, first, how all young children learn and, second, how teaching strategies can be adapted and fine-tuned to meet the needs of individual children with disabilities.

Motivation

One of the most powerful keys to learning is **motivation,** and it is one of the oldest notions in the field of psychology (Maslow, 1998). Motivation is an incentive or inducement to action. Human organisms behave and act on the environment for certain reasons. Young children with no disabilities are typically easily motivated; early childhood educators may not need to make a great deal of conscious effort identifying and understanding the motivations of such children. For young children with disabilities, however, the identification of **high-preference items**, people, and activities is crucial to intervention success. If children are not paying attention and are not engaged, they are not likely to learn. It is very challenging for practitioners to figure out what will attract and sustain a child's attention when it is difficult to "read" his or her signals, as is often true when children have multiple or severe disabilities. Cook, Richardson-Gibbs, and Dotson (2018, p. 20) give the following examples of cues that may be missed or misunderstood:

- Children sometimes do not look directly at a toy or event. They may use side vision rather than central vision, thus giving the impression of not visually attending.

- Children with disabilities may not reach or point even though they are interested. This could be due to motor difficulties and/or visual impairment.

- There are children with disabilities who may not smile often or may have a rather flat facial expression. This may be characteristic of children with very low muscle tone or visual impairment, or it may be a symptom of an emotional disorder. Other children who lack a social smile may smile unpredictably. This is sometimes a characteristic of children on the autism spectrum.

In contrast, Cook and colleagues (2018, p. 21) also remind us of other unique ways that children might express interest and attention:

- Children may become very still and quiet when they are interested in something but may not be looking at or even facing the object.
- They may flap their arms and hands excitedly when interested in something.
- They may stiffen and extend their arms and legs or turn their head away even though they are interested. In other children, this reaction may be a sign of rejection or disinterest.

As a result of these kinds of difference, it is also important to encourage early educators to conduct a **high-preference inventory** by interviewing families or caregivers and directly observing how children respond to the presentation of different activities, items, or persons and how they respond to the removal of such stimuli.

Effectance Motivation. It is also essential to view the two types of motivation: external and intrinsic. The techniques of behavior analysis and behavior modification rely primarily on externally provided motivators. These might include primary **reinforcers**, such as food and water, or socially conditioned reinforcers, such as praise or tokens. In addition to external motivation is **effectance motivation,** which is thought to depend on internal motivational factors, as discussed next.

The classic theory of effectance motivation holds that all young children innately have an internal drive toward effectance or achievement (White, 1959). Children internalize or feel personally responsible for the impact or effect their own behavior has on their environment. Typically, developing children easily feel pride in accomplishments they can attribute to their own effort or ability (Dweck, 2016). It is this personal feeling of control over oneself and pride in one's efforts that provides inducement to act (motivation). It is important to create and support these opportunities for children who have challenging disabilities.

The existence of an internal drive to have an effect on one's environment suggests the importance of encouraging young children to *initiate* interactions with both the animate and the inanimate world around them. For children without disabilities, the key to this type of motivation lies both in the opportunity for self-initiation and exploration, and in the existence of a responsive environment. Teachers and caregivers must learn to read a child's subtle signals that are often ambiguous and may occur infrequently. Being sensitive to these signals may help teachers identify situations in which a child with disabilities is attempting to act on the environment. For many children with significant disabilities, it will often be necessary to manipulate the child's environment in ways that increase the likelihood the child will initiate an interaction and experience success. All too often children with disabilities are placed in "respondent" rather than "initiator" roles. This frequently occurs as the result of a teacher's or therapist's use of repeated prompts and cues. However, more functional, generalizable skills—and ultimately greater independence—may be learned from certain self-initiated behaviors. Indeed, many behavior "problems" are self-initiations that may provide cues for successful child motivation and teaching strategies.

Verbally and in other ways, the teacher may have to call the child's attention to the fact that his or her actions really do make a difference. Only when the success of an action is attributed to one's own efforts can pride, resulting in motivation or the desire to try again, be realized. Dweck (2016, 2017) calls our attention to how important teachers can be in helping children to discover that it is the effort they put forth that really matters. By focusing on efforts rather than outcomes, we can help children achieve the growth mindset that leads to success and self-confidence. The following examples may help illustrate the importance of understanding that children's motivation can result from their realization that they can have an effect on their environment. Their efforts can make a difference.

Johnny is a healthy, energetic, typical 4-year-old. Most of his interest is in large muscle activities. He loves being outside, riding tricycles, and climbing. One rainy day, he wandered over to the cupboard where the modeling clay was kept, managed to climb up on the counter, and opened the cupboard. Mrs. Hunt's first inclination was to reprimand Johnny for climbing, but instead she said, "What are you looking for? Can I help you?" She then realized that he was trying to get the clay. This was uncharacteristic of Johnny because he typically had no patience for this kind of fine motor activity. So, Mrs. Hunt decided to encourage his interest. She immediately gave him some clay, assisted him with rolling it, praised him for his multicolored snakes, and invited a peer of his to join in. Thus, she was able to encourage participation in a new activity by taking advantage of Johnny's own drive to act on his environment.

Another child, Robert, has cerebral palsy. He has very limited movement in all four extremities. He cannot walk and is just beginning to reach for and attempt to grasp objects. Even though he has severe physical impairments, he has a great sense of humor and loves attention. During free-play time, he is placed prone on a cushion so he can watch two of his peers without disabilities, Maria and Jeff, playing with blocks. The teacher enters the group and begins to build a block tower just within Robert's reach. She demonstrates to Robert that if he reaches and contacts the block tower, he can knock it down. She pretends to be dismayed by the destruction of the tower. Robert beams. Now the teacher rebuilds the tower, and, without prompting, Robert reaches to knock down the tower again, thoroughly enjoying the game. Very shortly, Maria and Jeff want to get into the game, each building towers for Robert to knock down.

These scenarios demonstrate the use of effort and motivation and the importance of having an *effect on one's environment*. In the first example, the teacher recognizes Johnny's interest in the clay and responds to that interest, thus allowing him to have an impact on the objects and people around him. She then assists his development in a new skill area. In Robert's case, he becomes motivated by his effect on both the physical and social environment. He experiences *effectance* by successfully making the tower fall down and also by initiating a turn-taking game (social interaction) with both his teacher and his peers. This is a result that is often difficult for young children with disabilities to achieve.

Applied Behavior Analysis

The contributions of **applied behavior analysis (ABA)** to the field of special education have been substantial. The ABA teaching approach involves observation, assessment, task analysis, systematic teaching of skills, and ongoing data collection to monitor progress. The ability to describe behavior objectively, analyze antecedent events and consequences, and shape children's behavior is a basic skill requirement for all educators. Although space does not allow a thorough presentation of the principles and applications of applied behavior analysis in this text, early childhood special educators must acquire competence in the use of techniques such as conducting functional behavior assessments, providing positive reinforcement of spontaneous initiations of appropriate behavior (i.e., "catch them being good"), using contingent reinforcement, planning for generalization of new behaviors and skills across situations, fading prompts and supports to avoid "prompt dependence," and organizing classroom structure and ecological modifications (for more information, see Storey and Post, 2017).

Briefly, this approach is based on the principle that the immediate consequences of a specific behavior can either increase or decrease the occurrence of that behavior. Consequences that are pleasurable are called *reinforcers*. Consequences that are unpleasant or aversive are called *punishers*. The use of punishers or aversive control is not appropriate for infants and very young children. However, the use of **positive reinforcement** can be very helpful in increasing the strength and frequency of certain desirable behaviors. For example, giving a thirsty child a sip of juice each time he or she makes a sound might help increase vocalizations.

Whenever possible, the positive reinforcer should be a **logical** or **natural consequence** of the particular behavior, rather than an artificial one. An example of a logical consequence is the expectation that when a child spills a container of crayons, he will pick up the crayons. In other words, an adult has determined a consequence that is related to the child's behavior. The adult can then appropriately praise the child for knowing that he should and did make the effort to pick up the crayons. A natural consequence may occur when one of the crayons rolls out onto the floor and is smashed when stepped on. Therefore, the natural consequence is that the child cannot use the smashed crayon for coloring or drawing. However, if the child makes the effort to clean up the mashed crayon, he could be given another crayon as a logical consequence and positive reinforcer.

Another key component of applied behavior analysis is the planning and selection of specific cues and prompts. Again, whenever possible, the child should learn to respond to natural rather than contrived cues and prompts. Earlier behavioral programs used a highly structured approach aimed at so-called errorless learning. Teaching of specific skills was broken down into many small steps (a task analysis), beginning with highly contrived cues and prompts that were to be faded gradually until the child could perform the behavior without prompts. Unfortunately, the misuse of these procedures (e.g., the repeated use of exactly the same discriminative stimulus combined with lack of prompt fading) can often result in "prompt dependence." Generalization to other settings then becomes difficult. For example, a child could be taught to say the word "cookie" in response to the imitative prompt "Say cookie" but would not spontaneously request a cookie. Thus, more recently, emphasis has been placed on teaching children to recognize the appropriate situation in which to use the behavior and to respond to more natural cues such as an adult's expectant look or saying, "Do you want something?"

Still another key component of applied behavioral analysis is reinforcement of the child's **successive approximations**. This is a solid principle of learning based on recognition of the importance of starting with whatever the child can do and gradually encouraging closer and closer approximation to the correct behavior. For example, initially a child may be able only to swipe at a paper with a colored marker. Gradually, the child can be reinforced for making marks that come closer and closer to drawing a circle.

Discrete Trial Training (DTT).   Very specific target behaviors, such as naming objects or identifying colors, may be readily taught using *Discrete Trial Training/Teaching* (DTT) (Gongola & Sweeney, 2013). This approach also applies the principles of ABA by using very specific antecedents (instruction) and consequences (immediate reinforcement for correct response), repeated or "massed" trials until the skills are mastered, and careful data collection to assess learning progress. One of the common challenges encountered is functional generalization of the learned behavior in natural environments.

Pivotal Response Training (PRT).   An example of another ABA approach that addresses the challenge of function and generalization is *Pivotal Response Training (or Treatment)* (PRT) (Koegel & Koegel, 2012). This approach is particularly effective in teaching skills in the area of social-communicative behavior. It teaches the child to initiate interaction with the adult in order to gain access to a desired object or experience. PRT solves the problem of generalization often associated with DTT, because the training can easily be implemented with family members, within natural environments. The behaviors targeted and learned are inherently reinforcing and functional. And the process simultaneously strengthens the child's effectance motivation by reinforcing initiation. Both DTT and PRT are identified as interventions with an established level of evidence (National Autism Center, 2015). The principles of **positive behavior support (PBS)** are now being applied to whole classrooms and schools (Baker & Ryan, 2014). These principles are more thoroughly discussed in the following section and in Chapter 6.

Positive Behavior Support (PBS)

Behavioral principles are also useful in our attempts to understand certain behaviors by carefully observing both the **antecedents** of the behavior (i.e., the events that occur immediately prior to the behavior) and its **consequences** (i.e., what occurs immediately following the behavior). For example, a child who has tactile hypersensitivity (i.e., is very sensitive to touch) may have frequent episodes of crying. Careful recording may reveal that these episodes are brought on by situations in which the antecedent event is the child's being crowded or touched by other children. Observation may also reveal that the usual consequence of this crying is for the child's favorite adult to start talking to him. A simple intervention that may reduce the crying and increase the child's tolerance for crowding would be the following: When the preferred adult notices the antecedent situation (crowding) occurring, she could approach the child *before* he begins to cry, smiling and commenting that he's having such a good time with the other children.

Such a rearrangement of **contingencies** (i.e., what behavior or event follows or precedes another behavior or event) reinforces the child for participating without crying *and* conditions the child to associate crowded situations with the pleasant experience of having a friend engage him in conversation. This preventive approach focuses on identifying the conditions that encourage positive behavior, rather than concentrating on reactions to already displayed negative behavior. The teacher or caregiver provides what is termed *support resulting in positive behavior*. Chapter 6 offers a more thorough discussion of positive behavior support.

PBS techniques can be powerful influences on children's behavior. It is extremely important that they not be used in isolation from a thorough understanding of the *whole* child. For example, one would not use behavioral strategies to control tantrums without also exploring all possible causes of these tantrums (e.g., medication effects, pain, fear, or communicating other messages). Again, additional information on PBS is offered in Chapter 6.

Social Mediation of Experience

The literature in the field of developmental and cognitive psychology is rich with both theoretical explanations and empirical descriptions of the ways in which adults mediate (i.e., assist in making meaningful) the environment and the events that young children experience. Long ago, Feurstein, Rand, Hoffman, and Miller (1980) referred to these phenomena as **mediated learning experiences (MLE),** in which adults carefully enhance a child's understanding and mastery by translating events both physically and verbally as the child experiences them.

Another theorist, Vygotsky (1980), stated that cognition develops within a social context. He described the **zone of proximal development (ZPD),** which is the level of skills that the child is able to exhibit while interacting with a significant adult or more capable peer, but cannot perform independently. As sensitive adults interact with young children, they become aware of this zone and are able to facilitate development by providing just the right degree and type of support necessary to assist the child's progress toward independent mastery of a task. Bruner (1982) referred to this as **scaffolding,** or the "gradual release of responsibility from the expert to the learner" as the adult assists a child in problem solving or performing a difficult task. Such social mediation of the child's experience is important for all infants and young children regardless of their particular capabilities. Teachers of children with disabilities may need to use specific prompts to support the child's participation and then gradually fade these prompts to increase the child's independent behaviors. Note the two examples that follow.

José is a highly gifted, somewhat rambunctious 3-year-old. He is trying to use three blocks to build a sort of archway for his truck to go under, but it is too narrow. He glances around briefly for a solution but quickly gives up and starts to move on to something else. His teacher notices and says, "Huh, the space is too narrow, isn't it? The truck can't go under. The truck is too big. Hmm. What can we do?" While making these comments, the teacher finds a long piece of cardboard that, if substituted for the block across the top, will make it possible to widen the opening. She does not say this but simply offers the piece of cardboard to José. She waits, giving him the opportunity to discover the solution himself, which he promptly does. He pushes the truck through, and his teacher comments, "Oh, good. Now the opening is big enough for the truck to go through."

A second child, Min, has severe developmental delays and multiple disabilities. She is blind and uses a wheelchair. She is able to reach and grasp but does so infrequently. Her favorite activity is eating. She appears to be responsive to food aromas and sounds because she becomes much more alert as lunchtime approaches and food carts are moved through the hallways. Her teacher helps Min organize and understand her experiences around lunchtime, mediating the environment around her. As the teacher notices Min becoming alert to the smell of the approaching food and sounds of the food cart, the teacher says, "Lunch! It's lunchtime, Min. Let's get ready." The teacher first introduces Min's bib, encouraging her to touch and feel it, saying, "Here's your bib." The teacher helps Min put on the bib, encouraging as much independence as possible by getting Min to push her arms through the holes. Next, as the cart enters the room, she taps its side so Min can hear it, then moves her close to it so she can feel it. The teacher says, "Good, our food cart is here. Now we can eat. I'll push you over to the lunch table."

In this way, the teacher is mediating what might otherwise be simply a confusing blur of sounds, smells, touches, and position changes. By doing this consistently, the teacher will eventually assist Min in understanding and anticipating these events.

Responsive Adult–Child Communication Strategies

As you can see in the preceding examples, another critical factor in assisting children's learning is the use of language. How adults and older children talk to infants and young children has a major impact on their development, particularly in the areas of language and cognition. These strategies are discussed in some detail in Chapter 8. However, it is appropriate to summarize them here as well.

1. *Use referential language.* That is, use the names of things and actions; be specific and concrete. For example, a child enjoys rolling a ball down the slide. Teacher A might say something like "Wow! That's awesome. Look at it go." Although this is an enthusiastic and positive response to the child's involvement, it is not referential. This comment would have a less positive effect on the child's language development than would teacher B's response: "Wow! The ball's rolling down. Down the slide. That ball's rolling down fast!"

2. *Use redundancy and repetition of key words and phrases.* It is not sufficient to refer to something only once. Language needs to be redundant, mentioning key concepts and events several times. In addition, repetition of key words and phrases is important. Redundancy and repetition are important to all children and even more important for children with disabilities. In the preceding example, the word "ball" is used two times, "down" is used three times, and "rolling" is used twice. Ideally, these three concepts would be introduced again during the play situation in a slightly different context. For example, the teacher could roll a different ball down an inclined board, or the children could roll themselves down a hill, and so on.

3. *Use routines.* Some degree of routine and predictability is important for all children. For children with disabilities, the careful use of routines becomes an important instructional practice that builds the child's confidence, competence, and participation in daily activities. Repetition of key words and phrases within a familiar sequence of daily events facilitates language development. Both play routines and caretaking routines are effective strategies for encouraging many areas of children's development and are discussed in more detail later.

4. *Provide comprehensible input.* The comprehension hypothesis indicates that children learn language when they understand what they hear or see. This

comprehensible input results in the mastery of language skills (Krashen, 2017). It is important for children to be tuned in to and understand what you are talking about, even if they don't actually understand all the words. Several strategies facilitate this. For example, adults can follow the child's lead and talk about what the child is seeing, doing, touching, eating, or feeling by "mapping language onto experience" (MacDonald, 2004) or using parallel talk (Scanlon, 2012). Similarly, self-talk may be used by adults to describe what they are experiencing to the child. Another strategy is to talk about concrete things that can be seen, felt, or heard. In this way, words can be associated easily with their referents.

5. *Match adult language to the child's language level.* For children who are just beginning to learn language, adult language input must be short, consisting of one- and two-word utterances and short, simple sentences. As the child's language develops, adult language can become more complex to fit the child's understanding and language level. MacDonald (2004) referred to this as **matching,** "which means that the closer our behavior is to the form, content, and intention of the child's behavior, the more likely he is to respond to and learn from us" (p. 124). For example, John has just begun to use single words. As he is playing catch with his teacher, she says, "Catch. Catch the ball. Catch the ball, John." John's friend Theo, who speaks easily in simple sentences, joins the game. The teacher says, "Here, Theo. Catch the ball, and then throw it to John." In this way, the teacher models more complex utterances for Theo.

6. *Establish turn taking.* For very young children or children with severe disabilities, it may be necessary to first establish turn-taking skills before the strategies previously listed can be used effectively. Turn taking provides the social basis on which communication skills and conversations develop. In a child without disabilities, turn-taking skills are well established within the caregiver–infant dyad in the first 3 or 4 months of life. For some children, however, this may need to be established as a specific teaching goal. A systematic approach to encouraging turn taking with children who require intensive supports is described later in this chapter. Strategies include (1) imitating something the child is already doing; (2) engaging in an activity that the child enjoys, then interrupting that activity and waiting until the child makes some kind of response; or (3) physically prompting the child to take a turn. Chapter 8 elaborates on other ways to develop communication skills.

Routines

Recent research highlights the significance of predictable daily activities on parenting and children's development. For young children, these daily activities are often referred to as caregiving *routines*. Based on a longitudinal study with typically developing children, Monk and colleagues (2010) argued that consistency in daily activities may increase the predictability of infant demands that, in turn, enhances parent perception of infant cues and confidence in meeting the baby's needs. In turn, confident and sensitive parenting supports a baby's ability to self-soothe and self-regulate. Findings suggest that these early experiences influence a child's ability to handle changes during the early school grades.

The relationship of home routines to children's preschool and kindergarten skills was revealed in data from the Early Childhood Longitudinal Study (Ferretti & Bub, 2017). This study found that a higher level of family routines was associated with fewer teacher-reported behavior difficulties, greater gains in children's social behaviors from preschool to kindergarten, and a higher level of readiness for kindergarten.

Natural Routines.   Daily routines in natural environments are the kinds of routines that occur as part of carrying out the daily activities of life. For infants and toddlers, these daily activities are called *caregiving routines*. Young children have many natural learning opportunities to practice a variety of skills across developmental domains when they participate in home and community routines with their families (Keilty, 2010). However, families may vary in the extent to which their lives are characterized by a predictable routine or schedule. Although some home environments may be quite predictable (e.g., wake up, eat breakfast, go to school, come home from school, have a snack, take a nap, play with Dad, eat supper, watch television, take a bath, read a story, go to bed), others may be chaotic and unpredictable. Some degree of predictability is thought to be important to young children. It helps them feel secure and gives them a sense of mastery and control over their environment. As discussed in Chapter 6, a sense of control facilitates both emotional and cognitive development.

Predictable daily routines are also important in the center or classroom for the same reasons that they are important at home. In addition, they provide useful contexts for teaching across all developmental domains and classroom management (Lester, Allanson, Bolton, & Notar, 2017). A familiar routine also serves as a necessary background against which children with disabilities can experience novel and special events. For most children, a familiar routine helps them participate in new situations, for example, going outside for a fire drill, that are sandwiched between familiar activities. Some children with disabilities have great difficulty adjusting to any changes in their usual daily routine and will need more preparation and structure to support their participation. However, when such events occur as simply one of many unpredictable and unfamiliar events in a chaotic day, they are meaningless at best and sometimes stressful. Familiar, predictable routines provide ideal opportunities in which young children can learn self-help skills. The Center on the Social and Emotional Foundations for Early Learning (n.d.) identified these simple and effective strategies for teaching young children with disabilities to participate in self-help routines:

1. Obtain the child's attention (e.g., eye contact, touch, physical guidance, or joint attention) and get down on the child's eye level.

2. Break down the activity into small steps and provide clear directions for each step. Tell the child what to do rather than what not to do—for example, during hand washing, "hands under water" versus "stop tapping the sink." If needed, post a series of photos illustrating each step in the activity in the relevant location and show the child the steps in the activity.

3. Demonstrate each step for the child and encourage him or her to do the same by saying, "Look, do this." Once the child begins to learn the steps, take turns showing each other what to do next. If needed, remind the child what to do by demonstrating or physically guiding the child through the action.

4. If an activity is challenging for or disliked by the child, use a "first/then" direction. For example, "First wash hands, then eat cookies." Choices may also be offered, for example, with hand washing: "Do you want to use the vanilla soap or the orange soap?"

5. Be positive in your assistance to help the child be successful and let the child know that you understand his or her feelings. For example, "I know it's hard to wash your hands. Let me help." If the child likes songs, you might sing, "This is the way we wash our hands, wash our hands, wash our hands, this is the way we wash our hands and then we'll be ready for a snack."

Play Routines. Even though play is thoroughly discussed later in this chapter, it is important, at this point, to mention the important role of play routines providing repetition and routine in the classroom. Play routines can be designed specifically to teach language, concepts, and social skills. A play routine often revolves around a pretend play theme, such as shopping, going on a camping trip, finding something lost, hunting for treasure, or a birthday party for the child's favorite stuffed animal. The possibilities are endless. The purpose of a play routine is to provide a familiar activity sequence within which to teach specific concepts, vocabulary, social skills, or pragmatic communication skills. The play routine requires a great deal of work and planning initially, but as the routine is repeated over and over, it becomes easier to implement while it also becomes more powerful as a teaching strategy. The complexity and content of the play routine will depend on the needs and characteristics of the children in the class.

Exhibit 4.1 demonstrates how the general strategies discussed here can be incorporated into the medium of play, the context that is most normal to young children.

Exhibit 4.1

Use of General Instructional Strategies During Playtime

Event	Strategy
The children in Mr. Curtis's class have finished lunch. Mr. Curtis announces that it is time to clean up the tables and go to recess.	Signal for transition
The children are very familiar with this routine, so with little assistance they throw away their napkins and milk cartons and bring their cups and plates to the sink.	Use of routines
Andrea, a 4-year-old who has Down syndrome, heads out to the playground. On her way, she notices the bottle of bubble soap on the shelf. She loves blowing bubbles and tries to grab the bottle.	
Miss Chinn, the aide, notices and asks, "Would you like to take the bubble soap outside? OK. Can you get the bottle for us?"	Response to child's interest
Andrea reaches with one hand but has difficulty getting hold of the bottle. Miss Chinn gently moves Andrea's other hand toward the bottle, encouraging her to grasp with both hands.	Child chooses Scaffolding occurs
Andrea gets the bottle and carries it outside.	Child experiences success
Andrea's friend Alex notices that she has the bubble soap.	Peer interaction
He comes over and offers to help her get the top off. He blows some bubbles, and then hands the wand to Andrea so she can try.	
The teacher approaches and sits down on the grass with the children.	
He says, "Andrea, look at these bubbles. Many, many bubbles! Oops! One popped. The bubble popped. Pop! Pop!"	Repetition of key words. Use of short sentences
Andrea looks at Alex pointing to a bubble on the ground, saying "Buh!" Alex says, "Bubble. Right!" Then the bubble pops, and Andrea says, "Pop! Pop!"	Child's request is heard
Later that same day, Miss Chinn finds a balloon. She brings the balloon to Andrea, saying, "Let's blow up the balloon." Andrea does not seem interested at first, but she becomes intrigued as Miss Chinn starts to blow. She blows it up a little bit, and then stops. She looks expectantly at Andrea.	Generalization practice. Redundancy
Andrea waves her hand toward the balloon. Miss Chinn says,	Reading child's nonverbal cues
"Shall I blow some more?" Andrea says, "More."	Responsivity
The aide finishes blowing up the balloon. Then she says, "I'm going to *pop* the balloon. I'm going to *pop* it."	Foreshadowing events
Andrea looks at her quizzically. Miss Chinn then takes a pin and pops the balloon. She says, "It popped!" Andrea claps her hands excitedly. She runs off to find her friend Alex at the sand table. She looks at Alex and says, "Pop!"	Social interaction Use of language to describe past events

> **Enhanced eText** Application Exercise 4.1: In this exercise, you can apply what you have learned in this chapter and identify the importance of routine and repetition for young children.

Play as an Important Teaching Context

The skilled use of the instructional strategies described in this chapter requires the particular attention of the ECSE professional. There is no better context in which to use these strategies than the context of play. In fact, in many ways, play is probably the single most important concept in early childhood special education. It is important both as a teaching and learning context and as an end in itself. Play is an essential skill. Typical young children can often learn play skills with little guidance from adults. Many children with disabilities, however, must be assisted in learning these skills and ECSE professionals must provide play opportunities despite the current emphasis on academic skills in some preschool programs. For further understanding of the developmental sequence of cognitive and social interaction skills that are facilitated through play, see Chapters 6 and 9 of this text.

Many learning opportunities can and should be embedded within play activities. For example, pretend or creative play and manipulative or exploratory play provide opportunities to develop and practice social-emotional skills (e.g., cooperation, turn taking, following directions, group participation, increased attention span, learning through senses); language and literacy skills (e.g., increased verbalizations, vocabulary development, language comprehension, academic language, and categorization); and cognitive and academic skills (e.g., problem solving, curiosity, and creativity). Thus, play-based learning opportunities should be an integral part of the early education curriculum (Pyle & Danniels, 2017).

Play is an ideal context in which to discover and mobilize children's motivations. It also creates a rich environment in which teachers can use the interaction and mediation strategies described earlier. There are different types of play, including physical play, constructive play, language play, fantasy or pretend play, social play, and games with formal rules that provide opportunities for teaching and learning across all areas of development. Based on an analysis of the literature on play and observations of children at play, Gray (2017) identified the following four characteristics:

1. Play is voluntary. Children choose what and how to play and learn from this process. If anyone other than the "players" directs the actions during play, this is not truly play.

2. Play is intrinsically motivating, valued more for its means than its ends, and provides a context for practicing new skills.

3. Play is guided by structure or rules that allow for creativity. Rules provide limits for action during play but do not prescribe actions.

4. Play is imaginative and allows children to remove themselves from the present and real world. For example, in constructive play, children can pretend they are building a bridge.

These characteristics are a strong endorsement of the role of play in the education of young children and should motivate teachers to facilitate opportunities for play.

It is equally important to apply these concepts to the field of early childhood *special* education. This application requires some refinement. First, as mentioned before, some children with disabilities do not initiate spontaneous play easily. Thus, teachers must develop strategies not only for using play as a context but also for encouraging its occurrence—for example, providing a favorite peer model with preferred materials to engage the child with limited play skills. Second, it is necessary to understand how the elements of play can be achieved for all children.

Some 40 definitions are listed in the dictionary for the word **play.** An operational definition that might be useful for our purposes would be the following: *Play* is a situation in which an infant or child is actively engaged with his or her environment—either animate or inanimate—but for which there is not an intended or predetermined outcome or goal.

Several key elements in this definition parallel the principles and strategies discussed earlier and demonstrate why play is such a powerful teaching and learning context. First, the child must be engaged. This suggests that, at the very minimum, there must be some information processing occurring; the child is paying attention to something. Furthermore, active engagement requires initiating and acting on the environment in some way. The term *environment* refers not only to the physical world of objects, space, and sensory stimuli but also (and perhaps more important) to the social environment. The social, or animate, environment consists of the people (and pets), communication, emotions, facial expressions, touches, and so on that impinge in some way on the infant's or child's experiences.

The element of play that perhaps most distinguishes it from other contexts or activities is the final element: There is no predetermined outcome or goal. In play, goals may emerge and unfold or arise spontaneously; outcomes are discovered through exploration and trial and error.

Given this definition of play, it can range from the simple exploratory behavior of the infant to the complex pretend scenarios of the preschooler. Playing peekaboo or putting blocks in a can may be play for one child, whereas pretending to be an alien from outer space is play for another.

Thus, play must be viewed as an important and necessary component of early childhood special education. It is, of course, not the only component. Routine daily living events are equally important contexts for learning. For busy parents, these contexts are possibly more important than play. There is also an important place for more structured, traditional learning contexts, particularly as children reach preschool age or are enrolled in behaviorally designed programs that focus on particular skills or behaviors. But the hallmark of the competent professional in the field of early childhood special education is the ability to unleash the full potential of play not only to facilitate learning but also to enhance the joy and quality of life for young children with disabilities. The nature of play, the sequential development of social skills through play, and the impact of disabilities on play behavior are discussed in Chapter 6.

Music and Young Children

As every early educator knows well, music and movement activities are very enjoyable and motivating for all young children and can be easily considered a "general instructional strategy." In a study of how preschool teachers used music in their classrooms, Rajan (2017) found that most reported using primarily teacher-directed activities such as singing along to CDs during circle time, for transitions, or as background music. These teachers also used songs to teach new vocabulary and concepts, and had a variety of musical instruments available for children to use. However, teachers' use of music and songs was limited by their self-consciousness and lack of training and resources. Rajan suggests that teachers need additional training to embed the use of music within the curriculum and to develop child-centered activities.

An increasingly applied approach to working with children with disabilities is music therapy (Schwartz, 2008, 2012). Such increased application may have been promoted by the response of the U.S. Department of Education (2010, p. 25) in clarifying that music therapy can be considered an appropriate related service on a child's IEP under the following circumstances:

> If a child's IEP Team determines that an artistic or cultural service such as music therapy is an appropriate related service for the child with a disability, that related service must be included in the child's IEP under the statement of special education, related services, and supplementary aids and services to be provided to the child or on behalf of the child. 34 CFR §300.320(a)(4). These services are to enable the child to advance appropriately toward attaining the annual goals, to be involved and make progress in the general education curriculum, and to participate in extracurricular and other nonacademic activities, and to be educated and participate with other children with and without disabilities in those activities. 34 CFR §300.320(a)(4)(i)–(iii). If the child's IEP specifies that an artistic or cultural service such as music therapy is a related service for the child, that related service must be provided at public expense and at no cost to the parents. 34 CFR §§300.101 and 300.17.

Music therapy is based on the theory that, through music, certain areas of the brain can be activated or reprogrammed to assume various functions, particularly those associated with communication and language. In fact, LaGasse (2013) cites research that suggests "there is a sensitive window for music learning that affect[s] brain connectivity and sensorimotor abilities" (p. 31). Bailey and Penhune (2012) found that children who received music training before age 7 had rhythmic matching abilities and verbal abilities superior to those of children who had no involvement with music.

The statement of purpose of the American Music Therapy Association includes a summary of evidence-based practice for the use of music therapy in special education (American Music Therapy Association, 2010). This summary lists several areas in which music therapy has been effective, including improvements in attention, socialization, self-expression and language, auditory processing, behavior, and sensory motor skills. Even without these potential positive effects on children's behaviors and skills, opportunities for creative expression and joyful experience enhance learning for both adults and children! For example, Williams, Berthelsen, Nicholson, Walker, and Abad (2012) conducted a 10-week musical program with mother–child dyads. Pre- and post-program parental questionnaires found statistically significant improvements in parental mental health, child communication, and social skills. The use of music to decrease anxiety and increase sustained attention is also growing in popularity. Evidence suggests that the use of music in early intervention may be very promising. (For example, see a peer-reviewed study with a young child with pervasive developmental disorder by Nwora and Gee [2009].)

Enhanced eText Application Exercise 4.2: In this exercise, you can apply what you have learned in this chapter to identify the learning opportunities that a child may experience during play.

Arranging the Physical Environment to Maximize Learning

A well-designed learning environment promotes children's learning. In a center-based program, the learning environment is composed of the physical environment, the social-emotional environment, and the teaching–learning environment. The physical setting should be organized, developmentally appropriate, and motivating for the participation of young children. Social-emotional and teaching–learning environments are composed of adults and children who interact in the setting. The quality

Video Example from
You Tube

Enhanced eText
Video Example 4.1
Music Therapy Session
https://www.youtube.com/
watch?v=0xwf76MUkto
In this video of a music therapy session, there are many opportunities to facilitate listening, imitation, singing, social interaction, and communication skills.

Video Example from
You Tube

Enhanced eText
Video Example 4.2
Making Room for Play: The Preschool Room Play
https://www.youtube.com/
watch?v=9xCCBIvgWQ0

and quantity of social interactions are influenced by the philosophy of the program; the numbers of adults and children; the training and experience of the adults; and the developmental abilities, needs, and interests of the children.

The Physical Environment

The room should be examined for the physical layout, furniture, use of space, adaptations, and amount of light. Based on principles of Universal Design, the physical environment should enable all children to move around safely and accommodate different motor abilities and activity levels. Figure 4.1 illustrates one satisfactory environmental arrangement. Note that either the library corner or block area could be used for "circle time." The room should be uncluttered with well-defined and consistent activity areas. For example, a carpet, tape on the floor, shelves, or screens may mark certain areas to let children know where, when, and how to use materials. Traffic patterns between areas should be clear and easy to recognize, and there should be sufficient space between furniture to accommodate a wheelchair, walker, or child with a wide gait. Independent movement from one area to another should occur. The height of tables and chairs should enable children to sit well supported, feet flat on the floor, with their elbows above the table. Tables with semicircular "bites" out of them and rims around the edges allow children to get closer to materials while also preventing items from rolling to the floor. Figure 4.1 highlights optimal room arrangement.

For children with visual impairments, room arrangements should not be changed frequently. When changes must be made, it is important to orient these children to the new arrangement by walking around with them to identify the changes that have

Enhanced eText

Video Example 4.3

These videos illustrate different considerations for organizing the preschool classroom to facilitate developmentally-appropriate learning activities across curricular domains, classroom management, and learning through play.

Figure 4.1 Room arrangement

Source: Reprinted with permission from Teaching Research Division, Western Oregon State College.

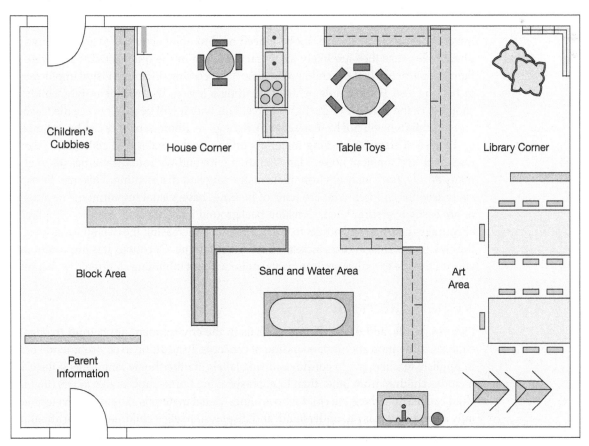

been made. For safety, doors should be either fully open or completely shut, and the sharp edges of tables should be padded. Learning materials should be of different sizes, shapes, and textures to encourage children's exploration and active manipulation. Toys and other objects might be rotated every month or so rather than keeping everything out all the time. Rotations are a means to facilitate environmental organization as well as to maintain children's interest.

Grouping Children

Grouping is also an important consideration in the teaching–learning environment. In a classroom that provides different centers or areas, the optimal number of children in a particular area depends on the space and availability of materials. If possible, there should be at least two children in a small group based on their interests to promote play and interactions. A system may be established (e.g., name cards, color cards, clothespins) to determine who can be in the area, to establish turn taking, and to organize small groups.

In a large-group activity, children need a specific place to sit with sufficient space between them. There should be different options for sitting on the floor (e.g., carpet square, mat, pillow, chair, or specialized equipment) as needed. However, if at all possible, children should be on the same physical level. Rather than having one child in a wheelchair and the other children sitting on mats, for example, all children should be seated in chairs. Other considerations for the teaching–learning environment include how to use peer models and promote peer interactions. For example, an experienced child could be asked to introduce a new child to the preschool setting or routine activity (e.g., show the child where to line up for recess or obtain materials for an art project).

Sound and Lighting

The noise level in the room should be monitored, and background music and adult–adult conversations should be reduced so as not to interfere with children's attention and ability to hear child-directed conversations. Noisy activities (e.g., sound toys and musical instruments) should not be placed next to quiet activities (e.g., book area or puzzles) because they are likely to distract children in the quiet activity. Be aware of lighting, particularly if the child has a sensory processing difficulty, visual impairment, or hearing loss. For example, when presenting a lesson, the teacher, not the children, should face the window or the light source. This way it will be easier to see the teacher, and the children will not be distracted by light glare. Room acoustics can be optimized by the use of sound-absorbing materials on the floors, walls, and ceilings to reduce resonance and ambient noise. Many children with and without disabilities (as well as many adults) find noisy environments distracting and disorienting. This may be especially true for children who are hard of hearing, have visual impairments or autism, or are easily overstimulated. Constant background noise from radios and CD players encourages children and adults to talk louder, thus increasing the overall noise level in the classroom. This, in turn, increases stress and fatigue. Of course, it is important that efforts be made to reduce environmental noise without inhibiting children's exuberance.

Visual Materials

Pictures, labels, and other visual materials in the environment are helpful to engage children's attention and understanding of concepts. In addition to environmental print in English, teachers might consider adding labels in other home languages if the class includes children from other than English-speaking homes, and Braille labels (that the child can reach) if there is a child who is blind. Visual materials should be developmentally appropriate, easy to understand, and displayed to elicit children's visual attention. Bright, clear, simple pictures and other props can be used to supplement stories, prepare children for transitions, review past activities, and learn new vocabulary. However, too many pictures or labels and those that are abstract or complicated just add visual clutter. An area is visually distracting if it looks cluttered, the child's visual attention is distracted, or the child cannot find the item needed for the activity because the area is too large with too many choices.

It is usually not necessary to make adaptations in facilities or equipment for children with cognitive, health, communication, or social-emotional differences. However, some children, such as those with autism, must have a well-organized and predictable environment in which to learn (Hall, 2017). Children who are experiencing difficulties in self-control or overreactivity do require more clearly defined limits and greater consistency in caregiving to feel safe. Nevertheless, opportunities for as much natural social interaction as possible are essential to the success of an inclusive program.

Special Considerations for Infants and Toddlers

Some special concerns may be considered in designing learning environments for infants and toddlers. Health and safety issues are of primary importance. To maintain sanitary floors that children sit and crawl on, some infant-toddler centers have a "no shoes" policy inside the facility and ask adults and children to remove their shoes and sandals before coming into the room. Floors need to be padded, sharp edges and table corners must be eliminated, and elevated areas should be no more than 2 feet in height. Sinks and soap for hand washing and diapering must be conveniently located to encourage proper hygienic practices. Diapering areas should not be located near food preparation centers. Young children tend to mouth, chew, and suck on toys and other items. When this occurs, those materials should be separated and sanitized before being made available again to children. Carpets of short pile material facilitate ease of cleaning. Storage areas that are easily accessible help avoid clutter and hazards in traffic areas.

Environments for infants and toddlers should be designed to encourage movement and interaction with one another. For example, young children are likely to explore and move along carpeted steps and ramps that lead to interesting play areas. Places to crawl through, such as tunnels, and cozy spaces to crawl into, such as a specially designed box or cubby, motivate movement. Use of multiple elevations also encourages easier interaction between very young children and their caregivers by facilitating eye contact. Beanbag chairs set on the floor are effective crawling/climbing motivators and can be comforting at the same time. Adult rockers and couches not only provide additional places for toddlers to climb into but also encourage adults' holding, reading, and talking to infants and toddlers.

Providing choices for infants and toddlers whose disabilities may restrict movement is essential. They need incentives, such as a variety of toys, to move their bodies. Toys and other interesting objects should be displayed clearly on shelves that are neutral in color so the objects are easy to see. To avoid visual confusion, only a few toys should be visible at any one time. However, it is wise to keep some interesting toys in cupboards or on high shelves to encourage children's communicative behaviors as they request objects they cannot reach. As mentioned previously, room acoustics to reduce sound reverberation and natural lighting are also important considerations for infant and toddler environments.

Creating a Positive Social-Emotional Environment

The social climate of a classroom is intended to facilitate participation of all children and build a sense of belonging through responsive and nurturing interactions. See Chapter 6 for key concepts and strategies for promoting social-emotional development in young children. It is important for adults to build a sense of classroom community and to set the tone for children and families. As discussed in Chapter 1 and throughout the text, all children are children first, and all children can learn to the best of their capabilities.

Anticipate Children's Questions

The arrival of a child with obvious disabilities (e.g., uses a wheelchair, is blind, or is nonverbal) may elicit some discomfort and questions from preschoolers without disabilities. Adults may ask simple questions to find out what children are thinking and to support a positive self-image of the child with a disability. For example, in a preschool setting, a child asked the teacher, "Why is Joey sitting in a wheelchair?" and another said, "What's wrong with Sally's eyes?" The teacher explained that Joey needed his wheelchair to move around and asked the children what they thought about that. After a few seconds, a preschooler answered, "Joey's lucky; he doesn't need to find a chair!" The teacher also explained that Sally was blind and then asked Sally if she wanted to tell the children anything. Sally piped up and said, "I don't see with my eyes; I see with my fingers!"

In addition to spontaneous conversations about a child's disability that may occur when children have questions, teachers might consider planning some structured activities if appropriate. Collaboration with the children's families and other team members may provide suggestions for conversations, simulations, and other developmentally appropriate activities to help a preschooler with a disability explain his or her learning needs to others and to help classmates understand another child's disability and the ways to interact with that child. Just as dolls in the play area should reflect the racial diversity of children in the class, dolls should also include those with disabilities, such as dolls wearing hearing aids, glasses, or leg braces or sitting in a wheelchair.

Encourage Children with Specific Positive Feedback

Children appreciate being recognized for completing tasks, participating in activities, and other everyday accomplishments. All too often, adults offer common, automatic, and nonspecific feedback (e.g., "Good job!"; "Great work!") in response to a child's everyday accomplishments. These words are intended to praise the child but may not be very effective.

Research indicates that sincere, behavior-specific, descriptive praise is more meaningful and motivating for children and has positive effects on their behaviors (Floress, Beschta, Meyer, & Reinke, 2017). Moreover, the use of specific and descriptive praise (e.g., "You put all of the trucks in the bin" or "How nice. You used so many colors!") provides appropriate language input and vocabulary that is likely to support children's language development and expressive communication. Furthermore, the child being praised should be able to perceive this as positive acknowledgment of his or her efforts in order for praise to be effective. In addition to using descriptive words to provide sincere, specific feedback, teachers might consider whether their attention, intonation, facial expression, gestures, and body language communicate their positive recognition of the efforts put forth by the child.

Provide Opportunities for Self-Efficacy and Decision Making

Choice making is a developmentally appropriate practice that helps children develop confidence, decision making, and social skills (Copple & Bredekamp, 2009). There are many natural opportunities for children to make choices (e.g., to select from snack options, choose the color of paper for a project, etc.) both at home and in the classroom. Adults can identify what and when options might be offered that are safe and appropriate for the child and when to offer them. For example, a child cannot choose to not take prescribed medication or choose to engage in an activity that is inappropriate or unsafe. Adults should respect the child's selection from the array of developmentally appropriate options that are offered.

Choice making not only creates a sense of efficacy and empowerment, it also is an evidence-based practice that promotes communication and other skills of children with a variety of disabilities (Clark & McDonnell, 2008). Opportunities for making choices can be easily embedded in typical preschool activities. Moreover, they provide natural interventions for children with disabilities for the following reasons (McCormick, Jolivette, & Ridgley, 2003):

1. A child can indicate a choice through speech, sign, eye gaze, gestures, or an augmentative and alternative communication (AAC) device.

2. Engagement in preferred activities is likely to promote the child's attention and learning.

3. Making choices draws on cognitive skills (e.g., asking for a choice or adding to choices that are provided), communication skills (e.g., verbally indicating or touching the selected object), motor skills (e.g. picking up the selected object), and social skills (e.g., negotiating with a peer).

4. Specific learning objectives can be addressed within high-interest activities.

5. Making choices is likely to decrease challenging behaviors.

6. Making choices supports the child's development of social competence, decision making, and autonomy.

Designing the Teaching–Learning Environment: Universal Design for Learning

Programs that implement the principles of **Universal Design for Learning (UDL)** promote access for children with a range of abilities and needs through flexible methods and materials that accommodate for individual, cultural, or linguistic differences. Teachers must consider whether classroom materials, bulletin board displays, and books reflect the full range of children's linguistic, cultural, and ability characteristics. Are key labels in the environment in English and home languages? Do books, music, songs, displays, and dolls represent different cultural and linguistic backgrounds, relevant home languages, and children with a range of abilities? Also, teachers must design and implement teaching methods that ensure access to the curriculum and to learning objectives for *all* learners, regardless of possible cultural, linguistic, and ability characteristics or challenges. The three key UDL principles—multiple means of engagement, representation and action, and expression (Center for Applied Special Technology [CAST], 2014)—are discussed next.

Multiple Means of Engagement

Multiple means of engagement make it possible to capture every child's attention, increase motivation, and accommodate a range of interests and learning styles. A variety of scaffolds and prompts may be used to engage and maintain children's participation. These are described here.

High-Preference Objects.   *High-preference objects* should be examined to identify characteristics (e.g., movable parts, different textures, lights, or sound making) that engage the child. Using this information, teachers may scaffold a child's participation in a less preferred activity through materials with high-preference characteristics that fit the activity (DiCarlo & Vagianos, 2009). Careful observation of a child's interactions with toys and other materials will reveal his or her preferences. For example, if a child enjoys playing with cars but resists scribbling and other emergent activities, the teacher might develop creative ways to incorporate "cars" in emergent literacy activities. A car could become a painting tool by dipping the wheels in print and rolling the car across paper. The child could be encouraged to draw a road and a parking lot and then drive and park cars or trace the wheels of the car.

High-Probability Requests.   *High-probability requests* (those to which a child is likely to respond consistently) may be used to increase the probability of a child's motor or verbal response to a new or challenging request (Chambers, 2006). For example, to encourage a very active child to sit down (low-probability request), the teacher might deliver a few high-probability requests (e.g., "Pat your head," "Clap your hands," "Stamp your feet"), and then say, "Sit down."

Child's Strengths.   *A child's strengths* (e.g., interested in visual information, very social, interested in other children, or easygoing temperament) and a "head-to-toe" assessment (e.g., to identify the area of the body over which a child has the most control) may also provide significant information on how to support a child's engagement (Chen, Rowland, Stillman, & Mar, 2009). For example, a child who is very interested in classmates might be more likely to follow a peer's model rather than respond to an adult's request. A careful head-to-toe assessment may reveal that a child with a significant motor disability has the most control over his left foot, so the AAC device should be positioned under that foot. More specific intensive support procedures with regard to working with children with intensive and complex needs are discussed in Chapter 5.

Multiple Means of Representation

Multiple means of representation involve providing information in a variety of formats and complexity levels that will enable various ways for children to acquire knowledge. The goal is to ensure that instructional content is accessible to every child. A range of formats may include English, home languages, manual signs, symbols, pictures, and the use of AAC devices, as needed. Content may be provided in various formats (e.g., verbal, print, pictures, video, or objects) as appropriate for children's learning needs. For example, directions or questions might be communicated through multiple means (e.g., speech, print, signed, modeled, or pictures) and teachers may repeat key words and phrases (e.g., home languages or signs) to facilitate each child's understanding.

Multiple Means of Action and Expression

Multiple means of expression refers to alternative ways for children to respond and demonstrate what they know and to express ideas, feelings, and preferences. For example, in response to a question about a story, children may say one word or a phrase, point to a picture, sign a word, hold up an object, or activate an AAC device. Some children may use gestures or actions to demonstrate their knowledge of selected topics. The purpose is to provide a way for every child to communicate and demonstrate learning. The provision of assistive technology is a mandate of IDEA 2004 in an effort to provide a variety of means for representation and expression.

Enhanced eText Application Exercise 4.3: In this exercise, you can apply what you have learned in this chapter to identify the purpose and principles of Universal Design for Learning.

Embedding Teaching and Learning Opportunities

When including young children with disabilities in educational settings, early educators must select and schedule activities that allow for a wide range of abilities as well as interests. There is no special time for working on children's learning objectives. Interventions should be embedded within the daily activities and routines (Sandall & Schwartz, 2012). **Embedded learning opportunities,** or those activities that originate out of natural play behavior, are very appropriate. For example, children can practice self-help skills in the dress-up corner, where they can learn naturally from their peers as the process of dressing and undressing occurs. In such an activity, each child's unique needs can be accommodated. One child can be encouraged to put on colorful socks while another is attempting to button his shirt and a third is tying her shoes. All throughout the activity, children have the opportunity to interact socially. This is even more likely if the teacher has contrived a purpose for the dress-up, such as "going out for lunch." Also see Exhibit 10.3 in Chapter 10 for more suggestions on how a teacher can plan for embedded learning opportunities.

As recommended, teachers might embed learning opportunities to work on specific objectives with a child during daily activities by using a format like that shown in Exhibit 4.2. When scheduling center-based activities, balance is the key: There should be

Exhibit 4.2

Objectives Within Routine Matrix for 4-Year-Old Maxine

Name: _____Maxine_____ Date:_____

Objectives	Routines			
	Circle	**Centers**	**Play Outside**	**Snack**
Maxine will make choices.	Offer Maxine two picture cards when her turn to choose song.	Offer Maxine two materials (e.g., different colors of paper or felt pens) for art project.	Have a peer show Maxine a set of three pictures of play equipment for her to make a choice.	Have a peer offer Maxine the daily snack.
Maxine will count objects up to 10.	Ask Maxine to count the number of children in the circle.	Ask Maxine to count the number of materials (e.g., shapes) used in activity.		Ask Maxine, "How many crackers do you want?"
Maxine will respond to peer interactions.	Ask peer to offer choice of two musical instruments to each child in circle.	Provide materials that children need to share (e.g., glue, scissors) and encourage children to ask each other for a turn.	Assist peer in asking Maxine for a turn on the tricycle or swings, when appropriate.	Encourage Maxine to respond to peer who is offering snack or making other offers.
Maxine will initiate interactions with peers.		Assist Maxine in asking peer for materials she needs to complete activity.	Assist Maxine in asking peer for a turn on the swings or tricycle, when appropriate.	
Maxine will identify and label five colors.	Ask children about the color of their clothing; use in song or as transition activity "everyone who has blue on. . . . ."	Ask Maxine to sort objects into three sets of colors or to name colors, as appropriate to activity.		Discuss color of snack foods and ask children to identify something else in the room with the same color.

a balance of large-group, small-group, and individual activities; structured and unstructured activities; and active and passive activities. Activities should address all areas of children's development. Exhibit 4.2 illustrates such a balance.

Carefully Planned Schedules Promote Consistent Daily Routines

As discussed earlier, daily routines provide the consistency necessary to help young children feel secure and experience a sense of mastery and control over their environment. Scheduled plans are one means of regulating activities and providing for consistency through the establishment of daily routines. We acknowledge that teachers planning for a group of preschoolers rarely have the luxury of hours for planning on school time. Teaching young children is demanding work at best. It is important to develop efficient, effective ways to plan. This requires a well-organized curriculum.

The first step in planning is to ask the following questions:

1. How will the day be divided into various activities?
2. How much time will be allowed for each activity?
3. Which routines and activities will be repeated daily (e.g., greeting the children as they arrive, circle time, bathroom routines, playtime, and outdoor time)?
4. How will themes be used to provide a focus for the activities?
5. What use will be made of small and large groups for specific teaching?
6. Which activities must be repeated frequently over time to allow for increasingly complex skill development?
7. Who will have to follow these activity plans?

Ms. McLynn's unique planning considerations are discussed in Exhibit 4.3.

Regardless of the materials used or specific activities, teaching is guided by the **specific objectives for each child.** For instance, if the teacher chooses to teach colors this week by baking cookies and icing them with the colors being taught, the activity can be individualized to meet different children's learning objectives. For example, she will tell one child, "Show me the blue icing" and ask a different child, who already knows the color "blue," to "use the yellow icing." For children who have already demonstrated they can *recognize* all the colors, the teacher will ask, "What color did Joe use on his cookie?," whose answer requires recall and expressive vocabulary.

Exhibit 4.3

Ms. McLynn's Lesson Plan Strategies and Sample 1-Week Plan

1. *Ms. McLynn plans activities a month in advance.* She is careful to choose activities that are highly motivating, including both novel and familiar materials. Vocabulary, concepts to be emphasized, and gross and fine motor activities, as well as music and stories, are chosen in relation to a theme.

2. *A monthly theme is more effective than themes that change every week.* Although it is common for teachers to identify a "theme of the week," these themes should be connected in some way. In addition to the scheduled plan, a lesson plan form with spaces to write specific activities, strategies, and vocabulary for each day is important.

3. *Key vocabulary, concepts, and activities should be repeated and continue to be practiced and elaborated throughout the year.* Teachers often spend a great deal of time planning and gathering materials for different daily and weekly activities. However, most children—especially children who are dual-language learners and children with disabilities—learn more efficiently when there are opportunities for repeated practice to achieve true mastery of new skills within familiar routines.

4. *Occasionally, introduce novel, unexpected experiences and materials.* Children's interest and motivation can be piqued via the occasional presentation of completely novel and unfamiliar activities and materials. (Helping children make sense of the unfamiliar and the challenge of making connections between the novel object or event and the child's existing knowledge base are great ways to apply both Piaget's constructivist approach and Vygotsky's concept of the zone of proximal development [ZPD], which are discussed in Chapter 9.)

> THEME: *"Learning about the different signs of spring"*
> ACTIVITIES:
> MONDAY: *Discovery walk to look for buds on trees and spring flowers*
> VOCABULARY: *Spring, season, weather, buds, flowers, petals*
> TUESDAY: *Plant seeds in individual pots*
> VOCABULARY: *Soil, seeds, damp*
> WEDNESDAY: *Make crepe paper flowers and learn a song about spring*
> VOCABULARY: *Crepe paper, flower, stem, petal, leaves*

5. To maximize the teaching and learning effectiveness, *each activity should be repeated at least once*, with interesting variations, as well as provide opportunities for repeated practice of key learning objectives.

6. Many of the objectives for each child require practice over time. **Equivalent practice** makes it possible for the children to practice the same skill, using many different materials and contexts. They are not bored, even though they are practicing the same skills daily. The needed repetition never becomes meaningless drill.

Just as learning activities are planned carefully, daily schedules must also be planned. Teachers should have a rationale for the order in which activities occur and the length of time spent in each activity. Research by Luke, Vail, and Ayres (2014) suggests that teacher-facilitated physical activity immediately before teacher-directed group time increases the on-task behavior of young children with significant developmental delays. Equally important is the *careful planning of transitions* from one activity to the next. This includes key words and phrases used by the teacher to mark the end of one activity and the beginning of the next activity—for example, *"We're all done with our morning circle. What do we do next? Right, it's time for outside play."* Teacher-created songs with simple repetitive refrains to familiar melodies may scaffold children's participation in transitions from one activity to the next. Copies of the daily schedule, including transition cues, should be readily available for visitors and substitute teachers. Exhibits 4.4 and 4.5 give examples of time-use plans.

Enhanced eText
Video Example 4.4
Transition Songs for Preschool
https://www.youtube.com/
watch?v=8_gd1JhV-B4
This video demonstrates how to create transition songs.

Equivalent Practice
Providing a Variety of Activities to Accomplish Any One Outcome or Objective

In choosing appropriate activities to achieve any one outcome or objective, educators are limited only by their imagination and creativity. For example, the following objectives might be chosen to achieve the goal "To learn the names of body parts."

Individualized Education Program (IEP) Goal

When the teacher points to any body part (eyes, ears, nose, mouth, arms, hands, or feet) and asks, "What is this?," Danny will name them correctly in 8 out of 10 trials. Each body part will then be checked on a doll, the child, and another child.

Exhibit 4.4

Example of a Daily Schedule: Preschool Classroom

Time-use plan and description of daily routines for both morning and afternoon classes.

8:30 a.m. Greeting. Greet children individually as they arrive. Welcome them by name, encourage a response by using eye contact, and smile and say, "Hi" or "Good morning." Assist them only as much as necessary to hang up their coats and get ready for their playtime. Ask whether they have brought a note from home. Some (as needed) go to the bathroom.

Active conversation by mapping language on children's experiences or parallel talk is essential, as their primary learning need is to develop social, language, and cognitive skills through their everyday experiences. Following arrival, children will play, some alone and some in small groups of *their choice.* This open classroom is an important teaching time because children choose from a variety of options including activity boxes with manipulatives, magnetic letters, or markers and paper, games, or toys. Teachers, assistants, and volunteers may facilitate the children's interactions with materials and other children, but it is each child's option to choose what to do. Encourage children to choose carefully, complete an activity, and then return toys and games to the shelves. They are not required to share what they have chosen and may play alone if they prefer. It is important to enjoy conversation with children about what they are doing, although this will be a bit one-sided at first. Interactive conversation and turn taking (which includes the adult's listening) are the optimum ways to model and promote speech and language skills.

Concepts to emphasize are listed on the weekly theme page and on the *concept board* behind the teacher's desk. The intent of the concept board is to provide a "prompt sheet" for adults in the classroom to use these words continually in appropriate ways throughout the day. Create opportunities for children to use these concepts correctly in the days ahead, not just the day on which they are taught.

8:40 a.m. Cleanup time. Children take turns ringing the bell to announce the end of playtime. Sing the "cleanup" song. All participate in cleaning up and moving chairs to form a semicircle facing the bulletin board. Reward with descriptive or behavior-specific praise those who arrive first with their work completed. Even physical activity of this level might contribute to on-task behavior during circle time.

8:45 a.m. Circle time. Sometimes children sit on their own carpet squares on the floor or on bean bag chairs to allow for variety. The purpose of this period is to give children practice in participating, listening, and controlling themselves in a large group. This takes time. Daily activities might include discussing who is at school and who is absent, a review of the daily schedule, a short story, and "show-and-tell." These activities not only help children become socially aware but also help them develop their language expression, memory, and just plain everyday knowledge. Teacher-directed movement activities help transition children to the next activity, such as listening for their names and moving quickly or in pairs.

9:00 a.m. Small-group time. Children choose from activities previously set up by the teacher or by an assistant during circle time. Activities may focus on language, emergent literacy, numeracy, and problem solving and may include a combination activity, such as cooking, which builds sequencing skills, language, and concepts. Some children may work individually with the teacher, paraprofessional, or therapist at this time. For children with disabilities, choices may be narrowed to develop target behaviors such as interactions with peers, language skills, and concept development. Children may rotate from the center to another depending on their interests. When the teacher signals the end of small-group time, the children clean up, use the toilet, and wash their hands.

9:30 a.m. Movement time. Depending on the weather, movement activities may take place inside the room, in the gym, or outside. Music may accompany such activities. The physical therapist or adaptive physical education instructor may work in a small group that includes some children with IEPs. After the movement activity, children wash their hands before eating a snack.

9:50 a.m. Snack time. Along with water, a variety of nutritious foods are provided to encourage the eating of healthy snacks, conversation, and an understanding of the foods' differences, for example, in color, texture, taste, and shape. As children finish, they brush their teeth and select a book from the shelf.

10:10 a.m. Story time. Sometimes, all the children "read" a selected book to themselves. At other times, some read to themselves, while others join a small group to listen to a story. When enough adults are available, they may read to small groups of children around the room.

10:30 a.m. Music time. Music, action songs, and finger-play activities occur in the circle.

10:50 a.m. Creative art time. Art and other creative activities are usually done in small groups. On occasion, parents share special interests with children at this time. Choices are provided, such as choosing among colors or materials, when possible. Children clean up after creative activity time and wash their hands or go to the restroom, if needed.

11:15 a.m. Dismissal preparation. Children clean up and then join others in the circle. This is an opportunity for the teacher to ask the children about their day, for example, to name a favorite activity or raise their hands if they liked the activity the teacher names. One at a time, children get their belongings and put on their backpacks, while others exchange feelings about the day and sing the closing song.

11:30 a.m. Dismissal. Children are released to their parents or bus drivers.

Note: Times suggested are approximate. Young children should not be rushed. Flexibility is necessary to capture "teachable moments" and to accommodate special events such as field trips.

Short-Term Sequenced Instructional Objectives

1. When the teacher points to any of the body parts listed and says, "This is a nose. Say 'nose' (etc.)," Danny will imitate the teacher's spoken model.

2. When the teacher says, "Show me your [names body part]," Danny will point to his own body part.

3. When the teacher points to any of the body parts listed, says, "This is a (name)," and waits for an answer, Danny will name the part. If he doesn't respond, she can provide a prompt, for example, "nnn."

4. When the teacher asks, "What is this?" while pointing to his or her own, another child's, or a doll's features, Danny will name the features correctly.

The following list of activities could be used to provide equivalent practice on any of the objectives just described.

1. Bathing a doll
2. Dressing a doll
3. Washing hands and faces
4. Doing a puzzle (that includes body parts)
5. Drawing a face or person at the chalkboard
6. Drawing a face or person on paper
7. Pasting features on a teddy bear made of construction paper
8. Singing a song ("made-up" chants are fun, such as "I touch my nose and blink my eyes. I clap my hands and say 'Surprise!'")
9. Making a gingerbread man

As illustrated in the following dialogue, these activities will allow children to work on their individual learning objectives while participating in an activity together.

The Activity: Bathing a Doll

Equipment: Aprons, warm water, soap, washcloths, towels, a doll bathtub, and a dirty doll.

TEACHER: Sally, will you help me wash our doll? She is so dirty. Look at those hands and feet. (Pointing.)

SALLY: I get the water and soap.

DANNY: Wa-er (water). (Points at water dripping on floor.)

Exhibit 4.5

Example of a Daily Plan: Parent Participation in a Toddler Center

This parent participation daily schedule helps prepare toddler-age children for more structured preschool classrooms, while also providing parents with access to staff and service providers along with parent-to-parent support.

Time	Daily Schedule	Notes
9:00	**Arrival**	Staff greets parents and children and assists children in finding a cubby.
	Facilitated play and exploration: small indoor climbing structure with stairs; goldfish; pretend cooking/dress-up corner (oven, sink, table, mirrors, hats); dolls and doll beds; tea set; stuffed animals; containers to dump and fill; large box to crawl in and out of; cause-and-effect toys; board books; stacking toys; blocks; sound-making toys (maracas, bells, drum, etc.).	Staff joins parents and children, chatting and observing children together, engaging in "triadic" interactions (i.e., parent–child–teacher/therapist). Reasonable physical activity should be included to encourage later on-task behavior.
9:25	**Transition to large-group circle**	• Use cues to signal this transition (e.g., sing "cleanup" song, use chimes, turn lights on and off, etc.). • Allow plenty of time to leave play areas and move to circle. Children who are reluctant to leave an activity they are enjoying will often join the circle time once most of the children are there and a familiar song begins. • Assist children who need help in moving to the circle and getting seated in adult laps or small chairs. A child who continues to be reluctant can be gently encouraged to observe the children and sing from a distance. For toddlers, "compliance" is not the goal. Rather, gradually learning to shift attention and recognize cues is the goal.
9:30	**Large-group circle** **A.** Music (with guitar): "Good Morning"/"Buenos Dias"; "Where Oh Where?" (sing each child's name); "Wheels on the Bus" (help toddlers learn motions). **B.** Activity (Very brief!): "What's in the Box?" (e.g., open box to find musical instruments). Music and movement using culturally familiar recorded and/or sung music.	**A.** Initially, parents should be comfortable sitting with their child, with the goal of gradually moving outside the circle as children become more comfortable with the routine. **B.** Objectives: Focused attention, movement activity, vocabulary and concepts, object permanence.
9:45	**Transition to developmentally appropriate centers:** Tabletop art activity (e.g., dot markers, finger paints), pretend kitchen or dress-up area, and Library Corner.	Remind parents of key vocabulary related to each center, and strategies of mapping language onto experience and expansion of child's utterances, etc. Parents attempt to engage toddlers in activities. When attention and interest wane, parents follow child's lead, transitioning child to outside play.
10:00	**Outside play yard: facilitated and self-directed play:** Large sandbox, water play. Trikes, wagons, toy cars, and ramps. Large wedges. Large balls; small plastic balls in wading pool. Medium-sized parachute. Playground equipment (slides, ladders, infant/toddler swings, hammocks, etc.).	• Objectives: improve gross motor skills; social interaction (encourage children with disabilities and those without to interact with toys, games, equipment); exploration through movement and space. • Parents are encouraged to participate and practice language input skills, and scaffold large motor skills of running, jumping, digging, pushing, pulling, throwing, etc.

Time	Daily Schedule	Notes
10:30	Snack	• Encourage self-help: wash hands, finger feeding, drinking from cup, requesting, making choices. • Attention to positioning and feeding techniques (as needed).
11:00	Cleanup/toileting	This is time for children to help clean up: put cups in tub, put trash in can, wash hands. As cleanup proceeds, individual children can be taken to the bathroom. Adults map language onto activities: "Trash in can. Then, wash your hands."
11:20	Closing circle	Parents, children, and staff join together in music, rhythms, rhymes, and relaxation.
11:30	Departure	Staff assists parents and children in gathering materials for departure.

Note: Important components underlying daily program

1. Physical, occupational, and speech therapists work in classrooms throughout the morning.
2. Parents participate in the classroom, spend some time with other parents for parent-to-parent support and socialization, and provide children with opportunities to gradually manage separation. Teachers and therapists debrief with parents, demonstrate techniques, and coach them throughout the day.
3. Bilingual interactions throughout morning activities. Stress importance of maintaining home language.
4. Each child has individual goals within daily activities.
5. Signal transition times.

TEACHER: Oops! Yes, the water is dripping! Get the towel, Danny.

VICKY: (Grabbing the doll.) I hold baby.

TEACHER: Hold the baby carefully, Vicky. Be gentle. (Pointing to the arm.) Look, Vicky, her arm is all wet. What should we do? Ask Danny for the towel.

VICKY: Towel please, Danny.

DANNY: Dere no (nose). (Pointing.)

TEACHER: Right, Danny, that's Dolly's nose. Her arm is wet and her nose is wet, too.

DANNY: Wha da? (What's that?)

TEACHER: That's her ear. (Pointing.) Can you find her other ear?

DANNY: Dere (there). Ear!

TEACHER: Right! Dolly has *two* ears.

The teacher's careful use of responsive interactions supports both Vicky's use of sentence expression and Danny's comprehension and expression of single-word vocabulary. Thus, instruction is individualized for each child within the same developmentally appropriate play activity.

Using an Activity to Achieve More Than One Objective

As discussed earlier, researchers in early childhood special education advocate an activity-based or routines-based intervention approach for planning and implementing programs for young children with disabilities (Jennings et al., 2012). This approach suggests that teaching strategies and learning goals must be embedded within daily routines that are *developmentally appropriate and motivating* and may be generalized across home and center activities.

Most activities can be used to achieve several objectives at the same time. For example, learning to follow two- and three-step directions is an important skill. Counting and learning colors and other concepts are goals included in every preschool curriculum.

In bathing the doll, the teacher might say, "Get the blue towel. It is under the sink" (emphasizing color and the preposition *under*). She might say, "Take off both socks. See, one sock is on her foot, and the other is on the floor" (emphasizing one-to-one correspondence, *foot*, and the preposition *on*).

Of course, most preschool teachers do many of these things spontaneously and without much conscious planning. However, when the program includes children with disabilities, this important emphasis on specific skills cannot be left to chance. These children require explicit examples, meaningful repetition, and a variety of related experiences. A single experience is inadequate. The ability to generalize from one experience to the next must be conscientiously planned and supported.

Several of the teaching strategies described in this chapter are highlighted in the materials from the National Association for the Education of Young Children (NAEYC) available on the NAEYC website at http://www.naeyc.org/ (select "DAP" under the Topics menu on the home page, then click on "10 Suggested Teaching Strategies" in the box on the right). These can be summarized as follows.

Ten Developmentally Appropriate Teaching Strategies

- Give positive attention to what children do or say.
- Acknowledge persistence and effort, rather than just praising and evaluating.
- Be specific when giving feedback, rather than just making general comments.
- *Model* techniques for ways to solve problems, rather than just talking about them.
- Demonstrate the correct way to do something (e.g., the motions to be made when stirring).
- Create or add a challenge to tasks so they are slightly beyond the child's current ability.
- Ask questions that challenge children's thinking.
- Give assistance (e.g., a cue or hint) to help children move beyond a comfortable level of competence.
- Directly provide new information and facts.
- Give clear directions to guide children's behavior.

Summary

Curriculum is a clear description of what we teach (goals) and how we teach (strategies). Goals and strategies are developed in accordance with a clearly defined philosophy based on evidence describing how young children learn. The philosophy of this text assumes that goals must be functional and ecologically relevant. Strategies will be built on what we know about each child's strengths and needs as well as the most effective techniques for helping each child reach his or her goals. Instruction must be embedded within daily routines and in the social interactions between children and significant others in their environment.

Universal Design for Learning provides a framework for developing and implementing instruction that provides multiple means of representation, expression, and engagement. In this way, children with a variety of abilities and learning needs can benefit from and participate in the learning environment. A wide body of research has contributed to the catalog of principles and strategies that make up what can be called general instructional strategies. The strategies that can be adapted and fine-tuned to meet the needs of children with disabilities have been described here. Play is seen as the most natural and important teaching context.

It is important not only to arrange the social environment but also to consider how the physical environment can influence both children and adults in ways that will enhance children's opportunities to learn and to interact socially with one another. Careful planning of daily schedules promotes desired consistency through routines and assists the staff in accommodating disabilities within daily activities.

Reflect and Apply

1. The curriculum we choose and strategies we use to facilitate development in young children should be derived from evidence-based practices. Reflect on what it means to be derived from evidence-based practices. Then choose a curriculum, research it, and identify what components (if any) of the selected curriculum are supported by evidence-based practices.

2. Select two different types of play, and for each type identify the developmental skills that children can develop and practice in these learning opportunities.

3. Outline and be prepared to discuss the elements that are critical in designing a classroom environment that will facilitate children's positive behaviors.

4. Identify an instructional objective for a specific lesson plan. Then describe the principles of multiple means of engagement, representation, and action and expression. Outline how each of these should be considered to support children's achievement of the instructional objective for the selected lesson.

5. Consider the usual morning routines/activities for a preschooler at home or in an early childhood classroom. Be specific in discussing what learning opportunities are embedded in these daily routines/activities.

Chapter 5

Considerations for Teaching Children with Specific Disabilities

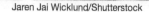
Jaren Jai Wicklund/Shutterstock

⌄ Learning Outcomes

After studying this chapter, you should be able to:

5.1 Discuss why children with disabilities require a coordinated and integrated team approach from professionals of different disciplines.

5.2 Define the principles of flexible participation.

5.3 Identify instructional prompts that are effective when they are individualized for the child's learning needs.

5.4 Describe how systematic instructional practices promote learning when children require intensive supports.

5.5 Explain how to prevent prompt dependence; prompt should be varied and faded as soon as the child masters the skill.

5.6 Generate adaptations for all children that increase participation in inclusive daily activities.

Three-year-old Hana Kim has been enrolled in the ABC preschool for 3 weeks and is still getting used to the daily routine. After about 2 minutes of sitting on the carpet at circle time, she lies on the floor or leans on other children. During center time, she does not respond to the teacher's requests and needs to be physically guided to participate in activities. Hana has Down syndrome, hypotonia, and severe myopia. She is legally blind and wears glasses for severe nearsightedness. Hana has a few vocalizations (consonant-vowel combinations) and some gestures (e.g., reaches toward a desired object and claps hands in an action song or at completion of an activity). She lives with her parents, who are bilingual (English/Korean), and her grandmother, who speaks Korean. The family speaks Korean at home, and the grandmother takes care of Hana while her parents are at work. At the individualized education program (IEP) meeting, the Kims indicated that Hana understands some words in Korean and says a few. Hana attends a state-funded preschool program that includes children with disabilities. Adults in the classroom include Judith, the early childhood general education teacher; Myrna, the early childhood special education (ECSE) teacher; and three paraprofessionals. No one in the program speaks Korean. There have been other children with Down syndrome in the class, but they had understood and used English or Spanish and did not have a visual impairment. Myrna arranges to make a home visit at a convenient time for the family so she can observe Hana in a familiar setting and obtain information about her likes, dislikes, strengths, and needs from the family. She also wants to find out how much Hana understands in Korean and whether she is exposed to English at home. Myrna also contacts the school district's speech-language pathologist, occupational therapist, and teacher certified in visual impairment to arrange a team meeting and to obtain their consultation in developing Hana's intervention program.

All children can learn and benefit from preschool. However, some children with disabilities require systematic instruction and specific supports to participate actively in everyday activities. It is up to early childhood special educators and other practitioners to identify and provide the individualized supports that each child requires. As illustrated in the preceding vignette, teachers of young children with disabilities must collaborate with the children's families and professionals of relevant disciplines to design and implement interventions that are both developmentally and individually appropriate for each child. This chapter identifies key strategies to obtain information about children with specific disabilities, and it describes ways to plan and implement selected instructional strategies that will support the child's learning and participation.

It should be noted that although certain instructional strategies are essential for children with particular disabilities to learn and participate in early childhood education programs, many of these supports are helpful for all children, including those with a range of learning needs. For example, visual supports benefit many different children, including those with limited English language skills, communication problems, challenging behaviors, and self-regulation difficulties.

Getting Started: Gathering Information about the Child

To develop and implement an educational program for a young child with disabilities, teachers need to gather accurate and comprehensive information about the child. This process requires skillful observation of the child, focused conversations with the family, shared information across disciplines, and careful review of available records. After conducting these procedures to gather information about a particular child, teachers may still have unanswered questions related to implementing effective instruction. In this case, teachers should identify other resources for support and professional development.

Learn from the Family

The family is the best source of information about a child's preferences, dislikes, strengths, and learning needs. A conversation about these topics involves questions as follows:

1. Tell me about your child.
2. What is the primary language used at home, and what language(s) does your child understand?
3. Under what circumstances is your child the most communicative?
4. How does this child make his or her needs and wants known?
5. What are his or her favorite toys, people, and activities?
6. Why do you think he or she likes them?
7. What are things that he or she does not like or finds difficult to do?
8. Why do you think he or she finds these tasks challenging?
9. What are his or her strengths?
10. What would you like him or her to learn?

It is important for teachers to reinforce information shared by families by discussing why this information is helpful, confirming when similar observations are made at school, and making intervention suggestions. For example, Myrna gained valuable insights from her visit and conversation with the Kims. She found out that Hana says some words in Korean such as "um ma" (mom), "ap pa" (dad), "mam ma" (food), and "kka kka" (cracker or snack). The Kims explained these are "baby words" used by Korean families. Before this conversation, Myrna had thought Hana was just babbling rather than saying actual words, so she made a note to listen more carefully and to respond accordingly. She also discovered that Hana enjoys her grandmother's singing and knows some hand movements to familiar songs. Myrna had noticed that Hana seems to like music time in the classroom, and the conversation with the family confirmed this preference.

Therefore, she suggested that they sing to encourage her to try less-preferred or new activities. Myrna said, "At school Hana doesn't like to use her hands to manipulate play dough or finger paint, so we sing 'This is the way we roll the play dough, etc.' while gently guiding her to interact with materials by encouraging her to put her hands on top of ours, helping her to feel our hand movements and the play dough."

Identifying the child's preferences and interests is an essential initial step in developing interventions and selecting reinforcers to motivate learning. A preference or reinforcement assessemnt will determine the items, activities, and situations that are reinforcing for a child (Da Fonte et al., 2016). For example, *Child Preference Indicators* (Moss, 2006) is one tool that is particularly helpful for gathering preference information on children with disabilities. It can be downloaded from http://www.imdetermined .org/ (click on "Educators," and then select "Child-preference indicators" from the Elementary box at the bottom of the page).

Collaborate with Team Members

Teachers can draw on the expertise of professionals of relevant disciplines by asking specific questions to obtain relevant suggestions for designing a child's individual program. The following sections provide sample questions to draw on the expertise of relevant discipline-specific service providers (e.g., speech-language pathologist, occupational therapist, physical therapist, teacher certified in visual impairments, and teacher certified in hearing loss). A comprehensive list of all potential team members is beyond the scope of this chapter. These sample questions are intended to illustrate how information might be obtained and then shared and used to develop interventions. To this end, key points of a hypothetical discussion among members of Hana's educational team are outlined after the selected sets of questions. Teachers of young children with specific disabilities are encouraged to identify and collaborate with service providers on the children's educational team.

Speech and language pathologists have a variety of roles and responsibilities as a member of an early childhood special education team. They also provide services in different locations, including in the preschool classroom or pullout from the classroom (Crais & Woods, 2016). Therefore, it is essential for a teacher to collaborate with the assigned speech-language pathologist in serving the child with an IEP.

Questions for the Speech-Language Pathologist

1. What are this child's receptive and expressive language and communication skills?

2. What specific messages or communicative functions does this child express?

3. What alternative and augmentative communication systems (AAC) are appropriate to enhance this child's expressive communication?

4. Is there any specialized equipment that he or she needs? If so, how do we obtain it? Will you help us learn how to use it?

5. What are specific intervention strategies that will promote this child's language and communication skills?

6. How will you provide speech and language services to children whose services are on their IEPs?

7. What opportunities will we have for collaboration?

Myrna shared what she had learned on the home visit about Hana's communication and language development with the team. They discussed the parents' concern that two different languages—Korean at home and English at school—might confuse Hana, especially because she has Down syndrome. Mr. and Mrs. Kim had asked whether they should speak English to Hana at home because they want her to succeed at school. Myrna had reassured the family that communicating with Hana in their home language and including her in family interactions was the best way to develop her language. She said they would work closely to support Hana's language development in both Korean and English. Diane, the speech-language pathologist, confirmed there was indeed research to support the view that children who have Down syndrome can learn two languages to the best of their capabilities. Such studies found that learning another language was not detrimental in any way and that these children's language skills in a second language were the same as those in the first language (Bird et al., 2005; Feltmate & Bird, 2008). They agreed to identify and use specific communication strategies to support Hana's understanding of language concepts (e.g., repetition, pacing, visuals, actions, and gestures) and to share these with the family as well (for details about these strategies, see Chapter 8 of this text, California Department of Education [2009], and Klein [2008]). The speech-language pathologist also suggested talking to the family about using some signs for key words such as *more, all done,* and *eat* to build on Hana's use of gestures and to help make her communication clear across both the home and school environments.

Occupational therapists vary in their service delivery models from one-on-one pullout sessions to embedding services within the child's typical routines and environments. However, one-on-one pullout sessions are not recommended for most children receiving early intervention or preschool services (Wakeford, 2016). Consequently, teachers of young children with disabilities should collaborate with the occupational therapist to embed learning opportunities in the classroom routine.

Questions for the Occupational Therapist

1. What are this child's sensory processing, oral-motor, and fine motor skills and needs?

2. What can we do to support the child's sensory processing to maintain self-regulation (e.g., if the child is hyperresponsive or hyporesponsive)?

3. Does this child have the fine motor skills to use gestures or manual signs, to indicate choice, or activate communication devices?

4. What can we do to encourage this child's eating and drinking skills?

5. What environmental accommodations are needed to support this child's participation?

6. Is there any specialized equipment that he or she needs? If so, how do we obtain it? Will you help us learn how to use it?

7. What are specific intervention strategies that will promote this child's sensory processing, adaptive development, and oral-motor and fine motor skills?

8. How will you provide occupational therapy services to children whose services are on their IEPs?

9. What opportunities will we have for collaboration?

Alice, the occupational therapist, indicated that she would observe Hana in class the next day during play, lunch, and transitions between activities, as well as downtime and structured activities to identify needed interventions (Holloway, 2008). After these observations, Alice would have a better idea about ways to encourage Hana's attention, play, fine motor, eating, and other adaptive skills in the classroom.

"Collaborative and integrated models are common for PTs providing services in ECSE settings" (Kennedy & Effgen, 2016, p. 408). Moreover, "the routine-based, task-oriented, or activity-based approach is much easier to be carried over for retention of skills as compared to the more isolated model" (p. 409). With this approach, teachers should anticipate that physical therapists will embed their services within activities during the classroom routine.

Questions for the Physical Therapist

1. What are this child's motor abilities and physical needs?

2. What handling and positioning techniques should we use to facilitate the child's interactions and participation?

3. What should we expect the child to be able to do without physical support or prompting?

4. What environmental accommodations are needed to support this child's participation?

5. Is there any specialized equipment that he or she needs? If so, how do we obtain it? Will you help us learn how to use it?

6. What are specific intervention strategies that will promote this child's motor skills?

7. Are there any cautions related to the child's positioning and physical needs?

8. How will you provide physical therapy services to children whose services are on their IEPs?

9. What opportunities will we have for collaboration?

Because a physical therapist (PT) was not a member of Hana's educational team, Alice would consult with classroom staff to facilitate Hana's motor development. For a child with severe delays in motor development or physical disabilities, collaboration with a PT is essential to implement positioning and handling techniques, strategies that promote motor skills, and ways to access adaptive equipment (Snell, 2008).

Questions for the Teacher Certified in Visual Impairment

1. What is this child's visual impairment, and what are the implications for his or her learning needs?

2. How close does this child have to be to see print, pictures, and objects, and what size should they be?

3. What is the best position (i.e., to the right or left side, or in front) for presenting items to the child so he or she can see them?

4. What material accommodations are needed to help this child see pictures and other visual targets?

5. Would this child benefit from corrective lenses or any magnification devices?

6. Given this child's severe visual impairment, how should we label classroom shelves where we have pictures for other children? Should we use Braille, textures, or tactile symbols?

7. What environmental accommodations are needed to support this child's participation?

8. Are there any specialized instructional materials that you will provide? For example, storybooks in Braille, a Braille writer, or magnification devices?

9. Are there specific strategies that will promote this child's use of functional vision or compensatory skills?

10. How will you provide services to a child with visual impairments in the class?

11. What opportunities will we have for collaboration?

Patty, the teacher certified in visual impairment (TVI), indicated that Hana was severely myopic (nearsighted) and should wear her glasses consistently. She suggested that visual materials should be presented not more than 12 inches right in front of Hana and that pictures should be simple ones on high-contrast backgrounds (Topor, 2014). She said there were tactile books, brightly colored toys, and other instructional materials from the American Printing House for the Blind that she would bring to the classroom to see how they worked with Hana. Patty also suggested that Hana hold an object that was relevant to the story during group time to maintain her attention. She and Alice would examine the characteristics of various objects to identify those that might fit Hana's visual, sensory processing, arousal, and fine motor needs.

Questions for the Teacher Certified in Hearing Loss

1. What is the child's hearing loss, and what are its implications for his or her learning needs?

2. Is this child able to perceive speech, vocalizations, or other auditory input?

3. If this child wears hearing aids or a cochlear implant, what do we need to know about how to check and monitor them?

4. Would this child benefit from an FM system? If so, will you help us learn how to obtain, check, and use the system?

5. What do we need to learn about encouraging this child's listening skills?

6. What should we learn about using manual signs with this child?

7. What environmental accommodations are needed to support this child's participation?

8. Are there specific strategies that will promote this child's listening and communication skills?

9. How will you provide services to the child with hearing loss in the class?

10. What opportunities will we have for collaboration?

Because Hana does not have a hearing loss, she does not have a teacher certified in hearing loss on her educational team. However, Deborah, the general education preschool teacher, mentioned that she was aware the preschool classroom was noisy. She said that background noise should be monitored and eliminated, when possible, so that Hana could hear and discriminate speech and associate its meaning with ongoing activities (Chen, 2014). Along that topic, Myrna, the ECSE teacher, said she would ask the Kims whether Hana had ear infections that could impede hearing and language development as well.

Identify Required Assistive Technology Devices

As discussed in Chapters 1 and 3, the Individuals with Disabilities Education Act (IDEA) requires that a child's needs for assistive technology (AT) to facilitate communication, mobility, and learning must be addressed in the individualized family service plan (IFSP) or in the individualized education program (IEP). AT includes any item or piece of equipment that may be commercially obtained, modified, or created to increase or support the functional capabilities of a child with a disability. AT ranges from simple, inexpensive materials (e.g., pictures, grips on spoons, rolled towels) to expensive digital technology (e.g., computer tablets and cochlear implants). AT includes augmentative and alternative communication (AAC). It is an umbrella term for a range of different communication methods, such as pictures, manual signs, or voice output devices. Augmentative communication is used to supplement limited or difficult-to-understand speech. Alternative communication is required for children who do not speak and need another means of communication. Children with disabilities may require and benefit from AT, as identified by the previous questions for service providers of various disciplines. Important issues are whether the child has the AT he or she needs, and how and when the AT is used during everyday activities at home and at school.

Questions to consider:

1. What AT have parents and professionals identified to meet the child's learning needs?

2. What funding is available for costly equipment or devices? Have these sources been contacted?

3. Who is responsible for repairs of costly AT?

4. How can the child receive an AT loaner to use while his or her device is being repaired?

5. Who is responsible for creating or modifying commercially available materials, for example, making a visual schedule, adapting writing implements?

6. Does the child have the required AT? If not, what can be done to rectify the situation?

7. How and when are the AT used at home and at school?

8. If the AT is not used consistently, why and what can be done to address this challenge?

The following three online resources provide information on assistive technology for infants, toddlers and preschoolers:

EZ AT Assistive technology (AT) activities for children ages 3–8 with disabilities: A guide for professionals and parents (2015) http://www.pacer.org/stc/pubs/STC-16.pdf

Describes instructional activities, ways to adapt the activity, and needed technology or materials.

EZ at 2 Simple assistive technology ideas for children ages birth to two. A guide for increasing young children's participation in activities and daily routines (2011),

http://www.pacer.org/stc/pubs/EZ-AT-book-2011-final.pdf

Provides photos and descriptions of devices to facilitate a child's participation at home, during meals, during playtime, while reading, around the community, and at special events and places.

Pacer examples of assistive technology for young children

https://www.pacer.org/stc/pubs/STC-29.pdf

Two-page handout describing assistive devices to encourage a child's participation during daily routines and activities and to promote social, fine motor, and communication skills.

Plan and Conduct Observations

To gather information about a child, it is also important to observe the child's reactions and interactions across different situations, activities, and environments (Chen, Rowland, Stillman, & Mar, 2009). These include home and school; indoors and outdoors; in quiet, focused situations and in noisy, distracting environments; during routine and unfamiliar activities using novel and familiar materials; in individual, small-group, and large-group settings that are adult facilitated and child directed; and during activities seated at a table as well as those involving movement and exploration. These observations will identify the child's strengths, interests, and learning needs. Consider the following:

1. How does the child communicate interests, enjoyment, needs, and wants?

2. How does he or she communicate various feelings of anger, frustration, or fear?

3. How does the child interact with peers?

4. Does the child initiate interactions? If so, how?

5. Does the child respond to initiations from peers? If so, how?

6. What activities and materials seem to interest and motivate the child?

7. How long will the child participate in preferred activities?

8. What activities appear to be challenging for or disliked by the child?

9. What supports/prompts/reinforcers are needed to scaffold the child's participation in nonpreferred activities?

10. How does the child respond to verbal information and requests in different situations?

11. How does the child respond to information and requests using visuals (pictures, gestures, signs)?

12. How does the child respond to different physical prompts (e.g., **hand-under-hand guidance** or **hand-over-hand guidance**)?

Guided by the questions just listed, members of Hana's educational team, including the three paraprofessionals, shared their observations and identified selected strategies they would use. They agreed to meet again in 1 month to discuss her progress and to determine what might be modified and what could be the next steps in Hana's program.

Enhanced eText Application Exercise 5.1

In this exercise, you can apply what you have learned in this chapter to identify recommended practices for teaming with professionals specializing in different disabilities to serve children with disabilities.

Suggestions for Teaching Children with Specific Disabilities

It is essential to remember that a child with a disability is first a *child* who benefits from learning opportunities that are developmentally, individually, and culturally appropriate. A child's educational objectives are derived from the information gathered from the child's family, members of the educational team, and a careful review of pertinent reports. Instructional strategies should build on the child's strengths, interests, experiences, and abilities to scaffold needed areas of learning and development.

Related to the importance of using the child's strengths to scaffold learning is the suggestion that children with different genetic disorders tend to show certain characteristic behaviors that may be used as a guide for developing interventions. To demonstrate how etiology-related behaviors might be used to develop strategies, Hodapp, DesJardin, and Ricci (2003) compared the strengths and weaknesses of children with Down syndrome with those of children with Williams syndrome.

Research suggests that children with Down syndrome tend to show strengths in visual short-term memory and imitating gestures. They seem to have difficulties in auditory short-term memory, expressive language, and articulation. In contrast, children with Williams syndrome demonstrate a strength in auditory and linguistic skills and have difficulties with visual-spatial and perceptual motor skills. Given these profiles, teachers might begin teaching a child with Down syndrome by including visual supports (e.g., visual activity schedules, picture books, signs and gestures to support spoken language) to enhance auditory memory and language development. However, for a child who has Williams syndrome, the emphasis might be on auditory cues, music, rhyming activities, and use of parallel talk and language expansion to support learning needs. Of course, every child is an individual and teachers should identify each child's unique strengths and needs in planning instruction.

Building on a child's experience is also an important instructional strategy. All children benefit from authentic experiences with real objects before they can fully understand the meaning of plastic models or appreciate pictures and stories about unfamiliar activities. For example, consider a story about "going camping" that is being read to a group of children with disabilities, some of whom are dual-language learners, in a classroom at an urban school with a high poverty rate. Without creative activities related to the concepts and vocabulary involved in "going camping," this story will not be very meaningful to these children.

The following suggestions are designed to address specific learning needs in order to promote learning and development. However, these selected suggestions *should be tailored* to meet each individual child's unique needs. Some children have combined or multiple disabilities, so interventions will need to address these complex learning needs. For example, almost 40% of children who are Deaf or hard of hearing have an additional disability (Guardino & Cannon, 2015), about 65% of children with visual impairments have another disability (Hatton, Ivy, & Boyer, 2013), and the Centers for Disease Control and Prevention report that 32% of children with ASD also have an intellectual disability (Christensen et al., 2016). Other suggestions can be found in appropriate sections throughout this text. We hope they will serve to stimulate problem solving and the development of many more effective instructional supports.

Health Impairments

Technological advances have led to the survival of many children with special health-care needs. Many of these children have intellectual, physical, and sensory disabilities. Furthermore, some children with special health-care needs have "medical complexity" or substantial health care needs, one or more chronic conditions, and/or "functional limitations often associated with technology assistance and health care use" (Elias & Murphy, 2012, p. 997). The many common chronic health problems include allergies, asthma, cancer, cystic fibrosis, juvenile diabetes, heart defects, and seizure disorders. They may result in limited alertness or strength and may have a negative impact on the child's availability for learning. For more details, see medical and nursing reference books. The suggestions made here are appropriate for almost any child with a chronic health impairment regardless of its specific nature.

Families and caregivers must work closely with health-care providers not only to ensure coordination of care of the primary disorder but also to assist in the maintenance of general health. Remember that children with health impairments are more prone to common illnesses such as colds, ear infections, or diarrhea than are other children. Children with chronic health needs usually have less energy, miss more school, spend more time convalescing at home, and are hospitalized more frequently than are children with most other disabilities. These repeated separations are stressful for the child and family. Great responsibility is placed on parents, who must continually monitor the child's health, transport the child to and from appointments, endure the anxieties of medical routines, and sometimes perform daily therapy. In addition, some chronic health problems are life threatening. Teachers and other service providers must be sensitive and supportive.

The following considerations will facilitate the successful inclusion of children with complex health-care needs in general education settings (Lehr & Greene, 2002):

1. Carefully developed health-care plans should be part of the child's IEP. These plans provide details of the child's medical condition, necessary procedures, documentation, and an emergency plan, and should include decisions about who will implement specific health-care procedures while the child is at school.

2. Identify sources of information and training for staff, and obtain them before the child begins to attend class.

3. Inform other children about their classmate's health-care needs in developmentally appropriate ways and involve the child in these discussions if he or she will be comfortable doing so.

4. Involve the child in whatever steps of preparation, administration, and cleanup procedures that he or she can help with.

5. Implement other supports required for the child with complex health-care needs, such as having arranged the environment for safety, having electrical outlets for required equipment, identifying backup equipment, and contracting with local fire departments regarding emergency plans.

Specific Strategies for Teaching a Child with Health Impairments

1. Find out as much as possible about any health problems experienced by the children in your program. Search the Internet for relevant information, and, if appropriate, contact appropriate health-care agencies. Develop a list of questions to ask and document the answers. Pay attention to dietary restrictions and requirements, medication, possible side effects of medication, physical restrictions, and behaviors indicating that a chronic illness is becoming acute.

2. Consult the child's parents and the primary care physician in planning the child's program. Become aware of what may cause a health crisis, such as a seizure or insulin reaction. Teachers and other service providers must be completely prepared to deal with any such health-related crisis. They must know what warning signs to look for, what accommodations are appropriate, and how to follow through on emergency measures.

3. Develop a list of typical classroom activities. Ask the parents and physician to note which activities should be avoided and to suggest adaptations so the child can participate as fully as possible.

4. Prepare classroom assistants and other children for the possibility of crisis events so that no one will be frightened and everyone will receive appropriate care. Perhaps a curriculum unit can be used to prepare children for what will happen in case of emergencies, including fire drills, earthquake procedures, and so forth.

5. Encourage the child to participate as actively as possible.

6. Some children fatigue rapidly. Arrange the class schedule so that vigorous activities are followed by less strenuous ones. Monitor the child's participation and energy level to determine when he or she needs to rest.

7. Help children understand the implications of their health problems. Be open and encourage them to discuss or use dramatic play to communicate their fears and anxieties. Children who understand what foods they can or cannot eat, what activities they must avoid, and so on can begin to make decisions for themselves and thus feel more in control of their lives.

8. Develop a plan for keeping in touch with children who must be absent for long periods. Telephone calls, cards (paper and electronic), and video chats can go a long way toward helping children maintain connections with teachers, classmates, and the community.

Hearing Loss

A hearing loss ranges from mild (hard of hearing) to profound (deaf). Specialists (audiologists, speech-language pathologists, and teachers certified in hearing loss) can assist teachers and other service providers in understanding the degree to which development of speech may be affected by a hearing loss (Chen, 2014; Waldman & Roush, 2009). Parents should be consulted to determine how much hearing the child does have and which communication method is used with their child—such as listening and spoken language (LSL) that focuses on listening to develop speech or simultaneous communication (SimCom) that uses both speech and manual signs at the same time. Total communication (TC) is a philosophy that embraces the use of all forms of communication, including signing, speech reading/lip reading, listening, written language, amplification, cochlear implantation, technology, and gestures. The goal of TC is to facilitate a child's speech and language development as effectively as possible.

Many developmental milestones for a child with hearing loss will be similar to those of the hearing child. The impact of a child's hearing loss is most obvious in language development. Children with hearing loss may exhibit inappropriate behavior because they lack understanding of social expectations that are conveyed through spoken language and auditory cues. Two technological advances have changed the current educational options of young children with hearing loss in the United States: the implementation of universal newborn hearing screening, which has led to earlier identification, and the option of cochlear implantation for children as young as 12 months old (Nittrouer, 2009). When children with hearing aids or cochlear implants are included in general education preschool classes, it is essential that the preschool teacher collaborates with the teacher certified in hearing loss, speech-language pathologist, and if available, an educational audiologist (Davenport & Alber-Morgan, 2016).

Specific Strategies for Teaching a Child with a Hearing Loss

1. Learn about the child's amplification equipment (e.g., how to check the child's hearing aids and change a hearing aid battery, how to use the FM system, what you need to know about a cochlear implant).

2. If the child wears an FM system, the teacher should wear a wireless microphone to allow the child direct access to the teacher's voice. Keep clothing and jewelry away from the microphone to eliminate scratchy noises. Turn the microphone off when out of the classroom without the child.

3. Involve the child in the care and maintenance of the amplification equipment as appropriate. Teach the child to report if the device is not working.

4. Provide preferential seating for the child so he or she has a good view of the teacher, activity, or other children depending on the goal and purpose of the activity. Encourage the child to move so he or she can see the person who is speaking.

5. Experiment to find out and check with parents or the teacher certified in hearing loss to determine how close in proximity a speaker must be to encourage the child's listening skills.

6. Provide learning activities that encourage the child's use of listening skills, if appropriate.

7. Speak at normal speed and volume without exaggerating lip movements.

8. Avoid speaking with your back to the child or with a bright light behind you. Don't inadvertently cover your mouth when speaking. Realize that moustaches and beards do interfere with the visibility of lip movements. Lipstick may make lip movements easier to see.

9. Use normal vocabulary and sentence structure. Be prepared to repeat, rephrase, point out, demonstrate, and use visuals and gestures if the child does not understand what is said.

10. Model for the child what to do if he or she does not hear or understand what a peer or adult says, for example "What did you say?"

11. When seeking the child's attention, be certain to use his or her name. Teach the child to attend to your face and wait for the child to look at you before speaking.

12. Use visuals and three-dimensional aids. Model the desired behavior whenever possible.

13. If appropriate, encourage the child to use spoken language in group activities by allowing time for him or her to start and finish speaking.

14. Work closely with the audiologist, speech-language pathologist, and teacher certified in hearing loss in planning instructional activities for any child who is Deaf or hard of hearing.

15. Adaptations made for children with speech and language delays are also effective with children with hearing loss.

16. If the child uses SimCom or manual signs as a primary means of communication, learn manual signs for frequently used requests, key vocabulary, positive feedback, and so on so you can communicate directly with the child. Also collaborate and plan with the educational interpreter to learn vocabulary in signs and to inform the interpreter about upcoming learning activities.

17. Help the child learn about his or her hearing loss and amplification device in a developmentally appropriate way and how to explain them to others.

18. Reduce background noise by keeping the classroom door closed, using rugs and wall and window coverings, and attaching padding (e.g., felt pads or tennis balls) to the bottom of chair and table legs.

Difficulties in Learning

Children with learning difficulties are those who may be at risk for the development of learning disabilities or who for some reason learn "differently." Such children may exhibit excessive motion, find it difficult to attend or concentrate, lack coordination, experience difficulties in visual or auditory processing of information, have poor memories, or have difficulty in abstract reasoning and in making generalizations. Such disabilities are often difficult to detect and accept because they may be invisible. Nevertheless, concerns about a child's learning difficulty should be addressed. Refer to Chapter 1 for a discussion on Response to Intervention (RTI). A referral for screening and enhanced learning opportunities should be provided; then, if warranted, evaluation and early intervention services should be obtained to address these children's learning needs (National Joint Committee on Learning Disabilities, 2006).

Specific Strategies for Teaching a Child with Difficulties in Learning

1. Be consistent in the use of positive behavior support (PBS) techniques to increase the child's attention and appropriate behavior. Structure and consistent classroom organization help children feel secure and respond appropriately to their environment.

2. Present content in short segments and provide information in multiple ways (e.g., auditory, visual, or through movements or manipulatives). Provide for repeated practice as necessary.

3. Analyze tasks. Break them down into as many small steps as needed for success. Use short sentences and simple vocabulary.

4. Use concrete examples and meaningful experiences when presenting new concepts. Choose functionally important concepts, not just those that are listed as the next steps on developmental scales.

5. Provide behavior-specific and descriptive praise for the child's progress, no matter how small.

6. Concentrate on each child's strengths, not weaknesses, and use interests to scaffold learning.

7. Be patient when it is necessary to show a child how to do something many times. Children learn through repeated and meaningful opportunities to practice skills. Do not expect children to generalize concepts easily without planned instruction.

8. Give one direction at a time until a child can handle more than one. Provide visual, gestural, and physical prompts if necessary.

9. If indicated, consult with the speech-language pathologist in planning the child's program. Suggestions for children with hearing loss, visual impairments, and speech and language impairments are also useful for those with learning disabilities.

10. Help parents understand that such children's difficulties are not indicators of lack of effort. Encourage the establishment of consistency and opportunities for learning experiences at home. Help parents recognize their children's small successes.

Physical Disabilities

Orthopedic impairments (of the bones, joints, or muscles) may be the result of conditions such as arthritis, cerebral palsy, muscular dystrophy, spina bifida, and spinal cord damage. Characteristics vary by the nature and severity of each condition. Children with physical disabilities acquire information and manipulate the environment in atypical ways. For example, children who have severe physical impairments may communicate through subtle body language, such as breathing changes and eye blinks.

Of course, the most obvious developmental challenges are in the motor area. Children with problems in this area may attain motor milestones at a different rate or in a qualitatively different way than typical children. They require specific interventions and equipment to develop selected motor skills (Snell, 2008). Certain aspects of language and cognitive development will be delayed because of motor impairment. For example, inability to grasp and manipulate the environment contributes to delayed problem solving. Delays in postural control and difficulties with oral-motor control or hand movements may hinder the development of speech and communication skills. Alternative responses using adaptive equipment may be necessary to enhance cognitive, communication, emergent literacy, and play skills (Sadao & Robinson, 2010).

Specific Strategies for Teaching a Child with Physical Disabilities

1. Review the suggestions for teaching the child with health impairments.

2. Proper handling and positioning of the child are extremely important. The child needs to feel comfortable, secure, and well balanced to be able to concentrate. Consult the parents and physical therapist to determine appropriate positions. For example, a prone position over a bolster will allow the child to make visual contact with the environment. A side-lying position may assist arm and leg movements. Each child's position will usually need to be changed every 20 to 30 minutes.

3. Arrange activities and the environment so the child's minimal movements will produce effects on the environment (e.g., to activate a communication device). This way, the child will develop a sense of confidence and competence.

4. Use adaptive equipment and both high- and low-tech assistive technology that allows the child to interact with the environment and across activities as much as possible. Consult specialists in making the most appropriate physical adaptations to the classroom and its equipment.

5. Become proficient in the use of wheelchairs, crutches, braces, prosthetic devices, and other adaptive equipment.

6. Consult speech-language pathologists and AAC specialists to identify a successful response mode for the child. Special communication devices may need to be constructed for some children.

7. Provide sufficient time for the child to initiate and respond to communication.

8. Work toward realizing the goal of active participation for each child. Self-confidence may be the key to future motivation and success.

9. Do not underestimate a child's capabilities or understanding while being realistic.

Video Example from
You Tube

Enhanced eText
Video Example 5.1
Morning Sign-In with Ethan and Amanda
https://www.youtube.com/
watch?v=gsfPetKpNZ8
This video shows how the teacher supports a child's participation in the morning sign-in routine.

Visual Impairments

A child who has *low vision* has a corrected visual acuity of no better than 20/70. The term *low vision* is used when there is enough usable vision for learning with the help of correction (glasses or contact lenses). A child who is legally blind has corrected visual acuity no better than 20/200 in his or her better eye. A child with 20/200 visual acuity sees at 20 feet what those with normal vision see at 200 feet. Vision loss may result from common refractive errors (nearsightedness or farsightedness) or from eye problems, such as amblyopia (lazy eye), cataracts, cornea damage, or detached retina, or from problems in the areas of the brain used for vision, such as cortical visual impairments (Topor, 2014). The teacher certified in visual impairments should provide classroom and instructional recommendations based on the functional vision assessment (FVA) and the learning media assessment (LMA) that he or she is qualified to conduct (Kran & Mayer, 2015).

The functional vision assessment (FVA) identifies how the child uses vision at different distances: for tasks or objects that are close (closer than 16 inches), intermediate (at a distance of 16–36 inches), and more than 3 feet away. The FVA report is based on findings from a variety of sources, including a review of the child's records, interview of teachers and the family, observations, and a variety of formal (e.g., visual acuity, visual field, contrast sensitivity, color vision, and light sensitivity) and informal (e.g., eye preference and finding an object in a picture) vision measures. The report provides recommendations for ways to support the child's effective use of vision through modifications or changes to the environment (e.g., additional lighting); adaptations (e.g., use of a high-contrast marker to outline drawings); and specialized instruction (e.g., learning to use a magnifier to look at pictures).

The learning media assessment (LMA) assesses a child's response to and use of visual, tactile, and auditory information. It is used to select general learning media (instructional methods and materials) and literacy media for reading and writing. IDEA (2004) requires that the IEP for a child who is blind or visually impaired include instruction in Braille unless the IEP team determines that instruction in Braille or the use of Braille is not appropriate based on an evaluation of the child's present and future literacy needs and skills.

Many of the children with visual impairments who are included in general education preschool programs have some functional vision. Visual impairments may affect other areas of development. Differences have been noted in motor milestones that require self-initiated mobility (such as creeping, walking, and exploration) and in hand use (handling and manipulating objects) that can affect a child's interaction with the environment and development of concepts (Chen, Calvello, & Friedman, 2015).

Depending on the severity of vision loss, there may be a corresponding delay in language and cognitive development due to the inability of the child to discern facial expressions, including the movement of lips, and decreased access to gestures and other visual information. The ability to associate concrete objects visually with verbal labels promotes early language development. Many children with severe visual impairments also experience difficulty understanding personal and possessive pronouns and will need specific instruction related to these concepts.

Specific Strategies for Teaching a Child with Visual Impairments

1. Consult with the child's parents, ophthalmologist or developmental optometrist, and teacher certified in visual impairment to determine just what the child can see. Many children can at least see shadows, color, and shapes.

2. Review recommendations on the child's FVA and FMA and collaborate with the teacher certified in visual impairments to implement them.

3. Encourage the child to wear prescribed eyeglasses and find out when he or she should wear them.

4. The peripheral (side) vision may be clearest for children with some types of visual impairments (e.g., cortical visual impairment). In these cases, a head position turned to the side may indicate a child's attention rather than inattention.

5. Be aware of lighting conditions and their effect on the child. Seek the optimal lighting needed to enhance each individual child's use of vision.

6. Orient the child to the classroom layout and location of materials. Provide a new orientation whenever changes are made.

7. Identify areas of the room by different floor coverings, signs in high-contrast colors, furniture with specific colors, and so on.

8. Provide the child with a rich variety of tactile, manipulative, and auditory experiences. Verbally describe key aspects of the activity (e.g., "Jenny's touching the rabbit. Feel the rabbit—the fur is soft.") in developmentally appropriate language.

9. Facilitate auditory localization, reaching for sound, and auditory discrimination skills. Label sounds that occur in the environment (e.g., telephone ringing, someone entering the room). If possible, take the child to the sound source so he or she will learn what made the sound.

10. Monitor and reduce the noise level in the classroom because a child with visual impairments relies heavily on auditory cues.

11. Encourage the child's autonomy and active participation both by your actions and in the way the room is arranged. For example, giving the child the cubby at the end of the row will make it easier to find. Label the cubby with a texture and the child's name in Braille.

12. Provide preferential seating for the child so he or she can see the teacher, activity, materials, or other children depending on the goal and purpose of the activity. Encourage the child to move to a different location, if necessary, so he or she can better see the focus of the activity.

13. Experiment with bright, shiny, and lighted objects of various sizes and shapes to encourage the child's interest and participation in relevant activities.

14. Encourage children to identify themselves when they approach a child with severe visual impairments. Facilitate interactions with peers and turn taking by verbally mediating children's actions and modeling language for children.

15. When seeking the child's attention, be certain to use his or her name. Use gestures and physical prompts to help the child understand the meaning of pronouns and possessive words (e.g., help Hana tap her chest to signify "me" or "I"; tap the hand of another child to signify "you").

16. Be alert to the child's need for physical prompts. When teaching new self-help skills, position yourself behind the child, use hand-under-hand or hand-over-hand assistance, as appropriate, and gradually reduce the amount of help provided.

17. Before beginning a new activity, simply state what is going to happen to prepare the child. If possible, provide the opportunity for the child to handle materials as they are introduced.

18. When possible, use real objects and provide authentic experiences to introduce concepts and build the child's understanding of plastic models and stories. For example, if the class is reading a story about making a fruit salad, having the children cut up real fruit (e.g., bananas and apples) to make the salad will help them understand the concepts of "banana," "apple," "salad" and the classification of "fruit."

19. Consult with specialists to develop adaptations for the child with low vision. For example, black pen marks on the edges of paper will help the child identify the boundaries of the drawing pad.

20. If a child does not have any functional vision, consult with the orientation and mobility instructor about the room arrangement and techniques to help the child locate where to sit, walk safely from one area to another, and use trailing and human guide techniques. Collaborate with the teacher certified in visual impairments about making tactile adaptations to visual materials and activities, how to obtain relevant equipment (e.g., a Braille writer, books in Braille), and when and where Braille should be used.

21. Provide activities for the child to develop the hand strength and dexterity (e.g., manipulating play dough) that will be needed to use a Braille writer.

22. Help the child learn about his or her vision loss in a developmentally appropriate way and to explain it to others.

23. Help the child develop self-confidence through active participation and a sense of accomplishment.

Autism Spectrum Disorders

Autism spectrum disorder (ASD) is a neurodevelopmental disability that ranges in levels of severity and in the amount of support that an individual with ASD needs (National Autism Center, 2014). No two individuals with ASD seem to have identical symptoms, and a symptom may be mild in one child and severe in another. Children classified with ASD vary widely in abilities. Some may demonstrate near- or above-average intellectual and communication abilities, whereas others may have severe developmental disabilities and never develop spoken language skills.

Difficulties with social interactions, communication, and restrictive and repetitive patterns of behavior are characteristics of autism. Some children with autism engage in repetitive, stereotyped behaviors (e.g., hand flapping) or ritualistic behaviors (e.g., sequentially touching certain objects on entering the classroom every day) and may become agitated in response to change. A child with ASD Level 1 requires support, ASD Level 2 requires substantial support, and ASD Level 3 requires very substantial support. For the official diagnostic criteria for autism, refer to the *Diagnostic and Statistical Manual of Mental Disorders,* Fifth Edition (DSM5; American Psychiatric Association, 2013). Some children on the autism spectrum tend to display strengths in rote memory, visual memory, and visual processing and are likely to pursue their special interests. Some of the specific strategies outlined next seek to build on these strengths.

Specific Strategies for Teaching a Child with ASD   The most recent report from the Centers for Disease Control and Prevention (*Autism and Developmental Disabilities Monitoring Network Surveillance Year 2010 Principal Investigators,* March 28, 2014) indicates that ASD occurs in about 1 of every 68 children aged 8 years old. This unprecedented increase in the numbers of children with autism in the United States has resulted in numerous interventions and approaches to teaching this population. However, it must be emphasized that such interventions have been used effectively for teaching other children with special needs, including developmental and intellectual disabilities (Downs, Downs, Fossum, & Rau, 2008).

In 2015, the National Autism Center published *Findings and Conclusions: National Standards Project, Phase 2* examining the research published between 2007 and 2012 on a wide range of interventions and treatments for children on the autism spectrum (National Autism Center, 2015). This report identified 14 intervention approaches (behavioral interventions, cognitive behavioral intervention package, comprehensive behavioral treatment for young children, language training, modeling, natural teaching strategies, parent training, peer training package, pivotal response treatment, schedules, self-management, social skills package, and story-based intervention package) as "established" by having sufficient research to establish their effectiveness; 18 as "emerging" interventions that offered some evidence, but not sufficient evidence of effectiveness; and 13 as "unestablished" or identified as having no sound evidence of effectiveness.

Numerous intervention approaches have shown positive changes in children who receive intensive services from an early age. It is important to note that these specific interventions tend to focus on different aspects of ASD and on various areas of development. Because of the variability in the targeted skill areas, the underlying theoretical assumptions, and the strategies employed, the selection of a particular approach (or combination of approaches) should depend on the needs and characteristics of the child and the needs and preferences of families, as well as evidence of effectiveness. Applied behavior analysis (ABA) implements specific principles of learning, such as the use of positive reinforcement and prompts to increase desired behavior. Current approaches based on ABA include Discrete Trial Training (DTT), also known as intensive behavioral intervention (IBI); Pivotal Response Teaching (PRT); and the Picture Exchange System (PECS). Exhibit 5.1 highlights selected intervention models. Although some

Exhibit 5.1

Selected Interventions for Children with Autism

Assumptions/Foci	Strategies	Outcomes
Discrete Trial Training (DTT)[1]		
Reinforcement strengthens target behaviors. Focuses on skill acquisition and compliance.	Intensive (25–40 hours/week). Analyzes tasks to break down into steps. Uses positive reinforcement for target behavior at each step. Adapted to individual child.	Child learns new skills and complies with requests.
Pivotal Response Teaching (PRT)[2]		
Pivotal behaviors will influence social, communication, behavior, and academic skills. Focuses on play, social skills, and communication.	Intensive (25 hours/week). Targets pivotal skills, including motivation and response to multiple cues. Allows child to select toys or activities. Uses natural reinforcer or consequences for each target behavior and for any attempts.	Child increases play, social, and communication skills.
Treatment and Education of Autistic and Related Handicapped Children (TEACCH)[3]		
Highly structured routines and environment support participation. Focuses on independent skills.	Organize and structure learning environment. Use visual supports (schedules, sequence charts, work areas). Adapted to individual child.	Child learns independent skills in daily activities.
Picture Exchange Communication System (PECS)[4]		
Learning to give a picture/icon to another to communicate a request will promote communication development. Focuses on communication development.	Use visuals for child to make requests for desired objects or activities. Uses natural reinforcer that is related to visual (picture/icon).	Child initiates picture exchange to communicate. Child learns functional communication and may use simple language structures.
Floortime (DIR)[5]		
Relationship-based interactions influence social-emotional development. Focuses on social-emotional development and interactions with significant others.	Follows child's lead and joining in his or her play. Supporting child in joint attention and turn taking. Encourages "circles of communication."	Child increases and initiates joint attention and social interaction with significant others; develops spontaneous communication.
Social Stories[6]		
An individually developed script (story) will help overcome difficulties with changes and perspective taking. Focuses on social behavior.	Uses a script or story to teach appropriate behavior in challenging situations. Individualized for each child.	Child improves social skills and ability to handle challenging situations.

[1] Cohen, Amerine-Dickens, and Smith (2006).
[2] Koegel, Bradshaw, Ashbaugh, and Koegel (2014).
[3] Mesibov and Shea (2010).
[4] Sulzer-Azaroff, Hoffman, Horton, Bondy, and Frost (2009).
[5] Greenspan and Wieder (2006a).
[6] Gray (2010).

occupational therapists provide sensory integration therapy (SI) with many children with autism and other children with developmental disabilities, this approach remains controversial. There has been little evidence of the effectiveness of sensory integration therapy (Lang et al., 2012; Leong, Carter, & Stephenson, 2015). However, more recent reviews of studies on SI therapy indicate that this approach is a promising practice requiring additional research (Bodison & Parham, 2018; Schaaf, Dumont, Arbesman, & May-Benson, 2018).

In addition, the following strategies reflect those that are necessary for the success-ful inclusion of all children with special needs, including those with ASD, regardless of the model or theoretical approach followed:

1. Collaborate with the child's family, because typically they are well informed about their child's difficulties and their child's unique characteristics. This will also help ensure smooth transitions between home- and center-based or school programs.

2. Interview the child's parents to determine those objectives and activities that their child really likes (high preference) and those that he or she really dislikes. These may include unusual fixations, either positive or negative. Understanding the child's fears and cravings helps in understanding the child's behavior.

3. Create a well-organized, predictable environmental space. Establish clear visual boundaries and minimize distractions. This may be the single most important strategy. Classroom areas must be well marked, and the daily schedule should be consistent. Transitions between activities must be clearly signaled by visual and/or auditory cues. Activities that are regular and routines that are familiar provide predictability for all children and are especially important for children who have ASD.

4. Capitalize on strengths in visual processing and special interests by individualizing visual work schedules with the use of objects, photographs, and icons.

5. Use visual aids whenever possible. Handing a child four placemats with the outline of the plate and silverware automatically tells the child that he or she is expected to set the table for four people. The mats show exactly where to place items.

6. Unplanned changes can cause behavioral outbursts in children who have challeng-ing behavior. Often, these behaviors can be minimized through simple redirection with **verbal prompts** (e.g., "We're going to go outside in a minute" instead of sim-ply saying, "Let's go, everybody").

7. Reduce the noise level of the classroom to the extent possible by using area rugs and wall hangings made of sound-absorbent materials. Use a quiet voice when speaking. If possible, use incandescent and natural lighting rather than fluorescent.

8. When touching the child, use firm pressure rather than a light touch. If touch is annoying to the child, firm pressure, especially if applied to the chest and back, can be soothing. Always provide some anticipatory cue so the child knows he or she is going to be touched and is not startled by the contact.

9. Be absolutely consistent about consequences for unacceptable behavior. It is very important to try to determine exactly what triggers the behavior and change the environment to reduce the likelihood of reoccurrence. Moreover, the function of the behavior must also be determined in order to teach the child an acceptable replacement behavior. For example, when Leon is upset, he screams, bites his hand, and falls on the floor. As much as possible, anticipate when Leon is about to get upset, give him a card with an image that says, "I need a break," and let Leon take that break. If he is already upset and screaming, ignore his behavior, give him the "break card," and then respond to that communication. Remember that behavioral approaches to positive behavior support are not inconsistent with sound develop-mental approaches and can be especially effective for children with ASD.

10. Verbal and visual cues are powerful tools to communicate with and help children with disabilities participate in regular everyday activities (e.g., pointing to the cubby and saying, "Hang it on the hook" to a child who needs to hang up his coat or allowing children to point to pictures to indicate their desires).

11. Sequence cards composed of pictures and/or objects that illustrate a series of connected actions or activities can help the child with disabilities. These may be semi-permanent or changed frequently, depending on individual children and programs. Such cards help a child know what to expect next.

12. Work closely with team members from other disciplines. Children with ASD frequently have unique needs across several areas of development. An occupational therapist and behavior specialist may help determine the cause of and interventions for certain behavioral difficulties.

13. Work with home-based program service providers to maximize the impact of intervention by helping the child generalize skills across settings. This is especially important when working with private agencies whose programming efforts need to be coordinated to minimize confusion for the child.

Fetal Alcohol Spectrum Disorders (FASD)

Alcohol use during pregnancy is clearly related to identifiable long-term outcomes in the child. FASD is a lifelong neurodevelopmental disability caused by damage to the fetus when a mother drinks alcohol during pregnancy. The developing brain is susceptible to alcohol damage throughout pregnancy (May et al., 2014). FASD is an umbrella term intended to encompass all individuals along a broad continuum of clinical deficits related to prenatal alcohol exposure. The range of disabilities spans the spectrum: from full fetal alcohol syndrome, with characteristic facial features and small stature, including microcephaly, cognitive disabilities, and central nervous system effects, to those who do not meet the full criteria for FAS and are said to have a Neurodevelopmental Disorder–Prenatal Alcohol Exposed or ND-PAE (Chasnoff, 2010).

Children with ND-PAE may have minimal to moderate facial characteristics or none of these characteristics at all. They might have normal intelligence and physical development. However, they do tend to have behavioral difficulties that have a negative impact on learning. The impact may not be apparent until a child reaches the second or third grade. The characteristics that are unique to FASD are largely behavioral, although many such children have sensory input issues that may cause them to be clumsy. Brain damage caused by alcohol exposure leads to the following:

1. Executive function disorder resulting in poor decision making. Diagnosis must include executive function ability.

2. Difficulty with cause and effect, which puts them in danger from those who would exploit them. They are overrepresented in the penal system because a "friend" asked them to do something illegal or they didn't think of the consequences of their actions. They may put themselves in dangerous situations and need to be kept safe.

3. Their behaviors may be interpreted as willful and belligerent.

4. Memory is impaired. What is mastered one day may be gone the next.

A recent study of FASD prevalence was conducted in four first grades around the United States. The researchers found that 1 in 20 of the children whose parents gave permission for testing could be diagnosed with FASD. This means FASD is 2 or 3 times more prevalent than autism (May, Chambers, & Kalberg, 2018).

Many children with FASD or the potential for ND-PAE are not formally identified in their early years because they do not show the classical facial characteristics or do not demonstrate a developmental delay based on standardized tests. Difficulty in getting a diagnosis is frustrating to parents and teachers. Pediatricians often will not give a definitive diagnosis of FASD without a history of alcohol abuse by the mother. Many affected children are in foster care or are adopted, so the mother's history may remain unknown. There is a stigma attached to harming one's child with drinking during pregnancy, which leads to denial and guilt in their families of origin.

Nevertheless, these children may present self-regulatory problems that cause them to be in need of early intervention services. For example, as infants, they may show early signs of difficulty regulating and controlling their behavior. They might be described as restless and difficult to comfort. They may easily become overstimulated and agitated.

During the preschool years, their self-regulatory difficulties will perhaps persist. Some children continue to be easily overstimulated and frequently have difficulty modulating their behavior. For example, giggles can turn into uncontrolled laughter, pleasant moods into sullen ones, or independence into extreme dependence. Particularly in the area of social-emotional development, these children may show delays and exaggerated reactions to events. For example, they often display more difficulty with transitions within the school day (e.g., changes in routine and changes in staff) than is expected for children their age. Such children may eventually be labeled as having learning disabilities or attention deficits.

Specific Strategies for Teaching a Child with Fetal Alcohol Spectrum Disorder Children with FASD may be served under several different categories, the most common being learning disability and attention-deficit/hyperactivity disorder (ADHD). However, appropriate services should include IEPs and IFSPs with behavioral as well as academic goals. Several strategies can be very helpful in working with young children who have been exposed to alcohol prenatally. The same strategies are useful for many children with other disabilities as well:

1. Be aware of the kinds of situations and events that trigger inappropriate behaviors:
   - Inconsistent, unstructured environments
   - New situations
   - Overstimulation
   - Internal changes, such as illness or extreme fatigue

2. When inappropriate behavior occurs, attempt to understand what triggers the behavior as well as what consequences may be maintaining it.

3. Increase predictability and consistency in classroom routines. Prepare children for what comes next.

4. Be very concrete with directions. Instead of "clean up," say "put the paper in the wastebasket."

5. Avoid making cognitive and social demands that are far beyond the developmental level of the child. It can bring on a tantrum or frustration.

6. Provide extra support during new or difficult tasks; use task analysis and teach in small steps.

7. Reduce unnecessary stimulation, especially background noise.

8. Respect children's play and work space by keeping unnecessary interruptions to a minimum.

9. Limit the number of rules; communicate them clearly and enforce them consistently.

10. Expect setbacks and regressions because this is a common problem for many children prenatally exposed to alcohol. They are inconsistent in their ability to perform skills previously taught to them. Also, be aware that home events such as family or neighborhood violence or a change in caregiver can have a major impact on children's behavior and learning.

11. Be vigilant! *Safety* is an issue with children with increased activity level, poor impulse control, and trouble understanding cause and effect. Repeat and reteach safety precautions continuously. Use of the strategies just described, over time, strengthens children's self-control and sense of mastery over the environment.

There is no cure for FASD, but those affected can be helped to stay safe, resist exploitation, and act appropriately. As with other disabilities, the earlier the intervention, the better the outcome.

Teaching Children with Severe and Multiple Disabilities

Children with multiple disabilities (those who have more than one disability such as a visual impairment and physical disability), those with severe disabilities (e.g., severe intellectual disabilities), and those with complex needs (e.g., medical problems and sensory impairments) require systematic and specialized instruction and a coordinated team approach across disciplines. In this way, necessary supports will facilitate these children's active participation in learning activities by providing a means of communication, opportunities to make choices, and the opportunity to develop a sense of competence and belonging. It is critical that the child's family and educational team access relevant informational resources to develop and implement the child's educational program.

One of the most heterogeneous groups with low-incidence disabilities are those who have both a visual impairment and hearing loss, and often fall under the IDEA eligibility category of "deaf-blind." They require specialized instruction and individualized strategies, particularly to develop communication skills. The National Center on Deaf-Blindness (http://nationaldb.org) provides many helpful publications on teaching children with both a visual impairment and hearing loss and contact information for the federally funded deaf-blind technical assistance project in each state.

When children require intensive supports because of medical needs and other severe and multiple disabilities, they may not have many opportunities to make choices or initiate an activity. These circumstances place them at risk for learned helplessness. That is, they may behave in a helpless way, having learned that their behavior has no effect on the environment. Selected strategies for supporting a child's active participation and development of autonomy are outlined next. They include providing opportunities for choice making, conducting ecological inventories and discrepancy analyses, developing an interdisciplinary support participation plan, analyzing a child's lack of response, considering the principles of partial participation, using a hierarchy of prompts, errorless learning, and using a step-by-step process for developing communication.

Provide Opportunities for Children to Make Choices

If a child is constantly being physically prompted, he or she may not initiate interactions or behaviors in a preferred activity or to obtain a desired outcome. This child may become prompt dependent. As discussed in Chapter 4, providing opportunities for children to make decisions is a valuable evidence-based practice that builds a child's self-confidence, competence, communication skills, and other areas of development. Children who require intensive supports may require systematic instruction to learn about making decisions, which begins with making a choice. Sometimes adults offer too many items at one time, or they begin with two or three high-preference items that confuse some children with disabilities. The first step is to identify the child's preferred activities, objects, and foods through systematic presentation of those items and careful observation of the child's responses to them, including facial expressions, gestures, and actions (Clark & McDonnell, 2008; Stafford, 2005). Once high-preference items are identified, they can be used to implement systematic instruction to teach the child how to make a choice by presenting pairs of items in this order (Stafford, 2005):

1. Preferred and disliked (e.g., two foods or two toys)
2. Preferred and neutral/meaningless (e.g., one food item and a block)
3. Preferred and preferred (e.g., two preferred foods or two favorite toys)

The child is likely to select the preferred item when it is offered with a disliked or neutral and meaningless item. Once the child learns through the natural consequence and positive reinforcement of his or her indicating behavior, two preferred items may be offered.

Ecological Inventory and Discrepancy Analysis

When a child needs intensive supports to participate in activities, one strategy to identify the types of required prompts and other interventions needed is to conduct an ecological inventory and discrepancy analysis. Procedures for conducting an ecological inventory and discrepancy analysis are derived from research on the instruction of children with severe disabilities in inclusive settings (Chen & Downing, 2006; Downing, 2010). An **ecological inventory** for a preschooler involves observing preschool environments, identifying the usual activities, and observing what children without disabilities are doing to participate in them. Once activities are identified, an ecological inventory of each key activity is needed to analyze steps in the activity and skills needed to participate. Exhibit 5.2 lists the sequence of steps in a painting activity at an easel and the skills required for a child to complete each step independently.

Exhibit 5.2
Ecological Inventory for Easel Painting Activity

Identified Steps	Skills Required for Each Step
1. Go to easels in art area.	Hear and understand teacher's directions.
	See and locate the easel art area.
	Move to it.
	Find empty easel.
2. Put on paint bib.	Get bib from hook on side of easel and put it on.
3. Select brush.	Pick up brush.
4. Choose color of paints on easel tray.	See containers of paints.
	Put brush in paint.
5. Paint paper on easel.	See paper.
	Grasp handle and move brush across paper.
6. Return brush to tray on easel.	Put brush on tray.
7. Remove bib.	Take bib off and hang on hook.
8. Go to sink and wash hands.	Hear teacher's directions: "Wash hands."
	See sink and go to it.
	Turn on water, use soap, wash hands, rinse,
	turn off water, get towel, dry hands, throw paper
	towel away.

A discrepancy analysis uses an ecological inventory of the skills needed for an activity and examines the child's participation in each step for differences between his or her actual and expected performance. A discrepancy analysis determines possible reasons for these differences or discrepancies that then become the focus of intervention. The task analysis process, as described in Chapter 3, identifies the steps in the activity and steps that the child is able to take independently, and then determines how to teach the steps that the child needs to learn (Snodgrass, Meadan, Ostrosky, & Cheung, 2017). Specific skills required for each step can be examined to determine what the child has to do to participate in each step. If the child cannot perform the skill, teach it, develop an adaptation, and instruct the child how to use it or a different or related skill. The strengths and skills of the child influence the type of prompts and interventions that are needed. Exhibit 5.3 illustrates a discrepancy analysis for skills related to easel painting for a 4-year-old with cerebral palsy.

Interdisciplinary Support Participation Plan

As discussed earlier, teachers should draw on the expertise of service providers of relevant disciplines given the complex needs of children with multiple disabilities. As shown in Exhibit 5.4, one way to address the child's individual objectives and identify adaptations within an activity is through the development of an interdisciplinary support participation plan.

Exhibit 5.3

Discrepancy Analysis for Easel Painting

Four-year-old Miguel has cerebral palsy and low vision and uses a wheelchair.

Identified Steps in Activity	What Miguel Does on His Own	Potential Reason for Discrepancy	Intervention Options
1. Go to easels in art area.	Sits in wheelchair.	Cannot move wheelchair on own.	Offer Miguel a paint bib; ask if he wants to paint. When he touches it, say, "OK, put it on; let's go paint." Help Miguel put on bib with Velcro tabs at neck. Push Miguel's chair to tabletop easel on table that is high enough for his wheelchair to fit under it.
2. Put on paint bib.	Waits for adult assistance.	Has difficulty putting on bib.	
3. Select brush.	Tries to grasp brush.	Brush handle is too small.	Provide a paint roller with built-up handle and with Velcro clasp or paint glove.
4. Choose color of paints on easel tray.	Looks at paint containers. Puts fingers in paint.	Has difficulty holding brush.	Place one small tray of paint on table; when Miguel looks at it, tap his wrist so he puts his painting tool in it.
5. Paint paper on easel.	Looks at paper.	Wheelchair does not fit under easel stand; Miguel too far from paper.	See adaptations 1, 3, and 4 that encourage Miguel to paint.
6. Return brush to tray in easel.	Did not use brush.		Ask Miguel if he is finished painting; if so, help him remove the painting tool.
7. Rmove bib.	Pulls at bib.	Cannot untie bib.	Undo Velcro tabs on bib.
8. Go to sink and wash hands.	Waits for adult assistance.	Cannot move wheelchair on own; sink is not accessible to child in wheelchair.	Set up wipes and tub of water on table beside Miguel's easel for all children to wash hands.

Exhibit 5.4

Interdisciplinary Support Participation Plan

Child: Three-year-old Hana is learning to participate in class activities. She has Down syndrome, is very nearsighted, is hypotonic, and tends to lie on the floor.
Activity: Singing during circle
Measurable objectives: During circle, Hana will sit upright for 5 minutes and imitate hand movements to action songs with physical assistance.

Steps in Activity and Specific Skills	How Hana Will Participate
Walk to carpet. Sit on carpet. Look at and listen to teacher. Imitate hand movements. Sing song.	Identify peer buddy who will walk with Hana to carpet while the assistant sings "walking, walking, walking to the carpet." Assistant helps Hana sit on the air cushion wedge close to teacher. Assistant gets down on Hana's visual level and signs LOOK, LISTEN. Assistant uses hand-under-hand guidance with Hana to model hand movements.

Interdisciplinary Team Members	What They Will Do
Preschool teacher Early childhood special educator Teacher certified in visual impairment Occupational therapist Paraprofessional	Selects action songs based on curriculum themes. Collaborates with preschool teacher to identify action song that builds on hand movements Hana uses (e.g., clapping). Uses animated vocal intonation and repetitive words and actions. Works with paraprofessional. Provides information about Hana's functional vision, best distance for vision use, and size and color of materials. Provides wedge pad to encourage Hana to sit up, suggestions for positioning, and ways to increase her muscle tone. Uses signs for LOOK, LISTEN and hand-under-hand and partial physical prompts to encourage Hana's hand movements to song.

Objectives Within Routine Matrix

As discussed in Chapter 4, embedding interventions within the daily routine is a significant, effective, and meaningful strategy for teaching young children. Teachers and other service providers, in collaboration with families, should identify specific objectives to address the learning needs of children with disabilities and provide relevant daily learning opportunities. An **objective within routine matrix,** a simple method for embedding interventions, is a list of the child's objectives that identifies when and how to provide learning opportunities during routine activities. This one-page document also guides classroom staff during their interactions with a child. To create a matrix, list each individual objective (e.g., will select a picture from a field of three to indicate a request) for a child in the left column and then list the different daily activities (e.g., circle, play, snack, recess, etc.) across the top row. Within each space at the intersection of the objective and activity, write down the strategy and supports (e.g., show the child three pictures to select a play area and ask, "Where do you want to play?"; sign PLAY) that should be used to facilitate the child's participation.

Exhibit 5.5

Objectives Within Routine Matrix for 3-Year-Old Hana

Name _____ Hana _____

Objectives	Routines			
	Circle	**Centers**	**Play Outside**	**Snack**
Hana will make choices.	Offer Hana a choice of two objects (e.g., spider or scarf) when it is her turn to choose a song. Begin with her favorite ("Itsy, bitsy spider") and a less preferred song.	Offer Hana a choice of two materials (e.g., strip of sponge or popsicle stick) for glue activity. Hana will hold onto either item; needs verbal prompting to dip in glue. Say "dip, dip, dip."	Help peer show Hana an object to represent the area they will play in together (e.g., plastic shovel for sandbox or piece of chain for swings).	Offer Hana the daily snack from a common serving dish. Be sure that the snack (e.g., crackers) is placed on a high-contrast colored dish or put dark-colored paper on dish.
Hana will imitate simple gestures, hand movements, and actions.	Sing songs that include movements that Hana will imitate (e.g., "Hands go clapping, clapping," etc.). Use hand-under-hand guidance or prompt from her elbow to imitate other movements (e.g., hands go up).	Demonstrate how to use materials (e.g., dip sponge into bowl of glue and then dab on paper or crumple tissue paper for project). Verbally prompt Hana to do the same.	Encourage peer to take turns with Hana in sandbox (e.g., by showing her how to scoop sand into a container, poke pegs into a mound of sand, etc.). When Hana seems to have had enough of the sandbox, help her imitate the sign for ALL DONE.	After Hana has eaten one cracker (her favorite), ask her if she wants "more" snack and sign MORE. If she looks at the cracker, prompt her from the wrists to make the MORE sign.
Hana will respond to her name.	Play a "name game"—"Where is xxxx?" Prompt Hana to pat her chest when she hears her name.		Use Hana's name and peer's name when facilitating turn taking in the sandbox.	Ask, "Hana, want snack?" and sign EAT. Wait for Hana to look at you.

The matrix may also include curriculum modifications and accommodations to support a child's participation (Sandall, Schwartz, & Gauvreau, 2016). Exhibit 5.5 shows how selected objectives for Hana are addressed during the school day.

Analyze a Child's Lack of Response

It is sometimes challenging to figure out why a child does not respond to a routine request or directions. Teachers may assume that a child's lack of response is due to his or her intellectual disabilities or complex needs. However, it is most important to hypothesize about possible causes for the child's lack of response, determine how to test what might be the problem, and then develop and use an adaptation or way to support the child's understanding and response, as follows:

1. The child does not understand what is being requested (language difficulty).

   Possible adaptation: Use clear and specific language and visual supports (e.g., object, pictures, signs, or peer model).

2. The child did not hear the request (e.g., was not paying attention or has a hearing or auditory processing problem).

   Possible adaptation: Move closer to child and face him or her when speaking, and use visuals, gestures, or signs to obtain the child's auditory and visual attention.

3. The child does not want to comply with the request (ignoring direction).

   Possible adaptation: Provide positive reinforcement whenever child follows directions, provide a natural reinforcing consequence to the targeted response, or use high-probability requests as momentum to encourage compliance with a low-probability request (see Chapter 4).

4. The child does not know what to do (e.g., hears and may understand the direction but does not have the skill to comply with the request).

   Possible adaptation: Provide a clear and specific model (e.g., peer model), and use appropriate prompts to guide the child's response so that he or she will learn what is expected.

This framework may be also used to analyze a child's challenging behaviors. Whatever the basis of the child's difficulty in responding, be sure to provide positive feedback and reinforcement when the child attempts to comply with the request. This way, the child becomes familiar with the routine requests and expected responses.

Principle of Flexible Participation

The framework provided by the Universal Design for Learning (UDL; see Chapter 1) to create accessible instructional environments for all children is particularly essential for children who have intensive learning needs. The principle of partial participation was developed many years ago to support the inclusion and participation of children with severe disabilities in home, school, and community activities through individualized adaptations (Ferguson & Baumgart, 1991) in four areas. An essential feature of this principle relates to social and attitudinal adaptations—that is, changing assumptions, beliefs, or judgments about a child's limitations and figuring out how to provide assistance in a respectful way (e.g., the adult asks Bob if she can wipe his mouth when he drools and waits for Bob to respond). Other adaptations relate to materials, the sequence or rules of a task, or personal assistance, as shown in Exhibit 5.6. More recently, the term "flexible participation" has been used by Parette and Blum (2014) to describe how to help children participate in everyday activities through technology using the multiple means of engagement, representation, and action and expression of UDL. The use of flexible participation strategies within the UDL framework provides a helpful tool for planning instruction for preschoolers with disabilities. See Exhibit 5.6 for examples.

Prompting and Fading Procedures

Instructional prompts are used to help children participate in activities and develop skills. Some children attend to natural prompts; others require more specific supports. Prompting and fading procedures are recommended by the Division for Early Childhood (DEC) to promote the acquisition of skills (Sandall, Hemmeter, Smith, & McLean, 2005). There are two ways to use prompts systematically, and both have advantages and drawbacks (Gaisford & Malott, 2010; Mueller, Palkovic, & Maynard, 2007):

- *Most-to-least prompting.* The adult has control over the behavior and ensures that the child responds correctly (errorless learning), particularly when learning a skill. The level of prompts should be faded to decrease the child's dependence on prompts and increase independent skills. Sometimes the child may receive more assistance than needed.

- *Least-to-most prompting.* The child is less likely to become prompt dependent because the use of less-intrusive prompts allows the child control over his or her behavior. However, adults may need to increase the level of prompts if errors continue to occur. Least-to-most prompting may produce high error rates in the

Exhibit 5.6

Flexible Participation Strategies with Universal Design
for Learning Examples in Preschool Activities

Flexible Participation Strategy	UDL Examples
Adapt or modify materials to fit the child's developmental and sensory needs.	**Engagement:** Add dowels on puzzle pieces or wooden tabs to pages so child can manipulate them. Add clasps to stabilize materials, or provide zipper extenders. Use child preferences for materials to promote participation. **Representation:** Change the size and complexity of pictures or photos so child can see and understand them. Use songs, movements, and objects. Use simple sentences and short phrases, repeat key words in English and home language. **Action and Expression:** Provide a sensitive switch to activate toys, a voice output device, or screen overlay on tablet.
Modify or alter rules or sequence of skills so child can actively participate.	**Engagement:** Use task analysis to reduce the number of items or components of a task that the child is expected to complete. Use first/then cards to motivate child's participation. **Representation:** Provide visual or object sequence cards related to the task. **Action and Expression:** Increase response options through pointing, eye gaze, gestures, or selecting object, picture, or printed word, or using key word signs or a voice output device. Provide additional time for child to respond.
Provide personal assistance from peers or adults using prompts to support child's active participation.	**Engagement:** Pair child with preferred peer in small-group activities. **Representation:** Ask peer to repeat directions or show child the visual or object sequence cards. Adult shows the child a spoon and cup to represent eating and drinking. **Action and Expression:** Target child's ability to participate, for example, child with severe physical disabilities will look at the cup or spoon to indicate that he wants the adult to feed him or give him a drink. Use least intrusive prompt in the prompt hierarchy to assist child's participation and fade prompts as appropriate.

child's responses and, in turn, low levels of reinforcement and increased emotional responses. See Exhibit 5.7 for a hierarchy of prompts. To decrease the likelihood of a child becoming prompt dependent, it is essential to fade or change prompts once a child has mastered the skill.

Teachers need to determine the appropriate type of prompt and whether a most-to-least or least-to-most sequence of prompting fits the child's learning needs and the target activity or expected response. DiCarlo, Baumgartner, Caballero, and Powers (2016) found that least-to-most prompting with the addition of teacher–child proximity and face-to-face positioning before beginning the prompts were effective in having preschoolers comply with teacher requests during free-choice time. However, Seaver and Bourret (2014) suggest conducting an individual assessment of prompt use with each child with a disability to determine what type is most effective. In a study of older students with autism, they found that a model prompt was efficient with 60% of the students. However, for some, the use of physical, verbal, or gestural prompts is the most efficient in learning daily living skills. Highbee (2010) provides additional considerations regarding the use of prompts. It is much easier to fade physical prompts than verbal prompts. Fading of physical prompts also includes shadowing the child and gradually increasing the adult's distance from the child. In visual learning activities (e.g., looking at photos of activities) where the goal is to focus the child's visual attention on the target (e.g., photo) to complete an activity independently, have the child tap or touch the target and eliminate distractions (e.g., verbal prompts, gestures, eye contact, praise, or other adult behaviors) from the visual task. This way, the child's attention is on the visual target and his or her own behavior.

Exhibit 5.7
Hierarchy of Prompts

Natural Cues
Child responds independently to request because he or she notices **natural cues** related to the activity. For example, child sees other children at the snack table and finds an empty chair to sit at the table.

Verbal Prompts
Specific verbal direction on required response is given. The verbal prompt (speech or sign) may be direct (e.g., "Find a place to sit") or indirect ("Time for snack"). Once a child understands and responds to a specific verbal prompt, consider varying the request and fading the verbal prompt so the child does not become dependent on the adult's verbal direction. For example, a child may become dependent on the verbal prompt "sit down" and stand by the chair waiting for the adult's verbal prompt.

Visual Prompts
Pictures, objects, and other visual means (e.g., gestures and labels) may be used as **visual prompts.**

Objects
An object is used to prompt the child's response (e.g., a cup indicates "Time for snack" and the child takes the cup to the table).

Pictures
A picture (photo or line drawing) is used to prompt the child's response (e.g., a photo of children at the table or drawing of a cup to indicate "Time for snack").

Words
The printed word is used to prompt the child's response (e.g., the label "Snack").

Gestures
Gesturing is used to prompt the child's response (e.g., pointing to the snack table).

Modeling
The expected response or action is demonstrated (e.g., another child is a model and walks in front of the child and finds a place at the table).

Physical Assistance
The use of physical assistance provides the most support and is the most intrusive type of prompt. It ranges from full physical assistance (e.g., using hand-over-hand guidance to take the child to the table, find a chair, and sit down) to a partial physical prompt (e.g., tapping the child's shoulder to remind the child of the expected response). For physical prompts to be effective, children should tolerate and cooperate with tactile input. Physical assistance is also called *manual guidance*. Spatial fading or graduated guidance refers to changing the location of the physical prompt (e.g., hand, wrist, forearm, upper arm, elbow, then shoulder) as the child becomes more independent in his or her response.

Errorless Learning

Errorless learning refers to teaching procedures that decrease the chance that various factors may influence the child's incorrect response and increase the likelihood that the child will respond correctly. Common activities include teaching a child to identify objects, pictures, words, colors, shapes, and numbers (Mueller, Palkovic, & Maynard, 2007).

Maximizing the chance that the child will respond correctly provides a foundation of correct responses on which the child can build. Furthermore, the teacher can positively reinforce the child for these correct prompted responses to motivate participation in learning opportunities. In this way, a child develops a sense of competence and experiences success. Procedures include reducing distracters and using physical prompts to elicit the correct response. After providing errorless learning procedures for a certain period of time, teachers can evaluate the child's progress by removing the prompt.

Errorless learning is effective in teaching children with severe intellectual disabilities or memory difficulties who make frequent mistakes, lack self-confidence, and do not remember learning experiences or feedback on their responses. In contrast, trial-and-error learning may be effective for children who are more often correct than incorrect in their responses, have self-confidence, are able to remember learning experiences, and can use feedback on their responses. Some children with disabilities require systematic and sequential instruction to discriminate, match, and sort pictures. Instructional strategies that support errorless learning include simple discrimination learning, match-to-sample, and sort-to-sample, each of which is described next.

Simple discrimination learning involves the ability to identify whether objects are the same or different. Initially, when teaching a child to discriminate between two items, begin with items that are very different in appearance and function (e.g., ball and spoon). Once the child can recognize these differences, then teach discrimination of two items (e.g., bowl and cup) that vary in one relevant feature (e.g., form) while other dimensions (i.e., size and color) are the same. Higher-level discrimination learning is achieved when the child can identify objects that vary on multiple dimensions (e.g., size, color). That is, a bowl is a bowl despite differences in size and color. Discrimination learning can be encouraged through natural activities, for example, in a nature walk, picking up leaves or stones.

Match-to-sample is an instructional format that teaches the child to select an item from an array of items that matches a sample item. The sample and array may be objects or three-dimensional items, or pictures or two-dimensional items (Gaisford & Mallot, 2010). The teacher provides a model of the "correct choice" (e.g., cup) from a number of "incorrect choices" (e.g., bowls) from which to select the one that corresponds to the model. In addition, it is important to build in opportunities for the child to generalize the skill across situations (e.g., identifying cups in creative play in the house area or setting the table, or pictures of cups). Match-to-sample is also one way to determine what concepts a child understands when he or she cannot communicate verbally.

Sort-to-sample is used to teach the child to sort a variety of items into two categories that are represented by models. The first step is to sort by "similarity" of characteristics on a single dimension such as color, shape, or size—for example, sorting blocks that are identical in size and color but are two different shapes. The next step is sorting on two dimensions, for example, a group of same-colored objects that vary on two dimensions (e.g., blocks that are different in size and shape). Sorting may be based on multidimensional differences such as sorting toys and clothing and then may progress next to differences in function (e.g., sorting things you eat and things that you wear).

Communication Strategies

Children with multiple and complex needs may be nonverbal and use idiosyncratic or subtle signals that may be difficult to recognize and interpret. They often require systematic intervention to develop and expand their communication skills. A means to communicate is a basic human right for everyone. As discussed previously, some children require augmentative and alternative communication (AAC) methods. Despite this urgent need, many young children do not receive AAC in a timely manner. Some professionals and parents believe that a child's use of AAC will inhibit speech development despite research to the contrary. For example, research has found that the use of manual signs with young hearing children with a range of disabilities not only increased the children's communication and language development, but also speech skills if the child had potential (Lederer & Battaglia, 2015).

To begin planning interventions, teachers and speech-language pathologists might assess the child's communication using an appropriate tool, such as the *Communication Matrix* (Rowland, 2004). This field-tested assessment was designed for children at the earliest stages of communication and who use any form of communication. The matrix has been used nationally and internationally with children who have sensory impairments and multiple disabilities and has been translated into several different languages. It provides a means for identifying a child's early communicative functions (refusing, requesting, engaging in social interactions, or seeking information) and communication levels (preintentional behaviors, intentional behaviors, unconventional presymbolic communication, conventional presymbolic communication, concrete symbols, abstract symbols, and language-combining symbols). An online version of the Communication Matrix is available at www.communicationmatrix.org and is currently free of charge.

The following strategies have been found to be effective in promoting the early communication development of young children who have sensory impairments, multiple disabilities, and other complex needs (Chen, Klein, & Haney, 2007; Chen, Klein, & Minor, 2008):

1. *Interpret the child's signals.* Carefully observe the child's behaviors to figure out how he or she expresses attention, interests, needs, and desires. Review the child's reactions and nonverbal communication during the daily routine and identify when the child seems alert. This way, teachers and parents may be able to identify, interpret, and respond to the child's subtle and sometimes puzzling signals.

2. *Identify the child's preferences.* Once the child's repertoire of communicative behaviors has been recognized, the child's preferences should be identified to motivate interactions and communicative initiations. Observe the child's responses to different people, objects, and activities. What does the child seem to prefer, and what does he or she seem to dislike? What are the characteristics of selected preferences? These characteristics may be used to scaffold the child's participation in low-preference activities and to promote a range of developmental skills. For example, Meiling dislikes table activities and prefers to sprinkle sand in the sandbox or beans in the tub. The teacher might develop a craft project that involves sprinkling colored sand (either with fingers or in a salt shaker) on contact paper or gluing beans on cardboard to encourage Meiling's participation at a table and her fine motor skills.

3. *Establish predictable routines.* All children benefit from repeated and predictable daily activities. Predictable routines are essential for children with medical and health concerns. Ask parents about daily activities that occur in a consistent order. For example, what happens before and after dinner? As shown in Exhibits 5.4, and 5.5, discipline-specific interventions may be embedded within these natural learning opportunities.

4. *Provide anticipatory cues.* Once specific routines are established, selected cues may be used to help children develop anticipation and confidence in everyday activities. Cues are the consistent use of specific words or sounds along with selected objects, visual stimuli, or physical stimuli—depending on the child's sensory abilities—just before beginning the activity. They should be associated with the activity so the child can understand what they represent. For example, for a preschooler who is blind and nonverbal, immediately before bath time, the parent gives the child the rubber duck that communicates "Bath time" because

the child plays with that toy in the bathtub. At school, just before recess, the teacher gives the child a piece of plastic rope that communicates "Let's go to the swing" because the swing is suspended by plastic ropes and the child holds onto them.

5. ***Develop turn-taking games.*** One way to develop early back-and-forth interactions is to wait for the child to vocalize (or perform an action, e.g., clap, roll a car), and when the child pauses, imitate the vocalizations (or actions), and then pause for the child to take a turn. Children learn to imitate vocalizations and actions that are within their repertoire before they can imitate novel or unfamiliar sounds and actions. You can also take a turn by speaking when the child pauses in an action. For example, when a child shakes a maraca and then pauses, you could take a turn by saying, "Shake, shake, shake" and then pause for the child to shake the maraca.

6. ***Encourage the child's communicative initiations.*** Once a child actively participates in preferred activities, you can use a *pause-and-wait* or *interrupted routine* strategy to motivate the child to initiate a request for more of the activity. For example, push the child three times on the swing and then stop. Pause and wait for the child to indicate a request for you to push the swing some more by wiggling his or her legs, or saying or signing "more." If needed, model the request or help the child make the sign to shape the child's communicative behaviors. The teacher can also support the development of true initiation by simply delaying the beginning of an expected routine. For example, the teacher helps Hana get seated at the lunch table, places an empty bowl in front of her, then walks away, and waits. Because this is a familiar routine, Hana begins to be aware of the delay. She looks around for her teacher and vocalizes. This is a true communicative initiation. Even better, *it is unprompted.* If the teacher responds immediately to Hana's communication by bringing her favorite food or drink and saying, "Oh, I see you're really hungry today!," there is a good chance Hana will learn the very useful skill of initiating a request.

Enhanced eText Application Exercise 5.2
In this exercise, you can apply what you have learned in this chapter to identify the principles of partial participation that can be used to support the inclusion of children with disabilities in settings with typically developing peers.

Enhanced eText Application Exercise 5.3
In this exercise, you can apply what you have learned in this chapter about the use of instructional prompts to help children participate.

Enhanced eText Application Exercise 5.4
In this exercise, you can apply what you have learned in this chapter about how specific and systematic instructional strategies promote learning when children require intensive supports.

Video Example from
You Tube

Tips for Promoting all Children's Participation

This section provides a list of tips for implementing simple adaptations that are consistent with the principles of Universal Design for Learning (UDL) to provide multiple means of representation, expression, and engagement. See Chapter 4 for a description of these components of UDL that are intended to support participation of all children.

Creative Arts Area

- If a child still puts things in his or her mouth, be sure to monitor the handling of small objects that may be choking hazards.

- Select activities that emphasize process rather than product and allow the child to create his or her own unique work of art.

- Choose activities that invite children's participation at varying developmental levels and sensory abilities (e.g., collage making, scribbling, painting, using clay or play dough).

- Provide a variety of painting utensils (e.g., gloves, sponges, squirt bottles, rollers, toothbrushes) that are easy for children to manipulate and use.

- Vary the position of surfaces to paint on (e.g., sidewalk, wall, easel, table, slant board) to fit the child's positioning needs and motor abilities.

- Support verbal instructions with demonstrations using materials and pictures so that the message is easy to understand.

- If needed, use the child's preferences (e.g., cars or songs) to scaffold participation in the art activity (e.g., dip a toy car in a pan of paint and roll across paper to paint, or sing a painting song).

- Adding textures or scents to paints and clay increases interest in handling the material. Be sure to monitor children who are likely to try to eat these materials.

- Use contrasts (e.g., dark paper with light-colored paint, chalk, etc., or light paper with dark materials) to increase visual attention.

- Provide additional lighting at work areas, if needed, to focus visual attention.

- Provide a tray, container, or area with edges so the child can easily organize and find needed materials.

- Reduce the amount of visual and physical clutter in and around the child's work area.

- If a child is hesitant about touching or handling new materials, use hand-under-hand guidance.

- Have the child place his or her hand on top of the teacher's hand to introduce new materials: The teacher holds the new material, object, or art media; the teacher encourages the child to feel the new material with his or her fingertips; and as the child becomes comfortable, the teacher gently rolls his or her own hand around so the child feels more of the material that the teacher is holding.

- Add Velcro to handles on brushes, markers, and other tools and make a Velcro hand holder for the child who has difficulty grasping materials.

- Freeze water colored with food coloring in ice cube trays with a popsicle stick in each cube. Once frozen, the popsicle stick may be built up with sponge and tape if needed. Use these colored "popsicles" to encourage children to draw or color on white paper. Use relevant vocabulary, including "cold" and "melting."

- Build up the handles of brushes, markers, crayons, and other implements with masking or duct tape so the child has a large enough handle to grasp.

- Melt leftover crayon pieces and pour into small paper cups; before the wax solidifies, add a length of ribbon or yarn across the diameter with several inches of excess on either side; when the wax is set, remove from cup; tie the ribbon around the child's hand to help him or her grasp the chunky crayon. The ribbon helps keep the crayon in the child's hand even if his or her grasp is not consistent.

- Use nonslip shelf liners, Dycem mats, suction cups, or mounting tape to help keep materials in place as the child works on a project.

- Use three-dimensional art materials to help facilitate grasp rather than pieces of cut-out paper that are difficult to pick up off flat surfaces (e.g., cut pieces of pipe cleaners rather than flat pieces of construction paper to make a picture of silkworms).

Library Area

- Use books with cardboard pages for younger children who are learning to turn pages.
- Glue or Velcro a small, thin piece of sponge or a small popsicle stick, or attach a small, plain hair clip at the lower-right corner of paper pages to help a child learn to turn pages.
- Include some push-button sound books that children can activate.
- Provide books that have repetitive phrases or refrains so children can predict and complete phrases.
- Select books that relate to a child's everyday experiences and preferences to increase participation and understanding.
- Modify the story and what is written (e.g., simplify or shorten) so the words are meaningful to the child.
- Add gestures or signs for key words in repetitive phrases (e.g., "fell down and bumped his head") that children can learn to imitate.
- Use books with clear pictures and high contrast between foreground and background and nonglossy pages so they are easier to discriminate visually.
- Select books with uncluttered pictures rather than cluttered pictures (e.g., too many things happening in the same picture, abstract pictures, or "busy" backgrounds).
- Select books that have tactile elements, such as shapes of objects and textures.
- Provide objects, manipulatives, or felt pieces that go along with the story to actively engage a child. These may be collected in a "story box" that accompanies the book.
- Place a tactile symbol on the cover of a book so the child with visual perception difficulties can discriminate and recognize it. For example, glue a small plastic cookie on the book *If You Give a Mouse a Cookie.*
- Provide tactile books with Braille or "twin" vision books (with both Braille and print) for a child who is blind so he or she can follow along with the story being read to the group.
- Give a child with low vision his or her own copy of the book to follow along while the teacher reads from the same book to the class.
- Provide developmentally appropriate storybooks in children's home languages.

Manipulatives Area

- Provide materials that children with a range of hand skills can handle and manipulate (e.g., puzzles with knobs, toys with dowels), or that provide auditory or visual feedback (e.g., rain sticks or light-up toys) or activate by a switch.
- If needed, make sure to stabilize materials (e.g., nonslip shelf liners) and provide a boundary (e.g., use a tray).
- Provide containers for a developmentally young child to put smaller items in and take out from, rather than asking him or her to create an end product from the items.
- Use see-through containers with lids that need adult help to open. This will keep materials organized and easy to find, and encourage the child's communication (e.g., to request help or say "open" or "off").
- Use sweater-size plastic storage containers and cut out part of one side so the child can slide his or her arms inside the container to play with manipulatives or other textures and won't "lose" materials.
- Cut out part of a small empty and clean plastic bottle to make a scoop; the child can scoop up smaller objects that he or she may not be able to pick up with fingers.

- Encourage the child to cross midline by offering items on the other side and to use both hands (even if very difficult) by playing with large objects (e.g., beach ball) that require two hands.
- Place selected materials on a tray so the child can easily find what is needed.
- Reduce clutter so the child can easily find items that he or she needs or wants to put together.
- Place objects in the child's work area with spaces between them so the child can find separate objects (if objects are clustered together, a child with low vision may not see several pieces, and a child with fine motor difficulties may have more difficulty picking up the desired item).

Pretend Play Area (e.g., dress-up, while awaiting transportation)

- Encourage a peer to show the child where objects are located in the play area (e.g., dolls and dress-up clothes; pretend food, cups, and plates).
- Provide plastic models of food and empty food packages that represent the cultural backgrounds of children in the class.
- Provide opportunities for the child to use representations of real objects (e.g., dolls, bottles, cars) to engage in imitative play.
- Use play scripts to help the child understand "what comes next" and learn key words associated with play.
- Encourage simple dress-up (e.g., putting on a hat, scarf, bag, and shoes), and have a mirror available for children to look at themselves.
- Provide dress-up clothes with Velcro (instead of buttons and zippers) that are easy for children with motor difficulties to put on and take off.
- Position the child on the floor, if needed, to encourage self-dressing from a stable and comfortable position.
- Provide paper, writing implements, small whiteboards, and markers to foster scribbling and early writing activities during play (e.g., making a grocery list, taking an order at a restaurant, etc.).

Gross Motor Activities and Outdoor Play

- Encourage the child to move around the playground to try different activities with peers by asking a preferred peer to show the child the selected play area and support their interactions.
- If a child tends to play only in one area (e.g., on the swing or in the sandbox), try to figure out why. Does the child feel safe in these areas? What skills does the child demonstrate? Is equipment available for the child's specific motor needs (e.g., are the tricycles appropriate in size and do they have proper seat support)? What skills and supports are required for the child to participate in different activities?
- Provide opportunities and supports for the child to engage in gross motor activities, such as sliding, swinging, and bouncing on outdoor equipment, but be aware of possible health concerns. For example, a child with Down syndrome may have serious problems with his spine and should never be encouraged to do somersaults. Children with shunts may not be able to tolerate being upside-down because their shunt may not work in that position. Children with seizure disorders or motor difficulties may need to wear helmets.

- Allow the child to use his or her whole body when interacting with objects from other areas (e.g., push the dolls in the cart or transport blocks in a small wagon).
- Add weights to the carts or wagons to provide sensory feedback when the child pushes wheeled toys.
- Adapt tricycles by using Velcro or straps to help keep the child's feet on the pedals, if necessary.
- Partially deflate beach-type balls to facilitate grasp in catching and tossing games.
- Use touch (physical prompts) and visual (gestures, pictures, objects) cues to obtain the child's attention if he or she does not respond to your verbal cues.
- To obtain the child's attention in a noisy environment, move closer to him or her rather than yelling. (*Note:* A child's hearing aid receives the clearest sounds from about 3 feet away.)
- When a child has a visual impairment, be aware that glare on a sunny day may negatively affect this child's use of functional vision. Furthermore, the visual contrast between rooms inside (darker) and the playground outdoors (lighter) can be exaggerated for this child, so he or she will need time to adapt to the change in lighting.
- A child with vision impairment may have great fear of the outdoors—the environment is larger and changing all the time. Provide extra time and support to orient the child and for him or her to become familiar and secure in moving around the outdoor environment.
- Use classroom equipment and furniture to create obstacle courses to promote spatial concepts and movement activities (e.g., on, in, up, over, under, through, etc.).
- Allow the child to stand, if preferred, when doing tabletop activities so he or she can move but still attend to the activity.

Large-Group Activities

- Entice children's interest in coming to the circle (e.g., use animated intonation, sing a song, chant, or shake a red "surprise bag"; distribute toys that sound).
- Allow the child to bring a transitional object to the circle that represents a favorite activity and helps ease the transition into a large-group activity.
- Use preferential seating to allow the child to make the most use of his or her vision, hearing, and body to engage the child's attention and provide access to sensory information.
- Be sure the child is seated at the same level as peers—for example, not in a wheelchair or stander if everyone else is on the floor.
- Determine the family's preference regarding the communication methods for a child with a hearing loss: signing, speech, or both.
- Make sure to check that the child's hearing aid or FM system is working properly.
- Be aware of the acoustic resonance and ambient noise in the room. Try to reduce background noise wherever possible (e.g., use carpets, sound-absorbent materials, and screens; do not seat the child near a noisy air conditioner or open window with traffic noise).
- Use objects with magnets such as letters or shapes so that if the child has fine motor difficulties, he or she can slide the objects around, rather than try to pick them up or accidentally knock them off the work surface.

- Add built-up handles or other adaptations to musical instruments or other group-time objects to allow the child who has difficultly with grasping to hold onto them more easily.

- Implement shorter group activities (e.g., 5 to 10 minutes long), rather than longer large-group activities (e.g., 20 to 30 minutes) in which the child may begin to lose interest.

- Provide photos, symbols, or objects in a "What's next?" format so the child can anticipate what will happen after circle time.

- Provide appropriate ways for the child to ask to leave a large group if it becomes too overwhelming (e.g., using words such as "out," signaling with a picture or symbol, going to a specific adult).

- Use music and movements. Nonverbal children and restless children may vocalize or move during music or singing.

- Use switches and other AAC devices to give the child a "voice" during activities and make sure that every child has a means of communication.

- Provide adaptations within the activity so every child has a way to participate. For example, to answer a question about the story, one child might say a phrase, another might sign a single word, and another might touch a picture of the object.

- Conduct a large-group activity in an area of the room with the *least* amount of distractions (e.g., avoid areas with open shelves with easily seen toys; walls with things to poke, rip, or pull; and large objects like rocking chairs to climb on or under). If needed, use screens or attractive cloth covers to conceal distractions; these can be easily removed when children are encouraged to use the items on the shelves.

Summary

This chapter focused on selected practices for teaching young children with specific disabilities and those who require intensive supports. Teachers and other service providers can begin by gathering information about the child's preferences, strengths, and learning needs and collaborate with the family and across disciplines to develop and implement effective learning opportunities. Selected intervention strategies include conducting ecological inventories and discrepancy analyses and providing individualized prompts and adaptations to support children's participation. Systematic planning, interventions, and supports enable children with specific disabilities and complex needs to play and learn alongside typically developing peers.

Reflect and Apply

1. Outline a circle time lesson and identify two systematic instructional practices, and discuss how you would implement them to facilitate the participation of a child who requires intensive supports.

2. Conduct an interview with a parent or classroom teacher to determine the preferences of a target child. Identify how you could use your findings to motivate the child's participation in a selected learning activity.

3. Outline a learning activity and identify the types of prompts that may be used to support the participation of a child with limited language skills and physical disabilities.

4. Develop four objectives for a preschooler with disabilities and develop an objective-within-routines matrix to embed learning opportunities during daily class activities.

5. Conduct an interview with a speech and language pathologist, occupational therapist, or physical therapist to discover that person's role and responsibilities in serving preschoolers with disabilities, where services are provided (e.g., in the classroom or pullout), and why that model was selected.

Chapter 6
Promoting Emotional and Social Development

Godfather/Fotolia

Learning Outcomes

After studying this chapter, you should be able to:

6.1 Discuss how a secure attachment—a strong, positive, and trusting relationship with a primary caregiver—provides the foundation for a child's healthy emotional development.

6.2 Describe how high-quality supportive environments facilitate the social-emotional development of young children.

6.3 Give examples of specific intervention strategies that could be used to assist young children develop positive social skills.

6.4 Explain the importance of and strategies for encouraging the development of play as a means of facilitating self-regulation and social development.

6.5 Identify techniques to reduce and replace challenging behaviors through careful environmental planning and positive behavior support.

Early social experiences and responsive relationships not only have profound influences on a child's brain development, but also on positive emotional health. This essential foundation supports a child's well-being in all areas of development and learning. The work of pioneers such as Bowlby, Ainsworth, and Erikson, as well as the more recent work of Stanley Greenspan, provides useful foundations for the understanding of early emotional development. From the initial attachment to a primary caregiver in infancy through the establishment of mutually responsive interaction patterns and communicative strategies, the emotionally supported preschooler achieves a strong and healthy sense of self and the ability to express and understand a wide range of emotional experiences and ideas.

With this emotional strength and healthy autonomy, the young child begins to develop effective social skills. For many children, preschool is their first experience in a group setting. They may need assistance to participate optimally in this new experience. All children are in the process of learning to recognize and to cope with their feelings in environments requiring that they also learn to regulate their own behavior. Typical social skill development is illustrated in Appendix A.

This chapter describes how adults can assist children in becoming emotionally and socially well adjusted. We present strategies for supporting young children's emotional needs, facilitating self-regulation, and decreasing challenging behaviors. We recognize the influence of the environment and emphasize the importance of play in the creation of secure and responsive early education experiences.

Becoming Emotionally Secure

Understanding emotional development in young children must begin by considering the dynamics of attachment. The infant's strong, positive feelings for a primary caregiver provide the seed from which all aspects of development can grow. More than 50 years ago, Selma Fraiberg (1974) coined the term **infant mental health** from her work with parents and their infants (birth to 3 years) when referring to practice

Enhanced eText

Video Example 6.1

Toxic Stress Derails Health Development https://www.youtube.com/ watch?v=rVwFkcOZHJw This video illustrates the importance of responsive nurturing and stable caregiving environments in children's neurological and social emotional development.

that supports early development within secure parent–infant relationships. Today, attention is being given to infant and early childhood mental health. Without a solid foundation, built on secure caregiver–child relationships, children will be at risk for problems in the area of social and emotional development. The concept currently has been expanded to include *infant and early childhood mental health* (IECMH) and is defined as follows:

> IECMH is the developing capacity of the child from birth to 5 years old to form close and secure adult and peer relationships; experience, manage, and express a full range of emotions; and explore the environment and learn—all in the context of family, community, and culture. Strategies to improve IECMH fall along a promotion, prevention and treatment continuum. (*Zero to Three*, 2016)

Ways to facilitate children's positive relationships, understanding of feelings, and learning through interactions and exploration are discussed in this chapter. For children with disabilities as well as those at risk due to adverse childhood experiences (discussed later in this chapter), such as prenatal drug exposure and/or early childhood trauma, the establishment of healthy, responsive caregiver relationships may be threatened. (For an extensive discussion of the topic of infant and early childhood mental health and mental health disorders, see Brandt, Perry, Seligman, and Tronick [2014].)

Attachment

One of the most important aspects of healthy social and emotional development is the concept of attachment. Psychologists believe the development of an attachment bond between the child and the caregiver to be perhaps the most significant early social and emotional event in the child's life (Brandt et al., 2014; Rathus, 2014). **Attachment** is the term John Bowlby used in the 1940s and 1950s to describe the bond of affection that develops between an infant and his or her primary caregiver. He found the infant to be biologically predisposed to turn toward the caregiver (as a means of survival) for a sense of security when venturing out. Infants are thought to develop secure attachments when their caregivers have been there to provide comfort and reassurance during times of distress. In the 1970s, psychologist Mary Ainsworth provided empirical evidence for Bowlby's attachment theory in her now famous "Strange Situation" research that demonstrated individual differences in the quality of attachment. The Ainsworth Strange Situation paradigm (Ainsworth, Blehar, Waters, & Wall, 2015) is a semistructured laboratory procedure used in studies to identify the quality of an infant's attachment to the primary caregiver. In the "Strange Situation," the infant's responses to a series of separations and reunions with a stranger and parent are carefully observed. The paradigm consists of the following seven 3-minute episodes:

1. The mother brings the infant to the playroom and puts down the infant.
2. A stranger enters the room and attempts to play with the infant.
3. The mother leaves the room.
4. The mother returns and the stranger leaves.
5. The mother leaves the infant alone.
6. The stranger returns.
7. The mother returns and greets and picks up the infant.

A reenactment of the Strange Situation scene can be found at http://www.parentingscience .com (select "Attachment" from the Babies menu on the home page).

As a result of early studies conducted by Ainsworth and colleague, three categories of attachment were defined. Group B infants greeted parents in an unambiguous manner on reunion. For example, the child might smile, greet, approach, or establish physical contact. These infants were considered to be *securely attached*. Group A infants demonstrated pointed avoidance of the caregiver on reunion, characterized by aborted approach, averted eye gaze, or ignoring. These infants were labeled *insecurely attached–avoidant*. Group C infants could not be comforted by caregivers, and on reunion they directed angry, resistant behavior at the parents through behaviors such as pushing away, kicking to be put down, or refusing a toy. These infants were labeled as *insecurely attached–resistant*. Later research by Main, a doctoral student of Ainsworth, identified another type of insecure attachment that could be described as *disorganized or disoriented attachment* (Duschinsky, 2015).

In her pioneering work, Ainsworth (1973) described the insecurely attached infant as a child who becomes greatly distressed when separated from the caregiver; at the same time, this child is not easily comforted by the caregiver. It is as if the child's sense of trust has been disturbed or never fully developed. More securely attached children, in contrast, fuss less when left and cease crying more quickly. There is an interesting parallel between Thomas, Chess, and Birch's (1968) classic descriptions of children with easy and difficult temperaments (discussed later in this chapter) and Ainsworth's description of children with secure and insecure patterns of attachment. Some children, then, may be predisposed by temperament to influence the attachment process negatively or positively.

The significance of the reciprocal relationship between the young child and the primary caregiver has long been recognized. The baby signals his or her need for some kind of care by crying or fussing, the mother responds by picking up the child, and the child responds in turn with some kind of bodily reaction, such as cuddling. The baby's bodily adjustments signal to the mother that the child is ready for the next step, be it diapering, feeding, bathing, or just cuddling and stroking. The baby responds to the caregiving by quieting, which reinforces the mother's behaviors. The importance of such a chain of cues and responses is readily apparent. Any breakdown in the signaling and response system may affect the whole bonding and attachment process. Fraiberg (1974), in her classic research on infants who are blind, noted that the babies' lack of visual access, eye contact, and mutual gaze and delay in the development of social smiles inhibited the parent–infant relationship. These parents were encouraged to frequently hold the babies, sing and talk to them, and use toys with sounds and toys that the child could hold. As a result, these infants developed social smiles and recognized their parents' voices. Other disabilities and difficult temperament can also delay the attachment process. Children with cerebral palsy may not be able to provide warm reinforcement to the caregiver because cuddling may be more difficult. Children with hearing loss cannot respond with eye contact and other attachment signals when the mother uses her voice. Resultant attachment patterns, then, are an end product of a complicated interactional process. Not only do the child's innate mannerisms influence the response of the parents, but, of course, the adult's natural tendencies help determine the child's view of self and environment.

An important goal of early intervention programs is to encourage and support the development of a strong affectional bond between caregivers and children, especially in those instances when a child's disability or/or quality of temperament might inhibit the attachment relationship with parents. Educators can help parents become tuned into the child's cues so that their contingent responses can produce an enjoyable response in the child. When parents can learn to understand unclear or confusing signals from their child who has disabilities, they have a chance to respond in appropriate ways, allowing them to develop feelings of confidence and competence. Comfort, Gordon, and Naples (2011) developed a practical tool for identifying the level of mutually positive and pleasurable interactions between parents and children from 2 to 71 months of age. Practitioners can use such an observation technique as they plan intervention strategies that may include acknowledging parents' recognition and responsiveness to their young children's signals and coaching parents in this practice.

Enhanced eText

Video Example 6.2

Developing Attachment: Rejecting a Child's Stress
https://www.youtube.com/watch?v=9u8ObYi_EB0
The importance of responsiveness to an infant's signals of stress and the potential consequences of ignoring or rejecting a child's signal are demonstrated in this video.

Erikson's Stages of Psychosocial Development

In his classic developmental outline, Erikson (1993) discussed three stages of psychosocial development thought to be characteristic of the young child. Each stage includes the solution of a problem involving conflicting feelings and desires. The resolution of the central problem of each state creates a favorable disposition for adjustment at the next developmental stage. Table 6.1 presents Erikson's stages of personality development, along with adult behaviors that can help children come to a healthy solution of each stage's problems of conflicting desires and feelings.

Sense of Trust Versus Mistrust. Erikson (1993) considered the first year of life to be the crucial time for the development of a sense of trust. During this time, an environment characterized by consistency and dependability fosters the development of trust in those responsible for the child's care. The quality of caregiving is more important than the quantity of food or love given. Caregiving that is basically consistent and sensitive to an infant's needs promotes a view of the world as dependable and safe. Negative, inconsistent, or insensitive caregiving, by contrast, stimulates a fearful, suspicious view of the world.

The child's development of a sense of trust (or mistrust) in the world is only one of the personality attributes developed during infancy. Erikson also discussed the importance of children's perceptions of their ability to control their own body movements. Through actions such as continuous repetition of grasping and holding objects, children learn that they can depend on their bodies to do their bidding. It is not difficult to imagine the frustration experienced by children with physical disabilities during their quest to develop a sense of trust in their own bodies. A curriculum that incorporates specific body movement activities encourages all children to become more trusting in their body control.

Practitioners who provide an environment of consistent, predictable, and responsive care will help to further a young child's development of trust in caregivers. Conversely, helter-skelter experiences in the program can make a fearful child even more fearful or a basically secure child question his or her relationship to others. An atmosphere of trust is easily developed through establishing reasonable, enforceable rules of conduct, the regularity of a basic schedule of activities, and sensitive, immediate responses to children's needs.

Table 6.1 Adult Behaviors That Promote Children's Personality Development

Erikson's Stage	Appropriate Adult Behaviors
1. To promote sense of *trust*	Be consistent and sensitive in caretaking. Respond contingently to child's signals and behaviors. Provide prompt relief of discomfort. Be warm, affectionate, and nurturing. Provide a stable and predictable caregiving environment. Avoid showing favoritism. Offer choices when appropriate.
2. To promote sense of *autonomy*	Allow opportunities to explore. Forbid only what really matters. Couple firmness with tolerance. Avoid shaming. Let child set pace and practice developing skills. Be accepting of individuality.
3. To promote sense of *initiative*	Encourage role-playing (pretend play). Talk about feelings and dreams. Facilitate problem solving and resolution of conflicts. Answer questions. Serve as an appropriate role model. Hold punishment to a minimum.

Sense of Autonomy Versus Shame and Doubt.   From the end of the first year of life through the second and third year of life, most children are busy exploring their environment and trying to establish some independence. Children who are primarily trustful usually do not hesitate to develop their own opinions as so-called "terrible twos" if encouraged to develop skills at their own pace. Children of this age who are given opportunities to make simple choices, to exercise their expanding sensorimotor abilities, and to experiment with their newfound verbal skills will become confident enough to assert themselves appropriately.

Children who are shamed (e.g., being called a "bad boy") or told "no" continuously will begin to doubt themselves and their abilities. They may react by defiance or act ignorant of authority. Children who are not allowed to make choices when they are young may become overdependent and fearful when they need to make major life choices. Some children may withdraw into their feelings of worthlessness, whereas others may strike out aggressively.

Practitioners can assist children in developing autonomy with a reasonable degree of self-control by creating opportunities for young children to explore, to make decisions, to ask questions, and to exercise appropriate self-restraint. Curricula and room arrangements that provide centers with materials to manipulate and a choice of activities will ideally promote children's autonomous, confident behavior. Establishing firm, reasonable guidelines for classroom exploration and conduct encourages autonomy while not letting children become overwhelmed by their need for independence and by their lack of mature judgment. Children of this age who are readily propelled by their more mature large muscles may be easily frustrated when their smaller muscles do not react so efficiently. Practitioners must lend assistance in ways that increase a child's self-confidence, such as asking questions to help a child problem-solve, or using the least intrusive prompt. Children with disabilities may need special incentives (such as using preferred items to scaffold unfamiliar activities) to venture into the activities so easily enjoyed by children without disabilities.

Sense of Initiative Versus Guilt.   Children who have developed a basic trust in their environment and in themselves and who have experienced a growing self-confidence in their ability to explore and experiment are ready to develop a sense of initiative. Around 4 or 5 years of age, children experience a heightened period of imagination and fantasy. It is a time for reaching out and intruding both physically and verbally. Children with healthy personalities and healthy bodies vigorously try out their developing ideas of themselves. They are great imitators, as evidenced by their "superhero" play and their use of any and all four-letter words.

Children of this age are also beginning to develop what is termed a *conscience*. Because they often have difficulty separating fantasy from reality, they may feel guilty about merely thinking unkind thoughts. Teachers who are aware of this tendency try to avoid overreacting to a child's characteristic statement of "I hate you." When difficulties occur in the home such as death or a divorce, children need to be helped to realize that their actions or thoughts did not cause the unpleasant event to happen. This is also an age of nightmares and dreams. These children need extra comfort and reassurance in separating fantasy from reality.

Teachers who allow leeway within secure guidelines for children's developing sense of initiative can contribute significantly to their motivation to achieve. This motivation is important to the next stage of industry versus inferiority, and it is necessary for the development of self-confidence and the desire to try out the freedom to explore, to imagine, to question, to help plan, to make choices, to participate in meaningful activities, to create, and to engage in role-playing behavior. Teachers of young children with disabilities must be aware of the need to teach some children to explore, to play, and to attempt what may be difficult. Children whose abilities or environments are limited may have to be helped directly if they are to develop feelings of trust, autonomy, and initiative.

Greenspan's Model of Affective Development

Over the years, Stanley Greenspan has been an important contributor to the understanding of infant–child emotional development. His work has been particularly important because he has addressed the specific needs of infants and young children with disabilities and developmental differences, including children with autism (Greenspan & Wieder, 2006a). See Chapter 5 for an outline of Greenspan's approach. Like the pioneer Erikson, Greenspan proposed a "developmental structural model" of the stages of emotional growth that are summarized here. Greenspan's model parallels Piaget's stage theory of cognitive development in many ways.

Six basic stages are represented in Greenspan's model. Note that in more recent writings, the last three stages (complex sense of self, emotional ideas' representation, and emotional thinking) are each divided into two substages. In most cases, the second substage simply represents greater elaboration of the particular emotional capacity being addressed. Thus, for the sake of simplicity, only the six basic stages are described here.

Self-Regulation and Interest in the World.   During the period from birth to approximately 3 months, healthy infants develop the ability to regulate their internal states in ways that allow them to take in and attend to the world around them. Through sight, vision, sense of touch, and smell, infants experience their environment. This experience is best achieved when they are in a calm, alert state.

Babies who are neurologically overresponsive and are easily overstimulated may experience great difficulty maintaining a calm, alert state. As a result, such babies have less opportunity to take in the world around them. They may not develop a natural interest in their world if that world is painful or irritating.

Infants who are hyperirritable need special handling techniques that assist them in self-regulation and maintenance of a calm, alert state. For example, swaddling them, placing them in a tucked and flexed position, applying firm pressure to the chest, using deep pressure massage (rather than light stroking), and rocking can be helpful in calming **hyperresponsive** infants. Some premature babies, babies who have been prenatally exposed to certain drugs, and babies who have experienced certain neurological insults may benefit from the use of such techniques.

Some infants may be **hyporesponsive**; that is, they are difficult to arouse. They have trouble becoming fully awake and maintaining an alert state. They are sleepy and passive. Such babies may respond more to certain types of sensory stimulation than to others. For example, a baby might remain sleepy through parents' exhaustive efforts to interest him or her in their sounds and funny faces. Such a baby might be more aroused by touch and kinesthetic stimulation (movement and position). Thus, it may be possible to assist the baby in reaching an alert state by massaging or tickling and frequently changing his or her position. Once in an alert state, the baby may find voices and faces more interesting.

In summary, during this early stage of development, infants must be supported in their efforts to achieve a calm, alert state and to experience the sensations provided by the world around them without being overwhelmed.

Falling in Love (Attachment).   During the period from approximately 2 to 5 months, infants who have been successful during the first stage in regulating internal states (homeostasis) begin to be very familiar with their primary caregivers. In addition, they begin to associate sensations of the primary caregiver—face, voice, odor, touch—with pleasurable sensations of being cuddled and fed. As a result, as Greenspan famously said, the babies "fall in love" (Greenspan & Greenspan, 1985, p. 16). This is the essence of infant attachment. The reciprocal of this experience for a caregiver, as an infant responds to the caregiver's presence and behaviors, is called **bonding**. As a caregiver bonds with the infant, he or she becomes more responsive to the infant, both behaviorally and affectively, and, in turn, strengthens the infant's attachment. As discussed earlier, the development of attachment and bonding progresses over time and is dynamic and interactive. Each partner influences the other in powerful ways.

Infants who have difficulty responding in positive ways to caregivers' behaviors (e.g., infants who are born very prematurely or who have been affected by prenatal exposure to drugs) may be in some jeopardy during this stage. For example, an infant who is hyperirritable may cry or turn away when his mother brings her face close or talks to him. He may look at her only fleetingly and may avert his gaze when she smiles. Such an infant may have difficulty developing a preference for the human world, which is an important outcome of this stage of attachment. According to the **transactional model,** understanding how infants and their parents influence each other over time is essential to the development of appropriate recommendations for treatment. "The treatment may simply involve augmenting the parents' ability to see the normal in the abnormal—for example, to recognize that preterm babies, although different in size, have cognitive and social-emotional needs and patterns of development similar to full-term babies" (Sameroff & Mackenzie, 2003, p. 18).

Intentional Two-Way Communication.   From approximately 3 to 10 months of age, as their behavior consistently elicits feedback from significant caregivers, one can observe the gradual development of intentionality in infants. They learn that they can do things that have an effect on the environment and particularly that they can use actions to communicate with the social world. Caregiver responsiveness to this intentional communication is crucial to infant development.

Specifically related to children's healthy emotional development is a type of caregiver response referred to as **affect attunement.** By the time infants reach 9 or 10 months of age, the nature of their caregivers' interactions begins to include mirroring of the infant's affect (emotional state). Parents no longer simply imitate or respond to the baby's behavior but also accurately reflect the baby's feelings. When the baby is happy, Mother smiles and reflects this feeling. When the infant is crying and upset, Mother may furrow her brow and frown, saying, "Oh, poor baby." When the infant is startled or surprised, Mother may pull back quickly, with her eyes opened wide, saying, "Oh, my goodness!" In this way, the infant can begin to learn that it is OK to express a wide range of emotions. As caregivers match and reflect their emotions, infants also learn to recognize emotions in others. Most important, they learn that not only their behavior but also their feelings can influence others.

It is extremely important that adults learn to read the affective cues of infants with disabilities. For example, an infant with severe motor impairment may have difficulty giving clear signals of joy or sadness. Parents may be very frustrated by not being sure whether the child finds an experience pleasurable. Sometimes only the greatest extremes of emotions, such as anger, can be understood easily. Early interventionists from several fields may need to work together as a team with parents to help make this kind of emotional communication clear so that parents can respond appropriately. Failure to do this enhances the risk that the infant will give up and become passive and withdrawn. Such a reaction will significantly interfere with the child's ability to fully realize the next stage of emotional development—an organized sense of self.

The Emergence of an Organized Sense of Self.   The period from 9 to 18 months (the transition from infancy to toddlerhood) is an important period of development in which infants achieve a clearer sense of themselves as individuals who are separate from others. They begin to be able to move away from caregivers by using **distal communication.** That is, they can crawl across the room and look back at their father, who, in turn, smiles and vocalizes to them. In this way, toddlers learn they can be separated from caregivers but still experience their love and support. Thus, they eventually learn that it is safe to be separated by physical space and that they, themselves, are separate beings.

Children with certain disabilities may need special assistance during this stage. For example, a child who is blind may need to be assisted in learning to communicate distally and in learning that he or she has a separate identity. A toddler with adverse childhood experiences may have been thwarted at every stage of emotional development. If the toddler's social environment has been unresponsive and he or she has not been successful in expressing and understanding a wide range of emotions, development of a sense of self will be significantly threatened.

As toddlers develop a sense of self, they become increasingly able to associate and use more complex chains of behavior around emotional events. For example, when their mothers return home, toddlers do not simply smile, but they smile, vocalize, toddle over, and reach their arms up to be held. They initiate and carry out these behaviors in competent ways. Their sense of ways of interacting in various circumstances begins to be internalized and organized. Their self-image is forming.

Emotional Ideas (Representation). From 18 to 30 months of age, toddlers become increasingly able to represent ideas and experiences internally (mentally). By 24 months, the toddler can create a mental image of basic feelings and needs (e.g., happiness, sadness, anger, fear). By 30 months, the child can mentally represent and express a wider range of needs and emotions as well as two or more emotions in one play episode or expression (e.g., baby's tired, baby hugs mommy). The emotionally healthy toddler develops a clear mental image of what these basic emotions feel like as well as what they look like in other people. For example, the infant can create a mental image of his or her own feeling of fear or anger as well as create images of Mommy or Daddy when they are angry or happy.

During this period, toddlers are becoming much more independent. They develop a more sophisticated understanding of themselves as emotional beings and of the emotional characteristics of significant others. That is, not only can they see themselves as "sometimes naughty and sometimes nice," but they also know that although mommies are sometimes happy and sometimes sad, they are still the same person.

Emotional Thinking. From 30 to 48 months, the child begins to understand and think about the logical connections between ideas. For example, the child understands causal relationships such as "The girl is sad because her mother is angry," "If I kiss my baby sister, she will be happy," and so on. The child learns that certain ways of behaving will make Mommy mad and others will make her happy. Children who have not experienced consistent reactions to their behavior or who have not been allowed to express a range of emotions are hampered in this stage of development.

During this stage, children's participation in pretend play has an important role in their development of emotional thinking. Pretend play is also a critical educational and therapeutic activity. Through pretending, a child can act out his or her own range of emotions as well as practice elaborated relationships between mothers and fathers, parents and children, brothers and sisters, and so on. Pretend play can provide the child with the opportunity to learn to say, "I'm really mad at you!" rather than hitting someone to express anger.

Children can also act out their own emotional crises and frustrations. Children from abusive and neglectful environments may learn important coping strategies by playing out themes of abandonment or violence. For these children, as well as children with severe emotional disorders, it will be important for the early educator to work in collaboration with mental health professionals in determining appropriate intervention strategies.

Building a Responsive Environment

Early education specialists have shifted their focus away from a skill-based approach to a more interactional view recognizing the importance of the child–environment fit. This **ecological perspective** recognizes the need to create a nurturing and responsive environmental climate conducive to promoting a child's healthy social and emotional development. Such a climate not only can prevent the occurrence of emotional and behavioral problems but also can be the major factor in resolving conflicts that develop between children and their environment. The following sections discuss characteristics that most researchers consider essential to optimum growth during the early childhood years. These are highlighted in Figure 6.1.

Structure and Consistency

Consistency means predictability. In instructing parents and teachers in techniques for effective child management, predictability can be equated with the feeling of being safe.

Figure 6.1 Building a healthy environment

Source: Illustration courtesy of Sandra Hovancik.

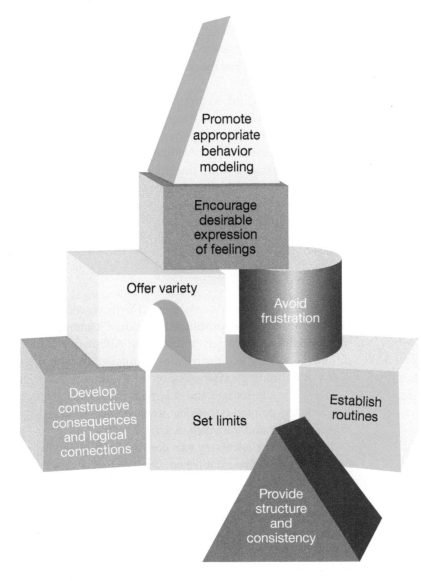

From a practical point of view, caregivers must be consistent for children to learn the rules of conduct for social acceptance. Children are as baffled by inconsistent rules as we would be if we were trying to learn the rules of baseball and the batter sometimes ran to third base instead of first base after a hit. If it is sometimes all right for a child to jump up and down on the sofa and if other times a reprimand results, the rule the child learns is to "try and see."

Instead of the "terrible twos," we should call toddlers the "testing twos." Given consistent responses to their testing, they learn the rules and usually try to function within them. At the same time, consistency fosters their understanding of the basic relationships between cause and effect. Also, as Jones, Higgins, Brandon, Cote, and Dobbins (2013) point out, "The consistency of an organized environment enhances the resiliency building process by providing students with routines" (p. 9). We discuss routines next because they provide children with a sense of stability that enhances their ability to manage the effects (or possible setbacks) of their behavior.

Routines

To develop Erikson's sense of trust or the feelings of being safe, professionals must plan carefully. Routines or schedules that allow children to predict within reason what will happen next help them to relax and handle transitions from one activity to another with relative ease. Although schedules should not be so rigid that teachers cannot take advantage of "teachable moments," children can be prepared for changes in routine and for the times between activities when movement, a change of pace, or grouping is required.

Misbehavior can result when children do not know when or how to transition to the next activity. Children should be given a signal such as a flick of the lights or a reassuring word that they will soon need to stop the activity in which they are engaged. Young children need time to become uninvolved just as they need time to become involved. Teachers should discuss obvious transitions in the daily schedule with children so they can develop the understanding that change is OK and can be predicted. Routines are essential for smooth transitions, effective classroom management, and a positive learning environment (Lester, Allanson, & Notar, 2017). Chapter 4 elaborates on the importance of daily routines.

Limits

Reasonable limits or directions help provide consistency. Developmentally appropriate and clear directions or limits not only contribute to children's emotional needs for security but also create conditions for safety and security. Although children have a strong need to be autonomous, they lack the cognitive judgment to control their own behavior enough to avoid harming themselves or others at times. Behavioral limits offer children guidelines they can imitate and internalize in their development of appropriate self-regulation. As pointed out earlier, teachers must establish a delicate balance between necessary limits and the freedom to explore.

Only limits that are absolutely necessary to a positive learning environment for both children and teachers should be established. Too often, teachers and parents establish so many limits or rules that none can be learned or enforced consistently. Teachers should remember that if children are to follow a rule or a direction and have no choice, they should not be given a choice. Inadvertently, adults sometimes make the mistake of saying something like, "It is time to go home. Wouldn't you like to put on your coat?" What if the child replies "No"?

In a well-quoted, classic text on child management, Smith and Smith (1976) suggested that an effective rule or direction should fulfill the following three requirements that are still applicable today:

1. *It must be definable.* Rules have to be at the developmental level of the children both in vocabulary and in expectations. They must state specific behaviors that are expected or not allowed. For example, we often hear parents or teachers tell children to "be good." What does "be good" mean to the child or to the adult? To the child, it may mean not running in the building because that is what he or she got into trouble for yesterday. To the parent, it may mean eating all his or her lunch because the parent has noticed many leftovers in the lunch box. Rules or expectations must be clearly stated in behavioral terms. If teachers want children to stay within a certain area while sitting on the carpet, then they should mark the area with tape so the child knows exactly what the limits are. Concrete visual aids help young children learn rules of conduct just as they help them develop cognitive skills.

2. *It must be reasonable.* Teachers must judge the developmental level of children before rules can be established. It is not reasonable to expect many 2½-year-olds to share toys with others to the extent that many adults may expect. A constant consideration of developmental appropriateness is necessary. It must be remembered that children with developmental delays require extra time and support as they learn to adapt to limits that others may adapt to more easily. For example, some children may be able to listen to a story for only 5 minutes, whereas other children may still be engrossed 20 minutes later.

3. *It must be enforceable.* Teachers and parents must assume that not all children can or will adhere to all limits. Some rules will be broken. For limits or rules to help children feel safe and trustful, any established rule must be enforceable. When children observe that teachers cannot or will not do anything about a broken rule, they cannot predict what will happen and become anxious. Children seek and enjoy limits. Some will break a rule just to see whether they can indeed predict what will happen. This is generally called "testing the limits," and it happens in every classroom. As suggested earlier, teachers should see a certain amount of this as typical in children's establishing predictability. Teachers should react firmly, consistently, and calmly. This reaction will define for children the consequences of their behavior. It will tell them what will happen if rules are broken. Seeking to avoid the consequences will motivate them to control their behavior. They feel secure when others are helping them develop self-restraint. Of course, only developmentally appropriate rules can be enforced. If a special circumstance causes a teacher to change the rules or limits, a discussion with the children will help them to understand the need for flexibility within consistency.

Constructive Consequences

An effective means of helping children develop social responsibility is through the use of natural and logical consequences. **Natural consequences** occur when an adult does not interfere at all and a child learns from what naturally happens in a situation. They are a direct result of actions taken by the child. For example, a child who comes late to the circle may not be able to sit by his or her best friend. If a child does not eat the prepared snack, becoming hungry may help him or her to learn to eat when food is available. Natural consequences help children to learn that their actions matter and that they have the power to determine outcomes. **Logical consequences,** conversely, are those developed by adults who find that natural consequences either are not readily available or are harmful. These usually help to keep or to restore order and avoid chaos. If so, they must be directly related to expectations or rules that are consistent and have previously been explained to the children. For example, for children who run from the table to the sink when they are supposed to walk, a logical consequence would be to ask them to go back to the table and walk to the sink. Consequences that help children to learn to control their own behaviors must be both logical and immediate.

If a consequence does not bear any logical relationship to the child's action, then it will be difficult for the child to learn the logical relationship between cause and effect. A consequence that occurs long after the child's action will not be associated with it by the child. If the child cannot remember what it was that caused the consequence, then he or she will not make the link between cause and effect.

Logical Connections

A **logical connection** between an act and its consequences provides a number of advantages to establishing and maintaining a healthy relationship between children and their environment. Children who are denied the use of materials immediately after being careless with them are more likely to realize that their behavior caused the consequence because the consequence was *related* to the child's action. However, if the child was simply told to sit in the corner, he or she might not realize that his or her behavior caused the consequence. Such a situation might cause the child to feel "picked on" because he or she might not understand why he or she is being sent to the corner. On the other hand, removing the materials can be seen as necessary to the protection of the other children. A logical connection helps children to focus on the behavior to be changed, making it easier to interpret their actions as the cause of the consequence.

A child who is also given some control over the extent of the consequence is more likely to feel the ability to do something about terminating or preventing such consequences in the future. For example, children who are asked to remove themselves from the group for being disruptive and told they may return when they feel they can control themselves have an opportunity to take part in their own rehabilitation. They can learn not only that disruptive behavior causes removal, but also that self-control can earn the chance to return. Conversely, children who are told to sit in the time-out area for 20 minutes or until the teacher comes for them feel that immediate self-control will not help and that only the passage of time changes events.

Variety

Careful planning to include a change of pace during the day is essential to motivating children to learn. A variety of both individual and group activities consistent with the children's developmental level should be included. Young children need to have active physical involvement interspersed with quiet activities. Children whose senses or physical mobility are limited fatigue more quickly and need an opportunity for rest. Others may need additional opportunities to move freely to release inner tension.

Because of their ages, young children generally have short attention spans. (Of course, there are exceptions.) This needs to be considered carefully when planning the daily schedule. If children's attention wanders and they are bored or frustrated, they become restless. This restlessness can become contagious, influencing the behavior of a number of children. This is one of the reasons why learning theorists recommend that practice of any kind be distributed over time.

Finally, a change of pace also means including activities that are just plain fun and full of laughter. Most adults are guilty of being in too much of a hurry or so intense that they miss the occasional opportunities to laugh with children or to turn a mistake into a learning experience. Even shoes on the wrong feet often appear funny enough for a chuckle and for encouragement to try again, rather than the usual response of "Your shoes are on the wrong feet."

Avoiding Frustration

Teachers who are astute observers of children are able to plan and implement a therapeutic environment. They are alert to individual signs of frustration and stress. Understanding the developmental level of each child makes it possible to plan appropriate activities. Even finely tuned activities, however, can produce frustration in a tired, hungry, or sick child. Teachers should quickly recognize subtle warning signs, such as nail biting, sighing, fidgeting, or thumb sucking, and those that are more obvious, such as fussing, crying, and tantrums. Usually, an immediate change of activity reduces the frustration and thus *prevents* disruptive behavior.

Frustration can be avoided by teachers' reducing clutter and noise. (It has been found that high levels of noise are related to stress and increased behavior problems [Kostelnik et al., 2015].) Quiet, organized environments are essential to promote learning in children with self-regulation and attention difficulties. Directions should be simple, activities need to be meaningful and relatively short, and the teacher should be available in case the child needs help. Teachers should analyze tasks and break them into manageable subskills that are appropriately sequenced. Efforts, regardless of outcomes, should receive recognition. Competition should be avoided. Activities that guarantee success can make not only a child's day but also the day of the teacher.

Transition times can be periods of frustration for children if not smoothly organized. Distractible children can become unruly if left to wander or wonder. Withdrawn children may become fearful. Routines for transition times must be explicitly taught. As discussed earlier, signals such as a timer with countdown sounds help children wind down from one activity to get ready for the next. Hurrying young children only frustrates the teacher who forgets that preschoolers have not developed the inner time clocks that often rule adults. Scheduling major activities to end at natural breaks during the day makes transitions smoother. For example, it is easier to gain children's cooperation in cleaning up art materials if they know lunch will follow.

Promoting Tolerance

From 3 to 5 years of age is the developmentally appropriate time to deliberately facilitate an understanding of differences and promote positive feelings toward diversity. A deliberate focus on what has become known as an anti-bias education (Derman-Sparks & Edwards, 2010) is extremely important. Too often, materials found in early childhood programs focus on children and families who represent what might be considered to be the mainstream culture in the United States of the past. That is, what is usually represented are Anglo, middle-class, able-bodied, English-speaking, heterosexual nuclear families dwelling in cities. There are too few books that accurately depict children from low-income families, that illustrate a variety of ethnicities, family structures, and lifestyles, or include adults or children with disabilities. The same is true of toys, songs, posters, and the like.

Derman-Sparks and Edwards (2010) recommend the following four anti-bias goals that allow all to benefit:

1. Facilitating the development of self-awareness, pride in family, confidence, and a generally positive view of themselves and their heritage.

2. Helping children to find joy and comfort in human diversity by learning to understand how they are different and how they are similar to one another. A simple lesson where eggs of different colors are cracked open and found to be alike on the inside develops this understanding.

3. Encouraging children to recognize unfair behavior, to be able to describe it, and to realize that it is hurtful. Not only can teachers reflect this in their actions, but they can deliberately assist children in understanding and labeling feelings in an effort to generate empathy.

4. Intervening when children need to learn how to act, by themselves or with others, to object to and stop prejudice or discriminatory actions, such as teasing or the exclusion of others.

Video Example from

Enhanced eText
Video Example 6.3

Anti-Bias Lessons Help Pre-Schoolers Hold Up a Mirror to Diversity
https://www.youtube.com/watch?v=s3iM7yIhde0
This video includes an interview with Derman-Sparks and anti-bias instructional activities in two preschool classrooms.

Teaching Emotional Literacy

The Center on the Social and Emotional Foundations for Early Learning (CSEFEL) defines emotional literacy as the ability to identify, understand, and respond to one's emotions and those of others (2009). Research indicates that children with emotional literacy are less lonely, less impulsive, have fewer behavior problems, tolerate frustration better, are healthier, and demonstrate higher academic achievement compared to children who lack emotional literacy. To promote emotional literacy, adults should express their own feelings, label children's feelings, play games, sing songs, and read stories that include vocabulary about feelings.

In spite of an appropriately planned schedule of activities, consistency, and well-defined limits, unpredictable things do happen. Children need to learn to cope constructively with feelings that arise from interpersonal situations. Anger, jealousy, depression, fear, and other unpleasant feelings are common interpersonal emotions. Teachers choose either to provide an opportunity for helpful expression or to insist on at least temporary suppression. To correctly perceive feelings in themselves and others, children must have words for those feelings. Children can be taught feeling words directly by pairing pictures of facial expressions of feelings with the appropriate affective label. Adams (2011) suggests that teachers make a list of feeling words for a range of emotions—positive (e.g., happy), negative (e.g., angry), and neutral (e.g., calm) words referring to changes in feelings—and not judge emotions as good or bad. Helping a child learn how to recognize a difficult feeling (e.g., frustration because a tower of blocks falls down) provides an opportunity to support the child in regulating these emotions (e.g., take a few deep breaths to calm down and then problem-solve a different way to build a tower so it won't fall down).

Sensitive teachers find many opportunities to help children accept and express their feelings incidentally in the context of daily activities. Practically any unpleasant experience in the classroom can be a source of discussion. Young children cannot assimilate long lectures explaining feelings or behavior. Short statements or a gentle reassuring touch helps a child know that having feelings is all right. A simple acknowledgment (labeling) of feelings and inquiry about coping behaviors help a child understand and express emotions appropriately while feeling accepted. For example, the teacher might say, "It is OK to be mad when Johnny rips your paper, but I can't let you hit him. Can you think of another way to let Johnny know how angry you are?" Adults can also clearly express their own emotions and model appropriate behavioral expression of those emotions.

Numerous well-written books are available that help children learn to identify, understand, and respond to their own feelings and those of others. Even difficult topics such as death and divorce are subjects of sensitive presentation. Puppets, role-playing activities, art activities, punching bags, and imaginative unstructured play also give children opportunities to work through their feelings acceptably. (See CSEFEL's website to download a variety of charts on feelings, problem solving, and solutions that may be used with preschoolers to teach emotional literacy: http://csefel.vanderbilt.edu/resources/strategies .html#teachingskills.) Exhibit 6.1 illustrates a lesson that can be planned to help children learn to understand, label, and constructively express their feelings.

Promoting Appropriate Behavior Modeling

Young children with disabilities often learn new and more adaptive behavior through imitating their peers without disabilities. The modeling effect is a strong argument for integrating children with and without disabilities in early education programs. In fact, one of the most important advantages of group instruction is the opportunity for **observational learning** (Noonan & McCormick, 2014). This form of learning has often been referred to as modeling and consists of imitation of another's actions. Observational learning cannot be left to chance.

Exhibit 6.1
Encouraging Thoughtfulness, Empathy, and Caring

Goal
To create daily opportunities to nurture thoughtfulness, empathy, and caring in children.

How to Begin

1. *Be* what you wish to see children express. If you want them to be thoughtful, be thoughtful yourself.
2. Notice nearly every expression of *that* quality. Call attention to the child who expresses it in a spontaneous way. Do not make a major production of it. Rather, touch the child gently or hug lightly. Say, "That's so thoughtful. You helped Susie with her coat." You may think that the other children are not paying attention, but they are. In no time, they will try to figure out ways to get you to tell them how they are being thoughtful. And, of course, they will be learning the subtle meaning of "thoughtful."
3. Avoid calling attention to thoughtlessness or lack of empathy or caring; unless it is truly hurtful to others, ignore it.
4. On the other hand, if you see a child doing something negative to another child, say, "Can you imagine how you would feel if someone did that to you?"

After a Few Days

1. Reduce the frequency with which you call attention to the target quality. Continue to do all the things suggested in the previous list but less often.
2. Make up short stories about children who are thoughtful. Use puppets, flannel boards, or pictures. Catch a child expressing thoughtfulness. Paste the picture on one page and write a brief story below it telling what happened: "Susie couldn't get by. Tommy moved his chair. Then she could get through. That was thoughtful." Or, "It was truly kind of Marco to sit beside Jordan and offer to share when he understood how upset Marco was when his ice cream fell out of the cup."
3. Read stories and comment about examples of thoughtfulness, empathy, and caring as you read (e.g., "Little Red Riding Hood was thoughtful. She shared her cookies with her grandma").
4. Occasionally, with puppets and stories, mention lack of kindness (or whatever quality you are focusing on at the time). Then ask the children to suggest a kind thing to do. Be careful. At this point, do not lecture. Do not try to relate it to something they should have done.

Note: Remember, you are not only nurturing thoughtfulness, empathy and caring, but also helping the children learn the names of their feelings and actions. All too often, adults tell children to "Be kind" or "That was a thoughtless thing to do." Instead, "That was so kind of you to give your chair to Sally" or "Taking all of the crayons for yourself was not very thoughtful" helps the child to understand what actions are kind actions and what actions are not thoughtful. Children may not have the slightest idea what it means to be kind or thoughtful. Labeling the good behaviors makes it easier for children to express them spontaneously and purposefully.

From Then On

1. Continue to call attention to examples of the qualities you wish to see expressed. Of course, as these qualities increase in number, it becomes impossible to call attention to each of them constantly. It also becomes unnecessary. There seems to be a special magic to the expression of positive qualities. If a once-established quality seems to be diminishing, however, merely begin to call attention to it again and do so regularly.
2. Introduce new targets regularly. Watch them expand. You may discover quickly that even some of the naughtiest children express some of the target qualities from the first day. You may not have noticed before.

The teacher's responsibility is to understand the dynamics of learning through observation and imitation and to ensure that appropriate models of desired behavior are available. Numerous variables help determine whether a child will reproduce the observed behavior. Researchers have found that simply placing children with and without disabilities together does not necessarily result in the desired peer imitation. Children are more likely to imitate or model their more competent peers and those they observe receiving direct reinforcement from their teachers and others in their environment. As Allen and Cowdery (2015) state, "Teachers of young children are powerful models for classroom behavior" (p. 323). Children will imitate the behavior of teachers as well as other children. If children are not allowed to yell in the classroom, then teachers should not yell either. Teachers are also in a position to be very obvious when they dispense reinforcement for desired behavior. They can encourage children to clap for one another, they can put or have another child place happy-face stickers on the paper of a child who has completed tracing his or her name, and they can distribute snacks to the first child who is seated and waiting patiently.

In addition to learning from live models, children may also imitate models provided on video, a method called video modeling. A video clip of the child, a peer, or an adult demonstrating the target behavior may be shown to the child followed by an opportunity to practice it. Video modeling is effective with children with a variety of disabilities who like to watch videos and has been found to be an evidence-based practice for teaching children with autism spectrum disorders (Wong et al., 2015). For a step-by-step guide to using video modeling in the classroom, see Wynkoop (2016).

Enhanced eText Application Exercise 6.1
In this exercise, you can apply what you have learned in this chapter to identify the characteristics of the environment that support young children's social and emotional development.

Facilitating Social Skills

The development of positive social skills is critical to the successful inclusion of children with disabilities in community-based settings. Social skills are also essential to the emotional well-being of young children because such skills enable them to develop friendships and self-esteem. (Appendix A outlines the developmental sequence of social skills.) It has been found that children with disabilities in inclusive preschool classrooms often do not participate in social behaviors as much as their peers without disabilities, and it is helpful to pinpoint where in the social interaction children are being challenged. Deiner (2013, p. 92) recommends that the following interactions be observed:

Gaining attention: How does the child go about getting the attention of others?

Initiating Interaction: Once she has their attention, what overture is made to them?

Responding to others: Do the children have skills that invite others to join them?

Sustaining Interactions: Are the children able to continue interactions and practice the give and take skills necessary to sustain interaction?

Shifting the focus of an interaction: Do children have the skills necessary to change roles to refocus the play when appropriate?

Ending an interaction: Do children have ways of closing interactions instead of leaving?

Early childhood educators understand the importance of their role in helping children with disabilities establish appropriate and effective relationships with their peers. They provide modeling, direct instruction, praise, token reinforcement, and social interaction activities. In addition, they also structure the environment to facilitate peer mediation in the facilitation of full social participation of young children with disabilities. Examples of this environmental structuring follow.

Use Environmental Structuring

1. *Keep the groups relatively small* (from two to four children) when structured learning activities are involved. Small groups make it possible for teachers to facilitate ongoing positive social interactions without interrupting them.

2. *Assign seats around tables or at group time* to encourage interaction. In inclusive environments, typically developing children can be seated next to children with disabilities.

3. *Provide materials appropriate to the skills or interaction desired.* Children must learn to use play materials before they can be expected to play with them in cooperative situations. Children who become frustrated because they do not have the skill to use a material in the expected manner for an activity may become disruptive or withdraw.

4. *Promote selection of materials that facilitate cooperative interaction.* Some materials are more conducive to positive social interaction than others. Promote the choice of social toys (blocks, balls, and puppets) rather than isolated toys (crayons, modeling clay, and puzzles). Simple table games such as Lotto or Candy Land, with specific rules, may be more conducive to cooperative play than more unstructured play materials such as sand, crayons, or puzzles. Children with disabilities who have not developed imaginative play may need to move gradually from structured to unstructured play when positive interpersonal relationships are a high-priority goal. Teachers will need to observe carefully to determine which materials are most conducive to fostering the desired behavior. See Chapter 4 and Appendix B for additional ideas.

5. *Make sufficient materials available to promote cooperation and imitation.* When children outnumber the materials available, cooperative play obviously depends on children's willingness to share. If sharing is not one of the priorities for the play activity, then abundant materials should be available. Imitation is also not immediately possible and cannot be reinforced if children must wait to use the materials. However, fewer materials should be available if the goal is for children to learn to take turns or make requests for materials.

6. *Plan definite activities that require cooperation.* That is, select tasks that require at least two children to communicate and cooperate to reach a mutual goal. Each one's actions should be indispensable to the other. For example, a color-sorting task requires one child to sit on each side of a screen. Each has three different-colored bowls and a number of objects. One child is the dispatcher, who describes what he or she is doing as objects are placed in the bowls (e.g., "I am putting the yellow car in the red bowl"). The other child attempts to follow these directions to imitate the actions of the dispatcher. Such an activity is particularly helpful to children who have difficulty cooperating and paying attention long enough to follow directions. Of course, the more verbal (e.g., using speech or manual sign) the children are, the easier the task. Remember, some children must be taught how to imitate or to model the behavior of others.

Use Peers Without Disabilities as Mediators of Social Skills

Intervention practices in which peers are prepared to interact and model appropriate behavior have been well researched and are now thought to be strongly supported by evidence-based practice (Koegel et al., 2012). Several authors describe strategies for using peers as mediators of social skill development. With peer-mediated strategies, coaching is provided to a peer to promote social interaction skills rather than having only adults prompt the child with disabilities. Strategies include asking a peer to demonstrate a skill or activity for the child with disabilities

Video Example from

You Tube

and training or prompting children (both with and without disabilities) to initiate interactions with one another. It is ideal to select coaching peers who have higher-level social skills than the children with disabilities. However, it is important that the more socially competent children are not too developmentally advanced for their less able play partners (Hollingsworth, 2005). Peers can be coached to share, request to share, assist, and compliment the attempts at social interaction made by children with disabilities.

When selecting peers to be trained to become mediators or "buddies," it is important to consider the following peer attributes:

1. Does the peer consistently follow the teacher's directions?
2. Does the peer demonstrate age-appropriate interactional skills?
3. Does the peer attend the program regularly?
4. Does the peer frequently play with the same toys and engage in the same activities that seem to be preferred by the child who is the target of intervention?
5. Has the peer expressed or shown interest in interacting with the "target child"?

Enhanced eText Application Exercise 6.2
In this exercise, you can apply what you have learned in this chapter by listing specific strategies that help young children develop positive social skills.

Encouraging Developmental Play Behavior

Although research on the significance of play for children with disabilities is limited, the contention that play is an important contributor to their development is widely accepted. Recognizing the critical role of play in the enhancement of every aspect of a child's development, researchers are now investigating play behavior from a variety of viewpoints. Play may be the single most important teaching context, as noted in Chapter 4 and elaborated on in this chapter.

The Importance of Play in Supporting Healthy Social and Emotional Development

The importance of play has been noted in the early literature as far back as Plato and Aristotle. Freudians view the repetition of experiences in play as a means of gaining mastery over painful events. Eriksonians consider play to be a method by which children organize and integrate life experiences. Piagetians see play as an essential means of mastering one's environment. Play develops creativity and increases the child's repertoire of responses. The importance of play as a context for teaching and learning was discussed in Chapter 4.

Furthermore, through play, children learn self-regulation, social, and language skills, particularly when adults scaffold children's language and learning (Wasik & Jacobi-Vessels, 2017). Increased attention is finally being given to the critical role of play in the development of children with disabilities. Lifter, Mason, and Barton (2011) state that play is important for three major reasons:

(a) Play increases the likelihood of placement and learning in natural, inclusive, less restrictive settings;

(b) play is adaptable and can be used in multiple settings as a context for embedding intervention, practicing new skills, and conducting authentic assessments, and it provides opportunities for social and communicative interaction with peers and adults; and

(c) play has predictive value for communication and social skills. (pp. 289–290)

The importance of creating an environment that promotes spontaneous child-directed play cannot be underestimated. Early childhood educators have long realized the need for play activities as a part of all preschool curricula. The issue of accountability, however, has jeopardized the role of spontaneous play in some classrooms. Teachers feel pushed to judge the value of a play activity by what is learned. Perhaps the challenge now is to create a three-way balance among less structured creative activities, freedom of choice, and directed tasks designed to promote learning and development.

The Nature of Play

Long ago, Piaget (1963) placed play into three broad categories. First, *practice play* accompanies the sensorimotor stage of cognitive development. Practice play is characterized by the exploration and repetition involved in mastering an activity. The game of taking things out and putting things in is typical practice play.

Symbolic play describes the second type of play, which occurs during the preoperational stage of cognitive development. Preschool children involved in symbolic play can be seen using one object to represent or symbolize another. A child might attribute the qualities of a smartphone to a small wooden block and go around "calling friends" and "taking pictures." The child's increased verbal ability allows imitating and reenacting experiences, thus facilitating pretending and dramatic play. The third kind of play is referred to as *games with rules*, which require more complex communication and cooperation. Whereas some children may engage in rule-oriented play during preschool, interest in this behavior is thought to heighten during the concrete operational stage of cognitive development near 7 years of age.

Development of Social Interaction Skills Through Play

A review of the literature on inclusion of preschoolers with disabilities highlights the positive effects of inclusion in general education preschools on the social and language development on children with disabilities (Lawrence, Smith, & Banerjee, 2016; Warren, Martinez, & Sortino, 2016). However, despite the good intentions of inclusion, we find again and again that children who are typically developing do not regularly include children with disabilities in their play. In their research, Diamond and Hong (2010) found that children with disabilities were included more often when teachers used intentional environmental strategies to support children's peer social relationships. Special intervention strategies are necessary to increase interaction and promote the social skill development of children with disabilities. They may require supports to develop the interpersonal skills that typically developing children may acquire through usual play behavior. To understand the developmental levels of social play behavior, we discuss a variation of the classic work of Parten (1932). Parten's six levels of social participation provide a sequence for reference, but they need more empirical support to be followed without caution. However, they do provide guidelines for the observation and selection of intervention strategies.

1. ***Unoccupied behavior.*** At this level, there is no interpersonal interaction. The child may watch anything that attracts his or her attention. Some children engage in self-stimulating behavior. Even at this level, children should be placed near other children and reinforced for manipulating a toy and staying within the social

environment. Teachers may identify and use the child's preferred toys, materials, and actions to redirect or shape repetitive behaviors into more acceptable behaviors (e.g., provide maracas for the child to shake as a replacement for flapping hands).

2. *Solitary independent play.* Again, the child plays alone and with toys that are probably different from those being used by other children. He or she may be within speaking distance of other children but is unlikely to interact with them. Based on the child's preferences, teachers should encourage involvement with toys even if the child is not interacting with others. Toys must be carefully chosen and reinforcement given for use in the expected ways for the activity. Encouragement of appropriate use of toys and objects not only will help children enhance their cognitive skills but also will make them better prepared for social and play interactions with peers.

3. *Onlooker behavior.* On this level, children are definitely observing the play of others and may even engage in conversation with them. As a step toward actual involvement with others, adults should position children where they can clearly observe other children and encourage any attempts at interaction. Teachers should identify common interests in toys and materials and preferences for classmates to motivate the child's observations. One promising approach to increasing the social interaction of young children with disabilities has been to teach peers without disabilities to be the initiators of social exchanges. Considerable success has been reported when peers are trained to use behavioral procedures to elicit social responses during play from young children with a variety of disabilities (Morales & Ledford, 2016). Opportunities for generalization to new settings should be identified and implemented. Success might be more assured when the peer without a disability uses "natural" initiations to which the children with disabilities might respond.

4. *Parallel activity.* Behavior on this level includes independent play among children using toys like those used by the other children. Teachers should identify the child's preferences for classmates and toys to structure opportunities for imitation of play actions and turn taking. To move children toward complete involvement, the teacher should encourage the children without disabilities to share toys with the children who have disabilities and to ask for toys from the children with disabilities. In this way, the children without disabilities act as initiators of social interactions. Children with disabilities must be positioned within the group to facilitate access to toys and their peers.

5. *Associative play.* On this level, children are playing with other children. There is borrowing, lending, sharing, engagement in similar activities, and interest primarily in association rather than activities. To facilitate such involvement, teachers must deliberately structure the environment. They must provide toys and objects such as blocks, dress-up clothes, and games that encourage interaction. Space must be adequate because crowding tends to lead to disruptive play. Teachers may support the child with a disability by providing prompts for him or her to make requests or share materials with other children. Peers without disabilities should be reinforced for conversation and sharing with playmates who have disabilities. Children with disabilities may need extra encouragement and redirection if they begin to wander from the group.

6. *Cooperative or organized play.* On the final level of Parten's continuum, children play in a group that is organized in some way. There are common goals and a division of labor. All members usually feel like part of the group even though it is led by one or two players. Typical activities include building structures during block play and dramatization. The teacher's role in facilitating cooperative play centers around preparation of the environment and providing appropriate space

and "social" toys requiring cooperative interaction between two or more children. Teachers may support the child with a disability by providing prompts for him or her to make requests or share materials with other children.

The Impact of Disabilities on Play Behavior.   Although it is very important to understand the normal progression of play behavior, it is also extremely critical that we carefully observe children with disabilities in order to understand what differences they might have in their play behavior. Macintyre (2010) points out the importance of careful observation before deciding if an intervention is needed and how to support children with learning differences in their play. For example, consider how to help a child with low muscle tone grasp an object or support a child who avoids eye contact and has trouble reading nonverbal cues engage in pretend play with a peer. After finding little literature on the play of children with disabilities compared with the large amount of work on typical play development, Kuhaneck, Spitzer, and Miller (2010) noted that children with disabilities progress through similar stages of play development as children without disabilities, but more slowly. In general, the development of play behaviors is closely tied to cognitive and motor development. Children with disabilities also tend to need greater assistance from adults. The difficulties in the play of children with autism, which include lack of symbolic play, limited imitation of others, and repetitive play with objects, are well documented (Lifter et al., 2011).

Some Ways to Facilitate Children's Play.   Education usually emphasizes structured, teacher-directed play when children do not appear to learn readily through spontaneous play. Some children with adverse childhood experiences (e.g., multiple foster placements in the early years or experiencing trauma) may not have had many opportunities for play. Teachers and caregivers need to provide these. Lifter et al. (2011) discuss the success that results when adults use systematic prompting and focus on appropriate play goals. It is important to recognize environmental factors that can impact children's involvement in play. For example, inappropriate toys and play materials may contribute to the limited play behavior of children with disabilities. Toys that are not durable fail to withstand rough treatment, and toys such as dolls designed for symbolic play are not developmentally appropriate for some children. Children who still need to engage in practice play must be provided with toys strong enough to accommodate repeated use. Children who lack attending, imitation, or communication skills cannot be expected to share or take turns. Developing these abilities takes time and is taught deliberately through modeling and reinforcement. Teachers need to assess a child's strengths and areas to be developed to encourage the most appropriate play activities.

Once the teacher notes that a child has begun to explore the environment and effectively uses a variety of different toy objects, it is time to encourage the development of more sophisticated and sustained toy play and play that requires more social interaction. Teachers should also observe children's interactions with different toys to identify preferences and also which toys facilitate what types of play (Trawick-Smith, Wolff, Koschel, & Vallarelli, 2015). Exhibit 6.2 suggests some guidelines to enhance productive free-choice play.

Imagining and pretending may be difficult for many children. Some children with cognitive or language differences may not understand the concept of "pretend" and need specific supports to develop this understanding. Granting this freedom to be somebody else or something else is often a good way to lead a withdrawn child out of his or her shell. Dress-up clothes, an assortment of hats (firefighter, cowboy or cowgirl, train conductor, or nurse), and old costumes left from Halloween are appealing motivators. However, it is important for adults to be aware of how they may promote gender stereotypes and to remember that some parents may be uncomfortable with their sons dressing up in stereotypical female clothing (e.g., a tutu) (Freeman, 2007). Furthermore, some parents may not want their children to wear costumes because they do not participate in Halloween for religious reasons. When there are differences between the beliefs and values of teachers and families, teachers should explain what children learn through dress-up activities, listen carefully to parents' perspectives and concerns, and problem-solve a solution with parents. Pretending to be animals during story times and participating in musical activities allow many children to romp and move freely. With freedom of movement comes greater ease in being around other children.

A large box with holes for windows provides a sense of protection. As the children crawl in and out, they discover new ways of looking at things. Looking through the window in the box restricts the view in unexpected ways. Moving becomes purposeful.

Exhibit 6.2

Creating Play Environments That Support the Development of Social Skills

A. *Arrange the play area thoughtfully.*

1. Provide adequate space indoors and out. Avoid crowding.
2. Arrange small play spaces separated by shelves or other dividers. Puzzles, books, and other things to do alone should be available.
3. Prepare larger spaces for cooperative play with blocks and other building materials.
4. A play kitchen in a corner encourages group play. Provide some full-sized pans and spoons and child-sized equipment.
5. Maintain the same basic room arrangement over time but vary or rotate the play materials available. Have a storage area where toys may "rest." Sometimes allow the children to choose what will be stored and what will be available.
6. Puppets, dolls and dollhouses, and barns and animals should be regularly available. These imagination stimulators require setup space, whether used alone or with a group.
7. Remove toys that appear to encourage an activity or a noise level incompatible with the behavioral and learning styles of all the children. In small areas, large cars and trucks usually generate too high of an activity level for safety.
8. Plan to alternate indoor and outdoor play whenever possible. Outdoor areas should provide safe climbing and running spaces as well as tricycles and structures for crawling in, over, and under.
9. Address children's disabilities; for example, provide special equipment and adapted toys that support participation of children with physical disabilities.

B. *Establish rules or guidelines from the beginning.*

1. Keep the rules simple and limited in number.
2. Just telling children rules is important but not very effective. They will need to learn the guidelines by observation and experience. But the teacher should have the rules firmly in mind.
3. Rules should be designed to establish thoughtful, kind, and courteous behavior. The following are some we have found useful:
   a. The child who chooses a toy first may decide whether he or she wants to play alone or with others. The child's decision will be respected.
   b. Sharing is not required, especially if the item to be shared belongs to a particular child. Sharing is encouraged, however. When more than one child wants a particular toy, a time limit may be used to give turns; for example, the teacher may set a timer for 5 minutes, and when the timer rings, the next child gets a turn. Teachers may also ask the children what they can do when two children want to play with the same toy. This question helps children problem-solve and come up with a solution.
   c. Children wanting to join an established group must be invited to join. The newcomer may ask to play but cannot move in without a welcome.
   d. Good manners are modeled and expected. "May I," "please," and "thank you" are routinely used by teachers. Children absorb these courtesies quickly.

e. When a child or a group is finished with an item, the item must be returned to its place on the shelf before a different toy or game is chosen.

f. Sometimes children like just to watch for a while. This wish is respected. Rockers and beanbag chairs are often used by watchers.

g. Just as child newcomers may not barge into an established group, so must adult (teachers or parents) newcomers ask permission and be accepted.

Seeing what is inside intrigues some children. If the box is large enough, a small carpet and a place for a snack will encourage some children to enter.

Teachers may want to tell stories using a flannel board or pictures. Then, as the teacher provides simple props and withdraws from the center of the activity, children usually accept the suggestion to "play the story."

Role-playing is a form of pretending and imagining. An apron and play kitchen equipment make it possible for children to be Mom or Dad. A plastic hammer or a wrench enables a child to be a carpenter or garage mechanic. Some children pretend to be their big brothers and sisters.

Much insight into fears and frustrations can be gained by encouraging role-playing without evaluating it. Of course, the insights gained may not be pleasant. Judgment about how to use such knowledge requires compassion, understanding, and wisdom.

Puppets are therapeutic and fun for most children. A box with a "stage" cut out, an old television with the insides removed, or a table with a curtain becomes the puppet theater. Of course, a real puppet stage can be constructed by a creative parent. The puppets can be made from socks or sewn from a simple pattern. Commercial puppets are enchanting, although most are expensive. Children enjoy merely playing with the puppets, but if a teacher puts on the first show, they will have a better idea of how to be puppeteers.

It is not unusual for withdrawn children to say their first words with a puppet on their hands. They may find it necessary to use the puppet for days whenever they want to talk. A change of puppets should be offered with care. If a particular puppet is effective, the teacher should not rush into expecting the child to assume many roles with other puppets. Some children require prolonged encouragement before they can venture out.

Peers and play often draw children out of their shells. Suggesting that one child help another by picking up a spilled puzzle leads to later spontaneous kindnesses. Some children notice the needs of other youngsters more completely than most adults believe. Consider the experience of Lance and Carla:

> Lance was enrolled in kindergarten, but continually preferred to stand quietly in a corner of the room. The kindergarten teacher was patient and experienced, but with 32 other children, the situation was overwhelming to Lance. Because of Lance's continued withdrawn behavior, his parents moved him to a preschool. When he entered school, his eyes were unsmiling, and his lips were taut. For several days the other children played around him. He refused snacks, special treats, and all efforts to involve him in play. Then Carla took over. She was 4 years old. She walked right up to Lance and said, "I like blocks. Play with me." Immediately, she pulled Lance abruptly to the floor, pushed the blocks to him, and began to build. Smiling and chatting away (definitely a monologue), she told him all about the wonderful house she was building. Lance stared emotionless, but Carla was not disturbed. After a while Carla said, "Help put the blocks back. We'll do a puzzle." Lance did not move. A few minutes later Carla announced, "Lance likes grapes." The teacher did not discover how Carla knew of Lance's liking for grapes but promised to bring the fruit the next day.

The following day, Carla asked for some grapes "for Lance." Carrying the grapes with one hand and dragging Lance with the other, she moved to the puzzle corner. She said, "We'll do a puzzle first." With the grapes plainly in sight but out of Lance's reach, they began a puzzle. "When we finish, we eat grapes," said Carla. Lance smiled and slowly pushed a puzzle piece to Carla. He also ate grapes with Carla.

Carla's mothering continued for weeks as she ignored Lance's rebuffs. She regularly told everyone, "Lance is my friend," and busily planned things to do with him. She alternately insisted and cajoled. Frequently, when Lance ignored her, she walked away, only to return as if nothing had happened a few minutes later. Carla literally planned and executed instruction with Lance. No doubt, Carla's natural inclinations accomplished more than many well-planned teacher-directed lessons.

Facilitating Play and Social Skill Development in Children with Severe Disabilities. Children with obvious or more severe disabilities may have had little opportunity to play with other children. Some may have spent much time in hospitals, whereas others may have very protective parents who fear their child might experience ridicule or rejection. Of course, many disabling conditions by their very nature make it difficult for children to play in ways that lead to social skill acquisition. For instance, children with severe hearing, speech, or cognitive impairments may not have the language necessary to make their needs known or to engage in appropriate spoken conversations. Children with physical disabilities or lack of behavior control may have problems making friends because their behavior or necessary adaptive equipment has become a barrier to social interaction. Children with autism spectrum disorders have difficulties with symbolic pretend play and social play. Therefore, practitioners must make special efforts to facilitate the effective opportunities for children with severe disabilities to engage in play with peers without disabilities. For example, Wolfberg (2015) has reported on the positive effects of the Integrated Play Group (IPG) approach on the social play skills of children with autism spectrum disorders. Teachers may help families identify community resources that will support the development of a child's play. For example, the local Lekotek Center offers a range of resources (such as play groups, a toy lending library, adaptive and assistive technology, and parent support) that may benefit the child and family. See the website of the National Lekotek Center for locations and services at http://www.lekotek.org/.

Recognizing the benefit of play for all children with disabilities, Sluss (2015) discusses the importance of early education in creating a responsive, effective environment that facilitates and supports play for children with disabilities. Teachers are encouraged to:

1. Remember that children with disabilities are children first and that play is an essential learning experience.

2. Recognize that some children may not initiate play, so teachers must intervene to encourage and support play.

3. As appropriate, help each child recognize how his or her disability might affect how he or she does participate in play.

4. Expect that all children can participate in play; establish this expectation with typically developing preschoolers.

5. Individualize the play experience to promote participation by making modifications to materials and in the environment as needed.

6. Realize that without adult intervention, children with disabilities may not have many opportunities for play experiences. For example, teachers may ask parents if they are interested in being on a list to organize play dates.

7. Use assistive technology to support children's participation in play activities.

Several strategies for developing these skills have already been discussed. Of course, it is necessary to begin by carefully observing to find out what social skills each child already has and which ones need to be developed. In addition, the transdisciplinary play-based approach to assessment presented by Linder (2008) provides comprehensive guidelines for assessing children's social skills through everyday play routines.

Physical Prompting and Fading.   Sometimes children with severe disabilities may not participate because they do not know how to play with the available toys or respond to others. When they do not react, there is no play behavior for the caregiver to reinforce and encourage. The caregiver, then, may have to physically guide the child through the desired response. For example, if the game is to roll a ball from one child to another, the caregiver or a peer model may gently guide the child's hand until the child can approximate the behavior on his or her own. The guiding hand should be gradually removed as the child's approximation becomes closer and closer to the desired behavior. If during this fading or gradual removal of the physical prompting the child becomes upset or apparently is not ready to continue alone, the fading should be discontinued temporarily. Such an approach can be very effective with children who experience severe physical, visual, hearing, or intellectual disabilities. It is much easier for these children to follow directions illustrated through physical prompting. It is also critical that the child receives a natural reinforcer for participating in the play behavior—for example, the rolling ball lights up or makes a sound, or the peer cheers on the child's participation and gives a high five.

Initiating and Sustaining Play.   Some children may need to be given a way to communicate their desire to initiate and sustain play behavior. When a child does not seem to have the words to invite another to play, the caregiver must supply them for the child. For example, when Darren wanted Brad to help him build a road in the sand, he kept looking and motioning to him. Brad, who often does not follow nonverbal cues, did not respond. Then Ms. McLynn said, "Darren, go up and say to Brad, 'Come help me build the road.'" Darren modeled Ms. McLynn, who, in turn, reinforced both Darren and Brad as both began to build a road. When another child began to step on the road, Ms. McLynn said to Darren, "Say, 'Stop!'" Darren again modeled Ms. McLynn, and the children played on. Some children may need AAC methods, such as communicating through manual signs or a voice output device to interact with peers.

Helping Children with Emotional and Behavioral Challenges

No matter how responsive and positive a teacher and the environment may be, there will be children who continue to need additional support as they strive toward healthy social-emotional development. There will also be behaviors that we perceive to be challenging just because our unique set of past experiences, values, instructional practices, and institutional guidelines lead us to perceive certain behaviors as challenging. Or, as Tomlin (2004) states, "'Difficultness' (often) lies in the eye of the beholder, rather than in the behavior of a given child" (p. 33). Perhaps further understanding of individual temperamental qualities will help us be less stressed and more tolerant in the face of challenging behaviors.

Individual Temperament

"Temperamental predispositions are necessary, but not sufficient, building blocks for the child's developing personality" (Sturm, 2004, p. 5). As these constitutionally based building blocks are influenced by experience, they evolve into the features of individual personalities. Temperamental traits determine how a child typically interacts with his or her environment.

Current writers often turn to the pioneering work of Thomas, Chess, and Birch (1968, 1970; Chess & Thomas, 2013) when they discuss concepts of **temperament** or early-appearing patterns of observable behavior. Through intensive parent interviews and observation of children, Thomas and colleagues identified nine characteristics of temperament that they clustered into three basic types describing approximately 65% of the children studied. The other 35% did not show a basic constancy of temperament or style of behavior.

They described the *easy* child as one whose behavior is low in intensity and who is adaptable, approachable, predictable in bodily functions, and positive in mood. This kind of child easily makes parents believe they are good at parenting. Obviously, such a child (accounting for approximately 40% of the sample studied) would be a pleasure in the classroom.

The second type of temperament is that of the *difficult* child, accounting for approximately 10% of the sample studied. This type of child is often negative in mood, adapts slowly to change, has unpredictable biological functions, and often exhibits intense reactions to environmental demands. Such a child not only requires that teachers and parents exercise extra effort and patience to keep the child's self-esteem intact but also behaves in such difficult ways that the self-confidence of involved adults is often threatened. When adults are unable to provide firm guidance by building the environment discussed throughout this chapter, they may experience a sense of helplessness when such children appear unhappy or out of control. The threat of becoming burned-out caregivers is very real. This possibility is even more acute in the case of at-risk children who have exhibited early developmental delays. When children are unable because of disabling conditions or prematurity to exhibit the social signals necessary to establish early attachment, their difficult behavior later on is even more of a challenge to parents who may already be feeling uneasy about their parenting skills.

The third type of child discussed by Thomas and colleagues is the *slow-to-warm-up* child, accounting for approximately 15% of the sample. Such a child typically exhibits negative responses to new situations but, given time and patience, eventually adapts. Patience and understanding of the child's tendency to withdraw seem to be the key to helping this child adjust and become comfortable with new situations.

The stability of these temperamental traits is thought to depend not only on characteristics of the child but also on the dynamic interplay between the child and caregiving environment. As Blackwell (2004) stated, "In other words, an adequate understanding of temperament must be one in which the child is regarded within the context of her environment" (p. 38). This is extremely important given that studies found that although behavior patterns do modify somewhat over time, they generally persist into adulthood (Soto, 2016).

It must be stressed that there is no "good" or "bad" temperament, and children should not be labeled as "easy" or "difficult" because of their behavior styles. Early educators may use other terms to describe children's characteristics, for example, "movers and shakers" have high activity levels and physical exploration, while "sitters" may prefer to explore by watching. A "dramatic" child has intense responses, while at the other extreme, a child may be "mellow." In terms of quality of mood, a "sunny" child is always happy and pleasant, while a "somber" child tends to be irritable and sad. It is the responsibility of caregivers to influence the child–environment interactional process to create a "goodness of fit" that supports a child's learning and development (Pelco & Reed-Victor, 2003). Therefore, the sections that follow suggest some practical methods of giving additional assistance to children whose behavior interferes with learning or can be described as disruptive or harmful.

Helping Children Develop Executive Function Skills

According to the Center on the Developing Child at Harvard University (2017, p. 3), "Executive function skills are crucial building blocks for the early development of both cognitive and social capacities." It highlights three interrelated dimensions of executive function skills:

Working memory: The capacity to hold and manipulate information in our minds for a short period of time. For example, working memory enables a child to follow multistep directions or take turns in activities.

Inhibitory control: The skill that enables selective and sustained attention before action. For example, inhibitory control enables a child to control impulses and emotions even when angry or frustrated and to ignore distractions and stay on task.

Cognitive or mental flexibility: The ability to adjust to changes in demands, rules, and settings. For example, cognitive or mental flexibility allows a child to use "inside" or "outside" voices in different settings and problem-solve how to resolve conflicts with peers.

Moreover, evaluations of preschool programs have found that interventions were effective if one of the following strategies was implemented:

1. Promoting children's emerging executive function skills, such as retaining and using information, focusing attention and resisting distractions, planning actions, and revising plans when needed.

2. Training teachers to use effective classroom management techniques, such as providing positive reinforcements for appropriate behavior, redirecting challenging behavior, and providing mental health consultation for the overall classroom and individual children.

3. Training teachers to focus on children's prosocial behaviors, problem-solving skills, understanding and expressing emotions in acceptable ways, controlling impulsive behavior, and organizing to accomplish goals.

Children who lack sufficient self-regulation are usually viewed as aggressive, hostile, overactive, impulsive, or hyperactive. Such children find it difficult to follow classroom limits. Some, such as hostile and aggressive children, may deliberately strike out at others or damage equipment. Others, such as hyperactive or impulsive children, may merely be unable to control extraneous movements. Although these behaviors are certainly challenging, it is important to remember that any behavior that continues over time serves a purpose or function for the child exhibiting the behavior. Such behaviors have a purposeful communication function. Miller (2016) suggests that these behaviors may be attempting to communicate a child's frustration due to the following:

1. Inappropriate expectations: "You're asking me to do something that is too difficult."

2. Misunderstanding expectations: "I don't understand what you want."

3. Immature self-control: "I want a certain thing, and I want it now."

4. Boredom: "I'm bored; pay some attention to me."

5. Group contagion: "This is so much fun—I just can't help myself."

6. Fatigue and discomfort: "I don't want to because I don't feel good."

7. Desire for recognition: "I am here, too."

The conceptualization of challenging behavior as being "functional" represents a change in how challenging behaviors are understood and dealt with (Dunlap & Fox, 2012). We now see that it is our responsibility to interpret what the child is trying to communicate and assist the child in learning socially acceptable ways to communicate his or her thoughts and needs. We are further encouraged to try to prevent undesirable

Enhanced eText

Video Example 6.6, Part 1

Flexible, Fearful, or Feisty: Different Temperaments of Infants and Toddlers
https://www.youtube
.com/watch?v=tkNyaOe-ty4

Enhanced eText

Video Example 6.6, Part 2

Flexible, Fearful, or Feisty: Different Temperaments of Infants and Toddlers
https://www.youtube
.com/watch?v=5p5IYWRB4iE
These videos provide an overview of the qualities of temperament, observations of toddlers in child care, and suggestions for caregivers who wish to encourage children's participation.

Enhanced eText

Video Example 6.7

Preschoolers with ADHD
https://www.youtube.com/
watch?v=fhQUK8lnoDE
This video discusses the controversy, diagnosis, and interventions
for preschoolers with ADHD.

attempts at communication by anticipating needs and preventing such behavioral episodes. Efforts at prevention include making sure activities are developmentally and
individually appropriate and requests are clearly understood, using highly desirable
toys and activities, and providing positive feedback. By removing antecedent situations,
we are able to prevent functional misbehavior from occurring.

It is only when aggressive behavior occurs with high frequency; involves extreme
behavior, such as the destruction of property or cruelty to animals or behavior that is
dangerous to other people; or increases after 3 years of age that we should consider that
serious problems exist that need a specialist's intervention.

Some children with challenging behaviors may be labeled as having attention-defi-
cit/hyperactivity disorder (ADHD). ADHD is characterized by the inability to maintain
normal levels of attention, extreme impulsivity, and high levels of activity. Whereas
many young children normally display these behaviors, children with ADHD exhibit
inappropriately high degrees of them (Wolraich, 2006). The onset of ADHD occurs
before the age of 7, and the disorder occurs more often in boys. Degrees of severity
differ, and symptoms can be exacerbated or ameliorated by environmental factors. Early
childhood special education practitioners should be careful not to ascribe the ADHD
label automatically to every child who exhibits extreme problems with behavior control. Only through complete assessment by professionals of relevant disciplines is the
diagnosis of ADHD warranted. As noted in Chapter 5, it is not unusual for children
with fetal alcohol spectrum disorders to be served under the designation of ADHD or
learning disabilities.

Any diagnosis involving attention span is especially difficult with young children
because many adults have unreasonable expectations. The literature has not been consistent in indicating what length of attention is normal in everyday contexts. Ruff and
Capozzoli (2003) hypothesized that two systems are responsible for attention in the
first 3 years and are important at different times. During the first year, infants give
most of their attention to novelty. As they develop neurologically, they start coordinating attention and activity, and their actions follow intentions. It is not until closer to
4 years of age that children can readily stay focused on a task and resist distraction.
Tomlin (2004) discusses the importance of the development of cognitive skills such as
self-talk in providing the mechanism that helps children develop the capacity to attend.
She reminds us that "it is useful to consider the ability to persist with tasks and give
sustained attention to activities and situations as a developmental skill that is at least
partially dependent on cognitive abilities and is influenced by situational factors, such
as what else is going on at the time and the type of activity" (p. 32).

Prevention Through Environmental Preparation.   Teachers need to prepare the child's
environment. Children who are hyperactive, anxious, or angry often find it almost
impossible to sit still, to take turns, or to wait for explanations. They may constantly
squirm, turn, or wiggle. Such children may be easily overstimulated if they have difficulty filtering out extraneous sounds or sights. Teachers must take care to limit the noise
level in their classrooms and the visual stimuli surrounding these children. Centers that
have minimal space or are associated with different activity or noise levels may create
too much confusion. The inability to filter out extraneous stimuli and to inhibit impulses
may be the reason some of these children can be so difficult for parents to handle when
shopping in department or grocery stores.

Concentration can be improved by providing a quiet place to work free from distraction. Ample equipment and materials should be available so these children do not
have to do too much waiting or sharing. Teachers should limit the use of toys or games
with many small pieces to manipulate that can create frustration. They must space
tables far enough apart so extraneous movements will not bother others. They should
eliminate toys such as guns and soldiers that elicit aggressive behavior. They should
place impatient children in a position to receive snacks or working materials relatively

early in the waiting time. As these children show signs of increasing their capacities for inhibitory control, waiting time can be increased.

Scheduling. As discussed earlier, predictable routines are essential to supporting young children's socially acceptable behavior. Schedules must be reasonably consistent for children to learn expected routines. By knowing what to do and when to do it, children are less likely to exhibit challenging behaviors. Predictability in type of activity, rather than sameness, is the key.

Carefully Consider Curricular Implementation. Teachers must carefully consider curricular implementation. When children are appropriately involved in activities with materials or people, they usually are demonstrating appropriate behavior as well. Children who find it difficult to concentrate may fall behind in developing preacademic skills and may be labeled as having learning disabilities later on. Sometimes their speech is so fast that words and thoughts become a jumble, resulting in excessive use of gestures. Children's frustrations may develop into aggressive behavior and a loss of self-esteem from being ashamed of their lack of inhibitory control. To avoid these frustrations, directions must be extremely clear and given one by one, often with visual aids. Teachers should analyze tasks and present them in sequential steps so they can reinforce success intermittently and frequently. Materials and activities must be interesting. Using the child's name often while working with a group helps the child focus his or her attention. A calm voice is a must. A raised voice will only create anxiety and heighten the child's level of activity.

Unstructured free playtimes or transition times can be especially difficult for impulsive children. Choices for these children may have to be limited. Transitions are clearly signaled and structured to minimize wait time, and are likely to facilitate children's appropriate behaviors. It helps to establish definite procedures for transition times, such as those suggested in Exhibit 6.3. A teacher or paraprofessional will need to stay with children with challenging behaviors until they have become involved in their new activities. Tasks that require eye–hand coordination can be especially useful for helping children learn to follow directions, complete activities, and regulate their behavior.

When such tasks are interesting and simple enough to complete quickly, children can readily experience success. Examples include picture puzzles, activities with stickers, and apps on tablets. When children are losing inhibitory control during either free play or work time, by directing their attention to tasks that require eye–hand coordination, children can self-regulate.

Using loud, lively CDs during music time can be upsetting for children who have difficulty with self-regulation. Some activities on CDs require children to be able to process auditory information quickly to participate. For children who lack inhibitory control, these CDs may be inappropriate or can be used for only a very short time. Teachers must remember that many behavior problems are simply children's responses to overstimulation or frustration. Why create or accentuate such problems?

Teachers can use visual aids to support children's inhibitory control. Carpet squares or pieces of tape on the floor give them a definite, visual, and tactile space in which they are to keep themselves. Having a definite location for their belongings is also important to all children. It provides a sense of security. While on field trips, overactive children should be in small groups and close to adults. If they are verbally engaged, they usually have better inhibitory control. Similar-style name tags for groups of two or three help these children feel a sense of belonging to a small group.

Maintain Guidance Through Physical Proximity and Touch. An adult's physical proximity or a gentle touch can help some children maintain inhibitory control. This is especially useful when young children are placed in situations that challenge their inhibitory control. Many publicly supported early childhood programs are placed within elementary schools. As a result, children may be expected to stand and walk

Exhibit 6.3

Daily Activity Transition Techniques

A. *When children are playing (free-play or free-choice activities):*

1. Five minutes before cleanup time, quietly say, "It's almost cleanup time." Speak to small groups and individuals—do *not* make a group announcement.

2. Have a child ring a bell to signal "Cleanup time, now."

3. Sing a "cleanup song."

4. Move among the children, helping them find containers and properly sorting and replacing toys. As children learn where things belong, teacher assistance should be reduced.

   Suggestions: Early in the year, have a limited number of toys and games available. As the children learn to replace those correctly, add new ones and remove some things. Avoid clutter. Provide variety, for example, puzzles, games, blocks, beads, and coloring materials. Have a specific container for each kind of toy. Provide a particular place to which each container is returned as the children clean up.

B. *Transition from circle time or a group activity to another directed activity such as a small-group lesson, snack time, or individual lessons:*

1. As the activity in progress draws to a close, tell the children, "It's almost time for _____."

2. Establish brief eye contact with each child—a look and a smile at the same time. Then say, "Listen for the directions. It is _____'s turn."

3. Give each child, in turn, specific directions for moving to the next lesson or activity location. For example:

TEACHER: Matt, clap your hands two times, touch your ear, and walk backward to the table for a snack. (Others watch as Matt follows the directions. The directions are given in one long sentence. Matt must wait until the teacher finishes speaking before he begins.)

TEACHER: (To Danny, who has a learning problem): Danny, jump two times. (Danny's directions are shorter and spoken more slowly.)

When the teacher gives specific directions for going to the table or the next activity location, children learn to listen to and follow directions while being able to "let off a little steam." The transition occurs in an orderly way and enhances a sense of appropriate behavior.

in lines and to behave in ways that usually are not expected until they reach kindergarten age. Teachers may even need to take the hands of some children to help them maintain the needed inhibitory control. This should not be done as a punishment for misbehavior but before problems arise. If the teacher uses hand-holding as a negative consequence, the teacher might become an aversive stimulus, and this will negatively affect the child's self-image.

Use Signal Interference to Prevent Loss of Inhibitory Control. Signal interference can be very effective with impulsive children if teachers have observed carefully to see what usually sets off such children. Sometimes patterns in behavior are obvious, such as excessive frustration or activity just before a snack, during circle time, or near the time to go home. Environmental factors such as overstimulation, lack of sufficient movement space, or lack of time to complete a task might be a part of the patterns. Nonverbal (and sometimes verbal) signals, such as a nod or wink, can be especially effective if used in the beginning stages of misbehavior and with children who are capable of understanding them and can remember why the signal is being given.

Signals must be used before a child becomes so emotional that he or she is unable to stop the behavior. A warm relationship between the teacher and child contributes to the effectiveness of this approach. As children mature, they can be taught to understand their own signs of impending loss of inhibitory control. They can then be encouraged to signal the teacher that they need a time-away or change in activities.

In addition, teachers should use and teach young children self-calming strategies, and have them practice these strategies during their daily routine. These strategies include taking five deep breaths, blowing or popping bubbles, listening to a favorite song or music, coloring or drawing, taking a drink of water, giving him or herself a hug by wrapping his or her arms around his or her body, playing with clay or sand, looking at a book, or taking a break from an ongoing activity (Meltzer, 2015).

Pick Your Battles.   Teachers and parents should pick only the most disruptive and aggressive behavior as targets for control. Those who work with very young children must be willing to tolerate a high level of activity. Otherwise, their negative reactions will exacerbate the child's behavior.

Do Not Permit Aggressive Behavior.   The first rule toward helping children control the expression of unacceptable, possibly harmful behavior is that teachers should not permit aggressive behavior. From the very beginning, adults must make it perfectly clear that hitting, kicking, pushing, and shoving will not be allowed. Then teachers and parents must act swiftly when such behavior is expressed to demonstrate consistently and firmly what the consequences of such actions will be. Children thus learn that these actions will not be tolerated because they lead to nonpunitive but effective consequences. Firm consistency helps children develop trust in themselves and in others.

Despite the teacher's best efforts toward preventive discipline, aggressive acts do occur and must be dealt with immediately. The key to dealing with aggressive children is for the teacher to be nonaggressive. Many consider nonpunitive discipline, such as a time-out (or time-away, as discussed in a following section), to be effective. Children learn that aggressive behavior will not be tolerated of anyone, not even the teacher. They also learn that the teacher can be trusted to be fair but firm. If teachers are to give attention, they should give it to non-aggressors. That is, the teacher should give attention to the victim rather than to the aggressor. Throughout this chapter, other examples of nonaggressive methods of behavior control are discussed. These merit consideration.

Deescalate Play Behavior.   Children need to be helped by active adult participation to deescalate their play when it gets out of hand. To illustrate the need to help children refocus their play when they become too energetic or physical, one can describe the all-too-familiar building blocks scene. Children begin innocently making block towers, and one child accidentally knocks against or otherwise destroys another child's creation. Then hostility erupts, and aggression occurs. Involved adults should not only try environmentally to prevent or catch the behavior before it escalates but also return children to positive playfulness by not making judgments and reading intent into every aggressive act.

Consider the Value of Time-Away.   It is generally agreed that everyone needs a break when a child has lost control. Therefore, Miller (2016) recommends *time-away* instead of time-out. Time-away acknowledges that everyone needs a breather once in a while. When a child loses inhibitory control, the caregiver can suggest that the child take a break until he or she feels better and wants to participate. This action should be considered as a brief respite and not punishment. The time-away area should be a pleasant place near a window, or a book or puzzle corner. Giving the child something to do will facilitate inhibitory control. There should be a rule that only one child can be in the area at any time, and children should be encouraged to go there when they feel the need for quiet time. Whenever possible, an adult should be available to provide support to the child.

Use Time-Away Effectively.   Although *time-away* has long been used to deescalate behavior, the disadvantages of this technique are being noted. These include the opportunity for the distressed child to damage the area of time-away, to make distracting noise, to leave the area, or to forget he or she is being punished. There is also concern that it might be too much to ask a very young child to regain inhibitory control alone and that appropriate behavior cannot be taught when a child is in isolation. If time-away is being used, Cook, Richardson-Gibbs, and Dotson (2018, pp. 85–86) offer the following important considerations:

1. Make sure the child understands exactly what behavior will result in a time-away.
2. Warn the child, calmly, only once.
3. Be sure the child is within the teacher's view at all times.
4. Keep the time-away very short.
5. Be positive at the end of the time-away; praise the child for being in control of him- or herself. Help the child choose and engage in another activity.
6. Monitor the behavior of other children to be certain they are not giving the child either positive or negative attention.

Deal Consistently with Temper Tantrums.   Temper tantrums that are only bids for attention may go away when they are consistently ignored. If the tantrums persist, then the child becomes a candidate for the six-step time-away process just outlined. Teachers should make calm and nonthreatening statements, such as "It seems that you are unable to play with us right now. I hope you will be able to work with us after some time in the 'thinking corner.'" Once the child is back and participating appropriately, reinforcement should be given for his or her participation in the activity.

Mutual cooperation with parents is essential to establishing firm, consistent guidelines. The adult reactions should not be punitive or display anger when firmly redirecting the child. Above all, adults must be certain that a tantrum does not result in the child's getting his or her own way in an inappropriate manner. The child's day should be organized so that numerous opportunities exist for the child to get attention in constructive ways.

Help Overactive Children Feel Good About Themselves.   Many children who overact are angry underneath and expend energy covering up feelings of insecurity or vulnerability. A possible primary objective for such children is to view themselves as capable of developing inhibitory control. Experience has shown that when these children begin to feel like responsible individuals, their need for demonstrating negative behavior diminishes.

Healthy young children enjoy pleasing adults whom they can trust. When these children misbehave, teachers should ask themselves whether something they are doing or not doing is causing the problem. Have the children been allowed to change activities frequently enough? Is too much being demanded? Are the children being allowed to constructively express their feelings verbally and physically by pounding clay or knocking down tenpins? Is the frequency of positive reinforcement at an optimum level? The teacher's responsibility is to prevent children from losing inhibitory and developing feelings of shame, guilt, and poor self-confidence.

The curriculum needs to be reviewed periodically to ensure realistic developmentally and individually appropriate expectations. Experts caution educators to beware of stressing academics to the detriment of social and emotional development. It is suggested that early educators avoid emphasizing academics during the preschool years. Instead, they are encouraged to concentrate on certain prerequisite skills, such as listening, being able to relate past experiences to present activities, and using and respecting the tools of learning.

Finally, helpful teachers (1) express their acceptance of children's feelings, negative and positive; (2) reassure overactive children that one of the teacher's jobs is to protect children from harming others or themselves; (3) exhibit confidence in children's abilities to improve inhibitory control; and (4) demonstrate that children will be allowed greater opportunities to control their own behavior as they exhibit increased self-restraint and appropriate expressions of feelings.

A Word About Medication.   Perhaps the most controversial method of handling children who lack sufficient inhibitory control involves using psychotropic drugs. The use of psychotropic drugs with preschoolers is increasing. Methylphenidate hydrochloride (Ritalin) and dextroamphetamine sulfate (Dexedrine) appear to be used most often with preschool-age children (Rappley, 2006). However, there is evidence to suggest that side effects may be stronger and different from those observed in older patients. It should also be noted that the Food and Drug Administration guidelines for methylphenidate-based products do not recommend use in children younger than 6 years (Kollins & Greenhill, 2006). Furthermore, the American Academy of Pediatrics recommends behavioral therapy as the first line of treatment for preschoolers (4–5 years old) with ADHD. The primary care physician "may prescribe methylphenidate if the behavior interventions do not provide significant improvement and there is moderate-to-severe continuing disturbance in the child's function" (Subcommittee on Attention-Deficit/Hyperactivity Disorder, Steering Committee on Quality Improvement and Management, 2011, p. 2).

Considering the diagnostic difficulties involving young children and lack of sufficient treatment studies, a cautious approach to the use of stimulant medication is definitely warranted. Medication should *never* be used as the only treatment. Its use should be considered only when the hyperactivity is extreme and when medication is part of a well-designed and well-monitored, multimodal management program.

Encouraging Children Who Are Reluctant to Participate

Children who are reluctant to participate in activities are rarely a bother to teachers and classmates. Shy or timid children are easily overlooked. Research suggests that social withdrawal in early childhood is a risk factor for a wide range of negative outcomes (Rubin, Coplan, & Bowker, 2009). Special attention is important for children whose behavior ranges from timid and inhibited to completely withdrawn; otherwise, their needs may go unnoticed. Such children usually separate themselves physically, avoid group activities and verbal interaction, seem afraid to try new tasks, sometimes appear disinterested, and may seek comfort through self-stimulation (e.g., rocking, twisting their hair, or thumb sucking). These children lack the very behaviors that would normally bring them into social contact, such as looking, talking, approaching, and playing with others. Teachers often find themselves responsible for helping these children develop approach and responsiveness behaviors.

In addition to lacking social contact behavior, some of these children may be preoccupied with self-stimulation or with daydreaming and fantasy (Miller, 2016). By being so absorbed in their imaginations or their repetitive acts of sensory stimulation, they miss social cues. This lack of attention interferes with opportunities for social learning available to children who are not isolated. Children who also experience language delays are at an even greater disadvantage. Even if they are paying attention, they may not be able to understand directions or to ask necessary questions. They have or take few opportunities to demonstrate what they know and understand. Skill and patience are absolutely necessary to help these children develop the trusting relationships they so desperately need.

Prepare the Child's Environment.   Throughout this text, the importance of thoughtful preparation of the environment is stressed as a means of preventing behavioral challenges. For reluctant or inhibited children, on the one hand, the teacher needs to establish a climate of safety, predictability, and consistency. On the other hand, the teacher needs to extend an acceptance of his or her responses, however limited, and provide nurturance, nourishment, and individual attention regardless of the quality or quantity of the child's initial output. By focusing on reducing stress and creating a nonthreatening atmosphere, the child may become more actively involved.

Children who are reluctant to participate appreciate a small safe place to which they can retreat. The place must not be like the time-out area. The child should be able to view the classroom activities from the safe place. Many inhibited children learn a great deal from watching others. Through watching, they may develop the confidence necessary to attempt a new or different task.

As the child becomes more trustful, the "watching chair" can be moved closer to the ongoing activity. At an intermediate point, identical play materials can be placed within the child's reach. The teacher should not coax the child. No attention should be given to the child unless he or she attempts the activity either alone or with the others. If this occurs, then positive reinforcement should be given immediately, quietly, and inconspicuously. The teacher must know what the child enjoys. A smile, rather than a public announcement of the child's participation, would probably be more appropriate.

These children feel more secure if materials are kept in the same place every day. They want a definite place for their own objects, including crayons and coats. The teacher should not force them to share until they are ready to do so. Consistency in routines and procedures helps them predict daily activities and therefore feel more comfortable. The children must be prepared in advance for any new or strange situations such as visitors, field trips, or fire drills.

Promote Peer Assistance.   Seating nonparticipating children near relatively quiet but competent children can do wonders in promoting peer assistance. Experience has shown that extremely shy children often respond to another child much more quickly than to an adult. Caring, concerned children who do not move too loudly or quickly are helpful peer models and facilitators, and they do not threaten the insecure child. Such children can be prompted to invite the reluctant child to participate without begging for involvement. As noted earlier in the story of Lance, sometimes the best approach is for the child or perhaps the teacher to ask for help—for example, "Johnny, will you please help me clean up this paint" or "Please hold the picture." Help can begin with an independent activity, such as passing snacks, and can graduate to a cooperative activity, such as two children going to get juice. Helping others gives the child an easy basis to establish relationships; at the same time, self-confidence can be enhanced.

Consider Curricular Adaptations.   Like most children, inhibited children need a predictable schedule that includes both group time and individual time. Group size can be increased as the child builds confidence. Some children who are unwilling to express themselves in conversation join in a song because they feel less conspicuous. They may sit on the edge initially. The teacher should not rush them. In the beginning, peripheral involvement such as holding pictures rather than naming them can be encouraged. Many of these children participate physically before they participate verbally. If a story is being read and followed by questions, call on the reluctant child last and then do not coax. Teachers must remember that the child must set the pace.

Some young children interact with pets before they interact with people. Letting such children take care of pets helps them feel that they are contributing to the welfare of the pets and to the classrooms. Their involvement also gives them a chance to receive the approval they seek.

Socially isolated children often respond to the social learning principles of modeling and imitation. Teachers should therefore seriously plan opportunities for these children to observe positive, pleasant social interaction, as discussed earlier.

Individual attention is sometimes the key to getting reluctant children to participate in instructional activities. Teachers should approach them calmly, speaking slowly and clearly, and state exactly what they expect. They should present activities that they are reasonably certain are interesting to the child. Teachers must try to couple their attention to the child with something pleasant. They should help children associate feelings of enjoyment when they see or think of their teacher. If the child refuses to become involved, then the teacher should merely place the materials nearby and let the child watch. This procedure should be followed at snack time as well. The teacher should not become anxious if the child does not eat. The more uncomfortable attention the child receives, the less he or she is likely to eat.

An effective strategy for facilitating engagement includes the following. Begin by staying close to the reluctant child. Then suggest that he or she join a group: "Tim and Laura could use someone to help build a bridge. Why not give them a hand, Bob?" At this point, the teacher should move away, returning to give positive attention if the child acts on the suggestion. Teachers then may wish to give additional suggestions if they seem to facilitate involvement.

Provide Opportunities for Expressing Feelings.   As mentioned earlier, the expression of a full range of emotions is essential to healthy emotional development (Greenspan & Wieder, 2005). Inhibited, withdrawn children typically experience many unexpressed emotions. Special encouragement thus must be given to self-expression. Drawing, painting, puppetry, clay, water play, finger painting, and music can provide opportunities for this expression. Of course, these children must not be forced, and their efforts must be rewarded without regard to their products. As trust develops, teachers can gradually encourage verbal expression by asking questions such as "Is the girl in your picture very upset or unhappy today?" Like active listening, this approach helps children feel understood and accepted. They can attribute their unpleasant feelings to the object in the drawing and thus find these feelings to be less threatening.

Pictures, especially photographs of the children themselves, are especially useful when talking about feelings. Pictures that show clear facial expressions, definite gestures, or obvious effects of the child's actions on others should be chosen. Such pictures help the child to perceive how another may feel and to discover cause-and-effect relationships. Guided discussion should focus on describing what is happening, what will happen, and how those in the picture might feel.

Strategies for Supporting Children Who Are Shy or "Slow to Warm Up."   Above all, teachers must be conscious of the need to help all children feel good about themselves so they may find the courage to develop the social contact skills critical to healthy social involvement. One factor to consider is temperament, which was discussed in more detail earlier in this chapter. Whereas some children have social-emotional challenges, others may simply be shy or "slow to warm up." The teacher should begin with step-by-step presentations of noncompetitive tasks that the child can achieve. Gentle positive reinforcement for effort coupled with the development of a trusting relationship is essential. When children participate little, it is extremely difficult to manipulate the environment to ensure an optimal reward-to-punishment ratio. Avoiding punishment may be the most efficient means of helping the child build confidence and trust in the beginning.

Because a child's inhibited, withdrawn behavior can be a developmental pattern later associated with serious disturbance, it is imperative that teachers work closely with parents, counselors, and psychologists. When a child's severe reluctance persists after a couple of months of consciously structuring the environment and creating nonthreatening opportunities for involvement, the teacher should not hesitate to seek help. After giving the child a reasonable time to become adjusted, considering the child's age and previous experiences (or lack of them), the teacher takes careful observational notes. The teacher should study these carefully to see whether any progress is being made, and he or she should discuss minimal progress with the school psychologist or another mental health worker to determine whether additional evaluation or a change in programming is necessary.

Strategies for Supporting Dual-Language Learners and Preventing Challenging Behaviors.   Given that it is natural to communicate through behavior, it is important that practitioners understand what children are attempting to communicate even when they are not using words. It is especially important to learn strategies to interpret a child's actions when English is new to a child. Understanding challenging behaviors that are temporary reactions to language differences is critical. Behaviors often misinterpreted include not talking, difficulty following directions, and difficulty expressing ideas or responding to questions. If the impact of learning a new language is not considered, such behavior might be attributed to developmental delays, innate behavioral tendencies, or something else other than language differences.

It is not unusual for children learning a new language to go through a nonverbal period during which they are gathering information about how to communicate in their new language. During this period, children may choose not to speak, may isolate themselves, or may pretend to understand, and, therefore, may be inconsistent in responding to directions. We must remember that behavior is a form of communication.

Nemeth and Brillante (2011) offered the following strategies for programs that include children who are dual-language learners:

- Decrease large-group sessions in favor of small groups and one-on-one interactions.
- Speak slowly, repeat key words, avoid slang, simplify sentences, and allow more time for processing and responding to what has been said.
- Enhance communication with nonverbal cues such as gestures and sign language.
- Encourage children who speak the same language or are just caring individuals to help one another.
- Provide a comfortable place where a child can be away from the constant pressure of trying to understand and be understood by others.
- Keep schedules predictable to help eliminate the stress of trying to anticipate what will come next.
- Develop collaborative relationships with bilingual and ESL colleagues as well as the families who can help make the child more comfortable. They can assist you in recognizing what a child is trying to communicate through actions and can be supportive of your efforts.

Effective Use of Reinforcement

Research suggests that lack of achievement may be related to children's failing to link acceptable performance with their own efforts or abilities. They may instead attribute their successes to chance, task ease, or powerful others (Weiner, 2005). Some children have the tendency to attribute successful performance to external causes. Therefore, teachers must be extremely careful in the wording they use to acknowledge children's positive behaviors. They must help children learn how to attribute success to themselves rather than to something outside of themselves, as discussed in the following section.

Give Credit Where Credit Is Due

Praise must describe in specific terms the behavior that the teacher wishes to have repeated either by the child being praised or by those who are watching at the time.

Furthermore, the praise must give the child credit for his or her efforts or abilities. Consider these statements: "Darren, I am proud of you. You listened carefully to my directions and then tried to do exactly what you were asked to do." If the teacher had said, "Thank you, Darren, for being good," Darren would have no idea what behavior to repeat in the future if he wished to "be good." By being specific, Darren learned that carefully following directions and trying to do what was asked of him are considered "being good." Such explicit statements point out to others what behavior is expected; at the same time, Darren is helped to realize that his efforts will be noticed and are of value. Note that effort rather than outcome was emphasized.

Young children, and especially young children with disabilities, must be encouraged to focus on *effort* rather than on outcome. After all, they may be able to control their efforts even though successful outcomes are sometimes out of reach. Consider this statement: "Darren, I'm so glad you have a new hearing aid. You were able to follow my directions." Darren now feels that he could succeed because of the hearing aid, not necessarily because of his effort. He may or may not put forth effort in the future, especially once his hearing aid is no longer a novelty. Consider how easy it would be for the teacher to say: "Darren, I appreciate how you followed my directions and stayed in your seat." Now, Darren will know that his *effort* to stay in his seat was noted and appreciated. He is more likely to put forth the effort to follow such directions again in the future. Chapter 4 elaborates on how to enhance effectance motivation and assist in the development of growth mindsets through appropriate reinforcers (e.g., specific praise).

Based on a review of studies related to the use of praise with preschoolers at risk for behavior disorders, Hester, Hendrickson, and Gable (2009) identified critical factors that help make praise effective. These include *contingency,* that is, when a target behavior occurs, praise must follow as well as *specificity* related to the target behavior. Praise must occur *immediately* and *consistently* after the occurrence of the target behavior. Teachers should also observe the *effect on the child* because not every child reacts positively to praise. Research also found that *characteristics of the consequence* are important because praise should be enthusiastic, varied, and matched to a child's behavior, developmental level, and preferences; and that *opportunities for children to respond* should be correlated with teachers' frequency of praise. Therefore, keeping in mind the importance of immediate praise that focuses on the child's **effort** and is sensitive to the child's developmental level of understanding is more likely to help the child repeat desired behavior (Dweck, 2016).

Ignore Minor Disruptive Behaviors

Some irritating behaviors will disappear if they receive no attention or reward from anyone. Teachers must be astute observers. Even though a teacher may ignore a behavior, it does not mean that other children are not giving attention to it. Simply ignoring the behavior does not work in such a situation. The child is getting attention of some kind and is possibly modeling inappropriate behavior for other children.

Some children use troublesome four-letter words, stick out their tongues, or tap their tables merely to get a reaction from the teacher. Observant teachers usually guess when this is the case. Ignoring behavior can be effective as long as the teacher realizes that the child may continue the behavior until some kind of attention is given. The answer is to find a way to give the child positive attention. This can be done by directing the child to an activity while simultaneously ignoring the undesired behavior. Depending on the child, ignoring alone may just bring on more disruptive behavior.

If the child's challenging behavior is intended to obtain attention, then "planned ignoring" is a strategy designed to decrease the target behavior by withdrawing the reinforcement of attention. Similar to factors related to the effective use of praise, Hester and colleagues (2009) also identified critical factors for effective planned ignoring from research with preschoolers at risk for behavior disorders. These include *pairing planned ignoring with reinforcement strategies, contingency, immediacy, specificity, characteristics of the consequence,* and *effect on the target behavior.*

Minimize the Use of Negative Consequences

Punishment may decrease the rate at which inappropriate behaviors occur, but it can also produce negative side effects, such as fear, tension, and withdrawal. Any aggressive acts by an adult also provide undesirable models for children to imitate.

Rewards are considered to be any action or statement that builds a child's self-confidence or anything that makes the child feel good about him- or herself. Punishment refers to any action or statement that decreases a child's self-confidence or makes him or her feel less worthy, so it should be used judiciously.

Careful preventive observation is essential. When a teacher sees a child begin to lose control or interest because of frustration, fatigue, or hunger, the teacher must quickly use redirection by changing the child's activity or focus of attention. Teachers can develop special nonverbal signals such as a "look" to be given as reminders to children who seem about to misbehave. Then immediate reward or reinforcement can be given when a child increases the effort to control his or her behavior.

Punishment in the form of *logical and natural consequences* can have an informative effect if used wisely. Punishment that is part of rule setting in the classroom can be a safe natural consequence predicted by those who do not follow classroom rules. When linked directly to their behavior, children can see the relationship between their causative act and the resulting effect.

If children know that hitting others or otherwise fooling around during circle time will cause them to be asked to leave a motivating activity, then they will see the consequence as justified and directly caused by their behavior. They will not see the teacher as arbitrary or themselves as not responsible for the outcome. They will know how to prevent the disliked consequence in the future if the teacher has specifically stated why they were punished. The teacher might say, "Vicky, you must take a break. You have hit Susie and we must not hurt others."

Walker, Shea, and Bauer (2006) provide the following guidelines to those who find it absolutely necessary to use punishment:

1. Specify and communicate the punishable behavior to the children by means of classroom rules for behavior.
2. Post the rules where the children can see them and review them with the group frequently.
3. Provide models of acceptable behavior.
4. Apply the punishment immediately.
5. Apply the punishment consistently, not whimsically.
6. Be fair in using the punishment (what is good for Peter is good for Paul).

Of course, these rules have to be adapted for use with very young children. Picture symbols might be used instead of words when listing the rules. Walker and colleagues also listed 14 reasons why teachers should avoid using either physical (spankings) or psychological (derogatory statements) punishment. Basically, other forms of behavior management are more effective and avoid damaging effects on children. More important, punishment bruises the already fragile developing self-confidence of children.

Punishment that is in any way derogatory or demeaning must not be used. Only punishments that are logical, safe, natural, and unattached to the child's person or personality should be used. Table 6.2 illustrates the importance of this suggestion. Acceptable punishments, when kept to a minimum and used as a last resort, include deprivation of privileges (including time-away) and compensation for intentional wrongdoing, such as picking up deliberately spilled puzzle pieces. Remember, however, that any form of punishment should be administered with firm kindness to avoid becoming derogatory or demeaning.

Positive Behavior Support (PBS)

Traditional approaches to the modification of behavior have concentrated on eliminating unacceptable behavior by applying negative consequences such as time-away. Recent approaches to encouraging appropriate behavior and decreasing challenging behavior focus on preventing challenging behaviors by analyzing the cause and/or purpose (function) of the unacceptable behavior. This approach, which is an important step in reducing challenging behaviors, involves determination of the communicative function of the behavior by conducting a functional behavior assessment in order to develop a positive behavior support (PBS) plan.

Note that the focus is on facilitating social and other functional skills by using strategies that are respectful and evidence-based and not only on decreasing challenging behaviors. A functional behavior assessment is a respectful evidence-based practice that involves (1) understanding the *antecedents* of behavior as possible triggers of inappropriate behavior, (2) analysis of typical *consequences* of the behavior (i.e., what usually happens as a result of the behavior), (3) identifying the *function* of the behavior, (4) determining those contextual conditions that might best support the positive behavior of a particular child, and (5) identifying appropriate *replacement* behaviors. See the additional discussion of PBS in Chapter 4.

According to Fox, Dunlap, and Cushing (2002), the PBS approach determines the function of a particular behavior and its relationship to specific antecedents and consequences. Through careful observation of the child in daily environments and working in partnership with the child's family, a PBS plan is generated. Rather than manipulating the consequences, a PBS approach focuses more on changing the antecedent conditions and on teaching appropriate communication and social skills as *replacement behaviors*.

Factors such as low frustration tolerance, emotional ability, lack of impulse control, and tactile and auditory hypersensitivity are common characteristics of children with disabilities. As a result of these characteristics, certain antecedent situations may be more likely to trigger unacceptable behaviors in children. Although any child, regardless of whether he or she has a disability, can develop patterns of behavior that are disruptive or are considered unacceptable, the characteristics of certain disability conditions may increase the likelihood that a child will develop a behavior problem.

Table 6.2 Logical Consequences Versus Punishment

The Behavior (What Happened)	Logical and Natural Consequence	Punishment
Child spills milk.	Child cleans up spill.	"You are so clumsy." "Don't you ever watch what you're doing?" "You messed up again."
Child grabs another child's toy.	Child returns the toy.	"You're a brat again." "Must you be so bad?" "You're always the selfish bully."
Child "forgets" to hang up coat.	Child hangs up coat.	"Can't you remember anything?" "How many times have I told you . . . ?"
Child yells loudly in supermarket.	Parent says softly, "Let's practice a soft voice." Child returns to the market and practices being quiet.	"Shut up; you're a bad girl." "Good girls are quiet in public." "I'll never take you to the store again."

Using Behavioral Analysis to Understand Disruptive Behavior

In preventing and managing a behavior that is truly disruptive (e.g., screaming) or potentially harmful (e.g., biting, hitting, or self-injurious behavior), it is helpful to use a systematic, functional behavioral analysis procedure to determine the function or purpose of that behavior. Any given behavior may have different functions. *The type of behavior does not tell you the function of the behavior. The same behavior in two different children may have two completely different functions.*

Challenging behaviors have four possible functions, as discussed below (Minahan & Rapport, 2012):

1. *To get attention.* Frequently, the primary motivation of unacceptable behavior is to gain attention and interaction from a caregiver or significant adult. An effective general strategy that can significantly reduce behavior problems is to *make sure you connect with each child on a supportive, one-on-one basis frequently throughout the day.* This means being at the child's eye level, patiently listening to both words and feelings. A young child's seeking interaction and attention from a significant adult should not automatically be considered inappropriate or atypical. It is the particular *way* in which the child obtains attention that may be problematic. For children who often engage in inappropriate behavior to get attention, an effective strategy is to provide the child with some brief special attention before the child engages in the inappropriate behavior. It is also helpful to attend to the child immediately when he or she engages in an appropriate behavior ("catch them being good"). The following are common attention-getting behaviors:

   - Running away
   - Leaving an activity
   - Picking on peers
   - Having a tantrum
   - Removing clothing
   - Destroying property
   - Turning water/lights on or off

2. *To escape something unpleasant.* In some cases, the child may be trying to escape an *internal state.* For example, the child may be in some kind of discomfort or may feel extremely stressed or anxious because of physiological or biological factors rather than external conditions.

More often, the child is trying to escape *environmental* conditions that cause stress, anxiety, or discomfort. For instance, a child with very sensitive hearing (often the case in children who have autism) may experience discomfort in a noisy room. Analysis of antecedent conditions and events is critical to understanding the escape function of a behavior. Common environmental conditions that may cause stress or discomfort for some children are the following:

   - Noisy or highly resonant acoustic environment
   - Too many children in close proximity
   - Cluttered or disorganized physical environment
   - Confusing, unpredictable environment and schedule
   - Large, open spaces with no boundaries

Some children may be trying to escape a specific task or activity they dislike. For example, a child may hate brushing his teeth or may dislike the tactile sensation of certain materials such as finger paint or sand.

Some "escape" behaviors are obvious, such as running away or refusing to stay seated. Just as often, however, the behaviors are less easily interpreted. Consider the following list of behaviors that are frequently caused by a need to escape:

- Screaming
- Throwing objects
- Hitting or biting
- Self-injurious behavior (e.g., biting own hand)
- Self-stimulatory behavior (e.g., hand flapping or rocking, which often serves to block out the environment)

3. *To gain access to something (tangible) the child wants.* In this case, the child engages in unacceptable behavior to *gain access* to a toy, activity, or area he or she finds pleasurable. Engaging in a negative behavior to obtain an object is usually fairly obvious. Gaining access to something less tangible may not be obvious. For instance, a child who frequently runs away may be running away not to escape or to gain attention but because she loves being outside.

4. *To obtain sensory stimulation.* In this situation, the child engages in a behavior that is internally pleasing or self-stimulating or to remove a sensation that is uncomfortable (e.g., pain, boredom). For example, rocking back and forth is enjoyable and may calm a child who is feeling frustrated; or for a child who is bored, blinking his eyes may provide sensory stimulation. A variety of behaviors that are visual, auditory, tactile, kinesthetic, olfactory or gustatory, proprioceptive, or vestibular may serve a sensory stimulation function.

Careful observation of the behavior, the antecedents, and the consequences can help accurately determine the function of a behavior. For example, a child may turn the lights on and off not because he wants the teacher's attention but because he loves the visual effect of the lights going off and on. Furthermore, it is important to remember that a behavior may serve more than one function for a child. Teachers should conduct a functional behavior assessment to determine the function of challenging behaviors and to implement relevant interventions to decrease the behavior or teach a replacement behavior or skill.

Designing Positive Behavior Support Plans for Young Children with Disabilities

Understanding Problem Behaviors as Communication. Often problems occur in children who cannot express themselves verbally. Many children with disabilities have limited language skills and frequently express strongly felt needs in nonverbal ways. All too often, these nonverbal communications are inappropriate and are then identified as behavior problems.

As discussed earlier, an important step in reducing problem behaviors is to determine the communicative function of the behavior. It may be helpful to view the child's behavior as an attempt to communicate the need to escape or the desire for attention, to request a desired object or activity, or to obtain sensory stimulation, as previously described. Once this is determined, a more appropriate communicative behavior can be taught. This new behavior is referred to as replacement behavior, as mentioned earlier.

Exhibit 6.4 depicts a step-by-step approach adapted from Cook et al. (2018) for designing and implementing a positive behavior support plan. By following this approach and providing support for positive behavior, practitioners are more likely to prevent or reduce challenging behaviors while promoting those that are positive.

The Pyramid Model

A current popular framework for promoting social-emotional development and addressing challenging behavior in young children is the Pyramid Model (Hemmeter, Snyder, Fox, & James, 2016). This model has been implemented widely in early childhood programs and consists of the four following levels going from the bottom to the top of the pyramid:

1. **Nurturing and responsive caregiving relationships** involve universal promotion practices, such as supporting children's play; responding to children's conversations; supporting communication of children with special needs; providing positive feedback and encouraging appropriate behavior; and building relationships with children.

2. **High-quality supportive environments** also involve universal promotion practices, such as providing adequate materials, defined play centers, a balanced schedule, structured transitions, clear directions, individualized instructions for children who need support; teaching and promoting a limited number of rules; and designing activities that engage children.

3. **Targeted social emotional supports** are secondary prevention practices that include teaching children to identify and express emotions, and teaching and supporting self-regulation, strategies for handling anger and disappointment, social problem solving, cooperative responding, and friendship skills and collaboration with peers.

4. **Intensive individualized interventions are tertiary interventions** that include convening a team to develop interventions; collecting data to determine the problem behavior; developing individualized behavior support strategies and implementing the behavior support plan; conducting ongoing monitoring of child progress; revising the plan as needed; and collaborating with families and colleagues to implement the plan.

Level 4 interventions are based on information gained from implementation of a "functional behavioral assessment" (FBA). This functional behavioral assessment allows staff to generate and test hypotheses regarding the following:

Characteristics of the target behavior: specific description of the behavior that the team agrees needs to be decreased or modified (e.g., *child hits only one specific peer with his closed fist*).

Antecedents of the target behavior: what occurs *prior* to the behavior (e.g., *children transition to circle time, where they are prompted to sit close to each other on the floor. "Victim" child sits near target child and leans sideways, against him. Target child hits him*).

Consequences of the behavior: events/circumstances that occur *after* the child engages in the behavior (e.g., *Adult scolds target child and moves "victim" child away, out of his reach*).

Based on this information, specific interventions are planned and implemented, with careful documentation as to their effectiveness. If necessary, Level 4 interventions and supports will be modified and documented again.

Differences in cultural values, expectations, and child-rearing practices (discussed in Chapter 2) may influence children's behaviors in a preschool classroom. Teachers may use a matrix across classroom routines to obtain input from families about behavioral expectations in order to discuss and minimize differences in expectations

Exhibit 6.4

Positive Behavior Support Procedure

Step 1:   **Conduct an "A-B-C" analysis to carefully observe the behavior over a period (at least 1 week).**

A is for "antecedent":
What happens just before the behavior occurs?
B is the inappropriate behavior:
What does the child do?
C is the "consequence":
What happens immediately following the behavior?

Step 2:   **Carefully describe the unacceptable behavior.**

What does the child actually do? Describe the sequence:
　　Child looks at teacher.
　　Child begins to scream.
　　As teacher approaches, child runs toward door.

When does child do it?
Where does the behavior occur?
Who is usually present when the behavior occurs?

Step 3:   **Hypothesize about why this behavior occurs.**

Is the cause internal (e.g., medication, illness, fatigue, low threshold, frustration)?
Is the child trying to escape?
Is the child trying to get attention?
Is the child trying to obtain a desired object or activity?
Is the child engaging in sensory stimulation?

Step 4:   **Determine a possible communicative value of the behavior.**

Is the child using this behavior to try to tell us something? For example:
"I'm in pain."
"Let me out of here!"
"Please touch me (look at me, talk to me, come close to me)."
"I would rather play with the Legos or be outside on the swing."

Step 5:   **Identify possible behavior "triggers."**
Use information from Step 1 regarding the antecedent. What sets off the child's behavior?

Step 6:   **Plan environmental changes or changes in antecedent events to reduce triggering behavior. For example:**

Place certain items out of reach.
Keep other children a certain distance away.
Change acoustic characteristics of room to dampen sound.

Step 7:   **Identify replacement behavior, if appropriate. For example:**

Child will make sign for "Stop" rather than hitting.
Child will point to card that says "Quiet Zone" when he or she needs "time-away."
Child will sign "All done" when he or she is full rather than dumping food on the table.

Step 8:   **Carefully plan with staff what the consequence will be if the behavior still occurs occasionally. For example:**

Teacher will remove child from the play area.
All adults will move away from the child. (If an extinction procedure—for instance, planned ignoring—is used as a consequence, the frequency or intensity of the negative behavior to obtain attention may initially increase before it begins to decrease.)

Step 9:   **Monitor the frequency and intensity of behavior to make sure it is decreasing.**

Note: Teachers must realize the behavior is not going to suddenly disappear overnight using this procedure. Thus, it is important to measure the behavior periodically (e.g., how many times per day the behavior occurs or how long the behavior episode lasts) to determine if it is gradually decreasing. Often teachers think the procedure is not working and abandon it too quickly.

between home and school. As discussed earlier, young children who are new immigrants to the United States may be at risk for developing challenging behaviors, particularly social withdrawal, because of their family's stressful immigrant experiences, lack of English skills, and low socioeconomic and political status (Allen & Steed, 2016). In these cases, children and families may also benefit from access to resources in their communities.

Enhanced eText Application Exercise 6.3
In this exercise, you can apply what you have learned in this chapter about techniques to reduce and replace challenging behaviors through careful environmental planning and positive behavior support.

Use of Social Stories

Once a target behavior has been identified through careful observation, a **social story** can be an effective intervention strategy that teaches self-awareness, self-management skills, and social skills. Social stories originated with Carol Gray more than 20 years ago as a way of helping children understand social situations, expectations, social cues, and socially appropriate behavior. This technique has come to be used readily with children with autism spectrum disorders. Nevertheless, it is a valuable tool for use with all young children who exhibit lack of inhibitory control, have difficulty in new situations, or otherwise need assistance in developing age-appropriate social skills. These are brief descriptive stories that provide accurate information about what to expect in a situation and how to act appropriately in it. They are usually written for a particular child who has difficulty when encountering specific situations, such as transitioning from one activity to another, being expected to share toys during outdoor time, or adjusting to a substitute teacher or new babysitter.

Social stories should be made up of the following four types of sentences (Gray, 2010):

1. *Descriptive sentences*—tell where situations take place, who is there, what they are doing, and why. *Example:* "At circle time, we find our carpet squares, sit on them, are quiet, and look at Mrs. Green so we can hear what she wants us to do."

2. *Directive sentences*—describe what behavior is expected of the child. *Example:*

   "I will look at Mrs. Green and listen quietly. When I want to talk, I will raise my hand."

3. *Perspective sentences*—describe the feeling and reactions of the child and others who are there. *Example:* "When I shout out, Mrs. Green and the other children get upset. When I wait to hear my name, everyone listens to me. It is fun to hear what everyone has to say."

4. *Control sentences*—After the social story is read, the child states or draws strategies to help him or her remember the information from it. *Example:* "When we take turns and listen to each other, we have fun and are happy."

It takes practice to write good social stories, and they should be created for an individual child's situation. Consult the Gray Center on Social Learning and Understanding at http://carolgraysocialstories.com/ and the work of Carol Gray (2010) if you are just beginning to use social stories as a tool to enhance social skills and facilitate self-control in young children. Examples of scripted stories of social situations can be found on the website for the Center on Social and Emotional Foundations for Early Learning at http://csefel.vanderbilt.edu/resources/ (from the home page, select *Practical Strategies* from the Resources by Type menu, then *Scripted Stories for Social Situations* from the resulting list).

Remember that especially for young children with limited language comprehension and for children with autism who often process picture representation better than spoken language, pictures or photographs should accompany social stories. It needs to be understood that this technique is totally different from the use of visual supports such as photos or picture cards to support daily routines and schedules. Some helpful hints are included in Exhibit 6.5; a sample Social Story is illustrated in Exhibit 6.6.

Special Considerations for Working with Children with Adverse Childhood Experiences

Adverse Childhood Experiences (ACEs) include categories of child maltreatment (e.g., physical, sexual, psychological abuse and neglect) and household dysfunction (e.g., substance abuse, mental illness, caregiver treated violently, and incarceration). ACEs have been found to have a life-long negative effect on health and the quality of life (Centers for Disease Control and Prevention, 2016). Research

Video Example from

You Tube

Enhanced eText
Video Example 6.8
Carol Gray: What Are Social Stories™
https://www.youtube.com/watch?v=vjlIYYbVIrI
Carol Gray's approach to social stories is illustrated in this video.

Exhibit 6.5
Developing a Social Story

1. Always be positive. Avoid words like *not, never,* or *always*.
2. Try to keep to one topic per story, and be very specific about what behavior you are trying to teach or change.
3. Carefully observe the child in the situation under concern. Try to view the situation through the eyes of the child.
4. Include feeling words that describe what the child might be feeling, should be feeling, or what others might be thinking or feeling.
5. For every directive or control sentence, there should be two to five descriptive and/or perspective sentences.
6. Write in the first person.
7. Depending on the child's cognitive level, you may want to address only one behavioral concept in each story.
8. If pictures are used to accompany the story, be certain that the pictures also fit within the child's developmental skill level.
9. Stories can be more effective when read just before a situation in which the problem behavior is likely to occur.
10. Modeling the desired behavior just after reading the story may help ensure positive results.
11. Observe carefully to be certain that the social story is successful. If not, try varying the time and setting in which the story is read.
12. If the story is successful, its use should be gradually faded away. The story can be reintroduced as needed.

Exhibit 6.6

Waiting for My Turn to Talk

Talking is fun. All of us like to talk.
It is hard to hear when lots of us talk. We need to take turns.
Mrs. Garcia, our teacher, likes us to raise our hands when we want to talk.
It is hard to remember to raise my hand but I will try.
It will feel good to get a turn after I raise my hand.
I will try to sit quietly and raise my hand so Mrs. Garcia will want me to have a turn.
It will be fun to have a turn.

with a sample of urban children found that ACEs in early childhood were associated with teacher-reported below-average academic and literacy skills and attention, social, and behavior problems in kindergarten (Jimenez, Wade, Lin, Morrow, & Reichman, 2016).

As discussed in Chapter 2, safe, stable, and nurturing relationships and environments have a positive impact on the development and learning of young children. Programs to ameliorate or prevent ACEs include home-visiting programs for pregnant women and families with newborns, parent-training programs, mental illness and substance abuse treatment, partner violence prevention, social support for parents, high-quality child care, and financial support for families living in poverty (Centers for Disease Control and Prevention, 2016).

Unfortunately, given the complexity and stresses of life and family situations, some children with disabilities are at risk for ACEs. For instance, children with disabilities are the most likely to be victims of abuse and neglect (Charlesworth, 2017). According to the Children's Defense Fund (CDF) (2014), every 47 seconds, a child in the United States is found to be abused or neglected. In addition, studies suggest that children with disabilities are more likely to be abused than their peers without disabilities (Stalker & McArthur, 2012). Therefore, it comes as no surprise that related legislation would be in place. The key legislation dealing with child abuse and neglect is the Child Abuse Prevention and Treatment Act (CAPTA), originally enacted in 1974 and most recently amended and reauthorized in 2003 within the Keeping Children and Families Safe Act (Public Law [PL] 108-36). Part C of the Individuals with Disabilities Education Act of 2004 (IDEA) contains complementary language requiring the referral for services of any child who "(A) is involved in a substantiated case of child abuse or neglect; or (B) is identified as affected by illegal substance abuse, or withdrawal symptoms resulting from prenatal drug exposure" (Part C, Section 637 [a][6][A & B]).

Probably the single most important intervention strategy for children with ACEs is the establishment of a predictable and safe environment. Over a period of time, a responsive, predictable environment may provide the child with the support necessary to enable him or her to build the resilience to explore the physical environment as well as relationships with others (Berson & Baggerly, 2009). Earlier discussions of classroom routines, both in this chapter and in Chapter 4, provide important suggestions for designing and implementing predictable environments. Programs that depend primarily on children's self-direction or that require children to accept major responsibility for their use of time may provide too much freedom and ambiguity for children who have been maltreated.

Research suggests that severe maltreatment can result in **reactive attachment disorder (RAD)** (Haugaard & Hazan, 2004). A basic feature of children with RAD is inappropriate social relating. These children either are indiscriminate in seeking affection or, at the other extreme, are reluctant to seek or accept affection. Haugaard and Hazan state, "The goals of intervention with children who have RAD are to give the child (a) a source of emotional security, (b) opportunities for corrective social experiences, and (c) better social skills" (p. 158). Therefore, for children with attachment disorders, it is extremely important to assign a **primary provider**—one person who is consistently available to greet the child, to assist with self-help skills, and especially to be available in moments of frustration and loss of control (Hanson & Spratt, 2000). By experiencing repeated and consistently warm responsiveness, children can learn to obtain comfort from a social relationship.

Children must learn how to influence people and events in appropriate and effective ways. Other important program goals for these children will be to assist them in learning inhibitory control and how to express and understand a wide range of emotions. Children who have been maltreated often engage in disruptive behavior that interferes with learning.

Discipline should be carried out in an affectively neutral environment so positive expressions are not paired with negative consequences. Children with ACEs often receive mixed messages from caregivers. For example, a parent may be physically abusive one moment and overly solicitous the next, or the parent may assume a false sweetness to induce the child to comply or perform some task. Thus, a teacher should not apply a discipline strategy such as removal from an activity while at the same time saying something positive such as "You know I love you very much."

In addition, staff members should be clear and consistent in their expression of such emotions as happiness, sadness, or fatigue. This assists the child with ACEs in understanding human emotions and provides models for the child's expression of his or her own emotions. Although the importance of consistency and routines was discussed earlier, it is critical to remember how an environment built on these attributes can contribute to the development of resiliency or the ability to cope with adverse experiences.

Particularly useful to consider when working with families of children with ACEs is the **transactional model** of intervention. All elements of the system (child, family, and environment) are viewed as exerting reciprocal influences on one another. "Children affect their environments and environments affect children. Moreover, environmental settings affect and are affected by each other (Sameroff, 2009, p. 18). A transactional model does not isolate one element of the system, such as the child, for intervention. Rather, such a model attends to all components of the family system, including child, family, and environmental characteristics. Thus, it is necessary for the classroom teacher to work in close collaboration with other team members and social service agencies to meet the many needs of the child with ACEs and his or her family. Exhibits 6.7 and 6.8 provide information on recognizing signs of physical abuse and following up after a case of abuse has been reported.

As thoroughly discussed in this chapter, children who have developed healthy self-concepts through nurturing environments develop more readily in all areas. Chapter 7 outlines the concerns and techniques most essential to the promotion of motor and self-help skills.

Helping Children in Poverty

While the impact of homelessness on families was discussed briefly in Chapter 2, teachers should understand how poverty impacts child development and academic performance. There is evidence that the circumstances and stress related to poverty can interrupt the development of the brain (Noble et al., 2015). Circumstances such as crowding, noise, violence, lack of stability, separation, and poor nurturing affect not only brain development, but also may result in less efficient auditory processing (Stromberg, 2013). Thus, learning and appropriate participation are impacted and the damage can last a lifetime.

Children in extreme poverty may also be homeless. When they lack a fixed, regular, and adequate nighttime residence, school may become one of the few safe, stable

Exhibit 6.7

Recognizing Signs of Physical Abuse

1. Be alert for signs of sadness or anger as well as bruises, burns, and cuts. Listen to what the children say. Be especially alert for changes in behavior that cannot be explained by impending illness or an event at school. Begin *at once* to record specific details of your observations. Be certain to make a written note of the date, time, and manner of observation. These may be necessary if a report must be made to authorities. Keep these confidential and under lock and key.

2. Cigarette burns are usually round. Small round burns should always be investigated.

3. Bruises on legs and buttocks can be the result of falls. The frequency and severity of the bruises are useful criteria. Even clumsy children are bruise free most of the time. If the child consistently has bruises, follow up.

4. Black eyes do result from bumping into things. So do bumps on heads. Again, the severity and relative frequency of the bruises should dictate the degree of teacher concern.

5. Little children usually "tell all," but even 3-year-olds can be frightened into lying about how they were hurt. It is not unusual for parents to tell little ones that if they say that Mommy and Daddy hurt them, a big bad person will come and take them away. When this happens, the children's explanations are usually and obviously "dictated." If the story changes, follow up.

places in their lives and might provide them with hope to one day be able to escape poverty (Council for Exceptional Children, 2018). Teachers should watch for signs of homelessness: wearing the same clothes every day, being unkempt, frequently being late, and lacking in school supplies. Through trusting relationships with children and their families, teachers can find out the family situation and be helpful in seeking support for them. In extreme conditions, such children may be withdrawn or depressed and often behave inappropriately. Absenteeism is often a problem. Laws require that such children be served. IDEA requires schools to seek out, identify, and evaluate ALL youth with disabilities. Schools must take the initiative to reach out to help families connect with community resources, provide transportation, if needed, and make every effort to involve homeless families in making decisions for their child.

Exhibit 6.8

Follow-Up

1. After a report to the proper authorities has been made, the teacher should seek help and guidance from the principal or director of the school. Next steps with the parents should not be decided by the teacher alone. Home visits should be discontinued at least for some time. This is a needed safety precaution for both the teacher and parents.

2. On subsequent visits, after conferences with persons who are competent to advise the teacher on what to do and how to do it, the teacher should not go alone to the home. A paraprofessional should accompany the teacher and should be alert to what is said. Confidential notes made by the teacher after the meeting should not become part of the child's file but kept in the teacher's personal possession. These can be destroyed when the need for them has ended.

3. Regardless of the nature or severity of the case, if the child continues to attend school, it is the teacher's responsibility to continue to try to encourage the parents to participate in parent meetings and volunteer at school. The teacher should have the assistance of persons trained and skilled in helping these parents. If the school or center does not offer this service, the teacher should insist on receiving it from some public or private source. Skill in teaching does not imply that the teacher must be all things to all people. Trying to be so can result in disaster.

Classrooms must provide structure, security, a nurturing environment, positive behavior support, and effective classroom management. The children must be helped to feel safe and accepted. Transitions may be difficult, especially for those with disabilities. Personal space and possessions might be very important to these children. A desk or "cubbie" might feel like their "home." As a result, some children could become territorial or highly protective of what they see as theirs. Be sure they are able to put their name on their possessions and/or spaces. Some understanding and empathy can make all the difference in the success of such children.

Summary

This chapter provided an overview of the essential elements of a home and school climate conducive to developing healthy personalities. Some of Erikson's growth stages were reviewed to emphasize the interaction between factors within the child and environmental conditions from without. Of necessity are early warmth and consistency in caregiving, encouraging autonomy within reasonable guidelines, and developing initiative tempered with gentle direction.

A more recent theory proposed by Greenspan has described five major stages of emotional development: self-regulation, attachment, intentional communication, an organized sense of self, and emotional thinking. Greenspan stressed the importance of a responsive environment and the infant's need to learn to express and recognize a wide range of human emotions. Using a Piagetian framework, such cognitive milestones as intentionality and pretend play assume important roles in affective growth.

The essential blocks that promote infant and early childhood mental health were illustrated and described. Teachers were urged to prevent inappropriate behaviors by building security through the use of a number of behavioral principles, including establishing limits, routines, variety, constructive consequences, avoidance of frustration, behavior modeling, and opportunities for appropriately expressing feelings.

Some children arrive at preschools and child-care centers with behaviors and emotional characteristics that interfere with learning. They may be too active or too withdrawn. They may be impulsive. Some are overly dependent on adults for direction, whereas others refuse all direction from their teachers. Techniques for working with unique ways of behaving were suggested. These range from effectively using time-away to using puppets and play. Throughout, the role of positive reinforcement and appropriate modeling of behavior was emphasized. Enhancing a child's self-confidence and emotional literacy are ever-present goals.

Guidelines were offered to promote the creation of an environment that facilitates spontaneous play behavior considered to be essential in the development of emotional well-being. The procedure for developing positive behavior support plans provides practitioners with a systematic approach to behavior management. The final section addressed the characteristics and needs of children with adverse childhood experiences.

Reflect and Apply

1. Assume that you are observing children involved in a creative activity such as painting at an easel. Think and be specific about what you could say to reinforce the child's efforts, rather than what might be perceived as the quality of the product.

2. Reflect on Figure 6.1. Be specific when stating at least five understandings for each block that a practitioner should keep in mind when building a healthy environment.

3. Consider the differences among natural and logical consequences. Create examples for each and determine when and under what circumstances each could be positive or negative.

4. Brainstorm with a couple of peers and come up with a list of possible impacts that various disabilities might have on play behavior. Then speculate on what could be done to minimize or alleviate the potential impacts.

5. Visit the Technical Assistance Center on Social Emotional Intervention for Young Children at http://challengingbehavior.fmhi.usf.edu/. Learn about the Pyramid Model. Carefully study and summarize the six steps of the process of building positive behavior support. Reflect on something new that you have learned that will help you to positively approach challenging behaviors.

Chapter 7
Helping Young Children Develop Motor and Self-Care Skills

Dave Clark Digital Photo/Shutterstock

∨ Learning Outcomes

After studying this chapter, you should be able to:

7.1 Explain how physiological maturation and environmental factors influence the rate and quality of physical and motor development.

7.2 Define the roles of physical and occupational therapists in promoting the motor and self-care skills of young children with disabilities.

7.3 Discuss why positioning and handling are so important for normalization of muscle tone, prevention of contractures, and stabilization of the body.

7.4 Explain why interventions should be embedded in self-care activities to encourage functional behaviors, including gross and fine motor skills.

7.5 Describe various strategies for teaching self-care skills and how family–professional collaboration is vital for designing and implementing self-care activities.

7.6 Recognize why adaptations of materials and environmental considerations are essential in program planning for children with physical disabilities.

Nikki

Nikki was born 2 months premature, weighing in at 2 pounds, 2 ounces. She remained in the neonatal intensive care unit for 8 weeks, during which time she experienced a life-threatening infection. As she recovered, it was clear early on that she sustained some brain damage with neurological impairment. Hearing and vision appeared to be within normal limits, but movement on the left side was limited. She was eventually diagnosed with cerebral palsy (CP) with spastic hemiplegia (involving the arm, trunk, and leg on the left side). She was followed in the CP Clinic at Children's Hospital and received home visits from a physical therapist who helped her parents with positioning and activities to maximize Nikki's gross and fine motor skills. Specific "exercises" were recommended to encourage use of her left arm and leg. Most of the therapy was embedded into daily living routines and playtime. As she began to walk, she was fitted with an ankle-foot orthotic (AFO) brace, which provided support and better balance.

At age 2½, Nikki was referred to an early intervention program that had both home- and center-based components. The team worked closely with her parents to develop strategies for interaction that would maximize use of her left side, maximize use of reciprocal movements (i.e., right and left together), and motivate self-help activities (eating, dressing, and toileting). Nikki's father is a musician, and he uses music to get Nikki to move and "dance." He ties bells, balloons, or ribbons on her left wrist or ankle to make sound and increase awareness. The teachers at school are also doing similar activities with Nikki as well as with other children in the program. When Dave, Nikki's father, visits the class, he brings his guitar and encourages all the children to "get their groove on."

As Nikki is getting ready to transition to an inclusive preschool program, a teacher and therapist from the program will help the staff members of the receiving class make adaptations (as needed) for Nikki's success.

Motor development refers to the changes related to voluntary physical movement that occur during a child's life. Coordination of movement skills contributes to children's development of self-confidence, a positive body image, competencies in physical activities, early literacy skills, play skills, and social development. For many children with motor problems or delays (e.g., cerebral palsy, other physical disabilities, developmental delays, and intellectual disabilities), movement experiences are often limited. Studies indicate that children with disabilities (e.g., autism, pervasive developmental disorders, and intellectual disabilities) have delays and differences in motor development compared to children without disabilities. Additional instruction, therapeutic intervention, and encouragement are essential to promote children's development in all areas (Emck, Bosscher, Beek, & Doreleijers, 2009; Matson, Mahan, Fodstad, Hess, & Neal, 2010; Lloyd, MacDonald, & Lord, 2013).

Motor skills are usually divided into at least two general categories. **Gross motor skills** refer to activities that involve the use of the large muscles of the neck, trunk, arms, and legs. These include basic body movements such as lifting the head, rolling, crawling, creeping, walking, running, leaping, jumping, hopping, galloping, and skipping. Large muscle strength and endurance are also important in climbing, pushing, pulling, hanging, and lifting.

Fine motor skills involve more precise movements of the small muscles, especially those of the eyes, speech musculature, hands, fingers, feet, and toes. Movements such as blinking, focusing, sucking, grasping, releasing, pinching, and writing are considered to be fine motor activities. Many fine motor skills, including cutting, pasting, copying, and writing, require the eyes to direct the hands. These activities are referred to variously as those that require perceptual-motor, visual-motor, sensorimotor, ocular-motor, or eye–hand coordination.

This chapter reviews normal motor development, including gross and fine motor skills and self-care skills. It suggests activities to enhance children's learning and development. Identification of problems in motor development is emphasized, with suggestions for intervention. Special efforts are taken to encourage the integration of movement skills into other areas of instruction as well as in daily routines.

The Development of Motor Skills

Babies learn from the sensations of movement, primarily from active rather than passive movements. Sensory input (such as tactile, proprioceptive, visual, or auditory) is sent through the nervous system and integrated at appropriate levels of the brain and spinal cord. As messages are received and processed, responses are sent back in the form of motor acts. Voluntary motor activity is controlled by upper brain centers located in the cerebral cortex, whereas involuntary or unconscious muscle movements (e.g., digestion of food, eye blinking, and reflex movements) are controlled by lower brain centers, that is, the cerebellum and parts of the brain stem.

In general, motor skills develop according to predictable sequences of physiological maturation, with the development of movement patterns progressing from simple arm or leg actions to highly integrated total body coordination.

The rate of development appears to depend not only on the quality of environmental stimuli, but also on the stage of brain development. Studies have identified gender differences in preschoolers' gross motor and object-related skills (Colombo-Dougovito, 2017; Goodway, Robinson, & Crowe, 2010). The extent to which this difference may be due to children's experiences is still being questioned. Parents' expectations and interactions with infants often differ according to the gender of the child. These expectations are reflected in play activities.

Environmental factors such as amount of sleep and exercise, quality of medical care, and adequacy of nutrition may influence the rate and ultimate degree of physical and, thus, motor development. Lack of access to playgrounds or opportunities to engage in motor activities may also affect children's motor skills (Goodway et al., 2010; Venetsanou & Kambas, 2010). In addition, child-rearing practices and opportunities for physical activity vary among cultures. This also should be taken into account when viewing differences in motor skill development. Teachers should learn about the family's values, concerns, and practices and develop a collaborative relationship with the family to identify ways to support the child's motor skills. In general, a child's potential for motor skill development is considered to be an interaction between genetics and specific environmental influences.

By the time a child is 5 or 6 years of age, many motor behaviors have been established and require only refinement and mastery at a higher, more complex level. During these early years, motor development follows a highly predictable sequential and overlapping pattern. Although the rate varies at which typically developing children progress, the sequence remains fairly constant. The literature on motor development contains many descriptions and timetables for the stage and age at which motor abilities are attained. Variation in developmental rate is well documented. It is not unusual to hear mothers compare walking age variations from 8 to 18 months. See Appendix A for a summary of typical gross and fine motor development.

Sequential Trends of Motor Development

Seven basic principles govern the sequence of motor development (Piek, 2006). These principles should guide expectations of children's motor skills and the development of relevant physical supports:

1. *Cephalocaudal pattern.* Muscular development proceeds from the head to the foot. For example, infants have voluntary control over their heads before lower parts of their body. Similarly, children can usually throw before they can catch.

2. *Proximo-distal pattern.* Growth and development tend to proceed from the spine (proximo) to the outer extremities (distal). That is, voluntary movement begins in the shoulder, then moves on to the elbow area, wrist, and finally the fingers.

3. *Mass-to-specific pattern.* The body movement of young infants is undifferentiated, involving the total body. Later, specific patterns of movement develop out of these generalized mass movements. When learning new skills, it takes time for children to inhibit the unwanted extraneous movements.

4. *Gross-motor-to-fine-motor pattern.* Children usually gain control over large muscle activity before fine or small muscle activity. In addition, a child must gain differential control. That is, movement of muscles on one side of the body should occur without similar movement on the other side of the body, unless desired.

5. *Maximum-to-minimum-muscle-involvement pattern.* Like the mass-to-specific pattern, body movement becomes increasingly more efficient. With practice, children learn to eliminate unnecessary expenditures of energy. Where it once took a whole bodily effort to catch a ball, children learn to catch with the use of just one arm and hand.

6. *Bilateral-to-unilateral pattern.* Children progress from undifferentiated use of both sides of the body to unilateral preference, referred to as the *establishment of laterality*.

7. *Orderly development pattern.* Children differ in the rate of their development but do tend to follow a similar pattern if environmental conditions are adequate and no organic deficits are present.

Helping Parents Understand

In discussing various aspects of child development with families, practitioners should seek ways to provide practical information that addresses family questions and concerns and assists them in promoting their children's development. Appendix A and other lists of developmental milestones can help guide discussions. Parents of a child with delays in motor development may have questions and express concerns about the child's motor skills. For example, parents may ask, "Cody is almost 2 years old. When will he walk?" The early childhood special educator should collaborate with the child's physical therapist to provide information about the child's motor development. They should discuss their observations of the child's motor behavior with the family—for example, "I notice that Cody is trying to reach that toy on the sofa. We can work on helping him pull to stand, bear weight, and cruise while holding on to the sofa. These are all skills that lay the foundation for learning to walk."

Reflexive Development

The early motor activity of infants is structured by a variety of primitive and automatic reflexes. Primitive reflexes are evident in early infancy at or soon after birth. There is a wide range of variation in reflex responsiveness among infants as well as within the same infant, depending on the behavioral states of the child being observed. These reflexes are expressions of the immaturity of the infant's nervous system and provide a basis for assessing the integrity of the developing neuromuscular system.

It is important for teachers to have some idea of how coordinated movement evolves and what factors may interfere with normal functioning. Concerned early childhood special educators may consult a physical or occupational therapist to assess reflexive behavior.

Developing Gross Motor Skills

Gross motor skills refer to the involvement of the large muscles of the neck, trunk, arms, and legs. Early childhood affords the time and practice for emerging skills to become accomplished before rapid bodily changes begin to occur. Children develop postural control and learn to walk, run, catch, and jump with relative skill. The extent to which children become proficient in these skills depends on muscle development as well as the opportunity for using their muscles. Children require safe and obstacle-free environments that encourage movement and exploration. Practitioners should provide regular opportunities for physical play during the school day by providing access to playgrounds and relevant equipment (Hyndman, Benson, & Telford, 2016). Moreover, parents' perception of children's motor skills and the family's lifestyle and various responsibilities may influence the amount and type of physical activities in which children with disabilities participate out of school (Siebert, Hamm, & Yun, 2017). However, surveys of teachers and caregivers of children with severe disabilities have found that many playgrounds at schools and in the community are not fully accessible to children with severe disabilities (Stanton-Chapman & Schmidt, 2016a, b). Practitioners should collaborate with families to identify resources and physical activities in the community that match the child's interests and abilities and the family's values and routines.

Program administrators and teachers should evaluate outdoor areas and playgrounds for possible barriers to accessibility for children with physical disabilities and then determine how to reduce or eliminate them, and support all children's participation. The Americans with Disabilities Act (ADA) requires that playgrounds be accessible to individuals with disabilities. Guidelines for accessible playgrounds include the following:

- Paths to playground equipment are wide enough for wheelchairs and have surfaces on which they can be easily maneuvered.

- Swings should provide adequate support (e.g., bucket seats with back and neck support and straps).

- Sandboxes should be elevated so children in wheelchairs can access them. Sand play and digging tools should be easy to grasp and manipulate.

- Tricycles have adapted seats with back support and straps on pedals to position the child's feet.

- Overhead rings and bars should be low enough so a child in a wheelchair can reach them.

- Transfer points (raised platform where a child can get out of a wheelchair) have handholds for the child.

Developing Fine Motor Skills

Fine motor skills involve small muscles. Most fine motor skills, as far as preparation for manual control is concerned, involve hands and fingers. Coordination of hands and fingers is built on dexterity, stability, and sensation that provide the foundation of dexterity (Bruni, 2016). Stability provides the positioning, control, and strength of the arms and hands; for example, opening cupboards. Bilateral coordination involves using both hands in movements; for example, to manipulate toys. Sensation provides feedback on what the hands are touching to guide movements; for example, playing with sand. Dexterity involves grasp and release skills, thumb control, wrist movement, and finger coordination. Some children with Down syndrome had difficulty with bilateral coordination because of low muscle tone, poor body stability, and delays in the development of handedness (up to 7 years). The coordination of looking to guide hand movements is referred to as eye-hand coordination, a visual-motor skill.

Practice Payoff.   Long before a baby can walk, her mother may report, "Sally picked up a raisin today." Surprised that the child could pick up something so tiny, mothers become more alert about leaving beads and other nonedibles around. Later, this ability to see small things and pick them up will become the foundation for grasping and holding crayons, pencils, and other small objects. Having things available to pick up is all that is necessary for most young children to learn important fine motor skills; however, they must have opportunities to practice. Building with small blocks, manipulating small toys, imitating action songs and finger plays, and using crayons, chalk, and scissors all lead to improvement of essential skills. Huffman and Fortenberry (2011) list activities that address the stages of fine motor development so important to success in writing: whole arm (e.g., making large movements with arms), whole hand (e.g., squeezing sponges and pouring activities), pincher (e.g., using thumb, middle finger, and index finger to pick up buttons or use eye droppers or tongs), and pincer (e.g., using thumb and index finger to pick up pieces of cereal) coordination.

Snap-together beads, geoboards, puzzles, beads for stringing, button and lacing boards, and large nuts and screws offer interesting and challenging fine motor practice for young children. Cooking activities help children develop skills such as stirring, cutting, pounding, and rolling while learning a variety of concepts. Table 7.1 provides a sample list of typical motor skill activities. A chart of normative expectations can be found in Appendix A. Research indicates that the fine motor skills of infants with

Video Example from

Enhanced eText
Video Example 7.2
Early Childhood Motor, Chapter 8
https://www.youtube.com/watch?v=6hBFcH2UyhQ
This video illustrates the fine motor development of toddlers and preschoolers who are doing puzzles, eating, cutting, painting, coloring, and drawing.

Table 7.1 Typical Motor Skills Activities

Gross Motor Development			
Eye–Foot Coordination	**Eye–Hand Coordination**	**Body Awareness**	**Balance**
Kicking	Climbing	Crawling in and out of things	Standing on tiptoe
Climbing	Hanging	Crawling through and around things	Walking the balance beam
Jumping	Striking balloons		Riding wheeled toys
Hopping	Throwing	Moving like an animal	Walking around tire edges or sandbox rails
Dancing	Catching	Imitation activities	
Walking the balance beam	Using tools	Playing "Simon Says"	Moving and carrying something without spilling
	Block building	Steering wheeled toys	
Jumping over ropes	Rolling balls	Pounding / Stirring	Walking with bean bag on head or shoulder
Fine Motor Development (Eye–Hand Coordination)			
Cutting	Lacing	Outlining with stencils or templates	Using eyedroppers, tweezers, turkey basters
Coloring	Geoboards	Copying	
Drawing	Tracing	Pasting	
Sewing	Painting	Building block towers	
Puzzle building	Paper folding	Stacking	
Bead stringing	Copying designs	Using tongs	
Self-Care Skills			
Dressing (buttoning, zipping, snapping, buckling)			Eating
Personal hygiene (brushing teeth, washing hands)			Toileting

developmental delays can be improved through play and manipulation of objects (Aparicio & Balaña, 2009; Sanz & Menéndez, 2010). Teachers of preschoolers should provide many learning opportunities for the development of fine motor skills through developmentally appropriate activities.

Scribbling and Drawing. A synthesis of studies that examined the marking and scribbling behaviors of infants and toddlers by Dunst and Gorman (2009) revealed the following implications for practice:

1. Easy-to-hold big crayons and markers that produce distinct visual effects resulted in an increased quantity and improved quality of markings.

2. Drawing surfaces that had an image (e.g., figures or faces of people or animals) on the background elicited more frequent and complex scribbles than blank paper.

3. Slant surfaces made it easier for children to draw using crayons and markers than flat surfaces.

4. Structured activities elicited the child's drawing upon an adult's request or the imitation of an adult's drawing.

5. Unstructured activities resulted in child-initiated drawings and longer periods of collaborative drawing episodes with an adult that were associated with more complex drawings.

6. More opportunities to draw and scribble led to increased engagement of children in these activities that, in turn, promoted the transition to a higher-level pre-representational drawing.

Bruni (2016) provides the following suggestions to help preschoolers move from a palmer (using the palm) grasp to manipulate a marking utensil to develop a tripod (the thumb and fingers) grasp by using (a) a "finger crayon" that has a round bulb to hold in the palm and a pointed end, (b) short pieces or chalk or crayons, (c) a triangular shaped crayon, and (d) thick markers.

Trivette, Dunst, and Hamby (2013) found that providing children with multiple opportunities in structured and unstructured activities and a variety of materials to engage in scribbling, drawing, and writing promoted emergent writing skills. The use of "Big Paper" (large sheets of paper) to cover tables or the floor encourages preschoolers to collaborate on drawings and talk about their drawings (Edmister, Staples, Huber, & Garrett, 2013). Teachers may provide a variety of writing tools (e.g., crayons, markers, and pencils with foam grips if needed; letter, shape, and object stamps with large handles) and rotate among groups to ask children about their drawings and promote peer interaction.

In another synthesis of research studies, Trivette, Hamby, Dunst, and Gorman (2013) identified a multiple step sequence of emergent writing between 12 and 60 months of age. Children progressed from making marks and dots, to scribbling (random then controlled marks), to line drawing (controlled lines and shapes), to representational drawing (figures of people and objects, invented drawing, and conventional pictures), to symbolic writing (conventional letters, invented spelling, conventional name writing and spelling). The sequence as shown in Figure 7.1 helps teachers determine the next step to expect and encourage in a child's development of writing skills.

Given the ubiquitousness of tablets with apps to encourage tracing and writing on the screen, teachers should consult with occupational therapists to determine the purpose of each activity and meaningful objectives for an individual child. For example, using the index finger to trace and draw is a different fine motor skill than using a writing tool. However, many children become motivated to engage in tracing and drawing through an app. Using a stencil on the tablet may serve as a transition to a more conventional writing tool.

Handedness. When observing children engaged in fine motor activities, the question of "handedness," or hand preference, usually arises. Although most children show a hand preference during the preschool period, some children without disabilities may not achieve hand dominance until they are beyond preschool. Even then, some children develop functional ambidexterity. Hand dominance reflects an interaction between genetic and environmental factors (Johnson, Nicholls, Shah, & Shields, 2010). A review of studies on handedness in children and youth with autism spectrum disorders found that 18% were left-handed and 44% had mixed handedness. There were no significant differences across age groups except that younger children tended to have more mixed-handedness (Rysstad & Pederson, 2016). Practitioners should allow the child to choose which hand he or she is comfortable using or to switch between hands. Left-handed children may take time learning to handle objects and writing independently. Teaching the child how to slant the paper slightly to the right makes it easier to maneuver. It is important to note that some children with disabilities may not demonstrate hand preference because they lack body stability (e.g., will use one hand for balance or have limited reach to maintain balance). Or, they have difficulty crossing the midline and may switch the toy from one hand to another when they reach the midline of the body (e.g., change toy car from one hand to the other when pushing the toy across the midline). They might just reach with the hand closest to the toy (Bruni, 2016). Careful observation and consultation with an occupational therapist (OT) or physical therapist (PT) are needed to address these issues. When children have hemiplegia (type of CP in which one side of the body is affected), they naturally use the unaffected (stronger) hand and need encouragement to use the weaker hand, when appropriate. Here are some suggestions:

- Activities in which the affected hand holds or stabilizes the material (e.g., affected hand "holds" a container such as a piggy bank or bowl) or paper and the unaffected hand "fills" the container with selected objects (e.g., coins, plastic bears) or cuts or colors the paper

Figure 7.1 Developmental sequence of emergent writing

Source: Elizabeth Leone.

	Accidental marking: Child makes marks without apparent intent. Marks on surface are the result of random movements while holding the marking implement.
	Dots: Child uses the tip of the marking implement to make tiny repetitive marks on the surface.
	Random marks: Child shows awareness that the implement causes the mark. The child experiments with different movements and pressures to see what types of marks are created.
	Controlled strokes: Child masters swiping the implement over the surface in opposing directions.
	Controlled marks: Child is increasingly able to control marks made and to arrange them in a planned way.
	Geometric shapes: Child makes closed forms that they may or may not verbally identify as a particular geometric shape.
	Written marks: Marks look letter-like but most do not represent actual letters. Can look like a combination of circles and lines or other simple marks. They are arranged in a row.
	Letter practice: Child uses a combination of letters, numbers, and letter-like markings without spaces.
	Copy environmental print or model: Child uses and copies letters in the environment as writing models.
	Invented spelling: Child understands the sounds associated with words and uses the sounds to write the words.
	Conventional: Child spells an increasing number of words correctly.

- Activities that encourage use of both hands, such as clapping hands, scrunching tissue paper into balls, batting a big balloon, finger painting with pudding, squeezing large Koosh or squishy balls

- Activities that encourage use of the affected hand, if appropriate, such as shaking an easy-to-hold/adapted musical instrument, popping bubbles, waving bubble wands, or removing small foam stickers that are stuck on the unaffected hand

Teachers and family members should consult with the child's PT or OT to develop motivating and developmentally appropriate ways to encourage hand use.

Developing Eye–Hand Coordination.   When encountering sensory stimulation of a particular kind for the first time, children *receive* (sense) the stimulation. Subsequent encounters usually result in their *perceiving* (interpreting) the stimulus. If any of the senses are impaired, even slightly, children may not be able to sense the initial stimulus accurately. If they do not receive an accurate first impression, later interpretations of that stimulus will be wrong or confusing to them. Thus for infants and young children, any limitation in movement may interfere with development of perceptual skills and have an adverse effect on other kinds of learning and social skill development.

We encourage the development of perceptual-motor skills as tasks in and of themselves and in association with language and concept development. There is no doubt that functionally and developmentally appropriate curricula for young children contain numerous activities that promote perceptual-motor development as part of the daily routine. Puzzles, marking pens, touching visual targets on tablets, scissors, buttoning and unbuttoning, and self-feeding are just a few that embed the development of eye–hand coordination.

Individualizing a Visual-Motor Activity.   By writing the goal and objectives for cutting with scissors on one page, as illustrated in Table 7.2, the teacher has a helpful one-page

Table 7.2   Example of Using Goals and Objectives to Individualize an Activity

Given (the teacher will provide or restrict) Goal:	The Child Will	Criterion
To develop cutting skills.		
Terminal objective: To cut along a line and cut out a circle		
Blunt-tip scissors; paper with a 3-inch straight line, a 3-inch curved line, and a 3-inch-diameter circle; and directions to cut on the line and cut out the circle.	Cut as directed.	Cut within ¼ inch of lines within 5 minutes.
Short-term objectives (least to most skilled): To use tongs (or tweezers) to grasp and release small objects		
1. Tongs, 5 small pieces sponge, 4-inch bowl with water, teacher's guidance in placing fingers and thumb and forefinger in cutting position, and help in opening and closing tongs.	Open and close tongs around sponge piece, lift it to bowl, and release it into bowl, accepting teacher's assistance as needed.	Keep fingers in correct position and accept help.
2. Same as before, except restrict teacher's help to verbal directions, encouragement, and reminders.	Same as before.	Keep fingers in correct position and complete action (no time limit and no penalty for "dropped" sponge).
3. Same as before.	Same as before.	Maintain correct position, lift and drop sponge into bowl (no more than one piece outside bowl within 2 minutes).
To use blunt-tip scissors		
4. Blunt-tip scissors and strips of construction paper 1 inch wide and 11 inches long.	Cut paper.	Cut at least 10 pieces within 5 minutes.
5. Same as before, with heavy black lines marked on paper at 1-inch intervals.	Cut paper on lines.	Cut within ¼ inch of lines, one cut per line (no time limit).
6. Blunt-tip scissors and construction paper 3 inches wide and 11 inches long, with heavy black lines at 1-inch intervals the width of the paper.	Make three cuts per line.	Cut within ¼ inch of lines, severing each piece within 10 minutes.
7. Same as terminal objective (except longer time criterion).	Cut as directed.	Cut within ¼ inch of lines within 10 minutes.
8. Same as terminal objective.		

Note: These examples of instruction on fine motor skills should be embedded within an art or game activity. For example, children can cut out shapes to make a collage or picture, or they can pick up sponge pieces and transfer them to a bowl of water during a counting game or one of "stop and start" to music.

reference to guide him or her in planning the lesson to be useful to a group of children with widely varying skills. The terminal objective of cutting with scissors is an appropriate skill for a 5-year-old, whereas lifting small pieces of sponge with the tongs can be accomplished by most 3-year-olds.

It is also important to remember that cutting is a higher-level fine motor skill that builds on several skills: (a) bilateral coordination, that is, adjusting the paper so that the dominant hand can align scissors with the paper to cut out the shape; (b) stability of the body and shoulder to help the child make accurate hand movements; (c) sensation for sensory feedback of the joint and muscles to help make adjustments for cutting; and (d) dexterity that involves wrist rotation for a thumb up, midline position of the hand (Bruni, 2016). Teachers should collaborate with occupational therapists to provide strategies to promote a child's fine motor skills within daily activities, including breaking the activity into small steps and developmental sequences. The following developmental progression for cutting with scissors may help adults support children's cutting skills:

1. Snipping short individual strips
2. Cutting across a 1-inch strip of paper and then wider strips
3. Cutting a piece of paper in half
4. Cutting along a straight line
5. Cutting along a corner or angle
6. Cutting along a curved line
7. Cutting out a complete circle
8. Cutting out shapes that combine corners, lines, curves, and circles

Adaptations for children with physical disabilities include squeeze or loop scissors instead of traditional scissors. For some children, scissors with four finger holes may be useful because they allow the teacher to cut with the child. Children with visual impairments should be provided buff-colored paper with a heavy brown line for necessary contrast or cut along a raised line made of dried glue or yarn glued on paper. Some children may learn to use scissors by snipping paper straws or a line of rolled play dough. Some benefit from experiences such as tearing paper strips with their fingers before using scissors. Within an art activity, children can learn to tear paper strips using the following steps to promote success:

1. Provide a piece of paper with a small tear at the top, hold one side of the paper, and encourage the child to hold the other side and pull it to tear.
2. Give the child the paper with the beginning tear to hold with both hands and tear without adult help.
3. Give a child a whole piece of paper to tear into strips.

Some 5-year-olds with developmental delays may find it difficult to learn to use the tongs. They may require help and physical guidance as well as encouragement and verbal guidance for many days or weeks before they can proceed to the second objective. By being included in the activity with children who can do the more difficult tasks, they observe and discover that they also can participate and succeed.

It is critical to remember that one of the reasons for the sequence of carefully planned short-term objectives or steps is to provide each child with a task until a criterion is reached. It is possible to develop complex skills gradually and without the fear of failure. Beginning by expecting all children to "cut on the line" guarantees failure for many of them. To teach five or more children to cut on the line, it is necessary to provide each one with the materials needed, demonstration at his or her level of performance,

Video Example from

You Tube

▶

Enhanced eText
Video Example 7.3
How to Teach a Preschooler to Cut with Scissors
https://www.youtube.com/watch?v=bDtupoBsp6o
This video shows important steps in teaching a preschooler to use scissors.

and continued encouragement. In this way, no one fails; rather, each child succeeds. Most will recognize the challenge of the next step and be eager to try it.

In addition to the usefulness of the clearly written behavioral objectives to the teacher, as the lesson is planned and conducted, these same objectives help in pin-pointing necessary smaller steps. The basic set of goals and objectives should be designed to be useful guides in teaching most children. But some children will need even smaller steps. By analyzing the existing objectives, the teacher can identify these more precise steps.

The format of the page of objectives is helpful in analyzing the task. If the child is not succeeding, where is the breakdown? Should a change be made in what the teacher is providing or restricting? Or, is the quantity of work or time allowed inappropriate? By evaluating the task, the criterion, and what the teacher does or does not do, it is possible to establish a much better sense of effective instruction for the teacher as well as the children.

Throughout all activities, teachers attempt to help children develop confidence, accuracy, patience, and persistence. These qualities are nurtured more successfully when sequenced steps/behaviors are clearly stated.

Recording Progress.   Figure 7.2 illustrates an easy way to record children's progress when a group includes children with varying skill levels focusing on the same goal. By placing the expected behavioral step on the left side of the page and the names of the children across the top, it is easy to record progress and to identify each child's current en route behavior. The teacher (or paraprofessional) simply records the date and level of accomplishment for each item. Some prefer to include only the date of achievement. Then the next item on the list becomes the current behavioral step to be practiced.

Figure 7.2 Recording progress in-group with varying skill levels

CURRICULUM DOMAIN: Fine motor

Goal: To learn cutting skills

Key: + = Skill already established
☐ = Current target behavior
▨ = Date achieved

	Meg A.	Mary C.	Danny D.	Bobby J.	Vicky M.	Eric R.
Tongs and cotton balls	+	+	+	+	+	+
1-inch snipping	10/11	9/11	10/11	+	☐	+
1-inch snipping on heavy line	☐	10/11	10/11	+		+
3-inch cutting on heavy straight line		☐	☐	10/11		+
3-inch cutting on heavy curved line				☐		10/11
Cutting out 3-inch-diameter circle, heavy line						☐

Atypical Motor Development

Atypical motor development or motor differences can occur for a variety of reasons. Brain damage, orthopedic problems, progressive diseases, congenital disabilities, developmental delays, and sensory impairments can potentially interfere with motor skill acquisition.

Deviations in movement patterns affecting the young child usually originate in the prenatal or perinatal period. Neuromuscular dysfunction originating in the central nervous system, specifically CP, is the most common motor disability among children of all ages. *Cerebral palsy* is a general term given to nonprogressive brain lesions. It generally causes complex problems in all aspects of development (Hoon & Tolly, 2013). Abnormal movement patterns seen in children with CP are related to primitive reflex retention and problems of motor coordination and muscle tone. A continuum of motor dysfunction due to insult to the brain may include on one end a child with clumsy and awkward movements and on the other a child with CP who has such severe impairments that any coordinated movement is next to impossible. In between are varying degrees of movement problems.

As suggested by Howard, Williams, Miller, and Aiken (2014), a diagnosis of CP is not very useful for the practitioner unless it includes a description of the degree of involvement or the extent to which a child is affected motorically. Table 7.3 lists descriptions of the general characteristics of children with mild, moderate, and severe CP. PTs and OTs using relevant measures may assess the severity of CP. For example, the Gross Motor Function Classification System (GMFCS) includes the following levels for preschoolers: (1) walks indoors and outdoors and climbs stairs and learns to run and jump; (2) walks short distances, climbs stairs while holding rails, and cannot run or jump; (3) walks using a hand-held mobility device on level surfaces and climbs stairs with adult assistance; (4) needs adaptive seating, self-mobility with a walker or wheelchair; (5) no independent movement, may be transported in a manual wheelchair (Palisano, Rosenbaum, Bartlett, & Livingston, 2007). The Manual Ability Classification System (MACS) provides the following classification levels: (1) handles objects easily and successfully; (2) handles most objects, but with reduced quality and/or speed of movement; (3) handles objects with difficulty, needing assistance to prepare and/or modify activities; (4) handles a limited selection of easily managed objects in adapted situations; and (5) does not handle objects and has severely limited ability to perform even simple actions (Eliasson et al., 2006). The levels of gross and fine motor functioning of

Table 7.3 Diagnostic Criteria for Severity of Cerebral Palsy

Degree of Involvement	Characteristics
Severe	1. Total dependence in meeting physical needs 2. Poor head control 3. Deformities, present or potential, that limit function or produce pain 4. Perceptual and/or sensory integrative deficits that prevent the achievement of age-appropriate motor skills
Moderate	1. Some independence in meeting physical needs 2. Functional head control 3. Deformities, present or potential, that limit function or produce pain 4. Perceptual and/or sensory integrative deficits that prevent the achievement of age-appropriate motor skills
Mild	1. Independence in meeting physical needs 2. Potential to improve quality of motor and/or perceptual skills with therapy intervention 3. Potential for regression in quality of motor and perceptual skills without intervention

Source: Based on Best, Heller, and Bigge (2005), *Teaching Individuals with Physical or Multiple Disabilities*, Pearson Education, Inc., Upper Saddle River, New Jersey.

a child with CP affect a child's self-care, mobility, communication, social interaction, problem-solving skills, and level of assistance required (Phipps & Roberts, 2012).

Problems in Muscle Development

Muscle characteristics of tone, control, and strength are significant concerns in development and eventual intervention. Causes of problems vary from central nervous system damage and genetic disorders to nonspecific delays in development (Bruni, 2016; Hoon & Tolly, 2013). Interventions should consider the range of differences in muscle development (Winders, 2014; Bower, 2009).

1. *Deficits in muscle tone.* The degree of tension in the muscle at rest defines muscle tone. There are three main types of muscle tone deviation. The first, **hypotonia**, refers to low muscle tone (lower-than-normal tension in muscles) that makes children appear "floppy." The child with hypotonia has difficulty learning to move into upright positions, maintaining balance in sitting while reaching for objects, or pushing with the fingers. The ligaments supporting the joints are also looser, allowing more movement in the joints (hyperextension or being double jointed), especially in the shoulders, fingers, hips, and ankles. The child with Down syndrome or Prader-Willi syndrome or those classified as having ataxic CP are examples of children with hypotonia. These children are usually less active than their peers and may become fatigued easily by motor activities. Winders (2014) suggests the following crucial gross motor outcomes for children with Down syndrome to have a solid foundation for fitness throughout life: (a) to walk efficiently with his or her knees and feet pointing straight ahead with a narrow base and long stride; (b) to have his or her hips, knees, and ankles aligned to support the walking pattern; (c) to have a strong upper trunk with strength balanced between the muscles of the back and abdomen; and (d) to have strong arms and shoulders with balanced strength so the shoulders and arms fall in the middle of the side view. Teachers and families should collaborate with physical therapists to work on strategies that address these outcomes.

   Motor milestones such as sitting, creeping, and walking are usually delayed because of the affected child's generalized low muscle tone. Other areas affected may be the chest and face muscles. Because of low muscle tone, breathing tends to be shallow. The child may also have difficulty sustaining sounds when attempting to cry, babble, or talk.

   Conversely, the child with **hypertonia** has too much muscle tone. Another name for hypertonia is **spasticity**. A high percentage of children with CP have spasticity. The affected muscles are characterized as feeling stiff and rigid. For instance, when the child tries to passively extend the flexed arm, it feels "locked," and a slow, steady pressure at the elbow is necessary to perform this motion. In children with spastic hemiplegia, one side of the body is affected. In spastic diplegia, the legs are primarily affected, but the trunk and arms may also be involved. In spastic quadriplegia, all four extremities and the trunk are involved.

   Children with hypertonia are frequently delayed in achieving motor milestones. They often have difficulty assuming and maintaining postures that go against gravity, such as sitting, creeping, and standing. Breathing may also be impaired because of decreased movement of the ribs and chest. If facial and oral muscles are involved, as is often the case in spastic **quadriplegia**, articulation, chewing, and swallowing also may be affected (VenKateswaran & Shevell, 2008).

   Fluctuating muscle tone can be seen in children who are generally hypertonic or hypotonic. In these cases, an attempt at voluntary movement usually sets off increased muscle tone. However, when the child is resting, muscles may be hypotonic. The incoordination of contraction and relaxation may be seen in

athetoid movement patterns, which are repetitive, poorly coordinated voluntary movements. The most common type of motor disability in which fluctuating tone occurs is athetoid CP.

2. *Problems with muscle control.* Writhing movements, tremors, and fluctuating muscle tone are abnormal motor characteristics that interfere with voluntary movements. As the child with CP tries to do something, for example, not only fluctuating tone but also uncoordinated movements and abnormal posture caused by increased or decreased tone are present. Involuntary facial movements (mouth opening and closing and the tongue moving in and out) are often related to general muscle tone fluctuation throughout the body. Attempts at fine motor activities tend to increase problems in overall coordination in some children with CP.

3. *Problems with muscle strength.* There may be differences in muscle strength among and within children. Certain degenerative diseases such as muscular dystrophy have a progressive effect on muscle strength. Paralysis of muscles related to spinal cord damage such as spina bifida or traumatic injuries often causes permanent loss of strength in certain muscle groups. The inactivity of a child wearing a cast for a broken bone will cause losses of strength and muscle tone that quickly return to normal with exercise and movement.

Assessment of Motor Abilities

In educational planning or therapeutic intervention, it is important to assess the young child in all developmental areas and to determine how the absence or delay of motor abilities will affect overall learning and social interactions. No matter what type of assessment approach is used (observation checklist or standardized tests), the information should be translated into designing optimal learning experiences.

As emphasized throughout this text, the responsibility for assessing the child should be a team effort. The parent, teacher, physical and occupational therapists, physician, and allied health professionals all contribute information essential in the identification, diagnosis, and remediation of motor problems. As with all assessment, care must be taken not to apply diagnostic labels until all pertinent information is obtained. The high-risk premature infant, for example, is too often given an early diagnosis of CP based on symptoms characteristic of an immature but developing nervous system. Imagine the effects of that incorrect diagnosis on the parents!

Early childhood special education practitioners often become coordinators and synthesizers of assessment information. Information from parents on early developmental milestones, family history, and current behavior; hospital records and diagnostic assessment from medical specialists; and observations of the child in familiar activities add up to a comprehensive view of a child's physical development.

Infants and Toddlers

The earliest assessment of motor development is performed routinely at 1 minute and at 5 minutes after birth. The newborn baby is assessed for appearance (color), heart rate, reflex irritability, activity, muscle tone, and respiratory effort to determine whether further medical assistance is needed. A practical scoring system frequently used to assess these attributes is the Apgar score (Apgar & James, 1962). Table 7.4 shows the five criteria (organized into an acronym for APGAR) and point values used to measure the effect of loss of oxygen and damage to the circulation in newborns. Each characteristic is rated 0, 1, or 2 (with 2 being the best). These are added together to obtain an overall score that varies from 0 to 10, with 7 to 10 indicating excellent condition. Although a typical Apgar 5-minute score has been shown generally to predict future developmental progress, an abnormal score does not necessarily predict developmental disability. For

Table 7.4 Apgar Scoring System

Points	0	1	2
Activity (muscle tone)	Limp	Some flexion	Active motion
Pulse (heart rate)	Absent	Below 100	Above 100
Grimace (gag reflex)	No response	Grimace	Sneeze, cough
Appearance (color)	Blue, pale	Body pink, extremities blue	Pink all over
Respiration	Absent	Slow, irregular	Vigorous cry

example, research found that Apgar scores of less than 5 at 5 minutes and 10 minutes correlate with an increased risk for CP. However, most infants with low Apgar scores do not develop CP (Committee on Obstetric Practice, American Academy of Pediatrics—Committee on Fetus and Newborn, 2015).

More extensive observation of the newborn may be accomplished through the Newborn Behavioral Observation (NBO) system (Nugent, 2015). This system is based on years of research using the Brazelton Neonatal Behavioral Assessment Scale originally published in 1973 (Brazelton & Nugent, 2001). The NBO system identifies the newborn's strengths as well as the challenges the infant will encounter in his or her new environment. It takes less than 10 minutes to administer and offers parents the opportunity to interpret the infant's cues and learn about the kinds of caregiving techniques and stimulation that are appropriate for their infant. The NBO is a helpful relationship-based tool with high-risk infants that may be used to promote improved parent–infant interaction and function, maternal well-being, and the infant's self-regulation and stress-coping mechanisms. It may be used in the neonatal intensive care nursery (NICU), NICU follow-up, and Part C early intervention home visits (McManus, 2015).

When infants or young children do not have an obvious impairment, it is much more difficult to detect possible problems related to motor development. Usually, a parent or early educator detects the more subtle behaviors that can be observed over time and are not seen in a short office visit with a medical specialist. Some of the behaviors that may be considered as indicators of the need for referral include the following:

1. Delayed motor milestones (although delay is an important indicator, typical developmental variations must be kept in mind)
2. Abnormal posturing of arms and legs during rest or activity
3. Tremor of hands or arms when performing a task
4. Significant difference in skill between right and left arms or legs
5. Early hand preference (before 13 months of age)
6. Poor balance and equilibrium
7. Difficulties in eye tracking
8. Poor coordination in gross or fine motor activities
9. Poor motor control of tongue, lips, or mouth muscles (e.g., drooling)
10. Inability to inhibit movements, as shown by jerking, mirroring, or fidgeting
11. Poor visual-motor integrative skills, often seen in drawing
12. Weakness or extreme fatigue during movement activities

The more of these signs a child displays, the more likely he or she is to have some type of neurological dysfunction. Any of these behaviors should be noted and communicated to the child's primary care physician. In addition, various medications can cause side effects that may appear to be symptoms of neuromotor or attentional problems. Early childhood program staff and parents should know about the possible side effects of any medication a child may be taking.

Severe Motor Impairments

It may be challenging to assess young children with severe physical disabilities, especially if cognitive or communication skills are also being evaluated. Because many assessment tasks require both fine and gross motor skills, the child with severe motor problems is penalized for inability to perform on standardized items. An understanding of primitive reflexes and abnormal movement patterns helps the educator place the child in the *best position* for achieving optimum voluntary motor responses. A PT or OT can provide ways to help the child improve motor performance and demonstrate skills in other developmental areas.

Video records of a child's behavior and performance in informal play settings can also be helpful in understanding the qualitative aspects of his or her ability. The evaluator may require several sessions to assess the child's strengths properly. Because the child's psychological and physiological state can drastically influence muscle tone and coordination, movement abilities may differ considerably from day to day.

General Considerations for Assessment of All Young Children

Effective observation of motor skills requires observers to keep in mind that the *process* of or *approach* to motor tasks is significant. How a child goes about trying to catch a ball is much more revealing than whether the ball is caught. There is a great difference in ability between the child whose eyes are following the path of the ball and whose hands are working together to attempt a catch, and the child who seems not to be looking at the ball and whose hands hang loose or do not seem to work together. Although neither one may actually catch the ball, their differences in attempts must be carefully noted and considered. They are clearly at different levels developmentally. A child's lack of experience in activities such as climbing stairs or using scissors also influences performance. The child's level of excitement or fear of strangers and/or new tasks could be further inhibitors to motor processes.

Because the quality of performance depends on physiological maturation and experience, assessment for the purpose of developing instructional objectives must depend on individually referenced criteria. Although comparison with group norms can provide the early childhood educator with a general frame of reference, it cannot determine whether individual progress is adequate in light of changes that take place within that individual. For example, a 3-year-old who has the body height and weight of a 2-year-old cannot be expected to perform balance tasks with the ease of most 3-year-olds. Considering lack of balance to be a weakness and including objectives to teach balance would be inappropriate until a shift in bodily proportion takes place. In short, educators are expected to combine knowledge from normative tests with the observation of individual differences and develop a set of *criterion-referenced* objectives.

Developmental Task Analysis.   Once a teacher has used a developmental checklist derived from normative expectations and has observed very carefully while considering individual levels of maturation, interests, and experiences, program activities can be determined. The checklist may include only broad curriculum objectives that may be stated more as goals, or it may contain a more specific task analysis that breaks each broader goal into teaching steps. The checklist then becomes a teaching as well as testing or assessment tool.

Play-Based Assessment

This approach provides many opportunities to observe a wide range of infants and young children in both structured and unstructured play activities. It is especially useful in observing movement behaviors. Linder (2008) has developed observation guidelines for sensorimotor development that encompass categories of (1) general appearance of movement, (2) muscle tone/strength/endurance, (3) reactivity to sensory input, (4) stationary positions used for play, (5) mobility in play, (6) other developmental achievements, (7) prehension and manipulation, and (8) motor planning. The **sensorimotor observations** are integrated into the overall transdisciplinary play-based assessment, which includes cognitive, language, and social development. Bricker (2006) also uses play as a means for curriculum-based assessment and, in addition, describes strategies for setting up play centers within a classroom to facilitate the assessment process.

Physical Therapy Intervention

What is the purpose of physical therapy intervention? Who should provide the therapy? How is it used in home- or center-based intervention programs? Early childhood special educators ask these critical questions when planning for children with physical limitations.

Intervention should focus on the development of **functional skills** that will enable the child to participate actively at home, at school, and in the community (Kennedy & Effgen, 2016; Noonan & McCormick, 2014). Work on functional motor goals should begin as early as possible, especially for young children with severe disabilities. Examples of functional goals might include picking up Cheerios, turning a doorknob, and holding a crayon during daily routines. Such skills enable the child to participate actively in his or her environment.

In planning intervention for an individual child, the therapist should look carefully at the child's functional level, considering activities for daily living, interactions within both home and community environments, skills needed to support other developmental areas (e.g., positioning for problem-solving activities or social interaction), and types of assistive devices needed to enhance performance. After reviewing this information, teachers have a better picture of the functional level and type of motor goals to be initiated for the child. Exhibit 7.1 illustrates the basic steps in facilitating motor development.

Exhibit 7.1

Example of Five Basic Steps in Facilitating Motor Development

Behavior: Child Rolls from Back to Stomach

1. *Decide which behavior you want to teach.*

   Debbie will roll from back to stomach without assistance.

2. *Decide on the cue you will use to prompt the child.*

   Say, "Roll over, Debbie" while physically assisting her. Favorite toys are lying out of reach in the direction Debbie will roll to encourage rolling.

3. *Decide on consequences to follow the behavior.*

   Debbie will play with the toy obtained by rolling.

4. *Break the behavior into small steps and order the steps (task analysis).*

   a. When Debbie is lying on her back, physically bring her right arm across her chest and, by bending her right knee, gently roll toward her left, all the way over from back to stomach.

   b. Debbie is physically rolled over one half of the way. She rolls the last half of the way on her own.

   c. Debbie rolls on her own from back to stomach.

   d. Debbie rolls on her own from back to front.

(continued)

Note: The verbal cue "Roll over, Debbie" is used during each step.

5. *Decide how well Debbie must do the behavior.*

a. The number of seconds you will wait following the cue: Debbie will roll within 30 seconds of the cue.

b. The number of times Debbie should perform correctly: Debbie will perform correctly 8 of 10 times. When Debbie does this 8 of 10 times for 3 days in a row, she can go on to the next step.

Role of Therapists

As part of the team approach in early childhood special education, the therapist must help teachers and parents understand the objectives and techniques for the development of functional motor skills. In consultation with physicians, the OT or PT will provide the expertise for implementing gross and fine motor activities and offer advice on positioning and use of therapeutic devices (braces, wheelchairs, etc.) as well as facilitating the development of feeding and other adaptive skills. He or she will also work with families in both home and school settings to help implement PT or OT interventions within the context of the child's daily routines at home and in school (Kennedy & Effgen, 2016; Wakeford, 2016).

In addressing the motor development of infants and young children, there may be overlap in the roles of PTs and OTs depending on their training and expertise. The responsibilities of PTs include: (1) explaining the child's diagnosis, implications for motor development, and relevant interventions to promote motor skills; (2) assessing the child's motor skills and development; (3) demonstrating handling and positioning techniques; and (4) providing adaptive equipment to support the child's motor development and skills (Snell, 2008). In contrast, OTs (1) assess a child's sensory processing abilities and neuromotor skills, including fine and oral-motor skills; and (2) identify their impact on play, activities of daily living, and participation in the family (Holloway, 2009). With older children and adults, the **physical therapist** is usually concerned with large muscle movement and gross motor activities, whereas the **occupational therapist** is more often involved in the evaluation and treatment of perceptual-motor (fine motor) functioning and activities of daily living.

Current recommended practices require the PT or OT to actually work in the classroom beside the teacher or in the home with the parents. In this way, the therapist also demonstrates how the therapeutic activities can be embedded into the daily routine of the classroom or the home so that interventions are learned within meaningful contexts and children are more likely to generalize new skills. In addition, the therapist can observe and participate in classroom or home activities that may lead to a better understanding of the child and other developmental concerns.

Interventions related to physical and occupational therapy should be embedded into the child's early childhood special education program, with the teacher understanding their rationale and implementing them within daily activities. Regular meetings are essential for a successful physical or occupational therapy program in classrooms. Ongoing staff training in the classroom or professional development for classroom staff should be a significant part of the therapist's responsibility. Teachers should identify their concerns related to a child's motor skills and draw on the expertise of the PT and OT to find out how best to include the child with physical difficulties in the preschool environment. Questions may include the following:

1. What is the child's motor difficulty or physical disability?

2. How does this problem affect his or her motor development and skills?

3. What types of adaptive equipment or assistive technology devices does this child need to participate actively in gross motor, fine motor, and self-help activities? How do we obtain and learn to use them?

4. Are there any specific considerations related to positioning and handling this child?

5. Are there any specific intervention strategies that we can use to support the child's motor skills?

Approaches to Therapy

Numerous widely differing therapeutic techniques are available to improve the motor performance of young children with physical disabilities, including exercise, skill instruction, use of adaptive devices, drug therapy, and often surgery.

Proper positioning, inhibition of abnormal reflexes, and facilitation of active movement are major concerns in working with a child who has CP or other neurological disorders. Among techniques for dealing with these, physical therapists continue to use the Neurodevelopmental Treatment Approach (NDT) originally developed by Bobath and Bobath (1984) as part of their treatment approach. Although an online search revealed few studies supporting the efficacy of NDT in improving the gross motor skills of young children with cerebral palsy (Tsorlakis, Evaggelinou, Grouios, & Tsorbatzoudis, 2004), the effectiveness of NDT remains inconclusive (Brown & Burns, 2001; Butler & Darrah, 2001). A summary of studies by the Neuro-Developmental Treatment Association (2015) found mixed results and questionable research rigor. NDT is currently used in many settings and has also been adopted by some OTs and speech-language pathologists (Howle, 2007). The use of the NDT approach requires extensive training. However, teachers and parents can apply the basic principles and practical applications under the guidance of therapists certified in NDT.

One therapeutic approach that continues to have significant influence in the field of early intervention is sensory integration. Even though sensory integration has become a very popular approach to working with young children with disabilities, it remains controversial. There is much anecdotal evidence of its positive effect in working with children who have a variety of disabilities, particularly with autism. However, there is as yet no widely accepted body of research demonstrating its effectiveness (Leong, Carter, & Stephenson, 2015). The following section provides a brief explanation of key components.

Sensory Integration

The theoretical model and therapeutic techniques of sensory integration originated with the work of Jean Ayres (2005). Sensory integration (processing) is the ability to take in, filter, and process incoming information from all the senses (Howe, Brittain, & McCathren, 2004). Information from the sensory systems (touch, movement, smell, taste, vision, and hearing) is integrated with stored information (e.g., prior experience, memories, and knowledge) and then organized into responses. Difficulty processing and organizing sensory information can result in sensory integration dysfunction, renamed *sensory processing dysfunction* (Miller, Cermak, Lane, Anzalone, & Koomar, 2004; Sensory Processing Disorder Network, 2010). The diagnostic label *sensory processing disorder* includes three categories: (1) sensory modulation difficulties (sensory overresponsivity, sensory underresponsivity, and sensory seeking/craving), (2) sensory discrimination difficulties, and (3) sensory-based motor difficulties, for example, postural disorders and dyspraxia (Miller et al., 2004; Miller, Robinson, & Moulton, 2004). The "sensory processing disorder" label is used by occupational therapists. However, the DSM-V does not recognize sensory processing disorder as a separate condition because of insufficient evidence. Similarly, in a policy statement about sensory integration therapies, the American Academy of Pediatrics stated that difficulties with sensory processing are associated with many developmental and behavioral disorders. Sensory processing disorder should not be diagnosed because there is no universal framework for its diagnosis (Zimmer & Desch, 2012). Studies with children who have ASD have

Video Example from

You Tube

Enhanced eText
Video Example 7.4
Routine in a Program—Rolling with Friends
https://www.youtube.com/watch?v=11StFJEzDf8
This video demonstrates how the PT involves peers while working on a child's motor skills.

revealed that their sensory responses are different from those of children without ASD (Tomchek & Dunn, 2007). Given the association of sensory processing problems with autism spectrum disorders and attention-deficit/hyperactivity disorders, as well as the common use of sensory integration therapy by OTs, the following discussion is intended to provide basic information for teachers to facilitate collaboration with OTs.

Sensory modulation difficulty is the most common sensory processing problem. Relevant intervention activities are designed to provide tactile (touch) and vestibular (balance) stimulation. The OT uses multisensory approaches that enhance the nervous system's abilities to organize and interpret sensory input in order to improve motor output effectiveness. Swings, rotary equipment, scooters, and other play equipment are used in the child's therapy. The two main types of sensory modulation problems are being oversensitive or hyperreactive and being undersensitive or hyporeactive (Miller, Robinson, & Moulton, 2004). These difficulties may result in the following.

Attention and Regulatory Problems.   Some children may have difficulty screening out or inhibiting their response to extraneous nonessential sensory information, such as background noises or visual stimuli. Such children may be easily distracted and have difficulty inhibiting their attention to these irrelevant stimuli. Therefore, they have difficulty maintaining attention to appropriate information. Some children may also have problems with **self-regulation**. That is, they may overreact to stimuli and have difficulty calming themselves once they are in a highly aroused state.

Sensory Defensiveness.   Most practitioners are familiar with children who demonstrate "tactile defensiveness" or hyperreactivity (oversensitivity) to touch. These children resist touching or handling common materials and textures. In addition, children may also be highly sensitive to other sensory stimuli, resulting in visual defensiveness (e.g., avoiding direct eye gaze or hypersensitivity to light or flashing lights) or vestibular defensiveness (intolerance of movement or unstable surfaces). Children can also be highly sensitive to oral sensations (e.g., certain food textures or temperatures), to olfactory stimuli (e.g., negative reactions to strong odors), or to auditory stimuli (e.g., avoidance of certain sounds or inappropriate behavior in the presence of too many people talking at once). Children's motor movements may be greatly inhibited by fears such as walking up or down steps or on uneven surfaces. This can result in an insistence on certain routines and behavioral rigidity (e.g., insistence on wearing certain clothing and eating certain foods or insistence on highly predictable, "safe" daily schedules). Children who are hypersensitive need calming sensory input such as predictable sensory input and routines; decreased visual and auditory stimuli; muted colors; indirect, low-intensity light; quiet, rhythmic sounds; rhythmic motor activities (e.g., swinging, patting, swaying, rocking); firm hugs; structured areas (e.g., room dividers or screens) for activities, with a small group of children in the same area; and sufficient notice when there will be a transition or change in the routine (Kurtz, 2008; Thompson & Rains, 2009).

Children who are hyposensitive or underreactive to sensory stimuli may appear withdrawn, disinterested, and difficult to engage. They may seem self-absorbed, passive, lethargic, and unresponsive to movement or sounds. These children require alerting sensory input such as varied sensory experiences to engage their interest; toys with sounds and lights; colorful visuals/pictures; music with varied intensity, pitch, and beat; animated and varied vocal intonation; different movements (e.g., rolling, bouncing, jumping); textured finger paints; stories that involve actions; scented and textured clay; and different colors and shapes of materials (Kurtz, 2008; Thompson & Rains, 2009).

Careful observation of children's behavior is critical to consider whether a child's response to sensory input can be viewed as one of two generalized responses: **hyperresponsiveness/hyperreactivity** or **hyporesponsiveness/hyporeactivity.** Those who respond in a hyperresponsive manner may avoid stimuli because they have a lower tolerance for it. Children who respond in a hyporesponsive manner may be slow to respond to stimuli and may seek more of it. Familiarity with these general categories will make the child's responses more understandable and will enable families and teachers to provide appropriate activities.

Therapeutic techniques are based on complex theories of neurology and require very specific training in sensory integration theory and interventions. Some advocates of "SI" therapy, as it is called, may be overzealous in their claims of the broad applicability of this therapeutic approach in treating a wide range of behavioral, educational, personality, and movement disorders. Recent reviews of studies on SI therapy indicate that additional research is needed. However, SI therapy appears to have significant promise in alleviating or managing certain attention and self-regulatory problems (Bodison & Parham, 2018; Schaaf, Dumont, Arbesman, & May-Benson, 2018).

Positioning and Handling

Although it is often important to encourage movement, there are times when the young child should remain in a static position. For infants and young children with motor impairments, one area of significant concern is positioning and handling. To modify excessive or insufficient muscle tone and to control the predominance of abnormal reflexes, certain positions and specific handling techniques should be integrated into the child's home and school activities.

Positioning is the placement of the child in carefully selected positions (e.g., side-lying, sitting, standing) to normalize muscle tone, prevent deformity, and stabilize the body. Careful positioning also allows a child to function more efficiently during toileting, feeding, play, and other functional activities. For example, if a child's trunk is not stabilized for sitting, control of the arms and hands for self-feeding and playing with toys may be compromised. Consult with the child's PT regarding the optimal positions for individual children in various activities. Children should be in stable and symmetrical positions. For example, when sitting in a chair, the child's pelvis should be in the center of the seat and against the back of the chair; the hips, knees, and ankles should be flexed approximately 90 degrees with the feet and ankles positioned slightly under the knees; and the feet should be flat and supported with the toes forward. Simple options for facilitating the proper sitting position include placing nonslip material on the seat (e.g., shelf liner) and using a block of wood or covered phone books to support the child's feet if they dangle above the floor. Furthermore, the table surface should not be too high or too low and the child's elbows should rest comfortably on the surface (Bruni, 2016).

Handling provides movement opportunities and sensory experiences. It provides control to promote normal movement experiences, such as shifting weight or eliciting a protective response. It is important to ask the child's PT or OT about the appropriate lifting and handling techniques to use with the individual child so the child is held and can move securely in a position that facilitates normal muscle tone and inhibits abnormal postures. According to Snell (2008), these are the benefits of proper positioning and handling techniques:

- Development of control over posture and movement
- Inhibition of abnormal muscle tone or posturing
- Provision of more normal sensory experiences of position and movement
- Provision of stable postures during the development of mobility
- Prevention of the development of joint contractures

Proper Lifting

In using correct lifting and carrying techniques, especially with young children who have severe motor impairments, the practitioner or parent has an opportunity to

Figure 7.3 Improper and proper lifting techniques

Source: Illustrations by Barbara L. Porter.

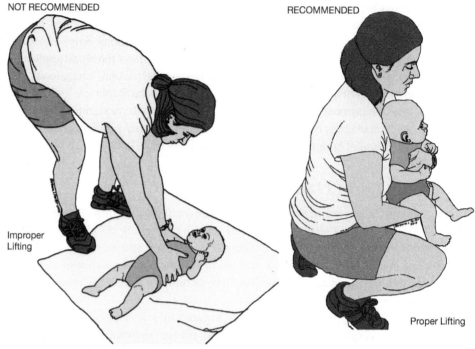

NOT RECOMMENDED

RECOMMENDED

Improper
Lifting

Proper Lifting

provide support as well as therapy. When a young child is lifted correctly, abnormal reflexes are not stimulated, and the child appears more normal and actually is under less stress. Some important steps in lifting and carrying are as follows:

1. Speak to the child, telling him or her what you are going to do and where you are going.
2. Wait for some response and encourage the child to assist in the process (e.g., "You need to help. Give me your hand").
3. Praise the child for any attempts to help.
4. Lift the child gently.

   To protect yourself from injury, practice the following:

1. Bend your knees and keep your back straight.
2. Avoid twisting; approach the child straight on.
3. Keep the child's body as close to yours as possible.
4. Do not try to carry the child by yourself if she is too large or too heavy.
5. Give the *least* amount of help needed.

Figure 7.3 shows proper and improper lifting techniques.

Adaptive Equipment and Assistive Technology Devices

Appropriate intervention program planning for children with motor problems may involve a diverse array of assistive technology devices or adaptive equipment. If needed, assistive technology devices should be identified on a child's individualized education program (IEP). The 2004 Individuals with Disabilities Education Act (IDEA) defines an assistive technology device as "any item, piece of equipment, or product system, whether acquired commercially off the shelf, modified, or customized, that is used to increase, maintain, or improve functional capabilities of a child with a disability. The term does not include a medical device that is surgically implanted, or the replacement."

This definition includes low-tech equipment (e.g., Velcro, bath seats, adaptive spoons and bowls) and high-tech equipment (e.g., computerized devices, powered wheelchairs) that can be used to support the motor and adaptive skills of young children (Campbell, Milbourne, Dugan, & Wilcox, 2006). Children may require *prostheses* (aids designed to function as limbs), *orthoses* (aids for assistance), *mobility devices* such as walkers and wheelchairs, positioning aids, or *academic aids* to help function in a classroom. The value and purpose of these types of devices are to help maintain normalized muscle tone, inhibit primitive reflexes, allow the child to use voluntary movements, provide optimal positioning to interact more effectively with the environment, and encourage independence. To become familiar with the adaptive equipment and assistive technology devices identified in this chapter, conduct an Internet search for images and information.

A child with a physical disability should be positioned to promote participation in activities with other children. If children are on the floor playing with blocks, the child with physical disabilities should also be positioned on the floor to enable eye contact, sharing, interaction, and turn taking (Judge, Floyd, & Woods-Fields, 2010). Wedges, bolsters, mobile standers, side lyers, and modified chairs should be used in a variety of ways as required. The choice of adaptive equipment should be made in consultation with a therapist, who can also help the teacher identify its purpose, explain its use for a particular disability, and describe any special precautions to be observed while the child is using the equipment. Teachers and families should advocate for the equipment their children need. Studies indicate that practitioners and families require information and training on the use of assistive technology for young children with disabilities (Judge et al., 2010; Kling, Campbell, & Wilcox, 2010).

Video Example from
You Tube

Enhanced eText
Video Example 7.5
Perl Using a Switch and Stander
https://www.youtube.com/
watch?v=cPqO8kKso4A
Simple adaptations to facilitate play between children are demonstrated in this video.

Enhanced eText Application Exercise 7.1: In this exercise, you can apply what you have learned in this chapter about the similarities and differences in the roles and responsibilities of physical and occupational therapists in working with young children who have disabilities

---

Development of Self-Care Skills

Self-care skills (such as feeding, dressing, grooming, and toileting) are part of adaptive development that comprises a large portion of the young child's daily living tasks. A family's culture, values, and child-rearing practices influence a child's development of self-care skills. Cultural values vary along a continuum from those that value independence of the individual and those that value interdependence or a mutual reliance on others within the family or community. It is important to determine the family's practices and expectations for the child's daily living skills so that interventions are family centered, routines-based, and culturally responsive. Using the following topics, a conversation with families can help practitioners gather information about a family's expectations and their child's self-care skills:

1. Please tell me about your child's daily routine related to self-care activities, that is, eating, dressing, tooth brushing, toileting, and hand washing.

2. Who helps your child with these self-care activities?

3. When does your child need help and what does your child do independently?

4. What activities are easy for your child?

5. What activities are difficult for your child?

6. What does your child like to eat and drink?

7. What foods or drinks does he dislike?

8. What would you like your child to learn related to self-care skills?

Certain motor skills, including a child's ability to control parts of his or her body, are important precursors for adaptive skill development. For example, between 9–12 months of age, children can pick up an object and bring it to the mouth if required for finger feeding (Bruns & Thompson, 2012). Although there are differences in when adaptive skills are acquired, development appears to follow a sequence. Knowledge of the steps in the adaptive domain is essential. This provides the basis for determining where to begin instruction and what prerequisite skills are needed. Table 7.5 presents the major milestones for adaptive skills.

Use of Task Analysis

Task analysis of adaptive skills is a process of breaking down a skill area into its component parts, as shown in Exhibit 7.1. Task subskills offer the specific information from which to assess and plan a developmental program for use by both parents and practitioners (Snodgrass, Meadan, Ostrosky, & Cheung, 2017). For example,

---

Table 7.5 Developmental Sequence of Adaptive Skills

Age in Months	Eating Skills	Toileting Skills	Dressing and Grooming
0–3	• Oral reflexes (e.g., sucking) present at birth • Coordinates sucking, swallowing, and breathing		
3–6	• Brings hand to mouth holding object • Begins to hold bottle with some assistance • May eat some solids—sucks from spoon • Begins to swallow from cup • Basic chewing begins to appear		
6–9	• Can hold bottle and bring it to mouth • Can hold and eat cracker • Uses tongue to move food in mouth • Eats infant food		
9–12	• More control over lips, tongue, and jaw • Holds spoon • Finger feeds	• Pays attention to acts of eliminating	• Holds arm out for sleeve
12–18	• Brings spoon to mouth • Drinks from cup with some spilling • Chews appropriately	• Indicates discomfort over soiled pants • Begins to sit on potty	• Takes off shoes and socks • Tries to put on shoes
18–24	• Sucks with straw • Scoops food, feeds self • Chews with rotary jaw movement • Uses cup with fewer accidents	• Communicates need to go to toilet	• Finds large armhole • Attempts to brush teeth
24–30	• Holds fork and begins to spear food	• Bladder trained during day	• Removes pull-down garments • Buttons large front button
30–36		• Becomes more routine-minded and sets time for elimination • Uses toilet independently	• Attempts to wash hands • Uses toothbrush • Opens front and side buttons • Closes front snaps

when teaching cup drinking, the steps may be broken into single teaching units, as follows:

1. Pick up cup with liquid from table with hands.
2. Bring cup to mouth without spilling.
3. Place end of cup on lower lip.
4. Close lips around edge of cup.
5. Tip cup to get sip of liquid in mouth.
6. Swallow liquid.
7. Remove cup from lips.
8. Lower cup to table.
9. Place cup upright on table.

The number of steps and substeps may depend on the child's cognitive level, the amount of physical mobility, and response to praise or rewards. For example, the child who enjoys drinks will be more motivated to learn to drink from a cup independently than one who is not interested in consuming liquids.

If the goal is too difficult or requires participation beyond the young child's physical abilities, a **partial participation task analysis** may be an alternative (Noonan & McCormick, 2014). In this approach, steps are broken down into even smaller increments to provide a flexible manner in which the child with more limitations can participate in a meaningful way. For example, the child's participation in cleanup after lunch may involve placing trash in a tub on the table, rather than moving to the trash can to throw things away (see Chapter 5 for a discussion of flexible participation).

A unique feature of task analyzing adaptive skills involves the use of **chaining,** which is based on the fact that one step must be accomplished before the next step can be performed. For assessment purposes, **forward chaining** (beginning with Step 1) yields the most useful information. **Backward chaining** or **reverse chaining** is more effective for teaching a skill to a child with developmental delays. With backward chaining, the adult does all but the last part of the task and lets the child complete the rest. Consider this example of backward chaining in which the child is first encouraged to complete Step 1 (last part) after the adult has completed Steps 5 to 2. After the child is able to complete Step 1, he or she will be expected to complete Step 2, and so on.

1. Child pulls on sock when just above heel.
2. Child pulls on sock when just below heel.
3. Child pulls on sock when toes have started in.
4. Child puts on sock when handed to her with heel in correct position.
5. Child puts on sock (heel in correct position).

Positive facial expressions and specific praise for each success combined with "you put your sock on!" encourage the child's development of self-care skills and build language. Tube socks may be easier for some children to put on because they do not have heels.

Dressing, toileting, and feeding are each a complex set of adaptive skills that are critical to a child's self-confidence and competence. Therapeutic and instructional procedures are emphasized in the next section.

Dressing

Whenever possible, instruction should be done at appropriate times and in natural situations, such as in the child's home when dressing and undressing normally occur. This will involve active family and staff participation in defining the goals, teaching procedures, establishing several types of reinforcers, and designing an easy data-keeping system.

As with all other adaptive areas, children with motor impairments have more difficulty learning dressing skills unless adaptations can be made. The following suggestions were offered by Finnie (1997) decades ago and are still applicable:

- Begin with the easiest garments and follow the typical sequential development of helping the child to accomplish undressing skills before learning to put on clothes.

- Clothes used for practice should be a few sizes larger than the child's normal size for ease of manipulation and putting on and off.

- Children may benefit from performing dressing or grooming tasks in front of a mirror.

- Children who have poor balance can complete many dressing skills while lying down. For example, a child may begin by side lying to pull pants on and then gradually turn as pants are raised to waist level. This positioning is especially useful when there is excessive motor tone.

- Children can sit in the corner of a sofa or use a corner chair to provide more stability while dressing.

- If the supine position on the caregiver's lap, changing table, or floor does not reduce extensor tone, the child may be placed prone over the caregiver's lap. Lower and upper extremity dressing can be done in this position. (Always consult with the child's PT.)

- Simple changes to a child's clothes may be the determining factor to enable self-dressing; for example, use of Velcro in place of snaps or buttons, elasticized waistbands, adding a metal ring through a zipper's tab to make it easier to grasp and pull, tube socks to eliminate the need of getting the heel positioned correctly, and slip-on shoes or shoes with Velcro closures.

- For all young children, use the opportunity to label clothing verbally and use parallel talk to describe the child's experience and actions in each step of the process (e.g., "Hold the sock, pull it up").

Toileting

Independent toileting skills are often an area of concern and frustration for both parents and children (and, yes, for the early childhood special education practitioner). Children without disabilities usually achieve bowel and daytime bladder control between 2½ and 3 years of age. Children with more severe developmental delay may take more time to develop toileting skills (Bruni, 2016). This does not suggest that younger children with developmental disabilities cannot be toilet trained. It does, however, point out the need for a coordinated team effort and consistent follow-through for both home and center programs.

Prerequisites to training include neuromuscular control and the child's awareness of discomfort when he or she has wet or soiled diapers. Then the child's pattern of elimination must be established. One way of doing this is to check every half hour to determine whether the child is dry or wet or has had a bowel movement. Over time, perhaps 7 days, a pattern of elimination may emerge if eating habits and activity levels have remained constant. This pattern guides the design and implementation of the toilet training program.

Other prerequisite skills that speed toilet training are the ability to walk with or without assistance, the ability to indicate a need to use the toilet, the ability to remain in a sitting position for at least 5 minutes, and the ability to comprehend and follow instructions. Some children may need to be encouraged to drink sufficient liquids so the need to eliminate is more predictable.

While the child is learning the prerequisites, Noonan and McCormick (2014) suggest that toileting needs are most easily managed through "timed toileting." This involves placing the child on the toilet for a few minutes at a time until elimination occurs. This way, the child becomes habit trained. If the child uses the toilet, provide positive reinforcement. If the child does not eliminate, remove him or her from the toilet without making a fuss. To further increase awareness of the toileting process each time the child eliminates, the adult can label the process by saying, "Megan, you did number one (or two)," using whatever label the parents and teacher feel are appropriate. (Terminology should be consistent.) See the American Occupational Therapy Association (2014) for a handout on tips for establishing a toileting routine. Other suggestions to facilitate the toilet training process include the following:

- Be calm and positive throughout the toileting process.
- Use the same child-friendly and culturally appropriate words for "toilet," "urination," and "bowel movement" consistently.
- Know that not all terms translate well across cultures. For example, the manual sign for toilet is shaking the "T" handshape, but in some Asian cultures, this gesture is viewed as very insulting.
- Read stories about a child learning how to use the toilet.
- Explain how to use the toilet in developmentally appropriate words the child will understand. For example, "You sit here and go pee-pee and poop."
- Empty the contents of the child's diaper into the potty chair or toilet so the child can see what is supposed to happen.
- Show the child what's in the toilet before flushing.
- Provide models so the child can see parents and older siblings use the toilet. Discuss this suggestion with families, as they may vary in their level of comfort regarding this suggestion.
- Teach boys to first urinate sitting on the potty chair; then once that habit is established, they can learn to stand and urinate.
- Establish a toileting routine. For example, always use the toilet after meals and before bath time or getting on the bus to go home from school.
- Praise a child's toileting success and calmly clean up accidents.
- Once the child is using the toilet regularly, teachers may discuss the switch from diapers to training pants with the family and announce that the child wears "big boy pants!"

When children have difficulty in maintaining trunk control while sitting on a potty chair, adaptations can be made to existing chairs by adding back and side supports or hip and shoulder straps, or using a commercial potty seat that includes these features. Fear or discomfort in sitting on a potty seat or potty chair will certainly make this a terrifying or frightening process for a child rather than a natural, relaxed experience. Relaxation can be achieved when the child feels secure with feet either on the floor or with some type of foot rest.

Supportive adults willing to work through the ups and downs of the training period are essential. Potty time, as well as diaper changing, is an opportune time to engage in language development activities, including nursery rhymes and songs.

Feeding

Mealtimes are natural opportunities for developing the child's social, communication, motor, and self-care skills. Children benefit from calm, predictable, and pleasurable mealtime routines. Teachers, therapists, and parents need to coordinate efforts to reinforce newly learned skills and develop others. The family dinnertime provides the best opportunity for a child to integrate language, socialization, and motor skills learned during the school day. Because of the time and attention required by the parent to perform the task of feeding, parents can consider feeding the child with a disability before the regular dinnertime. Then, during the meal, the child can be given dessert or a toy so that he or she may continue to participate and interact with the family without placing demands on the parents' mealtime. As the child becomes more independent, this schedule would probably change.

For infants and young children with severe disabilities, individualized plans for feeding must be a necessary part of the team's recommendation. This is especially true when there is a neuromotor disability, such as CP. Strategies may be needed to minimize the effects of oral-motor problems, including proper positioning and use of adaptive equipment. Positioning is critical in feeding the child with motor problems. If proper positioning techniques are not used during feeding, many children with abnormal muscle tone have problems with gagging, choking, or swallowing. Everyone who feeds the child must have an understanding of the child's movement patterns in order to respond appropriately to changes that may occur from day to day and hour to hour. Whenever possible, ongoing consultation with the OT or PT can offer important assistance in this process. Figure 7.4 shows the most usual positions for feeding: lap, arm, or chair.

In addition, consider the following suggestions, as adapted from Bruns and Thompson (2012) and Hooper and Umansky (2009).

Feeding Positions

- Positions in which a child can be fed will depend on age, physical size, postural tone, and movement patterns (see the examples in Figure 7.4).
- Unless an infant is still being bottle or breast fed, he or she should be positioned as upright as possible.
- The child should be comfortable and stable, and as upright as possible with the head, neck, and body aligned, and the body flexed.
- The child's head should be tilted slightly forward to encourage normal swallowing.
- Avoid hand pressure on the back of a child's head while feeding because this may elicit a primitive reflex that causes the child's body to extend.
- The child's legs should be relaxed and feet flat on the foot rest or on the floor when sitting in a high chair or adapted seat.
- Adults should sit in front of the child to encourage face-to-face interaction or beside the child with an arm around the child's head to support jaw and lip movements if needed. Standing over or behind the child will encourage neck extension and a poor position for the child to develop eating or drinking skills.

Sucking and Swallowing

- For bottle feeding, use nipples with regular-size holes. Larger holes in a nipple may cause choking if there is difficulty swallowing.
- When the child begins to suck on the nipple, "tug" gently at the nipple as if to pull it out. This can encourage the child to suck a bit harder. Also try thickening the liquid with a small amount of rice cereal for more suck resistance.
- A downward stroke on the cheek stimulates sucking.
- If the child requires jaw control, sit beside the child and place your thumb over the child's jaw joint with your index finger under the child's lip and your middle finger under the child's chin to gently push the chin up. If the child faces you, put your index finger over the child's jaw joint, your thumb between the lower lip and the child, and your middle finger under the child's chin to provide jaw control.

Figure 7.4 Most common positions for feeding

Source: Illustrations by Barbara L. Porter.

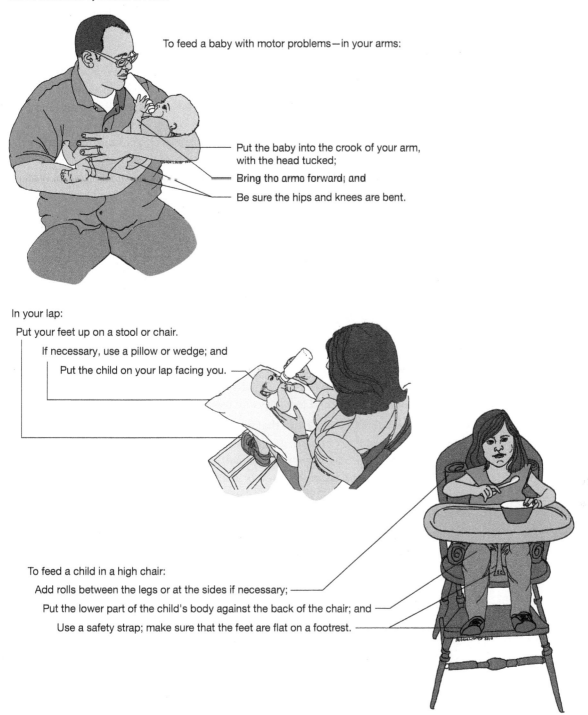

To feed a baby with motor problems—in your arms:

Put the baby into the crook of your arm, with the head tucked;

Bring the arms forward; and

Be sure the hips and knees are bent.

In your lap:

Put your feet up on a stool or chair.

If necessary, use a pillow or wedge; and

Put the child on your lap facing you.

To feed a child in a high chair:

Add rolls between the legs or at the sides if necessary;

Put the lower part of the child's body against the back of the chair; and

Use a safety strap; make sure that the feet are flat on a footrest.

- If there is a lack of normal swallowing, close the child's mouth (supported if necessary); stroke downward under the chin.
- Encourage mouthing and sucking of toys, hands, and pacifiers during nonfeeding times.

Self-Feeding

- When beginning to teach chewing, use foods that a child can digest easily.
- Place small amounts of food between the child's teeth on the inside of the mouth. Use lip and jaw control as necessary to keep the mouth closed. This should stimulate a chewing response.
- From pureed or baby foods, gradually introduce textured foods (e.g., bits of dry cereal, toast, soft cheese, diced potato, etc.).
- Finger feeding is the first step in self-feeding for very young children and may be encouraged by the following:
  - Caregiver holds food with own fingers and encourages child to bring caregiver's hand to mouth.
  - Caregiver holds food and encourages child to grasp food.
  - Caregiver places small bits of food on a flat surface for the child to pick up.
- Problems with finger feeding may require that the adult place a hand over the child's and assist his or her getting food into the mouth. Reduce support from the hand, to the wrist, to the elbow, and finally to no support. Use the same routine when a spoon is introduced.
- If the child has a hypersensitive bite reflex, use a small rubber-coated spoon for feeding. Place the spoon on the front third of the tongue and apply downward pressure. Remove the spoon at a 45-degree angle and avoid scraping food off with the teeth. Food should be removed with the lips.
- Children with severe eating and drinking problems are at risk for choking. Food may easily obstruct airways. If a child is coughing, the airway is not totally obstructed. Allow the child to cough and assist him or her to lean forward.
- Safety reminder: Cut up foods that a young child may choke on (e.g., grapes, hot dogs, and pieces of meat), and avoid hard foods (e.g., bacon, peanuts, popcorn, raw carrot pieces, nuts, or any small round food, such as candy) or sticky foods (e.g., popcorn, peanut butter, or marshmallows). These foods are easy to choke on.
- A nonslip rubberlike material, purchased by the roll, can be used for placemats under plates, toys, and so on, to keep them in place.
- Utensils should be easy for the child to grasp to encourage self-feeding.
- The child should be seated at eye level with other children in the group.

Drinking

- Offer broths or semisweet liquids (warm or cool) for the beginning stages of cup training. Milk and sweet liquids seem to impede the process.
- Place the rim of the cup on the child's lower lip. Do not place the cup between the teeth as this position causes abnormal swallowing.
- Use of a cutout cup (for child's nose) helps to observe lip closure and avoids bending the child's head back.
- Some children with disabilities may need thickened liquids or foods to encourage feeding and drinking skills. Applesauce or pureed vegetables may be used to thicken foods, and gelatin powder, yogurt, or commercial thickeners may be used to thicken liquids.
- Widely varying cups and eating utensils are available from several adapted equipment companies. Consult with therapists on selection of the most appropriate items for individual children.

Healthy Diets

A family's culture, values, and economic and educational levels determine their children's diets. Age-appropriate amounts of fruits, vegetables, proteins, grains, and dairy products offer a healthy and balanced diet for young children. In contrast, so-called junk foods, sugary foods and drinks, and foods with saturated and trans fats (cakes, cookies, bacon, and french fries) provide poor nutrition for everyone. With families, teachers may share information on healthy diets from the Mayo Clinic and the U.S. Department of Education:

> *Nutrition for Kids: Guidelines for a Healthy Diet* at http://www.mayoclinic.org/healthy-lifestyle/childrens-health/in-depth/nutrition-for-kids/art-20049335

> *Health Eating for Preschoolers* at https://wicworks.fns.usda.gov/wicworks/Topics/Preschooler.pdf

Some children may be picky eaters with limited food preferences. Other children may have limited exposure to a variety of foods, particularly those included in school lunches, and may not like them. Strategies to expand a child's diet include providing multiple opportunities for snacks during the day, a caregiver or peer showing pleasure in eating a bite of the new food, offering the child a bite of the new food with a preferred food, encouraging the child to taste the new food, finding creative ways to present the food (e.g., making a face out of fruit pieces), and praising the child's efforts to try new foods.

Practitioners must find out from families whether children have any food allergies and make sure that the diet of such a child is monitored at school. Common food allergies include milk, eggs, peanuts and other nuts, soybeans, wheat, fish, and shellfish.

Enhanced eText Application Exercise 7.2: In this exercise, you can apply what you have learned in this chapter about the benefits of embedding interventions in self-care activities to encourage functional behaviors, including gross and fine motor skills.

Adapting the Environment

Programs for children with disabilities should identify obstacles to the children's access to the environment and learning experiences, remove these obstacles, and facilitate the children's active participation. They should draw on the concepts of Universal Design and Universal Design for Learning (as discussed in Chapter 4).

The Classroom or Center

The early education classroom is a dynamic system that includes both physical and social components. Physical components include the actual classroom space, the arrangement of activity areas within the space, the furniture and fixtures, the play and work materials, the activities of the program and their sequence, the number of adult participants, the number and types of children (with and without disabilities), and the grouping of staff and children. Social components are the behaviors of and interactions between and among adults and children in the classroom setting.

The classroom environment can facilitate movement and independence by providing opportunities for children to determine their own behavior and manage some of their own materials. Accessible bathrooms, drinking fountains, and play materials encourage independence and learning. In collaboration with specialists (PT, OT, early childhood special education [ECSE] teachers), preschool teachers should evaluate their classrooms to determine how to accommodate a child with physical disabilities using the following considerations:

- Is the environment uncluttered, with ample space to move around? Is there room for a child using a wheelchair or walker, or a child who is learning to walk, to move in and out of the space and turn around?

- Are there interesting things for the child to see and touch, such as mirrors, mobiles, bulletin boards, children's work, and toys? Are labels at eye level for a child who uses a wheelchair?

- Are shelves and tables at an appropriate level for a child's height? Does the height of the table accommodate a child in a wheelchair? Can each activity area accommodate the child?

- Are shelves, tables, sinks, and other fixtures sturdy and stable enough to hold the weight of a child who may need to use them for support?

- Are materials and toys stored within easy reach of the child?

- Is the child's cubby and coat hook within easy reach?

- Are the visual cues (e.g., use of color, dividers, or labels) that designate different areas easy to discriminate and used consistently?

- What adaptive equipment and assistive technology devices are needed to facilitate the child's active participation in all activities?

In an effort to make inclusion classrooms appropriate for the young child with motor impairments, activities involving movement should allow the child to be involved as much as possible without accentuating the inability to move well. For example, the leader can combine movement activities with floor locomotion activities such as rolling or combat crawling. (These movement activities are enhanced by music or rhymes.) If a child is unable to perform movements voluntarily, an adult should provide the least amount of physical assistance needed to guide the child's participation in activities.

The Home

In home-based programs, the primary learning environment is the home and its surroundings. Although program staff may have little control over the child's home, the home visitor may recommend ways to make the home safe and facilitate learning. Burns, cuts, falls, electrical shock, and poisoning are some of the major home hazards. A practitioner who reviews such hazards with the family and explains what to expect from children at different ages promotes safety concerns. Other things that the home visitor may wish to explore with parents are the following:

1. The kinds of toys and objects in the home that facilitate exploration and learning

2. Toys that are age and developmentally appropriate and can be adapted to accommodate the child's learning needs

3. The level of visual and auditory stimulation in the home

4. Modification to the environment that may allow the child greater independence and freedom of exploration

5. Adaptive equipment, such as chairs, prone boards, and self-care aids, to encourage opportunities for social interaction and participation in family life

Exhibit 7.2 describes how to embed therapies within the home routine.

Video Example from

You Tube

Enhanced eText
Video Example 7.6
Routine in a Program—Playing "Red Light, Green Light" with a Voice-Output Device
https://www.youtube.com/watch?v=MybFrR79pTo
This video shows how a voice-output device assists a child to participate in a movement game.

Exhibit 7.2

Embedding Therapies into Home Routines

Because therapeutic intervention for young children with significant physical disabilities must include more than a weekly clinic visit or prescribed routines in a center-based program, emphasis on the integration of occupational and/or physical therapy interventions into the home routine is essential. Part C of IDEA emphasizes natural environments as the most appropriate context for early intervention services, as well as the need for family-centered services. Thus, it is essential that the therapist and family collaborate to identify the times and contexts within which to apply intervention strategies and work on goals that are relevant for the child and realistic for the family. By assessing the family's typical routine, the therapist and family can identify naturally occurring teaching opportunities within the child's home and community.

An example of embedding therapeutic interventions into existing family routines can be seen in the case of Frankie R., a 2-year-old boy with severe spastic quadriplegia. He is enrolled in a home- and center-based early intervention program, where he receives physical therapy on a weekly basis. The therapist and Frankie's parents identified several goals for the home and center. Two of the goals included in the family plan are the following:

1. To increase range of motion in shoulders and hips
2. To establish symmetry and head control while sitting

5:30 P.M.: Television, relaxing with Dad

Method: Position Frankie straddling Dad's leg, side lying on the couch, or prone-lying over Dad's lap.

Rationale: Mr. R. agreed that these procedures would not conflict with his need to relax and also would provide an opportunity for him to interact with Frankie. The physical therapist indicated that both goals were being addressed.

7:00 P.M.: Bath with Mom or Dad

Method: Stretch Frankie's shoulders and hips while bathing and drying him; also stretch his trunk by hip and shoulder rotation. Facilitate head control and reaching by playing in the water and touching body parts.

Rationale: The warm water and terrycloth towels tend to help Frankie relax, and, while he is undressed, this is a good opportunity to work on range of motion. Bath time provides a natural motivation to maintain head control and to move the arms in the water. It is also an excellent time for communication.

Using this approach for all home activities allows the maximum benefit from parent-identified activities that, with minimal intrusion, can be used to provide practice of important developmental skills.

Enhanced eText Application Exercise 7.3: In this exercise, you can apply what you have learned in this chapter to identify considerations for material and environmental adaptations to support the participation of young children with disabilities in settings with typically developing peers.

Video Example from

You **Tube**

Movement Education

Whenever infants and young children move any part of their bodies, there is potential for two kinds of learning to occur: learning to move and learning from moving. The relationship between movement and cognitive development has long been recognized. The classic cognitive theorist Piaget (1954) supported the belief that the child's first learning experiences are motoric. This realization emphasized the importance of movement for young children and allowing them to explore and experience the world.

Furthermore, research has found that movement/music intervention programs focusing on gross motor skills have a positive influence on the motor development of preschoolers (Venetsanou & Kambas, 2010) and encourage auditory discrimination, sound localization, and purposeful movement of children with visual impairments (Coleman, 2017). Teachers should collaborate with relevant related service personnel such as the adaptive physical education (APE) teacher, PT (for a child with physical disabilities), or orientation and mobility instructor (for a child who is blind) to develop a range of movement activities for preschoolers with disabilities in an inclusion class. Murata and Tan (2009) suggest a focus on imitation skills, bilateral integration and sequencing, and spatial awareness. Suggested activities include the following.

Imitation Skills

- Imitation of different body movements and actions (e.g., clapping hands or stamping feet)
- Imitation with objects (e.g., shaking a tambourine, tapping sticks together, putting a bean bag on your knee)
- Imitation using a tool (e.g., pointing to pictures with a stick or picking up small objects with tongs)
- Imitation of actions to songs and finger plays

Bilateral Integration and Sequencing

- Crawling on all fours, throwing, catching, or bouncing balls
- Marching to various rhythms, twisting, and reaching each hand to the opposite part of the body
- Rocking, swinging, and other activities that encourage crossing the midline
- Using instruments to set a beat and then asking children to tap their hands or stomp their feet in time to the beat

Spatial Awareness

- Move around in own personal space as defined by a carpet square or hula hoop (e.g., move right/left, forward/backward, step in or out)
- Walk, run, hop, or move toward a target without touching each other
- Go through obstacle courses that encourage changes in direction and position (e.g., going backward, crawling under, climbing over)

Movement education as a critical component of early education should also be viewed as a means of providing growth in critical thinking, problem solving, learning to think before acting, and paying attention to details (Marigliano & Russo, 2011). The next section highlights adaptations in movement education, including the significant role of music and imaginative play in young children's development.

Movement Skills and Music

Music, even without movement, enhances any program because it allows everyone to participate by listening, observing, or swaying. Dancing, marching, imitating, and imagining are often more enjoyable with music, and flexible participation does not detract from the positive experience.

Most songs on commercial CDs move a bit too fast for preschoolers, at least at first. If so, sing the songs without accompaniment and say the directions first. Using your voice also allows variation in pacing and intonation to engage children's attention, substituting words that are meaningful to children, and shortening or lengthening the song according to the children's interest. Gradually, as the children's ability to listen and move quickly grows, accompaniment can be added. Keep in mind that young children with mild hearing losses or perceptual problems may find recorded voices difficult to understand.

Rhythm bands, whether they include real instruments or pans with spoons, are exciting to children. Banging on something is an excellent way to develop awareness of body movement. Learning to make different kinds of noises by stamping feet loudly and tiptoeing quietly leads to other kinds of body awareness.

Numerous books are available to assist teachers in movement skills activities with the accompaniment of music. Because it is difficult to define dances or other rhythmic activities in terms of age, teachers must carefully think through their children's developmental characteristics. Even the most appealing jingle can frustrate children if the accompanying movements are too difficult (Palmer, 2001). For children with disabilities, beginning with the most simple and gradually working up to the more difficult songs or games is appropriate. Use a familiar tune and vary the words to focus on selected concepts, vocabulary terms, or situations—for example, when walking back to the classroom after recess, sing, "This is the way we march to class" to the tune of "Here We Go Round the Mulberry Bush." You may need to offer a personal invitation to reluctant children to join in by offering them your hand. If they do not accept, they should not be forced to join.

The Contribution of Music Therapy.   Informal use of music by teachers has long been used to increase children's attention, vocalization, and vocabulary, as well as motor coordination through singing and hand gestures. As introduced in Chapter 4, the field of music therapy is a growing contributor to the discipline of early childhood special education. It presents a positive, and increasingly evidence-based, way to build on the universal appeal of music and rhythm in supporting the needs of children who have disabilities. It has been demonstrated to increase brain plasticity and cognitive function to support memory (Thant, Peterson, & McIntosh, 2005). A meta-analysis conducted by Whipple (2004) found that music therapy is increasingly used with children who have autism spectrum disorder (ASD), with generally positive results. A review by Simpson and Keen (2011) reported somewhat more limited results of effectiveness. Rhythm activities (e.g., tapping, marching, and drumming) support coordination of gait and balance, and provide multisensory inputs (auditory, visual, tactile, and kinesthetic). Music therapy can also be used to target and support interactive turn taking with peers. As young children with disabilities develop preferences for familiar melodies and songs, music can also be used systematically to reduce anxiety and improve self-regulation.

Movement Skills and Imagination

According to Diachenko (2011), at about 2½ and 3 years old, children demonstrate two types of imagination. Cognitive imagination is used when children use dolls to reproduce familiar actions (e.g., feeding, putting a baby to bed). Affective imagination is used when children reproduce their feelings, (e.g., fear of a character in a story, such as a monster or wolf). Imaginary processes involve (a) creating an idea and (b) making a plan to operationalize that idea. Creating an idea requires restructuring images or words. Children may create an image of something they want to make. For example, children can convert a circle into a cookie or wheel, and so on. At 4 to 5 years of age, children's cognitive imagination promotes the development of role-play, painting, and construction games.

Children often need help in imagining things because some have had little opportunity to pretend or have not yet developed the language skills to engage in such play. Teachers can teach the concept of "pretending" by providing peer models, props, and role-play scripts. Children enjoy pretending to be what they have experienced in real life or seen in videos or books—for example, doctors examining patients, bus drivers, animals, and robots. Dress-up clothes add to the fun but are not necessary. Stories and flannel board materials can help stimulate ideas. Pretending to put out a fire with an imaginary hose is almost as exciting as the real thing and much safer.

Children discover the motions people make through seeing a combination of real people, videos, and pictures. Then they take turns pretending. Gradually, they become more creative. The firefighter has to put out a fire on the roof, so he stretches up high. Next, the fire is in the basement, so he aims the hose down low. A robot, walking with stiff legs, may move very slowly. Then, as someone turns the controls, he moves faster or even more slowly. Although the teacher may need to suggest ways to move at first, the children's use of imagination improves quickly.

Adaptations in Movement Education

Parents and early childhood educators are adept at using prompts (cues) when assisting children who are having difficulty developing motor skills considered to be age or developmentally appropriate. If a child does not respond to a normal verbal direction and modeling of desired responses, the verbal direction is repeated and accompanied by gestures. If there is still no response or an inadequate one, the verbal request can be accompanied by physically helping the child to perform the act. Positive reinforcement is given at whatever level the act is attempted. Of course, physical or gestural prompts are removed (faded) as soon as possible. Other adaptations are included in the following list and noted in Exhibit 7.3.

Exhibit 7.3

A Gross Motor Activity with Adaptations

Goal

To develop body image; to increase awareness of moving in different directions (directionality).

Objectives

Given directions to move forward, backward, and sideways, each child will do the following:

1. Do as directed when the teacher prompts (physically, with gestures, or with additional words, as needed).
2. As a member of a group, follow the teacher's spoken and gestured signal.
3. As a member of a group, follow spoken directions (no gestures).
4. Throughout this lesson, stop and remain still in the exact position he or she was in at that moment when asked to "freeze." (This condition helps children learn to inhibit unnecessary movements.)

Procedure

Begin with a small group of children sitting in a line facing the teacher. Then the activity may proceed according to the following steps (of course, variations will be determined by the individual needs of the children), using a "Simon Says" game format to provide individual practice and then a group learning opportunity:

1. "Simon says: Susie, come stand on the X" (point to the letter "X" made with masking tape on the floor).
2. "Good! Simon says walk forward, 1, 2, 3 steps" (physically prompting and gesturing to Susie).
3. "Right, you've walked forward. Great. Sit down. Tommy, Simon says it's your turn. Come stand on the X."
4. "Tommy, Simon says walk backward 1, 2, 3 steps." (Gesturing—but because Tommy begins to move backward, no physical prompting is needed.)
5. "Tommy, you did that just right. You walked backward."

6. Once each child has practiced the selected movements, provide an opportunity for the whole small group to play the game. Children can take turns being "Simon."

Procedural Notes

The teacher's enthusiasm and encouragement are of critical importance. The lessons will be individualized as each child's movements are observed. For example, children may need to wear a red band on their right hands to remember to distinguish left from right and have a familiar landmark in the room to learn directional movements, e.g., "Take two steps to the right, move towards the window." Use of landmarks, physical prompts, gestures, and demonstrations is faded as the children demonstrate understanding of concepts through appropriate responses. Children are encouraged to verbalize their understanding of their body movements through natural conversation as the activity progresses. Other considerations include the following:

1. Initially, each child should be given a brief individual turn. Children learn from watching. Begin with the child who is most likely to succeed with little or no help. This child serves as a model for the others to follow.

2. Next, pair two children at a time to follow the directions. The children may be given the same or two different directions, depending on their stage of development. (Keep the activity moving.)

3. As soon as possible (but for some children, this may take several days), have groups of three to five children moving at the same time.

4. To add variety, a 4/4 march or dance rhythm can be introduced with a drum, by singing, or using a CD. A square dance calling format can be included with the help of another adult. Guide children as needed, using modeling or prompting as well as calling out the directions.

5. New directions should be introduced following this same sequence, before incorporating them into the dance.

Lesson Adaptations

1. For the child with a hearing loss:
   a. Be sure the child can see your facial expressions and gestures.
   b. Place a child with good listening skills on either side of the child with a hearing loss.
   c. Let this child feel the drum or other musical instrument as the rhythm is played. It sometimes helps to set speakers on the wooden floor and let the child perform with bare or stocking feet.

2. For the child with a severe visual impairment:
   a. Use physical prompts until the verbal prompts can be followed. (Fade physical assists as soon as possible.)
   b. Assign a sighted peer "buddy." Holding hands may be helpful at certain times.
   c. Be certain the physical space for the activity is free from tripping and falling hazards.

3. For the child with a motor disability:
   a. Encourage as much active participation as possible.
   b. Use equipment (e.g., walkers, standers) as needed.
   c. Have an adult push the child's wheelchair, if necessary.
   d. Assign the child to be caller or drum beater.

4. For the child with an intellectual disability:

   a. Provide verbal and physical prompts as needed.
   b. Place excellent peer models beside the child.
   c. Give directions slowly and one at a time.
   d. Repeat directions as often as necessary (with enthusiasm).
   e. Demonstrate patience if the child cannot do what he or she could do the day before.
   f. Praise each small step of progress to reinforce and motivate the child.

1. When planning weekly lessons, incorporate some movement activities into each day's plan, alternate vigorous activities with more relaxing ones, and intersperse activities in a group with activities alone or with a partner.

2. Vary body positions in on-the-floor activities as well as during activities that involve locomotion, with the goal of giving attention to all attributes of movement.

3. Allow time for children to concentrate on their own bodily actions by using equipment and music with some but not all activities.

4. Facilitate the participation of those with perceptual or linguistic difficulties by providing repetition and modeling when giving directions and using simple vocabulary. Move from simple to complex and do not expect children necessarily to transfer meaning from one activity to another.

5. Break tasks into simple sequential steps and provide possible reinforcement at the accomplishment of each step. Avoid trying to cover too much or continuing an activity for too long.

6. Be conscious of each child's fatigue and attention levels. Maintain eye contact and do not allow outside distractions.

7. If a child has a visual impairment, be sure to use his or her name when verbally directing his or her activities.

8. Use of visual cues such as "stop" and "go" signs in red and green not only serve as attention getters but are essential to assist those with hearing loss or auditory processing difficulties. Avoid standing in front of a window to minimize the potential for glare when children look to you for direction. Be sure to get every child's attention before beginning to give directions.

9. Be creative as you include children with physical disabilities. Many activities can be done from a sitting position as well as a standing position. For example, children can touch their "heads, shoulders, knees, and toes" while sitting. Rather than run under a parachute, a "buddy" child may be selected to push their peer's wheelchair under the parachute.

10. To keep control, encourage only those activities that do not go beyond the level of movement or noise that adults and children can easily tolerate.

Chapter 8 conveys the complex nature of the development of communication skills. Its focus is on the importance of helping young children develop functional communication skills that will enable them to initiate and influence social interaction.

Summary

Professionals who work with children with a wide range of abilities and disabilities in various early childhood settings should understand physical and psychological factors that may interfere with the typical developmental process. Because young children are now being cared for in many programs as well as the home, knowledge of early behaviors is critical in planning intervention and assisting parents effectively. All early educators should study the development and interrelationship of the nervous system and motor skills.

The young child with a motor delay requires an interdisciplinary team approach involving the physician, therapists, nutritionists, parents, and teachers to address the child's learning needs at home and at school. Observations and team planning ensure consistency and selection of appropriate intervention strategies. Mutual understanding of therapeutic and educational goals facilitates the embedding of natural opportunities for motor skill development in everyday activities.

Adaptations of materials and environmental considerations should be a concern for all early education programs but more specifically when they include children who are medically fragile or have motor delays. Gross and fine motor skills, adaptive skills, and movement experiences must be an integral part of each child's day-to-day home and school activities. Its relationship to other aspects of development makes movement an essential component of an effective early education program.

Reflect and Apply

1. Outline the types of gross motor and playground activities that you would schedule during a school day for preschoolers and justify why you have selected these.

2. Develop a task analysis for a self-care skill that a preschooler can work on during the school day and identify opportunities for practice during the daily routine.

3. Interview a physical or occupational therapist and ask about the different approaches they use in therapy with preschoolers. Discuss what you found out from them in relationship to what you learned in this chapter.

4. Outline activities to facilitate a preschooler's scribbling and writing skills and identify opportunities to practice them during the daily routine.

5. Interview a caregiver of a toddler or preschooler about the child's self-care skills using the questions outlined in this chapter, and discuss what you found out and any suggestions you might make.

Chapter 8
Nurturing
Communication Skills

Dragon Images/Shutterstock

⌄ Learning Outcomes

After studying this chapter, you should be able to:

8.1 Understand that communication and language are very complex skills that are best understood as developing within predictable stages within a context of social interaction.

8.2 Recognize that the development of language during the preschool years consists of not simply more words and longer sentences, but pragmatic skills that enable the child to communicate effectively within a variety of social contexts.

8.3 Identify specific adult behaviors, such as careful listening and responding, mapping language onto a child's experience, and following the child's lead, that facilitate communication skills.

8.4 Discuss the ways in which ALL children communicate and explain some of the many alternative modes of communication available to children with multiple and complex disabilities.

8.5 Realize that two languages are better than one and the process of learning a second language proceeds in much the same way as first-language learning, within interactive social environments.

In recent decades, probably no aspect of child development has received more attention than the area of communication. Similarly, a great deal of interest has been generated regarding intervention strategies to facilitate the development and acquisition of speech and language skills. Much has been learned about which techniques and strategies best support the efforts of young children with disabilities to communicate with those around them.

This chapter considers several interesting areas of research and applies them to the design of early childhood curricula for children with special needs. We must first review some basic terminology used to describe the various subskills of language. (*Note:* For a thorough description of speech and language acquisition and the development of communication skills, see Fahey, Hulit, and Howard [2019] and Owens [2016].)

The Subskills of Language

The complexity of language is impressive. Language is often referred to as the most complex human function. To manage this complexity in discussing language, it is helpful to use the conceptual framework originally described by Bloom and Lahey (1978) and more recently by Loeb (2003). This framework defines three dimensions of language: *content, use,* and *form.* Each of these dimensions includes several traditional linguistic subskills, such as *semantics, syntax, morphology, phonology,* and *pragmatics.* These are described in the sections that follow.

Content, Use, and Form

The **content of language** is its vocabulary and meaning (semantics); that is, what it is about. **Use** refers to the purpose or function of language—what it is used for. The **form of language** refers both to its syntactic and morphological structure (i.e., the order and forms of words) and to the phonological form (i.e., the particular sounds, or phonemes, and the sound sequences that occur in spoken language). Every utterance can be analyzed according to these three dimensions. For example, take the child who, hoping for a second helping of ice cream, looks at his mother and asks, "Is there more ice cream?"

- The content of this utterance refers to the existence of a frozen sweet dairy product called "ice cream."
- Its use, or purpose, is to obtain a second helping.
- The structure of the utterance is a five-word interrogative sentence.

This theoretical framework is helpful in making clear the multidimensional and complex nature of language.

Semantics

Learning the *meanings* of words (**semantics**) is very dependent on interactions with adults who make their meaning clear. For example, talking about the ocean to a child who has never seen one will result in little understanding of *ocean*. Young children do not learn the meaning of words through vicarious experiences. Things they see must be named while they are looking at them and touching them. Activities must be described while they are happening. Then children must have the opportunity to experiment with the words to discover whether they have learned what each really means.

Examples of **semantic relations** are typically expressed in children's early two-word combinations. These include meanings such as *recurrence* (e.g., "more juice" or "'nother birdie"), *disappearance* (e.g., "cereal gone" or "no dollie"), *appearance* (e.g., "that Mommy" or "there ball"), *rejection* (e.g., "no want!" or "don't wash!"), *actions* (e.g., "baby fall" or "push Daddy"), *locations* (e.g., "cookie," "frigerator," or "doggie bed"), *possession* (e.g., "Teddy mine!" or "Mommy shoe"), and occasional *descriptors* (e.g., "cereal hot" or "pants dirty").

Syntax

Learning the rules for correct word order in sentences is one aspect of **syntax.** Syntax includes knowing that it is correct to say, "We are going to the ball game" rather than "game ball we are going to." Of course, children learning to utter syntactically correct sentences are really just trying to communicate. They are not consciously practicing the rules they are learning. But as they learn, children everywhere develop language in a similar sequence. Between 10 and 14 months of age, most typically developing children use single words to communicate. By age 2, they string together two or three words, and by age 4 they have mastered most of the syntactic rules and are creating grammatically correct sentences that follow the rules of the language they have been hearing and practicing.

Morphology

Children must also learn the rules for changing the *form* of individual words (the rules of **morphology**). For example, they discover when to add -*s*, when to add -*es*, and when to change the word *man* to *men*. They discover how to form possessives and how to use number and tense in verbs (e.g., *he walks, they walk, he walked, he is walking,* or *we walked*). Children learn comparatives (*long, longer, longest*) and how to add prefixes and suffixes to alter meaning. They use pronouns as possessives (*his* or *hers*), as subjects (*I, he,* or *they*), and as objects (*him* or *her*).

As they learn these rules of morphology, children make many interesting mistakes. They overgeneralize, saying, for example, "We wented" and "The mans." However, their errors are logical and confirm they are not just imitating what they are hearing. They are learning rules. Exceptions to the rules, such as irregular verbs and irregular plurals, will be learned in time. Often, very young children can be heard using irregular nouns and verbs correctly (*men, ran,* or *fell*). As they begin to internalize language rules, they may change to rule-governed forms (*mans, runned,* or *falled*). Then the surrounding adult models must help them discover these exceptions to the rules all over again.

Phonology

Learning the rules of the sound systems of speech and language (**phonology**) involves not only the individual speech sounds, or *phonemes,* but also discovering that pitch and rhythm changes make a difference. The intonation patterns (*prosodic* or *suprasegmental features*) are learned very early. Babies just a few months old babble in ways that sound almost like the patterns adults use. A conscientious listener can hear questions and statements in the intonation patterns of babies long before words can be heard. Careful listening will also detect exclamations!

As they near 6 months of age, many babies begin to babble in syllables that include some of the phonemes of the adult system. Their production is usually somewhat wide of the mark. By 1 year, they have learned to use some sounds accurately some of the time, and the first words begin to appear. However, the accuracy of children's production is highly dependent on being able to hear the sounds they are trying to produce clearly, accurately, and often. They do not need to hear the sounds in isolation. Hearing phonemes in a variety of words and connected speech (phrases and sentences) from responsive adults and older peers is sufficient for typically developing children. Most children learn to produce nearly all of the 44 phonemes of English by the time they are 4 years old.

Pragmatics

Learning how to use language in socially appropriate ways within various contexts is crucial to the successful development of communication skills. The term **pragmatics** refers to rules and conventions that govern how language is used for communication in different situations. Pragmatic communication skills also include many nonverbal behaviors (Fahey et al., 2019).

Speakers and listeners follow a set of unconscious guidelines as they talk to each other. According to Berko Gleason and Ratner (2013), it is possible to develop linguistic competence in semantics, syntax, and phonology, but lack the ability to use those skills in socially appropriate ways. These include behaviors such as looking at each other and glancing away and waiting for the speaker to pause before the listener begins to speak. These behaviors require attention to subtle cues. Facial expressions and body language appropriate to particular circumstances must be learned. The situation, the specific topic, the relation of the listener to the speaker, and many other variables determine *what* is said as well as *how* it is said. Children who have not acquired these pragmatic skills stand out as "different" in preschool groups almost as much as those whose speech is unintelligible. But it is more difficult for parents and teachers to pinpoint how and why they are different.

The following are ways in which the situational context influences how a person communicates: the people present, what was just previously said, the topic of conversation, the task that communication is being used to accomplish, and the times and places in which the communication occurs. Observation suggests that young children readily use these contextual clues to enable themselves to understand much more than words alone.

The acquisition of pragmatic skills begins to develop well before children's first words. Fahey et al. (2019) describe various **prelinguistic communication,** such as pointing and reaching, combined with vocalizations and directed eye gaze. These behaviors, which typically emerge in young children around the 10th month, lay an important foundation for later language development. See Table 8.1 for examples of developmental milestones in the area of pragmatics.

Table 8.1 Language Development: Expected Sequence and Approximate Age Norms

Approximate Age in Months	Pragmatics	Phonology	Grammar, Morphology, and Syntax	Semantics
1	Gazing, crying, "comfort sounds."	Begins to play with pitch change.		
3	Laughs, smiles when played with; looks at speaker; sometimes responds to a speaker by vocalizing.	Vocalizes two or more syllables.		
6	Babbles and smiles at a speaker; stops (begins turn taking) when someone speaks.	Babbles four or more syllables at one time; plays at making noises and labial (/p/, /b/, /m/) consonants emerge; vowels.		
8	Plays "peekaboo" and "pat-a-cake"; listens to adult conversations; turns toward speaker; understands gestures.	Uses intonation patterns for questions and commands; jargon includes vowels and consonants (five or more of each).	No real words, but vocalizing sounds as if forming a sentence or question.	Recognizes names of some common objects.
10	Follows simple commands; enjoys clapping to music; begins to "send message" by pointing.	Uses a varied jargon, with pitch and rhythm.		Says first words; tries to imitate words.
12	Responds to manner and attitude of speaker (e.g., joy, anger, or in a hurry).	Consonant–vowel and consonant–vowel–consonant jargon.	Holophrastic speech (one word stands for a whole sentence).	Uses two or more words; learns new words every few days.
12–18	Follows one- and two-step directions.	Imitates noises and speech sounds.	Some begin to use two-word sentences.	Recognizes and points to many familiar objects; learns new words almost daily.
18–24	Uses jargon and some echolalia; uses "dialogue"; uses speech to get attention; "asks" for help.	Uses /p/, /b/, /m/, /h/, /t/, and vowels.	Uses two- to three-word sentences, but omits articles and most modifiers; begins to use personal pronouns; telegraphic speech.	Says 10 to 20 words at 18 months, but some say as many as 200 words by 24 months; understands many more.
24–36	At age 2, speech is not used for social control, but at 2½ demands and attempts control.	Many begin to use additional consonants; add /f/, /k/, /d/, /w/, /g/; vowels 90% intelligible.	By 2½, grammatical morphemes begin to appear: -ing (present progressive); -s and -es (plurals); -ed (past tense); a, an, the (articles); my and 's (possessives); auxiliary verbs; prepositions.	Recognizes names and pictures of most common objects; understands 500 words.
	By age 3, language is linguistically and contextually contingent, and 70% of speech is intelligible, although articulation errors are still common. Short sentences (three to four words) are common. All vowels are correct, but /r/, /s/, /ch/, /j/, /v/, /l/, and /x/ are often incorrectly spoken. Vocabulary ranges to as many as 1,000 words. Sentence types include agent-action, action-object, and agent-object.			
36–48	Social control; whispers; tells name; "explains" what happened; asks questions; sustains topic; systematic changes in speech depend on the listener; some role playing; metalinguistic awareness (ability to think about language and comment on it); "hints" at things through smiles and gestures as well as words.	All vowels correct; although many children articulate most consonants accurately, articulation errors on the following are still within the normal range: /l/, /r/, /s/, /z/, /sh/, /ch/, /j/, and /th/; pitch and rhythm variations similar to adults, but this age enjoys extremes—yells and whispers.	Expands noun phrases with tense, gender, and number; conjugates "to be" correctly; uses pronouns, adjectives, and plurals; near age 4, begins using longer and more compound and complex sentences; begins to interrelate clauses (uses and, because, when, and then).	Vocabulary grows rapidly; actively seeks to learn new words; likes to experiment and makes many charming errors; continues process of differentiating lexical types; knows between 900 and 1,000 words.
48–60	Seeks information constantly; "why" is a favorite; becomes aware of behavior listeners attend to; begins to grasp relevance.	Begins to use stress contours; pitch changes purposefully; articulation errors still common, but diminishing; nonfluency not unusual; blends difficult.	Uses comparatives (big, biggest); uses all sentence types, including relative clauses; grammar approximates that of adults.	Size of vocabulary varies widely with experiences; many know 2,000 or more words.

Source: From Process: The Action of Moving Forward Progressively from One Point to Another on the Way to Completion, *Journal of Speech and Hearing Disorders,* v44, n1, pp. 3–30, by Carol A. Prutting. Copyright © 1979 by American Speech Language Hearing Association (ASHA).

Contribution of Social Interaction Theories to Understanding Early Communication Development

Social interaction theories maintain that language is learned primarily through social interactions (McCormick, Loeb, & Schiefelbusch, 2003). An important shift of interest has been away from the child in isolation and toward the dyad (significant pair of individuals): in this case, the parent–child or teacher–child dyad. The contributions of conversation and interaction to children's development of communication skills and the role of early caregiver–infant and caregiver–child interactions in children's development are well established (Sachs & Newman, 2013).

Another shift of focus in the study of children's development of communication has been toward the study of the purposes of children's communicative behaviors and the functional uses of communicative behavior within social contexts. These areas of emphasis have generated information and theories with important implications for the field of early childhood special education (ECSE). Several theories have evolved that reflect some aspect of this social interaction focus. Early on, Tannock, Girolametto, and Siegel (1992) described an **interactive model,** which suggests that parent responsiveness and the use of **motherese** or child-directed speech (described later in the chapter) are critical factors in the development of communication. This model also proposes intervention strategies based on the theory. These include following the child's lead and using strategies such as increased wait time to encourage communicative initiation and turn taking, as well as certain language modeling techniques, including describing what the child is doing, repeating key words and phrases, and syntactically and semantically expanding the child's utterances.

A third theory is a familiar one. This is Vygotsky's (1978) theory of the role of adult social mediation of children's learning experiences. This theory, which is applicable to all learning, not just language development, suggests that more capable adults or peers provide assistance to the child within social interaction contexts. When this assistance is provided within the "zone of proximal development," it provides the necessary "scaffolding" (see Chapter 4), or assistance to enable the child to master a particular skill and achieve independence.

Also critical to early language development is what is referred to as "joint attention," defined as happening when it is clear that both the caregiver's and child's focus of attention are on the same object or event at the same time (Campbell & Namy, 2003). By 6 or 7 months of age, the typically developing infant begins to respond to caregiver signals to focus attention on a particular object. This discovery of the infant's ability to follow the direction of the adult's eye gaze and establish joint attention was groundbreaking (Mundy, 2016). By 1 year, most infants are able to take control and direct adults' attention to something of interest. Adults enhance the establishment of joint attention by following the child's lead and commenting on something the child is attending to, pointing at, or commenting on. Also important is the concept of "coordinated attention," which describes the infant's and adult's attention both to each other and to another object (Akhtar & Gernsbacher, 2007).

Some children with disabilities (particularly those with autism) have difficulty responding to the caregiver's attempts to establish joint attention (see Bruinsma, Koegel, and Koegel [2004] for a review of this topic). Studies by Kasari, Freeman, and Paparella (2006) and Kasari, Gulsrud, Wong, Kwaon, and Locke (2010) have demonstrated the positive effects of training young children with autism to establish joint attention. Owens (2012) describes the importance of using a "functional language intervention model" that emphasizes utilizing teachers and family members as language "facilitators" within daily routines, and teaches communication skills through normal conversation and social interactions.

These social interaction approaches have provided a much greater understanding of the precursors of language development occurring during the child's first year of life. In addition, research and theories related to the effect of caregiver input and social interaction on children's development have important implications for intervention strategies and the design of early intervention curricula. It should be noted, however, that the study of joint attention has focused on the visual modality, and U.S. culture and child rearing. According to Akhtar and Gernsbacher (2007), word learning can occur without joint attention (e.g., in children who are blind) and varies by culture. They conclude the assumption that joint attention is necessary for language development is inconclusive.

Stages of Development of Communication Skills in Young Children

Early childhood special educators must thoroughly understand the development of communication skills in typically developing children. Several available texts provide detailed descriptions of typical communication development within each of the five subskills previously defined (see, e.g., Owens [2012]). Table 8.1 also provides development information for the major language subskills.

The following section briefly describes the major accomplishments in communication skills development from birth to 3 years of age. Because space does not allow a detailed description of this process, the section is intended only as an overview.

Prelinguistic Communication

It is important for early childhood special educators to recognize that the infant begins the process of learning to communicate long before the onset of true or conventional speech and language. Literally from the moment of birth, communication takes place between infant and caregiver. Research in the areas of mother–infant interaction and developmental pragmatics has suggested that the communication patterns established during the first year or two of life are crucial to children's later development in several areas, including language, cognition, and social skills.

During the first few months of life, the infant's communications are not really intentional. Nevertheless, they can be easily understood by those around the infant. For example, crying, smiling, cooing, looking, and eventually reaching are behaviors that often have great meaning for the infant's caregivers, even though the infant may not be using them "on purpose." A term used to describe these kinds of communicative behaviors is *perlocutionary* (Fahey et al., 2019).

These perlocutionary behaviors are responded to and interpreted by caregivers as though they *represented* intentions. As the infant gains greater control, voluntary behaviors eventually become *intentional* communicative acts. By 9 or 10 months of age, most children are engaging in a variety of intentional (but still unconventional) behaviors, such as pointing, use of directed eye gaze, and use of vocalizations to get attention, to exclaim, or to accompany their own actions or expression of wants and needs.

Prelinguistic Functions.   These types of intentional communicative behaviors are often referred to as **illocutionary behaviors.** In his now classic work "Learning How to Mean," based on careful observations of his son Nigel, Michael Halliday (1975) described several categories of communicative functions that infants may use even before the acquisition of first words:

1. The *interactional function* is also referred to as the "you and me" function. By using this function, the infant is attempting to elicit interaction and attention from others in his or her immediate environment. For example, an infant may look at his mother, clap his hands, and vocalize in an attempt to play "patty-cake." Or, he may wake from his nap and call from his crib to summon adult attention.

2. The *instrumental function* is also referred to as the "I want" function. Here, the infant uses communicative behaviors to obtain something he or she wants, such as food or a favorite object. For example, when an infant is looking toward his bottle, pointing, and saying "Uh," instrumental communicative behavior is occurring.

3. The *regulatory function* is the "Do as I tell you" function; it is used by the infant to control others' behaviors. For example, an infant may be requesting someone to push his stroller, remove him from it, or pick him up.

4. The *personal function* is called the "Here I come" function. The infant uses this function to simply express some emotion or have it accompany his or her own actions. For example, an infant tastes a spoonful of ice cream and says, "Mmmm," or drops something and says, "Uh-oh!"

5. The *heuristic function* is an important function because it sets the stage for the infant's use of communication to obtain information from adults in his or her environment. This is referred to as the "Tell me why" function. By use of strategies such as a vocalization with question-like rising intonation or raised eyebrows, the infant learns to solicit additional information, such as a label or explanation, from people nearby.

6. The *imaginative function* may be used by some infants during this pre-linguistic stage of communication development. The imaginative function is referred to as the "Let's pretend" function; it accompanies the older infant's pretend-play activities (e.g., car sounds).

The Onset of Language

Somewhere around 12 to 15 months of age, the infant learns his or her first "real" words. Communication becomes more symbolic and conventional. The toddler continues to use all the communicative functions just described, but now many of these functions are expressed using recognizable words such as *peek, bottle, up, oh-oh,* and *night-night.* In addition, a new function is now added to the toddler's repertoire: the *informative function.* Halliday (1975) called this the "Let me tell you" function because the child can now truly share information via symbolic language behavior.

Around this same time, the child also begins to move toward a new stage of cognitive development: the *preoperational stage.* Now the infant becomes increasingly able to represent things mentally. As a result, the infant can also use this newly found symbolic behavior to refer to things that are not immediately present in the environment and, very shortly, to events that happened in the past.

Thus, the onset of conventional speech and language skills also typically coincides with several other exciting milestones in the infant's development. The infant's communication is no longer tied to the here and now. In addition to using social interaction and manipulating the environment to meet his or her basic wants and needs, the child can now share his or her experiences with others.

It should be noted that the speech of a toddler at the early one-word stage is often unintelligible to anyone not involved with the toddler on a regular basis. Some words may even be idiosyncratic, bearing little phonemic relationship to the conventional word (e.g., "da" for bottle). Real words may also be combined with jargon or strings of unintelligible speech sounds (often consonant–vowel syllables, such as "da" or "tee"). The prosody or rhythm of these jargon productions may sound like the toddler is uttering whole sentences, although he or she really is not.

Combining Words

Sometime around 20 to 24 months, when the infant has learned approximately 50 to 100 words, he or she begins to put them together. Often, the first combinations will be words the infant already uses. For example, instead of saying "juice" or "more" to get another glass of juice, the infant will say "more juice." Just why the infant begins to combine words in this way is not clear. For many years, child language acquisition research focused on this process of learning to produce longer and longer utterances that conform more and more closely to adult language.

The *structure* of language refers to the way in which words are combined into sentences (syntax) and the various forms of words (morphology). The young child must learn to say, "I want juice" rather than "Want juice I" and "The boys are running" rather than "The boys is run." Much literature from the 1960s and early 1970s describes in some detail the evolution of children's grammar. Although teachers of young children need not be familiar with all the specific details of children's grammatical development, it is important that they know the major stages of language structure development as described in the following paragraphs.

1. *Telegraphic language.* When children begin to combine words, they are most likely to use only the words that have the most meaning. In earlier writings on child language acquisition, these utterances were called **telegraphic language** because, similar to a telegram, they omitted unessential words. Utterances such as "Want bottle!" rather than "I want my bottle" are typical of children in this stage.

2. *Grammatical morphemes.* Around 2 years of age, children begin to include **grammatical morphemes** in their utterances. Words such as *the* and *an*, word endings such as plural *-s*, present progressive *-ing*, past tense *-ed*, and others are gradually included. As a child first begins to use grammatical morphemes, he or she may often use them incorrectly. For example, the child may say "The boy runned" or "an apples." The teacher should be aware that incorrect use of grammatical morphemes nevertheless represents a more sophisticated stage of grammatical development than the earlier telegraphic stage in which grammatical morphemes were omitted altogether.

3. *Simple sentences.* Gradually, by the age of 3, children learn to produce sentences that resemble simple ones used by adults. These sentences contain a subject and a predicate and include the necessary grammatical morphemes, although still not always in the correct form. The 3-year-old says, "I want some milk, please," or "Let's go outside," or "My dollies is mad!" The 3-year-old has also learned to produce different kinds of sentence structures, to ask questions ("Where is my doll?"), and to give commands ("Give me my doll!"), as well as to make simple declarative statements ("This is my doll").

4. *Complex language.* By the age of 4, young children can easily combine words into sentences and produce them intelligibly. In addition, they can produce complex sentences such as "I don't want to go to the store if I can't buy a new toy." Perhaps even more important is their increasing linguistic flexibility.

Children's increasing skills in structure and vocabulary enable them to combine these skills with their emerging "pragmatic" skills. They can now adjust the structure and content of their language according to the nature of the situation and the age and status of the listener. For example, to his 2-year-old sister, the 4-year-old might say, "Give me the ice cream!" But when talking to an older adult, he would change the structure of his language (e.g., "Could I have some more ice cream, please?").

The 4- or 5-year-old child is also capable of carrying on a conversation: The child can take turns, extend the topic, and return the conversational floor to his or her partner. The following dialogue demonstrates these conversational strategies, which are so crucial to the young child's development of social skills:

DANNY: Erin, my turn to have the dinosaur puzzle!

ERIN: No, I'm not finished.

DANNY: But you promised.

ERIN: You can play with that Elmo puzzle.

DANNY: That's for babies.

ERIN: No, it's not. I'm almost done.

Finally, the 4- or 5-year-old child can also engage in *narrative forms*; that is, stories or explanations that have a beginning, a middle, and an end. The child is now able to use language not only to manipulate the environment and obtain social interaction but also to express emotions and to share experiences and ideas with others. Language and cognition now become inextricably woven together as a means of problem solving and learning about the world.

Many 4-year-olds have acquired the kinds of linguistic skills that will also support academic achievement. These autonomous or literate-style language skills are discussed in Chapter 9. The child's words and sentences can now stand alone. The child can tell a story or describe a situation clearly and successfully to a listener who has no previous knowledge or shared reference regarding the event being described.

Several of the milestones described in this section can be viewed as potential communication goals for young children with special needs. Strategies for helping children develop communication skills are described later in the chapter.

Necessary Conditions for the Development of Communication Skills

Because of the tremendous complexity of speech and language skills, several necessary conditions must exist for these skills to develop optimally. First, the peripheral sensory system must be intact. Hearing is of greatest importance, of course, for the development of language. In addition, vision and oral sensation must function well.

The central nervous system must also be intact. Speech and language development depends on the ability not only to receive incoming auditory information but also to process, organize, and store it. Of particular importance in the development of speech production (i.e., articulation skills) is the motor system. The production of speech involves very precise coordination of many muscles and muscle groups making up the speech production mechanism, including those involved in movement of the tongue, lips, jaw, velum, larynx, and muscles of respiration. The production of speech sounds in the rapid sequence necessary for the production of intelligible speech requires synergistic split-second timing and smooth control of these muscles. For children with motor impairments such as those associated with many forms of cerebral palsy, the production of speech is extremely difficult.

Cognitive abilities are crucial to the development of language skills. The content of a child's language depends on what the child is able to represent, organize, understand, and recall of the world around him or her.

Enhanced eText
Video Example 8.1
Speech, Language, and Hearing
Milestones: 1 to 2 Years—Preview
https://www.youtube.com/
watch?v=s69r5o7mfMk

Enhanced eText
Video Example 8.2
Speech, Language, and Hearing
Milestones: 2 to 3 Years—Preview
https://www.youtube.com/
watch?v=Tt42ZFmTjPk

Enhanced eText
Video Example 8.3
Speech, Language, and Hearing
Milestones: 3 to 4 Years—Preview
https://www.youtube.com/
watch?v=NX2UoZAHUP0
These videos from the American
Speech-Language-Hearing
Association highlight the key
milestones in early speech,
language, and hearing development
between 1 and 4 years of age.

Communication is first and foremost a *social* phenomenon. Communication development during the first year of life (and many of the precursors of language) depends on the infant's or young child's interest in the caregiver's social cues. This motivates the toddler to seek the attention of—and interaction with—others in the environment. The child who lacks this drive toward social interaction, as, for example, children on the autism spectrum, may be significantly challenged in the development of communication skills. Finally, the environment itself must be responsive to the infant and young child's needs. The linguistic input provided by caregivers must be appropriate to the infant's ability to process information. As mentioned earlier in this chapter, early caregiver–child interactions can enhance children's later development. These interaction strategies are also important to teachers in the field of ECSE, and they should be incorporated into the daily activities of the classroom. We discuss these interaction strategies in more detail later in this chapter.

Characteristics That Can Interfere with Language Development

Figure 8.1 summarizes the characteristics of common communication disorders. The following sections discuss these disorders in more detail. (See also the American Speech-Language-Hearing Association (ASHA) website at http://www.asha.org/public/Early-Detection-of-Speech-Language-and-HearingDisorders/.)

Hearing Loss. Hearing loss can interfere with both speech and language development. Even mild or intermittent hearing problems, such as those associated with otitis media, can interfere with the learning of speech and language. Children who are Deaf or hard of hearing can be taught to speak and to understand language, but the task is not an easy one and requires the help of parents and highly trained specialists. In the past, children with severe to profound hearing loss were likely to need to use sign language as their primary mode of communication. However, developments in electronic hearing technology, such as cochlear implants used with children as young as 12 months old, appear to be dramatically changing the speech and language developmental outcomes for these children.

With the increased use of newborn hearing screening protocols in hospitals, children who have severe hearing losses are usually identified early on. However, delayed speech and/or language development associated with *mild* hearing loss frequently goes undetected.

Children with mild hearing losses cannot hear all phonemes with equal clarity. It is important to recognize the possible long-term effects of mild, intermittent hearing loss from otitis media on language and literacy development. If a child fails to develop normal communication skills at expected ages, regardless of what other factors seem to be involved, the child's hearing should be checked and regularly rechecked by a competent audiologist. If any hearing problem is detected, the causes should be discovered and treated. When a significant hearing loss is detected, early intervention is critical. Without intervention (e.g., amplification or cochlear implantation, and development of listening skills or use of manual signs), children who are unable to hear normally during the first years of life may have difficulties in all aspects of language and speech development. The longer the hearing loss is undetected and untreated, the more serious will be the effects on the development of communication.

Visual Impairments. Although a visual impairment does not interfere with communication development to the same degree as hearing loss, it does affect concept and vocabulary development (Erickson, Hatton, Roy, Fox, & Renne, 2007). If the child cannot see clearly, it is difficult to recognize the things and events being discussed. Children who are blind, by virtue of their disability, have a different *experiential* base. They need some assistance in mastering certain aspects of language development, particularly in

Figure 8.1 Characteristics of common communication disorders

Source: From public information materials of the American Speech-Language-Hearing Association (1991). Reproduced with permission.

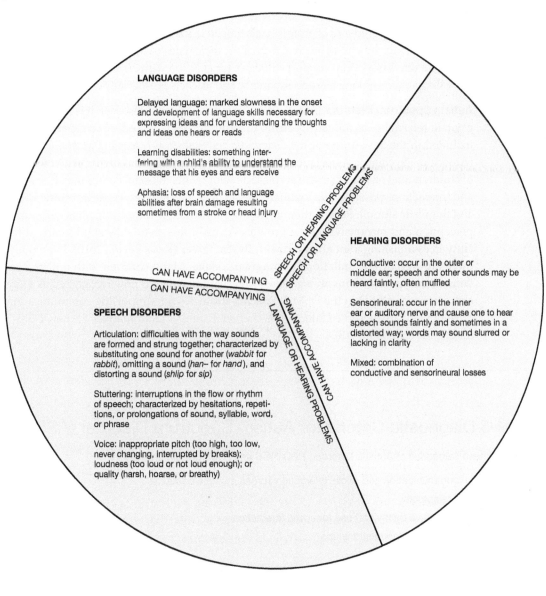

the areas of vocabulary and concept development and nonverbal pragmatic skills. Like children who are hard of hearing, children with low vision may have special needs related to social, concept, and language development that often go unnoticed.

Intellectual Disabilities.   Children with limitations in overall cognitive development need thoughtfully planned individualized opportunities and challenges. Children who have mild to moderate intellectual disabilities often are able to learn to talk and understand speech and language in the expected sequences, although at a slower pace. It is especially important to provide these children with a language-nurturing environment that gives input that is developmentally appropriate to their language and cognitive level.

The child with more severe intellectual disabilities poses very different problems and challenges for the ECSE teacher. When there is severe impairment of cognitive and perceptual processes, the impact on the development of communication skills is great. In many children who have severe or profound intellectual disabilities, rule-governed symbolic language skills may not develop. However, it is important to recognize that these children, too, must have some means of communication. Young children with severe and multiple disabilities are discussed in Chapter 5.

Emotional Disorders. In rare cases, atypical language development or the refusal to communicate at all may result from emotional factors. Although these issues require the skillful and caring guidance of professionals trained to identify and intervene with children and their parents, much can be done to support mental health in early education settings. Chapter 6 offers classroom support strategies for children with emotional or social problems. Cooperation among therapists, parents, and teachers is especially critical in this area.

Autism Spectrum Disorder (ASD). Autism is a "spectrum" disorder. It is more appropriately referred to as autism spectrum disorder or ASD. According to recent changes included in the 5th edition of the *Diagnostic and Statistical Manual of Mental Disorders* (American Psychiatric Association, 2013), or DSM-5, the core identifying characteristics of children who have autism are atypical developments in social communication skills and interactions possibly due to differences in how the child processes incoming social and linguistic stimuli. Recent attention has been directed toward difficulties with social perception and responsiveness. A growing focus in this area is the child's early difficulty in establishing joint attention with the caregiver (Kasari et al., 2010). Eventually, there are significant limitations in pragmatic skills. Many children with autism also demonstrate problems involving sensory regulation, which is now recognized as a key characteristic of ASD in the DSM-5. Specific strategies for supporting communication development are presented later in this chapter. Exhibit 8.1 summarizes the new DSM-5 diagnostic criteria for ASD.

Exhibit 8.1

Summary of DSM-5 Diagnostic Criteria for Autism Spectrum Disorder (ASD)

(*Note:* 2013 changes *eliminate* these categories of Autistic Disorder: PDD-NOS and Asperger Syndrome.)

A. Persistent deficits exist in social communication and social interaction across multiple contexts:
   a. Deficits in social-emotional reciprocity
   b. Deficits in nonverbal communicative behaviors' use for social interaction
   c. Deficits in developing and understanding relationships

B. Restricted repetitive patterns of behavior, interests, or activities, as manifested by at least two of the following:
   a. Stereotyped or repetitive motor movements, use of objects, or speech (e.g., flipping objects, echolalia, idiosyncratic phrases)
   b. Insistence on sameness, inflexible adherence to routines, ritualized patterns (extreme distress at small changes, difficulties with transitions)
   c. Highly restricted, fixated interests
   d. Hyper- or hyporeactivity to sensory input, or unusual interests in sensory aspects of the environment

C. Symptoms are present in early developmental period.
   a. May not be fully manifest until social demands exceed limited capacities, or may be masked by learned strategies

D. Symptoms cause clinically significant impairment in social or occupational areas of functioning.
E. Symptoms not better explained by intellectual disability or global developmental delay.

Source: American Psychiatric Association. (2013). *Diagnostic and statistical manual of mental disorders* (5th ed.). Arlington, VA: American Psychiatric Publishing.

Characteristics That Can Interfere with the Production of Speech

The following subsections describe characteristics that can interfere with the production of speech.

Structural Abnormalities.   Craniofacial deformities of any kind interfere with speech skill development. A child who cannot imitate and reproduce speech sounds is less skilled in using language as well. For example, if deviant oral structure precludes placing the tongue and teeth in the correct position to pronounce /s/, as in *boys* and *shoes,* the child cannot use the language rule "Add /s/ to form plurals."

Hypernasality, often associated with cleft palate, also interferes with speech production. Only three English speech sounds should be characterized by nasality: /m/, /n/, and /ng/ (as in *ring*); so when most of the sounds in a child's speech production are nasalized, listeners usually characterize the speech as unintelligible. Conditions other than cleft palate can cause this. If a child seems to be "talking through the nose," the causes should be discovered and corrected.

Motor Problems.   Normal control of the muscles necessary for speech is needed for correct articulation. This develops so spontaneously in most children that its significance is not recognized. Playing the violin skillfully is far less complex than pronouncing a word correctly. (*Note:* To appreciate this muscular achievement, shut your lips lightly and focus on the movements of your tongue as you try to say, "Look at Larry's new green coat.")

Cerebral palsy interferes with muscle coordination. It also can create problems with respiration, which, in turn, affects speech. Injury, other physical problems, and certain drugs also interfere. Teachers will want to work closely with therapists when children have problems of this kind. For some children with severe motor disorders, some form of augmentative technology will be critically important to ensure development of communication skills.

Voice Disorders.   The effect of a cleft palate and/or lip may result in a nasal voice even if a surgical repair was accomplished early in the child's life. Children who have frequent respiratory infections may lack nasal resonance. Children who scream a lot may be hoarse as a result of vocal cord abuse. All these problems deserve skillful attention and remediation from professionals.

Stuttering.   Stuttering is a disturbance in the rhythmic flow of speech in which a speaker repeats a sound or syllable, prolongs it more than is typical of other speakers, or "blocks" (i.e., completely halts the speech flow). Some individuals who stutter develop patterns of grimaces and gestures in an effort to avoid disturbing their flow of speech. These are sometimes referred to as *secondary characteristics*; that is, motor behaviors that become conditioned responses over time.

Stuttering usually begins between the ages of 2 and 4 years, although it may happen later. It should be noted that many children in this age range display intermittent disfluency as part of the normal process of mastering more complex communication. All speakers normally repeat, hesitate, and sometimes prolong sounds. This is especially true of young children. Finding the right word may be difficult for young children, and this is reason enough for them to hesitate and repeat. These common behaviors are referred to as *developmental disfluency* (Fahey, Hulit, & Howard, 2018).

Some speech-language pathologists believe that calling attention to the normal disfluencies of young children may result in more repetitions. Telling children to slow down or to think before they speak may actually increase rather than decrease disfluency and cause them to stumble even more. When you wish to encourage speech, it is very important to slow down, convey with your body language that you have time to listen, reduce the number of questions asked, and, in general, give your undivided attention. Guitar (2014) provides guidelines for effectively handling children's stuttering. (See http://www.asha.org/public/speech/disorders/stuttering.htm.)

Nurturing Speech, Language, and Conceptual Skills

A large body of information is available to the ECSE professional regarding ways of facilitating the development of communication skills in young children. Some of this information is presented in the following sections. ECSE practitioners are fortunate to be members of a field that has long been committed to "evidence-based practice" (EBP) as delineated by the early childhood special education (ECSE) professional organization, the Division for Early Childhood (www.dec-sped.org). Many of these "EPBs" are highlighted throughout this text. In addition, another invaluable ECSE practitioner resource is the *Handbook of Early Childhood Special Education* (Reichow, Boyd, Barton, & Odom, 2016).

The Important Role of Caregiver–Child Interaction

The importance of the early caregiving environment—and particularly caregivers' use of responsive communicative interactions—has been well established. Research demonstrating the positive impact of adult communication and responsiveness dates back to the 1970s (*Note:* The use of the term "caregiver" here refers to any adult who has the opportunity to observe and interact with young children within daily contexts. These contexts may include daily routines of home, child care, and schools. It can also include shopping trips, riding in the car, and visiting the zoo—or the doctor's office.)

It is almost impossible to overstate the positive impact of caregiver language input—and particularly important, caregiver *responsiveness*—on infant and child language development. This was dramatically demonstrated in a study by Caskey, Stephens, Tucker, and Vohr (2014) that investigated the possible effects of parents talking to their preterm infants while visiting them in the neonatal intensive care unit (NICU). The study found that increased amounts of parents' talking (i.e., higher word counts) predicted better language and cognitive scores of infants at 18 months! Another study (Hoff, 2003) demonstrated that the frequently observed effects of socioeconomic status (SES) on early vocabulary development are *mediated* by maternal use of language. Higher-SES mothers used more words, longer mean length of utterance, and more topic-extending replies, which in turn predicted greater child vocabulary. In addition, research by Karaaslan and Mahoney (2015) also demonstrated the impact of certain kinds of caregiver–infant and caregiver–child interactions on the development of young children with disabilities. Such studies have found that maternal responsivity appears to be *the critical factor.*

Effects of Lack of Parent–Child Interaction. Lack of appropriate caregiver–child responsive interaction may limit communication development. Some parents may not be aware of the importance of talking to young children and may think it silly to talk to their infant or toddler before he or she learns to talk. A recent study by Richards, Gilkerson, Dongxin, and Topping (2017) also found that parents tend to overestimate the amount of time they spend talking to their young children. As Weiss (2009) pointed out, it is important to keep in mind that intervention approaches based on parent–child interaction need to be adapted to the different cultural, linguistic, and child-rearing styles of families. Nevertheless, a strong case can be made for the *critically* important role of adult responsiveness, *particularly* with children who have communication difficulties. Thus, when a child is not developing language skills,

Video Example from
YouTube

Enhanced eText
Video Example 8.4
Serve-and-Return Interaction Shapes Brain Circuitry
https://www.youtube.com/watch?v=m_5u8-QSh6A
This video demonstrates how caregiver–infant interactions play a significant role in building and strengthening the neural connections that facilitate early social and communication development.

the early childhood educator must be alert to helping parents create a language-nurturing environment.

Parents can learn to use everyday experiences to teach communication skills. Cooking, cleaning, and gardening are excellent experiences for children. Conversation during these activities becomes an excellent language-teaching time. Washing the car or doing household chores provides great opportunities for fathers to foster speech and language learning. Parents and other caregivers can easily provide encouragement, examples, and thoughtful reminders within daily routines to easily ensure their child's language-learning environment and opportunities throughout the day.

Particularly important to the development of children's language skills are caregivers' uses of certain communicative interactions, which we describe in the following section. For more detailed understanding of this important area, see descriptions of field-tested intervention programs designed to assist caregivers and teachers of young children with multiple disabilities (e.g., Chen, Klein, & Haney, 2007), developmental delays, or autism spectrum disorder (e.g., Mahoney & MacDonald, 2007) in developing and refining these skills to support children's early communication development. Figure 8.2 gives examples of the kinds of interactions often targeted for infants and very young children.

The caregiver–child interactions within daily routines described in the following sections are equally important for teachers and early interventionists in other disciplines. Early interventionists must not only develop the ability to recognize and

Figure 8.2 Communicative interaction checklist

Source: From "Facilitating Mother–Infant Communicative Interaction in Mothers of High-Risk Infants," by M. D. Klein and M. H. Briggs, 1987, *Journal of Childhood Communication Disorders, 10*(2), pp. 95–106. Reprinted with permission.

OBSERVATION OF COMMUNICATIVE INTERACTION (OCI)
Mother-Infant Communication Project

Infant's Name _____ Birthdate _____ Age ____

Setting _____ Date _____ Adjusted Age ____

Observer _____

	Rarely/Never	Sometimes	Often	Optimally	Not Applicable
1. Provides appropriate tactile and kinesthetic stimulation (e.g., gently strokes, pats, caresses, cuddles, rocks baby).	1	2	3	4	N/A
2. Displays pleasure while interacting with infant.	1	2	3	4	N/A
3. Responds to child's distress.	1	2	3	4	N/A

    a. changes verbalization.
    b. changes infant's position, attempts to distract.
    c. provides positive physical stimuli (e.g., patting, rocking).
    d. avoids negative physical or verbal response.

	Rarely/Never	Sometimes	Often	Optimally	Not Applicable
4. Positions self and infant so eye-to-eye contact is possible (e.g., facing and 7 to 12 inches away).	1	2	3	4	N/A

    a. attempts to make eye contact.
    b. reciprocates eye gaze.

	Rarely/Never	Sometimes	Often	Optimally	Not Applicable
5. Smiles contingently at infant.	1	2	3	4	N/A

    a. consistently returns infant's smile.
    b. smiles in response to infant vocalization.

	Rarely/Never	Sometimes	Often	Optimally	Not Applicable
6. Varies prosodic features.	1	2	3	4	N/A

    a. uses higher pitch.
    b. talks more slowly.
    c. exaggerates "intonation."

(Continued)

FIGURE 8.2 Communicative interaction checklist *(Continued)*

7. **Encourages "conversation."**	1	2	3	4	N/A

    a. uses rising intonation questions.
    b. waits after saying something to infant, and looks expectantly, providing infant turn.
    c. imitates child's vocalizations, or words.
    d. repeats own sounds, words, or phrases (e.g., "Here's the bottle. Bottle.').
    e. answers when infant vocalizes (e.g., "Oh, yeah?" , "Okay.", "Is that right?").

8. **Responds contingently to infant's behavior.**	1	2	3	4	N/A

    a. touches or responds with facial expression within 2 seconds after infant vocalization.
    b. vocalizes within 2 seconds after infant moves arms, head, etc.
    c. vocalizes within 2 seconds after infant vocalization.
    d. stops own activity or verbalization in response to interruption by infant's vocalization or movement.
    e. responds vocally to infant from a distance of more than 2 feet.

9. **Modifies interaction in response to negative cues from infant.**	1	2	3	4	N/A

    a. changes activity.
    b. reduces intensity of interaction.
    c. terminates attempts at interaction.

10. **Uses communication to teach language and concepts.**	1	2	3	4	N/A

    a. interprets infant's behavior appropriately (e.g., "Oh, you're hungry, aren't you.").
    b. re-casts own sentences (e.g., adult says, "Shall we turn on the light? Turn on the light. There's the light.").
    c. comments on infant's attention to immediate environment and *labels* objects (e.g., "You see the doggie? That's the doggie.").
    d. matches infant's vocalization, or word with slightly more elaborate language (e.g., baby says, "Ball," and adult says, "That's a ball." or "Big ball.").

encourage the use of interactive behaviors between parents and children, but also, just as important, demonstrate and use these strategies consistently themselves.

Encouraging Conversation.   The early literature on mother–infant interaction described several specific strategies mothers use to encourage and maintain a dialogue with their infants. These include behaviors such as (1) use of rising intonation "yes/no" questions (e.g., "Wanna eat now?" or "Is baby tired?"), (2) pausing expectantly after each utterance to give the infant a turn, and (3) imitating the infant's vocalizations or responding to them as though they were intelligible (e.g., "Oh yeah?," "Is that right?," "No kidding!," etc.). Originally, this communicative style was called "motherese" (Cross, 1984); currently, it is termed *infant-* or *child-directed speech*. A research synthesis conducted by Dunst, Gorman, and Hamby (2010) found that children demonstrate increased attention to, preference for, and social responsiveness to infant-directed speech compared to adult-directed speech, and this promotes language development.

Responding Contingently to Child's Behavior.   Caregiver responsivity has frequently been found to be a robust correlate of later development in young children. Particularly important for caregivers and professionals is sensitivity to all communicative attempts on the part of the child. For example, a child with severe disabilities who is nonverbal and rarely initiates interaction or attempts to get attention should receive *immediate* attention for any communicative effort, including gestures, changes in body position, vocalizations, and so forth. The child who typically communicates only by crying or pulling the teacher's sleeve should receive an enthusiastic response for making a "duh duh" sound and pointing in order to request a drink of juice because this is a new behavior for the child. MacDonald and Stoika (2007) described an interaction strategy called "upping the ante," in which the teacher or parent encourages a slightly more sophisticated response than the one the child typically uses.

Modifying Interaction in Response to Negative Cues.   Another important aspect of maternal responsivity, albeit a more subtle one, is the ability to change or terminate interaction with an infant in response to such cues as gaze aversion, changes in body tension and facial expression, or lack of response from the infant. Interventionists, too, must be able to read children's cues of disinterest, overload, or distraction. Continuing a particular cue or prompt, such as "Show me the doll," when the child is clearly not attending to the stimulus is wasted effort and may eventually teach the child to "tune out" as a generalized strategy in responding to overwhelming or meaningless stimulation.

Using Communication to Teach Language and Concepts.   Much has been written about the language patterns that are typical of middle-class mothers and other caregivers as they interact with their young children. Some of these communicative interaction strategies appear to be correlated with later language development (see Exhibit 8.2). Caregivers and professionals should use these interaction strategies **contingently**; that

Exhibit 8.2
Talking to Young Children in Ways That Support Communication

Essential Communication *Input* Strategies

1. Interpret and respond to the child's communicative cues (e.g., *following child's eye gaze, caregiver hands the child his bottle, saying "Bottle, here's your bottle"; or the child cries after being seated in a swing and the adult takes the child out, saying "OK, no swing"*).

2. Follow the child's lead/respond contingently (e.g., *the child moves to the book corner, and the teacher follows and helps the child select a book; or the infant looks in the mirror and says, "ba ba ba," and the teacher responds, "Yes, you see the baby!"*).

3. Identify the child's interests (e.g., *the teacher carefully observes the child's preferences in class; surveys caregivers with high-/low-preference inventory*).

4. If the child does not engage in joint attention, the teacher establishes joint attention by controlling access to the desired object or activity (e.g., *the teacher holds the child's favorite toy near her face until the child looks at her and reaches for it*).

5. Encourage pleasurable turn-taking routines (e.g., *the teacher plays imitation games during circle time, using both silly sounds and physical movements*).

6. Build on spontaneous opportunities for "conversation" with the child (e.g., *the child holds up paper with scribbles, and the teacher asks, "Did you draw that for Mommy?" The child shakes his head "yes." The teacher then says, "Oh, I think she'll love your drawing!" The child points to the cubby. The teacher says, "Yes, put it in your cubby now, and later take it home to Mommy."*).

7. Use prosody appropriately: avoid rapid pace, and modulate intonation.

8. Interpret the child's communicative behavior (e.g., *"OK, I know you're getting hungry" or "It makes you sad that Daddy can't stay at school."*).

9. Map language onto the child's experience (e.g., *when building block structures with the child, the teacher says, "Oh look. This tower has all blue blocks. Uh-oh. I think our tower might fall down. Oops. It fell down."*).

10. Consistently use key words and phrases in daily routines and activities.

11. Engage in self-talk, describing your *own* actions, and parallel talk describing the *child's* actions (e.g., *"Mommy's making soup now"; "I see you're eating all of your peas!"*).

12. Repeat/emphasize key words and recast your own words and sentences (e.g., "<u>Bear</u>. Here's <u>Bear</u>. You love your <u>bear</u>.").

(continued)

13. Respond to the child's words with semantic and syntactic expansion (e.g., *the child says, "Car." The teacher says, "Yes, that's a car." "That car goes fast."*).

14. Use progressive matching (e.g., *the child feeding a doll says, "Eat"; the adult says, "Baby eat."*).

15. Limit "test" questions (e.g., *the teacher can say, "Your painting has so many beautiful colors! Can you tell me about your picture?"* rather than *"What's this? Who is that? What color is that?"*).

16. Using the child's interest, create opportunities and motivation for *functional* communication.

---

is, in response to the infant's or toddler's interest and attention as demonstrated by the child's eye gaze, gestures, and vocalizations or words. These interaction strategies include the following:

1. *Commenting* on what the infant or child appears to be attending to (e.g., "Oh, you hear that doggie barking, don't you?"), also referred to as "mapping language onto experience" or "parallel talk" (McCormick et al., 2003).

2. *Repeating and recasting* one's *own* words or phrases in different ways to emphasize important words (e.g., "*Doggie*. That's the *doggie*. Hear the *doggie*? *Doggie!*"), or using "self-talk" to describe one's own actions (e.g., "*Mommy is cooking chicken soup for you!*").

3. *Matching* the child's vocalization or word with a slightly more elaborated response, thereby interpreting the utterance (e.g., the child says, "buh" and the teacher says, "Bottle, yes, bottle"). This is also referred to as **progressive matching** by MacDonald and Stoika (2007).

4. *Expanding* the utterance syntactically (e.g., the child says, "cookie" and the teacher says, "That is a cookie") or *semantically extending*; that is, adding meaning to the utterance (e.g., the child says, "doggie" and the teacher says, "Yeah, that's a *big* doggie!").

Many of these kinds of responses are referred to as "following the child's lead." Following the child's lead has the obvious advantage of ensuring that the adult's language input is directly related to something the child is interested in and paying attention to. This increases the likelihood that the child will associate the word with the object or activity in which he or she is directly engaged.

General Classroom Strategies That Encourage and Support Communication

Social interaction theories of language development, and knowledge about the stages and major achievements of language acquisition, help the early childhood practitioner generate a useful approach to early language intervention. Before describing some of the specific strategies suggested by this approach, let us consider three important principles related to the development of communication skills:

1. *Interaction* is the first key to the development of communication skills. Infants and young children must learn to experience the pleasures of turn taking and reciprocal interaction.

2. True communication skills must be *functional* and powerful for the child. The ability to provide rote answers to stereotyped questions is not really communication. Infants and children must have opportunities to *initiate* communication and make things happen! Observation of early childhood special education classrooms reveals that young children are too often placed in a *respondent* role; that is, they are taught to respond to specific prompts and cues provided by

the teacher. Communication used only in this way cannot be a learning tool for young children. They must be encouraged to initiate interaction, and to use language and other communicative behaviors to *control* the environment appropriately, to ask questions and obtain information, and to solve problems. Particularly important for children with disabilities is the discovery that "language is power." Children must learn to use language for purposes other than simply answering questions.

3. Language develops best in a *responsive environment*. The teacher who is most sensitive to the infant or child's communicative intentions will be most successful in facilitating language development. Many specific ways of responding are suggested by the literature describing infant-directed speech or motherese (the speech and language characteristics typical of mothers' communication with infants and young children described earlier).

Beginning Where the Child Is

An understanding of appropriate practices in nurturing receptive and expressive language suggests that teachers should attend to children's levels of development. Thus, if 4-year-old Sean does not yet try to tell adults anything, one skill to nurture is the "telling" of things as very young children do. If Susie cannot produce any speech sounds distinctly, she may need to be encouraged in simple vocal play and babbling. If Tommy does not try to ask for things, perhaps he should be expected to make some kind of sound before he is given what he wants.

Developmental scales of speech and language can be checked to determine whether a child has a developmental lag. Speech-language pathologists can assist as questions arise. Table 8.1 can be used as a basis for constructing an informal checklist for evaluating language development. However, instructional objectives for language development should also be based on the *functional needs of the child,* which are most likely to be motivating. They should not be limited to items on a developmental checklist.

Conversing with the Child

Conversations about familiar things that interest young children are a critical tool in helping them to learn communication skills. Children's first verbal labels or names are of objects, people, events, and actions they know and can associate with. Unless they are truly interested and can make associations, they will not attend, and attention is a prerequisite for learning.

Choosing What to Talk About

Communication skills develop around objects and events that interest children. For the reluctant talker, food can be a good place to begin. For example, while sitting around a table with children, the teacher can cut an apple into pieces and describe such details as the name of the fruit, the smooth red skin and small black seeds, the sharp knife, and how the apple will taste. Pragmatic skills also can be nurtured in this social situation (e.g., turn taking and the use of polite requests).

Any game, dollhouse, play kitchen, or even rocks and dirt can be used as the conversational focal point. At first, the teacher should join the children in an ongoing activity with toys they have chosen, following the children's lead. Later, when rapport has been well established, the teacher may choose the activity. Introducing variety is important, but at first, joining in the children's choice of activities is best. The following are general suggestions for engaging in conversations with young children:

1. Listen attentively. Even if the sounds children are making are unintelligible, look at them with interest and listen.

2. Speak clearly and not too fast, especially if the child has very limited language ability. Use natural or slightly exaggerated intonation patterns (prosodic features), emphasizing key words. Avoid chronic use of very high pitch.

3. Avoid long and complex sentence structures. Recast words and phrases (e.g., "Where's your *ball*? Oh, there it is! There's your ball.").

4. Avoid one-sided conversations that usually result from the adult asking too many questions. Questions asked one after another do not constitute conversation. In fact, too many questions will often result in no conversation. But *good* questions can facilitate learning.

5. Talk mostly about the here and now. Make sure references to the past and future are very clear and contrast them with references to the present. For example, "Today it's raining, but *yesterday* it was sunny," or, "*After* we finish our snack, *then* we will go outside."

6. Use a calm and pleasant tone of voice. Bring fun to every conversation.

7. Use words the children are interested in because they can see or understand what they refer to as you talk. Tell them the names of actions as well as objects.

8. Pause between sentences. Don't be in a hurry.

9. As the children understand and speak more, gradually make your sentences longer and use a larger vocabulary.

10. For children who have mastered simple sentence structure, model complex relationships through more complex sentence structure. For example, "Oh look, now the sand sticks together *because* we mixed it with water" or "*If* we put one more block on top, *then* what will happen?"

Listening

While adults frequently remind children to "listen," it is often more important that adults listen carefully to children with great interest. This is especially true if the children have not developed speech and language skills at the expected rate. For children who have speech and language challenges, communication requires a great deal of effort. The adult response most likely to accelerate the growth of speech and language is an interested, responsive listener! Presenting responsive facial expressions and giving the child your patient, undivided attention are important strategies. Also, an adult's use of slightly exaggerated gestures and facial expressions can increase the salience of key words, as well as help convey word meanings to the child.

Developing Pragmatic Skills

Pragmatic skills are the social skills of language. Taking turns during a conversation, refraining from interrupting, and saying the appropriate thing cannot be learned in isolation. Children require social experiences and depend on social interaction. By **modeling** appropriate pragmatic skills, adults can direct attention to courteous and effective ways of conversing. Also, role playing is a very useful strategy for helping children develop such pragmatic skills as the use of polite forms, initiating conversations, and topic extension.

Expanding Skills

Children's language skills ideally are expanded through increasingly complex conversations with responsive adults who model more complex sentences and vocabulary. Some children may need more targeted models to support expansion, such as the use of "progressive matching." For example, if the child is using two-word phrases, such as "Dog water," the adult can model a slightly more complex structure: "Yes, the dog is drinking water." The strategies included in Exhibits 8.3, 8.4, and 8.5 can encourage communication in *all* children, regardless of the nature of their learning challenges.

Exhibit 8.3
Some Ways to Promote Syntactic Development

Tony uses many two-word sentences and some three-word sentences, and he loves to talk. Both his parents and his teachers have many conversations with him throughout the day. They *listen* to him with obvious interest. Some of the time they *expand* what he has said. When he says, "Falled down," they may say, "Your big tower fell down. That was noisy." They do this in a way that suggests, "You're right, it fell down" and not in a manner that indicates the child has said something wrong.

As the adults do things while Tony is present, they may use *self-talk*. They talk about what they are feeling and doing, as they do it: "Time for supper. I'll take the plates to the table now. The meat and the green beans are almost ready. It's time to make the salad. I'll cut the carrots first." The speaker pauses after each sentence and *listens and responds* if Tony comments. To intensify these naturalistic input strategies, adults can also create repeated syntactic patterns, for example, "I'm mak<u>ing</u> the salad. I'm mak<u>ing</u> the dressing. Now I'm pour<u>ing</u> the milk."

Sometimes his teachers and parents use *parallel talk*. They talk about what Tony is doing: "Tony, you put the toys on the shelf just the right way. I like the way you are picking up those blocks. You put the biggest ones on the bottom."

When Tony says something incorrectly, they rarely correct him directly, but they do use *corrective echoing*. If he says, "Her throwed dat ball," they might say, "You saw Susie. *She threw* the ball." And although they may exaggerate the "she" and the "threw" slightly by saying them slowly, they also confirm that they understood the meaning.

Exhibit 8.4
Arrival Time to Build Language Skills

The Scene: Children are arriving, and the teacher and aide are greeting them individually.
The Teaching Strategy: A warm greeting and a brief conversation with each child are designed to make each child feel welcome and expected. Modeling, expanding what the children say, and listening to them are some of the potential strategies to promote communication skills. Direct correction of articulation errors or grammatical mistakes will be avoided.

Ms. McLynn: Good morning, Sally. I am so glad you brought your doll. Do you want to take her coat off?

Sally: Me do. Coat dirty.

Ms. McLynn: I know you can take her coat off. Her coat *is* dirty, isn't it? We can brush the dirt off.

Sally: Wed shoes. (Pointing to her new shoes)

Ms. McLynn: I like those new red shoes. They are shiny.

Timmy: Hey, looka dat! Dat nose wiggles.

Ms. McLynn: I see our *rabbit*. She *is* wiggling her nose!

Nancy: Ms. McLynn, my mommie said that she couldn't come today but she will call you after while. She has to go to the supermarket 'cause we're having company tonight.

Ms. McLynn: I'm glad you told me she couldn't come. Would you like to pretend that you are at the supermarket too? We have lots of things in our store, too.

Exhibit 8.5

Promoting Specific Reasons for Talking

Using Language to Find Out About Things

Curiosity is expected of young children. Hide something in a box or bag and then encourage them to ask questions in order to guess what is inside (e.g., "Is it round?" or "Can it swim?"). This can teach how asking questions leads to answers. If "why?" and "how?" questions are not being used by some children, games and experiments with different toys can initiate them.

Using Language to Get Involved

As young children often play beside each other rather than with each other, sand, water, and block play encourage "getting involved." As they learn to express intentions, tell others what to do (directing), and report what has happened, they learn new language quickly. Combining verbal children and those who speak less well provides a natural language-learning opportunity.

Using Language to Get Help

Wanting something that is put away or too high to reach creates the need to ask for it. Zippers that stick and shoes that come untied create the need to ask for help. This becomes the opportunity for you to reinforce vocalization and use of language while ignoring gestures, helpless looks, and even tears. However, any attempt to say something should be rewarded. (Of course, for the child who usually does not even make nonverbal attempts at communication, *any* effort should be rewarded.) Modeling "Tie my shoe" and accepting the child's "Tie oo" at first encourage greater effort. Gradually, if you are absolutely certain that the child is able to say it better, you may appear to be puzzled until the child makes a better attempt.

Using Language to Get Attention or Approval

Some children poke and pull at adults as well as other children. Children need something to take the place of a habit that needs to be changed. For example, the words "Look" or "Watch me" can be used in many situations. If the child attempts to get attention in inappropriate ways, avoid responding immediately. Turning away, ask, "Do you want me to look?" (pause) "Tell me (pause) *look.*" Then refuse to watch unless the child says *something.*

Using Language to Tell Something

If there are interested listeners, most children want to tell them something. Asking parents to write a note about interesting events at home is helpful. Then you can initiate the discussion. Sometimes a picture or favorite toy from home serves this purpose. Formal show-and-tell is not usually effective with young children, but informally telling the teacher or a friend is popular.

Using Language to Defend Themselves

"Stop that" needs to be learned early. "Move, please" is better than shoving. Teaching children how to defend themselves verbally instead of with a push or shove results in more pleasant homes and classrooms. They need examples, models, and teachers' insistence that saying something is better than just shoving.

Using Language to Learn New Things

Children who know how to express themselves in one way are quicker to learn other ways to talk about things. When a wide range of new experiences is provided throughout the year, new ideas and new words are learned. The vocabulary of taking care of the science corner is not the same as the vocabulary for music time. For children with very limited speech and language, initially focus on things they need to know and say in the classroom and at home, and then expand to new topics and situations. See the following video that demonstrates strategies to support the language development of infants and toddlers.

Using Any Utterance or Gesture to Begin Communication

For some children with severe disabilities who have no recognizable means of communication, any attempt to make a sound or gesture needs to be rewarded with instant encouragement. If it appears that a child wants something and is attempting to ask for it, give it to the child immediately. If you know what word was attempted, model (say) it to confirm you understood. First efforts should never be the occasion for an attempt to improve the child's production. That comes *much* later. But let the child know that he or she has, in fact, communicated.

Communication Interventions for Young Children with Intensive Needs

Enhanced eText

Video Example 8.5

Language for Learning: Infants and Toddlers

https://www.youtube.com/watch?v=97B__Cwk7vY

Ways to provide developmentally appropriate language input to infants and toddlers are shown in this video.

Children with severe and complex disabilities typically experience significant communication challenges. Many cannot develop the use of intelligible speech. Some may never be able to use a formal symbolic system of communication such as signing or graphic symbols. Nevertheless, these children *can* learn to communicate using nonverbal, nonspeech systems of communication or speech-generating devices.

In planning communication instruction programs for children with multiple disabilities, it is perhaps easiest to consider two types of children. The first group includes those who have the cognitive skills necessary for the development of language (i.e., some formal system of symbolic communication) but do not have the fine *oral-motor skills* required for the production of intelligible speech. The largest number of children in this group would be those with severe cerebral palsy or other motor disorders but who do not have severe intellectual disability. The focus for these children is to design appropriate augmentative and alternative communication (AAC) systems to ensure that the ongoing development of language and literacy skills is commensurate with the child's cognitive level.

Other children may have greater cognitive and intellectual impairments that produce a poor prognosis for the development of any formal symbolic system. This group includes children with severe and profound cognitive disabilities and some who demonstrate *multiple* sensory impairments (e.g., a child with deafness, combined with severe visual and motor impairments and moderate intellectual disabilities). For these children, the goals of intelligible speech production and a symbolic system of communication such as sign language or graphic symbols may be unrealistic. A classroom teacher who is unfamiliar with infants or young children who have severe multiple disabilities is often initially overwhelmed with the apparent challenges, especially in the area of communication skills. However, these children *can* learn to use specific behaviors in functional ways to communicate basic wants, needs, and feelings.

Communicating with Children Who Have Complex or Multiple Disabilities

The following strategies are recommended for communicating with children who have complex disabilities, often referred to as "intensive needs."

Respond to Child's Behavioral Cues.   Many of the input strategies discussed earlier are also appropriate for children with severe disabilities, but they need to be used in more intentional, targeted ways. When an infant or young child demonstrates a low response rate (i.e., just doesn't seem to "do much"), the teacher's immediate and consistent *response* to the child's cues of interest and attention—and to any attempts to communicate—becomes crucial. Teachers must be more vigilant with such children and ready to respond with appropriate communicative input. (For strategies for working with infants and young children who have limited intentionality and multiple disabilities, see Chen et al. [2007].)

For example, let us consider a child, Joshua, who has severe motor and visual impairments. Joshua's voluntary behavioral repertoire consists of moving his head from side to side and a few vocalizations. He does not appear to understand any verbal input, but he does respond to sudden loud sounds, to the sound of his mother's voice, and occasionally to food odors as lunch is prepared. The teacher must be very alert to cues from Joshua that he is recognizing and processing some incoming stimulus. For example, if another child in the classroom drops her tray on the floor, the child with severe disabilities is startled and begins moving his head from side to side. The teacher should provide some verbal input appropriate to the situation and its meaning to the child. In this case, the teacher might say something like, "Uh-oh! That was loud, wasn't it? That was a loud crash! Maria dropped her tray." The teacher comments on the most salient aspect of the situation (in this case, the sound because Joshua has low vision), recasts her comment in a slightly different way, and semantically extends her own comment by adding information about the source of the sound.

Use Repetition and Predictable Schedules.   Repetition, redundancy, and responsiveness are important input strategies in working with infants or young children with severe disabilities. Certain key words and phrases should be used repeatedly to make significant the events of the day. Certain verbal cues should always be associated with certain actions and events. In this way, the teacher establishes **verbal routines,** which are important as children begin to learn to decode language. Classroom strategies that build on the child's focus of attention can establish "joint action routines" in which the adult engages jointly in an action with the child while associating key words and phrases with the activity.

For example, the greeting activities that begin the classroom day should include parts that are always repeated. The transition from music time to lunch should always be accompanied by many predictable cues, such as "OK, who knows what time it is now? It's lunchtime. It's time to eat," followed by a sequence of predictable events (e.g., wash hands, chairs moved, table set, etc.). After lunch, the input might be, "OK, we're all done. All done eating. Let's go outside. We'll play outside." Tables are cleaned, chairs pushed in, coats put on, and so forth, while appropriate verbal input strategies accompany these key events. Use of manual signs for key words can also be helpful, as it adds a visual cue to the spoken message.

Techniques for Teaching Expressive Communicative Behaviors: Output Strategies

As described earlier, careful verbal input in response to cues provided by the child that indicate interest and attention or attempts to communicate is an important key to facilitating communication development in *all* children. However, for children with more severe disabilities, the adult's use of input strategies is not enough. For these children, caregivers and teachers must also create the opportunities and the need to communicate. In addition, teachers must be aware of the array of specialized programs, techniques, and strategies that can encourage and teach expressive communication and language skills. Some of the strategies for doing so are described next and summarized in Exhibit 8.6.

Identify High-Preference Objects and Activities to Make Communication Functional.   Typically, developing young children first develop communicative behaviors around the objects, activities, and persons they are most interested in and most desire. Owens (2016) describes the importance of the *functionality* of communicative behaviors within natural social contexts. The young child's call for "Mama" and requests for "bottle" and "cookie" reflect the importance of high-preference events as motivators for the development of communication skills. The desires and preferences of the typical child are numerous and easily identified. However, identification of **high-preference items and events** for a child with severe disabilities can often present a major challenge. Nevertheless,

Exhibit 8.6

Strategies That Support Communicative Expression for Students with Intensive Needs

1. Teacher vigilance in responding quickly to a child's *initiated* request or comment (e.g., child points to spilled paint and teacher says "Oops! The paint spilled!")
2. Pause and wait ("interruption strategy"; e.g., stop swinging until child says or signs "more")
3. Delay of anticipated event (e.g., delay passing out lunch tray until child initiates)
4. Choice making (e.g., the teacher holds up a cookie and a carrot and asks, "Which one, cookie or carrot?")
5. Create need to request help (e.g., place toy on high shelf; tighten top of cookie jar)
6. Cloze technique ("completion prompt"; e.g., "Now it's time for _____.")
7. Violation of routines (teacher makes a "mistake")
8. Experience stories (describe familiar routines, using key vocabulary and syntactic structures)
9. Social stories (depict targeted social skills)
10. Script training (teacher creates script to accompany specific play routines, e.g., camping trip)
11. Applied behavior analysis approaches such as DTT, PRT, PECS, and functional behavioral analysis (FBA)
12. AAC systems (e.g., high-tech computerized voice-output devices and low-tech picture communication systems)

designing an environment that creates a need to communicate is not possible without first determining those things about which the child is most likely to communicate.

Thus, it is necessary to devote time to the systematic identification of high-preference items and activities (a **preference inventory**) for each child. To do this, parents should be interviewed carefully with regard to their child's schedule and activities at home. This effort may uncover clues related to possible preferences. In addition, the teacher should devote time to identifying high-preference items and activities systematically. Food is often assumed to be a high-preference item, and indeed it often is for many children. But the teacher should be aware of many other objects, persons, and activities that may motivate the child who has severe disabilities to communicate. Table 8.2 lists some examples

Table 8.2 Examples of High-Preference Activities for Preschoolers with Severe Disabilities

Motor/Kinesthetic	Manipulables
Bouncing	Playing with cause-and-effect toys
Riding in a wagon	Operating knobs
Swinging in a blanket	*Setting Changes*
Auditory/Visual	Going outside
Singing	Reduction of discomfort
Listening to CDs	*Tactile/Physical Interaction*
Listening to radio	Stroking
Watching television	Hugging
Operating a music box	Tickling
Playing with percussion toys	Brushing hair
Listening to recordings of familiar voices	Blowing air
Watching flashing lights	Playing with water
Watching mobiles	Playing with sand
Playing with a jack-in-the-box	

of these. The teacher must also be aware that, as with all individuals, children's preferences change over time and vary with circumstances. The search for high-preference motivating objects, activities, and persons to use in teaching functional communication skills must be a continuous process in any program that includes children with severe and multiple disabilities. See Moss (2006) for a preference inventory.

High-preference objects and activities can be identified and verified using a number of strategies. These same strategies can simultaneously be used to determine what voluntary behaviors a child with severe disabilities may be capable of using in a communicative way. The teacher must realize that the mere presentation of a potential high-preference object or activity will not necessarily evoke a positive response from the child. In many cases, interrupting or withholding an item or activity will be much more effective in determining the child's desire for it.

Identifying Behaviors That Can Be Used Communicatively

Whether to activate some augmentative communicative system or simply to find a communicative signal, the teacher must identify which behaviors the child can voluntarily control. Even in a child with the most severe disabilities, probably some behavior can be voluntarily controlled, such as directed eye gaze, head turning, reaching, or vocalization. *Any* behavior can be used as a communicative signal.

Three simple procedures can be used to determine which behaviors the child may be able to use communicatively:

1. *Presentation.* An obvious technique is simply to present an object to the child and observe the child's behavior. However, the presentation of an object or event, even if desired by the child, may not evoke any voluntary response.

2. *Interruption.* Another way is to present an object or activity believed to be high preference and then to stop the activity or remove the object. For example, a child who enjoys being pushed in a wagon is pushed for a moment or two, and then the wagon is stopped. The child's behavior is carefully observed in the event that he attempts to reinstate the activity. He may vocalize, move his head, change his body position or tension, attempt to reach out, and so on. The teacher can systematically observe which behaviors are under some degree of voluntary control.

3. *Withholding an anticipated event.* If there are regularities and predictable events in the child's daily life that he enjoys and if the child is able to anticipate those events given certain cues, then withholding such an event may also be a way of evoking the same kinds of behaviors as those described in item 2. For example, assuming that snack time is a high-preference activity for that child, seating everyone else at the snack table and "forgetting" the child would provide another opportunity to observe potential communicative behaviors.

Another strategy that can be used to create motivation for spontaneous communication is called "violation of object functions" or "violation of routines." Examples would be using a shoe to brush your hair, or putting a cup on a doll's foot. Such ridiculous situations may serve as powerful elicitors of communicative behavior, and perhaps a chuckle.

Teaching Communicative Behaviors by Creating Opportunity and Need for Communication

The simple strategies just described are powerful basic tools for both assessment and beginning intervention. Presentation, interruption, and withholding of an anticipated event are simple and systematic procedures. They can be used to identify and verify high-preference items and activities as well as to begin *teaching* rudimentary communicative behaviors. When a child's preferences have been inventoried and at least one voluntarily controlled behavior has been identified, the environment can be systematically designed to provide opportunities for the child to use the important communicative function of *requesting*.

Several techniques that can be easily incorporated into the child's daily activities are described next.

Requesting "More."   Even a child with the most severe impairments can be taught to request more of a desired object or activity, as described previously. It is not necessary that the child make this request again and again in each setting. For example, the child need not request every single bite of a favorite food. Rather, four or five opportunities could be provided several times per day. There is some evidence that this *distributed practice* is more effective than intensive training blocks of what are called *massed trials.*

Making Choices.   Another important technique is to provide *choices.* In as many situations as possible throughout the child's day, give opportunities to make choices. Choices of activities, food items, toys, and people can easily be incorporated into classroom programming.

Time Delay.   This procedure is another powerful technique to encourage functional communication (Mancil, 2009). Similar to a **pause-and-wait strategy,** when a child expects that something will occur and it does not, a strong need to communicate can be created. However, when using this technique, all too often teachers bombard children with questions, commands, prompts, and cues without giving them ample time to respond. Many children with severe disabilities require a longer time than others to process incoming information and organize a response. An expectant look on the teacher's face accompanied by silence can often be an amazingly powerful provocateur for communicative behavior once the desire to communicate exists.

Communicative Initiation.   Finally, it is extremely important to make sure the child with severe disabilities, particularly the child who is not ambulatory, is provided with some means of getting adults' attention. A child who is at the mercy of others to initiate communication cannot really engage in functional dialogue. Some children are unable to produce an audible vocal signal as an attention-getting device, and they need some other type of auditory signal, such as a bell or buzzer. The ability to *initiate* communication is critical to the success of any communication instruction program.

Teaching Communication Behaviors Through Applied Behavior Analysis

Many of the techniques described earlier can also be applied within highly structured, more intensive interventions using the principles of *applied behavior analysis*, or ABA. Generally, ABA procedures include the following elements: (1) a specific target behavior expected of the child (response), for example, saying "car"; (2) the specific conditions under which the behavior will be taught, including the antecedent (discriminative) stimulus (e.g., adult says, "Point to car"); and (3) the reinforcer to be given immediately if the child responds correctly (e.g., child receives a fruit snack).

Several traditional, highly structured ABA approaches are widely used with young children who have disabilities to support the development of specific language skills, such as following commands and labeling. One of the most widely used is *Discrete Trial Training (DTT).* DTT is a highly structured, programmed approach developed by Lovaas (2003). When used with young children, target behaviors are typically selected from a bank of predetermined, developmentally sequenced behaviors, and it requires very specific data collection within massed trials. Any changes in procedures (e.g., reinforcement schedule, prompts used, expected child response, etc.) are tied closely and continuously to a careful examination of the graphed data.

One common challenge of DTT is that the behavior specialist may not adequately program for generalization of the learned behaviors (Myers & Johnson, 2007). Also of some concern is that the "bits" of observable "discrete" behavior selected as targets for implementation of DTT may not support the development of complex communication processes and may actually interfere with language growth (Owens, 2016). Another concern is the overreliance of DTT techniques on imitative elicitation procedures, rather than more natural facilitative strategies such as responsive expansion and recasting within natural communicative contexts. Seiger-Gardner and Almodovar (2009) discuss studies comparing these two approaches. Although both approaches can produce increases in the target behavior, more naturalistic approaches promote greater increase in spontaneous language and faster generalization. Owens characterizes these two different approaches as directive versus facilitative.

Another applied behavior analysis approach used increasingly is referred to as *functional behavior analysis or assessment* (FBA). The purpose of this analysis is to determine the cause and *function* of a particular behavior. As shown in Exhibit 6.4, this approach carefully observes the *antecedent,* (i.e., *what happens just prior to the behavior*), describes the topography (specific elements) of the behavior, then carefully notes the *consequence* of the behavior. This is often referred to as **A-B-C analysis**, for *antecedent, behavior, and consequence*. For example, an FBA might reveal that the function of a child's noncompliance and running from circle time is related to his desire to escape loud sounds, or to avoid close proximity to other children. The disruptive behavior is viewed as the child's way of communicating that he finds the sounds and other children too loud and uncomfortable. FBA is a key component of a behavior management approach referred to as *positive behavior support* (Dunlap, Wilson, Strain, & Lee, 2013). An important element is determining the *communicative* function of the inappropriate behavior and teaching a more acceptable "replacement" behavior by which the child can achieve the same consequence in a more appropriate way. For example, the child could be taught to use a manual sign or picture card that represents *"want break"* to ask permission to move outside the circle, rather than screaming and running. In this way, FBA can be used not only to manage inappropriate behaviors, but also to support the development of communication skills.

More Naturalistic ABA Approaches.   Several communication interventions have emerged that maintain the basic elements of applied behavior analysis. These use opportunities within the natural environment to teach the target behavior and increase the functionality and generalization of learned responses. These approaches also have the advantage of being somewhat more "family friendly" in that they can be implemented within naturally occurring daily routines. Two examples of such approaches are milieu teaching and pivotal response treatment (Koegel & Koegel, 2012).

Milieu teaching is a term used to refer to a variety of semistructured behavioral techniques that are used in the natural environment to teach specific communication skills. Milieu teaching techniques include three basic elements: (1) arranging the environment in ways that increase the *need and opportunity* for communicative behavior (e.g., the child's favorite toy is placed on a shelf where he cannot reach it); (2) identifying specific target behaviors (e.g., child must point to the toy); and (3) applying carefully planned teaching steps and prompting procedures (McCormick et al., 2003). Examples of these training steps include the mand-model technique, incidental teaching, and the time-delay procedure. Detailed descriptions of several of these procedures can be found in Mirenda and Beukelman (2013) and Downing (2010). (Appendix C describes a common sequence of steps used in milieu approaches.) An important feature of milieu teaching is that it takes place during regularly occurring opportunities in daily routines. Being in the context within which the child will actually need to *use* the response might support generalization of the communicative behavior.

Pivotal Response Treatment or Teaching (PRT) is an increasingly used naturalistic ABA approach. PRT focuses on key "pivotal" behaviors (e.g., initiation and establishing joint attention) that, when increased, lead to changes in many other behaviors. Behavioral targets are typically spoken requests. A common example is teaching the child to initiate and establish joint attention with a caregiver and initiate a request for a preferred object or activity. For example, a child who rarely makes eye contact and infrequently vocalizes loves to go outdoors. Mother stands in front of the door until her child looks at or touches her and vocalizes. Mother then opens the door. Training establishes "shared control" of the desired object or activity, and it allows for successive approximation of targeted communicative response.

The **Picture Exchange Communication System (PECS)** was developed by Bondy and Frost (2001, 2011). PECS combines elements of several applied behavior analysis approaches and is discussed later in this chapter. Exhibit 8.6 summarizes these more intensive communication interventions.

Augmentative and Alternative Communication Systems

For many children with severe and multiple disabilities, the development of an **augmentative and alternative communication (AAC) system** will be necessary (Beukelman & Mirenda, 2013). Such a system involves the use of nonspeech communication strategies. Examples of these include signing, pointing to pictures, use of electronic communication devices and computerized speech-output systems, and so on. The system can "augment" existing communication skills and behaviors or may provide an "alternative" to speech production for a child who has no means of communication.

In recent years, AAC has come to be associated in many people's minds with high-technology equipment such as adapted computer keyboards that can be activated by a touch or laser beam to produce a communication printout or synthesized speech. (For a list of resources related to AAC technology for young children, see Sadao and Robinson [2010].)

It is important to understand, however, that AAC can include both high-tech and low-tech systems and is often multimodal. Low-tech systems are non-electronic. They include strategies such as simple adaptations of manual signs, use of photos or black-and-white line drawings arranged on a communication board or in a communication book, and letters of the alphabet printed on a card.

Particularly for very young children, it is important to begin training with very simple low-tech strategies and devices. These include several techniques already discussed, such as PECS, communication boards, and manual signing systems. Also important is the introduction of simple switch-operated toys. Although the development of high-tech computerized communication systems continues at a rapid pace, for some children low-tech strategies and devices may be more appropriate for their individual needs. However, in a short period of time, the explosion of low cost, easily accessed high-tech communication devices has been extraordinary. Historically, there was some reluctance to begin the use of augmentative communication strategies and devices for young children because of beliefs that the use of devices and nonspeech (i.e., "augmentative") strategies would somehow interfere with speech development. However, this notion has been thoroughly debunked (Romski et al., 2010).

Early interventionists should not wait to see whether efforts to teach speech to the child with multiple challenges will be successful before introducing augmentative communication instruction. Teaching nonspeech communication strategies does not appear to interfere with speech development. Such instruction may actually facilitate rather than decrease vocalization and speech development. In addition, many of the skills necessary for successful use of an AAC system are also beneficial and motivating for children who do *not* have severe disabilities. Use of pictures or line drawings as representations of real objects and activities is important for print recognition and use of computer keyboards.

The development of an AAC system for a particular child requires a team approach. Such a team ideally might include the parent, early childhood educator, occupational or physical therapist, and speech-language pathologist. In addition, if high-tech devices are being used, technology support will be critically important (although rapid development of high-tech, but simple-to-operate, low-cost devices of all kinds continues to amaze!).

Although space does not allow for a thorough discussion of the strategies and procedures for developing an AAC system, the following section briefly outlines a typical sequence of training steps.

Developing a Low-Tech AAC System

1. *Determine the child's communicative needs and opportunities.* Together with the child's family, it is important to determine in what situations and for what purposes the child currently needs or attempts to communicate. (If the child does not *attempt* to communicate, then the primary goal becomes creating the motivation necessary to encourage communicative initiations.)

2. *Determine the child's current communicative repertoire.* If the child does attempt to communicate, how does he or she do so? What does the child do to communicate wants and needs, express emotions, or share information? What movements can the child voluntarily control? Does the child use his or her eyes, vocalizations, or gestures, such as reaching or pointing?

3. *What are the barriers to successful communication?* Determine why the communication is not successful. Are vocalizations unintelligible? Are hand gestures poorly controlled? Is the child trying to refer to things that are not immediately present, such as something that happened yesterday?

4. *Determine the best "indicating response" to be used.* Of what behavior does the child have the best control? For many children with severe physical disabilities, eye gaze may be the only reliable voluntary movement. Other children may be able to touch or point to a picture successfully. Some children may not be able to use their hands but may have sufficient head control to point with a head stick (pointer) mounted on a headband or may be able to move the head to activate a switch.

5. *Determine the best "symbol system."* The symbol system depends largely on the child's cognitive level. Some children need to begin with the actual object, moving step by step to more abstract representations. Others may be able to begin immediately with photos or black-and-white line drawings of concrete objects. Occasionally, a child may actually prefer printed words rather than picture representations.

6. *Design the "display."* Once the indicating response and symbol system have been identified, it is then necessary to determine how the symbols will be displayed. For the child who cannot walk but who can point to pictures, a common display would be a communication board mounted on a wheelchair. For a child who uses eye gaze as an indicating response, the most common display would be pictures arranged on a clear Plexiglas frame called an "E-tran" board. For a child who is mobile, the display might be a picture book or laminated cards on a large ring. Other considerations are visual acuity and visual field factors. One child may need symbols to be enlarged, another may need the display positioned on the child's left side, and so on.

7. *Design training steps.* Teaching a child to use an augmentative communication system requires careful planning of the training steps. Exhibit 8.7 is an example of the

Exhibit 8.7

Training Angie to Use an AAC System

Angie was a 2½-year-old girl with spastic cerebral palsy. There was severe involvement of all parts of her body. She was unable to sit unsupported, reach or grasp, or bring her hands to midline. She also had some difficulty with head control. She was unable to produce speech sounds, although she occasionally vocalized. One day her mother mentioned to her early interventionist that Angie had recently begun to stare intently at things she wanted. Together, the early interventionist and parent, in consultation with a speech-language specialist trained in augmentative methodology, planned the following intervention.

1. ***Carefully describe current communicative behavior.*** In Angie's case, the most reliable communicative behavior was "directed eye gaze."

2. ***Identify high-preference and low-preference objects and activities.*** Angie loved to eat, so her favorite foods were identified as high-preference items, especially strawberry yogurt, ice cream, and orange juice. One low-preference activity identified was having her face washed, which she had always hated.

3. ***Establish "indicating response."*** The logical indicating response in Angie's case because she really had no other consistent communicative behavior was the use of eye gaze. Angie's mom began to give her lots of practice in using her eyes to track her glass or spoon before giving her a bite or drink.

4. ***Offer choice of a high- or low-preference item.*** Angie's mom or her teacher would hold up two items, a glass of juice and a washcloth, saying, "Which would you like, Angie: juice or washcloth?" Whichever item she looked at for more than a fleeting glance was the one she received. Initially, she would occasionally stare at the washcloth. She immediately got her face washed a bit, even though her mom knew this was not what she really wanted. This step was necessary to help her understand the communicative nature of her eye gaze. Quickly, she learned to scan the items right away to look for the item she wanted and then immediately fix her gaze on that item.

5. ***Offer choice of two high-preference items.*** The next step was to offer Angie a choice of two high-preference items. This represents a true communication situation. Her communication partner really does not know which of two foods she wants. Her eye gaze communication puts her in control of the choice.

6. ***Pair pictures with items.*** Next, the objects, such as a glass of juice and bowl of yogurt, were paired with pictures. In Angie's case, black-and-white line drawings of a glass and bowl were used. (Photos of the objects could have been used, but Angie's mom felt she could learn to recognize the line drawings easily, and they were easier to produce than photos by simply using a magic marker on a 3-by-5-inch index card.) The name of the item was printed at the bottom of the picture.

7. ***Fade objects.*** Gradually, the items were removed from sight, and only the pictures were presented. Angie learned that the picture *represented* the object. This was the beginning of Angie's comprehension of symbols, which is an important cognitive skill for the use of an augmentative communication system.

8. ***Reduce picture size and design display.*** Now the pictures could be made somewhat smaller and placed on a see-through Plexiglas board that could be attached to her wheelchair. The teacher and occupational therapist experimented to determine the best position of the board and how far apart the pictures needed to be to tell reliably what Angie was looking at.

9. ***Add vocabulary; expand system.*** From this point on, it was a fairly easy matter to add new pictures representing key vocabulary (e.g., "bathroom" and "TV") and whole sentences (e.g., "What's your name?"). Angie eventually developed better control of her hands and arms and learned to activate an adapted keyboard to produce synthesized speech.

Note: Parents can easily adapt these basic strategies to use with electronic devices such as cell phones and iPads, and inexpensive widely available communication devices.

training steps to teach a young child with cerebral palsy to use directed eye gaze. (For more detailed information on the development of AAC systems, see Drager, Light, and Finke [2008] and Sadao and Robinson [2010].)

Classroom Strategies That Facilitate Augmentative Communication Skills

Several activities that facilitate the development of low-tech augmentative communication skills can be built into the everyday activities of an early childhood program. These activities can be both fun and meaningful for all children, not just for the child with severe disabilities. Examples of these include the following:

1. *Use of switch-operated toys.* Battery-operated toys can be included among the play materials in the classroom. The switches can be adapted to be more easily operated by children with severe motor impairments. Cause-and-effect toys can be adapted with pressure switches, large toggle switches, heat-sensitive touch switches, and so on. Such switches are intriguing to all children and facilitate the learning of cause-and-effect relationships. In addition, for the child with severe motor impairments, they provide the motivation and opportunity to practice the fine motor movements required for activating various communication devices.

2. *Use of computer tablets and computers.* Thousands of software games and activities are available that are interesting and appropriate for very young children. These should be selected for inclusion in the early childhood classroom, and every effort should be made to familiarize the child with disabilities with the action on the computer tablet screen that activates the app or the operation of the keyboard and the relationship to the monitor display on a computer. This is a particularly good activity for peer interaction and modeling. (*Note:* Children should be taught keyboard skills rather than just allowed to use computers as self-stimulating, cause-and-effect toys.)

3. *Use of picture representations and symbols.* An important skill in the development of a successful AAC system is the ability to recognize that pictures and abstract symbols have representational meaning—that they stand for some real object or activity. Many young children, with and without disabilities, have not acquired this understanding. This symbolic representation skill is obviously necessary for the eventual development of literacy. Thus, whenever possible, functional use of pictures and symbols (including printed words) should be demonstrated in the classroom. Black-and-white line drawings can be pasted on cupboard doors and boxes to show their contents.
   - Bathroom signs should be similar to the adult bathroom signs.
   - Lunch menus should be posted and referred to at appropriate times.
   - Children can choose a favorite toy by choosing the appropriate laminated card or by pointing to a picture on a grid that corresponds to that toy.

   Visual discrimination and matching skills can also be encouraged by the use of picture-matching games and name recognition. (For more cognitively advanced children, shapes and letters could be matched.)

4. *Conversation starter strategies.* Many communication training strategies rely on teaching the *child* to request something. Although this is an important starting point, it is equally important to find ways to assist children who cannot speak in sharing information and experiences with others. These conversation strategies are very important and help prevent overemphasizing the communicative function of requesting. It is relatively easy to teach a child to request wants and needs. Thus, this is the communicative function that is most often emphasized in work with children with severe disabilities. Beukelman and Mirenda (2013) describe three conversation starter strategies: collections, remnant books, and topic-setter cards, as discussed next.

Collections.   Children can be encouraged to collect things of interest to them, such as bracelets, toy cars, pictures of friends, and so on. Both teachers and peers can be encouraged to notice and comment on the items in the collection as well as new additions to the collection. Again, this is an activity that all children can enjoy. For the nonspeaking child, it provides an excellent communicative context in which others can easily participate.

Remnant Books. Remnant books provide a way for the nonspeaking child to share past experiences. For example, a child may save various scraps and reminders—"remnants"—from a weekend trip to the zoo. The teacher and parent should help the child construct the book. The remnant book might have a postcard with a picture of the zoo, a ticket stub with the price of admission, a hamburger wrapper from lunch, photos of the most interesting animals, and a parking ticket next to a drawing of the family car. The book should be easily accessible so that the experiences can be shared at any appropriate time.

Topic-Setter Cards. For children who have difficulty initiating conversations, topic-setter cards may be useful. A simple line drawing or symbol that has meaning for the child is drawn on an index card. On the back of the card facing the prospective communication partner there is a message—for example, "What's your favorite TV show? Mine is *Power Rangers.*"

Using the Picture Exchange Communication System

Perhaps the most widely used approach to communication training for young children with significant disabilities and minimal functional communication skills is the previously mentioned Picture Exchange Communication System, commonly referred to as PECS (Bondy & Frost, 2011). PECS is a low-tech system that uses ABA principles to teach the child to *instigate* requests or comments using pictures representing high-preference objects, activities, or topics. PECS is particularly appropriate and effective with children who have autism spectrum disorder (ASD) because it requires an "exchange"; that is, the child must select the appropriate picture card and *approach* another person in order to *exchange* the picture for a highly desired object or activity. The system begins with careful observation of the child in order to determine high-preference objects and activities. It is deceptively simple, and is commonly used inappropriately without proper training.

Before training can begin, a careful assessment of the child's high-preference objects, people, and activities must be conducted. Input from family members and teachers, as well as direct observation of the child, are required. Each highly motivating activity or object is identified, and a photo or line drawing is produced and placed on a card. These are each attached to Velcro strips in a binder.

Unlike other low-tech AAC picture systems, the child does not *point*. Rather, the child is taught, in *Phase 1*, to remove the Velcro-attached picture from a book or binder, approach another person, and hand the picture to that person. The individual receiving the picture responds with appropriate language and gives the child the desired object or activity. Careful physical prompts (not verbal prompts) are provided *by a second trainer, not the recipient of the card*, until the child learns the following sequence:

1. Finding the correct picture
2. Removing the picture
3. Approaching the adult
4. Handing the picture to the adult
5. Waiting for the adult's response/compliance with the request

A significant advantage of PECS is that it requires initiation of *social interaction* for the communication to be successful. Eventually, the child may learn to combine sequences of pictures to represent word combinations and sentences. A brief overview of the PECS training phases is presented in Exhibit 8.8.

Exhibit 8.8

Picture Exchange Communication System (PECS)

Brief Overview of Training Phases

Identifying High Preferences

Prior to beginning training, high-preference objects, persons, activities, and topics will be identified. This phase must be completed carefully. The PECS procedure cannot be effective if these are not truly high preferences! Careful data collection throughout PECS training will ensure the identification of items that are no longer reinforcing.

Phase 1 Goal: Child will look for, select, pick up, and hand the picture/symbol card to the communication partner. (*Note:* Prompts are provided by a second trainer, *not* by the "communication partner," i.e., the recipient of the card.)

Phase 2 Goal: To increase the child's spontaneity and generalization of the picture exchange. This includes decreasing the use of prompts and increasing the frequency of initiations and the number of high preferences. (*Note:* If children only use PECS cards when prompted, or during certain activities, and do not make requests *spontaneously throughout the day,* the system is not being used/trained correctly!)

Phase 3 Goal: Child will discriminate among more than one picture. This requires the child to scan two or more pictures and discriminate the desired icon from the distractor icon(s). (*Note:* If the child selects the "wrong" picture, the communication partner does not correct at that point, but gives the child the corresponding item. This would be the "natural consequence," teaching the child to better discriminate among pictures.)

Phase 4 Goal: Child will spontaneously request using simple sentence structure. Once the child can discriminate among a substantial repertoire of pictures (icons) of high-preference items and activities, he or she will learn to create a "sentence strip" by combining an icon for "I want" with a familiar preference picture.

Phase 5 Goal: Child will be able to answer the question "What do you want?" Child will learn to answer the question "What do you want?" by answering with an "*I want*" icon plus the picture of the desired high-preference item.

Phase 6 Goal: Commenting in response to a question. Here the goal is for the child to comment on something *other* than what he or she wants, by responding to the question "What do you *see*?" using an icon for "*I see*" and an icon for an object that is *not* one of the child's highly preferred objects. In this case, the child does *not* receive the item. It is hoped that this new skill of labeling (rather than requesting) will eventually lead to spontaneous commenting as a new communicative function, and the important pragmatic skill of *answering.*

Note: Extensive training steps, not described here, are required to reach the goal of each phase. See Frost and Bondy (2001, 2011).

Enhanced eText Application Exercise 8.2: In this exercise, you can apply what you have learned in this chapter about alternative modes of communication available to children with multiple and complex disabilities.

Supporting Communication in Children with Hearing Loss

A preschool teacher whose class includes a child with a hearing loss must work in close collaboration not only with the child's parents but also with specialists trained to work with infants and young children with hearing loss. These specialists may include an audiologist (if the child wears a hearing aid), a speech pathologist trained to work with children with hearing loss, or a teacher with certification in deafness.

An important decision for every family of a child with a significant hearing loss is the selection of a primary communication modality: speech or manual sign (or a combination of both), and, increasingly in many cases, a decision about using the cochlear implant as a way to maximize learning and access to spoken language.

The use of American Sign Language (ASL), or the "manual communication" approach, is strongly endorsed by members of the Deaf community as well as by many teachers of students with hearing loss who believe that ASL is the most easily and naturally acquired language for children with significant hearing losses. Although the early introduction of signs enables the child who is Deaf to achieve major *language* milestones without delay, the process of teaching *speech* skills is often slow and tedious.

There are several different systems of sign language. ASL is the system that most members of the Deaf community prefer. It is a language in its own right. Its structure does not correspond to the structure of English: Rules of word order are different, and there are no signs for grammatical markers, such as *-ing* or *-ed*. Because of the belief that ASL does not facilitate the learning of spoken English and literacy skills, other sign systems have been developed that more closely match the grammar and vocabulary of the English language. These systems can be signed simultaneously with speech. Examples of such systems (referred to as "manually coded English") are Signing Essential English (SEE).

Proponents of the oral approach believe that the individual with a hearing loss must be given the skills to function comfortably in a hearing world. Approaches that emphasize speech (sometimes referred to as "auditory-oral" or "listening and spoken language (LSL)" approaches) stress the importance of teaching the child with a hearing loss to produce intelligible speech and to use his or her residual hearing to be able to understand the spoken language of others.

The Increasing Use of Cochlear Implants

In recent years, technological improvements in the **cochlear implant** have greatly increased the use of oral approaches in promoting the understanding and use of spoken English in children who have even severe to profound hearing loss.

The controversy over which approach is best has raged for more than 200 years and continues to be an emotionally charged debate. Overall, the research findings on efficacy are mixed. One consistent finding has been that for Deaf children of Deaf parents, the early use of ASL clearly facilitates *language* development. Adults who are Deaf and who identify strongly with the Deaf community are proponents of the notion that children who are Deaf should be viewed not as deficient or having a pathology, but as members of a different culture that has its own language, traditions, values, and literature. Most individuals within the Deaf community view ASL as their natural native language (Ladd, 2003). Spoken English is an optional second language.

The parents must make the decision regarding the language modality to be used with the child who is Deaf or hard of hearing. If parents have already made this decision, it is the responsibility of the early childhood professional to understand and support that approach. In those cases in which parents are in the process of trying to decide which approach is best, the early childhood professional can direct them to specialists who can give them accurate and reliable information about the characteristics of each approach. Regardless of the approaches involved, Spencer and Marschark's (2010) review of evidence-based practices offered the following statement: "Children who are identified early and receive early intervention have been found to demonstrate language development in the 'low average' level compared to hearing children" (p. 42).

Specific Strategies for Working with Children with Hearing Loss

The following are suggestions for early childhood preschool teachers whose classes may include a young child with a hearing loss. Additional suggestions are included in Chapter 5.

1. For children learning to sign, ask parents to teach you signs used at home; teach parents new signs introduced at school.

2. Teach signs for key words to *all* the children in the classroom.

3. Be sure windows or other light sources are not behind you or shining into the eyes of the child. For the child to read lips or signs, the light must be on the speaker or signer, not in the child's eyes.

4. As often as possible, include adults and older children with hearing loss in your classroom. It is important for all young children (not just the child with a hearing loss) to observe role models who wear hearing aids and/or use sign language. Such an individual might sign and speak a story or song or simply assist with daily routines.

5. Include in your classroom books that include the signs for key words in the story. (Many such materials are available from Gallaudet University Press in Washington, D.C.)

6. When the child does not appear to understand, repeat the sentence or say it in a slightly different way. Then add visual cues (e.g., gestures, facial expressions, or pointing to an object or picture).

Facilitating Comprehension of Speech

Use the following suggestions to facilitate the development of the child's ability to comprehend speech:

1. Don't talk too fast. You may need to slow your speech rate slightly. Be careful not to distort the rate and rhythm of your normal speech pattern.

2. Do not exaggerate lip movements or pause after each word. This does not make lip-reading easier and provides inappropriate speech models for the child. However, do avoid mumbling, chewing gum, or keeping your hands in front of your mouth.

3. Stand or sit still. It is hard for children to focus on a moving target!

4. Don't ask, "Do you understand?" Children often say "yes" regardless. Rather, discover how much has been understood by asking questions or giving directions and observing the child's responses.

5. If the child does not appear to understand, repeat the sentence or say it in a different way. Then add visual cues such as facial expression, gestures, or pointing to an object or picture.

6. Be aware of the child's potential for use of residual hearing. Help the child learn the meaning of various sounds in the environment by drawing his or her attention to them, for example, the sounds of musical instruments or the sound of a timer bell.

7. Perhaps most important, follow the suggestions made in this text for nurturing the development of speech and language in all children.

Hearing Aid. It is critical that the early childhood professional be aware of the child's potential for the development of **residual hearing**. Even children with the most severe losses usually have some hearing and with assistance can eventually learn to use this hearing. The *meaning* of sounds must be learned and does not happen automatically.

We have experienced unprecedented changes in both early identification of young children with hearing loss as well as major advances in biomedical technology (Spencer & Marschark, 2010). In the past, the average age of diagnosis of a hearing loss was 24 months, well beyond a critical developmental period for learning to recognize sounds of speech. Increasingly, states are implementing comprehensive early hearing detection programs in which all newborns are routinely screened. In addition, major advances in technology have resulted in improved instrumentation for assessment, thus increasing the reliable identification of the incidence of hearing loss as well as the type of deficit.

Equally significant is improved amplification technology, such as digital programmable circuitry, resulting in major improvements in the performance of hearing aids. As a result, hearing aids can be programmed to match specific characteristics of the child's hearing loss and minimize the effects of background noise.

Ideally, the young child with a hearing loss will have been fitted with a hearing aid in infancy to maximize the use of residual hearing. The challenge of supporting the very young child's use of a hearing aid is an important one. With the assistance of the audiologist, the teacher and parent must work together to ensure optimal use of the hearing aid. *Ensure that the child wears the hearing aid consistently in the center and help the family to expect the same at home.* Also consult with the audiologist to determine the types of sounds the child can perceive most easily.

The following suggestions may be helpful in encouraging the child's use of a hearing aid:

1. Check the batteries daily; have extra batteries on hand.

2. Cover the controls on the hearing aid so they remain set at the proper levels; keep ear molds cleaned (do not clean with alcohol); keep the receiver away from water or extreme heat; avoid dropping the receiver.

3. Work with parents to teach children to care for and insert their own aids as part of their daily self-care routine.

4. At home, have a special place where the aid is always kept, away from pets and siblings.

5. For infants and very young children, behind-the-ear aids may need to be secured with tape or a "huggie aid" loop to keep the aid on the child's ear.

6. Be aware of the acoustic characteristics of your classroom and the child's home environment. For optimal use of amplification, the acoustic environment must be appropriate; that is, relatively free of extraneous noise (such as background music, playground or hallway noise, etc.) and reverberating surfaces. When speech sounds are reflected off hard surfaces, they are more difficult to comprehend. Dampen noise by use of carpets, wall hangings, acoustic tile, and so on.

Cochlear Implants: Amazing Advances in Technology

Increasing numbers of children with severe or profound sensorineural hearing losses are being treated via cochlear implants (Spencer & Marschark, 2010). A cochlear implant is a surgically implanted electrical device that directly stimulates the auditory nerve, thus bypassing the damaged nerve fibers in the cochlea. A cochlear implant consists of four components: a microphone, a signal processor, a receiver, and the surgically implanted electrodes (see Figure 8.3). A cochlear implant does not restore hearing; however, with intensive auditory training, children can develop significant auditory skills and, in many cases, spoken language skills within normal limits.

The improvements in cochlear implant technology have been very dramatic, making it possible to program many more channels of discrete stimulation, thus more closely mimicking the neural input frequency band of the normal ear. Some research has demonstrated that the language development of children with cochlear implants is superior to that of children with hearing aids. This is particularly true for children with

Figure 8.3 Components of a cochlear implant

Source: © 2018, provided courtesy of Advanced Bionics LLC.

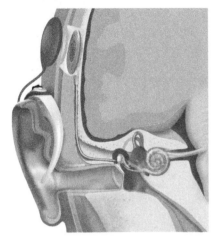

profound hearing loss who are identified early. Before the development of cochlear implants, the achievement of intelligible speech in children with profound hearing loss was very limited—even when the mode of communication was oral plus conventional amplification (hearing aids) (Yoshinaga-Itano, 2006). Currently, though some controversy remains around the use of this technology, many children with significant hearing loss are receiving cochlear implants at younger and younger ages, in some cases well before 12 months of age (see *Advantages of Early Cochlear Implantation: Parent Guide* at www.medel.com/us/children). As of the publication of the current edition of this text, there appears to be a growing consensus that earlier implantation results in superior speech development. Nicholas and Geers (2006) conclude there is research evidence that children who receive cochlear implants before age 2 have a greater chance of achieving normal spoken language development than children receiving the device later. However, in a more recent review of the literature, Spencer and Marschark (2010), as noted earlier, state: "Even with early cochlear implantation, language abilities remain on average below those of hearing peers" (p. 56).

Supporting Spoken English

Regardless of the mode of communication, Yoshinaga-Itano (2006) recommends the following to support the child's development of **spoken English:**

- Frequent assessment to ensure that intervention strategies are, in fact, promoting age-appropriate expressive language skills.
- A team-based approach to ensure that amplification is fitted at the earliest possible age and adjusted to the specific characteristics of the child's hearing loss.
- Incorporation of auditory skill development into families' daily routines and meaningful opportunities to teach listening skills (e.g., doorbell, telephone, or car pulling into driveway) and use of specific sounds for certain events (e.g., "oh oh" for something falling, "up up up" for lifting the child up, or "whoo whoo" while moving the toy train).
- Furthermore, for young children with **profound hearing loss,** "early cochlear implantation and a high quality early stimulation program results in expectations that are similar to those for early-identified mild-to-severe hearing loss and the use of conventional amplification." (p. 323)

In the early childhood classroom, especially if there is a student with a cochlear implant, it will be extremely important for the teacher to identify the key service providers, for example, audiologists, teachers with Deaf and hard-of-hearing certification, speech-language pathologists, and families. (For information related to meeting the needs of young children with cochlear implants, see the resources and frequently asked questions available at http://www.asha.org.)

Also, because the appearance of cochlear implant receiver technology is unusual, it may be important for teachers and staff to learn not only how to support the child, but also how to assist peers with some level of understanding of the implant. Children's books addressing this, such as *Abby Gets a Cochlear Implant* (Riski, 2008), can be useful.

Children with Intermittent Hearing Losses

Some young children have hearing losses that come and go. Fluid in the middle ear, wax in the ear canal, and frequent colds, no matter how mild, may result in a hearing loss that comes suddenly and remains for some time. Physicians are usually unaware of this condition unless parents report it to them, and parents are unaware because the child is not complaining. However, they often report that "Johnny has been so stubborn this week. He doesn't come and do what I tell him unless I yell at him." Or they may say, "Sandy has been so grumpy all week. She won't listen. She just pretends not to hear me." It is important to recognize that these mild intermittent hearing losses may place children at risk for language differences (Roberts & Zeisel, 2004).

Supporting Communication in Children with Visual Impairments

Early childhood professionals must work collaboratively with specialists who have expertise in the area of visual impairment in infants and young children. This collaboration can provide the early interventionist with important information describing the nature of the child's functional vision and ensure that optimal adaptations are made. It is also critical to involve orientation and mobility specialists as well as teachers certified in visual impairments (Dote-Kwan, 2014). The orientation and mobility specialist can support the development of walking and moving safely in the environment. Equally important is the support the specialist can offer families and ECSE practitioners related to "orientation," which helps the young child make sense of the world around him or her, thus supporting important sensory and cognitive development.

The following suggestions may be helpful in facilitating communication skills in children with visual impairments:

1. Use the strategies already described in this text.

2. During vocalizations, touch the child to let him or her know you are there listening. Use the child's name to initiate conversations and interact with the child verbally just as you would with any other child of the same language development level.

3. Use auditory and tactile cues to help the child *anticipate* what will happen next; for example, before you wash the child's face, touch his or her hand with the washcloth and say, "Let's wash your face now."

4. Talk about and describe the child's actions as well as your own and others' actions as they happen.

5. Be certain the child uses vision to the maximum extent possible and then combine looking with touching and talking.

6. Be certain that children with visual impairments see and feel all parts of an object and understand the relationship of parts to the whole and to the context in which it is used.

7. Spatial relations are difficult to demonstrate. Place the child in various positions and encourage touching and manipulating. Sometimes use toys to demonstrate concepts such as on–off, up–down, and in–out.

8. Use language and the auditory modality to facilitate the child's beginning understanding of directionality and distance; for example, say, "I'm across the room, far away. Now I'm coming closer!" so the child can hear the difference in your voice as you approach.

9. Avoid "bombarding" the child with too much talk. Use key words and descriptions but don't describe every possible object and action. Pause frequently and avoid talking too rapidly.

10. Teach the child to localize sounds and recognize their source, direction, and distance.

Supporting Communication in Children with Autism Spectrum Disorder

Increasingly, it is clear that the label "autism" is used to refer to a group of individuals who, although they share certain core characteristics of social communication deficits, present a wide range of skills and cognitive abilities. Children with "autism" as a group represent a broad spectrum of strengths and needs. Thus, the term *autism spectrum disorder,* or ASD, is currently used to refer to these individuals.

We have mentioned previously the challenges associated with young children with ASD in establishing joint attention. This social perceptual difficulty also interferes significantly with the development of language. Important intervention goals related to communication interaction include turn taking, social initiation, and the development of instrumental and regulatory functions of communication—that is, using gestures and words to express wants and needs and to influence the behaviors of others (Prizant, Wetherby, & Rydell, 2000). More recent studies have demonstrated the positive effects of increasing joint attention in children with ASD. Kasari et al. (2010) conducted a randomized, controlled study of caregiver use of joint engagement with their toddlers who have ASD. Parents were successfully trained to support their child's joint engagement, which in turn increased children's gains in attention and responding.

An important prospective study by McDuffie and Yoder (2010) examined how different kinds of parent verbal responsiveness predicted child vocabulary development in their children with ASD. The children whose parents more frequently used responsive "follow-in" comments relating to the child's focus of attention or to the child's verbal communicative behaviors had greater gains in spoken vocabulary. As a result of such findings, interventions for language delays often target parent responsiveness. Particularly with children who have autism spectrum disorders, the establishment of joint attention becomes essential. See, for example, Kasari and colleagues' joint attention and symbolic play intervention program, referred to as Joint Attention and Symbolic Play Engagement and Regulation (JASPER) (Goods, Ishijima, Chang, & Kasari, 2013).

Use of Applied Behavior Analysis Approaches with ASD

By far the most frequently used intervention methods with children on the autism spectrum are methods that apply the principles of ABA. According to a report of the National Autism Center (2015a), the most empirically validated forms of intervention for children with autism are those derived from ABA. The use of traditional direct elicitation approaches to language instruction that rely on elicited imitation, typical of ABA procedures, may be problematic, particularly in those children with ASD who rely on **echolalic speech** (i.e., the immediate or delayed exact repetition or "parroting" of another person's speech). Although they may respond easily when the teacher models a cue such as "Say 'cookie,'" generalizing the response to functional and meaningful spontaneous use of the word *cookie* is often extremely difficult. Techniques that may be more helpful include strategies that limit the use of imitative prompts and increase opportunities for initiated functional communication. Some of these were presented earlier in the discussion of strategies for children with severe disabilities. Children with autism often handle visual or graphic information more easily than auditory or verbal information. One successful approach to developing communication behaviors is the use of PECS, described earlier in this chapter.

Communication intervention programs for young children with autism should be both structured *and* functional rather than one or the other. Historically, approaches have emphasized one or the other. For example, Lovaas's "discrete trial" approach (Jennett, Harris, & Delmolino, 2008) has been criticized because of its lack of generalization across partners and situations, its emphasis on the child as a respondent rather than an initiator, and its focus on specific language forms rather than on functional communication skills. In contrast, naturalistic teaching strategies such as an incidental teaching approach described by McGee and Daly (2007) and Pivotal Response Training (Koegel & Koegel, 2012) can be very effective in promoting language skills in young children with ASD. These approaches are both structured and functional. Functionality is established by working with the child within meaningful contexts such as play and daily routines and creating the need and opportunity for communicative behaviors that can be generalized to other situations. Structured teaching steps and careful data recording described in various ABA applications can then be used to monitor the child's progress and the effectiveness of the intervention.

Another approach frequently used with young children who have autism is the Developmental Individual Differences Relationship Based (DIR) model (Weider, Greenspan, & Kalmanson, 2008). See Hess (2013) for an in-depth description of DIR, including case examples. This approach directly addresses the core characteristics of the disability of ASD: functional emotional developmental capacities, communicative development, and parent–child relationship and interactions. It also considers individual differences in sensory, motor, and cognitive skills. Thus, it differs substantially from ABA approaches in that it focuses on underlying processes and relationships rather than symptoms and discrete behaviors. See Exhibit 5.1 in Chapter 5 for a list of intervention methods for children with ASD that include these communication approaches.

As the numbers of young children with ASD continue to increase, it is crucial that we identify the interventions that can best address the social communicative needs that so often cause lifelong challenges for these children and their families. There are many approaches and therapies recommended for children with autism. Unfortunately, there is no magic bullet or cure, and professionals disagree on the most effective communication interventions. For a comprehensive model within which to view the complex needs and intervention approaches for children with ASD, see the SCERTS discussion by Prizant (2015). As mentioned earlier in this chapter, individuals who work with children who have or are suspected of having ASD should also be familiar with the updated diagnostic description in the DSM-5 (American Psychiatric Association, 2013).

Supporting Communication in Children with Severe Motor Disabilities

Infants and young children who have significant motor challenges, such as those associated with cerebral palsy, spina bifida, or traumatic brain injury (TBI), may or may not have cognitive disorders or intellectual disabilities. Many children with severe motor disorders present highly complex challenges, particularly in the development of communication. Many of the communication strategies already discussed in this chapter will be very useful.

Those children who have significant motor challenges but who have relatively intact cognitive skills present a particular challenge and responsibility for the ECSE practitioner. Many of these children have the capacity for development of good language and academic skills. However, because of the serious limitations in the production of intelligible speech, this potential will not be realized without the concerted efforts of an interdisciplinary team focused on the development of an efficient and effective augmentative or AAC system, discussed previously in this chapter. The earlier this process begins, the better. This places a great responsibility on early educators to develop knowledge and skills in this area and to work collaboratively with other professionals (e.g., physical therapists, speech-language pathologists, technology specialists, and educational specialists in the area of physical and health impairments) and with family members.

Although the focus on the development of an effective alternative communication system will be critical for speech output for children with severe motor disabilities, *it is equally important that careful high-quality language input be provided by adults who will support the ongoing development of language comprehension in the child.* The ongoing development and modification of AAC systems will be lifelong and important. But it should not overshadow the importance of the adults' role in providing excellent language input, using the many suggestions presented throughout this chapter.

Supporting Communication in Children with Language Differences

Because demographics in the United States are changing so dramatically, professionals working with young children must be prepared to respect and celebrate diversity while at the same time preparing children to succeed in the mainstream. According to the 2017 U.S. Census Bureau American Community Survey, the percentage of the U.S. population age 5 and older in 2016 speaking a home language other than English was 21.6% (some 40.5 million people). The survey also notes that 8.6% of the American population is limited English-proficient. By far the largest subgroup is Spanish-speaking, and in many parts of the country, it is commonplace for early childhood settings to include at least one staff member who speaks fluent Spanish. Increasingly, however, there may be many different home languages represented in our communities: for example, Cantonese, Vietnamese, Korean, Filipino (Tagalog), and Hmong. Early educators must be able to support all children's English language development. Fortunately, we have already described many strategies in this chapter that not only support first-language acquisition in young children with and without disabilities but also will support children's learning of English as a second language. Currently, these children are referred to with various terms, such as "dual-language learners" (DLLs), "English learners" (ELs), or "English-language learners" (ELLs).

Educators and service providers who offer interventions and supports for young children with disabilities whose home language is other than English are often concerned that exposure to more than one language may interfere with the important goals of language development and learning English. However, there appears to be little evidence that this is the case (Duran, Hartzheim, Lund, Simonsmeier, & Kohlmeier, 2016; Genesee, 2016).

In an exhaustive longitudinal analysis of 39 children who are dual-language learners and whose first language is not English, Bailey and Osipova (2016) provide an exhaustive study of families and educators who successfully sustain these children's linguistic development in two languages: their home language and English. These authors begin by presenting (and debunking) common myths related to possible negative effects or challenges of dual-language exposure and learning. These well-debunked myths are summarized in the following list:

1. Learning more than one language is detrimental to children and causes late talking.
2. Multilingual learners have accents and limited vocabularies, and struggle with grammar.
3. Some children will never be able to learn a second language.
4. Children with disabilities may not be able to learn, and should not be taught, additional languages.
5. Learning more than one language will lower children's chance of academic success.

6. Learning more than one language puts children's social development at risk because they will not be experts in either culture.

7. Complete immersion is necessary for second-language acquisition.

In addition, the very common, but incorrect, assumption that children with disabilities and challenges in learning a first language will be further disadvantaged by exposure to a second language is addressed in Paradis, Genesee, and Crago (2011). The Pyramid Model (discussed in Chapter 6) also provides a framework and strategies for supporting the language development of DLL children with disabilities or challenging behaviors (Brillante & Nemeth, 2017). From infancy, the human brain is hardwired to learn speech and language. Therefore, infants can sort out differences in language and distinguish between phonemes, such as between "puh" and "buh."

Learning a New Language

The most efficient way to help young children learn a second language will begin by using the same adult–child **responsive** interaction strategies discussed previously in this chapter that support **first-language** development and learning. For example, engaging the child in conversations about the things they are interested in throughout the day, and following the child's lead, provide effective support for language development and learning, at very low cost to the caregiver or teacher. Tabors (2008) contended that the same principles that undergird the fostering of language in all children should be the basis of teaching children who are learning English as a second language. The dialogue between teacher and child should occur in situations that maintain the child's interest and attention and should be *responsive to the child's interests* rather than a directive.

The ways of talking to young children that have been demonstrated to be effective in supporting children's first language must also be used by early childhood educators to support young children's learning of English as a second language. In order to support home-language maintenance, parents should be encouraged to use their first (native) language when speaking to their infants and young children (Chen, Klein, & Osipova, 2012). This practice is also reinforced in the 2009 California Department of Education resource guide for working with preschool ELLs. In addition to these strategies, teachers should be aware of additional classroom practices that are particularly important for DLLs in that they *link* English-language learning to home language and to familiar experiences and materials. These include the following:

1. Incorporate key words and phrases in the child's home language throughout the day, such as in storybook reading and conversations.

2. Use materials (e.g., storybooks) and activities (e.g., rhymes, songs, snacks) that reflect the child's home culture and practice.

3. Use visual cues and media, such as pictures, objects, and video, to make clear the topics to which the teacher is referring.

4. Create shared *interesting* experiences, such as science projects and field trips, to establish communicative contexts in which to practice the new language.

5. Make the concepts of "bilingualism" explicit and positive, not only for the child who is learning English, but for the **whole** class! *In modern U.S. society, the ability to speak two languages, and the concepts associated with that learning process, are invaluable for everyone.* For example, a Spanish-speaking child points to the picture of a dog and says, "Perro!" The teacher says, "Yes, in Spanish the word is 'perro' and in English we say 'dog.' You can speak two languages! Let's all say 'dog' in Spanish: Perro! And how do we say it in English? Dog, yes 'dog'!"

In this way, the teacher helps all children in the class develop a meta-awareness of two different ways of saying the same thing. *Children can be encouraged to suggest other words to compare in English and Spanish.* Taking this impromptu lesson one step

Video Example from

You Tube

Enhanced eText
Video Example 8.6
Bilingual and Monolingual Baby Brains Differ in Response to Language
https://www.youtube.com/watch?v=N7Gn_ImK4_Y
This video demonstrates the early language–related abilities that result naturally.

further, the teacher can ask, "Who knows what sound Perro starts with? Yes, 'puh.' What letter says 'puh'? Right! The letter 'P.' Who can find that letter on the board?" The same process can be repeated for the English word "dog."

To support the language development of DLLs, teachers should also use the many strategies discussed earlier in this chapter. Cheatham, Jimenez-Silva, and Park (2015) identified the following intentional teaching strategies to provide developmentally appropriate and respectful feedback to children who are learning English:

1. **Recasts.** Provide the appropriate language model that communicates the child's intent (e.g., correct pronunciation of a word); or to model the correct use of "he/she" "him/her," as some languages do not have grammatical rules regarding gender (e.g., Tagalog, Turkish, and Korean).

2. **Repetition.** Repeat the child's mispronunciation or incorrect sentence structure and provide the correct language model.

3. **Clarification requests.** Ask, "What do you mean?" when the child's request or comment is not understood.

4. **Elicitation.** Support the child's language use by (a) using a completion prompt (teacher stops before completing a sentence) for the child to complete the teacher's sentence; (b) asking a question (e.g., "What is it called?"); or (c) asking the child to restate what he or she said.

5. **Direct feedback.** Indicate that the child has made a language mistake and then model the correct utterance.

6. **Translation.** The teacher translates his or her directions in English into a child's home language for the child who needs more home language support, or asks a child who uses his or her home language, "How do you say that in English?"

Helping young children whose first language is not English be proud of the fact that they are learning two languages, as well as developing understanding of important literacy concepts important to the whole class, are examples of simple ways to embed complex concepts into everyday, repeated classroom routines and novel events. Also important will be the frequent visits and participation of fluent adult speakers of the children's home language and, if possible, at least one regular staff member. Teachers and staff should explicitly celebrate the multicultural/multilingual characteristics of the classroom. (For practical classroom suggestions for developing rich learning environments and activities for young dual-language learners, see Garcia and Garcia [2012].)

Stages of Second-Language Learning

Children progress through stages of second-language acquisition that are similar in many ways to the stages of first-language acquisition discussed earlier in this chapter. Initially, children do not attempt to use English and are either silent or use their home language. During this period, children are observing and listening, and it is an important time for teachers to concentrate and use clear, comprehensible language as they talk to children. During the second stage, children may begin to use some single English words, interspersed within their first language. In the third stage, use of telegraphic language (e.g., use of word combinations, such as "Doggie eat hot dog") and "formulaic" speech patterns begin to emerge (e.g., "I gonna_____" or "Gimme_____"). The final stage includes acquisition of grammatical morphemes and mastery of syntactic rules for different sentence patterns. (*Vocabulary* development will continue into adulthood.) The *typical* English-language learner acquires basic *social/communication* skills within approximately 3 years. However, in their classic work, Cummins and Swain (2014) found that the ability to achieve academic proficiency in English may take 5 to 7 years! Children who have disabilities may progress through these stages at a slower rate, but the sequence of acquisition will be similar (Morrow, Roskos, & Gambrell, 2016).

Dual-Language Learning and Home-Language Maintenance

It is often assumed that, in young children, exposure to two languages makes language development more difficult. This assumption may seem even more logical if the child has a disability that already interferes with language learning. This leads to two important questions for the ECSE practitioner:

1. Should families of young children who have language-learning challenges avoid using the home language, and, if possible, switch to English-only input when communicating with their child?

2. To what extent is it possible for young children with language-learning challenges to learn a second language?

Genesee (2004) has examined evidence related to the possible negative effects of "dual-language learning," including the second-language development of young students with learning disabilities and specific language impairments. No evidence was found that exposure to the second language interferes with development of the first language. Genesee states that "dual language learning is not a cause of language impairment" (p. 212). He further suggests that children with language-learning difficulty experience the same difficulties in learning a second language, but that learning a second language does not make the first-language-learning process more difficult or interfere with the achievement of proficiency in the first language. Support for this position was also provided by a study by Bird and colleagues (2005) that examined the second-language development of several children with Down syndrome. In addition, a review of studies of dual-language learning in children with autism, Deaf children with cochlear implants, and children with speech and language impairments also found that home-language maintenance did not impede their language development in English (Chen & Gutiérrez-Clellen, 2013). Also relevant to this discussion is the fact that a strong first language can support both language and literacy learning in the second language.

In short, there is no evidence to suggest that parents should stop using their home language with young children who have disabilities (Genesee, 2008) or that children with disabilities who are learning English should not be exposed to a second language (Chen et al., 2012). Although there continues to be some debate, it appears that children with disabilities can acquire proficiency in a second language at a level commensurate with their language-learning and intellectual levels.

The case for maintenance of the home language within the school setting is further strengthened by certain sociocultural factors. One is the desire and value of ensuring the maintenance of one's home language as a way of strengthening ties to the family and to its cultural heritage. Families are no less committed to the importance of this simply because their child has a disability, and they should not be persuaded to abandon this ideal. *Note:* It is sometimes the case that child-rearing patterns in some cultures may not include the adult–child communicative interactions discussed earlier in this text that support and enhance language and literacy development. Early childhood educators and special educators must clearly share with parents the **importance** of communicating in their native/preferred language with their children on an ongoing basis, within daily routines. Also important will be the teacher's offering of storybooks written in the family's language so that parents can easily engage their child in shared book reading and related conversation.

There is an increasing realization in our society that bilingualism is actually an advantage. Gollnick and Chinn (2009) point out the career and economic advantages of speaking more than one language in our increasingly multicultural communities and in an increasingly global economy. Evidence of the positive *cognitive* effects of being fully bilingual also exists.

Despite the erroneous concern of some that children's home language may be interfering with their acquisition of English, the more worrisome trend may be the *loss* of the home language. Maintenance and continued development of the home language do not happen automatically and must be intentionally nurtured by families. Genesee (2004) concludes that the cognitive advantages of bilingualism can best be achieved when both languages are nurtured to high levels of proficiency, thus adding even more strength to the case for maintenance of a home language.

It should also be noted that Hyter, Rivers, and De Jarnette (2015) in a research synthesis of studies on the pragmatic language of African-American children differentiated between their use of general American English (GAE) and African-American English (AAE). They found that African-American children who spoke AAE demonstrated just as strong emergent literacy skills as peers who spoke GAE, and that AAE speakers who learn to shift between dialects in literacy activities have better outcomes than children who do not.

A Note on Cultural Dialects

Even when everyone in a school, community, or country speak the same "language," subcultures within the larger group may speak that language with different *accents* or *dialects*. Accent refers to differences in word pronunciation, while dialect extends beyond pronunciation to include differences in vocabulary and grammar. Occasionally, children who speak with accents may be misdiagnosed as having speech disorders. Perhaps even worse, individuals who do not speak "standard" English may be viewed negatively by members of the dominant culture. Unfortunately, this has been the case with African-American dialects, referred to as "Ebonics" or African-American English.

As we have emphasized throughout this chapter, consideration of each child's unique language development needs is important, whether the child is a first- or second-language learner. The specific strategies discussed earlier related to children with disabilities will also be important for children learning English as a second language.

Enhanced eText Application Exercise 8.3: In this exercise, you can apply what you have learned in this chapter to identify the strategies that facilitate dual language learning in young children.

Planning Communication Intervention: Collaborative Consultation with Speech-Language Specialists

It should be clear to the reader that nurturing the development of communication skills in young children who have significant disabilities requires a team approach. Major contributions can be made by a qualified speech-language pathologist (SLP) who has received training in early intervention and early childhood education. The SLP can make a particularly important contribution in the area of assessment, using both formal and informal measures. The American Speech-Language-Hearing Association Practice policy (2010) on the roles and responsibilities of speech-language pathologists in schools emphasizes the use of collaborative relationships. The collaborative model acknowledges the importance of the relationship among the teacher, the speech-language pathologist, the parents, and other service providers who work as a team. Each of these key players contributes different skills and information to the processes of

Exhibit 8.9

Communication Intervention Plan

CHILD'S NAME: _____ DATE: _____
TEACHER: _____ CLASS: _____
TEAM MEMBERS:
FAMILY MEMBERS: _____
SLP: _____ OT: _____
PT: _____ VI, DHH SPECIALISTS: _____
PARAPROFESSIONAL: _____

1. ***SELECT A GOAL AREA:*** (e.g., prelinguistic [illocutionary] initiations; language content [vocabulary]; expansion of language structure [syntax and morphology]; pragmatic skills [appropriate use/function of communication]; etc.) _____

2. ***DESCRIBE THE TARGET BEHAVIOR:*** (e.g., Sara will use vocalization + pointing to request snack or favorite toy; Alfredo will increase vocabulary to select favorite song ["spider"] and favorite snack ["cookie"]; Sung will use the sentence "Could I play with you?" to initiate social interaction appropriately with peers during recess; etc.) _____

3. ***SELECT APPROPRIATE COMMUNICATION MODE:*** (e.g., speech, picture communication system [e.g., PECS or communication board], manual signs) _____

4. ***IDENTIFY CONTEXTS:*** (Examine daily routines to identify opportunities for embedded practice of targets, i.e., "embedded learning opportunities" (ELOs); e.g., Alfredo will be given opportunities to request "spider" song during circle time and free play, and to request "cookie" at snack and during pretend scenarios in the dramatic play area; etc.) _____

5. ***CAREFULLY DESCRIBE TEACHING STRATEGIES AND ADAPTATIONS:*** (e.g., discrete trial, Pivotal Response Training, violation of routines, natural cues, decreasing/increasing verbal/visual/tactile prompts, use of music, cloze technique, social stories, etc.) _____

6. ***DESCRIBE GENERALIZATION PLAN:*** (e.g., Sung will learn to use phrase with siblings and cousins at home; Sara will use vocalization and pointing during outside play to request placement in swing or help getting into the sandbox; etc.) _____

7. ***PLAN PROGRESS-MONITORING SYSTEM:*** (e.g., Record child's use of target behavior every Friday.)

_____

assessment, planning, intervention, and problem solving. As part of the assessment, the speech-language specialist should carefully interview the classroom teacher regarding the child's communicative behaviors and observe the child in the classroom. Innovative teaching strategies and activities might be demonstrated in the classroom by the speech-language pathologist, who, in turn, would receive feedback and suggestions related to curriculum standards and goals from the classroom teacher.

Exhibit 8.9 presents a sample planning form that the teacher might find useful in the systematic selection of target behaviors, intervention approaches, and key personnel. A collaborative partnership with the speech-language specialist will be critical to the successful planning and implementation of communication interventions.

Summary

As should be evident in this chapter, the array of effective interventions—if skillfully applied—offers tremendous potential for positive impact on the development of language and communication in young children with disabilities.

Communication, language, and speech are highly complex skills that develop as a function of many underlying processes, including cognitive, fine motor–perceptual, and especially social interaction. There is perhaps no area of development as crucial to the young child with special needs as communication skills. The early educator, in close partnership with parents, can have a major impact on this area of development. For the child who has less severe disabilities, providing language input finely tuned to the child's perceptual and cognitive level, in a style that follows the child's lead and within a context of social interaction, can greatly facilitate communication skills development.

For the child who has more severe and multiple disabilities, in addition to these input strategies, it will also be necessary to structure the environment in ways that encourage the child to communicate his or her basic wants and needs. Once this important motivational factor has been provided, specific communicative behaviors can be shaped. Often, these are not conventional speech or language behaviors. Nevertheless, they can be used in functional ways and can form the basis of augmentative communication systems.

With careful planning, the strategies that facilitate communication can be incorporated into all classroom activities. Furthermore, monitoring of children's communicative behaviors within a variety of *naturally occurring contexts* can provide the most meaningful assessment of progress.

Chapter 9 addresses the development of cognitive skills and literacy. The areas of cognition, language development, and literacy are inextricably interwoven. Understanding of the dynamics of language development will assist in obtaining insight into children's developing mental capacity as they journey toward becoming literate beings.

Reflect and Apply

1. Explain the three broad dimensions of language originally described by Bloom and Lahey.

2. Define and give an example of each of the linguistic "subskills" of language.

3. Outline why it is important that young children learn to *initiate* communicative behavior and note the conditions that are necessary for optimal development of communication skills.

4. List and describe several *adult* communicative behaviors that encourage and facilitate language development in young children.

5. Discuss and demonstrate ways in which young children with severe disabilities might be able to communicate, even if they are unable to produce speech.

Chapter 9
Encouraging the Development of Cognitive Skills and Literacy

Rnl/Fotolia

∨ # Learning Outcomes

After studying this chapter, you should be able to:

9.1 Give examples of how the processes of attention, perception, and memory work together to enable the child's development of cognitive skills and acquisition of knowledge.

9.2 Understand the development of thinking and reasoning, from the infant's first reflexes to the 5-year-old's problem-solving strategies.

9.3 Discuss why it is important to facilitate critical early cognitive skills such as intentionality, means–end discovery, trial-and-error exploration, object permanence, and imitation.

9.4 Recognize that critical cognitive skills for the preschool child include symbolic representation (particularly pretend play), expansion of referential language skills to support early literacy, and exploration and problem solving to support emergent math and science skills.

9.5 Illustrate how programs can be designed and learning environments adapted to support emergent literacy, math, and science within naturalistic daily activities.

9.6 Describe the variability in children's home cultures and experiences with literacy and literate oral language styles (e.g., narrative), with explanation of the implications for instruction.

> KIM: When we talk on the phone, how does our words get to the telephone pole wires and to our house?
>
> MOM: Well, that is hard to explain. Our voice travels by what we call sound waves.
>
> KIM: Oh, it must be like on the ocean. Our talk rides like a surfer.

As this interaction between mother and child demonstrates, the cognitive development of young children is evidenced in their attempts to use what they know to solve new problems. New information is taken in and related to what was learned earlier. New knowledge and old knowledge are adapted to solve problems more efficiently. Cognition can be thought of as how the individual makes sense of his or her world.

What Is Cognition?

Cognition is defined in the *Oxford English Dictionary* as "the mental action or process of acquiring knowledge through thought, experiences and the senses." Decades ago, Piaget (1977) referred to the development of cognition as the child's construction of reality. These simple definitions belie the great complexity of human cognitive processes. How the young child develops the ability mentally to represent and understand the world around him or her is by no means simple. Understanding the evolution of thinking and reasoning, from the infant's first reflexes to the development of complex problem-solving strategies, is critically important to being effective educators of young children. Many children with disabilities have cognitive differences or intellectual problems that interfere with the development of the conceptual and reasoning skills necessary for mastery of academic skills. The early childhood special education professional can recognize these challenges and provide the necessary supports and adaptations for the achievement of important cognitive skills.

Basic Cognitive Processes

Three basic processes related to information processing are important to the development of cognition: attention, perception, and memory. Infants must be able to pay attention to the world around them; they must also be able to receive, recognize, and discriminate stimuli. Eventually, they must be able to organize and interpret those stimuli and store them for later retrieval.

Attention

Attention is the focusing of the individual's perceptual processes on a specific aspect of the environment. Learning cannot take place unless the individual is able to focus attention on the important elements of a task or situation. Attention is basic to many cognitive tasks and a prerequisite for effective intervention. Attention in the form of concentration requires that the developing child learn to master two somewhat contradictory skills: (1) the ability to focus on those aspects of the environment that are relevant and have the greatest functional value to the task at hand and (2) the ability to ignore the multitude of surrounding irrelevant stimuli. *Selective attention* begins almost at birth, and the kinds of stimuli and the way babies look at them change in predictable ways. When a child attempts to attend and respond to too many irrelevant stimuli, the child may be labeled as distractible.

Perception

Perception is the process of receiving and interpreting sensory information. Perceptual abilities depend on the sensory systems of touch, taste, proprioception, smell, hearing, and vision. These systems actually develop in utero, thus enabling the newborn infant to begin the processes of perceptual development at birth. Each sensory system (tactile, visual, auditory, olfactory, and gustatory) is associated with a different mode of perception. For perception to occur, some information must be stored in the nervous system. Sensations are then interpreted in the context of stored information.

The interpretations or perceptions of individuals may differ, depending on what is stored and on the strength of the perception modality, such as visual and auditory, which develop unevenly. Thus, one child may perceive more accurately through the visual channel, whereas another may gather information more efficiently through the auditory channel. As stated earlier, young children may find it easiest to interpret physical cues, followed by visual and finally verbal cues. Unfortunately, most teachers tend to teach predominantly through talking and expecting responses to verbal directions. Teachers who attempt to match teaching input to the developmental needs of their children contribute greatly to the progress of children with perceptual disabilities, who usually have difficulty interpreting and obtaining accurate meaning from their environment.

Discrimination

Discrimination is the perception of the similarities and differences among related stimuli. This is an important aspect of information processing. For example, the young infant's ability to discriminate change and novelty in the repeated presentation of a stimulus increases attention. Later, children who learn to discriminate characteristics visually such as shape, size, distance, and color while in preschool will be prepared for the subtle discriminations required to identify printed letters, numbers, and words in kindergarten and first grade. Likewise, children who learn to perceive the differences and similarities in pitch, loudness, rhythm, melody, rate, and duration of sound will likely be successful in learning to read through a phonics approach. Children with disabilities also benefit from a phonics approach. For example, systematic phonics instruction has resulted in positive reading outcomes for children with developmental disabilities and significant cognitive disabilities (Ahlgrim-Delzell et al., 2016; Finnegan, 2012). For children with hearing loss who use sign language, a visual phonics strategy involving hand shapes for each sound to provide a letter-sound correspondence is effective in building phonological awareness skills (Easterbrooks & Trussell, 2015).

Most reading readiness activities, by design, assist children in developing discrimination skills. For example, when asked to find a picture illustrating a spoken word, the child must discriminate among visual details in the picture and speech sounds while also practicing association and memory skills. Most of the activities discussed in this book, and highlighted in Appendix B, give children practice in developing perceptual efficiency and accuracy.

Memory

The third basic cognitive process is memory, the process by which information received through attention and perception is stored in the central nervous system. Memory is an extremely complex phenomenon composed of the following features:

1. Incoming sensation is perceived briefly (about 1 second).

2. If attended to, it is placed immediately in short-term memory, where it can be stored for 10 to 15 seconds.

3. If information in short-term memory is processed, it is referred to as "working memory."

4. Depending on a number of factors, some information from working memory will be placed in long-term memory, where it can be stored indefinitely, retrieved at a later time, and associated with other information.

Very young children have few memory strategies and usually need repeated pattern experiences of an event or information before it can be stored in long-term memory. The ability to learn is highly associated with memory. Many factors can interfere with memory storage and retrieval. For example, environmental conditions such as noise, visual clutter, excitement, emotional factors, and fatigue may interfere with retention. Also, content that is not interesting or meaningful, or is too complex or too long, might not be developmentally appropriate and therefore might be difficult to remember. This point is a pivotal one when thinking about interventions for children who have disabilities or developmentally delays. Also relevant is the type of response required from the child. Is it immediate or delayed? Does it require recognition or recall, or a motor or vocal response?

In reality, the three processes of attention, perception, and memory are interdependent. Individuals cannot pay attention if they are unable to perceive incoming stimuli, they cannot store information they are unable to perceive, they cannot further develop perceptual skills of recognition and interpretation if they are unable to store the information in memory, and so on.

Development of Cognitive Skills

The Developmental Theory of Piaget

Historically, the most prominent cognitive theorist to influence the fields of child development and early education was Jean Piaget, a Swiss scientist interested in epistemology, or the study of human knowing. He was neither a learning theorist nor a maturationist. Rather, he combined these two views and believed that human cognitive development is a product of the interaction between the environment and the infant's biological capacities.

Two now-classic concepts developed in Piaget's theory are the **schema** and the process of **adaptation**. The schema can be defined as a psychological structure that provides the individual with a template for action in similar circumstances (Piaget & Inhelder, 1969). **Schemata** (or "schemes"), which initially are infant reflexes, gradually become differentiated, combined, organized, and under the child's control. They also eventually become internalized; that is, they become mental processes. This occurs through adaptation, a twofold process made up of **assimilation** and **accommodation**.

During the assimilation part of adaptation, experiences are taken in by infants or young children through the application of existing schemata. For example, the infant applies her "sucking schema" to her thumb. However, not all experiences can be assimilated to existing schemata. For example, if the infant tries to apply her existing sucking schema to the corner of her blanket, she will not be successful. The infant must change, or "accommodate," her existing schema to adapt to this new situation. Thus, through the complementary processes of first using existing schemata and then modifying them to adjust to new experiences, the infant adapts to the world around her. In Piaget's view, this is the process of learning.

In addition to his important theory of cognitive development, Piaget also contributed an important research methodology that included naturalistic observations of infants and young children combined with presentation of situations in which to test his hypotheses. Information related to the sensorimotor and preoperational periods was based on his observations of his own children. His descriptions of the development of mental operations were based on his observations of schoolchildren.

Piaget described several stages in the development of cognition. Each stage of development builds on the previous one. As children mature and interact with their environment, they construct and reconstruct reality through the processes of assimilation and accommodation in accordance with their cognitive capabilities at each stage. Piaget's approach is often referred to as "constructivist" because of its premise that knowledge is constructed by connecting new experience or information to what the child already knows. In some sense, the child constructs his or her *own* knowledge using his or her existing cognitive processes (depending on developmental stage) to make sense of new experience and information and to add them to existing schemas, thus increasing his or her own complexity of knowledge and skills (Slavin, 2017).

The Sensorimotor Stage.   The most creative and rapid period of human development is between birth and 18 months of age. The sensorimotor stage is divided into six substages. The first five of these stages lay the foundation for the beginning of representational thought—the mental representation of objects and events. The sixth stage, with its full achievement of object permanence, marks the transition from sensorimotor "knowing" through patterns of action to mental knowledge and symbolic ability.

Sensorimotor Substage 1: Use of Reflexes (0–1 Month).   During the first month of life, the infant interacts with the world primarily through reflexes. As the nipple touches her lips, she sucks; she "roots," or turns automatically to the side of the cheek that is touched; sudden loud sounds or loss of support elicit a startle, or "Moro," reaction; and so on.

Sensorimotor Substage 2: Primary Circular Reactions (1–4 Months).   During the second substage, the infant's reflexive behavior leads accidentally to new experiences. For example, the infant discovers her thumb and assimilates this experience to her existing nipple-sucking schema. She accommodates to the new object (her thumb) and thus *learns* to suck her thumb. Such primary circular reactions are always centered on the infant's own body.

Sensorimotor Substage 3: Secondary Circular Reactions (5–8 Months).   During this substage, the infant becomes increasingly interactive with events and objects in the external environment, outside her own body. Secondary circular reactions are those behaviors in which the infant engages in order to repeat an interesting event. For example, the infant accidentally hits a mobile hanging above her crib, which provides the visual experience of seeing the mobile move. The infant then tries to hit the mobile again to re-create this experience.

Sensorimotor Substage 4: Intentional Adaptations (8–12 Months).   During this substage, the infant begins to use and coordinate her secondary circular reactions to achieve a specific goal. This represents a major milestone in the development of cognition: the development of intentionality. Now the infant can look at the mobile and use the "looking-and-swiping" schema acquired through her secondary reactions of substage 3 and *intentionally* activate the mobile. She now has the goal in mind *before* she engages in the behavior. She has discovered the means–end relationship.

Also, during this stage, the baby demonstrates the earliest ability to search for hidden objects. However, she will search in the place in which she last discovered the object. For example, an interesting object is covered with a blanket, and the infant is assisted in rediscovering the object. In full view of the infant, the object is then hidden under a box. Despite observing this, the infant again searches for the object under the blanket. She does not engage in a systematic search based on where she sees the object disappear.

Sensorimotor Substage 5: Discovery of New Means (12–18 Months).   In substage 5, rather than simply repeating a behavior to re-create an interesting event, the infant searches for novelty through tertiary circular reactions. She systematically changes her behavior and observes the effect. This is sometimes called trial-and-error exploration. The following is a familiar example of this type of behavior. A 15-month-old infant, sitting in a highchair, drops and then tosses her food onto the floor, first from one side of the tray, then from the other. Although parents may interpret this as willful naughtiness, it is actually evidence of the growing cognitive abilities of the infant. It enables her to learn about cause and effect. Through such trial-and-error behavior, the infant discovers new means, or strategies, for achieving goals. For example, the child learns that she can crawl *around* a barrier to reach something on the other side if she is unable to crawl *over* it.

Continued development of the concept of object permanence can also be seen during this substage. Now the infant more systematically searches for the object at the place where she sees it disappear. However, if the infant does not see the object being moved, she will not search for it.

Sensorimotor Substage 6: Rudiments of Representational Thought (18–24 Months).   Substage 6 marks the end of the sensorimotor period. By the end of this substage, the toddler has mastered the full concept of **object permanence.** She clearly understands that objects exist whether or not she can see them. She searches systematically for an object even when she has not seen it disappear. This important cognitive capability now frees the infant from her dependence on sensorimotor actions for discovery and understanding. It frees her from the "here-and-now" world and enables her to develop memory skills.

The 18- to 24-month-old toddler now has the capacity for **mental representation**—the ability to think. This mental representation ability is particularly evidenced in two types of behavior observed toward the end of substage 6: deferred imitation and pretend play. The ability to imitate something observed at an earlier time reflects the toddler's mental representation and memory for that event; deferred imitation also provides a mechanism for learning.

The ability to act out previously experienced events through pretend play (e.g., putting the doll to bed or pretending to serve breakfast) also is clear evidence of the ability to think about and remember such events. Like deferred imitation, pretend play provides important contexts in which to learn.

The Preoperational Stage.   The second major stage of cognitive development in Piaget's theory is called the preoperational stage. This term simply reflects the fact that although preschool children are clearly more capable than sensorimotor infants, they are not yet able to perform the mental operations required of logical thinking and reasoning. Piaget was more intrigued with what the preoperational child could *not* do than with the important achievements of this period. In Piaget's later writing, this stage was divided into two periods: the preconceptual and the intuitive.

The Preconceptual Period (2–4 Years).   A major accomplishment during this period is the development of **symbolic ability.** The child learns that one thing can represent another thing. This symbolic ability is evidenced both in her pretend play and in increasing language development. The child can now use a block as a truck, or she can *imagine* that a cloud is a bear floating in the sky. Language becomes freed from the immediate context. Words as symbols can now be used to describe and share experiences that occurred in the past.

The Intuitive Period (4–7 Years).   During this late preoperational stage, the child begins to demonstrate certain precursors of the next cognitive stage. For example, she can now categorize objects on the basis of certain features (e.g., the red balls and the blue balls or forks and spoons). However, children are still unable to focus on more than one feature or dimension at a time.

Piaget was very interested in the mental operations that children could *not* perform during this stage. The classic "conversation experiment" demonstrates the child's inability to decenter: Two identical beakers are filled with equal amounts of water. The water from one of the beakers is poured into a narrower, taller beaker. When asked whether the tall beaker now contains more or the same amount of water as the short, wide beaker, the child invariably responds "more" despite repeated demonstrations of pouring water back and forth. According to Piaget, the preoperational child lacks the ability to attend to both height and width and centers only on height (tallness). She also lacks reversibility of thought and cannot realize that the width of the shorter beaker would compensate for its lack of height and vice versa.

The lack of ability to decenter is also observed in the preschooler's egocentrism. She has difficulty taking another person's perspective and views the world in relationship to herself. She does not understand that someone else may not be able to see what she can see, and her language is often insufficiently referential. This inability to take the perspective of others relates to the concept of "theory of mind." (See Slaughter and de Rosnay [2017] for a discussion of how environments help shape a child's ability to take the perspective of others.) Later in the preoperational stage, the child's *representational* skills become more elaborated, as is particularly demonstrated in dramatic play episodes. The preschooler can orchestrate long and complex interpersonal sequences that provide opportunities for practicing social routines and solving problems. Another characteristic of children during this period is their inability to think *logically*. Children's thought is sometimes referred to as *transductive*. Although truly logical thought is either inductive (proceeding from the specific to the general) or deductive (from the general to the specific), young children's thought often proceeds from the particular to the particular, with no logical connection. For example, a 4-year-old trips as she comes in the door and announces, "I just ate a whole candy bar so I can't walk too good!" Although the child cannot think logically at this stage, she clearly recognizes that events have causes and perceives the need for explanations.

The Stages of Concrete Operations and Formal Operations.   Once the child moves into the stage of **concrete operations** (which extends from the ages of 7 to 11 years), she has achieved the mental flexibility necessary to perform the operations required in reading and mathematics and the ability to think logically. In the conversation experiment described earlier, the child at this stage has no difficulty understanding that the volume of liquid is the same regardless of the height of the beaker. The child no longer centers on only one dimension. This significantly enhances her problem-solving capability. The child in this stage of cognitive development is able to decenter and to consider many dimensions of an object or a problem simultaneously.

The final stage of **formal operations** is achieved somewhere between 11 and 15 years of age. The young adolescent is now capable of performing the mental operations mastered during the concrete operations stage on more abstract material. She can now think about complex moral dilemmas that often have more than one "right" answer, depending on the situation. She can also think scientifically, using processes of the scientific method, such as hypothesis testing.

Alternative and Neo-Piagetian Views of Cognitive Development.   The developmental theories of Piaget and his associates spanned a time period from the early 1930s to the 1970s. Their influence on the field of early childhood education continues today. It must be noted, however, that "neo-Piagetians" and many contemporary theorists and cognitive scientists continue to build on or revise his work, incorporating new evidence from research on information processing and cultural influences. For example, Case (1985) suggested that Piaget's stages of development are influenced by the development of information-processing skills. Bidell and Fischer (1989) discussed the roles of cultural and social interaction on cognitive development, an approach consistent with the social-constructivist views of Vygotsky (1986). Bjorklund and Causey (2018) describe how biological factors interact with children's experiences in both the physical and social worlds.

Video Example from

YouTube

Enhanced eText

Video Example 9.1

Piaget's Stages of Development
https://www.youtube.com/
watch?v=TRF27F2bn-A
Piaget's stages of development are
the topic of this video.

Demonstration of Cognitive Skills Through the Developmental Stages of Children's Play

One of the easiest ways to observe the development of children's cognitive skills is through the observation of their play. The stages of cognitive development can be readily observed using the following taxonomy: simple manipulation, exploratory play, functional play, and symbolic play.

Simple Object Manipulation

Simple manipulative behaviors such as mouthing, poking, waving, banging, or throwing are examples of secondary circular reactions that are typical of sensorimotor substage 3. As the infant reaches substage 4, around 8 to 10 months, these sensorimotor schemata become combined and under intentional control. The child now clearly *intends* to bang or throw. For example, the infant notices a ball and purposely moves toward it, picks it up, and throws it.

Exploratory Play

As the infant moves into the fifth substage of sensorimotor development, she engages in trial-and-error exploration. She notices some blocks and a can. She picks up the can and bangs it on the floor, and then puts it on her head. She picks up the block and puts it in the can. She dumps the block out of the can. She is also capable of inventing *new means* to achieve her goals. For example, she cannot reach a ball that has rolled under the sofa, so she takes her mother by the hand to solicit her help. The means–end behavior also signals the beginning of problem solving.

Functional Play

By the end of the fifth substage, the child can demonstrate appropriate object use. She pushes the truck, pounds with the hammer, dials the telephone, combs her hair, and so on. She may also demonstrate autosymbolic play, pretending to engage in some familiar activity such as sleeping or eating.

Symbolic Play

By the end of the sixth substage, the child has achieved the ability to represent objects and events internally and to engage in symbolic behavior. Symbolic play develops through several stages from the end of the sensorimotor period through the preoperational period.

Initially, the child engages in pretend play activities in which she is the actor, engaged in some highly familiar activity such as going to sleep. During the next stage, she focuses the pretend play activity on some inanimate recipient of her actions, such as a doll or teddy bear. Now she pretends to put the doll to bed or pour coffee for the bear. Next, the doll will be the agent, not just the recipient, of the child's actions (e.g., the doll washes herself or puts the teddy to bed).

After 24 months, there is a gradual increase in the preoperational child's ability to use nonrealistic objects to represent real objects as symbolic skills improve. Eventually, after 36 months, the child may use imaginary objects or people in play activities. There is also an increase in the length and complexity of pretend play sequences in the preoperational period. After 24 months, the child can play the roles of different individuals and reenact events from the past. After 36 months, the child begins to plan pretend scenarios in advance and organize who will do what. Play sequences begin to look more like a story, with a beginning, a plot that evolves (e.g., a problem to be solved or a special occasion), and an ending. By this stage, language becomes an essential element of play.

By age 4 or 5, the child begins to act out possible *future* scenarios (i.e., "what would happen if . . . ?" situations) and can act out multiple roles (e.g., play the mother who is also a doctor).

Supporting the Development of Cognitive Skills in Young Children

Several cognitive milestones are particularly important targets for early intervention. Certain disabling conditions may begin to interfere with children's achievement of these important cognitive skills early in infancy. For example, a child who is blind may have particular difficulty with the achievement of object concepts and object permanence.

A child with motor impairments may have difficulty discovering means–end strategies, and his or her opportunities to practice trial-and-error exploration will be limited.

The following section describes several key cognitive milestones during the period from birth to 3 years of age and provides suggestions for facilitating these cognitive skills. In addition, we encourage you to review other chapters that describe generic strategies such as scaffolding (Chapter 4), communicative interactions (Chapters 4 and 8), and naturalistic milieu approaches to intervention (Chapter 8). These strategies are particularly effective in the development of cognitive skills. Many of the specific suggestions in this chapter reflect those approaches.

Another key point mentioned previously is that teaching *must be activity based.* That is, intervention goals and objectives are integrated and incorporated into pleasurable, developmentally appropriate *play* activities. They are *not* isolated as bits of behavior to be learned, but embedded into enticing play routines. (See Barton [2016] for an analysis of research on teaching play to young children with disabilities.)

Intentionality

As discussed earlier, somewhere around 8 to 10 months of age, typically developing infants achieve the ability to do things intentionally. They no longer must discover things by chance in order to repeat them. They can now perform an action on purpose. Achievement of **intentionality** is a prerequisite to almost every other skill. The ability to act deliberately on the environment is an important key to continued development.

Some children with severe disabilities may need assistance in the development of intentionality. For such a child, the importance of intentionality cannot be overemphasized. Learning that the individual can produce a behavior volitionally and that such behavior has an effect on the world around him or her is a major accomplishment. The following strategies are examples of ways to facilitate this important cognitive milestone.

1. *Increase motivation by use of high-interest objects and activities.* As discussed in Chapters 4, 5, and 6, the development of an intervention program for an individual child should begin by taking a careful inventory of high- and low-preference objects, people, and activities. It will be necessary to interview caregivers to obtain a good understanding of the child's likes and dislikes. Once these are identified, they may be used to create the need to communicate in order to act on the environment in some way.

2. *Create the desire or need to perform intentional acts.* The following are examples of strategies:

   (a) Place a high-preference object within the child's view but out of reach.

   (b) Begin a pleasurable activity and then abruptly stop it. Wait for the child to do something in an attempt to continue the activity. For example, push the child in the swing, and then stop the swing. Wait for some kind of signal from the child that she wants to continue, and then resume the activity.

   (c) Engage in an unpleasant activity, such as washing the child's face, and then discontinue the activity if the child indicates rejection (e.g., pushes your hand away).

   (d) Interpret even unintentional cues such as head turning or arm waving as intentional; respond as though the child did it purposely. For example, if the child inadvertently moves her arm toward a toy, respond by handing the child the toy.

   (e) Adapt favorite toys, music players, television sets, and so on so they can be activated by a switch requiring only minimal movement from the child.

3. *Allow ample time for the child to initiate a purposeful behavior.* Some children appear not to demonstrate intentional behavior simply because they have learned there will

not be enough time to organize a response. Adults frequently anticipate children's needs or perform actions for them, interfering with their initiation of intentional acts.

Means–End Behavior

As infants learn to act intentionally on their environment, they discover that these actions have certain effects on objects and people. As they become familiar with these causes and effects, they are able to engage in an action intentionally to bring about a desired end and, when necessary, to modify that action to create new means to achieve the desired end. For example, a child may use a stool to help her climb onto a countertop so she can reach the cookies, or she may pull at mother's hand and take her to the counter to get the cookies.

These kinds of behaviors are important manifestations of the child's ability to associate cognitively certain events with their consequences. Children with disabilities often need assistance with both understanding these relationships and engaging in **means–end behaviors.** It may be necessary to structure the environment carefully in ways that clearly demonstrate cause and effect and consistently reinforce the child for attempts to achieve certain goals.

Simply constructed toys and devices that produce an interesting response to a specific type of manipulation can be effective. These include infant toys such as a busy box, a jack-in-the-box, and an easily activated musical toy.

Equally important is the contribution of a responsive social environment. Caregivers who respond quickly to an infant's signals of discomfort or to an older child's bids for attention will support the development of means–end behaviors.

Trial-and-Error Exploration

The ability to explore objects and space systematically is crucial to the development of the child's ability to learn from experience and develop problem-solving skills. Systematic manipulation of objects and modification of the individual's own actions, referred to as **trial-and-error exploration,** lead to self-directed learning and the discovery of new behaviors and solutions.

In attempting to assist children in learning these exploratory strategies, teachers must understand they are teaching a *process* rather than a specific behavior. For example, a jar containing pieces of candy is offered to a child. The jar has a tightly fitted lid. To teach the child to take off the lid would simply require task analyzing this skill and teaching it step by step until the child had mastered unscrewing the lid. Encouraging trial-and-error exploration, in contrast, requires a different approach. It is necessary for the teacher to use several of the generic strategies described in Chapter 5. The teacher must assist the child in initiating different attempts to open the jar and reinforce *persistence,* not just success. The teacher must be able to read the child's cues of boredom or frustration and know when to finally scaffold successful unscrewing of the lid. Other opportunities must be created later on in which to generalize this trial-and-error process.

The following example demonstrates a way of encouraging trial-and-error behavior as a problem-solving strategy.

> *Nathan is sitting at the snack table with several peers without disabilities. Each child is handed a fruit roll in a wrapper as a special treat. The children eagerly tear open their wrappers. Nathan has motor coordination difficulties and typically cannot manage such a task. He has become accustomed to seeking help in such situations, so he makes the manual sign for "help" and hands the package to his teacher. This time, the teacher does not immediately open the package. She hands it back to him and says, "I'm sorry Nathan, I can't help right now. I'll help in a few minutes." She signals to the aide to sit next to Nathan. Nathan fiddles briefly with the wrapper, then looks at the aide, who says, "Well, try it this way." She turns it around and hands it back to him. He tugs at one end of*

the wrapper unsuccessfully. The aide says, "Boy, that's hard to do, isn't it?" He pulls at the other end of the wrapper, again to no avail, and then bangs it on the table. At this point, the aide takes the package and makes a small tear in one corner. She hands it back and points to the torn corner. Nathan pulls at that corner and opens the wrapper. The teacher then approaches Nathan, saying, "Well, you got that unwrapped all by yourself, didn't you!" It is hoped that this child has learned something about the value of trying different solutions and the importance of persistence.

Object Permanence

The achievement of the concept of object permanence is critical to the child's continued development of important mental processes including memory and mental representation. Throughout the first year of development, children learn about the existence and properties of objects. As they continue through the sensorimotor period, they eventually discover, by the end of the second year, that objects and people continue to exist even when they are out of sight and their removal was not observed.

At this point, which marks the end of the sensorimotor period, children have the ability to represent objects and events internally. They can conjure mental pictures in their minds; they no longer must see an object to know it exists. This is obviously important for the development of memory skills.

Object permanence can be demonstrated in many simple ways for young children. Perhaps one of the first such activities introduced to infants is the game of peekaboo, a simple way to demonstrate that a person continues to exist even when the infant cannot see the person's face. Other ways to demonstrate object permanence include searching for something missing from its expected storage container, playing hide-and-seek, or hiding cookies in your pocket and asking children to guess what you have.

Deferred Imitation

The ability to re-create an action observed at a previous time reflects the development of important cognitive skills. It requires an understanding of object permanence, the beginning development of memory skills, and the ability to represent a sequence of events mentally. **Deferred imitation** eventually plays an important role in the development of pretend play and language development.

The development of imitation skills, both immediate and deferred, may be encouraged by using the following sequence:

1. Begin by imitating the child's behavior, encouraging turn taking, and then encouraging the child to continue the game. Children who have no disabilities happily see this as a sort of "Simon Says" game.

2. Next, introduce a variation of the behavior to see whether the child will attempt to follow suit.

3. Once the child can do this easily, you can be the initiator of the imitation game rather than imitating the child's behavior first. (Over the years, many programs have been developed that teach imitation at this level, using modeling, physical prompts, and reinforcement techniques.)

4. When the child has acquired a generalized imitative response (i.e., the child will attempt to imitate novel behaviors in addition to those that have been trained) and has developed the concept of object permanence, it may be possible to teach *deferred* imitation. The length of time between presentation of a model and imitation of the model can be increased gradually. For example, at recess, the teacher can model how to "walk like a duck," encouraging the children to imitate her. Later, the teacher can say, "Can you remember what we did at recess?" This requires the child to use both memory and imitation skills.

> **Enhanced eText** Application Exercise 9.1: In this exercise, you can apply what you have learned to identify strategies to facilitate critical early cognitive skills in young children with disabilities.

Supporting the Development of Cognitive Skills in Preschoolers

Developing Symbolic Representation Through Play

As children enter the preoperational stage of cognitive development, two major achievements reflect emerging symbolic skills: (1) increasing use of language to represent objects and events that are not present in the immediate environment or that occurred in the past and (2) the ability to engage in *symbolic pretend* play. Much has already been said about play in this text. Play is important as a *context* for teaching, as discussed in Chapter 4. Play is also an important social goal as an end in itself in the development of social skills. It also facilitates healthy emotional development, as described in Chapter 6. Through symbolic play, children express their understanding of the world around them and the interrelationships of people and events. In addition, symbolic play provides an important context within which to experience and express emotions, both one's own and those of others.

In this chapter, we discuss symbolic play as an important cognitive milestone. The ability to allow one thing to stand for something else, such as a block representing a car or a tissue representing a blanket, is evidence of the child's developing symbolic representation skills. Eventually, children can represent complex scenarios and sequences in their play. Other evidence of symbolic skills can be observed in drawing, language, mental images, and eventually in reading, writing, and mathematics, as will be described later in this chapter.

Cognitive Developmental Stages of Play

The early childhood special educator must be aware of the importance of facilitating play skills, in general, and pretend play, in particular. As we discussed earlier in this chapter, symbolic play moves through various stages. The first is **autosymbolic play,** in which children themselves are the actors. These play episodes reenact highly familiar activities such as pretending to eat or go to sleep, and they incorporate materials that are real (e.g., a pillow) or that closely resemble real objects (e.g., a small plastic spoon or tiny cup from a tea set). For children who are functioning developmentally at the end of the sensorimotor period, these are the kinds of activities that can be modeled both by the teacher and by other children. The use of play routines discussed in Chapter 4 can be helpful in establishing this early type of pretending.

The simple level of pretending can also be encouraged in group activities. For example, the teacher can say, "Let's pretend to be a snake" or "Let's pretend to swim." It will be important to select pretend activities that represent very familiar activities or concepts. Children who are just learning to pretend will have difficulty pretending to do or be something they have never experienced.

The teacher should gradually introduce pretend play scenarios that involve other actors, such as dolls and stuffed animals, as well as other children acting out familiar roles of relationships to one another. The classroom should include dramatic play centers that include materials that encourage pretending, such as dress-up clothing, a toy stove, a sink and cupboards, dishes, brooms, telephones, dolls and doll beds, and so on.

Also, the teacher should gradually encourage the use of objects that are more and more abstract. For example, instead of toy cars that look exactly like real cars, that crash and have to go to the amazingly accurate replica of a garage for repairs, wooden blocks can be used for cars and an upside-down box can become a garage. The ability to use the same blocks for a fence and the box for a doll bed represents the emergence of *mental flexibility* (e.g., reversibility and understanding of transformations). This is a hallmark of the next stage of cognitive development, the stage of concrete operations that typically emerges between the ages of 5 and 7 years. The current LEGO® phenomenon in children's play supports the development of creativity, mental flexibility, and fine motor skills, as children create, destroy, and re-create everything from spaceships to monsters using only small plastic bricks! (*Note to teachers:* With adult scaffolding, this can also create narrative scenarios and complex problem solving!)

The following example demonstrates the facilitation of symbolic play skills in a child with severe disabilities.

> Jason and Monique love to play house in the dramatic play center. Andrea, who has many repetitive, stereotypical behaviors, loves to sit in the rocking chair in the classroom and rock. The teacher decides to move the rocking chair into the dramatic play area and suggests to Jason and Monique that maybe Andrea could be the mother today: She could help the baby go to sleep by rocking her. After rocking for a while, while Jason and Monique are "cooking," Andrea is encouraged to put the doll in the doll bed. Now it is time for everyone to go to sleep. Jason and Monique lie down with their pillows, and they encourage Andrea to do the same. The baby then wakes up crying in the night, and, because Andrea is the mother, she must rock her back to sleep.

A scenario such as the one just described could also be incorporated into a play script that is illustrated through peer modeling and pictures of actions that are repeated several times. In this way, Andrea could be assisted not only with pretending but also with language development and cooperative play.

Problem Solving

As preschoolers face increasing demands to develop greater and greater independence, the cognitive skills that enable them to engage in problem solving become increasingly important. Typical preschoolers often have little difficulty *recognizing* problems to be solved; they may need help only with generating more effective solutions. Children who have disabilities or are at high risk, however, may need assistance not only in the development of problem-solving strategies but also in recognizing that a problem exists and that they have the capability to solve that problem through their own focused efforts. As discussed in Chapter 6, problem solving is related to executive function skills.

Problem solving is distinctly different from academic learning. Academic skills represent external knowledge that must be taught; problem-solving opportunities during early childhood encourage the child to create new mental relationships by interacting with the environment. Meaningful problems stimulate children's mental activity as they relate new understandings to previous ones.

Conditions Necessary for Problem Solving to Occur.   It is all too easy to structure activities with young children so carefully that they never have the opportunity to solve problems or to realize the relationship between cause and effect. Alert parents and teachers often prevent problems so consistently that young children seldom have the chance to recognize a problem, let alone solve it. Yet everyday activities at home and at school can offer many opportunities to teach children these important skills. Even if problem-solving opportunities are readily available, children will respond only when the following conditions are met.

Freedom from Fear of Failure.   Taking risks is natural to young children. That is why they must be watched so carefully. But taking risks in trying new things requires courage for some children. This is especially true if their early explorations resulted in painful or negative consequences. The child with visual impairments may be physically insecure and may resist exploring. Some children with disabilities may be overprotected, and children with adverse childhood experiences may be excessively wary. If children have had limited opportunities to play, to use a variety of different toys and materials, and to make discoveries, they need encouragement and support to explore their natural talents and curiosity.

Opportunities to Experience Cause and Effect.   Young children readily learn the relationship between cause and effect through inquiry and experimentation. Teachers and caregivers must take time to listen to and act on children's questions. Safe conditions, inside and outdoors, should allow for experimentation. Noise and mess often are a sign of cognition in action. Children learn from digging and piling up things. Pouring and stirring with sand and water teach new concepts. Opportunities for discovery are limitless. But the freedom to imitate, explore, and "do it myself" must be systematically taught to some children.

Encouragement and Reinforcement.   Encouragement and reinforcement are also necessary for cognitive learning. Cognitive learning is disrupted if children fear negative responses. The logical consequence of making a mess should be cleaning it up, never a teacher's scolding or saying, "I warned you not to do that." Encouraging experimentation may merely require making the materials available, but some children need to be told repeatedly that it is all right to play with things that may be forbidden at home. Children and their parents need to understand that some things are appropriate at school and not at home.

Teachers should be ready to provide social and tangible rewards for progress in expressions of curiosity and resilience and for the learning achievement. Just as structured, sequential lessons are needed for children to learn to recognize shapes and colors, so prompting and supporting are needed for children to learn qualities such as curiosity, experimentation, and problem solving.

Problem-Solving Skills to Be Nurtured.   In illustrating how to solve problems with everyday materials, Segatti, Brown-DuPaul, and Keyes (2003) see problem solving as a collection of skills to be nurtured: analyzing the situation to determine the problem, brainstorming possible solutions, envisioning the steps involved in solving the problem, and anticipating the consequences of these solutions. Not only is problem solving a natural logic, but the motivation to overcome obstacles appears to be natural as well.

Children basically enjoy solving problems. Deciding where to have a snack or the best place for playing with clay presents opportunities to talk about why one place is better than another. This is the beginning of problem solving. "Staging" or contriving problems to solve is a useful addition to those problems that occur spontaneously. Having too few cartons of milk at snack time creates the need to count the children before going to get the milk. Losing pieces of puzzles can become the occasion to talk about how this problem could be avoided in the future. Children can then be helped to see that puzzles should not be put away unless they are finished and complete. Discovering that the taller children can reach things whereas others cannot leads to problem solving, a math lesson, and a lesson on concept comparatives (e.g., "Who is tallest? John is tall, but Timmy is taller. Bill is the tallest child in the class").

Although problem solving itself is considered to be a cognitive (thinking) skill, it involves language learning, social awareness, and motor activities. The alert teacher sees the distinct opportunities to develop many skills from the simplest situations.

Teaching Children Who Have Intellectual Disabilities

Some young children demonstrate significantly delayed or impaired cognitive functioning early in life. The primary identifying characteristic of these children is a significantly slowed development of cognitive skills; hence the earlier term *mental retardation.* In the 1980s and 1990s, the term *developmental delay* was commonly used to refer to this disability. (Note that parents often found the term "developmental delay" misleading because it implies that the child will eventually "catch up" and that development is just proceeding at a slower pace.)

In August 2017, "Rosa's Law" officially stripped all references to "mental retardation" in federal health, education, and labor policies, changing the language to "intellectual disability" (www.wrightslaw.com). The law is named after a 9-year-old child with Down syndrome, Rosa Marcellino. Rosa's parents sued to remove the wording "mentally retarded" from her school files, because they viewed it as pejorative. The term "mental retardation" was eventually changed to the current "intellectual disability."

As mentioned in the introduction to this text, parents and society, in general, are often very uncomfortable with cognitive/intellectual limitation and disorder. This discomfort has been reflected in the variety of labels used. Historically, the earliest labels included terms like "idiot," "moron," "feebleminded," and "retarded." Ironically, many terms were originally intended to be *less* pejorative or offensive than a previous term. But over time, each term became pejorative.

For example, the term "retarded" was introduced in 1895 as a more respectful term than the earlier words previously mentioned. But by the 1960s, the term "retarded" had become a term commonly used to insult someone. This illuminates the fact that over time even new words associated with the condition take on a negative social stigma (Reynolds, Zupanick, & Dombeck, 2013).

For the purposes of our discussion here, we are referring to those cognitive processes and skills described by Piaget and, in this section, to children who, very early in life, demonstrate significant difficulty with the kinds of early developmental skills discussed in this chapter. These cognitive challenges can be caused by many factors, including genetic disorders (e.g., Down syndrome), prenatal injury to the fetus from toxic substances (e.g., alcohol) or viral infections (e.g., rubella), perinatal complications (e.g., anoxia), and postnatal influences such as traumatic brain injury (TBI), asphyxia (e.g., near drowning), and poisoning (e.g., lead poisoning). Although these factors do not always cause significant cognitive impairment, it is a possible outcome. We are referring to global developmental or cognitive deficits, not impairments of specific neurological processes.

Characteristics of Children with Significant Intellectual Disabilities

"Intellectual disability" is described in the Individuals with Disabilities Education Act (IDEA) as "significantly sub-average general intellectual functioning, existing concurrently with deficits in adaptive behavior and manifested during the developmental period, that adversely affects child's education performance" [34CFR 300.8(c)(6)].

The following are characteristics commonly associated with children who have significant intellectual disabilities. (*Note:* Prior to 2010, the terms *mental retardation* and *cognitive disability* were commonly used.)

1. One of the most obvious and defining characteristics of young children with intellectual disabilities is their slower rate of cognitive development, as well as slower development in other areas, such as self-care and communication, which will typically be commensurate with their cognitive level.

2. In addition to slower rates of development, children may experience significant difficulties with the kinds of basic cognitive processes described earlier in the chapter. They may also experience short-term memory deficits and difficulty attending to relevant stimuli.

3. Children with intellectual disabilities experience particular difficulty with language development. Whereas for most developmental domains the child will function at a level similar to his or her mental age (i.e., cognitive level), language achievement may be below the child's mental age.

4. Many children process information more slowly and require more time to produce a response.

5. Children with significant delays often do not demonstrate newly learned skills spontaneously and have difficulty generalizing skills to new situations.

Adapting Instruction

In light of these learning characteristics, practitioners should use intentional teaching strategies and have high expectations for all children. Several strategies that can be effective in assisting young children who have significant cognitive impairments are summarized in Exhibit 9.1. Also see Chapter 4 for a discussion on the Universal Design for Learning (UDL). These adaptations are easily incorporated into any preschool program. Peers without disabilities can often benefit from them as well. For example, during activities designed to facilitate classification skills, familiar functional materials can be used, such as forks, knives, and spoons or different-colored socks. Another simple adaptation is to remind all staff to avoid using rapid speech patterns and increase the length of pauses. This adaptation will make it easier for all children to understand, and it will provide ample time for children to organize their ideas and expressive communications. Particularly important are the use of repetition, creating a predictable environment, and facilitating active learning by teaching the child to initiate.

Exhibit 9.1

Special Considerations for Children Who Need Extra Time and Spaced Practice

1. ***Provide concrete or multisensory tasks.*** Preschool-aged children naturally learn more easily when tasks are three-dimensional and concrete rather than abstract.

2. ***Find the child's most efficient mode of learning.*** Observe carefully to determine each child's strongest mode of learning. If it is visual, then use visual cues to assist auditory directions. If auditory, then accompany visual tasks with auditory assists. If motoric, then use movement as much as possible to teach language and cognitive skills. However, some children may learn new tasks better with unisensory input rather than multisensory input (i.e., they can only pay attention to one type of sensory stimuli at a time).

3. ***Monitor pacing.*** Children who must work extra hard to concentrate or to process information usually tire easily. The amount of effort exerted should be varied to allow for occasional rest times, quiet activities, or soft music. Children who process information more slowly should receive less information or should receive it over a longer time.

4. ***Provide repetition.*** Some children need to try things again and again or need to have something repeated several times before it can be grasped. Intermittent practice helps children remember skills they have learned.

5. ***Plan for modeling and imitation.*** Some children do not acquire information incidentally. If a specific response is desired, plan experiences in which the behavior is demonstrated and positively reinforced. Once the child imitates the desired behavior, be certain to give the expected reinforcement.

6. ***Analyze tasks.*** Use *task analysis* to break down tasks into simple short steps that can be sequenced from the easiest to the most difficult. Complex task sequences may need to be broken into simple, short steps that are taught one at a time.

7. ***Give explicit directions.*** For some children, it is necessary to give specific directions slowly and one at a time. One step can be completed before the next direction is given.

Facilitating Cognitive and Information-Processing Subskills Related to Academic Achievement

For the preschool child, one of the greatest concerns regarding the development of cognition has to do with the cognitive skills that will ultimately support the learning of the academic skills of reading, writing, and mathematics and classroom language skills. Many of the mental operations and thinking skills that evolve throughout the preschool years will be critical to school performance and the development of academic skills. This section addresses the teaching of these cognitive subskills.

However, it is important to realize that the development of academic skills—and literacy skills in particular—does not depend on levels of cognitive development alone but also on the social and linguistic experiences of the child. Thus, to truly understand academic readiness and to develop strategies for facilitating academic skills in young children, it is also necessary to understand the role of the social context of the young child's family and culture.

The early caregiver interactions described in Chapters 4 and 8 also play a critical role in children's later development of cognitive and academic skills. The preschool years can be viewed as a period of preparation for the formal academic achievement that must take place in the early elementary school years in reading, writing, and mathematics. In addition, a fourth area is now realized to be crucial to children's academic success: *school language.*

Significant debate exists regarding to what extent academics should be stressed during the preschool years. Preschool programming approaches often reflect one of two polar views. One view suggests that academic skills should be directly taught in preschool programs emphasizing learning the alphabet, sound–letter relationships, counting, and reading and writing numbers and letters. At the other end of the continuum are programs stressing that neither academics nor academic readiness skills are appropriate for the preschool classroom. These programs emphasize self-directed play and exploration and exclusively child-centered activities.

In light of the continuing concern regarding the lack of school preparedness of millions of young children from impoverished environments who are at risk for a variety of biological and social reasons, there is probably an important middle ground somewhere between the two views.

Recently, research has addressed whether or not success in kindergarten is dependent on success in preschool readiness tasks that focus on social-behavioral skills (such as following directions, playing and communicating appropriately with others) versus preliteracy skills (writing one's name, counting, letter recognition, etc.). Findings from four studies follow.

Pentimonti and colleagues (2016) focused on children with language impairments and found that preliteracy readiness was more predictive than social-emotional development for success in kindergarten. Bierman et al. (2014) followed low-income Latino and African American students, emphasizing both social-emotional skills and emergent literacy and language skills. Results showed gains in both social and literacy skills in kindergarten.

Loughlin-Presnal and Bierman (2017) included an emphasis on teaching **parents** the academic expectations for success in kindergarten. Not only did children make significant gains in emergent literacy and self-directed learning, but perhaps equally important was the result that parents' beliefs about their child's academic potential, and parents' support for child learning, increased.

Pears, Kim, Fisher, and Yoerger (2016) targeted preschoolers with developmental disabilities. Results showed significant improvements in literacy skills in kindergarten, with several children improving from "significantly at risk for literacy development" to just "at risk."

While the findings of these studies were somewhat mixed, the case can be made that much may be done within a child-centered program to enhance the child's cognitive, social, and linguistic foundations for the development of academic skills. It is extremely important that the early childhood special educators understand the potential of these academic foundations and be able to design educational environments and programs that facilitate those skills. Equally important, these programs must be child centered, developmentally appropriate, engaging, and supportive of children's creativity, exploration, unique learning styles, and sense of self. (See Exhibit 9.2 for an example of an adapted approach to "calendar time" for preschool students with significant disabilities that promotes cognitive development while accommodating for the reality that time concepts such as months and days of the week are highly abstract concepts. These are often not grasped by 3- to 4-year-old children.)

Exhibit 9.2

Making Calendar Time Meaningful for All Children

Calendar time is an almost universal activity in preschool programs. Because of the abstractness of concepts of time, children with special needs often have difficulty relating to this activity. The following is an example of how calendar time might be made more meaningful for children with intellectual disabilities.

1. Rather than presenting the entire calendar month, highlight only the current week. Each day should be a different color, with Saturday and Sunday easily distinguishable from the days of the school week (e.g., they might be pastel, whereas the weekdays are primary colors).

SUNDAY	MONDAY	TUESDAY	WEDNESDAY	THURSDAY	FRIDAY	SATURDAY

2. Identify one activity for each school day that is done only on that day. For example, Monday is "Pudding" day, Tuesday is "Walk-to-the-Park" day, Wednesday is "Popcorn" day, Thursday is "Hat" day, and Friday is "Cleanup" day.

3. Each of these days has a special symbol or picture representing that activity. The symbol is placed on a cardboard square of the same color as the corresponding day on the calendar and with the name of the day printed on the bottom.

4. Introduce the calendar activity by saying, "Who knows what day it is today? Right! It's Monday. What do we do on Monday? We make pudding. It's Monday, and we're going to make pudding. Who can find the Monday card?"

5. Teach the children to learn to recognize the appropriate day-of-the-week card by relating the activity symbol to its matching color and word.

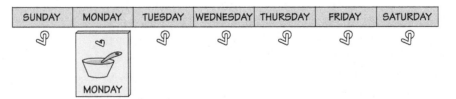

(For children with severe disabilities, show a duplicate of the activity card during the actual activity. Actual objects may also be used to represent the activity for children with visual impairments, visual processing difficulties, or severe intellectual disabilities. The use of pictures, symbols, and objects will help with symbolic representation and memory.)

6. At the end of the day, again say, "What day is it today? It's Monday and we made pudding." Then foreshadow a *future* event by saying, "Who knows what day it will be tomorrow? It's Tuesday. And what do we do on Tuesday?" Encourage the children to find the Tuesday card, but do not hang it on the calendar until the next day.

7. At the beginning of the next day, begin by asking, "Who knows what day it was *yesterday*? What did we do?" Point to the Monday activity card already placed on the calendar the previous day and review the Monday activity. This facilitates children's learning of past tense.

8. Repeat Steps 4, 5, and 6 for Tuesday, and so on.

9. As the week progresses, have the children mark the sequence of days and the passage of time as the activity cards fill up the calendar. As the week comes to a close, briefly review the week's events and talk about weekend plans.

   With this activity, a child who has severe intellectual disabilities can work on matching and eventually associate the activity symbol card with the activity and a particular day of the week. Children without disabilities can learn the days of the week; use language to describe past, current, and future events; and learn to read the names of the days of the week.

Basic information-processing skills such as attention and memory, as well as certain mental operations such as seriation, categorization, one-to-one correspondence, and logical thinking, form the cognitive bases for academics. The following sections provide developmentally appropriate classroom strategies for facilitating these processes and concepts.

Facilitating Children's Engagement

Some appropriate techniques for facilitating children's participation are discussed in the following section.

Assessing Problems of Attention.   To help young children develop appropriate capacities for focused engagement, the teacher must identify the factors that may be contributing to lack of attention. *However,* as discussed in Chapter 4, *the most fundamental factor in establishing attention and engagement in children is to identify high-preference activities that are intrinsically interesting and motivating to each child.* The teacher must also be certain that the child has no health problems and there is no interference with normal vision or hearing. Obviously, many young children with special needs do have physical problems that affect their concentration. The guidelines in Chapter 5 offer some assistance in developing an environment most responsive to particular special needs.

Assuming that their attention expectations take into consideration each child's special needs, teachers will want to assess whether tasks match the child's abilities and are broken into manageable steps, directions are clear, vocabulary is at a developmentally appropriate level, and the amount of stimulation is reasonable.

Stimulus Selection.   Teachers should analyze the amount and complexity of stimuli to which the child is being asked to respond. Some distractible children may not be able to attend to a very colorful puppet with a very high voice while seated on the floor in a large group far away from the teacher. The same puppet might get a totally different response in a small group with two or three children seated at a table with a paraprofessional who uses a soft voice. Decreasing the amount and complexity of impinging stimuli will make it easier for the child to separate relevant from irrelevant stimuli.

When children have difficulty figuring out what stimuli are relevant, using novelty in the form of concrete objects, touch, and movement can help focus and sustain attention. It is believed that infants first learn to interpret stimuli received through the sense of touch (tactile). Then around the age of 3 or 4 months, they integrate information presented visually and auditorily as well. Even so, for many children, touch continues to help isolate the relevant features of a stimulus and increase the child's ability to focus on them. When trying to teach children how to walk across a street safely, giving each child a teddy bear to "instruct" in role-plays might be an effective means of focusing attention and recall.

Duration of Attention.   Initially, the amount of time required for a task should be in keeping with the child's natural ability to sustain attention. Then, using positive reinforcement and in some cases a timer, the *time on task* requirement can be increased. Remember that often children do not sustain attention because the task itself is inappropriate because it may be too easy, too difficult, or boring. For the very young child, learning tasks need to have visually concrete (obvious) beginnings and endings. Because some children just do not know how to start an activity and have poor visual organizing skills, they are easily distracted. Through careful structuring of environmental demands, teachers can help children have productive contact with early learning materials.

Goal Selection and the Zone of Proximal Development.   Perhaps the greatest factor that interferes with school readiness and academic achievement of young children with intellectual disabilities is failure to identify short-term goals that are reachable, that is, within Vygotsky's "zone of proximal development" or ZPD. By selecting the appropriate starting point, frustration can be minimized and involvement sustained. Puzzles exemplify a type of material that often places inappropriate demands on children. There is a wide range of difficulty of puzzles that are supposedly designed for young children. Perhaps an appropriate puzzle is just not available when the child decides to visit the puzzle corner. He or she tries several different puzzles but is unsuccessful. So this child may try to take another child's puzzle or perhaps begin to wander aimlessly around the classroom.

This child's difficulty with engagement and sustained attention may be related more to the characteristics of the activity than to the learning characteristics of the child. Teachers can scaffold the child's engagement, as well as task persistence and a sense of mastery, by helping the child select toys and materials that are developmentally appropriate and *just beyond the child's current level of competence (what the child can do independently), that is, within the zone of proximal development (what the child can do with help).* Repeated attempts to teach the child a task that is *not* within the child's ZPD will more often than not lead to frustration, and perhaps to the child's generalized disinterest, rather than learning a new skill. Equally important, once a new skill *is* learned by teaching within the child's ZPD, the teacher must create a new, more challenging short-term objective to ensure continued movement toward the final goal. In the example here, that might be independent focus of attention and success in completing preschool-level puzzles.

Active Looking and Listening.   Active attention through looking and listening is critical to learning. Engagement can be more easily sustained through individualized, highly engaging activities such as cooking. For example, nearly all children (and adults) love to make cookies or popcorn. Children are presented with the steps of a recipe: first demonstrated verbally with actual ingredients and utensils and then with a large written display including both print and pictures.

The teacher demonstrates each step of the recipe, and then children participate in each step (with as much active hands-on participation as possible). Each child should be encouraged to describe what he or she is doing and, later, what was done. Children can count and measure and practice scooping and pouring. They can observe and describe the properties of the ingredients used. They can describe how ingredients are transformed as they are combined (e.g., change in color or change from dry to wet or sticky). They can anticipate/predict how the ingredients might change as they are heated—that is, "cooked" or "baked." They can observe the final product to test their predictions and review the process. Finally, they can eat and savor their snack! When demonstrated and talked about, cooking is a literacy lesson, a language lesson, a fine motor lesson, a science lesson, and a math lesson all rolled into one. Furthermore, children's attention and engagement are easily maintained. Exhibit 9.3 discusses why snack time is a perfect activity in which to embed cognitive skill development.

Structuring Learning Experiences

Young children who have not yet developed adequate attention, concentration, perceptual, or memory skills may not be making effective contact with their learning environment. By structuring the curriculum, teachers can help these children become active problem solvers and effective learners. Attention must be given to the scheduling of a structured, isolated, small-group instructional session by restructuring the periods of the day traditionally called "free-play time" or "center time." In an inclusive early education class, there might be 4 or 5 children with disabilities in a group of 20. Even though there may be only one or two teachers, paraprofessionals are usually available so that one adult can be involved in each of three small groups. Ideally, each group would contain a mix of children with and without disabilities. The children without disabilities function as models and often spontaneously assist a child who is having difficulty with a particular task.

Many activities such as puzzles, cutting, and drawing are easily adapted. Children can work side by side with puzzles of differing level of difficulty or can cut with scissors designed to accommodate different levels of skill. If necessary, a particular child may be seated closest to the adult at the table so that sufficient opportunities for reinforcement and prompts are available.

Exhibit 9.3

Snack Time: A Perfect Time to Develop Concepts

Most early education centers focus on teaching children how to enjoy a wide variety of foods. They stress good nutrition and encourage social manners. In addition, snack time provides a unique opportunity for developing concepts. Although different foods are eaten, the routine remains essentially the same each day: arranging the table, deciding how much food is needed, and discussing the qualities of the food. Eating is a multisensory experience that should not be taken for granted.

Unlike nouns, concept words cannot be taught directly because they are not objects with names. Instead, concepts must be experienced. Then appropriate concept words must be applied to the experiences. Snack time provides an ideal opportunity for many children to become directly involved in concepts related to math and science. For example, a child's glass may be *full* or *empty*, the grapefruit is *larger* than the apple, there are *not enough* straws, *how many more* do we need. An apple can be cut in half, which creates two pieces, and so on. Through lively conversations, observations can be guided, comparisons made, and concept words practiced. Meaningful questions readily bring light to number, size, and placement concepts.

Of course, snack time is not the only time to focus on concept development. It is just one of the best and often overlooked times. The ability to attend is greatly enhanced when touchable favorite foods can be smelled, seen, and tasted. Even children who are very easily distracted become intently involved when they have good things to eat.

Another approach includes having half the class group come to the work area, while the other half continues in free play. The second group comes to the work area after the first group has completed a designated number of individually prescribed tasks. In this way, children who need extra support always have peer models available.

Supporting Children's Planning Skills.   Many young children with special needs have difficulty *planning*. They need to learn how to begin a task, stay with it, and recognize when it is completed. They may see a task as endless and fail to recognize when they should take pleasure in a product or in the process of learning to learn. To promote successful contact with the task and recognition of accomplishment, it may be best to begin with learning tasks that have a visually concrete beginning and ending. Functional activities such as picking up all the blocks after play time, putting them in their proper container, putting the top on, and returning the blocks to the shelf can be broken down into small units that are gradually combined as children develop increasing attention and concentration skills.

Arranging Materials.   The following suggestions will be helpful to the child who has difficulty organizing his or her own work area. Such a problem is common to children who have delays in perceptual development.

1. Limit materials in the area to only those needed to complete the task.

2. Arrange initially needed materials before the child arrives or ask the child to bring the tub that contains the necessary materials to the center. This prevents distractible children from having to wait and possibly beginning to lose interest.

3. Be certain that all materials are within the child's reach and at eye level.

4. Put loose materials in a container to avoid spills and their resulting distraction.

5. Use visual supports and guidelines such as the placement cardholders that come with some visual matching cards to help the child develop necessary organization skills such as left–right progression.

Emergent Math and Science

According to an updated joint position statement by the National Association for the Education of Young Children (NAEYC) and the National Council of Teachers of Mathematics (NCTM), "high-quality, challenging, and accessible mathematics education for 3- to 6-year-old children is a vital foundation for future mathematics learning" (NAEYC, 2002a, p. 1). No doubt the same can be said with regard to early science instruction. There is increasing concern that children in the United States are falling behind in the areas of math and science, according to a report from the National Research Council (2005). Early childhood educators are encouraged to implement developmentally appropriate research-based preschool science curricula (Gelman, Brenneman, MacDonald, & Roman, 2010). Teachers should promote the math, science, and technology skills of preschoolers through instruction and curricula that are developmentally appropriate (Clements & Sarama, 2016). A 2009 National Academy of Sciences report called for an initiative to improve math and science education for preschoolers. The report emphasized that young children have a natural strong interest in learning about the world around them and that early success in mathematics leads to later success in both math *and reading.* To give every child a strong foundation in math and science, this effort must begin well before entrance to formal schooling (National Academy of Sciences, 2009). A strong case can be made for teaching mathematics and scientific inquiry together. The processes of scientific inquiry and children's natural intellectual processes and interests are completely intertwined. According to Gelman and colleagues (2010), the components of scientific inquiry for preschoolers include observation, prediction, experimenting, counting, measurement, and record keeping. Each of these components is certainly dependent on mathematics!

It is important for early childhood educators and special educators to realize that many of the early cognitive skills described by Piaget can be enhanced and used in early childhood classrooms to prepare children for successful learning in math and science. Indeed, all children—including children with disabilities—are fascinated by the world around them. Children love engaging in hands-on exploration and experimentation with every kind of "flora and fauna" and are sensitive to interesting characteristics of shape (e.g., "big," "round") and quantity (e.g., "one," "lots") and similarities and differences (e.g., "more," "bigger"). The inherent appeal of elements associated with math and science should not be underestimated. For many toddlers and preschool children with disabilities, activities associated with premath and scientific inquiry may be more engaging and more accessible than language and literacy. Teachers must not overlook the possibilities of accessing language and literacy *through* science and math. (For an extensive presentation of early childhood teaching strategies in math and science inquiry, see Epstein [2007].)

In the past, activities related to classification (grouping)—including sorting and matching, categorization, and seriation (ordering); concepts of space, time, and number; and comparisons (similarities, differences, and opposites)—were common in early childhood curricula. In recent years, there has been a move away from this focus to a very strong focus on early literacy. Perhaps this has resulted in less emphasis on early math and science. Clearly, *both* are extremely important.

Classification, Seriation, and Concept Development

Matching (a form of discrimination) and putting things together that are the same or alike are among the first of the expected skills. Initially, identical things are matched. Then several things that are alike in some way are *grouped*. *Sorting* is also a form of discrimination, followed by separating according to differences. Both matching and sorting activities are described within the broader context of **classification** (distinguishing characteristics of things, then sorting, matching, or otherwise grouping them). Note that the ability to understand the concepts of "same" and "different" is essential to performing on tests and following directions. Teachers should carefully teach the verbal labels of *same, alike, different, not the same,* and *not alike*. As children learn to classify, they are encouraged to begin with concrete, multisensory objects. Attention must be called to the various *attributes* (features or characteristics) of the objects. It is a pleasure to watch children as they move from the concrete to the abstract or from the simple to the complex in their thinking. For example, very young children are dominated by what they see, hear, smell, or touch. This is known as being "perceptually dominated." They will describe an orange as something that is orange in color, round, or rough (depending on the words within their vocabulary). Later, they will be interested in its function and will classify it as "something to eat." Finally, it will become part of a whole class labeled "fruit." In general, expectations move from the concrete to the abstract, from the simple to the complex, and from the here and now to the remote in time and space (Hohmann, Weikart, & Epstein, 2008).

Seriation is the ability to order according to relative differences (e.g., smallest to largest, lightest to darkest, etc.). Practice in seriation helps children coordinate relationships. They begin to understand relative size, position, and time comparisons. Teachers move gradually toward the discrimination of finer and finer differences by increasing the number of objects compared.

Making comparisons to see what goes together and what does not enhances thinking skills. *Grouping* and *regrouping* in many different ways require flexibility of thought. This flexibility is basic to successful reasoning, judging, and problem solving.

Once critical preacademic skills are identified as preschool objectives, the next step is to embed them into meaningful and engaging activities within the curriculum. The following sections present suggestions for teaching and developing necessary preacademic skills in young children. Exhibit 9.1, presented earlier in the chapter, can help teachers implement their curriculum with children who need extra time and spaced practice.

Classification. Classification activities should not simply teach children to group or sort by similar features but should also encourage children to organize (group or sort) the same information in different ways. This will encourage more *flexible thinking*. Most preschool curricula emphasize teaching colors, shapes, and sizes. Initial classification of things by these attributes should include a wide range of items. As children become adept at sorting things by color, they should be introduced to colored shapes. As they learn to sort by shapes, they can be provided with shapes of different sizes and thicknesses. The teacher can also encourage children to think of different criteria for grouping. In this way, children can be rewarded for divergent and creative thinking.

Children with disabilities may first enjoy *functional* sorting and matching familiar objects such as shoes, cups, cars, and so forth, before they can sort more abstract features such as shapes, colors, and size. The simple, familiar activity of matching socks of different colors and sizes may initially be more effective than less meaningful abstract materials such as attribute blocks of various shapes and colors. Cleanup time in the classroom is an opportunity to help children who may be having difficulty understanding the concepts associated with sorting. The teacher can remind the child to sort out the dinosaurs and blocks and put them in the right containers.

Using Attribute Blocks. Once children learn the concept of grouping iconic objects such as cars, a good set of attribute blocks (red, yellow, and blue circles, squares, rectangles, and triangles) can be introduced. Each shape is provided in two sizes and two thicknesses. At first, the children are taught to put all the red shapes together, mixing all the shapes in the same container but keeping the color constant. The blocks are mixed together on the floor in a pile, in equal amounts of red, yellow, and blue. The teacher begins by saying, "Let's put all the red ones here" and then picks up three or four red blocks one at a time, saying, "This one is red" each time. Next, a child is directed to "Find another red one" and place it into the correct box. The process is continued until all the blocks have been sorted according to color.

After a few days of doing this, circles and squares are contrasted. Blocks of all three colors and both shapes are mixed in a pile on the floor. The teacher sets the stage in the manner just described, except that now *shape* is the criterion.

When children are secure in this simple classification by a single attribute such as color *or* shape, multiple attributes can be introduced. Increasingly challenging games and "rules" can be created. They sort the blocks according to color *and* shape. For example, blue squares can be placed in one box and blue circles in another. Later, big blue squares and little blue squares may be sorted, and so on. Sorting and categorizing tasks can also be used to create "games with rules." Learning to play games and to understand that games have "rules" is an important achievement in preschool. For children with disabilities, the concept of "rule" can be supported using sorting tasks.

Adapting Instruction. Individualizing behavioral objectives is critical because, as in all teaching activities, the teacher's skill in making the activity interesting and enjoyable is important. There should never be a sense of solemnity or serious importance with games. The teacher must be ready to support each child at his or her success level. If the lesson includes children of more than one skill level (and it should), all the suggestions made for individualizing within the group should be followed.

A well-organized set of performance objectives enables the teacher to move forward or backward in providing the appropriate challenge while avoiding the overwhelming obstacle of failure. For example, the teacher may hand a red circle to Willie and say, "Let's put this big red circle with the other big red circles here" as she points and guides Willie's hand to the right box.

But she may say to Susie, sitting next to Willie, "Susie, what should go into this box?" as she points to the box with big red circles. Susie likely will respond, "Big red circles." In this way, each child is challenged, but no child fails. They also learn from each other.

Seriation.   Introducing children to serial ideas such as first and last should be done in the context of everyday activities, especially those that involve whole-body movement. *First* and *last* may refer to place in line or when one does something. These concepts are critical for young children entering kindergarten. Most of the problems involved in lining up or being allowed to do something are caused by children's lack of understanding and experience with these terms. Understanding the concept (cognition) and using the correct label (language) cannot be separated. Without the concept words, one cannot talk about the concept. Without the idea, the word is useless.

True seriation is more complex than simply understanding *first* and *last*. "Nesting" toys are typical seriation materials. Hardware stores often provide sample paint cards that can be used to seriate from dark to light. Household measuring cups, spoons, or variously sized screws or buttons can be used to practice seriation tasks. Graduated sizes and colors provide easy opportunities for learning observation and comparison, and terms such as *bigger* and *biggest, more* and *less*, and *most* and *least*.

Concept Development.   Learning abstract concepts such as *many, different, whole, taller, tallest, in front of*, and so on is often a special challenge for children with disabilities. Clearly identifying the teaching targets (concepts) to be learned and using intentional teaching to make sure they are mastered will be important. A system for teaching concepts includes the following features:

1. Identify the concepts to be taught.

2. Plan a large number of activities and games that make explicit the idea of each concept.

3. Look for "teachable moments" to reinforce the meaning of a particular concept throughout the daily routines. For example, children may be lining up toy animals and pretending they are walking back to the barn. The teacher could comment that the cow is first in line. She could suggest that the animals decide to turn around and go back to the field and have the children turn each animal around. She can then ask, "Now what animal is *first?*" Children will be intrigued to discover that the one that was first is now last!

4. In addition to taking advantage of teachable moments, teachers can also contrive ways to embed and practice concepts in daily routines.

5. Even after children appear to have mastered a concept, it is important to plan opportunities for regular review to make sure the skill is firmly established and generalized.

An examination of teachers' manuals for kindergarten and first grade yields a large number of necessary concept words. These should be introduced through real-life and play activities at least 2 years before the children encounter them in school. "Put your finger at the top of the page" is a much harder direction to understand if children have not learned about "the top shelf" or "the top of the page" in a book as someone reads a story. A review of the Boehm Test of Basic Concepts (Boehm, 2001) is helpful in selecting target spatial and directional concepts.

Teaching Number Concepts

Exhibit 9.4 presents early prenumber and number concepts. Some prenumber concepts are included in the skills just described. Important prenumber concepts are *many, few, more, less than,* and *another one*. Also, it should be noted that even infants can readily perceive differences in quantity (although, of course, they cannot *express* this number sense).

Exhibit 9.4

Emergent Math Concepts

Prenumber Skills

Sorting and classification

- Describing attributes
- Attribute games

Patterning

- Pattern replication using objects
- Describing pattern
- Completing pattern using objects
- Translating pictured pattern to objects
- Creating a pattern

Relations

- Comparing two objects (bigger/smaller; same as)
- Comparing substances (more/less than; same as)
- Ordering objects (seriation; smallest to largest, etc.)
- Equivalence sets of objects: one-to-one correspondence

Spatial relations (near, far, under, outside, next to, etc.)

- Understanding self in space
- Relation of self to objects
- Relation of objects to other objects

Time relations

- Understanding time periods have a beginning and end
- Ordering events sequentially
- Time relation concepts (e.g., *first, last, before, after, next, yesterday, today, tomorrow*)

Conservation

- Understanding that quantity and volume remain unchanged if arranged differently (e.g., viewing liquid in different-shaped containers)

Number Skills

- Rote counting
- Rational counting: identifying number in group by *cardinal* number (e.g., "There are *three* ducks" [answers "How many?"])
- Ordinal numbering (e.g., *first, second, third*)

Operations

- Adding one more
- Subtracting: one less; "take away"

Geometry

- Recognizing shapes
- Spatial characteristics of objects (e.g., *above, inside, top, bottom, right, left, edge,* etc.)

In teaching numbers and counting, it is common to teach rote counting from 1 to 5 or 10. Many children with disabilities learn this verbal pattern fairly easily. However, repeated rote counting without matching the number to each item counted (e.g., pointing or touching each item) may interfere with the development of one-to-one correspondence and true understanding of the concept of number (number sense). While stacking and counting blocks, for example, the teacher should assist the child in actually picking up and placing each block as the child or the teacher says each number. Also, counting to see how high the blocks can be stacked helps demonstrate the usefulness of number as a way of measuring quantity (e.g., "Oh wow! You stacked *nine* blocks this time!"). This approach supports the development of *rational counting*, that is, matching each numeral named to an object, and identifying the number of things in a group (the *cardinal* number, i.e., highest/last number stated). This can then lend itself to the development of understanding *ordinal* numbers (*first, second, third*, etc.).

Avoiding Stereotyped, Labored Teaching of Concepts

Regardless of specific behaviors identified as required school readiness skills, teachers must understand and be able to support the child's development of flexible, analytical, logical thinking. The examples in this chapter support this process. Teachers should provide frequent opportunities for children to learn the concepts through experiences appropriate to a particular setting (see Exhibit 9.3 for an example). They should not leave the learning of important concepts to chance, nor should teachers depend on rote repetition of songs or chants, such as the ABC song or rote counting. Rather, the daily schedule must provide repeated opportunities throughout the day in which children can use inquiry, discovery, and problem solving to master important prerequisite concepts of math and science. Teachers should keep in mind the following instructional approach:

- Identify the concepts.
- Use the concepts in both carefully planned activities *and* within spontaneous embedded opportunities throughout the day.
- Make meanings clear. Check for understanding.
- Review and recycle lessons periodically.
- Monitor progress frequently (what has each child learned?).
- *Make it fun!*

Development of Literacy

The previous section considered certain cognitive skills related to academic readiness. In this section, we consider social and linguistic factors related to literacy.

Literacy is certainly a hot topic today. Debates about the best instructional approaches to literacy have intensified in recent years. This is at least partly in response to the fact that millions of Americans are functionally illiterate. It is also related to the growing numbers of children who enter school without the necessary prerequisite communication skills and early experiences that prepare children to participate in formal literacy education. The Center for Early Literacy Learning (Dunst, Trivette, Masiello, Roper, & Robyak, 2006) describes a three-phase model of literacy development—preliteracy (birth–15 months), emergent literacy (12–42 months), and early literacy (36–60 months)—that may provide a framework for learning experiences. The emergent literacy phase from approximately 12–15 to about 36–42 months of age includes the acquisition of first words and use of communication functions (e.g., requesting, attention getting, and describing), increased receptive and expressive language, symbol and print recognition, and other emergent literacy skills. The early literacy phase from about 30 to 60 months of age includes an understanding of word units and speech sounds, "playing" with language, inventing spelling, echoing a reading model, and recognizing letters and words. A term that reflects the emphasis on the relationship of early experience to literacy is *emergent literacy*. "Emergent literacy refers to the developmental precursors of formal reading that have their origins early in the life of the child" (Whitehurst & Lonigan, 2002, p. 12).

Literacy is not simply an accumulation of the specific skills related to reading and writing but rather evolves through both social and cognitive processes that begin at birth. Literacy evolves gradually as a function of early interactions with adults, exposure to and interaction with print materials, and exposure to other children and adults who are *using* print in various "literacy events." Examples of literacy events include the following:

1. *Daily living activities,* such as making lists for grocery shopping; reading labels and recipes; going to various public service offices such as the departments of welfare, employment, and motor vehicles; and paying bills

2. *Entertainment,* such as reading newspaper movie listings, television guides, and books; doing crossword puzzles; and reading subtitles or credits on films or videos

3. *Religious activities,* such as attending Bible study groups, singing hymns, and reading daily devotional books

4. *Work-related activities,* such as writing checks, reading instructions, following delivery instructions, and stocking shelves

5. *School-related activities,* such as doing homework or playing "school"

6. *Interpersonal communications,* such as writing and reading notes, letters, and birthday cards

7. *Storybook time,* in which children are read to, primarily for their own entertainment

8. *Explicit focus on literacy teaching,* including activities in which reading or writing is the specific focus of the interaction. Such activities are often initiated by the child (e.g., the child asks: "What is this word?" or "How do you make a *T*?").

Van Kleeck (2004) pointed out that mere exposure to literacy materials and experiences is not sufficient for the development of literacy. *Rather, it is the adult–child interaction around such events that is important.*

The Precursors of Reading and Writing

Increasingly, researchers in the area of literacy development acknowledge the relationship between certain early skills and experiences and the development of reading and writing (National Institute for Literacy [NIFL], 2008; Strickland & Shanahan, 2004). According to the NIFL report (2008), the best early predictors of eventual competency in literacy appear to be knowledge of the names and sounds associated with printed letters, phonological awareness, the ability to rapidly name a sequence of random letters or digits, the ability to write letters in isolation, and the ability to remember spoken information for a short period of time.

Writing. Several developmental domains relate significantly to the beginning development of children's writing skills. The development of fine motor and visual-motor skills is obviously critical to the child's ability to eventually use pencils and markers to draw the abstract forms that make up the letters of the alphabet. Specifically, the following are important:

- Children's early experiences with art materials such as paints, crayons, and markers
- Adult encouragement and assistance in controlling print tools to make lines and circles

- Noticing similarities and differences in shapes and configurations

Also important is the cognitive skill of representation:

- Recognizing that pictures represent real things
- Attempts to use drawings as representation
- Adult assistance in learning to draw faces, body parts, houses, flowers, grass, sky, and so on

Early social experiences are also critical in the emergence of writing. Particularly important is the opportunity for involvement in adults' functional uses of writing, such as making a grocery list or writing a letter.

Reading.   Certain experiences and achievements both at home and in the preschool classroom are also critical to the eventual development of reading. As already established, by far the most important precursor of reading skills is access to rich, interactive experiences with caregivers and teachers that support children's *language development*. Print is a visual representation of language. In young children, reading ability is inextricably related to speech and language development, particularly vocabulary and phonological skills. (Note that as children get older, reading *comprehension skills*—particularly the ability to comprehend expository text—also depend on the ability to decode complex syntactic structures [Bernstein & Levey, 2009].) In the area of language and literacy experiences, the following are important:

- The development of oral language, particularly the development of narrative (e.g., storytelling) skills
- The development of a rich vocabulary
- Phonological and phonemic awareness and skills such as sound segmentation and rhyming

Early exposure to literacy events in the home is also critical to learning to read:

- Exposure and access to children's books
- Being read to regularly
- Observation and participation in adults' functional uses of reading (e.g., reading recipes, mail, menus in restaurants, etc.)
- Adults' attention to the alphabetic principle (e.g., reference to printed words and letters in storybooks, naming letters, teaching letter sounds, etc.)

Emergent Literacy Goal Areas

Exhibit 9.5 presents an example of the sequence of development of emergent literacy skills for one child.

Print Awareness

- Recognizes environmental print (e.g., fast-food logos on napkins, empty food containers, and wrappers; stop signs; bathroom signs; etc.).
- Understands functional uses of print (e.g., name on belongings, daily attendance, lunch menus, job assignments, treasure hunts, letter-writing center, pretend mailbox, etc.).

Concepts of Book Print

- Recognizes parts of a book (cover, pages, back).
- Understands book orientation (turning pages from front to back, top and bottom of page, reading left to right).
- Understands vocabulary labels related to print (e.g., *letter, word, sentence*).

Video Example from

Enhanced eText
Video Example 9.2
Five Predictors of Early Literacy
https://www.youtube.com/
watch?v=HqImgAd3vyg
This video identifies five predictors (oral language, phonemic awareness, alphabet awareness, concepts about print, and early writing with inventive spelling) of early literacy skills and evidence-based practices that support their development.

Exhibit 9.5

Sample of Emergent Literacy: Sequence of Emergence of Reading and Writing for One Child

Writing

1. Scribbles with marker and crayon.
2. Makes lines and circles.
3. Draws a face.
4. Adds stick figure arms and legs to face.
5. Writes own name.
6. Pretends to write letters to friends using wavy lines.
7. Practices making letter-like forms.
8. Includes some real letters.
9. Practices writing other common words (e.g., "Cleo" [dog's name], "DAD," "Dear Mom").
10. Attempts writing "I luv yoo," using *invented spelling,* reflecting phonemic awareness.

Reading

1. Enjoys looking at books.
2. Listens carefully to story while looking at pictures.
3. Holds book right side up; turns pages from front to back.
4. Talks about pictures; pretends to "read" book.
5. Retells favorite stories by looking at pictures.
6. Recognizes environmental print (e.g., McDonald's and Coca-Cola logos).
7. Recognizes own printed name.
8. Tries to rhyme words; likes books with rhyming words.
9. Segments spoken word into syllables (e.g., "ca-ter-pill-ar").
10. Recognizes each occurrence of the word *caterpillar* in favorite book.
11. Begins to learn some sound–letter associations (e.g., "*M* says 'mmm'").
12. Associates the letter B with the initial sound and letter in *boy*.
13. Can segment spoken word into initial sound (onset) and rest of word (rime).
14. Tries to sound out words (e.g., says "mmeena" for printed word *men*).

Story Sense

- Recalls main story elements (e.g., characters, main event, ending [resolution]).
- Can retell well-structured story (e.g., maintains main story elements in sequence).

Vocabulary Development

- Demonstrates steady increase in vocabulary.
- Enjoys learning to understand and use new words throughout all daily activities.
- Can define and discuss meanings of words.

Phonologic Awareness

- Can separate spoken words (e.g., knows that "I love you" contains three separate words).

- Can identify the beginning sound ("onset") of a word and separate the beginning sound from the rest of the word ("rime").
- Can hear and produce syllables and words that rhyme.
- Can segment spoken words into syllables (e.g., can break up the word *elephant* into "el-e-phant").
- Can break syllables into phonemes, or sounds (e.g., *pup* has three sounds: "p-uh-p").

Alphabetic Understanding

- Can name letters.
- Understands that letter combinations/sequences represent words.
- Understands that individual letters represent speech sounds (phonemes).

Speech/Print Match

- Can follow print while listening to a familiar story.
- Has some sight vocabulary.
- Can make initial sound–letter associations (e.g., knows that printed word *door* starts with "d" sound, although does not recognize entire word).

Control of Reading/Writing

- Tries to read and write.
- Identifies letter names.
- Can write some letters when given their sounds.
- Uses invented spelling (i.e., makes up spelling; writes words like they sound, e.g., "bk" for *book,* "luv" for *love*)

Developing Literacy in Daily Classroom Activities and Routines

Literacy-rich activities and materials should be embedded into each component of the preschool classroom. Here are a few suggestions (see also Hemmeter, McCollum, & Hsieh, 2005; McCathren & Allor, 2005).

1. *Opening Circle Time*
   - Have children find their own mats for circle time by identifying their names on the mats or their own picture symbols.
   - Assign children to daily jobs by hanging a nametag next to the duty assigned (e.g., "Jon—Pass out cups").
2. *Story Time*
   - Repeat interesting stories frequently.
   - Select stories with concepts that are developmentally appropriate to the child's cognitive level and interest.
   - Select books with rhymes and predictable phrases.
   - Provide extra copies of the book in the reading corner for individual use.
   - Make sure books used in circle time are large enough and have pictures and print that are easily seen and recognizable from a distance.
   - Encourage children's *active* participation in story time, both motorically and cognitively (e.g., invite children to act out parts of the story or to match pictures or objects to pictures on a page, and ask children what they think will happen next). Use "dialogic reading" strategies (McCathren & Allor, 2005) in which the child comments and asks questions and the adult responds.

- Ask children to find letters in words that are also in their own names or a friend's name. Or, count certain letters on a page (e.g., "How many letter *B*s can we find in this sentence?").

3. *Literacy Exploration*
   - *Art and writing center:* Provide drawing and writing tools, stationery, envelopes, blank pages, and albums for making books and other works.
   - *Role-playing center:* In addition to the usual dress-up materials and housekeeping toys, also include pads and pencils for shopping lists, a mailbox and envelopes, TV listings, cookbooks, checkbooks, and so forth.
   - *Book and library center:* Include books with CDs, copies of books read in circle time, predictable books, newspapers, and magazines. Make sure seating is comfortable and inviting for both adults and children.
   - *Word Wall:* Create a whiteboard or bulletin board where "interesting words" and words that match a child's experiences (such as feelings) can be posted daily. Throughout the day, adults should be mindful about the discovery of new words and remind children about them. Each word should be written and posted on the Word Wall, and "honored" by acknowledging, defining, practicing, and revisiting the word.

4. *Snack Time*
   - Find letters in alphabet soup.
   - Read labels on food containers.
   - Follow recipes.

5. *Outdoor Activities*
   - Modify "Simon Says" using large word cards or pictures. Combine a name card with an action card to encourage reading two words at a time (e.g., "Sandra—Jump").
   - Label storage areas (e.g., "BIKES," "BALLS").
   - Use traffic signs. Check frequently for word recognition.

6. *Closing Circle/Music Time*
   - Create a poster with pictures and/or words representing favorite songs. Children choose closing songs by pointing to the appropriate picture.
   - Send notes home with children for parents to read.
   - Have children find their own art project to take home by looking for their names.

See the website of the Center for Early Literacy Learning at http://www.earlyliteracylearning.org/index.php for reviews of research on early language and literacy development for infants, toddlers, and preschoolers with and without disabilities, as well as practical activities for families and practitioners.

Oral Language and Literacy for School Readiness

Much has been written about the relationship between oral language skills and literacy (e.g., Kamhi & Catts, 2012) as well as the nature of the school discourse style, or school language, that is required for successful performance in schools. Young children need to be familiar with certain types of language, sometimes referred to as **literate-style language,** to learn to read and write. This type of language is more decontextualized than language used in the home. Language used in the home often has a great deal of shared understanding among speakers. Such language does not depend solely on the *words* used in the communication but also on gestures, facial expression, and intonation as well as the shared knowledge and experience of the speakers. In addition, school classrooms require certain kinds of communication skills. These include answering questions, using language to "show and tell," raising hands before speaking, using language to talk about language and thinking, and so on.

The Nature of School Language

To be successful in school, children must be able to demonstrate certain kinds of communication skills. Some of these skills are linguistic, and some are social or pragmatic.

Certain kinds of interactions required in classrooms may be unfamiliar to some children. The following are examples:

- Children are required to raise their hands before speaking.

- Children are expected to answer questions individually, addressing the group at large. (Many children may be more accustomed to demonstrating their understanding through action rather than words.)

- Children are expected to respond very quickly.

- Teachers ask questions that are "test questions"; that is, the teacher already knows the answer and is using the question to evaluate the child's knowledge. Such a format is unfamiliar to many children.

The linguistic skills required are those that have been alluded to earlier in the chapter, including the following:

- The child must use and understand language in the classroom that is often decontextualized (i.e., not embedded in the immediate context). For example, the teacher often gives instructions using only words, or the child is asked to describe a past event.

- Vocabulary is expected to be specific and precise.

- Syntax and grammar are used to carefully mark the relationships among sentences (e.g., *if, but, because,* etc.).

- Narratives are expected to reflect sequence accurately and be coherent.

These literate language skills are built on the symbolic, referential language concepts that emerge during the preschool years. In turn, reading and writing skills, which must be learned in the primary grades, will be based on literate-style language. Many children do not have the kinds of early language experiences that prepare them for success in the early grades. In part, this may be due to cultural differences.

The following section addresses some of the ways in which children's early experiences with language and literacy may be different from what is expected in the classroom.

Enhanced eText Application Exercise 9.2: In this exercise, you can apply what you have learned in this chapter to adapt the previous list of literacy events for children and adults and identify developmentally-appropriate literacy events for preschoolers.

Cultural Differences in Early Language and Literacy Experiences

The influence of cultural and linguistic differences on early language development and school achievement continues to be the focus of much attention. Infants and young children are exposed to a wide variety of early experiences related to language use and reading and writing. In her classic work *Ways with Words*, Heath (1983) reported some of the most important research related to cultural differences in these early experiences. Using the ethnographic research method of participant observation, Heath carefully observed families in two communities in the Piedmont area of Appalachia. Heath provided detailed descriptions of the interactions between adults and young children in a working-class white community and in a rural African American community. She compared these interactions with the types of interactions that are typical of what she referred to as white middle-class "mainstream" families. We have much to learn from her work today.

Differences in Children's Early Use of Narrative

Decades ago, according to Heath (1986), differences were found in the types of narratives that young children were encouraged to use. Narratives are important both because they are believed to form the foundation for learning to read and write and because children are expected to be able to perform certain types of narratives when they enter school.

In her landmark research describing the cultural influences on children's use of different types of narrative, that is, "narrative genres," Heath summarized the kinds of narratives most common among different cultures as follows:

1. *Recounts.* A recount is a report of an experience from the past. It is commonly parent initiated (e.g., "Jenny, tell Daddy about your field trip"). Recounts are the most common form of narrative required in the public school. Unfortunately, they are the least common form of narrative in nonmainstream cultures. In middle-class mainstream families, however, children are encouraged not only to produce recounts frequently but also to use literate-style language—that is, language that is precise, highly referential, and in proper sequence.

2. *Eventcasts.* An eventcast is a description of a current activity. It describes situations or activities that are immediate or obvious, such as "I'm building a tower" or "Mommy's making pudding now." This type of communication is also common in mainstream families and in public schools (e.g., "John, tell us what the boy in the picture is doing"). However, it is very uncommon in many nonmainstream cultures, in which it is often considered ridiculous to talk about the obvious. Consider the effect of the following classroom scenario on a child who is not accustomed to the use of eventcasts. Paul is making a ball out of a piece of clay. The teacher notices and says to Paul, "Oh Paul, tell us what you're making!" Whereas a middle-class child might easily launch into a detailed description of what he was doing, Paul is somewhat bewildered and probably not sure he understood the teacher's question. He might even be concerned that describing such an obvious thing would be insulting to her.

As children get older, they learn to use eventcasts in **metalinguistic** and **metacognitive** ways. In other words, they use *language and thinking to talk about language and thinking* (e.g., "Let me think about how to do that" or "Oops! I said that wrong")! This is an important school language behavior and cognitive achievement, and it is essential in "learning how to learn."

Somewhat related to eventcasts is the kind of response required by the typical classroom test-question format consisting of a question–reply–evaluate sequence that predominates in school classrooms. The following is an example. Sean is playing with a truck, his favorite toy:

TEACHER: *Sean, what are you playing with?*

SEAN: Looks at teacher with blank expression and does not respond.

The child is being asked to answer a question that he is sure the adult already knows the answer to. He has not yet learned about the test-question format. Many young children who are not accustomed to this genre find it confusing and may not answer such a question.

3. *Accounts.* Accounts are similar to recounts in that they tell about a past event. However, accounts are initiated by the child rather than by an adult. Accounts are often accompanied by communication strategies designed to get and hold the listener's

attention (e.g., "Hey, ya know what?"). Although these types of narratives are much more common in nonmainstream families than are recounts and eventcasts, they are discouraged in many public school classrooms and often punished as interruptions or off-task behavior.

4. *Stories.* According to Heath (1986), the most common type of narrative among nonmainstream families is the story. Stories are often handed down from generation to generation, or they may evolve over a period within the child's early experience. Family stories may begin with an adult teasing a child about a particular event. Stories evolve and change over time, and eventually some parts may be fictionalized. Stories contain strong elements of performance—the narrator's style is important, and listener participation in the story is often expected. Needless to say, such language activities do not follow the rules of school language, and they may be viewed as lying or attention-getting behavior.

Teachers may misinterpret a child's behavior as indicating inattention or misbehavior because of differences between classroom expectations and a child's home experiences. For example, children from diverse cultural and linguistic backgrounds may not respond to the question and response format or instructional questions about stories (used in most preschool classrooms) because these types of questions are not used at home. Moreover, some children may discuss different topics related to the same theme rather than discuss a single situation in a linear way (Cheatham & Santos, 2005).

A study of Head Start preschoolers found differences between African-American and European-American children in their responses to questions about a story in a wordless picture book (Curenton, 2011). African-American preschoolers performed better on questions that required inferences about a character's motives and internal states. This difference may be related to the types of storytelling practices in the children's home communities (Curenton, 2011). These findings emphasize the need for teachers to gather information from families about the child's experiences, interests, and skills.

Cultural Differences in Early Caregiver–Infant Interaction

Long before children learn to use narratives, important cultural differences can be observed in how parents interact with their infants and young children. These differences can determine whether young children have opportunities to learn literate-style language prior to school entry.

Middle-class caregivers are typically verbally responsive to their infants and young children. This may not be the case in certain other cultures. Although caregivers from other cultures may be responsive physically through touch or through facial expression, they may not respond verbally. Hart and Risley (1999) documented many such differences between middle-class and non-middle-class families, and more recent research has found similar differences (Fernald, Marchman, & Weisleder, 2013). Middle-class caregivers are also more likely to use highly referential language than are caregivers who are members of some non-middle class or nonmainstream cultures. **Referential language** is characterized by the use of frequent labels and precise vocabulary with clear referents. Thus, typical middle-class communication practices expose children to both a large quantity of language and the quality of language that facilitates eventual development of literate school language skills. Examples of these different kinds of caregiver–child interactions are presented in the following dialogues.

Sample 1. Jason, 12 months old, sitting in his high chair, starts to whine.

MOTHER: Jason, what's wrong?

JASON: (Looks down at the floor.)

MOTHER: Oops! Your cookie, huh? You dropped your cookie. (Mother picks up the cookie.) Yuck. This cookie's all dirty. See, it's dirty 'cause it was on the floor.

Sample 2. Alice, 12 months old, sitting in her high chair, starts to whine.

MOTHER: (Looks up at Alice.)

ALICE: (Looks and reaches toward the floor.)

MOTHER: (Picks up the cookie and hands it to Alice.) Here it is.

In both these examples, the caregiver is responsive to her infant's cues. However, in the first example, the mother is both verbally responsive and referential. She uses the word *cookie* several times and other key words that specifically refer to the key features of the experience—*dropped, dirty,* and *floor.* In the second example, although the mother is responsive, her language is limited. When she does verbalize, it is nonreferential in that she does not explicitly name the object (*cookie*) or the location (*floor*). Instead, she uses the words *here* and *it*.

Cultural Differences in Uses of Print

Cultural differences can also be observed in children's early experiences with reading and writing. Even though reading books for pleasure or information and using writing for communication are common in middle-class homes, they may not be common in some non-middle-class and nonmainstream homes.

In the twenty-first century, teachers increasingly encounter children whose home language is not English, and the native language of the child is often not the only difference. Many factors can create a serious mismatch between teacher and child. The ways in which non-middle-class and nonmainstream families provide early language and literacy experiences for their children are simply sometimes different from those expected in our school systems. It is particularly important that teachers of young children with disabilities understand these differences and be aware of educational strategies that can help children make a successful transition to the language structures and functions used in classrooms.

Enhanced eText Application Exercise 9.3: In this exercise, you can apply what you have learned in this chapter about the different narrative types that preschoolers may experience or use depending on the culture of their homes and schools.

Specific Strategies That Support Emergent Literacy Skills

In early childhood programs, the major goals related to the development of early literacy range from development of a rich vocabulary and literate-style oral language skills to learning the subskills of literacy (e.g., phonological awareness, learning the alphabet, and beginning to learn sound–letter associations). Teachers can use the knowledge and strategies generated by years of research on the role of caregivers in supporting emergent literacy (Neuman & Dickinson, 2011).

To help children achieve the necessary foundations, teachers must begin by determining which kinds of language and literacy activities are already familiar to the children in their classes and then building on these experiences. As Heath (1986) stated, educators must find ways "to use what children do with language in their homes and communities to extend and enrich the school's repertoire of narrative genres" (p. 93). In addition, teachers must help young children understand the *value* of reading and writing. The following are examples of such strategies. (See also Exhibit 9.6 for an example of embedding emergent literacy goals into a project approach to preschool science.)

Teacher Strategies for Developing Children's Appreciation for the Value and Function of Literacy

- *Demonstrate the functional uses of print.* This is one of the most powerful strategies teachers can use in the classroom. It includes such activities as reviewing the daily schedule, reading the daily menu to see what will be served for lunch, listing on the board the names of children who are present or absent, writing notes to themselves as reminders to do something later, writing notes to other teachers, and so on. In these activities, children are *not* expected to read; more important, they are developing an understanding of the *functions* of reading and writing. As they observe the power of the printed word, children develop a fascination with decoding the mysterious symbols.

Exhibit 9.6
Supporting Emergent Literacy and Math Through Science: Planting Seeds

Planting seeds is a common early childhood theme or unit lesson. Many features of this activity make it inherently engaging for young children. It is a hands-on activity involving familiar and interesting sensations and materials, such as digging in dirt and pouring water. And it usually involves being outdoors. Once the seeds are planted, it offers an ongoing opportunity to observe changes and make predictions. It provides a great science lesson (e.g., the transformation of a seed into a plant, identifying the different parts of the plant, comparing different kinds of plants, etc.) and opportunities to develop prenumber skills and early math concepts (e.g., How many new plants have emerged? Which one is biggest? How many inches tall is it? How many days since the seed was planted?). The possibilities are limitless. This would be an example of the "project approach" to early childhood curriculum referenced earlier in Chapter 4.

Although this activity is typically intended to support science-related goals in the curriculum, a creative teacher can easily embed the components of emergent literacy into this activity. Consider adding the following elements to the seed-planting project:

1. First, books and discussions are provided related to plants, growing things, and seeds.
   (book reading; concepts of print)
2. As children are outside at recess or on a "discovery walk," the teacher points out different plants (grasses, flowers, etc.) to make sure that children's expressive and receptive vocabularies include key words.
   (vocabulary development)
3. Children can draw the various plants they have observed or even take pictures.
   (emergent writing)
4. The teacher introduces the planting project so that children can anticipate the activity.
5. Seed packets are supplied. Children are encouraged to not only look at the pictures of the plants on the packages but to read the labels as well.
   (functional print)
6. Three types of seeds are provided: beans, mums, and daisies (one vegetable and two types of flowers).
7. The key words related to the project are printed on cards—*Seeds*, *Plants*, *Beans*, *Flowers*, *Mums*, and *Daisies*—and placed on a bulletin board.
   (print-rich classroom)
8. Children say the words and analyze their sounds and segments:
   a. /sss/ plus /eeds/ rhymes with *beads*!
   b. "Dai-sies," "Flow-ers"—each have two syllables.
   c. *Mums* starts and ends with same sounds as *Moms*.

   *(phonological/phonemic awareness)*C

(continued)

9. The word cards (with no pictures) are placed on the bulletin board in a hierarchical configuration:

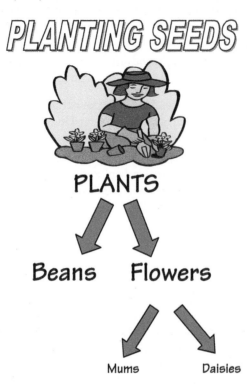

PLANTING SEEDS

PLANTS

Beans   **Flowers**

Mums   Daisies

10. The soil is prepared in a small space outdoors. Children check to make sure the garden location will get plenty of sunlight. Three sections are marked off for planting the three different types of seeds.

11. Children participate cooperatively in making small holes, pinching just a few seeds, placing them in the holes, and covering them with soil.

12. As the children place the seeds in the soil in each section, the empty seed packets are attached to a stake to make three signs representing where the different seeds are planted. Children predict which of the seeds (beans, mums, or daisies) will produce the most plants.

    (functional print)

    (science inquiry: prediction)

13. Children are assigned responsibilities for watering.

14. As the plants begin to emerge, each week the children observe each section of the garden to see which plants are growing.

    (science inquiry: observation and data recording)

15. Key words are reinforced. New words are added in response to children's questions and comments.

    (vocabulary enrichment)

16. On the bulletin board, each week a mark is made under the name of each plant as new seedlings emerge. Numbers of plants are tallied periodically:

    (a) How many bean plants?
    (b) How many mums?
    (c) How many daisies?
    (d) How many flowers?
    (e) How many plants altogether?

    (science inquiry: observation, documentation, classification)

    (mathematics: counting, addition, grouping)

17. The teacher points to each word, asking, "Which plant is this?" Over time, she draws children's attention to the following:

    (a) The letters in each word
    (b) The letters the words have in common
    (c) The letters that match letters in the children's names
    (d) The sounds of the initial letter in each word
    (e) Long words and short words

    (alphabetic principle)

18. Children may also document the planting process and growth of plants by taking photos of the steps in the process, such as preparing the soil and placing the seeds in the holes, the emergence of the first shoots and first leaves, and the change in the height of the plants.

    (science inquiry: documentation)

19. A book is then made of the photos. Children generate a phrase or sentence for each page.

    (narrative, grammar, concepts of print)

20. As the garden matures, new words are added to the vocabulary list, such as *water, leaves, stems, pick, prune,* and *bouquet*.

    (vocabulary and knowledge enrichment)

- *Collaborate with parents to identify the ways in which print is used in each child's home.* This might include such activities as reading the television guide, recipes, food labels at the grocery store, comic books, and so on. Similar activities and materials can easily be incorporated into the classroom.

- *Incorporate literacy events into children's play.* Treasure hunts are exciting ways to demonstrate the use of print. Again, children are not expected to actually read the clues but to experience their effectiveness in leading to the treasure. Other examples of play activities include playing postal service (letters are "written," placed in the mailbox, and delivered); going to the grocery store with a shopping list; and pretending to read a bedtime story to a doll. Reading recipes during cooking activities and writing notes that have been dictated by children to take home to parents are other good activities.

- *Play games that require referential language to facilitate literate-style oral language.* For example, two children can be separated by a screen. The child who is "It" draws a picture and instructs the other child to draw the same thing (e.g., "Make a big circle and color it blue. Now put two black eyes on it"). The object of the game is to see how closely the pictures match. Success requires the ability to use language in specific and precise ways. The same format can be used in playing with different shapes and colors of blocks or setting up a dollhouse. For children with severe disabilities, the game can be made simpler by using familiar objects and performing very simple tasks, such as selecting objects like a cup and a shoe to be placed in a box, and then comparing to see whether both children end up with the same objects in the box.

- *Structure other activities that facilitate literate language style.* These might include helping children explain the rules of a game to someone else, go to the school office and deliver a verbal message, describe an exciting event to a student who was absent, and play the "telephone" game. Simpler versions might include having children feel objects in a sack and guess what they are or playing "Simon Says." These activities facilitate the use of specific autonomous language. For children who are less verbal, they demonstrate the functional uses of language for the purpose of sharing information and regulating others' behavior.

- *Read stories to both large and small groups and to individual children.* The importance of reading stories cannot be overestimated. The stories selected must be meaningful to the children. They should be short, and they should be *repeated often.* Stories should also include props, such as items on a flannel board, or actual objects to highlight important story points. Involving children's actions at key story points is also important. Including props and actions will make story time more interesting for all children. Be sure to include print referencing (e.g., pointing out repeated words, sounding out certain words with the group, noticing words that

Video Example from

Enhanced eText
Video Example 9.3
Visual Support Video Series—How to Use Picture and Object Schedules
https://www.youtube.com/watch?v=POySP6A-4bo
This video shows how to use picture and object schedules that also introduce children to sequencing and print.

start with the same letter) in some portions of the storybook reading (hence the importance of using books with very large print in large groups). As stories are repeated, pause at key points to allow the children to fill in the familiar phrases. Familiar storybooks should also be available to children during free play so they can "read" the stories to themselves or to a friend or doll. (This will require having several copies of favorite books available.)

- *Help children create their own "little books."* One of the most motivating and flexible literacy activities is among the simplest. A reading program originally developed by Oelwein (1995) for children with Down syndrome suggests a simple and fun introduction to literacy referred to as "The Little Book." As shown in Exhibit 9.7, a sheet of paper, folded in fourths and stapled at the "spine," can produce a "little book" of eight pages. The teacher or child can "draw" or "write" on the pages or paste pictures and photos onto the pages. The child then turns the pages and "reads" the words and pictures he or she helped create! This is a very dynamic and quick activity guaranteed to capture the child's attention. There are several good websites on making books and creating stories.

Whole-Language Versus Phonological Approaches to the Development of Literacy

During the 1980s and 1990s, the field of reading instruction was dominated by a **whole-language approach** (Goodman & Goodman, 1986). In this approach, reading, writing, speaking, and listening are viewed as interactive and interdependent. The following are examples of common activities in a whole-language approach:

- Language experience stories that children dictate to the teacher based on shared experiences. Teachers should write stories on flip charts so they can be read again and again by the class. Students may copy the stories for their own reading later on.

- Choral reading of familiar stories or poems. Choral reading can play the same positive role that singing favorite songs plays for younger children. Choral reading combines this pleasurable repetition and predictability with written words.

- Use of predictable storybooks that include repetitions of sentences and key words.

- Journal writing and writing picture captions on students' own pictures.

Sometimes referred to as the "reading wars," the debate between phonological approaches and whole-language approaches will probably continue to flare up from time to time.

Current approaches to early literacy emphasize that the child's ability to discriminate and recognize the sound segments of words (phonological and phonemic awareness) and early learning of sound–letter relationships (alphabetic principle) are critical subskills in learning to read. (For a classic discussion of developmentally appropriate practice in teaching reading and writing, see Neuman, Copple, and Bredekamp [2000]; for reviews of the research literature in early literacy, see Neuman and Dickinson [2011].) It should be noted that several studies have found that the consistent factor in children's reading success is *access to excellent teachers* (Blair, Rupley, & Nichols, 2007; Reutzel & Cooter, 2015).

Phonological awareness refers to the ability to recognize and discriminate certain sound segments of language, including words, syllables, rhyming words, initial sounds, and individual phonemes, as well as the realization that these segments can be separated, linked, and moved around.

Phonemic awareness refers more specifically to the ability to perceive and manipulate (i.e., segment and blend) phonemes, which are the smallest linguistic units—that is, the speech sounds that make up the language. An example would be a child's awareness that the word *pin* contains the three phonemes /p/, /I/, and /n/. Children

Exhibit 9.7

Learning About Reading and Writing by Creating a "Little Book"

1. Fold a single page of paper into fourths.
2. Cut along the folds to make an eight-page "little book."
3. Write a title on the book based on the child's preference.
4. Involve the child in selecting pictures or creating drawings and writing the book.

must ultimately learn the relationships between phonemes and letters of the alphabet in order to learn to read (i.e., sound–letter association, referred to as the alphabetic principle). Learning to read by focusing on these sound–letter associations is referred to as **phonics.** Phonemic awareness does not come naturally to most young children and must be painstakingly taught. A preschool child will find it much easier to segment a word into syllables than into phonemes. Many children—even those without disabilities—have not developed this kind of sound awareness by the time they enter kindergarten. It is also important to note that a child's ability to *pronounce* words correctly does not ensure phonemic awareness or the ability to segment and blend sound. Needless to say, children with auditory-based learning disabilities often have difficulty with phonemic awareness.

Early childhood programs can make a significant contribution to the development of these skills. Mihai and colleagues (2005) suggest that activities working on the following skills will build phonological and phonemic awareness:

- *Environmental sound awareness:* Responding to sounds and associating them with items in the environment (e.g., *"woof-woof"* becomes associated with a dog).
- *Word awareness:* Identifying individual words and recognizing that some words are composed of two words (e.g., the words *back* and *pack* compose *backpack*).
- *Syllable awareness:* Discriminating sound segment within words. Some words have one syllable (e.g., *dog*), some have two syllables (e.g., *pup/py*), and some have three or more (e.g., *re/trie/ver*).
- *Rhyme awareness:* Identifying words that have the same ending sound (e.g., *stone* and *phone*). Some ending sounds look alike and others not so much (e.g., *rough* and *stuff*).
- *Onset-rime awareness:* Separating one-syllable words into two parts: beginning (onset) and ending (rime) sounds (e.g., /c/a/t/, /m/a/t/, /h/a/t/).
- *Phoneme awareness:* Associating sounds with letters (e.g., the word *mat* has three separate phonemes /m/ /a/ /t/) and combinations of letters (e.g., /ch/ in *chair*).

Although these are primarily listening skills, the principles of UDL (see Chapter 4) should be used so that all children can participate and learn. Early childhood programs can make a significant contribution to the development of these skills with the following types of activities:

- **Develop listening skills.** Children must first learn to *listen* (i.e., to concentrate and actively process auditory information). A wide variety of simple sound awareness games can be helpful in developing children's ability to listen, such as the following:

   1. With their eyes closed, ask children to identify different *environmental* sounds (e.g., running water, guitar, bell, drum, scrunching paper). Increase the difficulty of the game by asking children to identify the location of the sound and then the *sequence* of two or three sounds. Duplicate instruments or pictures of the sound-making items may be provided for children with severe disabilities to identify the sound source.

   2. Ask children to imitate or identify "soft" or "quiet" sounds versus "loud" sounds.

   3. Select a child to be "It." While the child closes his or her eyes, an item with a subtle noise, such as a ticking clock or timer, is hidden somewhere in the room. The child then has to listen carefully and try to find the item.

   4. Ask children to listen carefully and try to identify softly whispered words.

- **Help children perceive onsets and rimes.**

   1. Bring the child's attention to the beginning sound and the rest of the word (e.g., *pat* = /p/ plus /at/; *top* = /t/ plus /op/). Use the printed words and touch the letter that makes the beginning sound as you say it, and point out the part of the word as you make the ending sound. Provide children with duplicate labels so they can imitate saying the sounds and finding the corresponding letters.

- **Develop rhyming skills.** Learning to produce and recognize words that rhyme is a first step in phonological awareness.

   1. Use ample nursery rhymes, poetry, and rhyming books in group activities. For example, songs like *Willoughby, Wallaby, Woo* are favorites of many preschoolers. Allow children to fill in the rhyming words and to make up new rhymes.

2. See how many words or nonsense syllables children can generate to rhyme with a certain word (e.g., "What rhymes with *bike?*").

3. Complete rhyming pairs (e.g., *pie–sky, pin–fin, wig–?, fire–?,* etc.).

- *Develop the concept of a "word."* Children do not automatically know what a word is.

1. Ask children to list different words (e.g., "Say all the color words you know").

2. Say a short sentence (e.g., "John ate pizza"). Ask children to listen carefully and count the words. Explain that there are three different words: "John" "ate" and "pizza".

3. Help children identify "long" versus "short" words (e.g., *cat* versus *refrigerator*). Use hand movements to correspond to the duration of the word.

- *Teach recognition of syllables.* Children must be taught to recognize that words are made up of syllables.

1. Ask children to count and say syllables in a word (e.g., *re-frig-er-a-tor*).

2. Have the children make movements (e.g., clap their hands, stomp their feet, or pat the table for each syllable they hear in a word).

- *Help children synthesize words by combining syllables.* Help children listen to individual syllables in a word and synthesize them into the correct word.

1. Say "Who can figure out what word I'm saying: *tel-e-vi-sion?*"

- *Help children listen for initial sounds in single-syllable words.*

1. Listen to the word *pin.* What is the first *sound* in the word? What other word starts with the "puh" sound?

2. Which word starts with "puh": *cow, hat,* or *pig? Use pictures to engage children's attention.*

Note: Many of these activities can be readily adapted for children with disabilities. Use of repeated rhymes that include movement and identifying the sources of environmental sounds, for example, can be highly motivating activities even for children with severe disabilities.

Finally, another critical emergent literacy skill—and an important predictor of reading achievement (Whitehurst & Lonigan, 2001)—is referred to as the **alphabetic principle.** This includes naming the letters of the alphabet and understanding that each alphabet letter (or sometimes a letter combination) is associated with a particular speech sound (phoneme) and that printed words are made up of sequences of letters representing the sounds in words. It is acknowledged that, as with phonemic awareness, the alphabetic principle must be *taught* and often presents significant challenges to students with disabilities (Kluth & Chandler-Olcott, 2008; O'Connor & Bell, 2004).

Early childhood special educators must become aware of the opportunities to support reading development. As mentioned earlier, teachers can point out phonological and phonemic elements of words by making specific and frequent references to letter names and their associated sounds, both in storybook reading and in everyday encounters with environmental print. Several studies conducted by Justice have demonstrated the positive effects of teachers' targeted references to print during storybook reading (Justice & Kaderavek, 2009). Another literacy activity that is both simple and effective is the use of **dialogic reading,** described by Zevenbergen and Whitehurst (2003) and shown in Exhibit 9.8. Note the use of the acronyms C.R.O.W.D. and P.E.E.R. as reminders of the strategies. The teacher's ability to motivate and activate the child's interest in books and literacy, and in identifying letters and sounds in words, is a simple, but important, evidence-based strategy. It provides important support for the child's eventual realization that he or she can use these sound–letter associations to sound out words—indeed, *to read!*

Video Example from

Enhanced eText
Video Example 9.4
Dialogic Reading with Kathy
https://www.youtube.com/watch?v=T_IIMZq8nJU
This video demonstrates a teacher's use of dialogic reading strategies and explanation of vocabulary with a group of preschoolers in reading *Something from Nothing.*

Exhibit 9.8

Dialogic Reading

Prompted Reading Interaction Strategies

P.E.E.R.

Prompt the child to say something about the book.

(*Select from prompts listed in this exhibit: C.R.O.W.D.)

Evaluate the child's response: *"You're right! He only has one shoe!"*

Expand the child's response using topic extension or rephrasing:

Child: "I see there." (pointing to puppy)
T: "You see the puppy there? He's hiding in the box!"

Repeat the prompt to determine if the child learned from your prompt.

C.R.O.W.D.

(*Suggestions for use of prompts)

Completion prompt: The adult hesitates on a familiar word or phrase to see if the child can complete it—for example, *"Ready, set, _____" (Go!)* or *"One, two, buckle my _____" (shoe).*

Recall prompt: *"Can you remember where the puppy is hiding?"*

Open-ended prompt: *"What's happening here?"* or *"I wonder what that bear will do."*

Wh- **question prompt:** *"Who is that?"; "Where did he go?"; "Why is he mad"; and the like*

Distancing prompt: The adult makes reference to something *outside* the book—for example, *"We saw a spider like that yesterday, didn't we!"; "Did you ever go to the ocean?"; "Does your kitty look like this one?"*

Source: Zevenbergen & Whitehurst (2003).

Enhancing the Value of Storybook Reading

It has been well established that adult–child book reading is an important contribution to children's development of literacy skills. However, for some children who have significant disabilities, such as children with autism spectrum disorders, storybook reading may not be immediately engaging. Zimmer (2017) describes the following simple strategies to enhance children's interests and attention to book reading as well as increase reciprocal (turn-taking) interaction.

1. Select stories and pictures that are related to the child's strongest interests, such as trains, animals, TV figures, and so on. (Or, create a "book" using photos of family members and pets.)

2. Establish a consistent time and place routine for story reading (in a particular chair at bedtime in the child's bedroom or on the couch after watching a favorite TV show, etc.).

3. Use attention-getting prompts to direct a child's attention to the book (e.g., tapping the cover of the book, saying, "Oh look! Let's read this book about Thomas, the train!").

4. Use various types of questions to direct the child's attention to the pictures:

   (a) Labels: "What's this?" "That's the kitty, right?"

   (b) Choice question: "Is this a kitty or a puppy?"

   (c) Fill in the blank: "Look! The mouse ran up the _____."

   (d) Request name of an action: "What is that bear doing?"

   (e) Open-ended: "What do you think will happen next?"

Developing Print Awareness and Sight-Word Vocabulary

Helping any student discover the ability to sound out words is a tremendous motivator along what is often (for children with disabilities) a challenging path toward learning to read. Although there is currently wide acceptance of the importance of a phonics-based approach to literacy, for young children with disabilities the development of a meaningful sight-word vocabulary, particularly early on in the process, will be an invaluable skill. Often children with phonological and auditory processing challenges are able to develop phonological skills eventually but at a much slower pace. *This should not mean that young children with severe disabilities cannot experience the "joys of reading."* Recognition of names of family and friends, the ability to read environmental print (e.g., "Train Crossing," "Stop," "Restroom"), and recognition of common phrases (such as "Happy Birthday" and "I love you") or printed names of music and storybook choices will be invaluable.

Research indicates that through systematic instruction, children with significant cognitive disabilities have developed a functional vocabulary of sight words for use at home, school, and in the community (Browder, Wakeman, Spooner, Ahlgrim-Dezell, & Algozzine, 2006). Many children with Down syndrome develop reading skills through sight words and phonics approaches (Cologon, 2013). See the website of Down Syndrome Education International at https://www.dseinternational.org/en-us/ for current research and practice on promoting the literacy skills of children with Down syndrome.

As teachers and caregivers become more sensitive to the phonological and phonemic elements of words, they can make specific and frequent references to letter names and their associated sounds throughout the child's daily routines. For example, one of the authors was able to support her young grandson's awareness of initial sounds by playing a word-to-object matching game while making lunch. She placed three objects on the table (a spoon, a bowl, and milk). Then she wrote the name of one of the objects on a card. Showing the card to the child, she asked, *"Does this say spoon, bowl, or milk?"* emphasizing the initial sound. He quickly began trying to use the first letter in the word to "crack the code" so he could select the correct object. The procedure was then reversed. Three label cards were placed on the table, and one object was presented, requiring the child to find the matching card. This version of the game could serve to increase the child's visual scanning and letter-discrimination skills.

Preschool teachers often use a simpler version of this activity when taking roll in a large group, by holding up a name card and asking the group, "Whose name is this?" Children try to guess or decode, then the card is turned over to reveal the picture of the namesake. The teacher turns the card back to the print side and sounds out the name while pointing at the letters, then spelling the name, encouraging a whole-group choral response—for example, "It's Kim! K-I-M. Kim is here today!" Many preschoolers with severe disabilities have quietly learned to read this way! Taking attendance is a perfect opportunity to use print referencing as well as practice sound–letter association. Another simple and effective strategy is to keep small whiteboards available, both for the teacher and for children. Whenever an interesting word or name comes up, the teacher or child can quickly write the word on the whiteboard for further exploration, and begin to make the connections between words, letters, and sounds (phonemes).

While sight word recognition offers an important, readily accessible, early introduction to literacy, and encourages children's interest in letters and reading, there is increasing evidence that many children with significant intellectual disabilities can, in fact, learn to read with a phonics-based approach (see, for example, Browder et al. [2009]).

A Brief Note on Early Writing

For some reason, discussions about literacy, at any age, have a tendency to focus primarily on reading rather than writing. However, that may be a mistake when working with very young children who have disabilities. As mentioned several times previously, successful early childhood special education requires teachers' ability to gain children's attention and *actively* engage them in ways that help them experience *efficacy*. One of the challenges of helping developmentally young children learn to read is that it requires very focused visual and auditory attention and the processing of fairly abstract stimuli.

Learning to *write* (before it becomes a tedious and demanding fine motor activity), on the other hand, begins with drawing and creating and can be very active and exciting. See Chapter 7 for a discussion of the developmental sequence in emergent writing. The drawer/writer selects a "tool," chooses the colors, and completely controls the "attack" of lines, shapes, and strokes on paper (or walls and sidewalks!). The use of these motions and materials to produce something beautiful or to represent an iconic face with eyes, nose, and mouth (or a house with windows, a door, a sidewalk and Christmas lights outside, as in Exhibit 9.9) is nothing less than spectacular and empowering for a 3-year-old child. This is a cognitive "aha" moment. The child realizes he can autonomously create a representation of the world around him, and then proceed to create new worlds from his own imagination—eventually through both art and *writing*. Teachers can then take advantage of the fact that because of their egocentrism, young children will be very interested in something they themselves

Exhibit 9.9

Three-Year-Old's Drawing of His House at Christmas Time, with Lights, Windows, Door, Sidewalk, and Plants

Photograph by M. Diane Klein

have drawn or written. Similar to many adults, children are very taken by their own work! Teachers are encouraged to enthusiastically and frequently assist each child by using careful scaffolding techniques to write his or her name on schoolwork, utilizing prompts (e.g., "Your name is 'Tim,' right? OK. What's the first letter you hear in TIM? Right! It's a T! Can you write a T?") and gradually decreasing prompts until the child can independently write his own name. Teachers can use this as a scaffold on which to create opportunities for the functional use of *reading* by having children search for their names, which they have written themselves, to identify their own artwork or belongings. Recognizing one's own name is highly motivating for all children and is an effective strategy for teaching letter recognition to children with significant cognitive disabilities (Greer & Erickson, 2018).

Eventually, children become interested in "cracking the code" by *sounding* out new words! It's extremely important that children understand the "alphabetic principle" (i.e., letters represent sounds,) and that if you know those sounds, you can "break the code" and figure out a word! It should be noted, however, that there is one particular challenge related to learning the English language that teachers must be prepared to deal with. Many words do NOT have a phonetic spelling; that is, each letter does *not* predictably represent one sound—thus, the vexing "exceptions to the rules" that are so common in written English. One can only imagine a child's consternation when trying to sound out the word "through"!

Note: One of the author's grandsons, after proudly learning all the letters of the alphabet and mastering phonics, began to experience letters in some words that didn't "make their sound." As he attempted to read environmental print (e.g., street signs, grocery labels, etc.) or chapter books from the library, he felt tricked and went through a period in which he refused to read. When his grandmother explained that there are some "really annoying things about the English alphabet that he would just have to get used to and that he was not making 'mistakes,'" he quickly adjusted and discovered that he could use contextual cues to figure out the vexing words that didn't follow the rules!

An excellent resource for specific teaching and learning activities is *The Creative Curriculum for Preschool* briefly discussed in Chapter 4. It presents detailed teaching strategies and activities in several categories including literacy, vocabulary/language, phonological awareness, print, letters and words, and comprehension. For each of these categories, there are descriptions of teacher methods and activities, as well as a section titled "What Does the Research Say?" for each of the seven categories.

Summary

All preschool and child-care teachers share the responsibility of developing cognitive, active learning, and problem-solving skills, together with academic readiness, in young children. This task is especially important for teachers of children with developmental delays or disabilities. This chapter focused on practical, naturalistic ways to identify and teach these skills within daily activities and routines.

Piaget's stages of cognitive development were reviewed, as were ways of observing cognitive development through children's play. Strategies for supporting early cognitive skills were described. Cognitive skills in preschoolers can be enhanced readily within the natural environment through play and curiosity. Understanding the processes of children's cognitive development can lead to strategies to stimulate problem-solving skills and academic readiness in math and science.

By giving children the freedom to explore and opportunities to learn from failure while remaining free from anxiety, early childhood educators can easily incorporate both problem-solving cognitive skills and emergent literacy into the curriculum. Examples and rationales are provided to illustrate how children can develop the skills to identify and define problems, consider alternative solutions, choose among alternatives, and evaluate results with flexible judgment. The relationship between problem solving and academic readiness becomes apparent as concepts and abstract images are translated into words that facilitate movement through the stages of problem solving.

The section on emergent literacy describes the importance of encouraging children's development of symbolic function through pretend play, storybook reading, and early writing activities. Also important is the development of the literate-style language skills and phonological and alphabet skills that are so critical to school success. Teachers should also be aware of the possible cultural differences in children's early language and literacy experiences. These differences can influence children's social adjustment and academic success in school. Finally, a brief focus on writing ends this chapter, as it is often forgotten in our zest to be sure we have prepared young children to become good readers.

Reflect and Apply

1. Explain *Rosa's Law* and clearly elaborate on what it might mean to children and families today.

2. Using the information and strategies discussed in this chapter, design a daily preschool schedule of activities in which the key literacy, language, and math skills are embedded in daily routines.

3. Discuss functional uses of print and give examples of how learning opportunities with print might be embedded throughout the school day.

4. Discuss how you would explain the importance of early literacy skills to a preschooler's family and list the type of activities that you could suggest for the home and community.

5. Identify a familiar storybook for preschoolers and use dialogic reading strategies to list specific questions that a teacher could ask children about the story. Explain the advantages of dialogic reading for young children with disabilities.

Chapter 10
Teaming

Collaboration, Problem Solving,
and Inclusion Support

Monkey Business Images/Shutterstock

⌄ Learning Outcomes

After studying this chapter, you should be able to:

10.1 Describe why successful inclusion of young children with disabilities requires establishing collaborative relationships among all key players.

10.2 Discuss the critical role of conflict resolution and communication skills in successful problem solving and program planning for young children in inclusive settings.

10.3 Explain a variety of service-delivery models that are used to facilitate inclusion and support children with disabilities in early childhood settings.

10.4 Understand why paraprofessionals are critical to the effective support of children with disabilities in inclusive environments and why special educators must develop skills to support and supervise paraprofessionals.

10.5 Identify the specific challenges and possible solutions involved in effective use of paraprofessionals as one-to-one assistants.

Earlier chapters in this text focused on understanding the needs of young children with disabilities and delineated the theories and strategies that are useful for supporting children's learning and adaptation across all developmental domains. We also discussed ways to support families. As important as these areas of knowledge and skill are, training in the area of early childhood special education cannot be complete without an appreciation of the skills and dispositions necessary for the successful inclusion of young children with disabilities in typical early childhood settings. Early childhood special educators must learn to engage in effective collaborative teaming with all key players in children's lives. This chapter examines four broad areas: collaborative teaming and problem solving, models of inclusion support, and teaming that includes management of paraprofessionals.

In Support of Inclusion of Preschoolers with Disabilities

The inclusion of children with disabilities in early childhood programs with typically developing children is a mandate of the Individuals with Disabilities Education Act, a policy of federal agencies, and supported by national professional organizations and research. The U.S. Department of Health and Human Services and the U.S. Department of Education (2016b) jointly issued the *Policy Statement on Inclusion of Children with Disabilities in Early Childhood Programs* in September 2015. Derived from a joint position statement of the National Association of the Education of Young Children (NAEYC) and Council for Exceptional Children's Division for Early Childhood (DEC), this policy statement is intended to provide recommendations to state and local educational agencies as well as the variety of early childhood programs across the country to increase inclusion of all children. It summarizes the following:

- The benefits of including young children with disabilities
- Acknowledgment that inclusion is a basic right
- Realization that inclusive programs are NOT more expensive than segregated programs
- Understanding that inclusion in high-quality early childhood programs helps children reach their potential

The policy takes the position that "all young children with disabilities should have access to inclusive high-quality early childhood programs" (p. 3). It describes both the research base and legal foundation for this position. Also included in the policy statement are the challenges common to inclusion along with a refutation of each. Each state is expected to create an interagency task force to focus on early childhood inclusion.

In support of early childhood inclusion efforts in the United States, Guralnick and Bruder (2016) reviewed the goals that were identified 15 years ago. They discussed the current status and provided recommendations for the future. It was found that the basic goal of universal access to inclusive programs had not been met. Only 38% of children were found to be fully included in early childhood classes, while the majority spend varying amount of times with typical peers in educational settings. The second goal of providing accommodations to children with disabilities and feasibility is also in process. Differentiated instruction, data-based practices, and accommodations are an integral part of many early childhood curricula. However, the feasibility of inclusion programs has been challenging given differences in the philosophies and training of early childhood and early childhood special educators. The third goal is related to developmental progress. Research has found that children with disabilities benefit from peer models. They do demonstrate developmental progress in social communication, language, and literacy skills. The final goal involved the social interaction between children with and without disabilities. Although friendships have developed in educational settings, there is still concern about the maintenance of relationships among children with diverse characteristics.

To continue progress in achieving the four goals, Guralnick and Bruder (2016) recommended a unified administrative structure for all early childhood programs, adaptation of standards for university personnel preparation programs, alignment of state early childhood certification with national standards, implementation of a team approach, and expansion of inclusion practices to community settings.

After reviewing the research on preschool inclusion programs, Lawrence, Smith, and Banerjee (2016) found that typically developing children in inclusion programs have more positive attitudes toward children with disabilities and scored higher on measures of emotional understanding compared to typically developing children who had no social contact with children with disabilities. This review identified many instructional practices that have been discussed in this text that improve the quality of preschool inclusion programs. These include use of naturally occurring routines, embedded instruction, peer-mediated strategies, social stories, and shared storybook reading.

A unique challenge to the inclusion of preschoolers with disabilities also arises from the fact that early childhood education is not typically part of public schools in the U.S. (although this is now beginning to change). As a result, while U.S. schools are mandated to provide early education to preschool age children with disabilities, there may be no logical inclusive placement within a family's neighborhood school. Administrators may be faced with the challenge of creating an inclusive classroom that may be viewed as an anomaly and not directly related to normally conceived administrative responsibilities.

A Note on "TK" (Transition Kindergarten)

A current U.S. trend is beginning to provide a possible solution to the inclusive preschool placement dilemma. Because of increasing academic demands characteristic of current kindergarten curricula (partly the result of the implementation of "Common Core" standards), many states have chosen to implement what is referred to as *transition kindergarten* (TK). This program allows states to change the age eligibility cut-off for entry into kindergarten and to offer a year of state-funded preschool education referred to as TK. Parents of children who have disabilities may be able to enroll their children in TK. Thus, they participate in an extra year of state-funded preparation before enrolling in formal kindergarten. (For more information regarding transitional kindergarten, see "Transitional Kindergarten FAQs" at the California Department of Education website: https://www.cde.ca.gov/ci/gs/em/kinderfaq.asp.)

Collaboration, Problem Solving, and Shared Decision Making

The Division for Early Childhood (DEC, 2014) recommends that "practitioners representing multiple disciplines and families work together as a team to plan and implement supports and services to meet the unique needs of each child and family" (p. 14). Effective teaming requires collaboration and communication. Friend and Cook (2017) consider **collaboration** to be a style of interaction. Thus, the first major component of skillful collaboration is effective communication. Becoming aware of one's own communication style, reading the communication cues of others, and mastering the communication skills and styles necessary for effective collaborative consultation and teaming can be a major challenge. Second is problem solving. Truly collaborative problem solving and shared decision making do not occur just because a group of people have agreed to work together. An effective team, even a friendly team, must have a step-by-step process in place for solving problems and making difficult decisions. A third important component of collaboration involves the skills related to **conflict resolution.** Sometimes teaming and problem-solving processes cannot proceed because of significant conflict and resistance. Insights into the sources of conflict and resistance and the knowledge of strategies to manage and resolve conflict are essential skills for the early childhood special educator. It is also important to realize that sometimes conflict and resistance occur because participants may not realize that it is normal for individuals from a variety of disciplines to have differing perspectives and often lack an understanding of each other's discipline.

Communication Strategies: The Key to Successful Teaming

Increasingly, one of the greatest challenges faced by early childhood special educators working in roles that require collaborative teaming and consultation is the need to develop effective communication skills and to understand the problems and barriers that can arise from certain communicative behaviors. Effective collaborators are aware of and use their own verbal and nonverbal communication in ways that encourage collegiality and consensus building. Effective teaming and collaboration also require the ability to read the communication cues of others to understand their perspectives and concerns. Sometimes a person can be well-meaning, only to be undermined by his or her own communicative behaviors, interpersonal style, or inability to listen to others.

To become aware of their own communication behaviors, early educators must carefully examine their own communication styles via recording, self-reflection, or feedback from a colleague. Then they can seek to eliminate interfering behaviors from their professional repertoire. There are several common barriers to effective communication that can undermine communicative effectiveness. These can lead to less effective communication or even breakdowns in communication. For example, giving advice too quickly or too emphatically, false reassurances, not paying attention, making abrupt topic shifts, or asking unrelated questions can quickly undermine collaboration and problem solving. Another common barrier to consensus building is trying to arrive at a "quick fix"—arriving at a solution too quickly and not taking the time to ensure genuine buy-in from team members.

Nonverbal Communication Behaviors.   Particularly important are **nonverbal communication behaviors** that speakers are often not even aware of. The old saying "It's not what you say but what you do" holds a great deal of truth when it comes to effective communication skills. Surprisingly, nonverbal communication can often have a greater effect (both positive and negative) than what the speaker actually says!

The impact and meanings of nonverbal communication are culturally determined. The positive or negative impact of a particular behavior or expression is influenced by the conventions and rules of social interaction in any given group. The successful collaborator has a good understanding of other people's cues and develops a keen awareness of the impact of his or her own nonverbal behavior. Amazingly, body language can either inflame or diffuse conflict. Thus, it is important to learn to avoid sending certain negative messages with nonverbal behaviors and to use other nonverbal behaviors to help deescalate potential conflicts. Equally important is learning to read the body language of others to better understand their perspectives and feelings. Of course, it is also possible to use body language to reduce tension and resistance. Several nonverbal elements facilitate positive interaction: facing the speaker with arms open and relaxed, mirroring the speaker's affect and movements, and providing nonverbal acknowledgment of what is being said by smiling and nodding. These acts of nonverbal communication tend to reduce conflict in mainstream culture in the United States. However, given the country's diversity, it is likely that a child's educational team may be composed of practitioners and family members representing differing cultural and linguistic backgrounds with different interpretations of nonverbal communication behaviors. For example, although smiling and nodding commonly signal understanding and agreement in U.S. mainstream culture, some Indonesians may view bared teeth as aggressive. Similarly, nodding the head may have a different meaning "among some Asian, American Indian, Middle Eastern and Pacific Island groups. It often means, 'I hear you speaking.' It does not mean that the listener understands the message [, nor] does it suggest that he or she agrees; however, because disagreeing would be impolite" (Lynch & Hanson, 2011b, p. 66). Therefore, the meaning of nonverbal behaviors may be misinterpreted.

Verbal Communication Behaviors.   Verbal communication behaviors can also have negative or positive effects on group processes and the establishment of relationships. For example, simply talking too much or interrupting can significantly interfere with collaborative efforts. Also, rather than focusing on defending one's own position, it is important to focus sincerely on understanding and reflecting on the meaning of what each person says. Perhaps one of the most effective conversational strategies is simply to stop talking and listen! Other effective strategies include use of restatements, reflection, use of "I" messages, and so on. These communication efforts and skills can have very positive benefits for children and families. *It is important to note, however, that these specific strategies are not effective in the absence of a genuine concern for the best interests of the child and family and a genuine respect for the contributions of all the **individuals involved in the inclusive setting.***

A reader of this text who is new to the topic and experience of inclusion of young children with disabilities in general early education settings might wonder why the topic of "conflict resolution" is included. How can "conflict" arise within the context and mission of providing support, acceptance, and positive experiences for very young children who have disabilities? To be sure, the sources of conflict are rarely the challenges or characteristics presented by the child. Rather, conflict is most often related to the strong passions and differing perspectives of **adults** related to how services and instruction are best delivered to children. These include challenges related to the attitudes and demands of school and program administrators, differing approaches and priorities of various service providers, and family expectations about their child's educational experiences. The following information provides only an introduction to a substantial body of knowledge and practice. The ideas and strategies described are deceptively simple; however, they are difficult to implement effectively without a great deal of practice and patience. Effective collaboration is both an art and a science.

Problem Solving and Conflict Resolution

Problem solving and shared decision making are critical processes of effective teaming. Using collaborative strategies within a problem-solving process can also be a way to reduce conflict on an ongoing basis, particularly when problem-solving techniques are routinely incorporated when making difficult decisions. Even though such a process may admittedly be time-consuming, it can be very helpful in resolving difficult issues. It will be most effective if the whole team is familiar with the process and agrees to use it in those situations where there are significant differences of opinion or when important decisions need to be made. It should also be noted that there will be some cases where use of the problem-solving process is not appropriate (Friend & Cook, 2017). For example, the problem may be outside the responsibility of the team, or there may be a general lack of willingness and commitment on the part of the team to tackle the problem.

A Traditional Problem-Solving Approach.   Many problem-solving approaches are discussed in the literature on consultation and conflict resolution. The approach presented here is adapted from the pioneering work of Kurpius (1978). It is intended as a simple but systematic way to approach situations that are interfering with the effectiveness of the team process. The following steps are recommended in this well-accepted, collaborative problem-solving process. (They are demonstrated in greater detail in the case of Paulo presented in the next section.)

- *Identify the problem.* Objectively describe and agree on the behavior or situation that is problematic. This step makes it clear what each team member knows about the solution. *Failure to agree on just what the problem is often leads to failure to solve the problem.* One helpful strategy in problem identification is to identify the discrepancy between the current situation and desired situation. (For example, the current situation is the child bites other children once or twice each day. The desired situation is that he not bite anyone at all.) Then phrase the problem in the form of a question: "What strategies can we implement to reduce the frequency of biting?"

- *Generate potential solutions.* It is important for team members to understand that the "right" solution is not yet known. Team members bring a variety of perspectives, experiences, information, expertise, and experience that can contribute to identifying solutions to a specific problem. They also share strategies and resources. Brainstorming possible solutions, with all ideas being placed on the table without being judged, can be a productive process in generating ideas.

- *Discuss and select a solution to implement.* The team formulates a plan and agrees to try a particular solution. Generally, the person who will actually have to carry out the plan should have the opportunity to select the solution to try.

Video Example from
You Tube

Enhanced eText
Video Example 10.1
Conversation with Examples of Attending and Active Listening Communication Practices https://www.youtube.com/ watch?v=pxQ?xk1s8hU This video demonstrates attending and active listening communication practices involving a speech-language pathologist in collaborative consultation with a Head Start teacher. (Also, see Video Examples 10.2 and 10.3, which also focus on collaborative skills.)

- *Implement the solution.* Write an action plan including who will do what and by what date the plan will be executed and monitored to determine effectiveness of the solution.

- *Evaluate the outcome.* Reflection and evaluation determine what worked and what did not. Based on this process, identify the next steps. If necessary, revisit the process and select another solution.

Dealing with Conflict: Perspective Taking and the Process of Conflict Resolution

Often, because there are many players and many perspectives and sometimes because successful inclusion is truly challenging, conflicts arise. The inability to resolve conflict successfully seriously undermines the consultative process and makes it more difficult to implement the problem-solving steps presented earlier. The following sections briefly describe conflict and outline conflict resolution strategies.

The Nature of Conflict.   Conflict is inevitable in any true team process. Teams of individuals bring very different backgrounds, goals, values, and perspectives to a planning and decision-making process where there are seldom definitive solutions or "proven" techniques. The more complex and intensive the child's needs, the greater the variance in the range and configuration of optimal support.

There are two main types of conflict based on targeted tasks and interpersonal relationships (DeChurch, Mesmer-Magnus, & Doty, 2013), as follows:

- **Task conflict** arises from intellectual differences and is content based. It arises because individuals naturally differ in viewpoints, opinions, priorities, intervention strategies, curriculum, philosophy, instructional practices, service-delivery models, and so on. A task conflict may be related to the less common *process* conflict that is related to disagreements about how to achieve goals or who should do what. Task conflict is inevitable and when managed properly can make a healthy contribution to the team process.

- **Relationship conflict** is personal in nature. It involves issues of ego, gender, values, culture, and status. Such factors as personality differences, fear of loss of status or control, grief, and so on can create the most difficult conflict to resolve. Frequently, relationships influence task conflict, resulting in a most challenging situation.

Sources of Resistance.   Often, an important component of conflict is **resistance**. Individuals may resist participating and cooperating in the problem-solving process or in implementing solutions. This, in turn, causes conflict. There are many possible sources of resistance. In the early childhood inclusion situation, the following are common:

- *The attitude of "If it ain't broke, don't fix it."* Sometimes an individual simply believes the situation is as good as it can be and there is no reason for change or problem solving.

- *Fear.* Individuals may be fearful of change. Job responsibilities may change. The individual may feel incompetent to take on a new role. The most common example is the early childhood educator teacher who has little or no training with young children with disabilities. Often, the teacher simply fears not knowing what to do. This is seldom a comfortable situation for anyone. An individual who fears failure or incompetence should not be viewed as a "bad" person.

- *Social resistance.* Many individuals find a great deal of comfort and social support in their jobs. Anything that threatens this feeling of security and comfort can create anxiety. In the inclusive situation, such as a day-care setting, one of the benefits of these often low-paying jobs may be social camaraderie and support. Inclusion may result in several other professionals (often more highly trained) intruding into this comfort zone.

To understand resistance, it is very important to try to understand the perspectives of other key players. For example, in many communities, early education programs are understaffed. Including a child with even a mild disability requires some kind of accommodations and increased workload (if the child's needs are really being met). Early childhood staff may resent that they are being asked to meet the needs of children with disabilities with no additional resources or income.

A lead teacher in an inclusive setting may be accustomed to being in control of the "domain": the center or classroom environment, the children, and the staff. She may feel a significant loss of status if bombarded by advice and suggestions from therapists, special educators, and parents.

Understanding Resistance. People in a variety of professions usually consider the negative consequences of change for themselves before deciding to resist it. Resistance behaviors include speaking out with opposing points of view, ridiculing the change process, boycotting meetings, and sabotaging behaviors (Hendrickson & Gray, 2012). The first step to resolve the resistance is to try to identify the fears and concerns that are the source of the resistance, as previously mentioned. The next step is to try to understand how these fears are influencing the individual's behavior (e.g., doesn't return phone calls, becomes aggressive and emotional at team meetings, does not follow through). Next, try to determine what the "resistor" wants (e.g., to feel respected, to maintain authority) or seeks to avoid (e.g., feeling humiliated, admitting a lack of expertise, taking on extra work). Finally, help the resistor achieve what he or she wants while still achieving the group's goal (e.g., give credit for good ideas, acknowledge validity of concern, etc.).

To be effective in dealing with resistance and supporting the collaborative group process, team members must be willing to let go of their own needs to control, to be given credit for having the best ideas, or to be acknowledged for being proven "right." In our competitive American culture, this is often one of the most difficult strategies to master. Most of us have a deeply ingrained need to win—to be better than the next person, to stand out from the crowd. Collaboration requires letting go of these needs.

Conflict Avoidance. Resistance can lead to conflict. Everyone has experienced the frustration and emotionality that arises out of conflict. Almost everyone (with the exception of those few individuals who "love a good fight") vigorously seeks to *avoid* conflict. However, sometimes avoidance of conflict can be as deleterious as conflict itself. The following are examples of avoidance:

Withdrawal (e.g., "Just leave me out of it")

Compromising in such a way that no one is happy

Accommodation (e.g., "OK, just do whatever you want")

Majority rule (e.g., "Let's take a vote")

In any situation in which there is a need for relationship building and ongoing collaboration, conflict avoidance usually undermines the consultation process.

Conflict Resolution Strategies. So the key question is this: How *does* one manage and resolve conflict? Several strategies can offer immediate short-term solutions.

- *Pause and take a breath.* In any situation where either you are experiencing strong emotions related to conflict or you observe it in others, do nothing and say nothing for a short period. Take a deep breath. Don't be impulsive. Assess your own emotions. Try to listen carefully to the concerns of others before speaking.

- *Try to state the issues or sides of the conflict in a neutral way.* State, for example, "Let me see if I can summarize the two different ideas here: Mrs. Rivera, you are fearful that your daughter is going to be hurt; that there are too many children and the staff cannot really protect her every moment. Janice, you seem to feel that

Mrs. Rivera is being somewhat overprotective and her concerns are not really warranted. Am I right?" This approach allows individuals to restate their position if you have not captured it correctly or to acknowledge that your statement is correct. Either way, it can be a nonconfrontational method of encouraging and valuing honest expression of differences.

- *Assess your own role honestly.* Be aware of your own role in the conflict whenever you are not truly neutral (which will probably be most of the time!). Say, for instance, "You know, I have to admit I have some of the same concerns about whether the staff are really able to monitor the situation carefully enough. I get frustrated when I think they're ignoring her."

- *Attempt to move the group toward a problem-solving approach.* Ideally, when conflicts are full-blown, an attempt should be made to use the same problem-solving approach described earlier to resolve the conflict. However, because of the emotions that are often involved, getting to this point may require significant skill on the part of the consultant.

- *Use your sense of humor.* Humor can sometimes defuse and de-escalate a tense situation.

Although these strategies may offer some short-term management of conflict, longer-term ongoing strategies must be incorporated. Certain behaviors and practices, over time, will create a collaborative atmosphere, such as the following:

- Clarifying issues before misunderstandings can occur.

- Encouraging all players to express opinions as a general operating procedure.

- Focusing on needs (e.g., child's needs, teacher's needs, parents' needs, etc.) rather than focusing too quickly on solutions.

- Facilitating open discussion by expressing your *own* feelings and biases (e.g., "I have to admit I'm really uncomfortable with this").

- Giving feedback that values others' opinions (e.g., "Oh, I see where you're coming from on this").

- Encouraging members of the group to see others' perspectives. They don't have to agree, but just acknowledge or understand. Support the notion that understanding many different perspectives results in a better understanding of the situation and generates better solutions.

Also, critical to establishing a collaborative relationship and preventing conflict is *establishing trust.* Exhibit 10.1 lists some suggestions for establishing trust.

Finally, an important longer-term strategy for dealing with conflict is for the team to incorporate a systematic problem-solving process and be willing to use it when necessary (it is hoped before a conflict crisis arises). The problem-solving process described earlier in this chapter is applied to the case of Paulo that is next presented. It provides examples of perspective taking, resistance, and effective conflict management.

Problem-Solving Case Study: Paulo

The following case sets up a typical challenge faced by key players within an inclusive setting. Critical to resolving such a problem is the process of perspective taking. Adults who are given the responsibility of implementing and evaluating effective intervention and educational programs for children like Paulo may have very different perspectives on what is best.

The "Problem" with Paulo.   Paulo has recently been enrolled in a neighborhood childcare program. The family has arranged for a one-to-one assistant for him. Marie, an early childhood special educator, is the inclusion support specialist assigned to Paulo. Paulo has autism. He has little communication ability, and his speech-language pathologist

Exhibit 10.1

Establishing Trust in Collaborative Team Problem Solving

- Listen to understand, with unhurried attention. Use phrases such as "Correct me if I'm wrong . . . " or "Let me see if I understand what you're saying . . . ."
- Keep your word.
- Learn what matters to people and try to respect that.
- Share yourself honestly.
- Share your expertise without dominating the conversation.
- Solicit others' opinions.
- Trust others; trusting others often results in them trusting you. (Don't push others to trust you more than you trust them.)

Source: Information adapted from Bridges (2009), *Managing Transitions: Making the Most of Change*, Nicholas Brealey Publishing, 2011.

believes his tantrums are related to his inability to communicate. Therefore, she has introduced an alternative communication procedure known as the Picture Exchange Communication System (PECS) originally developed by Frost and Bondy (2002). This system uses specific procedures to teach the child to select and give the adult a picture (or pictures) in exchange for a desired object or activity. The inclusion support specialist is teaching Evelyn, the one-to-one assistant, to implement the procedure. She believes that if the rest of the staff would also learn the PECS procedure, two important objectives could be achieved: Paulo would have a functional communication system, and his disruptive behavior would decrease (Sulzer-Azaroff, Hoffman, Horton, Bondy, & Frost, 2009).

The early childhood staff is fairly skeptical of the effectiveness of the recommended PECS procedures. They believe Paulo's tantrums are increasing and are frustrated about whether Paulo can be successfully included in their center. The team has reached a crisis point.

Possible Perspectives of Key Players in Paulo's Case. Members of this team clearly bring different perspectives to the table. The following sections describe these perspectives.

Inclusion Support Specialist.   Marie, the special educator on the team, strongly believes that Paulo's behavior problems are related to his lack of functional communication. She wants Paulo to be successful in this setting. She is highly invested in teaching Paulo to use the PECS procedure but believes it will require the cooperation of the staff and time to train them. She believes she knows how best to support Paulo, but she is frustrated by the staff's lack of commitment to learning the PECS procedure and their narrow concern about how to control his disruptive behavior. She believes they are moving toward a single agenda: to have him removed from the program. She feels Paulo's mother expects her to be able to solve this problem as well as teach him to communicate. Marie is starting to feel like her credibility is on the line.

Paulo's Mother.   Mrs. Johnson, Paulo's mother, does not think he belongs in a special education class, but she realizes his behavior is jeopardizing his inclusive placement. She has an additional burden in that she needs to work and requires child care for Paulo. She is worried that she has seen little progress. It was her understanding that Marie would know how to help Paulo, but now she is not so sure. Mrs. Johnson is beginning to sense some negative feelings from Jenny, the teacher, and suspects she dislikes Paulo.

Early Childhood Teacher. Jenny is a very committed early childhood teacher. She enjoys her work and accepted Paulo willingly into her classroom. However, she has little experience with children with disabilities. She was definitely not prepared for the challenges presented by Paulo. She is amazed that even with the one-to-one assistant, he is totally disrupting the classroom. She feels overwhelmed and is beginning to dread going to work each day. She feels pressure from Marie to implement the communication training procedures. Although she knows Marie is the "expert," Jenny can't see how the procedure will reduce his temper tantrums. She's beginning to see reactions from the other children in the class. Jenny also feels guilty. She knows how much Mrs. Johnson wants Paulo to stay in the program.

Child-Care Administrator. Ms. Murillo, the child-care program administrator, understands that legally there is increasing pressure on the center to enroll children with disabilities. She is resigned to doing this and interested in putting mechanisms in place to support these children. However, she had no idea what would be involved and how time-consuming it could be. She hopes Paulo is an unusual case. She is amazed at how much effort is being expended for this one child. She is increasingly concerned about the effect it is having on Jenny, the best teacher at the center. Ms. Murillo is aware that the pressure on Jenny and Jenny's feeling that she is being critiqued and falling short of other people's expectations could lead her to resign. Ms. Murillo is also starting to feel some resentment toward Marie. Mrs. Murillo's limited experiences with school district personnel and therapists have not been particularly positive. She believes they look down on child-care staff. She feels generally frustrated that she has to manage the child-care program on such a meager budget. She feels it is unfair.

One-to-One Assistant. Evelyn has worked with just one other child. He was nothing like Paulo. She is increasingly unhappy with this job. The PECS procedure is complicated, and she's not convinced it will work. She realizes the early childhood education (ECE) teacher thinks she should be able to control Paulo's tantrums. She also gets the impression that Marie is not satisfied with how she is doing the communication training. She sees her only once a week. She is starting to feel paranoid that she is not pleasing anyone. She's also not sure who her boss is. A job at Starbucks is sounding better all the time.

Speech-Language Pathologist (SLP Consultant). The SLP, although not involved in Paulo's support on a regular basis, is very confident that her insights and recommendations are valid and should be implemented. She is surprised that Marie, the special education itinerant, is having such a difficult time getting the staff to implement the PECS procedure.

Enhanced eText Application Exercise 10.1: In this exercise, apply what you have learned in this chapter to identify different types of conflict and strategies to address them.
Enhanced eText Application Exercise 10.2: In this exercise you can apply what you have learned in this book about challenging behaviors and generating possible solutions using the problem-solving process.

Models for Supporting Children with Disabilities in Inclusive Settings

Children with disabilities who are served in typical community-based group settings are supported in a variety of ways. As discussed earlier, there is strong agreement on the value and importance of fully including young children in programs with their typical peers. However, currently there are no generally accepted standards or guidelines for whether, when, and how inclusion *support* is to be provided for children from birth to age 5. The requirement for "individualized" services remains a key component of both the individualized education program (IEP) and the individualized family service plan (IFSP), regardless of *where* the child is served. The particular model of support for a child in an inclusive setting must also be individualized and will depend on several factors, including the strengths and needs of the child, preferences of the family, and characteristics of available settings.

Richardson-Gibbs and Klein (2014) describe a variety of service-delivery models for support within these settings. These include itinerant direct teaching, itinerant collaborative consultation, team teaching, in-service training of the early childhood teacher, a reverse mainstreaming model with a special educator as the teacher, and use of a paraprofessional as a one-to-one assistant (with or without supervision). Also, for various reasons, some children are placed in early childhood settings with no support. The features and advantages of these service-delivery models are considered next.

No Support

There does not appear to be agreement among decision makers as to whether a young child with a disability placed in a community-based setting *always* needs some kind of support. For example, the early childhood staff may be considered highly skilled and quite capable and willing to make whatever modifications are necessary for the child to participate. Another example might be a case where parents feel that their own communications with the staff are sufficient to support the child in a given setting. (There are also cases where a child and the staff need support, but the support simply is not available or has not been appropriately requested.) A challenge in these situations is determining who is responsible for progress toward achieving the child's IEP goals.

Use of One-to-One Assistant

Many issues have emerged around the use of one-to-one assistants (also known as shadow aides, inclusion support aides, therapeutic companions, coaches, etc.). In this model, a specific adult is assigned to a particular child for the purpose of providing some specific assistance or support to the child that the existing program staff cannot readily provide. Issues include lack of training, need for supervision, roles, and responsibility—and the possible deleterious impact on children's independence and peer interactions (Giangreco, Suter, & Doyle, 2010). In some cases, the one-to-one assistant is the only support. In others, the one-to-one assistant is trained for a specific role and works under the supervision of an early childhood special educator or other professional. It has been our observation that in a quality early childhood setting, when appropriate support and consultation are provided by a specialist in a collaborative spirit, the need for one-to-one assistance can often be eliminated or significantly reduced to a short-term basis.

Staff In-Service Models

In-service training of early childhood program staff is frequently the primary vehicle for ensuring support for a young child with disabilities. In these cases, the staff is provided with training related to the kinds of strategies and specific interventions that are often helpful in working with young children with disabilities. However, for the most effective outcomes, in-service training should be provided in conjunction with other models of support such as coaching, performance feedback, and ongoing monitoring of instructional practices including analysis of videos (Lawrence, Smith, & Banerjee, 2016).

Itinerant Consultation Model of Inclusion Support

One of several models of inclusion support is the itinerant approach. As stated earlier, an **itinerant** is an individual who travels from one site to another to provide support for children with disabilities at each site. A typical itinerant caseload might be 15 to 20 children, depending on the number of targeted children at each site and the distances from one site to the next. Frequency of visits typically ranges from once a week to once a month.

As Dinnebeil and McIneney (2011) pointed out, some itinerants simply engage in the same kinds of direct instruction activities they used when they were teachers in specialized settings. They may provide the direct intervention either on a pullout basis or within the inclusive classroom. Although there is often some communication with the early childhood staff, little interaction occurs with children without disabilities, and the primary focus is on children with disabilities. This *itinerant direct instruction* role (also sometimes referred to as an *itinerant teacher*) tends to isolate the children with disabilities from the rest of the class and unfortunately may further the belief of the early childhood staff that the children must receive specialized services in order to be included. Appendix D contains several forms designed to ensure success with an itinerant consultation model.

Another itinerant model—one that in most cases is more appropriate as an ongoing support model for young children in inclusive settings—is an **itinerant consultant model**. The consultant role is a relatively less familiar role for most early childhood special educators than is a direct teaching role. The complexity of consultation includes working across a variety of settings, with multiple people, to address a range of concerns. An effective consultant requires not only professional competence, but also strong interpersonal skills, ethics, and cultural sensitivity (Wesley & Buysee, 2006).

The traditional role of the special education teacher in a special education preschool classroom or early intervention center–based program is *very different* from the role of an itinerant consultant. As a consultant, the early childhood special educator does not have direct responsibility for the teaching and learning of the children in a classroom. Instead, he or she has a more *indirect* responsibility for assisting children within a larger group of typical peers *via his or her relationships with other adults*. In addition to the skills and knowledge required for working with children with specific needs in a traditional special education class setting, additional skills are needed to engage children with disabilities successfully with their typical peers in inclusive environments. Furthermore, because the implementation of these teaching and support strategies will be carried out by the early childhood staff, the ability to work effectively with a variety of other adults, in a variety of settings, is also essential.

Collaborative Consultation Model.   A well-established consultation approach in education today is the **collaborative consultation model** (Buysse & Wesley, 2005). This model is best used when a group commitment is needed for the successful performance of the child and when more than one solution may resolve the problem. For example, if there are a number of possible approaches to reducing the tantrums of a child in a preschool setting, it may be necessary to assess the preferences, skills, and philosophies of all the individuals who are involved in working with the child before obtaining a commitment to a particular intervention plan. Because a collaborative consultation approach involves a group, there are two dimensions to consider in this type of consultation: the development of a resolution to the problem (the task) and the social dynamics and effects of effective group interaction (social dimension).

A key feature of collaborative consultation is the reciprocity and mutuality that must exist between the consultant and the consultee. According to Devore, Miolo, and Hader (2011), collaborative consultation involves a relationship involving a team of specialists and early childhood providers. In this relationship, each person contributes particular expertise to solving specific problems. DeVore and colleagues recommend identifying a lead consultant who will share information and obtain feedback from relevant others. This also implies that effective consultation must be an *ongoing process.* The effective consultant must collaborate in the processes of gathering information, identifying goals and strategies for implementation, and monitoring progress.

Each player (in our case, the early childhood inclusion support consultant and the early childhood teacher or caregiver) brings something of equal value to the problem-solving process. Although their contributions may be quite different, the collaborative process produces solutions that could not have been generated by either party independently. The process may often require the leadership and facilitation of the itinerant consultant, but the problem solving must occur as a result of mutual contribution and reciprocal interactions.

According to Friend and Cook (2017), collaboration must include parity in the relationship, shared goals, shared accountability, trust and respect, shared resources, and shared responsibility for decision making. Critical prerequisites to successful collaboration include effective communication skills and the ability to engage in interactions that support the processes of shared problem solving.

A Note on Disability Specialists and Therapists in Itinerant Service-Delivery Roles

This discussion of appropriate itinerant roles and practices is also relevant to many disability specialists and therapists who provide on-site services to children. Each specialist is typically focused on one particular developmental area. Even though the role of these specialized service providers is not necessarily to support and monitor the overall achievement and well-being of the child or the quality of the child's daily participation in the inclusive setting, the model of service delivery used is an itinerant model: either a direct service or a consultant model, or a combination of the two. Thus, much of the discussion here, including the specific strategies described in the next section, can also be applied to these very important members of the team.

Specific Support Strategies Provided by Itinerants

The itinerant consultant must view inclusion support as a shared venture, that is, a collaborative partnership with the early childhood staff. Within that context, the following are examples of specific support strategies and activities used by itinerant consultants. It should be noted that these same strategies are often used by co-teachers as well.

Providing Information.   Obviously, a significant portion of the itinerant consultant's job is to provide information to the early childhood staff. It is important to realize that not all information is wanted or useful and therefore may not be ultimately beneficial for the child.

The following guidelines are suggested for providing information to staff:

- Always follow up on staff requests for information. If you don't have the information, attempt to obtain it.

- Provide information in the most efficient, unobtrusive ways possible.

- Ask the staff for their preferences for receiving information—for example, do they prefer a brief discussion during your visit or after the visit? In the classroom or outside the classroom? Verbally or in writing? On NCR forms or in a notebook? During a team meeting, via e-mail, or over the phone?

Enhanced eText
Video Example 10.2
Conversation with Examples of Seeking and Verifying Information
https://www.youtube.com/watch?v=mUPG5Thlux8

Enhanced eText
Video Example 10.3
Conversation with Examples of Joining and Supporting
https://www.youtube.com/watch?v=5Z3PuPxjUq8
These two videos complete the demonstration of communication skills (that began with Video Example 10.1) involving a speech-language pathologist and Head Start teacher in collaborative consultation.

- Offer mini-in-services on topics of interest or importance to staff.
- Determine the best way for staff to provide you with information or observations and to ask questions. Information *must* flow in both directions.

Observing. Observation is an important activity for the itinerant consultant. The itinerant must carefully observe to understand the rules, routines, and culture of the classroom. She must observe the child's behavior in different activities and with different individuals. She must also observe how others interact with the child and the antecedents and consequences of the child's inappropriate behaviors.

Modeling. In a **modeling** strategy, the itinerant demonstrates a particular strategy while a staff member watches. For example, he or she may demonstrate how to fade a hand-over-hand prompt or how to scaffold a difficult task to provide just the right amount of assistance for the child. Simply modeling a procedure may not be sufficient to enable the staff to actually carry it out on their own, however. Modeling is best used in combination with coaching. That is, the inclusion specialist would demonstrate the procedure, then step back and encourage the staff member to do it. (It will be difficult for early childhood programs with limited staff to incorporate intensive complex procedures on a daily basis. Unrealistic expectations may result in staff feeling guilty or resentful.)

Coaching. **Coaching** can be an effective technique to assist staff members in learning specific strategies that may be helpful in supporting or teaching the child. However, coaching requires a positive trusting relationship between the itinerant and staff member. Coaching may be more effective following ample use of modeling, described earlier. The itinerant observes the staff member and child in the activity of concern (e.g., free play or snack time) and makes direct suggestions in real time as the activity proceeds. This is an example of an expert consultation approach and can be threatening if not done carefully.

Using Developmentally Appropriate Activities. Sometimes the early childhood staff may not realize that a child's disruptive behavior or reluctance to participate may be due to the fact that the child is developmentally younger than the other children in the class. In this case, the materials, curricular objectives, and behavioral expectations in the class may be inappropriate for the child. Beginning with *developmentally appropriate* expectations and activities may ease the challenge of certain activities or situations in the classroom. The following is an example:

Tina and the Blocks

Tina is reluctant to engage in any interactions with the other children. She tends to isolate herself and sometimes engages in repetitive self-stimulatory behaviors. Marie, the itinerant consultant, notices several very large blocks piled in one corner of the room where other children are playing with smaller blocks. Marie moves to the corner and begins to pile up the large blocks. Tina is intrigued by this simple activity, and she approaches Marie's large tower and immediately knocks it down. Tina claps with excitement. A little boy in the vicinity joins in the activity, piling the blocks again. When the tower is precariously tall, Tina knocks it down again. The typical peers clap and shout along with Tina. They continue taking turns in this thoroughly enjoyable game.

Admittedly, this game is developmentally much younger than might be considered appropriate for the typical peer. But it is appropriate for Tina and provides an entry for her into a turn-taking game with peers the same age.

Using Direct Instruction. Occasionally, even in a consultation model, direct intervention may be necessary to work on a particular skill to enable the child to fully participate in a particular activity. The itinerant may spend time directly teaching the child a skill or may implement a specific behavioral consequence over a period of time. Generally, however, because the itinerant is not consistently present in the classroom, this strategy may have less-than-satisfactory effects.

Adapting Curriculum or Materials. As Guralnick (2000) long ago pointed out, it is not feasible to assume that an existing program can or should totally modify its curriculum in an effort to accommodate the needs of one child. In some cases, however, the itinerant may suggest relatively unobtrusive adaptations. The following example demonstrates such an adaptation with Tina:

Tina Learns to Pretend

The typical children in the class are participating in a tabletop activity that supports the school readiness goals of sorting, grouping, and matching. The materials include various figures (e.g., animals, adults, and children) and cars and small colored blocks of different shapes. Because Tina has Down syndrome and is developmentally younger, she is not interested in the activity and tends to simply push the small figures around the table, annoying the other children. When Marie, the itinerant consultant, notices this, she places two large, flat blocks on the table. She takes one of the figures and lays it on the block, saying, "Look. This boy is sleepy. He's sleeping on his bed. Night night!" Tina immediately focuses her attention. She shuts her eyes and pretends to sleep, and says, "Night. Go sleep." The itinerant prompts her to take another figure. Tina immediately places the figure on the second block and says, "Her night, night." At this point, a typical peer next to Tina places a dog figure on the bed and says, "This doggie's tired too! He wants to go to bed."

Here, Marie has demonstrated for the staff that by introducing a more cognitively appropriate (and consequently more engaging) adaptation, she can encourage a pretend play activity, which is an appropriate developmental objective for Tina.

Another example of an adaptation is a simple physical adaptation:

Good Positioning for Tina Encourages Participation

Tina is smaller than the other children, and the chairs in the classroom are too big for her. Tina's feet do not touch the floor. Although she is able to sit in the chair without her feet flat on the floor, she is less stable and more likely to fidget and swing her feet. This may interfere with her ability to focus on the activity at hand and may even interfere with her fine motor skills. Marie suggests that taping together phone books to place under Tina's feet might stabilize her and make it easier for her to maintain a solid sitting position. The staff was unaware that the size of the chairs might be contributing to Tina's fidgeting, and they were appreciative of this suggestion.

It is important for the itinerant to offer to make these adaptations herself rather than simply telling the teachers how to do them. In many cases, the early childhood staff does not have the time or resources to make modifications, even if they are simple. In an itinerant model, staff buy-in of suggested procedures or adaptations is critical. The itinerant is in the classroom on a limited basis, for relatively short periods. If staff do not become invested in a particular strategy, if the strategy is too difficult, if they do not have sufficient resources and time to implement it, or if they do not think it makes sense, then it is likely that the procedure will not be used consistently or appropriately. In other words, the expert consultant approach without good communication and a strong, collaborative relationship will probably not be effective.

Adapting the Environment. In some instances, adaptation of the environment is critical to a child's successful inclusion. Take, for example, a child who is partially sighted or blind. Creating clear, well-marked pathways from center to center will be essential. For the child who is blind, marking key materials and areas of the room with different textures or Braille labels will provide important cues and—together with collaboration with an orientation and mobility specialist—will contribute to the child's independence.

Coaching Peers.   It is no surprise that, particularly for children with more severe disabilities, typical peers need some assistance in learning how to relate and establish friendships. Thus, coaching peers is another useful strategy that the itinerant can demonstrate for the staff. Tina has very limited communication ability. She is able to select photo representations of desired objects or play activities. Marie is coaching two little girls who have taken an interest in Tina to use the photos for communication. Because Tina has been trained previously to use this communication strategy, it results in a very positive (and genuine) engagement among the girls.

Assisting Staff in the Classroom.   The itinerant consultant should sometimes be available to provide assistance in the classroom. This can be valuable to the staff when they are shorthanded. It also provides an opportunity for the itinerant to participate with the other children while at the same time observing the child with a disability from a distance.

Involving Parents.   Parents are essential to the successful inclusion of a child with a disability in a community-based setting. Early childhood staff may not be accustomed to facilitating active involvement of the family in the day-to-day progress or activities of the child in the center or ensuring clear and consistent communication. The itinerant can provide crucial assistance in involving the parents in ways that best meet the family's needs. In some situations, families may prefer that the itinerant consultant serve as a liaison between the parents and the early childhood staff. She should communicate with the family via phone calls and provide them copies of her written notes after each visit. Family members must also be viewed as important team members and be invited to attend all team meetings.

The itinerant can provide assistance to the family in many different ways. For example, she may need to help parents understand the difference between the early childhood setting and a child's special education setting (e.g., limitations on resources, differences in philosophy, curriculum, etc.). She may need assistance determining if the child needs a one-to-one assistant. The itinerant also may need to serve as a liaison between the parent and early childhood staff. The itinerant should also clarify with the parents what the expectations are for the setting: Is it primarily to provide a safe child-care environment? Is the goal to provide social interaction opportunities with typical peers? Or, is the family assuming that all the child's IEP goals and therapeutic needs can be met in the early childhood program?

Coordinating and Meeting with the Team.   Although admittedly difficult to schedule in many early childhood programs, the itinerant must recognize the importance of regular meetings, including as many of the key players as possible. (Key players might include teachers and paraprofessionals, one-to-one assistant, program administrator, inclusion support specialist, therapists, and family members.) Such meetings are often difficult for early childhood programs whose budgets may not allow for the necessary time allocations. However, some kind of regular meeting schedule can often prevent many problems and may actually save time in the long run. It should be assumed that from time to time problems and conflicts are inevitable. In this event, it is critical to have a systematic way of addressing them.

The early childhood staff should be asked for their suggestions and preferences for when and where meetings might best be conducted. The itinerant must be realistic and not have expectations for the early childhood staff that cannot be met.

One of the challenges of serving children in inclusive settings is the increased number of key players and the need for and difficulty of coordinating the services and communication among them. Even when the special education services are housed within one agency or program, placement of a child in a community-based program by definition results in the need for coordination between two agencies. The more intense or complex the child's needs, the greater the coordination challenge.

In addition, when numerous specialists and therapists are involved in attempting to provide services on-site, a stressful situation can sometimes result for the early childhood program staff (and perhaps the child). Thus, the need to coordinate the activities of these service specialists becomes a significant priority. In many cases, however, no single individual has the responsibility for coordinating the team. An early childhood special education inclusion specialist may be in the best position to understand all the service-delivery needs of the child and family, and thus in the best position to coordinate them. Note also that genuine and effective team collaboration takes effort, skill, and practice.

Building a collaborative relationship within an itinerant model does not occur automatically, even when all parties are friendly, willing participants. It is an ongoing and continuously evolving process. Certain itinerant practices enhance this process, whereas others impede or undermine it. Ideally, the itinerant consultant develops mutually satisfying relationships with the key stakeholders at each site. Over time he or she can contribute to increasing the knowledge, skill, and comfort level of the early childhood staff in ways that enhance their own confidence, acceptance, and enjoyment of the child with disabilities.

Enhanced eText Application Exercise 10.3: In this exercise, you can apply what you have learned in this chapter about models of service delivery for teaching children with IEPs in preschool inclusion programs.

Co-Teaching Approaches to Inclusion Support

Much of the previous discussion related to itinerant consultant service delivery can also be applied to another common inclusion support model: that of co-teaching. But there are also some key challenges and strategies that are particularly characteristic of co-teaching support arrangements.

Co-Teaching Defined

In a **co-teaching** approach to inclusion support, an early childhood educator and a special educator share the classroom responsibilities. Co-teaching involves "general and special educators planning, delivering, and assessing instruction together in a single classroom" (Brown, Howerter, & Morgan, 2013, p. 85).

Friend and Cook (2013, 2017) suggest the following definitive characteristics of co-teaching:

- Two or more professionals
- Joint delivery of instruction (a co-teacher is not just an "extra pair of hands")
- Students with diverse learning needs
- Shared classroom space

The roles and responsibilities of each co-teacher in this model depend on several factors, including child needs, teacher preferences, classroom configuration, the nature of the activity, and the availability of other staff.

Challenges of Co-Teaching

Some unique challenges are associated with co-teaching. First, individuals must *work closely* with one another daily. (Experienced co-teachers often describe the relationship as being similar to a marriage [Murawski, 2009]). This requires team members to become aware of their own work style. For example, one teacher may be highly organized and have difficulty with change, whereas another may be creative and easily bored. Persons who have a strong need to be the leader rather than a follower and need to feel in control may have difficulty sharing the leadership and working collaboratively.

Co-teaching partners must often negotiate their differences in teaching *philosophy and values,* such as their attitudes toward inclusion, their knowledge and understanding of the characteristics of specific disabilities, or their beliefs about the most effective strategies and accommodations for children with disabilities. Probably more important than any other single factor is that *co-teachers must value and respect one another's philosophy and skills.* When this mutual respect is lacking, the effectiveness of the strategies suggested in this text will be significantly weakened.

Another significant challenge of co-teaching is the need for *planning time.* Successful co-teaching cannot occur without careful planning, debriefing, and evaluating results. In most cases, finding sufficient time for these activities (especially for hourly child-care staff) requires the support and involvement of program administrators. In fact, experts on co-teaching repeatedly point out that without co-planning, teachers tend to teach without differentiation strategies and resort to a one-teach/one-support model (Murawski, 2012).

Components of Effective Co-Teaching

Co-teaching has four critical components. The first is *adequate planning,* including adequate time, as mentioned earlier, and the development of appropriate preparation procedures. Another is the design of appropriate *co-teaching structures* (i.e., who does what in which activities). Another component (essential for all effective teamwork, not just a co-teaching approach) is an ongoing commitment to effective *collaboration and conflict resolution.* Finally, obtaining *administrative buy-in and support* is essential. Each of these is discussed briefly.

Planning and Evaluation.   The co-teaching team must consider two areas. The team must plan the specific adaptations and supports that are likely to be needed by the child to ensure maximum participation and achievement of IEP goals. In addition, they must determine who will do what (i.e., specific co-teaching structures). Although some support activities become routinized, others vary depending on the activity, needs of the child, and available personnel.

Co-teaching teams should plan together (professionals and paraprofessionals) and plan the role of each adult. For daily routine activities, teams may wish to assign standing responsibilities and simply revisit them periodically to make sure the team members are happy with their assignments. For atypical events (such as a field trip, a special presentation in the classroom, etc.), potential challenges need to be identified and specific adult roles and responsibilities planned and written down. (In some cases, peer roles can also be planned, such as the assignment of a peer buddy.) This will help maximize the learning and participation of each child with disabilities without hovering over children and providing *too much* support. The following are some of the critical steps that should be included when collaborating:

1. Identify a *consistent* time to meet. Consistency is a key, even if the meeting is for a short period or every other week rather than every week. If it is impossible for all team members to attend every meeting, rotate participation. Meet in an environment that can be free of distractions.

2. Begin the meeting by reflecting on the events and experiences since the previous meeting: What worked? What went wrong? What should be changed? What new understanding can be gleaned related to the child's needs or learning style?

3. Plan activities in detail: What activities and strategies will be continued with no change? What are new activities? When are they scheduled? Who will do what? What materials are needed?

4. Plan accommodations and teaching strategies to both support the child's full participation and reach the child's IEP or IFSP goals—within the daily schedule and daily routines or within a specific activity. *Do not lose sight of specific IEP goals for each child. Participation in daily activities is not enough.*

5. Plan or revise co-teaching structures based on each child's needs, the nature of the activity, resources available for support, and teacher styles and preferences (i.e., what roles or tasks does each adult do best and enjoy the most?).

6. When preparing a new or unique activity (e.g., visiting a bakery), consider possible challenges or negative reactions from children. (See the example of Elijah later in this chapter.) How will they be handled?

7. Evaluate the plan. Carefully debrief results and revisit plans during the next meeting.

The form presented in Exhibit 10.2 may be helpful in conducting efficient preparation. In addition to considering each staff member's role in a certain activity, it will also be necessary to plan for the implementation of certain teaching strategies to help children master specific skills and reach IEP goals. In addition, it is wise to procure specific accommodations as necessary to ensure the child's fullest participation in classroom activities.

Exhibit 10.2

Co-Teaching Planning Form: Assignment of Roles and Responsibilities

Date: _____   Child: _____

Members Present: _____

I. Review of previous period:

    What worked?

    What went wrong?

    What should be changed?

II. Evaluation of IEP progress:

    Goals:

    #1

    #2

    #3

    Etc.

III. Planning for the next period (who will do what and when?):

    A. Regular procedures to continue:

    B. Special events, new activities coming up:

        Possible challenges for this child:

        Specific support strategies (Who will do what?):

        Any preparation/preteaching necessary?

IV. Date of next meeting: _____

Designing Co-Teaching Structures.   Different methods of configuring the co-teaching roles and responsibilities are referred to here as structures. There are no limits on the types of **structures** that can be designed. Also, as mentioned earlier, some structures may be routinized, whereas others need to be specifically planned for certain activities or children. The types of co-teaching structures, or configurations, are determined by the needs and creativity of each inclusion team. The following are examples of common co-teaching structures (Friend, 2016).

One Teaching–One Supporting.   The easiest co-teaching structure is the one teaching–one supporting structure. In this case, one teacher (usually, the early childhood teacher) leads the activity, while the early childhood special education (ECSE) teacher provides assistance to children with disabilities as needed. This co-teaching structure is clearly the easiest because it requires the least planning and collaboration. The disadvantage of this commonly used structure is that often the special educator plays the role of a paraprofessional rather than a true collaborating teacher (Scruggs, Mastropieri, & McDuffie, 2007). Decisions about the nature of supporting activities or accommodations may lack careful consideration. Although this structure may be effective in encouraging some level of child participation and for immediate troubleshooting, it may be less effective in meeting specific and challenging IEP goals.

Complementary Teaching.   In complementary teaching, the ECSE teacher provides highly specialized support to one child, teaching very specific skills. These skills are carefully selected to enable the child eventually to participate in the activity independently. Complementary teaching can be best used when the required assistance is not so intrusive as to require the intensive teaching strategies of preteaching (described later). The ECSE teacher performs a task analysis for the required skill and teaches the skill by using various decreasing prompt strategies during the activity. The prompts are faded, and the strategy eventually leads to the child's ability to perform independently. The following is an example:

> Joshua was not able to clear his table setting after snack and tended to wander and engage in disruptive behavior. Usually, an adult would provide total assistance to Joshua to try to encourage him to participate in learning to clear his table. But there had been no improvement in his ability to perform the task independently. The ECSE teacher and the early childhood teacher discussed the need to prioritize teaching Joshua this skill. Using a complementary teaching structure, the ECSE teacher was assigned to provide direct instruction to Joshua each day after snack time. By using such teaching strategies as backward chaining, hand-over-hand assistance, and decreasing prompts, Joshua quickly learned to clear his table and throw waste materials in the trash.

Preteaching.   Another example is preteaching. Occasionally, there is an activity that requires skills too difficult for a particular child to learn within the context of the activity via complementary teaching. Or, it may be necessary to prepare a child to participate in a new activity or some novel event. In this case, the team may design a structure in which the special education teacher provides direct one-to-one instruction on the skill briefly each day until the child is sufficiently independent to be able to participate within the activity with minimal prompts and cues. An example might be working with a child to learn to set the table a few minutes each day before children come in for snack until the child can do it quickly and independently at the typical time. Consider the following example:

Elijah Gets Ready for Picture Day

> The annual "Picture Day" is coming up in 1 month. Elijah has great difficulty handling flashing lights, strangers, and changes in routine. Picture Day will pose a significant challenge for Elijah! His teachers meet with Elijah's mom to develop a preteaching plan. The ECSE teacher will develop a small-group Picture Day play script with pretend cameras. Several children

play Picture Day during free play over the next few weeks. In addition, the ECSE teacher develops a simple program to help Elijah learn to sit still on a stool and tolerate the flash of a camera. She uses successive approximations. She does this each day, just before snack, which is Elijah's favorite activity. At home, Elijah's mom begins to mention Picture Day frequently to Elijah, using positive affect and counting the number of days until the day the pictures will be taken. Use of this preteaching structure not only helped prevent a disaster on Picture Day but also introduced a very popular pretend play scenario in which Elijah was a willing participant.

Station Teaching.   Station teaching is used to support children's learning and participation in centers. In this co-teaching structure, the ECSE teacher is strategically assigned to the center that will pose the greatest challenge for certain children. For example, if several children need assistance and support for development of fine motor skills, the art center may be the most logical center to which to assign the teacher. Or, if there are children who experience particular behavioral challenges in more open-ended activities, the ECSE teacher is assigned to the block area or dramatic play area. The ECSE teacher can share specific strategies or techniques with other adults so over time they will feel comfortable implementing the interventions themselves. The following is an example of station teaching:

Having a Picnic

In circle time, the teacher will read a book about going on a picnic, ask questions, and use props to involve the children's active participation and teach new vocabulary. To follow up on the picnic theme, three centers are planned for the week before the summer break. One is a play area with a blanket on the floor and play food items to put in baskets for a "pretend" picnic outdoors. The second is a center for voting for favorite foods to take on a picnic. Five easels, each with a large chart with a different picture of food on it, are arranged in a row; children are told to identify three favorite foods by writing their name or initials on relevant charts. The third is a collage activity that involves pasting pictures of food on paper plates and feathers.

Of the three centers, the voting for favorite foods activity requires the greatest understanding of language, number concepts, task sequencing, persistence, and fine motor skills. Two of the children with disabilities will need considerable encouragement to participate in this activity. In addition, both children have IEP goals related to identifying and naming familiar foods, learning to count from 1 to 10, and writing their name. Thus, the ECSE teacher is assigned to this "station." She carefully plans the support techniques and accommodations that will assist each child in participating as fully as possible and in making progress toward IEP goals.

The IEP: The Key to Successful Inclusion

Improvement of social skills in daily activities obviously is a common and important IEP goal for many children in inclusive settings. Social skills can be readily supported simply by supporting full participation and peer interactions in daily activities. However, some IEP goals require careful consideration and implementation of a variety of teaching strategies (and perhaps collaboration with other disciplines) to ensure their achievement. Modifying certain behaviors (e.g., encouraging a child to wear eyeglasses or a hearing aid), making progress toward mastery of specific skills (e.g., learning to recognize one's name in print), and achievement of certain developmental milestones (e.g., self-feeding) require consideration and design of specific teaching strategies, including the embedding of teaching opportunities and practice within daily activities, referred to as *embedded learning opportunities* (Horn & Banerjee, 2009). Early educators not only must be able to identify and plan opportunities in which IEP goals can be addressed, but they must also go a step further and design specific teaching or adaptation strategies that will move the child closer to mastering each goal. The Objectives-by-Activity Matrix in Exhibit 10.3 is an example of such preparation using embedded learning opportunities.

Exhibit 10.3

Embedded Learning Opportunities Objective-by-Activity Planning Matrix

Child's Name LISA (L)   **Date:** _____

Goals Adaptations/Strategies

Goals / Activity:	Social Increase tolerance for proximity to peers. Acknowledge peers using social communications.	Language Increase functional communication (requests). Increase use of spoken vocabulary.	Motor Develop motor planning and accuracy to increase efficiency and independence in play and daily routines.	Preacademic Enjoy looking at books. Develop alphabetic principle; understand relationship of print to language.	Self-Care/ Independence Move through daily routine without prompts. Use utensils and cup for self-feeding without assistance.
Arrival Transition Cue: Natural cue to play area	Teacher (T) greets L and provides imitative prompt for L to say "Good morning" to peer.	T uses pause-and-wait strategy to encourage L to request help taking off her backpack.	T uses physical scaffolding to help L hang jacket and backpack on hook.	T says, "Find your cubby," directing L's attention to name/ picture card on the cubby.	T uses backward-chaining procedure to help L motor plan her sequence of entering room, placing items in her cubby, and walking to play area.
Free Play Transition Cue: Lights on/off for cleanup	T helps L tolerate proximity of peers by inviting peer to sit on mat at a comfortable distance from L, commenting to L, "It's great to have a friend to play with, isn't it!"	T uses violation-of-routines strategy by placing L's favorite musical toy out of sight. When L approaches teacher and vocalizes her distress, T immediately says, "Oh my—let's find your music box!"	If L has difficulty activating a toy she has selected, T provides (then fades) physical prompts.	T directs L's attention to labels on LEGO bins and plastic dinosaur bins, encouraging choice.	T waits for L to select toy.
Circle Transition Cue: "Let's line up for recess" (T points to door)	T allows L to remain outside the circle until all children are settled, then moves her closer to the group, prompting her to "show me where you'd like to sit."	T uses verbal imitative prompt for L to request her favorite song "Little Red Caboose" by saying, "Train song" (L already uses the word *train* when playing with the train in the block area).	For songs with motions, T provides physical prompts as needed. During an active dancing activity, L is allowed to move away from the circle if she prefers.	T makes sure L's favorite storybook is one of the story choices during circle time. T does not ask L to come to the front of the circle but places three name cards directly in front of her, asking her to "find your name; LI-SA," exaggerating the /li/ sound at the beginning of the word, saying, "Lisa begins with L."	T prompts L to move toward the circle area only if necessary. T waits until all other children are seated. If L still does not move toward the circle area, T directs L's attention to table closest to circle, if necessary taking her to that spot. (See "Social" goals.)

Goals Adaptations/Strategies

Goals	Social Increase tolerance for proximity to peers. Acknowledge peers using social communications.	Language Increase functional communication (requests). Increase use of spoken vocabulary.	Motor Develop motor planning and accuracy to increase efficiency and independence in play and daily routines.	Preacademic Enjoy looking at books. Develop alphabetic principle; understand relationship of print to language.	Self-Care/ Independence Move through daily routine without prompts. Use utensils and cup for self-feeding without assistance.
Activity:					
Outside Transition Cue: T rings bell to go inside.	T prompts J (typical peer) to invite L to play on teeter-totter (L's favorite outside equipment), reminds L it requires two people.	T asks L before going outside, "Where do you want to play?" If no response, T prompts, "Teeter-totter or water table?"	T scaffolds L getting on teeter-totter by herself by first waiting to see what L does, then saying, "First grab onto the handles." T pauses. "Next, put your leg over." Use physical prompts only if necessary. Reduce prompts over time.	T points out interesting letters on playground equipment, particularly the letter "L." T also writes L's name in the sand, then goes to the paint easel later and uses the hand-over-hand technique to help L paint her name.	(See "Motor" goals.)
Snack Transition Cue: Children clean up table; sing goodbye song.	T places L and J with two other peer volunteers at small four-person table. (Over time, the small table is moved closer to the rest of class at the large table.)	L's favorite snack, grapes, is in the cupboard. If L eats at least two bites of a less preferred food, T says, "What would you like for dessert?" If L does not respond or points, T asks, "Apples or grapes?" If L still does not respond, T busies herself with another child briefly.	T scaffolds fine motor tasks (e.g., opening milk carton, removing wrapper from cheese and crackers, peeling banana, taking sandwich from baggie) as appropriate, using verbal and physical prompts; decrease prompts over time.	T reads labels to identify juice versus milk. T points out letters on labels that match the "L" in L's name. Prior to lunch, T should take L to look at a printed lunch menu.	(See "Motor" goals.)
Departure	T asks peer J to hold L's backpack while L puts on her jacket. T provides imitative prompt for L to wave goodbye to friend J. If L does not respond to imitative prompt, T provides physical prompt.	As L gets on bus, T says, "See you tomorrow," using exaggerated intonation. Then says to L, "Tell me, 'See you tomorrow,'" repeating the exaggerated intonation pattern. T does this every day, in the same way. If L vocalizes in any way, T says, "Right! See you tomorrow!"	T uses backward chaining to assist L's motor planning to walk to her cubby, take her jacket off the hook, put on her jacket, and remove her backpack from the cubby. T uses scaffolding to help L put on her jacket.	T gives cue, "Find your cubby, Lisa." Points to wrong name printed on other child's cubby, saying, "Does this say Lisa? Nope, the first letter is 'P'— must be Paul's." T shows L a note to take home to her mother, saying, "Ask mommy to read this, OK?"	(See "Motor" goals.)

Communication and Collaboration in Co-Teaching Models

Co-teaching arrangements can place intense pressure on teachers to develop collaborative relationships. Good communication skills and the ability to solve problems and resolve conflicts are critical skills in successful co-teaching. Teaming and co-teaching can place great demands on individuals' communication and problem-solving ability. However, conscientious efforts to work collaboratively can create a sense of "family" and satisfying work environment.

It is helpful for all members of the team to be aware of their own temperament, communication style, and preferences. They must also be able to articulate their own program philosophies and understand how they are similar to or different from those of their co-teaching partner or other team members. Some of the personal characteristics and interpersonal skills that are important to successful teaming and co-teaching include the following:

- Open communication
- Self-awareness
- Satisfaction and enjoyment of one's role
- Mutual respect and acceptance of each team member
- Team spirit and empathy
- Flexibility
- Willingness to share the spotlight
- Ability to work within clearly defined roles
- Professionalism
- Commitment to planning and evaluation

Note: There is often a natural tendency in co-teaching models for the ECSE teacher to focus primarily on the children who have disabilities and for the early childhood teacher to focus on the children without disabilities. It is extremely important that the ECSE teacher and his or her co-teaching partner each take ownership for all children in the classroom.

Problem Solving and Conflict Resolution in Co-Teaching Models

Problem solving and conflict resolution are discussed in more detail in another section of this chapter. However, some problem-solving considerations are particularly important in co-teaching situations. First, it is important to develop a general agreement that problems must be solved, not avoided. The intensity of day-to-day contact in a co-teaching model requires that problem-solving strategies be used as a matter of course. Checking on the degree of congruence or difference should become part of the daily routine. It is also important to understand that conflict is inherent within any group process. Expecting that disagreements will occur, finding ways to encourage team members to express their disagreements, and dealing with disagreements on a regular basis are much more effective in team building than trying to avoid conflict.

Second, team members need to realize that personal friendships may make communication and problem solving more difficult rather than easier in some cases. When real differences occur between friends, there may be a tendency to avoid any interactions that might jeopardize the relationship. This may interfere with effective problem solving.

A third point is the realization that genuine problem solving can be time-consuming, especially during the early phases of team building. It takes time to analyze a problem and understand others' perspectives. Rushing to find solutions often results in failure to solve the problems. In turn, this failure can interfere with team building.

Administrative Issues

In order for inclusion to be successful, it is essential that administrators understand the dynamics involved and be supportive of all staff involved (Giangreco & Suter, 2015). Their support is needed for successful early childhood inclusion using a co-teaching model (or any model, for that matter). Many of the co-teaching strategies and practices described in this chapter require collaborative processes that are very time-consuming. If there is not adequate administrative support, the collaborative team process is significantly at risk. Furthermore, in some administrative situations, administrators from two agencies may be involved (e.g., a state-supported preschool program and local school district). Richardson-Gibbs and Klein (2014) have described factors that may enhance administrator support for early childhood special education inclusion practices and structures:

- *Establish clear, open lines of communication with administrators.* Understand that administrators may be dealing with "fear of the unknown." Early childhood special education inclusion may still be relatively new in some areas, and it is different from K–12 inclusion. Administrators bear the ultimate responsibility for program success and should be clearly informed of practices and challenges. Administrators also should be given credit and appreciation for their support.
- *Encourage "thinking outside the box."* Because of the nature of their job demands, administrators are often conservative. Staff members who understand the two points just listed will have greater success in encouraging administrators to be creative, to join in the problem-solving process, and to risk trying entirely new ways of doing things.

(For a thorough description and evaluation of the critical roles of administrators in successful inclusive schools, see Billingsley and McLeskey [2014].)

Stages of the Co-Teaching Relationship

Effective co-teaching relationships do not develop quickly. Depending on personalities, values, preferences, habits, and so on, it may be a slow process. Co-teaching has been compared to a marriage. Different phases in the relationship have been identified. Sileo (2011) described the following three major stages that occur as the co-teaching relationship matures:

- The preliminary relationship-building state involves getting started as co-teachers by discussing the basics of the relationship and shared classroom responsibilities. There may be feelings of discomfort with new job roles and guarded communication. Co-teachers should understand the definition of co-teaching, determine their roles, and communicate about their relationship in order to keep the focus on children's growth and development.
- Next, the marriage/co-teaching stage addresses curriculum planning and instruction, chooses co-teaching structures, and identifies progress monitoring procedures. Communication has become more open. There is now give/take and compromise in the co-teaching relationship.
- Finally, in the ongoing relationship stage, problem solving occurs along with continued compromise and collaboration. This stage is characterized by open, honest communication, humor, and a high degree of comfort. There is true collaboration with each partner contributing equally. Boundaries and role definition become somewhat blurred. Teachers no long refer to "your kids" and "my kids." At this stage, there is often mutual admiration and respect for one another.

Remember that effective co-teaching relationships are not free of problems and disagreements. The beauty of effective teams is that they can usually deal with these potential conflicts as a matter of course, in collaborative ways, before they become crises. In order to facilitate inclusion of children with disabilities within the general education classroom, the co-teaching team often consists of a special educator and a general education teacher. Appendix E offers a vision of the roles and responsibilities of the special education staff as related to the general education staff in inclusive educational settings (Inclusion Collaborative, Santa Clara County, California, Office of Education, 2018).

Effective Teaming with Interdisciplinary Specialists

We have discussed a variety of service-delivery structures for involvement of family members, early childhood teachers, special educators, and paraprofessionals in effective inclusion support. However, children with unique or intensive needs also require input, support, and evaluation from a variety of specialists. These include discipline-specific therapists (e.g., occupational therapists, physical therapists, and speech-language pathologists) and disability-specific specialists (e.g., teachers with certification in visual impairment and the Deaf and hard-of-hearing areas).

Incorporating this input into the inclusive setting and coordinating their efforts can be a significant challenge. Specialists may provide services to children in inclusive settings in a variety of ways. Typically, the specialist works as an itinerant. In this model, itinerant specialists may work directly with the child or in a consultation role, working primarily with the staff, or a combination of these two models. Communication with the specialist is critical. There is little evidence that working directly with a child for an hour each week can be effective if the specialist's intervention strategies and goals for the child are not understood and incorporated into daily routines. Furthermore, specialists' own efforts are enhanced only via their collaboration with other key players in the child's life.

Each specialist visits the center according to his or her own availability and scheduling. Ideally, the ways in which the services of specialists are organized should be carefully planned and coordinated. Specialists should meet regularly with the team at the center. However, this may be unrealistic. One possible model for using and coordinating the input from a variety of specialists in an inclusive setting is for the early childhood special education co-teacher or itinerant to serve as a sort of "conduit" for their input. He or she assumes the primary responsibility for working with the specialists and conveying information to other staff and to families. Because the well-trained ECSE co-teacher is likely to be familiar with the strategies used by specialists, this model can be quite efficient and can facilitate communication across team members even when meeting together as a group is difficult.

Teaming with Paraprofessionals

The Individuals with Disabilities Education Act and its amendments have recognized an important role for paraprofessionals in addressing the shortage of personnel by requiring that states develop training for paraprofessionals. The shortage of service providers is further complicated by the recognition that cross-cultural competence is essential to providing family-centered practices. As paraprofessionals tend to come from the local community, they often speak the primary language of the children and families being served and can provide a cultural bridge, helping to create a more collaborative relationship between school professionals and the communities they serve.

In addition, the frequent use of one-to-one assistants to support children in inclusive settings has further increased the use of paraprofessionals in early childhood special education. Realizing this, many states have integrated paraprofessionals into their service-delivery system and have established new occupational categories for paraprofessionals. Even though early childhood special educators find themselves responsible for supervising paraprofessionals, they typically have little preservice preparation in this area. Therefore, this text ends with a focus on guidelines for effectively developing and using paraprofessionals in the early childhood center or classroom.

Paraprofessionals increasingly play crucial roles in early childhood service delivery, regardless of the setting (Brown & Stanton-Chapman, 2017). They are essential members of any early intervention or preschool education team. However, the supervisor–supervisee relationship between the paraprofessional and early childhood educator or early childhood special educator presents a unique set of challenges, somewhat different from the challenges of teaming and collaboration described earlier. In a study examining paraprofessionals' job experiences and satisfaction, Brown and Stanton-Chapman (2017) observed and interviewed paraprofessionals and their teachers in early childhood and early childhood special education classrooms. Key findings with implications for practice include:

1. There is a relationship between a teacher's receptiveness to relinquish control and allow a paraprofessional to complete tasks and paraprofessional motivation to perform classroom tasks. There may be high or low teacher receptiveness and paraprofessional motivation. A mismatch in these levels (e.g., low teacher receptiveness and high paraprofessional motivation) will inhibit effective teaming. Teachers and administrators should work to increase teacher receptiveness and paraprofessional motivation.

2. The context, setting, and task also determine the responsibilities of paraprofessionals and influence training needs. Teachers and administrators should be aware of these differences and provide required training.

3. The paraprofessional–teacher relationship may be influenced by a power dynamic where the paraprofessional priority is to please the teacher before attending to other tasks. Teachers should be aware of this dynamic and strive to provide clear expectations and promote collaboration.

4. Paraprofessionals tend to be dissatisfied with their salary, whereas teachers may believe that paraprofessional pay and benefits are adequate. Paraprofessionals may be encouraged to increase their professional competencies and discuss their salary levels with administrators and relevant parties.

5. Teachers vary in their level of appreciation and recognition (nonmonetary compensation) of their paraprofessionals' efforts. Lack of appreciation or recognition contributes to the job dissatisfaction of paraprofessionals. Conversations between teachers and paraprofessionals regarding nonmonetary compensation would be helpful.

Who Are the Paraprofessionals?

Paraprofessionals are individuals who by their assistance extend the capacity and effectiveness of teachers and other interventionists. By definition, paraprofessionals do not have the training and expertise of professional teachers and they receive less in monetary compensation.

Various terms have been used to refer to those persons who participate in early education programs, but lack the full training and certification necessary to function as fully as teachers or clinicians. Terms such as *teacher aide, early intervention assistant, paraeducator, special education program aide,* and *instructional* or *therapist assistant* are common. In this text, the term *paraprofessional* generally refers to all those who provide assistance within early education programs and are not fully certified or credentialed. This is in keeping with the No Child Left Behind Act (NCLB; Public Law 107-334), which only includes the term *paraprofessional* and mandates these restrictions:

- A paraprofessional "may not provide any instruction to a student unless the paraprofessional is working under the direct supervision of a teacher."
- A paraprofessional may not provide one-on-one tutoring when the teacher is available.

Given that there is no federal legal definition for an "aide," IFSP or IEP documents must request the assistance of a *paraprofessional* rather than an aide when needed. Noting the legal stipulation just mentioned that assigns the educational responsibility to the teacher, the paraprofessional should be written into the documents as a support to the teacher rather than to a child. (See http://www.wrightslaw.com/health/parapro.aide.htm for more information.)

Designing and Defining Jobs

All paraprofessionals readily state, right from the beginning, they would like to have their role within a center or classroom explicitly defined (Austin, 2014). Designing and defining jobs is the starting point for effectively involving paraprofessionals. There are two primary reasons why job design is the appropriate point of departure. First, careful consideration of job design elements provides the criteria for recruiting and selecting paraprofessionals. Second, people work more effectively when they know what they are supposed to do and how and when they are supposed to do it. Thus, job design frames the expectations that are so important to job functioning and role relationships.

Because this responsibility falls on teachers, it clarifies in their minds the purposes, tasks, and conditions in which paraprofessionals are to be part of the classroom team. Similarly, a clearly defined set of tasks, responsibilities, and relationships establishes for paraprofessionals the framework within which they are expected to work.

Framework of Activities, Interactions, and Sentiments.   Job design refers to specifying the content and relationships of any job, be it the job of paraprofessional, volunteer, teacher, principal, or director. Properly conceived, job design considers both the jobholder as a person and the performance contributions expected on behalf of the organization (or classroom). A simple way of thinking about job design characteristics is to borrow concepts from a classic study of group dynamics in which Homans (1992) conceived of any work group (e.g., teacher, paraprofessionals, and pupils) as a social system. Homans identified three features common to any small work group: activities, interactions, and sentiments. With slight modification, the following are the basics for defining essential job design elements in education:

1. *Activities or tasks.* This feature defines the content of what a jobholder is to do. What is the scope or breadth of tasks? To what degree are they to be standardized and routinized instead of creative? How often are they to be performed? What results are expected? How are results to be recognized (by both the paraprofessional and teacher)?

2. *Interactions or role relationships.* This defines with whom the jobholder is expected to interact, how often (or under what conditions) this is to happen, and the quality of that relationship. What relationship is the paraprofessional to have with the children? With other staff members and parents? What are the paraprofessional's responsibilities and limits of authority relative to the teacher? How much autonomy or self-initiative freedom is given to the paraprofessional for certain types of tasks? To what extent is teamwork instead of individual action expected?

3. *Sentiments or values and attitudes.* Sentiment defines the conditions under which work is to be performed and sources of satisfaction available to the jobholder.

By calling attention to sentiments, the teacher is forced to anticipate and build on essential questions that affect the quality of the paraprofessional's involvement in the classroom, such as the following: What personal rewards are meaningful to the paraprofessional? How is the paraprofessional expected to view sensitive issues such as discipline methods and toilet habits? What values and attitudes held by the paraprofessional will contribute best to the program's objectives and be compatible with those of the teacher?

Developing Job Task Descriptions.   Because each paraprofessional brings different skills and expectations to the job and each teacher's or classroom's needs are different, the paraprofessional's job description must be designed to reflect the unique interaction desired. A clear understanding of paraprofessional roles and responsibilities is essential to ensure that paraprofessionals are being used appropriately. Tasks are only appropriate when the paraeducators have sufficient training, knowledge, and skills to carry out the tasks. Of course, clarity of instructions provided by the teacher and sufficient supervision are essential.

The job task descriptions should be expressed in writing, with each participant keeping a copy for reference and review, and in line with the program's or school district's policies. These should be rewritten at least once each year following performance evaluation and any time a significant change in assignment occurs. This job description typically conveys more than a trite list of "responsible for" statements and should reflect the philosophy and practices of the program. As previously suggested, a written job description provides both the criteria for screening candidates (in the case of paraprofessionals) and a picture of the job for the candidate. For a starting point in creating a useful statement of job task design, the supervisor should think about the ways in which a paraprofessional or volunteer can be useful. One of the easiest ways to develop such a list of task possibilities is to jot down ideas as they surface during the day. Some possible roles and responsibilities of paraprofessionals are listed in Exhibit 10.4.

Exhibit 10.4
Possible Paraprofessional Tasks

- Preparing the room, including setting up centers, organizing materials needed for special projects, and locating daily supplies
- Greeting the children and assisting with all routines
- Supervising activities in the classroom and on the playground
- Nurturing appropriate behavior, including dealing with misbehaviors appropriately and effectively
- Directing specific activities planned by the teacher
- Assisting children at mealtime and with toileting
- Charting behaviors during the implementation of behavior management programs
- Helping to order or create adaptive equipment
- Following specialists' instructions in helping to position or transport children
- Providing appropriate prompts to help ensure positive social integration
- Preparing, cataloging, and filing intervention games and materials
- Setting up media equipment
- Facilitating the use of assistive technology
- Contacting parents to set up conferences
- Helping with end-of-the-day routines, including cleanup

Once the teacher has identified desirable tasks, it will be necessary to clarify (1) who is to conduct the activity, (2) how often it is to be performed, (3) the manner in which it is to be performed (if standardization or consistency is desired), and (4) how all concerned can recognize successful performance.

Visualizing Role Relationships.   After the teacher has defined activity areas, he or she should think carefully about the role visualized for the paraprofessional. Will the paraprofessional be a creative contributor to the children's learning or merely the person behind the scenes who prepares materials? Will he or she be encouraged to suggest activities or be relegated to doing only what the teacher has planned?

The answers to such role relationship questions reflect the philosophy and style of the teacher. Figure 10.1 depicts the extreme views of interaction that teachers have of themselves in relation to support personnel. A teacher who wants to be the boss and run a tight classroom or center ought to be aware of this philosophy. Such a situation will definitely restrict the range of freedom and autonomy given to paraprofessionals (and may also interfere with the development of collaborative relationships).

It is helpful if the teacher thinks carefully about her role-relationship philosophy and leadership style before developing specific guidelines for the paraprofessionals who may be assisting him or her.

Translating Sentiments into Policy Guidelines.   Dedicated teachers generally work with some form of lesson plan or curriculum guide. Similarly, the teacher plans in advance the essential performance tasks expected of paraprofessionals and clarifies intended relationships. For optimum effectiveness, however, the teacher should also plan for and codify the *affective* behavior expected of paraprofessionals. This means in part explaining (in writing, when possible) not just the duties of the paraprofessional but the affect and tone of his or her interactions with children as well as the level of intrusiveness versus responsiveness that is expected.

Particularly important are guidelines for responding to unacceptable child behavior. For example, if a child spits at another child, what is considered an appropriate

Figure 10.1   Range of role-relationship philosophies between teacher and paraprofessionals

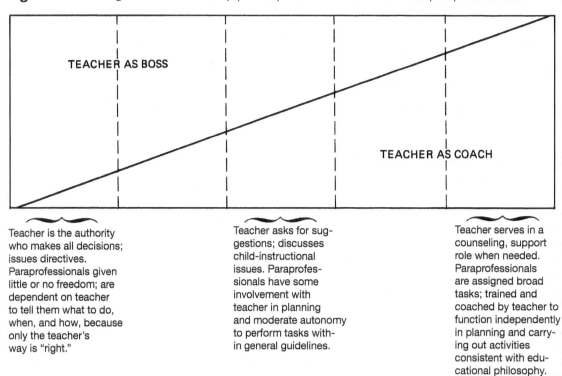

response? Gentle redirection? A stern facial expression? Saying, "Jason, I see you're angry at Philip" is not necessarily a clear "right" or "wrong" response, but there may be certain expectations that have become part of the culture within a given setting. The paraprofessional must understand these kinds of affective expectations. Clarifying roles includes not only clear expectations regarding the scope of work but also the nature of the paraprofessional's authority to act. Exhibit 10.5 features examples of written guidelines for interacting with young children.

Because they serve as a frame of reference for feedback, job design guidelines not only help in redirecting a paraprofessional's behavior when necessary but also stimulate job satisfaction. The paraprofessional knows when he or she has done a good job or has handled a difficult situation successfully and consistently within the program's standards. Guidelines also permit teachers to reinforce appropriate behavior. To the extent they allow the paraprofessional to make discretionary choices, the guidelines can help her or him feel more "professional" about being involved in the learning process.

Communicating Expectations

The socialization process of building an effective working relationship is genuinely a mutual responsibility. Both people have to learn about each other. In the process of

---

Exhibit 10.5

Child Interaction Guidelines for Paraprofessionals

1. *Create a pleasant atmosphere.* Tense children cannot become effectively involved. Help them feel comfortable by being warm and enthusiastic. If you relax and enjoy yourself, the children will feel this and follow your example.

2. *Your voice is your asset.* A soft, confident voice elicits a child's attention more quickly than a high or loud one. First gaining eye contact with a child and then speaking directly and softly to him or her will be more effective than shouting across the room.

3. *Be positive.* Instead of saying "Don't spill your milk," it is better to say, "Hold your glass with two hands." "Good builders put their tools away carefully" is a better response than "Don't throw your tools."

4. *Labels are for jelly jars, not for children.* Labels and phrases such as "naughty boy" or "bad girl" make children feel ashamed and unworthy. Children with these feelings cannot learn.

5. *Keep competition out of the classroom.* Nothing is to be gained from fostering competition among young children. Discourage children when they say, "I can draw better than Susie" by offering, "Each child can draw in his or her own special way."

6. *Choices are for choosing.* When it is time to clean up, do not ask the children whether they want to clean up. Instead say, "It is time to clean up now." If you do not intend to accept no for an answer, do not give them a choice. Give them a choice only when you really want them to choose.

7. *Sharing is not simple.* Preschool-aged children are just learning to share. If they are playing with something, in their minds the toy belongs to them at that moment. Children should be encouraged to ask whether they can have a turn and to tell others when they are through playing with something.

8. *Keep your eyes on the children.* Children must be within the visual range of supervising adults at all times. They need and deserve alert supervision, which is not possible when the responsible adult is engaged in conversation. If too many children are entering any one play area, redirect some to other areas.

9. *Do not dominate children's activities.* Children should be allowed to use their active imaginations as they experiment with ideas and materials. Unless you are teaching a specific lesson, stay in the background with supportive but not suppressive comments.

10. *Prevention is perfect.* Be alert so you can redirect behavior that can become a problem. Remember that children should not be allowed to hurt themselves or others.

communicating (verbally, in writing, and through behaviors), they begin to expand their clarification of mutual role relationships. At its very essence, *a role is a set of expectations about what is appropriate to do and what is to be avoided*. For paraprofessionals, the role can either be reasonably well defined and stimulating or ambiguous, conflicting, and stifling with unpleasant jobs and oppressive supervision.

Both the teacher and paraprofessional must communicate their expectations. The relationship between teacher and paraprofessional can make the experience rich and fulfilling or miserable and tedious. Perhaps more important, negative relationships can interfere with program effectiveness.

If only one teacher and one paraprofessional are involved, the orientation may take place in a pleasant corner of the classroom, or it can take place at a restaurant during a planned lunch hour. The number of people involved will influence where the meeting takes place and how it is conducted, but it should not influence what is discussed.

Stressing the importance of communicating common goals, Carroll (2001) identified several key items to be addressed immediately as paraprofessionals are oriented to a new position. She suggests putting together a packet that includes information on such important policies as when the day begins and ends, parking dos and don'ts, maps with critical sites such as a cafeteria noted, emergency procedures, attendance and confidentiality policies, and schedules for both children and staff with the paraeducator's schedule highlighted.

One could add to this list the importance of professional conduct. Paraprofessionals who are expected to behave as professionals usually do so. This includes being prompt, appropriately dressed, and respectful of all aspects of **confidentiality** regarding children's characteristics and behaviors.

Discovering and Using Special Skills and Talents

To make the orientation truly an opportunity for two-way communication, the resourceful teacher should encourage new paraprofessionals to reveal their special interests, skills, and talents. Asking about previous work experience is important. Parenting and homemaking skills, however, are equally important in preschools and child-care centers. Very few skills cannot be adapted to useful and interesting classroom activities. Everything from sports to needlework fits in somewhere. Hobbies can be the source of exciting lessons. Baking, gardening, sewing, and cleaning can be the basis for science and mathematics lessons.

One effective method of discovering the special skills and talents of paraprofessionals is to develop a simple questionnaire that potential paraprofessionals can fill out. Many teachers ask parents to complete the questionnaire to encourage parent involvement. Others use the questionnaire with hired paraprofessionals and with volunteers. The questionnaire in Figure 10.2 was designed to incorporate the needs of an early childhood center while allowing the respondents some latitude of choice.

Once the special interests, skills, and talents of the paraprofessional are known, the teacher may plan to adapt activities to them. A paraprofessional in one class loved to garden. An outdoor garden provided lessons in many concepts. Children learned about *straight*, *front*, and *back* rows. They learned about plants that grew *taller* and things that were *shorter*. They discovered the *shortest* stem and the *longest* vine. That garden was the basis of science lessons and nutrition themes as well as a source of beauty and joy.

One paraprofessional is bilingual in Spanish and English and so a valuable resource in a class with some children whose home language is Spanish. Because the teacher does not speak Spanish, the paraprofessional contributes in many ways. For example, he is asked to lead familiar songs in Spanish, to identify how to say key vocabulary words in Spanish, to add labels in Spanish to the English words on bulletin boards, and to help the teacher communicate with Spanish-speaking families. In fact, paraprofessionals

Figure 10.2 Samples from a parent volunteer checklist

Name _____

WOULD YOU LIKE TO:

1. [ ]   Read a story to some of the children?

2. [ ]   Lead a song or some other musical activity?

3. [ ]   Help children create something in art?

4. [ ]   Bring the family pet to visit the center?

5. [ ]   Help set up or supervise a field trip?

6. [ ]   Make a book of a child's story?

7. [ ]   Work puzzles or play games?

8. [ ]   Share your hobby with the class? Hobby:

9. [ ]   Show children how to use simple carpenter tools?

10. [ ]   Bring a guitar (or other instrument) and demonstrate?

11. [ ]   Help cut and paste pictures?

12. [ ]   Teach the children something about your occupation?

13. [ ]   Conduct a simple science experiment?

14. [ ]   Wear clothing from another country and tell about it?

15. [ ]   Bring necessary materials and plant some seeds?

16. [ ]   Demonstrate rug weaving, leather tooling, or other crafts?

17. [ ]   Make jam or churn butter?

18. [ ]   Decorate a bulletin board?

19. [ ]   Sew dress-up and/or doll clothing?

20. [ ]   Construct special toys or equipment?

And if none of these appeals to you, what would you like to do?

are twice as likely to speak a language other than English at home than their teacher counterparts. These multilingual paraprofessionals may be an answer to our shortage in the bilingual teacher population.

Another paraprofessional was particularly interested in puppets. She made sock puppets for each child and taught them basic puppeting skills. Puppet shows enlivened nutrition lessons and language lessons. Puppets sang the opening song and learned to say "please" and "thank you." Puppets helped with everything, and the paraprofessional felt proud of her accomplishment.

When the teacher gives special thought and care to matching classroom responsibilities with the paraprofessional's skills and talents, everyone benefits. Ideally, a paraprofessional will be ready for anything, and many of them are. But even when paraprofessionals are willing to do "anything and everything," relationships and performances are better when interests are allowed to blossom.

Defining the Teacher's Responsibilities to Paraprofessionals

Relationship building is a two-way process. We have stressed the importance of the teacher's responsibility for mentoring and guiding the paraprofessional. Exhibit 10.6 summarizes a few of the commonly accepted responsibilities for teacher leadership and guidance. However, this genuine caring must not interfere with the teacher's awareness of his or her role as the person on whom ultimate responsibility rests. A tug of war for the affections of the children or their parents is destructive and dysfunctional. Differing philosophies of what is best for children lead to subtle and disruptive experiences. Teachers who encounter paraprofessionals who refuse to accept the teacher's responsibility and authority must consult with program administrators about how to resolve these challenges.

Just as the teacher avoids embarrassing or criticizing the paraprofessional or volunteer in front of parents and other adults, so must the paraprofessional avoid undermining the teacher. It is the teacher's responsibility to make this clear from the beginning. The teacher must be alert to recognize any overt or covert attempts to interfere with behavior management or teaching methods. Such interference should be dealt with immediately. If free and open discussion of the importance of consistent attitudes and management of children is established in the beginning, future problems will be minimized.

Exhibit 10.6

Some Responsibilities of Teachers to Paraprofessionals

1. To exert active leadership and guidance to build a team of coordinated service providers.
2. To create an atmosphere in which paraprofessionals feel accepted and motivated to perform effectively.
3. To provide ample structure and direction so paraprofessionals know what is expected of them.
4. To hold an orientation session with new paraprofessionals to discuss program goals, procedures, and policies and what to expect of children with disabilities.
5. To plan work in advance of the workday and to build variety into the tasks paraprofessionals are assigned to perform.
6. To provide adequate information so that paraprofessionals can carry out their tasks and to provide feedback so they know how they are performing.
7. To have on hand the resources paraprofessionals will need to carry out assigned tasks; to show them where to find materials, how to set up an activity, and how to operate any special equipment; and to make known any restrictions or special requirements to accommodate particular children.
8. To assign tasks within the range of competency of a paraprofessional while providing increased responsibility and autonomy as performance indicates increased competence.
9. To provide opportunities for regularly scheduled meetings between the teacher and the paraprofessionals. (Such meetings will allow for adequate planning and avoid waiting for a crisis to force communication. Impromptu meetings should not become substitutes for regularly scheduled meetings.)

Being an Appropriate Role Model

Teachers must be appropriate role models. Saying one thing and behaving in a different way is inexcusable. What teachers *do* speaks louder than what they *say*. Also, teachers must be clear about their intent to demonstrate a particular procedure and their expectation that the paraprofessional will practice and learn the procedure. The teacher should explain what will be done and why it will be done. Sometimes a particular procedure should be written and available for reference. This is important for new activities. Teachers should consider directly explaining simple teaching strategies such as "prompt fading," "upping the ante," and "pause and wait."

After the teacher completes a specific demonstration of a strategy or directing an activity, the paraprofessional will want to practice the skill on his or her own. It is helpful for the teacher to observe the paraprofessional's use of the strategy when the paraprofessional feels ready—for example, "Tomorrow when you feel ready for me to watch you, let me know."

Part of a teacher's responsibility as a role model is to build up, not undermine, the desires and productive energies of paraprofessionals. Just as the teacher's responsibility toward children is to help them become more fully functioning independently rather than dependently, the same applies to paraprofessionals. But development of the independent skills and motivation of paraprofessionals does not occur through abandonment. A disorganized teacher whose actions reveal that he or she has given little thought to how paraprofessionals are to serve confuses and discourages those who seek to help. Perhaps one of the most effective ways in which a teacher can help develop the skills and motivation of the paraprofessional is through the eyes of someone working in the paraprofessional role. So, actively listening to the paraprofessional at appropriate and private times facilitates reflection and ongoing collaboration.

Allowing for Sufficient Planning Time

Another facet of paraprofessional motivation and effectiveness comes from the teacher and the paraprofessional prioritizing planning time. Many federally funded programs in the early days allowed for whole days for teachers and paraprofessionals to plan together each week. Money was available for regular evaluation and collaborative sessions. Few programs today include this necessity. Time for planning is a luxury.

As with everything else, teachers must do what they can. Day-to-day planning may need to be squeezed into very limited time segments. The time after school, lunch periods, and so-called breaks become the scarce moments for planning. These daily time constraints make it necessary for the teacher to do overall preparation before the school year begins. Attention needs to be given to designing record-keeping systems, choosing basic activity plans, organizing the classroom, scheduling activities, preparing materials, and assigning responsibilities. The paraprofessional's responsibilities within the daily schedule should be written out. There is rarely enough time before and after school for such comprehensive planning, no matter how dedicated the teacher and the paraprofessional may be.

Over time, however, paraprofessionals should be encouraged to plan some of the specific activities. The teacher identifies the goals and objectives, but the "equivalent practice" can be suggested by paraprofessionals. For example, one paraprofessional raised tropical fish. With her help, the children planned an aquarium. They learned colors as they chose the stones for the bottom. They discovered water temperature as they planned for the fish. Feeding the fish developed measuring skills and a sense of responsibility.

During the months that the aquarium served as an excellent teaching tool, the teacher and paraprofessional discussed many different ways in which it could be used. More than half of the excellent teaching ideas that evolved originated with the paraprofessional. The teacher continued to pinpoint specific objectives that could be achieved, but it was uniquely successful because of the paraprofessional's knowledge and enthusiasm to take charge of this project.

Providing Constructive Feedback: Coaching and Mentoring the Paraprofessional

Just as routine preparation time boosts effectiveness, so also does regular and constructive feedback and coaching from teacher to paraprofessional. One strategy is to use side-by-side coaching in which the paraprofessionals receive instruction from the teacher during their practice (Stockall, 2014). The teacher must also build in feedback about how the paraprofessional is doing. This is especially critical for paraprofessionals who are inexperienced in working with young children with disabilities. Informal feedback should not be the occasion for a great deal of discussion. It should be specific, clearly stated, and timely. The teacher should identify strengths, behaviors, and attitudes to be changed or developed. The more straightforward the feedback, the more effective it will be. Friend and Cook (2017) indicate that to be effective, feedback should be descriptive, specific, directed toward changeable behaviors and situations, concise, and checked for clarity.

In addition, Stockall (2014) emphasizes that teachers develop and use effective communication strategies (e.g., listening, using open-ended questions, clarifying, paraphrasing, acknowledging, and providing reflective feedback) to build a working relationship with paraprofessionals. French (2007) suggests that written feedback is more useful than verbal information, especially if it is accompanied by exact words or actions—for example, the precise words used by a paraprofessional that might have caused confusion when directions were being given. Brown, Gatmaitan, and Harjusola-Webb (2014) recommend organizing procedures for providing feedback to paraprofessionals and using a variety of methods (e.g., verbal, written, graphic, video). Finally, Stockall (2014) suggests a direct instruction training model (i.e., identifying a training goal; providing instruction, demonstration, and guided practice; observing independent practice; and providing performance feedback) as a systematic process for training paraprofessionals.

Avoid focusing on personalities. Conduct firsthand observations that focus on task behaviors and procedures that are changeable. For example, telling the paraprofessional that she is disorganized is not helpful. Explaining why the crayons and scissors should be placed within the reach of each child instead of at the end of the table, however, will help her understand precisely how to become more organized and efficient. The teacher should discuss why specific things are important or how a certain strategy might work better for a particular child's learning style. If necessary, the teacher should reteach and demonstrate again. It is especially important for the teacher to evaluate and provide suggestions to the paraprofessional with no other adults or children present or within hearing distance. The teacher's goal is to support and develop the paraprofessional's skills. Do not exaggerate the negative effects of a particular behavior. Rather, state what is wanted, why it is desirable, and how it can be achieved.

The teacher should not forget to reward effort and abilities as part of success. Things that are easy for the teacher may be difficult for an inexperienced paraprofessional. The teacher should not expect everything to be learned at once! Time is needed for practice. Recognition by way of a "thank-you" for regular role-appropriate behaviors is as important as special rewards for exceptional success. But such spontaneous or informal feedback opportunities do not eliminate the need for periodic formal evaluation of paraprofessional behaviors. It is also essential that the early childhood special education teacher be willing to acknowledge the contributions and strengths of the paraprofessional that the teacher him- or herself may not have. Every paraprofessional—even if inexperienced—brings his or her special knowledge and insights to the team. Such insights are invaluable. Encouraging the paraprofessional's ideas and input regarding children's behaviors, children's preferences, and the like results in that person's feeling more valued as a team member.

In addition to providing ongoing feedback and encouragement to the paraprofessional, the experienced professional engages in mentoring and staff development. Providing interesting written materials, encouraging attendance at conferences and workshops, observing other classrooms, and coaching the paraprofessional in learning difficult or unique teaching methods or procedures are examples of teacher activities that extend beyond good supervision. This mentoring relationship can often enhance collaborative problem solving and the team processes in the classroom.

Challenging Situations with Paraprofessionals

A positive teacher–paraprofessional relationship is essential for effective instruction and successful classroom experiences for young children. However, in the authors' experiences, novice teachers seem to be assigned the least competent or "difficult" paraprofessionals. McGrath, Johns, and Mathur (2010) identified 10 challenges with paraprofessionals that teachers may encounter. The following five are selected based on the authors' discussions with novice teachers:

1. *The paramother* whose parenting behavior conflicts with the teacher's style and practice. For example, the paramother may try to dominate a younger teacher or have difficulty setting boundaries with children. The teacher should draw on his or her professional competencies, clarify expectations for behaviors and boundaries, and reinforce the paraprofessional's skills and assets.

2. *The paraprofessional who has "been there, done that."* A paraprofessional who has years of experience in the program and so considers him- or herself an expert in all program-related areas. Moreover, this paraprofessional may have liked working with the previous teacher and is not open to new practices. The teacher should clarify expectations, stress the need for teamwork, respect the paraprofessional's knowledge, and clearly establish the role of the teacher in implementing classroom practice and structure.

3. *Working with Mrs. Administrator and company.* A paraprofessional may be a relative or close friend of a program administrator and the teacher finds that what happens in the classroom is bring shared with that individual. In this situation, a teacher may consult an administrator or union representative about any concerns. Furthermore, the teacher should remember and demonstrate his or her own professional competencies.

4. *Setting parental boundaries.* Paraprofessionals may develop relationships with families and reveal confidential information. Teachers should make sure that paraprofessionals have training, coaching, and supervision about how they are expected to communicate with parents.

5. *Multiple paraprofessionals in the same room.* Sometimes there may be conflicts between paraprofessionals in the same classroom. When this happens, the teacher should provide clear instructions to prevent disagreements from interfering with class time. Disagreements should be discussed at the end of the day when solutions can be reached. If problems continue, then the teacher should inform the paraprofessionals that the next step will be to request the principal or administrator's involvement. The teacher should also remind the paraprofessionals that they are all in the classroom for the benefit of the children.

Paraprofessionals as One-to-One Assistants

Increasingly, as mentioned earlier, paraprofessionals—or **paraeducators** as they may be referred to in school settings—are being used as one-to-one assistants in inclusive settings. They are sometimes referred to as a *shadow aide*. The assignment of a one-to-one assistant exclusively to a specific child can have definite drawbacks. The early childhood educator often assumes that the assistant has been well trained to work with the designated child, when usually this is not the case. Another disadvantage is that the child often becomes very attached to the assistant because of the intensity and exclusivity of the relationship and may avoid interacting with peers and other adults. Also, when peers try to approach a child with a disability, at times the paraprofessional unintentionally interferes with the peers' efforts to be friendly or helpful to the child with disabilities (Giangreco, 2009).

In some situations, such as in the case of a child who is extremely aggressive, self-injurious, or medically fragile, it is necessary to assign a one-to-one assistant, or the child would have to be removed from the program. However, the use of a one-to-one assistant may be just as restrictive as a segregated special education setting.

Giangreco and colleagues (2010) discussed the use of paraprofessionals in K–12 educational settings. Research suggesting that the unnecessary proximity of instructional assistants to children with disabilities in general education can actually impede children's progress is discussed. The following areas of concern related to the "hovering" of instructional assistants were some of those noted:

1. The general educators tended to avoid assuming responsibility and ownership for the education of students who have one-to-one assistants.

2. The assistant tended to separate the child from the rest of the group.

3. The prolonged close proximity with assistants fostered dependency of the child on the adult.

4. The excessive proximity sometimes interfered with peer interactions.

5. The unrealistic instructional expectations or lack of training of the assistants led to inadequate academic instruction of the children under their care.

6. Students who had difficulty communicating often found their assistant speaking and making decisions for them.

7. The student's gender became secondary to that of the assistant in such matters as toileting.

8. Students may express their embarrassment/discomfort about having a paraprofessional by displaying inappropriate behaviors.

Even though cited research typically involves older children, the results present many cautions for early childhood educators. The authors urge reconsideration of the growing tendency to assign one-to-one assistants. They also recommend that whenever feasible, assistants should be hired for groups of children rather than an individual child. They urge the development of definite guidelines to ensure the fading of prompts, the use of natural supports such as peer support, avoidance of excessive proximity (hovering), clarification of role responsibilities, and added training of both the paraprofessional and supervisor.

Supervision of One-to-One Assistants in Inclusive Settings

When a child is assigned a one-to-one assistant, one of the most serious issues is supervision. In community-based inclusive settings, one-to-one assistants may be employed by a different agency or school district than the early childhood teacher or special educator. As a result, the responsibility for training and supervision of one-to-one assistants may be unclear. Lack of clarity on this issue can be a potential source of conflict in the inclusive setting. Determining who is responsible for employing the assistant may or may not indicate who will provide supervision. Whereas some one-to-one assistants have developed skills in providing appropriate support, many have had little or no training.

Another issue that must be clarified is the role of the one-to-one assistant. Who determined that this level of support was needed and for what purposes? What are the one-to-one assistant's specific duties? Early childhood specialist teachers will want to know their role in terms of training and supervision. Will they have time? Do they have the knowledge and expertise? Do they want the added responsibility of supervising another adult in their classroom?

Guidelines for Use of One-to-One Assistants

The following are suggested as guidelines for the use of one-to-one assistants in early childhood settings:

- Clearly define the purpose of the one-to-one assistant.
- Make it clear to the one-to-one assistant that she or he should provide *only* the degree of intervention necessary to support the child's learning and participation and ensure the child's safety.
- The one-to-one assistant must not interfere with the child's opportunity for interactions with other children and must not become a constant barrier or buffer between the child and his or her environment.
- The use of a one-to-one assistant must not interfere with the child's development of independence.
- Avoid stigmatizing the child as the only child in the class who requires an attached adult.
- Put the specific daily responsibilities and activities of the assistant in writing.
- In consultation with parents, gradually decrease the intensity and proximity of the assistant.
- Gradually include more and more children in the target child's space.
- Whenever possible, view the one-to-one assistant as a temporary assignment.
- Encourage the child's attachment to other staff. The assignment of a one-to-one assistant must not discourage the other staff from interacting with or taking responsibility for the child with a disability.
- The use of a one-to-one assistant must not become even more restrictive than a segregated setting!

Successful Use of a One-to-One Assistant

James was a 30-month-old child with developmental delays. Mealtimes were very challenging for James because of occasional choking. He was also sometimes aggressive toward other children. He was fully included in a large day-care setting, and both his mother and teacher were concerned that the staff ratio and skill level did not provide adequate support for him in this environment. The decision was made to employ a one-to-one assistant for James. Initially, there were problems because the one-to-one assistant hovered over him every moment, even though he had choking episodes only when eating, and his aggressive behavior was unpredictable.

In a team meeting including the mother and the assistant, it was decided that the only time close proximity of the assistant was necessary was at mealtimes. A careful functional behavioral analysis revealed that the aggressive behavior occurred only when other children were crowding James. Rather than shadowing the child all day, the assistant simply watched for and managed those situations that typically triggered the aggressive behaviors.

Within 6 months, James was no longer choking, and the staff had learned how to prevent aggressive behavior, significantly reducing the need for one-to-one assistance. At this time, the use of the assistant was terminated.

Enhanced eText Application Exercise 10.4: In this exercise, you can apply what you have learned in this chapter to identify the specific challenges and possible solutions involved in effective use of paraprofessionals as one-to-one assistants.

Evaluating Paraprofessional Services

Evaluating paraprofessional services is a critical step in developing improved and successful programs for young children. Informal daily feedback helps create an atmosphere in which the paraprofessional feels secure, worthy, appreciated, and professional. This is especially true when teachers freely and sincerely express their appreciation of the paraprofessional's efforts and input.

Early childhood programs and school districts have policies concerning the schedule for evaluating professionals. If possible, the first evaluation should occur not too long after initial employment to focus on and correct misunderstandings and confused expectations. If within program policy, it may be helpful to begin with a 1-month probationary period, which can be extended or dropped, depending on the results of this initial evaluation. Such a clarification serves the interests of both parties because an effective evaluation acknowledges that the teacher, as well as the paraprofessional, can learn from the experience. The time between subsequent evaluations is lengthened to 3 or 4 months. For an experienced paraprofessional, once a year may be adequate.

Using Self-Evaluations

One formal technique is to allow paraprofessionals the opportunity to evaluate their own contributions and feelings. If the paraprofessional feels comfortable in sharing this self-evaluation with the supervising teacher, chances for growth and development can be enhanced. Perceptions of self-performance are tested against the teacher's observations and expectations. The teacher has the opportunity to provide constructive feedback, to offer encouragement, and to coach. The self-evaluation process may be open-ended, or it may be guided by a checklist such as the one illustrated in Figure 10.3.

As noted in the directions in Figure 10.3, using recent critical incidents is typically a practical technique for clarifying role behaviors and learning. By contrasting a successful event with a not-so-successful one, a problem-solving approach can emphasize conditions necessary for future success rather than belabor criticism of a past problem. When a paraprofessional or volunteer has not been doing something believed necessary (e.g., has failed to listen to children), the teacher can probe the consequences of such behavior. The teacher should be prepared to provide an example of when such a failure or neglect led to an inappropriate consequence. Then both the teacher and paraprofessional should work toward a plan of action for reducing the frequency of the undesirable behavior.

Teacher-Initiated Evaluations of the Paraprofessional

Teacher-initiated evaluations of paraprofessionals are necessary because some people see their own behavior in a more positive light than do others. Thus, the self-evaluation conference potentially must deal with distortions in perception between the

Figure 10.3 Self-evaluation worksheet for paraprofessionals

Name: _____   Date: _____

Check the appropriate box for each question as it applies to you. On the back of this page, note briefly two examples (contrasting if possible) of recent experiences for each question.

HOW OFTEN DO I . . .	Usually	Some-times	Seldom
1. Follow directions of the classroom teacher?	[ ]	[ ]	[ ]
2. Observe closely techniques used by the teacher and put them into practice when working with children and groups?	[ ]	[ ]	[ ]
3. Offer my services to the teacher when there is an apparent need for help?	[ ]	[ ]	[ ]
4. Plan for assigned tasks with children rather than wing it on a hit-or-miss basis?	[ ]	[ ]	[ ]
5. Observe closely to realize individual children's likes, dislikes, interests, and limitations?	[ ]	[ ]	[ ]
6. Allow children time to think and act on their own before giving directive help?	[ ]	[ ]	[ ]
7. Find opportunities for giving children choices in daily activities?	[ ]	[ ]	[ ]
8. Really listen to what children have to say?	[ ]	[ ]	[ ]
9. Acknowledge children's successes and appropriate behaviors and minimize failures or inappropriate behaviors?	[ ]	[ ]	[ ]
10. Accept suggestions and criticisms without becoming emotionally upset?	[ ]	[ ]	[ ]

paraprofessional and teacher. As long as the primary reason for evaluation is personal and team improvement, the dangers of conflict due to differing perceptions are reduced. An evaluation initiated by the teacher overcomes the potential clash between views, especially when the teacher uses a form or checklist. However, teacher-initiated evaluation can generate anxiety and defensiveness on the part of the one being evaluated. Success in either case hinges on the manner in which the teacher handles the conference.

It is better for the teacher to focus on specific behaviors rather than on generalities such as dependability or interpersonal relations. To do this effectively, the teacher needs to take the time to describe specific behaviors of the paraprofessional that are helping or hindering performance effectiveness. An easy technique for organizing a face-to-face evaluation conference is for the teacher to list a select few behavioral descriptions under the following three focal areas:

1. To enrich your performance, consider increasing or doing more often the following.
2. To help maintain your performance, keep doing the following things much the same as you have been doing them.
3. To avoid diminishing your performance, decrease or stop doing the following.

The teacher and the paraprofessional then discuss each of the behaviors to be increased, decreased, or maintained. Specific incidents are used to interpret and demonstrate why the change (or maintenance) would be helpful. The lists for each category should not be too long. The objective is to identify a few important behaviors that conceivably could be changed with concentrated effort. The teacher encourages commitment to some plan of action for changing, but improvement of the paraprofessional's performance may mean that the teacher has to change also if she or he is part of the cause of the problem.

The key to a meaningful evaluation is not what is written but rather the discussion of the recorded comments between the teacher and paraprofessional. The conference is the basis for developing objectives or intended targets of change (and behavior maintenance) in the future. In a "management by objectives" fashion, any objectives and action plans agreed on by the teacher and his or her paraprofessional can be briefly written, dated, and signed by both. Each subsequent review considers progress toward attaining the previously formed objectives. Collectively, these periodic evaluations are the basis for the year-end evaluation required for paraprofessionals in most school districts. As a psychological benefit, however, the periodic conferences reduce the chances that the teacher will take the paraprofessional for granted, and they encourage professional-like involvement.

Paraprofessional's Evaluation of the Teacher

Teachers who are dedicated to developing an effective use of paraprofessional services find it valuable to evaluate themselves as responsible models of instructional excellence and supervisors of paraprofessionals. If teachers and paraprofessionals have developed a relationship of trust and professionalism, teachers can gain much from the paraprofessionals' evaluative feedback. Teachers need to know when their directions are not clear, when they are expecting too much, and when they have been unappreciative or unresponsive. Most teachers do not wish to be negative or ineffective. They are human, however, and do err from time to time. Everyone will benefit from a two-way communication of constructive feedback and positive reinforcement.

Because the objective of a paraprofessional's evaluation of the teacher is to improve their role relationship and team performance, the process needs to be kept simple. Paraprofessionals need to be given an opportunity to capture their thoughts on paper, however, before any face-to-face meeting. This provides the paraprofessional the security of having reflected on and organized thoughts about the quality of the role relationship. A time should be scheduled, and the paraprofessional should be requested to bring in some written comments or feedback. A most effective way of promoting such preparation is to use a simple three-part variation of the technique mentioned in the previous section. Such an evaluation focuses on the following three items:

1. You could help my performance and our team effort if you would *increase* or do more often the following things.

2. I could do a better job of helping you if you would *decrease* or stop doing the following things.

3. To help maintain good performance, *continue* doing these things much the same as you have been doing.

If both the teacher and paraprofessional use a variation of the same three *increase, decrease,* or *continue* role-behavior issues, the process is enhanced. The simplicity of this form of evaluation enables the teacher and paraprofessional to think in parallel terms, considering what each of them can do to help the other so they both benefit. The concept of increasing, decreasing, or maintaining certain behaviors is easily understood. Not using scales, scores, or rating points reduces the defensiveness and anxiety of either party. The conference focuses on the three levels, inviting objectives and strategies for dealing with the specific identified behaviors.

Preventing Paraprofessional Burnout

Teachers are expected to both supervise and support paraprofessionals assigned to their classrooms or centers. Direct supervision expects the teacher, not the paraprofessional, to design and develop all aspects of instruction, including structuring the environment, creating staffing arrangements, selecting behavioral interventions, and so forth. Direct supervision does not mean that the teacher must have an eye on the paraprofessional at all times, but it does mean that the teacher knows how the paraprofessional is going about supporting instruction at all times (Austin, 2014). As discussed, direct supervision also means that teachers will be supportive, as evidenced in encouragement, feedback, and structure, so that paraprofessionals can more easily perform their jobs. Nevertheless, the tendency toward extreme disillusionment with one's job—professional burnout—is common among paraprofessionals.

Early educators will benefit from considering the following list of reasons for burnout:

1. Inadequate training of the paraprofessional for allocated responsibilities and inadequate training of teachers to provide the required supervision; this combination could make it more difficult to form a productive, professional team.

2. Stagnation resulting from lack of opportunity for professional development and advancement.

3. Poor organizational structure due to undefined role descriptions and unclear understanding of lines of authority.

4. Poor salaries for those who do not have the opportunity to advance.

5. Lack of recognition, especially when highly competent paraprofessionals are a threat to those in positions of authority.

6. Assignment of inappropriate responsibilities.

7. Lack of support from and time to communicate with partner teachers.

For additional information on ways to build effective teacher–paraprofessional relationships, see "Power Teaming: Strategies to Enhance Teacher–Paraeducator Partnerships," available at http://www.thearcoftexas.org/site/DocServer/Friday_Lasater_Power_Teaming.pdf?docID=1104.

Even though teachers may not be in a position to implement a career ladder, they can provide opportunities for paraprofessionals to feel valued and needed. We have discussed the importance of clear job descriptions, the need to discover and incorporate special skills and talents to help the paraprofessional feel like a contributing member of the team, and some helpful ways to show appreciation. Even these basic strategies will go a long way toward preventing burnout for those paraprofessionals who have become credible members of early education teams.

The effectiveness of paraprofessionals, whatever their role, depends greatly on not only their skills, but also their motivation. Because paraprofessionals work more because of a desire to help young children than for tangible rewards, the jobs they are expected to do should allow for the growth of their abilities. Paraprofessionals should feel that their supervising teacher values their attempts to enhance their skills. That is, supervising teachers should encourage them to pursue their interests by attending relevant conferences, taking courses, and so on.

Career Ladders for Paraprofessionals

Paraprofessionals who may be reading this text and who are motivated to seek teacher certification should investigate career ladder opportunities. Given the severe shortage of teachers with certification in special education, state agencies have created a pathway for paraprofessionals to obtain teacher certification. This is one way to recruit and retain teachers in high-need specializations, such as special education and bilingual education, plus increase the cultural and linguistic diversity among teachers. Some universities have state or federal funding in partnership with school districts to create and support an alternative certification route for paraprofessionals (Morrison & Lighter, 2017). When funding is available, states have provided funds to school districts to create a career ladder for paraprofessionals. In collaboration with local universities, school districts often provide financial support for paraprofessionals to complete undergraduate degrees and teacher certification (Commission on Teacher Credentialing, 2015).

Morrison and Lighter (2017) identified certain challenges such as (a) paraprofessionals that did not meet the entrance requirements for the university, and (b) figuring out how to give credit for previous learning experiences through documentation. Advance tutoring helped some paraprofessionals pass required tests, and taking courses at community colleges increased their GPAs. Benefits of this alternative route program include the tendency for paraprofessionals (a) to have connections in the communities that motivated them to want to teach there, (b) to have real-world experiences and insights to contribute to class discussions, and (c) to be able to apply what they learned in university courses to the classrooms where they are employed.

Summary

This chapter has dealt with a wide range of topics related to providing support for young children with disabilities in inclusive settings. Central to effective inclusive support are the processes of teaming, collaboration, problem solving, and conflict resolution. Two common approaches to inclusion support are itinerant consultation and co-teaching.

The role of the paraprofessional is expanding via the use of one-to-one assistants. Paraprofessionals are valuable resources for extending the teacher's care and development of young children. The extent to which this potential is realized depends primarily on how the teacher communicates expectations and develops a working relationship with paraprofessionals.

To be effective, teachers must have the confidence necessary to optimally supervise and support those under their direction.

As young children with disabilities are included in community-based early childhood education classes, the set of approaches and strategies described in this chapter will be increasingly critical to the promotion of the learning, development, and well-being of young children with disabilities and their families.

Reflect and Apply

1. Describe the advantages and challenges of inclusive early childhood special education programs compared with specialized programs that serve preschoolers with disabilities.

2. Discuss the elements of "conflict resolution" and why these skills are important in high-quality inclusion programs serving children with disabilities.

3. Explain the "models of service delivery" for teaching children with IEPs in preschool inclusion programs. Discuss the advantages and disadvantages of three different models.

4. You are asked to design a new early childhood special education program. What methods will you use to ensure effective, high-quality guidance and supervision of paraprofessionals in your program?

5. Assume you will be in a position to supervise and support a one-to-one teaching assistant. Consider some of the challenges that will likely evolve and describe what you will do to make certain the paraprofessional is not only effective but also an important, valued member of the team.

Appendix A
Chart of Typical Development

	Gross Motor Skills	Fine Motor Skills	Language Comprehension	Expressive Communication
0 to 3 months	Holds head up in prone position. Lifts head when held at shoulder. Kicks reciprocally. Rolls from side to supine position.	Moves arms symmetrically. Follows with eyes to midline. Brings hands to midline in supine position. Activates arms on sight of toy.	Responds to voice. Watches speaker's eyes and mouth. Searches with eyes for sound.	Cries when hungry or uncomfortable. Makes comfort sounds.
3 to 6 months	Holds head in line with body when pulled to sitting. Bears weight on hands in prone position. Sits with light support. Holds head steady in supported sitting position. Rolls from supine position to side.	Follows with eyes without moving head. Keeps hands open most of time. Uses palmar grasp. Reaches and grasps objects.	Quiets to mother's voice. Distinguishes between friendly and angry voices. Responds to own name.	Coos variety of vowel sounds. Laughs. Takes turns. Responds to speech by vocalizing. Expresses displeasure and excitement.
6 to 9 months	Exhibits body-righting reaction. Extends arms protectively. Sits independently, but may use hands. Stands holding on. Pulls to stand. Crawls backward. Gets into sitting position without assistance.	Transfers object. Manipulates toy actively with wrist movement. Reaches and grasps with extended elbow.	Looks at pictures briefly. Looks for family members or pets when named. Responds to simple requests with gesture.	Babbles to people. Produces variety of consonants in babbling. Babbles with adult inflection. Babbles reduplicated syllables, "mama," "baba," etc. Vocalizes loudly to get attention.

Sources:

Adapted from the following:

The Carolina Curriculum for Infants and Toddlers with Special Needs, by N. M. Johnson-Martin, S. M. Attermeier, and B. Hacker, 2004, Baltimore: Brookes.

The Carolina Curriculum for Preschoolers with Special Needs, by N. M. Johnson-Martin, B. Hacker, and S. M. Attermeier, 2004, Baltimore: Brookes.

Help 3-6 Assessment Manual, by P. Teaford, 2010, Palo Alto, CA: VORT Corp.

HELP Hawaii Early Learning Profile, by Stephanie Parks, 2006, Palo Alto, CA: VORT Corp.

Transdisciplinary Play-Based Assessment, by T. W. Linder and T. Anthony, 2008, Baltimore: Brookes.

Cognitive Skills	Self-Help Skills	Social Skills
Inspects surroundings. Shows anticipation. Inspects own hands.	Opens mouth in response to food stimulus. Coordinates sucking, swallowing, and breathing.	Regards face. Enjoys physical contact; molds, relaxes body when held. Makes eye contact. Expresses distress.
Begins rattle play. Repeats/continues familiar activity. Uses hands and mouth for sensory exploration of objects. Plays with own hands, fingers, toes.	Brings hand to mouth holding toy or object. Swallows strained or pureed foods. Inhibits rooting reflex.	Smiles socially. Discriminates strangers. Demands attention. Vocalizes pleasure or displeasure. Enjoys social play, e.g., "This Little Piggy." Lifts arms to mother.
Works to obtain desired out-of-reach object. Finds object observed being hidden. Touches adult's hand or toy to restart an activity. Plays 2 to 3 minutes with single toy. Follows trajectory of fast-moving object. Shows interest in sounds of object.	Uses tongue to move food in mouth (4 to 8 months). Holds own bottle. Mouths and gums solid foods. Bites voluntarily; inhibits bite reflex. Feeds self a cracker.	Recognizes mother (4 to 8 months). Displays stranger anxiety. Smiles at mirror image. Shows anxiety to separation from mother.

	Gross Motor Skills	**Fine Motor Skills**	**Language Comprehension**	**Expressive Communication**
9 to 12 months	Creeps on hands and knees. Moves from sitting to prone position. Stands momentarily. Walks holding on to furniture (cruises).	Takes objects out of container. Uses both hands freely. Tries to imitate scribble. Puts object into container. Releases object voluntarily. Pokes with index finger. Uses neat pincer grasp.	Understands "no no." Listens selectively to familiar words. Enjoys looking at books.	Babbles single consonant–vowel syllables, e.g., "ba." Responds to certain words (e.g., "wave bye bye") with appropriate gesture. Uses behaviors and vocalization to express needs.
12 to 18 months	Stands from supine position. Walks without support. Throws ball. Creeps up stairs. Pulls toy while walking. Carries large toy while walking. Moves to music.	Uses two hands in midline, one holding, one manipulating. Scribbles spontaneously. Places pegs in pegboard. Builds two- to three-cube tower.	Responds to simple verbal requests; identifies one body part. Understands many nouns. Brings objects from another room on request.	Combines gestures and vocalizations to express a variety of communicative functions. Says "Dada" or "Mama" purposefully. Uses single words. Uses exclamations, e.g., "Oh, oh!" Says "no" meaningfully. Uses 10 to 15 words (by 18 months).
18 to 24 months	Moves on "ride-on" toys without pedals. Walks upstairs holding railing, both feet on step. Picks up toy from floor without falling. Runs.	Imitates circular scribble. Imitates horizontal stroke. Holds crayon with fist.	Identifies three to six body parts. Matches sounds to animals. Understands personal pronouns, some action verbs, and some adjectives. Enjoys nursery rhymes.	Uses intelligible words about 65% of the time. May use jargon (syllable strings that sound like speech). Tells experience using jargon and words. Uses two-word sentences. Names two or three pictures. Attempts to sing songs with words. Imitates three- to four-word phrase.

Cognitive Skills	Self-Help Skills	Social Skills
Overcomes obstacle to obtain object. Retrieves object using other material. Imitates gestures. Unwraps a toy. Enjoys looking at books.	Finger feeds variety of foods. Holds spoon. Cooperates with dressing by extending arm or leg. Chews by munching.	Enjoys turn-taking games. Resists supine position. Shows like and dislike for certain people, objects, or situations. Shows toys to others; does not release. Tests parents' reactions at feeding and bedtime by new and mischievous behavior.
Understands adult's pointing. Hands toy back to adult. Matches objects. Places round and square pieces in form board. Nests two or three cans. Identifies self in mirror.	May refuse food; appetite decreases. Brings spoon to mouth. Drinks from cup with some spilling. Indicates discomfort over soiled pants. Removes socks.	Displays independent behavior; may be difficult to discipline. May display tantrum behavior. Demonstrates sense of humor. Is easily distractible; has difficulty sitting still.
Finds object not observed being hidden. Activates mechanical toy. Matches objects to pictures. Sorts objects. Explores cabinets and drawers. Remembers where objects belong. Recognizes self in photo.	Scoops food, feeds self with spoon. Chews with rotary jaw movements. Plays with food. Removes shoe when laces undone. Zips/unzips large zipper. Shows awareness of need to eliminate.	Expresses affection. Expresses wide range of emotions, including jealousy, fear, anger, sympathy, embarrassment, anxiety, and joy. Attempts to control others; resists control; peer interaction is somewhat aggressive. Engages in parallel play. Enjoys solitary play occasionally.

	Gross Motor Skills	Fine Motor Skills	Language Comprehension	Expressive Communication
24 to 36 months	Runs forward well. Jumps in place, two feet together. Stands on one foot, with aid. Walks on tiptoe. Kicks ball forward.	Strings four large beads. Turns pages singly. Snips with scissors. Holds crayon with thumb and fingers, not fist. Uses one hand consistently in most activities. Paints with some wrist action; makes dots, lines, circular strokes. Rolls, pounds, squeezes, and pulls clay.	Points to pictures of common objects when they are named. Can identify objects when told their use. Understands question forms *what* and *where*. Understands negatives *no*, *not*, *can't*, and *don't*. Enjoys listening to simple storybooks and requests them again.	Joins vocabulary words together in two-word phrases. Gives first and last name. Asks *what* and *where* questions. Makes negative statements (e.g., "Can't open it"). Shows frustration at not being understood. Sustains conversation for two or three turns.
36 to 48 months	Runs around obstacles. Walks on a line. Balances on one foot for 5 to 10 seconds. Hops on one foot. Pushes, pulls, and steers wheeled toys. Rides (i.e., steers and pedals) tricycle. Uses slide without assistance. Jumps over 15-centimeter (6-inch)-high object, landing on both feet together. Throws ball over head. Catches ball bounced to him or her.	Builds tower of nine small blocks. Drives nails and pegs. Copies circle. Imitates cross. Manipulates clay materials (e.g., rolls balls, snakes, cookies).	Begins to understand sentences involving time concepts (e.g., "We are going to the zoo tomorrow"). Understands size comparatives such as *big* and *bigger*. Understands relationships expressed by *if . . . then* or *because* sentences. Carries out a series of two to four related directions. Understands when told, "Let's pretend."	Talks in sentences of three or more words, which take the form agent-action-object ("I see the ball") or agent-action-location ("Daddy sit on chair"). Tells about past experiences. Uses *-s* on nouns to indicate plurals. Uses *-ed* on verbs to include past tense. Refers to self using pronouns *I* or *me*. Repeats at least one nursery rhyme and can sing a song. Speech is understandable to strangers, but there are still some sound errors.

Cognitive Skills		Self-Help Skills	Social Skills
Selects and looks at picture books, names pictured objects, and identifies several objects within one picture. Matches and uses associated objects meaningfully (e.g., given cup, saucer, and bead, puts cup and saucer together). Stacks rings on peg in order of size. Uses self and objects in pretend play.	Can talk briefly about what he or she is doing. Imitates adult actions (e.g., housekeeping play). Has limited attention span; learning is through exploration and adult direction (as in reading of picture stories). Is beginning to understand functional concepts of familiar objects (e.g., that a spoon is used for eating) and part/whole concepts (e.g., parts of the body).	Gets drink from fountain or faucet unassisted. Opens door by turning handle. Takes off coat. Puts on coat with assistance. Washes and dries hands with assistance.	Watches other children; joins briefly in their play. Defends own possessions. Begins to play house. Participates in simple group activity (e.g., sings, claps, dances). Knows gender identity.
Recognizes and matches six colors. Intentionally stacks blocks or rings in order of size. Draws somewhat recognizable picture that is meaningful to child, if not to adult; names and briefly explains picture. Asks questions for information: *why* and *how* questions requiring simple answers. Knows own age. Knows own last name.	Has short attention span; learns through observing and imitating adults, and by adult instruction and explanation; is easily distracted. Has increased understanding of concepts of the functions and grouping of objects (e.g., can put doll house furniture in correct rooms); part/whole (e.g., can identify pictures of hand and foot as parts of body). Begins to be aware of past and present (e.g., "Yesterday we went to the park. Today we go to the library").	Pours well from small pitcher. Spreads soft butter with knife. Buttons and unbuttons large buttons. Washes hands unassisted. Blows nose when reminded. Uses toilet independently.	Joins in play with other children; begins to interact. Shares toys; takes turns with assistance. Begins dramatic play, acting out whole scenes (e.g., traveling, playing house, pretending to be animals). Comforts peers in distress.

	Gross Motor Skills	Fine Motor Skills	Language Comprehension	Expressive Communication
48 to 60 months	Walks backward toe-heel. Jumps forward 10 times without falling. Walks up and down stairs alone, alternating feet. Turns somersault.	Cuts on line continuously. Copies cross. Copies square. Prints a few capital letters.	Follows three unrelated commands in proper order. Understands comparatives such as *pretty*, *prettier*, and *prettiest*. Listens to long stories, but often misinterprets the facts. Incorporates verbal directions into play activities. Understands sequencing of events when told (e.g., "First we have to go to the store, then we can make the cake, and tomorrow we will eat it").	Asks *when*, *how*, and *why* questions. Uses modals such as *can*, *will*, *shall*, *should*, and *might*. Joins sentences together (e.g., "I went to the store and I bought some ice cream"). Talks about causality by using *because* and *so*. Tells the content of a story but may confuse facts.
60 to 72 months	Runs lightly on toes. Walks on balance beam. Can cover 2 meters (6 1/2 feet) hopping. Skips on alternate feet. Jumps rope. Skates.	Cuts out simple shapes. Copies triangle. Traces diamond. Copies first name. Prints numerals 1 to 5. Colors within lines. Has adult grasp of pencil. Has handedness well established (i.e., child is left- or right-handed). Pastes and glues appropriately. Uses classroom tools appropriately.	Demonstrates preacademic skills.	There are few obvious differences between child's grammar and adult's grammar. Still needs to learn such things as subject–verb agreement and some irregular past-tense verbs. Can take appropriate turns in a conversation. Gives and receives information. Communicates well with family, friends, or strangers. Retells story from picture book with accuracy.

Cognitive Skills		**Self-Help Skills**	**Social Skills**
Points to and names four to six colors. Matches pictures of familiar objects (e.g., shoe, sock, foot, apple, orange, banana). Draws a person with two to six recognizable parts, such as head, arms, legs; can name or match drawn parts to own body. Draws, names, and describes recognizable picture. Rote counts to 5, imitating adults. Describes what will happen next. Dramatic play is closer to reality, with attention paid to detail, time, and space.	Knows own street and town. Has more extended attention span; learns through observing and listening to adults as well as through exploration; is easily distracted. Has increased understanding of concepts of function, time, part/whole relationships. Function or use of objects may be stated in addition to names of objects. Time concepts are expanding. The child can talk about yesterday or last week (a long time ago), about today, and about what will happen tomorrow.	Cuts easy foods with a knife (e.g., hamburger patty, tomato slice). Laces shoes.	Plays and interacts with other children. Plays dress-up. Shows interest in exploring gender differences.
Names some letters and numerals. Rote counts to 10. Sorts objects by single characteristics (e.g., by color, shape, or size—if the difference is obvious). Is beginning to use accurately time concepts of *tomorrow* and *yesterday*.	Begins to relate clock time to daily schedule. Attention span increases noticeably; learns through adult instruction; when interested, can ignore distractions. Concepts of function increase as well as understanding of why things happen; time concepts are expanding into an understanding of the future in terms of major events (e.g., "Christmas will come after two weekends").	Dresses self completely. Ties bow. Brushes teeth unassisted. Crosses street safely.	Chooses own friend(s). Plays simple table games. Plays competitive games. Engages in cooperative play with other children involving group decisions, role assignments, and fair play.

Strategies for Helping Children with Specific Disabilities Participate in Inclusive Settings

The following suggestions have been field tested and are based on discussions with inclusion specialists and professionals in the fields of special education and low-incidence disabilities. The information is organized according to different play or work areas and group settings typically found in child development centers and preschools. Suggestions are listed by disability (cognitive delays, physical disabilities, deafness or hard of hearing, visual disabilities, etc.). While most of these strategies are also included in Chapter 5, the authors hope that this format may be useful in and of itself.

Tips for Helping the Child with Cognitive Delays

Art Area

- Be aware of small objects that may be choking hazards to the child with developmental delays who still puts things in his or her mouth.
- Choose activities that emphasize process.
- Choose activities that the child can participate in at varying developmental levels (e.g., collage making, scribbling, painting, using clay or play dough).

Manipulatives Area

- Be aware of small objects that may be choking hazards to the child with developmental delays who still puts things in his or her mouth.
- Provide containers for the child to put smaller items in and take out, rather than assembling to create an end product.
- Use see-through containers with lids that need adult help to open. The child needs to ask for help, resulting in less dumping and more control within manipulatives area.

Block Area

- See suggestions for the manipulatives area.

Pretend Play Area (e.g., dress-up, transportation)

- Provide opportunities for the child to use representations of real objects (e.g., dolls, bottles, cars) to engage in imitative play.
- Use play scripts to help the child understand "what comes next" and learn key words associated with play.
- Use simple dress-up items (hat, scarf, bag, purse, shoes) and have a mirror available.

Gross Motor Area or Activities and Outside Play

- Allow the child to use whole body when interacting with objects from other areas (e.g., push the baby in the cart, transport blocks in a small wagon).
- Weight the carts or wagons for sensory feedback.
- Allow the child to stand, if preferred, when doing tabletop activities so he or she can move but still focus on activities.
- Use classroom equipment to create obstacle courses: on, in, up, over, under, through, and so on.
- Give the child opportunities to engage in sliding, swinging, and bouncing on equipment but be aware of possible health concerns: for example, *a child with Down syndrome may have serious problems with his or spine and should never be encouraged to do somersaults.*

Large-Group Activities

- Try to have shorter group activities rather than longer activities in which the child may begin to lose interest.
- Allow the child to bring a transitional object to the circle that represents a favorite activity and helps ease the transition into a large-group activity.
- Provide photos or symbols in a "What's next" format so the child can see what will happen after circle time.
- Suggest appropriate ways for the child to ask to leave a large group if it becomes too overwhelming (e.g., using words, such as *out*; signaling with a picture or symbol; going to a specific adult).
- Use music! Even a silent child will often vocalize during music or singing.
- Use switches and loop tapes to give the child a "voice" during activities.
- Use preferential seating for the child to make the most use of his or her sight, hearing, body, and so on.
- Try to conduct a large-group activity in an area of the room with the *least* amount of distractions (e.g., avoid areas with open shelves with toys easily seen, walls with things to poke at or rip or pull, large objects like rocking chairs to climb on or under, etc.).

Books

- Choose books that have repetitive phrases or refrains.
- Choose books that relate to the child's everyday experience.
- Choose books with clear pictures and high contrast between foreground and background.

- Choose books with uncluttered pictures (e.g., many things happening in same picture, "busy" backgrounds, etc.).

Tips for Helping the Child with Physical Disabilities

Art Area

- Use Velcro handles on brushes, markers, and so forth and make a Velcro hand holder for the child.
- Build up handles of brushes, markers, crayons, and so on with masking or duct tape so the child has a large enough handle to grasp.
- Melt leftover crayon pieces and pour into small-sized paper cups; before wax solidifies, add length of ribbon or yarn across diameter with several centimeters (inches) excess on either side; when wax is set, remove from cup; use ribbon to tie around the child's hand as he or she grasps the chunky crayon. Ribbon helps keep the crayon in the hand even if grasp is not consistent.
- Use Dy-Cem mats, suction cups, mounting tape, and so on to help keep materials in place as the child works on projects.
- Try to use art materials to help facilitate grasp rather than pieces of cutout paper, which are difficult to pick up off flat surfaces (e.g., cut pieces of pipe cleaners rather than flat pieces of construction paper to create a picture of silkworms).

Manipulatives Area

- Use large Rubbermaid-type containers (sweater sized) and cut out part of one side so the child can slide arms in to play with manipulatives or other textures and won't "lose" material.
- Cut out empty bleach bottle to make scoop; use the Velcro idea noted earlier if needed; the child can scoop up smaller objects that he or she may not be able to pick up with fingers.
- Encourage the child to cross midline and use both hands, even if very difficult.

Block Area

- See suggestions for the manipulatives area.

Pretend Play Area (e.g., dress-up, transportation)

- Provide dress-up clothes with Velcro instead of buttons and zippers.
- Use simple dress-up items (hat, scarf, bag, purse, shoes) and have a mirror available.
- Position the child on the floor to encourage self-dressing from a stable position.

Gross Motor Area or Activities and Outside Play

- Weight the carts or wagons for sensory feedback.
- Adapt tricycles by using Velcro or straps to help keep the child's feet on the pedals.

- Give the child opportunities to engage in sliding, swinging, and bouncing on equipment but be aware of possible health concerns: for example, a child with shunts may not be able to tolerate being upside down because the shunt may not work in that position.
- Partially deflate beach-type balls to allow easier grasp for catching and tossing.
- Consider purchasing adapted bikes that may be propelled by using arms instead of legs.

Large-Group Activities

- Use preferential seating for the child to make the most use of his or her sight, hearing, body, and so on to help maintain the child's attention and access to sensory cues.
- Be sure that the child is seated at the same level as peers—not in a wheelchair or stander if everyone else is on floor.
- Use objects with magnets such as calendars so the child can slide the objects around, rather than try to pick them up or knock them off the work surface.
- Add prosthetic devices to musical instruments or other group-time objects to allow the child to hold onto them more easily.

Environment

- Arrange the environment so there is space for the child to independently manipulate the walker or wheelchair to different areas of the room.

Tips for Helping the Child Who Is Deaf or Hard of Hearing

Circle Time/Story Time

- Determine family's preference regarding communication modality: signing, speech, or both.
- Seat the child close to the speaker in the best position to see and hear.
- Be aware of acoustic resonance and ambient noise in the room. Try to reduce wherever possible (e.g., use carpets, sound-absorbent materials, and decorations; do not seat the child near a noisy air conditioner or open window with traffic noise; etc.).
- Make sure the child's hearing aid is working properly.
- Use music with a strong bass beat.

Outside Play

- Use touch and visual cues to obtain the child's attention if he or she doesn't respond to your verbal cues.
- To increase the child's hearing in a noisy environment, move closer rather than yelling. (The child's hearing aid transmits clearest sounds from near distance.)

Art and Crafts Activity

- Support verbal instructions with demonstrations and pictures.

Tips for Helping the Child with Visual Impairment

Art Area

- Emphasize textures to increase interest and awareness.
- Emphasize contrasts (e.g., dark paper with light-colored paint, chalk, etc. or light paper with dark materials).
- Use additional lighting at work areas.
- Confine the child's work to the tray or an area that has edges so the child can organize and find needed materials.
- Reduce the amount of clutter in and around the child's work area.
- Have the child place his or her hand on top of the teacher's hand to introduce new materials: the teacher holds the new material, object, art media; the teacher lets the child feel the new material with his or her fingertips; and as the child becomes comfortable, the teacher gently rolls the child's hand around so the child feels more of the material that the teacher is holding.

Manipulatives Area

- Use large Rubbermaid-type containers (sweater sized) and cut out part of one side so the child can slide arms in to play with manipulatives or other textures and won't "lose" material.
- Reduce clutter so the child can easily find what he or she needs to build.
- Place objects in the child's work area with spaces between them so the child can find separate objects (if objects are clustered together, a child with low vision may think it's one solid object and not several pieces).
- See suggestions for the art area for ideas about lighting, space, and so on.

Block Area

- See suggestions for the manipulatives area.

Pretend Play Area (e.g., dress-up, transportation)

- Use play scripts to help the child understand "what comes next" and learn key words associated with play.
- Help the child learn where objects are: dolls, dress-up clothes; pretend food, cups, plates; and so forth.

Gross Motor Area or Activities and Outside Play

- Weight the carts or wagons for sensory feedback.

- Be aware of how glare from a sunny day may slow down a child with vision impairment. Contrast between darker inside rooms and outside can be exaggerated for a child with vision impairment.
- Encourage the child to move around the yard—discourage the child from playing only on the swing or in the sandbox (the safest places on the playground!).
- A child with vision impairment may have great fear of the outdoors—the environment is larger and changing all the time. Provide extra time and support to dispel the "fear factor."

Large-Group Activities

- Use preferential seating for the child to make the most use of his or her sight, hearing, body, and so on.
- Purchase and use a Braille lap calendar during calendar time for an older child.

Environment

- For a blind child, label all parts of the environment in Braille (that the child can reach).
- Use texture cues (e.g., a piece of sandpaper, cloth, rubber) to identify the child's chair, cubby, and so on.
- Use color to maximize visual contrast between different areas of the room.

Books

- Choose books that relate to the child's everyday experiences.
- Choose books with clear pictures and high contrast between foreground and background.
- Choose books with uncluttered pictures (e.g., many things happening in same picture, "busy" backgrounds, etc.).
- Use Braille imprint and tactile books.
- Give a child with low vision his or her own book (the same one the teacher has) to follow along in while the teacher reads to the class.

Appendix C

Common Sequence of Training Steps Used in Milieu Approaches

Step 1. Conduct high-preference inventory.

Identify the objects, persons, and events that interest and motivate the infant or young child.

Step 2. Create the need or opportunity to communicate.

Using procedures like time delay or violation of routines, manipulate environmental variables to encourage attempts to communicate. Keep in mind that identifying the objects, persons, and events that interest and motivate the infant or young child is a critical prerequisite to this step.

Step 3. Pause and wait. Give the child an opportunity to initiate communication.

For children with severe disabilities, this may take 10 to 20 seconds (as opposed to children without disabilities, who can organize and produce a behavior in 1 or 2 seconds). There are two ways in which the pause-and-wait strategy can be used. Early in teaching, it is often helpful to look expectantly at the child. Many teachers will find it very difficult to look at a child without saying anything for 10 to 20 seconds. However, in some cases, the use of this time delay can produce previously unseen communicative behaviors. When the child has acquired the behavior (e.g., directed eye gaze, pointing at an object, pointing at a picture, etc.), instead of looking expectantly at the child during the wait period, the teacher can move or turn away as though busy doing something else. This procedure can be used to encourage the use of an attention-getting behavior such as vocalizing or activating an augmentative and alternative communication (AAC) switch. Initially, this procedure will require two teachers: one teacher to implement the delay while another observes the child's unsuccessful attempts and provides prompts and cues.

Step 4. Provide a natural cue.

Initially in teaching a communicative behavior, cues and prompts can be provided when the child is unable to respond or responds inappropriately during the pause period. It is important, however, that cues and prompts *not* be provided every time, lest the child learn to simply wait through a series of prompts to eventually obtain the desired communicative consequence. Occasionally, the opportunity to communicate should simply be terminated until a later time during the day. This is particularly appropriate for optional situations such as choosing a toy or dessert. When a child does not respond during the pause period, employ a *natural* cue. A natural verbal cue is one that is likely to occur in the natural environment, for example, someone asking, "What do you want?" or "Can I help you?" or "Tell me what you want to do now." If the child still does not respond, prompts may be used.

Step 5. Use prompts and assistance.

A wide variety of prompts may be used to assist the child in communicative behavior. Many of these are borrowed from behavioral teaching strategies. Perhaps the most commonly used prompting strategy is the use of **modeling**. Modeling can be an effective prompt for children who have a generalized imitation strategy and who will attempt to imitate the teacher's model. Unfortunately, many children with severe disabilities do not have a generalized ability to imitate a model. For these children, physical prompting and shaping may be necessary.

Physical prompting involves physically guiding the child through the behavior. For example, if you are teaching a child to reach or point toward a desired object, a physical prompt moves the child's hand and arm through the motion of pointing. Using traditional behavioral methods, gradually fade this physical prompt until the child can produce the behavior on his or her own.

To use physical prompting effectively, the "topography" of the behavior must be accessible. Unfortunately, vocalization—one very important communicative modality—does not lend itself to physical prompting. Control of vocalization is completely internal. A teacher cannot force or assist a child in vocalizing other than by use of an imitative prompt. Thus, it is important to realize that when physical prompts must be used, communicative behaviors other than vocal behaviors must be selected.

Step 6. Comply with the communicative request.

Within this sequence of steps, provide the desired object or activity at any point at which the child produces an acceptable approximation to the targeted communicative behavior. That is, the child should get the toy, be moved to a favorite location, have the CD player turned on, or whatever is desired.

In addition, the teacher should always accompany his or her compliance with the appropriate verbal input. The input strategies described earlier are very important here, particularly the use of repetition and recast sentences. As the teacher provides the desired item, he or she should say, "Oh, you want the *doll*, huh! Here's your *doll*. What a beautiful *doll*." If the child then appears to be paying attention to the doll, the teacher can semantically expand these utterances by adding a bit more information. For example, "Oh, the *doll* has a new *dress*. Look."

Appendix D
Inclusion Support Itinerant Procedures

The following section provides specific suggestions for establishing an itinerant inclusion support program. Forms referenced in the text are found at the end of this appendix.

I. Getting Started
   A. Gather information from referral sources (include individualized family service plan [IFSP] and individualized education plan [IEP] progress notes and assessment data).
   B. Meet with the family:
      1. Discuss family's concerns, priorities, and resources.
      2. Remember, parents know their child better than anyone and will have accurate perceptions of both the challenges and potential benefits in the inclusive setting.
   C. Determine who the contact person is at the site (e.g., administrator, teacher) and make an initial phone call.
   D. Contact any other support providers (e.g., therapists, behavior specialist, disability specialist, etc.).
   E. Explain the kinds of services you can provide to all parties involved; determine their expectations and needs. (*Note: For many communities, inclusion support may be a relatively new and unfamiliar service. Families may not understand your role, and early childhood educators [ECE] may believe you will be critically evaluating them in some way. It is extremely important to clarify these issues before beginning your visits to the site.*)
   F. Using the "Inclusion Planning Checklist" in conjunction with the "Possible Modifications for Effective Inclusion" (see the forms at the end of this appendix) may be helpful in working out specific details of how you will provide service, including:
      1. Frequency of visits and written reports
      2. Strategies and times for providing feedback
      3. Opportunities for suggestions and questions from parents and ECE staff

II. The First Visit
   A. It is important that the initial contacts above be made before you observe the child at the site.
   B. Set up a time for the initial visit:
      1. Be sure to touch base with the site administrator.
      2. Ask him or her to show you to the classroom and introduce you to the staff.
   C. If the initial contact described above was not with the classroom teacher, you will need to briefly explain your role.
   D. If possible, provide written material describing the possible services and activities you can offer. (*Keep in mind that you may be the first person the teacher has had contact with who has expertise and knowledge related to the nature of the child's disability.*)

Note: Be prepared to answer questions and be willing (if necessary) to obtain additional information to share with the staff.

E. During the first one or two visits, it may be best to just observe the child, take careful notes, and (without being intrusive) chat with the teacher. This is a critical time for building trust. The inclusion consultant must be aware of two important issues at this point:

    1. ECE staff are extremely busy and often shorthanded.

    2. They are unsure of your role. (Common misperceptions of your role can range from believing you are there to directly teach the child or do therapy to suspicions that you are there to evaluate their setting and their teaching skills.)

F. Document each visit. Develop a form similar to the "Inclusion Observation/ Support" form at the end of the appendix so that you, the ECE teacher, and the parent have a record of your visit and your suggestions.

    1. The form can include:

        a. Date and time of visit

        b. Your observation of the child's progress (be as positive as possible, giving credit to ECE staff for supporting the child's adjustment, using adaptations, etc.)

        c. Specific suggestions to address problems identified by staff or parents

        d. A statement of what you will do (e.g., make communication board, help with behavior analysis, make referral, discuss something with parents, etc.)

        e. Date and time of your next visit

        f. Your name and phone number

    2. A hard or digital copy of the completed form should be provided to the parents and ECSE teacher.

Note: Observations documented using the "Inclusion Observation/Support" form should emphasize the itinerant consultant's observation of the *child* and related supports, not the teacher.

G. During initial visits, try to learn other children's names. Developing relationships with several children in the class can be a helpful strategy for encouraging peer interactions.

Note: It is important that the children in the class become comfortable with you. Also, try not to highlight the fact that you are there to help a particular child—although children will eventually figure this out.

III. Ongoing Visits

A. Individualize your inclusion support activities.

    1. Determine the child's needs.

    2. Determine what is most comfortable for the ECE staff. Remember, it may take time to feel comfortable in the setting. You will react differently to different sites because of personality factors, program philosophy, location, physical characteristics of the site, and so on.

    3. Select strategies that best fit the needs of both the child and the staff:

        a. Observing and giving written or verbal feedback/recommendations

        b. Providing direct instruction with the child

        c. Modeling intervention procedures for the staff

        d. Coaching the staff

        e. Coaching peers

        f. Making adaptations of equipment and materials

        g. Obtaining resources

    4. Use the "Individual Support Schedule" form at the end of the appendix to plan how the child's goals can be met within each daily activity.

B. Adjust the frequency of visits as needed in consultation with parents, staff, and the funding agency.

C. Learn to balance the needs and expectation of the family and the ECE staff.

    1. One of the most difficult challenges for many inclusion consultants is the feeling of being "caught in the middle" of differing perspectives and priorities of key stakeholders.

    2. The inclusion consultant must prioritize family preferences yet must work within the existing parameters and realities of the inclusive setting.

    3. Often, it will be necessary for the inclusion support specialist to set aside individual biases about what is best for the child or the desire to change the practices or the philosophy of the community setting.

D. When conflicts arise that are not easily solved, learn to use conflict resolution strategies.

E. At least quarterly, write a detailed report documenting the child's progress and current needs and agreed-upon next steps and short-term goals. The "A Quick Look at the IEP" form at the end of the appendix may be useful in simplifying the IEP for use in the inclusive setting to be sure that all IEP goals are being met. Revisiting the "Inclusion Planning Checklist" and the "Inclusion Action Plan" can also assist the team in assessing planning specific revisions to ensure steady progress toward achievement of IEP goals and objectives.

F. At transition ages or as the need or desire arises for the family to consider a new placement, assist the family in this often difficult decision-making process.

G. Provide ongoing team coordination support. More often than not, the inclusion support specialist must take the lead in coordinating the activities and communication of other team members (e.g., parents, disability specialists, therapists). This is a logical role for two reasons: (a) Coordination is a very time-consuming activity, making it difficult for ECE staff to take on this responsibility, and (b) the inclusion support provider often has the most regular contact with the child and family.

Possible Modifications for Effective Inclusion

Personnel

_____ No extra support necessary
_____ Part-time extra support (specific parts of day)
_____ Full-time extra support (1:1 aide)

Physical Assistance

_____ No physical help necessary
_____ Physical help as needed
_____ Partial physical help
_____ Full physical help

Curriculum

_____ Adapt for younger cognitive level
_____ Adapt for vision impairments
_____ Adapt for hearing loss
_____ Adapt for physical disabilities

Pacing and Amount of Time for Activities

_____ Same pace and time as all other children
_____ Less time than other children (e.g., less attention)
_____ More time than other children (e.g., goes slower)
_____ Slower pacing necessary for understanding (e.g., more wait time for comprehension and/or action)

Hierarchy of Prompts

_____ Full physical help to complete activities
_____ Partial physical help to complete activities
_____ Direct verbal reminders to complete activities (e.g., "Sit down")
_____ Indirect verbal reminders to complete activities (e.g., "What do you need to do?")
_____ Gestures to complete activities (e.g., pointing)

Environment

_____ Seating adaptations (e.g., chairs too high, child does better sitting next to specific peers, etc.)
_____ Reduce or minimize distractions or stimulation
_____ Define limits (e.g., physical and/or behavioral)

Behavior

_____ Define limits (e.g., physical and/or behavioral)
_____ Use positive reinforcement
_____ Determine behavior plans through use of ABC (antecedent, behavior, consequences)

Inclusion Planning Checklist

Child: _____ **Inclusion Site:** _____

I.   Planning for inclusion *(Have you compiled, received, or had access to the following information?)*

_____ IEP/IFSP
_____ Relevant reports about child
_____ Types of available supports or resources

II. Planning for teaming *(Have you developed an ongoing communication plan?)*

_____ Who is part of the "team"?
_____ When will we meet?
_____ How often will we meet?
_____ Do all people have to be present for all meetings?
_____ How will agendas be developed and by whom?

III. Designing modifications *(How do we determine when, what, and how much?)*

_____ For each part of the daily schedule (large- and small-group periods, free play, meals, etc.), answer the question "What should the child gain from this part of the routine?"
_____ Review modification options and levels *(What needs to be changed or added to help child learn during each part of routine?)*

IV. Implementation *(How can we follow through with modification plans?)*

_____ Who will make/develop the modification or alternative material/activity?
_____ What implementation steps are involved?
_____ Determine material and personnel needs for modification.
_____ Determine allocation of supports (e.g., need for 1:1 aide).
_____ How will modification be used/explained to child and peers?
_____ How will we determine modification is working?

V.   Evaluation *(How well did modification[s] work?)*

_____ Was (were) the modification(s) and implementation successful for child?
_____ Will you keep it, reuse it, change it, or throw it out?

Individual Support Schedule

Child: _____ Date:

Teacher(s): _____ Center:

Inclusion Consultant:

Schedule	Specific Supports/Adaptations (what staff will do for child that will help child be part of activities)
Arrival	
Morning Activities (Free Play)	
Cleanup	
Toilet/Handwash	
Snack	
Circle Time	
Small Group (Work Time)	
Outside Play	

Inclusion Observation/Support

Date: _____ Child: _____ Center: _____

Teacher(s): _____ Inclusion Consultant: _____

Schedule	Observations (what consultant observes)	Supports/Adaptations (suggestions for teachers that may help child be part of activities)

Note: A hard or digital copy of the completed form should be shared with parents and staff after each visit.

Appendix E

Roles and Responsibilities of the Special Education Staff as Related to the General Education Staff in Inclusive Educational Settings

INCLUSION
COLLABORATIVE

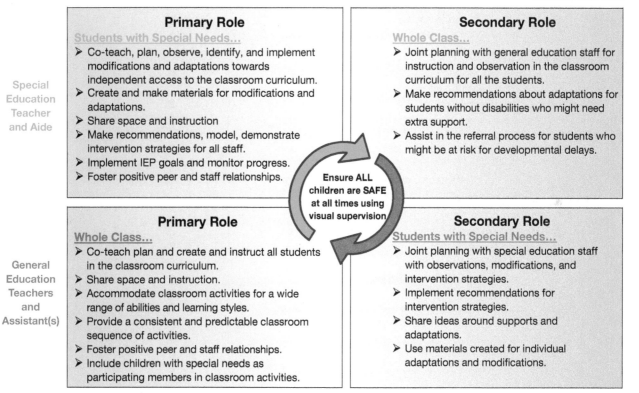

Special Education Teacher and Aide

Primary Role
Students with Special Needs...
➢ Co-teach, plan, observe, identify, and implement modifications and adaptations towards independent access to the classroom curriculum.
➢ Create and make materials for modifications and adaptations.
➢ Share space and instruction
➢ Make recommendations, model, demonstrate intervention strategies for all staff.
➢ Implement IEP goals and monitor progress.
➢ Foster positive peer and staff relationships.

Secondary Role
Whole Class...
➢ Joint planning with general education staff for instruction and observation in the classroom curriculum for all the students.
➢ Make recommendations about adaptations for students without disabilities who might need extra support.
➢ Assist in the referral process for students who might be at risk for developmental delays.

Ensure ALL children are SAFE at all times using visual supervision

General Education Teachers and Assistant(s)

Primary Role
Whole Class...
➢ Co-teach plan and create and instruct all students in the classroom curriculum.
➢ Share space and instruction.
➢ Accommodate classroom activities for a wide range of abilities and learning styles.
➢ Provide a consistent and predictable classroom sequence of activities.
➢ Foster positive peer and staff relationships.
➢ Include children with special needs as participating members in classroom activities.

Secondary Role
Students with Special Needs...
➢ Joint planning with special education staff with observations, modifications, and intervention strategies.
➢ Implement recommendations for intervention strategies.
➢ Share ideas around supports and adaptations.
➢ Use materials created for individual adaptations and modifications.

1290 Ridder Park Drive • San Jose, CA 95131 • (408) 453-6756 • www.inclusioncollaborative.org

Professional Competencies in Early Childhood Special Education

	Nonexistent	Poor	Satisfactory	Good	Excellent
I. *Appropriately and competently assesses children's strengths and needs.*					
A. Selects appropriate formal instruments.	1	2	3	4	5
B. Selects a variety of informal strategies appropriate for child's characteristics.	1	2	3	4	5
C. Collaborates with families and other professionals to gather information.	1	2	3	4	5
D. Monitors child's progress systematically to identify objectives and revise instruction as needed.	1	2	3	4	5
E. Reports assessment results in a manner useful to families.	1	2	3	4	5
F. Evaluates family involvement and satisfaction with assessment process.	1	2	3	4	5
II. *Plans effective instruction.*					
A. Works collaboratively with families in selecting goals and objectives and strategies.	1	2	3	4	5
B. Goals are related to assessment results.	1	2	3	4	5
C. Goals and objectives are clear and relevant to high-priority child and family needs.	1	2	3	4	5
D. Plan is communicated to families and other team members clearly, both verbally and in writing.	1	2	3	4	5
III. *Demonstrates understanding of how children learn and ability to utilize generic teaching strategies, including the following:*					
A. Role of social interaction.	1	2	3	4	5
B. Motivation (e.g., identifies high-preference objects, people, and events).	1	2	3	4	5
C. Arrangement of physical environment.	1	2	3	4	5
D. Use of play as both context and method.	1	2	3	4	5
E. Behavioral analysis (including task analysis and identification of antecedents and consequences).	1	2	3	4	5
F. Behavioral analysis (including use of positive reinforcement, use of cues and prompts, shaping, fading, chaining, and stimulus generalization).	1	2	3	4	5
G. Use of repetition and routines.	1	2	3	4	5
H. Appropriate caregiver–child interaction.	1	2	3	4	5
I. Critical role of family in child's development.	1	2	3	4	5

	Nonexistent	Poor	Satisfactory	Good	Excellent
IV. *Manages classroom environment to optimize learning.*					
A. Effectively arranges physical environment.	1	2	3	4	5
B. Creates appropriate classroom schedule.	1	2	3	4	5
C. Utilizes daily routines for instruction.	1	2	3	4	5
D. Creates effective play routines.	1	2	3	4	5
E. Provides opportunity for rest and quiet time.	1	2	3	4	5
F. Creates comfortable atmosphere for family involvement.	1	2	3	4	5
G. Takes responsibility for children's safety.	1	2	3	4	5
H. Effectively manages, coordinates, and involves paraprofessionals, volunteers, and consultants.	1	2	3	4	5
I. Selects highly motivating activities.	1	2	3	4	5
J. Utilizes individual as well as small- and whole-group formats appropriately.	1	2	3	4	5
K. Integrates all developmental domains (i.e., language, cognition, motor, social-emotional, and self-help) into each activity.	1	2	3	4	5
L. Applies Universal Design for Learning principles in instruction.	1	2	3	4	5
M. Acquires or creates required assistive technology to support children's participation and learning.	1	2	3	4	5
V. *Facilitates the development of communication skills.*					
A. Recognizes and correctly interprets communicative cues.	1	2	3	4	5
B. Understands the stages and characteristics of language and speech development.	1	2	3	4	5
C. Establishes turn taking.	1	2	3	4	5
D. Is responsive to child's communicative intents; follows child's lead.	1	2	3	4	5
E. Uses repetition and recasts.	1	2	3	4	5
F. Uses appropriate pacing and speech rate; waits for child's response.	1	2	3	4	5
G. Appropriately labels objects and key events.	1	2	3	4	5
H. Expands child's utterance.	1	2	3	4	5
I. Knows how to "up the ante" (e.g., prompt for better turn).	1	2	3	4	5
J. Utilizes play routines.	1	2	3	4	5
K. Selects relevant and functional communication goals.	1	2	3	4	5
L. Develops augmentative communication systems and skills as needed.	1	2	3	4	5
M. Provides opportunity for choices.	1	2	3	4	5
N. Facilitates literate, autonomous uses of language (e.g., narrative, explanation, story-telling).	1	2	3	4	5
O. Uses strategies to support English- and home-language development of dual-language learners.	1	2	3	4	5
VI. *Facilitates the development of cognitive skills.*					
A. Understands the stages and characteristics of typical cognitive development.	1	2	3	4	5
B. Creates opportunities for all children to experience "effectance" (i.e., to develop intentional behavior), and assists child to understand cause and effect.	1	2	3	4	5
C. Effectively encourages exploration and trial and error behavior through modeling, scaffolding, and use of cues and prompts.	1	2	3	4	5
D. Teaches object permanence in play and other natural activities.	1	2	3	4	5
E. Utilizes activities and materials that encourage mental representation and memory.	1	2	3	4	5
F. Develops symbolic behavior such as pretend play and recognition of graphic symbols.	1	2	3	4	5
G. Creates opportunities for problem solving and assists children in discovering solutions.	1	2	3	4	5

		Nonexistent	Poor	Satisfactory	Good	Excellent
VII.	*Facilitates emotional and social growth.*					
A.	Understands stages of social and emotional development.	1	2	3	4	5
B.	Engages in positive reciprocal interactions with child.	1	2	3	4	5
C.	Models and labels a wide range of emotions.	1	2	3	4	5
D.	Interprets and validates child's emotional reactions and states.	1	2	3	4	5
E.	Facilitates child's use of self-regulation skills.	1	2	3	4	5
F.	Uses symbolic play to enhance social and emotional development (at appropriate developmental stage).	1	2	3	4	5
G.	Builds self-confidence through emotional nurturing and encouraging trust, mastery, and independence.	1	2	3	4	5
H.	Sets appropriate limits and consistent, yet flexible, behavioral guidelines (i.e., "rules").	1	2	3	4	5
I.	To the extent possible, assists in providing a stable caregiving environment for child.	1	2	3	4	5
J.	Effectively fosters peer–peer interaction, with both peers with disabilities and nondisabled peers.	1	2	3	4	5
K.	Encourages altruistic behavior and "manners" in developmentally and culturally appropriate ways.	1	2	3	4	5
VIII.	*Facilitates development of motor skills.*					
A.	Understands stages and characteristics of typical motor development.	1	2	3	4	5
B.	(In consultation with appropriate therapists if necessary), *positions* child appropriately for each activity in order to encourage optimal fine and gross movement and to maximize participation and independence.	1	2	3	4	5
C.	Changes child's position frequently.	1	2	3	4	5
D.	Effectively builds child's motor competence and self-confidence by supporting child's independent movements.	1	2	3	4	5
E.	Utilizes appropriate assistive devices.	1	2	3	4	5
F.	Utilizes effective teaching strategies to encourage functional fine motor skills and eye–hand coordination.	1	2	3	4	5
G.	Utilizes outdoor activities for development of large muscle skills such as running, climbing, and throwing.	1	2	3	4	5
IX.	*Facilitates learning of self-care skills.*					
A.	Creates positive mealtime environment.	1	2	3	4	5
B.	Assists child in development of chewing and swallowing a variety of foods and textures; finger feeding; use of utensils (adapted as necessary).	1	2	3	4	5
C.	Establishes appropriate toileting schedule.	1	2	3	4	5
D.	In cooperation with family, develops consistent and appropriate toilet training procedures.	1	2	3	4	5
E.	Provides frequent opportunities in natural contexts to learn dressing skills.	1	2	3	4	5
F.	Adapts clothing as necessary to support independence.	1	2	3	4	5
G.	When necessary, applies task analysis and behavioral techniques in teaching self-care skills.	1	2	3	4	5

	Nonexistent	Poor	Satisfactory	Good	Excellent
X. *Facilitates academic readiness.*					
A. Uses developmentally appropriate techniques and materials and every-day contexts to teach cognitive operations such as classification, conservation, and seriation.	1	2	3	4	5
B. Demonstrates functional use of print (e.g., teacher models use of writing and reading in ways that are meaningful to children and displays print throughout classroom).	1	2	3	4	5
C. Creates opportunity for children to experience function and relevance of literacy behavior (e.g., treasure hunt clues, playing mail carrier, etc.).	1	2	3	4	5
D. Teaches important preacademic concepts such as opposites ("same" and "different," "big" and "little"); comparative terms ("taller," "tallest"); spatial terms ("in front of," "beside," "behind"); and quantity ("many," "few," "more") in *natural* contexts.	1	2	3	4	5
E. Teaches number and quantity concepts in meaningful ways (i.e., teaches "twoness" and "threeness," not simply rote counting).	1	2	3	4	5
F. Teaches auditory recognition, discrimination, and rhyming of sounds and sound combinations.	1	2	3	4	5
XI. *Promotes inclusion experiences.*					
A. Creates opportunity for involvement with peers without disabilities.	1	2	3	4	5
B. Creates opportunity for child and family to participate in and utilize community resources.	1	2	3	4	5
C. Develops child's ability to engage in age-appropriate and culturally appropriate activities through instruction and environmental adaptation.	1	2	3	4	5
XII. *Demonstrates collaborative and interpersonal skills.*					
A. Facilitates team approaches and works collaboratively with other disciplines.	1	2	3	4	5
B. Facilitates the development of children with low-incidence disabilities and medical risk conditions in consultation and close collaboration with disability specialists.	1	2	3	4	5
C. Understands roles of each discipline in providing early intervention services.	1	2	3	4	5
D. Effectively manages staff and develops competence and self-confidence of each staff member.	1	2	3	4	5
E. Develops positive work relations with both professional and paraprofessional staff.	1	2	3	4	5
F. Establishes appropriate partnerships with families.	1	2	3	4	5
G. Communicates with families in clear and culturally responsive ways.	1	2	3	4	5
H. Demonstrates flexibility and approaches difficult situations with joint problem-solving strategies.	1	2	3	4	5
I. Uses modeling and coaching strategies with families and paraprofessionals.	1	2	3	4	5
J. Reflects on professional practices and identifies areas for professional development.	1	2	3	4	5

Glossary

AAC   Abbreviation for augmentative and alternative communication.

ABA   Abbreviation for applied behavior analysis.

A-B-C analysis   Method of observation and evaluation of a challenging behavior that describes the antecedent, behavior, and consequence.

access   Providing a range of activities and environments by removing physical barriers, making adaptations, and promoting engagement and learning.

accommodation   Changes to the environment, materials, response modes, assessment, or instructional procedures that allow children with disabilities to demonstrate their knowledge and skills.

abduction   Movement of a limb outward (away) from the body.

acquired   Referring to a feature, state, or disease that happened after birth (acquired conditions are not inherited but rather are a response to the environment).

acquired immune deficiency syndrome (AIDS)   A communicable disease that reduces the body's ability to fight some types of infection.

activity-based instruction   Use of daily activities or routines to embed instructional goals and strategies.

active listening   Listening intently for feelings as well as content, being impartial, and reflecting back what is understood of the feelings and content.

acuity   Degree to which one is able to hear sounds and see visual images.

ADA   Abbreviation for the Americans with Disabilities Act of 1990.

adapt   To change or modify while retaining the basic model.

adaptations   Special teaching techniques or equipment that enable children with special needs to participate in an activity.

adaptive behavior   The ability to adjust to new situations and to apply familiar or new skills to those situations.

adaptive equipment   Any device that is modified to enhance the independence of the user.

adduction   Movement of a line inward (toward) the body.

advocate   One who acts on behalf of another.

affective   Pertaining to emotion, feeling, or attitude.

affective conflict   Emotional clashes between individuals.

affective domain   The state of feeling and expression of feelings.

ambient noise   Surrounding, extraneous sounds in the environment.

anecdotal record   A factual account of a child's behavior.

anomaly   Abnormality.

anoxia   The lack of oxygen.

Apgar test   An assessment of the health of newborns measuring appearance, pulse, grimace, activity, and response developed by Dr. Virginia Apgar.

apnea   A pause in breathing that lasts 20 seconds or longer.

apnea monitor   A monitor that sounds an alarm when an infant has a period of apnea.

apraxia   A loss of the ability to perform voluntary, purposeful movements due to damage to the brain (e.g., inability to perform movements of a command such as "Clap your hands").

arena assessment   The process of one professional conducting assessment while other team members, including the family, observe and contribute.

arthritis   Inflammation of a joint or joints.

articulation   The manner in which speech sounds are produced.

assessment   Either a test or an observation that determines a child's strengths or weaknesses in a particular area of development.

association   The process of relating one concept to another.

asthma   A complicated pulmonary symptom characterized by obstruction, labored breathing, and wheezing.

asymmetrical   Unequal; lack of similarity in form between two sides of the body.

Assistive Technology (AT)   Use of a device or service to maintain or improve the functional capacities of a child with disabilities.

ataxia   Characterized by disturbance of balance and awkward movements caused by damage to the brain or spinal cord.

ataxic   Unbalanced and jerky.

athetoid movement patterns   Moving uncontrollably and continuously.

atrophy   Wasting away or diminution in size.

atypical   Not typical. Different from the norm or average.

audiologist   A trained professional who measures hearing acuity, diagnoses hearing impairments, and assists in planning for remediation, including hearing aids and educational adaptations.

auditory discrimination   The ability to distinguish one sound from another.

auditory memory   The ability to retain and recall what has been heard.

augmentative communication (AAC)   Any method of communicating without speech, such as using signs, gestures, picture boards, and electronic or nonelectronic devices.

backward chaining   Teaching the steps of a skill backward, beginning with the last step.

behavior modification   Systematic, consistent efforts to change an individual's behavior. Carefully planned consequences for specific behaviors are designed to help a learner develop new and more appropriate responses to situations and experiences.

behavioral objective (or performance objective)   Identifies exactly what the teacher will do, provide, or restrict; describes the learner's observable behavior; and defines how well the learner must perform.

baseline   Refers to the level at which a child performs before intervention.

best practices   Strategies recommended by members of a profession usually derived from evidence-based practices.

bilateral Both sides.

biological risk Insult to bodily systems that makes typical development problematic.

body awareness (image) Awareness of one's own body and its position in time and space.

bolster or therapy roll A cylindrical piece of equipment (often made of foam) on which an infant is placed to help develop muscle strength, balance, and protective reactions.

bonding The establishment of a bond of affection between child and caring adults.

case management Responsible for coordinating services for a family and ensuring that individual family service plans are written and carried out. Currently referred to as service coordination.

categorical placement Placement of children according to classification of their suspected disabilities. Classrooms that are categorical usually group children according to disability labels, for example, classes for children who have learning disabilities or emotional disturbance.

catheter Small flexible tube inserted into a body channel to distend or maintain an opening to an internal cavity.

cerebral palsy Disorder of posture, muscle tone, and movement resulting from brain damage.

challenging behavior A repeated pattern of behavior that interferes with the child's interaction and learning in situations with others.

child-find The process of finding and identifying children with special needs.

choreoathetosis Type of cerebral palsy in which there are uncontrolled muscle movements in all four limbs of the body and sometimes in the face.

chromosomal abnormality A genetic disorder caused by too few or too many chromosomes or by chromosomes with extra or missing pieces. Down syndrome is caused by a chromosomal abnormality (an extra chromosome 21).

chronological age (CA) A child's actual age in years and months.

classification Distinguishing characteristics of things, then sorting, matching, or otherwise grouping them.

cochlear implant A device to treat severe sensorineural hearing impairment in which electrodes are surgically implanted in the inner ear to electronically stimulate undamaged inner ear nerves.

cognition Thinking skills including the ability to receive, process, analyze, and understand information. Also includes skills such as attending, discriminating similarities and differences, remembering, reasoning, and problem solving.

cognitive or mental flexibility The ability to adjust to changes in demands, rules, and settings.

collaboration Interactive relationships between two or more co-equal partners voluntarily working side by side with mutual respect and cooperation to reach a common goal through shared decision making.

combat crawling Pulling oneself forward with one's arms while letting one's belly and legs drag on the floor.

concepts Mental images or ideas.

confidentiality Records and other information about children must not be shown to anyone other than those who have been approved to have access to that information. Parental consent in writing must be obtained before information can be released to other individuals or facilities.

conflict resolution A systematic process for managing disagreements and conflicts that seeks a "win-win" outcome.

congenital Presumed to be present at birth.

consequences What happens immediately following a specific behavior.

consultation Involves professionals providing training, technical assistance, and feedback on effective instructional practices.

contracture Permanently tight muscles and joints.

coordination Harmonious functioning of muscles or groups of muscles in movement.

corrected age (of infants) Calculated by subtracting the number of weeks of prematurity from chronological age.

correlation The relationship between factors.

coteaching A form of teaming in which a general educator and a special educator jointly design and implement educational activities for children in a single classroom.

Council for Exceptional Children (CEC) A national professional organization for anyone working for and with children who are gifted and children with disabilities.

criterion A norm or standard for a behavior or item.

criterion-referenced tests Tests or observations that compare a child's performance on a particular task to a standard established for that specific task. Such tests identify what a child can and cannot do.

cross-categorical program A program designed to serve children who have differing disabling conditions.

curriculum All the specific features of a master teaching plan that have been chosen by a particular teacher for his or her classroom. Curricula may vary widely from school to school, but each curriculum reflects the skills, tasks, and behaviors that a school has decided are important for children to acquire.

custodial care Usually refers to the constant supervision and care of bodily needs provided in institutional settings.

cystic fibrosis A chronic disorder often causing respiratory and digestive problems.

decibel Unit used to measure hearing intensity or loudness.

decoding The act of deciphering or obtaining meaning from what is seen or heard.

developmental age The age at which a child is functioning (demonstrating specific abilities) based on assessment of the child's skills and comparison of those skills to the age at which they are considered typical.

developmental curriculum checklist A checklist of behavior often prepared by choosing items from standardized tests or scales. Duplicate items are deleted and those remaining are arranged in a developmental sequence. The checklist is then used as a guide in designing curriculum and in providing a record of individual children's progress through the curriculum.

developmental delay Classification for children with or without an established diagnosis who perform significantly behind developmental norms.

developmental quotient (DQ) A score similar to an IQ that describes an infant's developmental level.

developmentally appropriate practices (DAP) Strategies and activities that are appropriate for the child's age and developmental level.

developmentally disabled A term to describe the disability of persons who have an identifiable delay in cognitive or physical development compared with established norms.

diabetes mellitus A metabolic disorder related to insufficient insulin.

diagnosis A diagnosis is an effort to confirm the presence or absence of a delay or disability by observing the child and considering the results of tests.

dialogic reading An interactive reading method that uses verbal prompts and questions to elicit children's responses about a story.

diplegia Condition of cerebral palsy with major involvement of the legs and minor involvement of the arms.

discrepancy analysis Identifies the difference between a child's actual performance and the expected performance in daily activities to determine the possible cause for these differences and to determine the focus of intervention.

directionality The ability to know right from left, up from down, forward from backward, and other directional orientations.

discrimination The ability to differentiate among similar stimuli.

distal Further from the point of origin. For example, the fingers are distal to the shoulder, whereas the elbow is proximal to the shoulder.

divergent thinking Thinking that is unusual, different, and searching.

dual-language learners Children who are learning two or more languages at the same time, including those learning a new language while continuing to develop their home language.

dyskinesia Difficulty in performing voluntary movement, usually due to damage to the basal ganglia of the brain. Examples are *chorea* and *athetosis*.

dystonia (1) Abnormal muscle tone, either increased or decreased. (2) A genetic disorder in which a child experiences severe muscle spasms and exhibits abnormal movements and postures, especially when walking.

dystrophy Weakness and degeneration of muscle.

early intervention Services for children (and families) from birth to 36 months of age.

echolalia A habit of repeating (without meaning), or "echoing," what is said by others.

eclecticism Method or practice of selecting what seems best from various theories, systems, or programs.

ecological inventory A list of key activities that occur during a child's day.

ecological validity Occurs when assessment includes observations in natural settings that reveal what demands are made on children and what skills are demonstrated during daily routines with familiar caregivers.

ecologically relevant Skills that are functional; skills that assist the child with coping with daily environmental demands.

ECSE Abbreviation for early childhood special education.

efficacy Positive effects or impact of a program, strategy, or procedure.

emerging skills As children learn, they may use a new skill some but not all of the time. A skill observed at least some of the time is said to be emerging.

emotional literacy The ability to identify, understand, and respond to one's own emotions and to those of others.

empathy An active process in which one tries to learn all he or she can about another person in order to vicariously experience that person's feelings, thoughts, and experiences.

empowerment (empowered) A state of control over one's life; being able to take action to get what is wanted and needed.

en route behaviors Tasks to be mastered or behaviors to be demonstrated as the child moves from one level of functioning (entry behavior) to a designated goal or objective (terminal behavior).

encoding The act of expressing oneself in words or gestures.

entry behavior The level of functioning or behavior already acquired before beginning a series of tasks.

environment Everything the child encounters. The rooms, furniture, toys, the opportunity to experience new and different places, and the behaviors of those around the child constitute the environment.

environmental risk conditions The presence of factors in the family or community that lead to experiences that may result in developmental delay.

epilepsy A brain disorder frequently resulting in seizure activity that may be very mild or severe enough to cause loss of consciousness.

equivalent practice To prevent boredom in repetition, the teacher provides equivalent practice by offering a variety of materials and activities that are designed to develop the same skill. The task must also be at the same level of difficulty and provide the same kind of practice to be equivalent.

errorless learning An instructional method ensuring that a child makes the correct response when learning a skill, for example, by using visual or physical prompts to guide the child's response.

established risk condition The presence of a diagnosed physical or medical condition that is likely to lead to developmental delay.

etiology The study of the causes of diseases or disabilities.

evaluation (1) The process of making value judgments based on behavioral information about the effectiveness of a program in meeting the needs of children enrolled. (2) Under Part H, the term *evaluation* refers to the assessment procedures used to determine a child's eligibility for services.

eversion Turning out.

evidence-based practice (EBP) Practice based on integration of the best available research evidence with family and professional wisdom and values.

expansion Adults expand a child's utterance by stating the child's idea in a longer phrase or sentence.

expressive language What is said or written to communicate an idea or a question.

extension Stretching or extending the trunk and limbs of the body.

extensor pattern A pattern of muscle movement that causes a straightening out of a limb.

eye–hand coordination The ability to use visual input to assist in manipulation of an object with hands.

fading Slowly phasing out prompts with until no prompting is needed.

family-centered approach to assessment A practice of involving family members as primary decision makers on the assessment team.

family-centered practices Practices that are respectful, individualized, flexible, and responsive to each family's situation. Complete and unbiased information is provided to families so they can make informed decisions and be involved in making choices to strengthen both the child and the family.

family-focused early intervention Concentrating intervention equally on the child's family and on the child.

family functions One of the elements of family systems theory that refers to interrelated activities (outputs) necessary for the family to function effectively (i.e., affection, economics, daily care, socialization).

family subsystems The relational or interactive subsystems according to family systems theory, including the marital (adult partners), parental (parents–children), sibling (child–child), and extended family (nuclear family–relatives).

family systems perspective The family is viewed as an interactive unit; what affects one member affects all.

FASD Abbreviation for fetal alcohol syndrome disorder.

feedback The receipt of knowledge of results (the effect) of one's own behavior.

figure–ground discrimination The ability to attend to one aspect of a visual or auditory field while relegating other aspects of the environment to the background.

fine motor skills Activities with the fingers and hands.

First Chance programs Preschool programs for children with disabilities funded by the Bureau of Education for the Handicapped.

flexion Bending of elbows, hips, knees, and so on.

floppy Loose or weak posture and movements.

forward chaining A method of teaching a skill in an activity in which it is broken down into steps, beginning with the first step in the activity.

fragile X syndrome An X-linked disorder that often but not always causes mild to severe mental retardation. Some children with fragile X have average intelligence, with or without a learning disability.

free appropriate public education (FAPE) Designed by Public Law 94-142 to mean special education and related services provided at public expense. Such services are to be described in the individualized education program, appropriate to the child's individual needs, and meet requirements of the state agency.

FVA Abbreviation for functional vision assessment conducted by a teacher certified in visual impairment to identify how a child with a visual impairment uses vision at different distances.

functional skills Skills that will be immediately useful to the child and that will be used relatively frequently in the child's typical environment.

genetic Having to do with the principles of heredity.

gestational age The age of a fetus or infant stated in weeks from first day of the mother's last menstrual period before conception until the body reaches term (40 weeks).

goals The measurable statements on the individualized education program that identify the knowledge, skills, or behaviors a child is expected to demonstrate once the goal is achieved.

grammar The linguistic rules of language.

gross motor skills Activities such as running, climbing, throwing, and jumping that use large muscles.

hand-over-hand guidance Physically guiding a child through the movements involved in a fine motor task (e.g., placing your hand on top of the child's hand to help him or her grasp a spoon and bring it to his or her mouth).

hand-under-hand guidance Physically guiding a child though the movements involved in a fine motor task (e.g., grasping a spoon and having the child place his or her hand on top of yours).

hemiplegia Condition of cerebral palsy with major involvement of one side of the body.

hereditary Referring to a trait (such as eye color) or defect or disease (such as cystic fibrosis). Not all hereditary disorders are apparent at birth and not all birth defects are hereditary.

high-preference inventory Identification of a child's high-preference items determined through caregiver interviews and careful observation of a child's likes and dislikes; information can be used to identify ways of motivating, engaging, and reinforcing a child.

high-preference items A child's most preferred activities, objects, and people.

high-risk signals Those signs that when observed in very young children have been known to be predictive of more-than-normal likelihood of future disabilities or developmental delays.

hydrocephalus Congenital condition in which the accumulation of fluid in the brain causes enlargement of the skull.

hyperactivity Exceedingly active behavior not typical of most children.

hyperresponsive Unregulated reactive behavior. Children who are hyperresponsive may actually avoid stimuli as if they have a lower tolerance for it.

hypertonicity Condition in which muscles are stretched and constantly excited.

hypoactivity Opposite of hyperactivity; lethargy.

hyporesponsive Lack of appropriate reactive behavior. Children who are hyporesponsive may be slow to respond to stimuli and actually seek more of it.

hypotonicity Condition in which muscles are limp and do not exhibit resistance to stretching.

IDEIA Abbreviation for Individuals with Disabilities Education Improvement Act of 2004.

identification The process of finding and screening individuals to determine whether they might benefit from specialized services.

inclusion Another term used for integration of children with and without disabilities.

inclusive settings Sites, classrooms, and programs with typically developing children where inclusion of children with disabilities takes place.

individualized education program (IEP) A collaborative process that culminates in a written program plan that includes the child's present level of functioning; specific areas that need special services; annual goals; short-term objectives; services to be provided; and the method of evaluation to be implemented. An individualized education program is required for every child receiving services while P.L. 101-476 is in effect.

individualized family service plan (IFSP) A collaborative process that culminates in a written service plan that includes the child's present level of functioning; a statement of the family's concerns, priorities, and resources; measurable results or outcomes expected to be achieved for the child and family; the criteria, procedures, and time lines to determine progress; specific services to be provided; natural environments; dates of service initiation; and name of the service coordinator.

individualized instruction Instruction that is tailored to meet a child's background, needs, interest, and learning level.

infant and early childhood mental innate The capacity of the infant, toddler, or preschooler to form close relationships with adults and peers and to experience, manage, and express a range of emotions.

inhibitory control The skills that enable a child's selective and sustained attention before action.

inner language The language in which thinking occurs. The process of internalizing and organizing experiences that can be expressed by symbols.

instructional objectives These define specific accomplishments to be achieved. See "behavioral objective."

integration Education of children with disabilities together with their classmates without disabilities to the maximum extent appropriate.

interdisciplinary team approach Professionals from different disciplines work together to assess and provide intervention based on mutual decision making.

interindividual differences Differences between individuals.

intraindividual differences Differences in performance within one child on different factors or on the same factor at different times.

inversion Turning in.

involuntary movements Unintended movements that are not under the individual's control.

itinerant consultant model An individual who travels from place to place, providing direct services to a child with an IEP and collaborative consultation to the classroom teacher and other staff.

kinesthesia The muscle sense by which the child is aware of his or her body position and his or her movements in relation to the environment.

kinesthetic learner A child who learns best through movement and touch.

labeling Giving a categorical term (label) to a disabling condition and to those who exhibit such a condition, for example, "emotional disturbance" or "intellectual disability."

laterality Awareness of sidedness; left and right of the body.

LEA Abbreviation for local education agency.

least restrictive environment (LRE) A concept inherent in Public Law 94-142 that requires children with disabilities to be educated with peers without disabilities in general educational settings to the maximum extent appropriate.

least-to-most prompting A prompting procedure in which the prompts are provided with the lowest level of assistance to help the child correctly perform the target behavior, followed by a gradual increase in assistance if the child cannot correctly perform the behavior.

litigation The act or process of contesting by law through lawsuits.

LMA Abbreviation for learning media assessment conducted by a teacher certified in visual impairment to assess the child's responses and use of visual, tactile, and auditory information. It also selects instructional methods, materials, and media to facilitate reading and writing.

locomotor Pertaining to movement from one location to another.

low tone/low muscle tone Hypotonia.

LSL Abbreviation for listening and spoken language that focuses on listening to develop the speech of children with hearing loss.

mainstreaming The practice of integrating children with disabilities into general education classrooms whenever appropriate.

medically fragile Referring to an infant or child whose health status either is unstable or renders him or her at risk for developmental delay (often due to poor health or limitations on the infant's ability to participate in typical activities).

mental age Level of mental functioning. A child with a mental age (MA) of 4–0 is thought to be mentally functioning like a 4-year-old.

metacognition Having knowledge of one's thought processes and how to regulate strategies for thought or learning.

microcephaly An abnormally small head size, resulting in poor brain growth and mental retardation.

midline The vertical center line of the body.

milieu teaching A conversation-based early language intervention that uses child interests and initiations as learning opportunities in everyday activities. Milieu teaching includes arranging the environment, identifying specific target behaviors, and carefully planned teaching and prompting procedures.

mixed-type cerebral palsy A form of cerebral palsy in which both spasticity and choreoathetoid movements are present.

modality The pathways through which an individual receives information and thereby learns. Some individuals are thought to learn more quickly through one modality than another; for example, some process auditory information more efficiently than visual information and would thus be classified as auditory learners.

modeling An instructional strategy that provides a demonstration of an expected behavior.

most-to-least prompting A prompting procedure in which the prompts are at a level of assistance to make it possible for the child to correctly perform the target behavior, followed by gradual reduction of assistance until the child performs the skill independently.

motor planning   The ability to organize sensory information in order to plan and carry out the appropriate sequence of movements required to complete a task.

multidisciplinary team approach   Individuals from different disciplines carry out evaluations, and intervention may be offered with little opportunity for professional interaction or integrated planning.

multiple sclerosis (MS)   A progressive central nervous system disease affecting motor control.

multisensory learning   A technique to facilitate learning that employs a combination of sense modalities at the same time.

muscular dystrophy   A central nervous system disease that affects skeletal and respiratory functions.

narrative   The linguistic ability to combine words and sentences to recount an event or story sequence.

natural environment   Settings in which children without disabilities naturally participate.

neonatal intensive care unit (NICU)   The hospital unit staffed with specially trained medical practitioners who care for critically ill newborns, both premature babies and sick full-term babies.

neurological examination   An examination of sensory or motor response to determine whether there are impairments of the nervous system.

noncategorical   Grouping children together without labeling or categorizing according to suspected disabilities.

nonlocomotor   Lack of movement from one place to another.

nonverbal ability   Having skill to perform a task that does not involve using words.

norm-referenced tests   These tests report a particular child's performance in relation to other children of the same chronological age. Such tests are highly standardized and usually do not include individuals with disabling conditions in the normative sample against which behavior is being compared.

norms   A sample of a large number of people's behavior against which a particular behavior can be compared.

observable behavior   Behavior that can be seen, heard, or felt.

observational learning   Learning by watching those around us.

occupational therapy   Treatment given to improve movement for daily living.

ocular pursuit   Following an object with the eye.

olfactory   Pertaining to the sense of smell.

on-task behavior   The behavior of a child who is attending to or engaged in an appropriate, purposeful activity.

ophthalmologist   A physician trained in the diagnosis and treatment of diseases of the eyes.

optometrist   A vision specialist trained to measure refraction and prescribe glasses but not licensed to treat eye diseases.

oral motor skills   Skills involving muscles in and around the mouth, including chewing, swallowing, and forming speech sounds.

oral stimulation   Referring to the natural mouthing of toys that emerges in the infant between 3 and 6 months of age or to the specific activities (such as massaging the gums or lips) designed to help the child with *oral tactile defensiveness* tolerate having things placed in his or her mouth.

orthosis   Any assistive device used to support, align, prevent, or correct bone, joint, or muscle deformities.

orthotic   A custom-made orthopedic appliance (such as a brace, splint, or cast) used to promote proper body alignment, to stabilize joints, or to passively stretch muscle or other soft tissue.

OT   Abbreviation for occupational therapy or occupational therapist.

otitis media   Inflammation of the middle ear; a common infection.

otolaryngologist   A medical doctor who specializes in the diagnosis and treatment of disorders of the ear, nose, and throat.

otologist   A physician trained to treat problems of the ear.

parallel play   Typical play of the 18- to 24-month-old in which the child plays beside other children instead of actually interacting with them.

parallel talk   Parents of young children often talk about what their children are doing as it is happening. Their "talk" occurs parallel to what the child is doing. This practice appears to help young children learn language.

paraplegia   Paralysis of both legs.

paraprofessional   A trained assistant to a professional teacher, often referred to as a teacher aide or paraeducator.

parity   Equality of value or standing.

patterning   Guiding the child's arms or legs through a series of passive movements in order to stimulate normal movement patterns.

PECS   Abbreviation for Picture Exchange Communication System.

pediatrician   A physician whose specialty is working with and treating infants and young children.

percentile rank   The percentage of persons in a normal distribution who score below a particular point.

perception   The process of interpreting what is received by the five senses.

perceptual-motor   The interaction of various channels of perception with motor activity; for example, the act of kicking is a perceptual-motor interaction between sight and gross motor responses.

performance objectives   See "behavioral objective."

perinatal   Around the time of birth.

perseveration   Continuous repetition of the same action characterized by the inability to shift readily from one activity to another.

person-first language   The respectful practice of identifying people with disabilities as people, first, rather than labeling them. For example, saying "a child with autism," rather than "an autistic child."

phoneme   The smallest unit of sound found in speech.

phonetics   The system of speech sounds in a particular language.

PT Abbreviation for physical therapy or a physical therapist.

physical therapist A therapist who assesses gross motor skills and treats disorders of movement and posture.

physiotherapy Treatment of disorders of movement.

pincer grasp Coordination of index finger and thumb.

positioning Placing a child in certain postures in order to promote symmetrical body alignment, normalize muscle tone, and promote functional skills.

positive behavior support (PBS) Behavioral technique that focuses on the *prevention* of problem behaviors and providing support for more positive behaviors by identifying the *function* of the problem behavior and teaching the child a *replacement* behavior that is more acceptable. The technique also identifies the antecedents of problem behaviors as clues to possible "triggers" or causes of the behavior and attempts to modify or eliminate those causes.

postictal sleep The sleep that occurs naturally after seizures.

pragmatics The use of language in social contexts, including how language is used for communication.

premature infant A baby born before 37 weeks' gestation.

prenatally exposed to drugs (PED) Referring to an infant who was exposed to drugs as a fetus due to maternal substance abuse.

primitive reflex A reflex response to a stimulus such as touch or movement that is normal in infants. The word *primitive* refers to the fact that these are involuntary survival responses with which infants are born.

prognosis A forecast of the probable course of disease or illness.

prompting Using assistance to help a child perform desired behavior. Verbal prompting often involves saying a single sound or word to help a child remember what to say or do. Physical prompting that involves physical assistance or touch can be helpful to initiate a motor or self-help skill. Prompts should be reduced gradually (faded) until they can be eliminated.

pronation Turning of the palm downward or backward.

prone Lying on the stomach.

prosthesis Artificial device that replaces a missing body part.

psycholinguistics The field of study that combines psychology and linguistics to create an understanding of the total language process.

psychomotor Voluntary motor activity.

punishment A consequence after a target behavior that decreases the future likelihood that the target behavior will occur again.

Pyramid Model A framework of four levels (from the bottom to top: nurturing and responsive relationships, high-quality supportive environments, targeted social emotional supports, and individualized interventions) for promoting social emotional development and addressing challenging behavior.

quadriplegia Condition of cerebral palsy with major involvement of arms and legs.

range of motion The total distance through which a joint can be moved in natural directions.

rapport A harmonious relationship. When working with a child, establishing rapport involves developing a climate or atmosphere in which the child feels comfortable enough to perform as well as possible.

receptive language The ability to understand the intent and meaning of someone's effort to communicate.

reciprocal movement Alternating movements of arms and legs, such as movement involved in walking or in creeping on the hands and knees.

reflexes Postures and movements completely out of the child's control.

reinforcer An event or consequence (reward) that increases the likelihood of a behavior that it follows being repeated. May be concrete or social.

reliability Extent to which a test measures a given performance consistently. The degree to which it is dependable, stable, and relatively free from errors of measurement.

remission Period during which the symptoms of a condition disappear for an unpredictable period.

residual hearing Auditory acuity of an individual with hearing loss without amplification.

respite care Skilled child-care service for a child who is seriously ill or has a disability to provide relief for the family.

Response to Intervention (RTI) A multi-tiered approach to early identification and support of students with learning and behavior needs.

retarded An outdated term that was used to describe any individual who was slow to learn or difficult to teach. The current term is intellectually disabled. Legally, test scores, adaptive behavior, and other factors must be correlated to determine an intellectual disability.

retinopathy of prematurity (ROP) An eye disorder that can develop in premature infants. There is an increased incidence in infants who are given high levels of oxygen for long periods.

reversal A transposition of letters.

reverse chaining Begin by teaching with the last step of a task sequence and work backward to the first step. Particularly useful with self-care skills.

reverse mainstreaming Children without disabilities are integrated into classes composed primarily of children with identifiable disabilities.

righting Ability to put in or restore the head and body to a proper position when in an abnormal or uncomfortable position.

rigidity A type of cerebral palsy characterized by widespread continuous muscle tension. Muscles of the body become very stiff.

role release The systematic training of other professionals in one's own discipline-specific skills.

routines-based approach Use of daily activities to embed instructional goals and strategies; similar to activity-based instruction.

schemata Patterns.

scissor pattern Body movement in which one leg crosses over the other.

screening The process of sorting out from a total group those children who may have problems. It is often part of a total program called child-find or child-check. The intent is to test all children with specially designed screening instruments to determine those who need further diagnostic testing and to determine if a problem really does exist.

self-fulfilling prophecy The tendency for individuals to behave in accordance with views they perceive others to have of them.

self-regulation The capacity to control one's emotional state (e.g., impulses) and to organize an appropriate behavioral response to a stimulus (e.g., stop doing something or begin doing something as needed). In infants, self-regulation refers to the ability to attain an optimal level of arousal.

sensorimotor The combination of input of sense organs and output of motor activity.

sensory integration The ability of the central nervous system to receive, process, and learn from sensation (such as touch, movement, sight, sound, smell, and the pull of gravity) in order to develop skills.

sensory overload The condition that occurs when one or more senses have been overstimulated beyond the child's level of tolerance. It may occur as a result of too much noise, light, or movement.

seriation Ordering according to relative differences.

service coordination Professional assistance designed to help families procure, coordinate, and manage the diverse services needed by a child and family. (See "case management.")

sexually transmitted disease (STD) A contagious disease transmitted through sexual contact. STDs can also be transmitted in other ways, such as through blood contact (as with drug users who share needles).

shaping A technique of behavior modification in which behaviors that are successive approximations of the target behavior are reinforced until the target behavior is acquired.

sickle cell anemia A hereditary condition in which misshapen blood cells clump together in the blood vessels, causing varied symptoms: painful joints, chronic ulcers of the ankles, episodes of abdominal pain, and neurological disturbances.

SimCom Abbreviation for simultaneous communication that uses speech and signs at the same time for the language development of children with hearing loss.

small for gestational age (SGA) A newborn whose weight is low (below the 10th percentile) for his or her gestational age.

soft sign Any of several neurological indicators that collectively suggest the presence of damage to the central nervous system. They include disturbance of balance, visual motor difficulties, a lack of motor coordination, and so on.

sorting Discrimination and separation according to differences.

spasm Sudden tightening of the muscles.

spasticity Muscular incoordination resulting from sudden, involuntary contractions of the muscles; a type of cerebral palsy.

spatial relationships The ability to perceive the position of two or more objects in relation to oneself and in relation to each other.

spina bifida A disorder of the spinal column that may affect motor coordination and body functions.

standardization The procedure of having standard directions and scoring so that normative data about others who have taken the test can be used.

standardized tests Tests that are administered in a specifically described standard way, scored in a particular way, and then compared with the performance of a standard group.

standards-based practices Strategies and activities based on professionally determined expectations for the learning and development of young children.

stanine A single-digit derived score based on the normal curve. It ranges in value from 1 to 9 with a mean of 5.

status epilepticus Refers to a situation in which a person has two major seizures, one right after the other; signals that an ambulance should be called immediately.

stimuli Information that can be received by the senses.

stoma Opening in the abdominal wall, created through surgery, to allow the urine from the kidneys to drain into a collecting bag.

strabismus A condition in which the eyes do not work together, in that one eye deviates (wanders) from its position relative to the other eye. It may go inward (cross-eye) or outward (walleye).

stuttering A speech impairment evidenced by hesitations, repetitions, or spasms of breathing.

substantive conflict Arises from intellectual differences and is content based (e.g., differences in philosophy, priorities, etc.).

successive approximation The process of gradually increasing expectations for a child to display behaviors that are more like the desired target behavior; used in shaping behaviors not previously a part of the child's behavior pattern.

sudden infant death syndrome (SIDS) The unexpected and sudden death of an infant who has appeared to be healthy. SIDS occurs during sleep and is the most common cause of death in infants 1 month to 1 year. Cause is still unknown.

supine Lying on the back.

symmetrical Similarity in form between two sides of the body.

syndactyly A congenital anomaly in which there is partial or complete webbing or fusion of fingers or toes.

systematic fading The gradual removal of any support that assists a child's learning.

systemic Refers to a disease that can exist throughout the body (e.g., arthritis).

tactile Refers to the sense of touch.

tactile defensiveness An abnormal sensitivity to touch, indicated by infant's avoidance or rejection of touching and handling.

target behavior The terminal objective or final desired behavior that is the goal of shaping when using behavioral (performance) objectives. This same term, when used in relation to behavior modification, refers to the negative behavior to be changed.

task analysis Breaking down a difficult task into small steps that lead to completing the task. En route behaviors are behavioral objectives that state the individual subskills leading toward the terminal objective or the difficult task.

terminal objective The behavioral objective that a particular teacher has chosen as the highest level of skill he or she intends to strive toward to help a child or children achieve.

tiered instruction Refers to a framework of multi-tiered gradually increasing supports for children with behavioral and learning needs. Also known as RTI or response to intervention.

tone Firmness of muscles.

tongue thrust The strong involuntary (reflexive) protrusion of the tongue. It may be seen in some forms of cerebral palsy.

tonic neck reflex Uncontrollable movement in which turning of the head causes one arm to straighten and stiffen and the other to bend.

total communication A philosophy involved in teaching individuals with hearing loss that includes using speech, listening, and manual signs to ensure effective communication.

tracking Following an object with one's eyes.

transdisciplinary team approach The use of a team approach to services in which team members work across disciplinary boundaries to plan and provide integrated services. This approach includes sharing of roles through support and consultation with other team members.

transition The purposeful, organized process of helping children who are at risk or have developmental disabilities move from one program to the next, such as from an infant development program to an inclusive preschool program.

trauma The condition, physical or mental, that results from shock or a violently produced wound or injury.

tremor Involuntary vibration in large muscles.

Universal Design for Learning (UDL) A framework that promotes access to instruction through providing multiple means of engagement, multiple means of representation, and multiple means of action and expression.

utterance Something that is said or produced orally. It is not necessary that an utterance be spoken correctly to be counted in the child's mean length of utterance (MLU).

validity The extent to which an instrument measures what it is supposed to measure or what the test giver needs it to measure.

verbal expression The ability to express one's ideas verbally.

vestibular stimulation An activity that stimulates the vestibular apparatus (the structures contained in the inner ear that provide the sense of balance) and helps the child develop awareness of body position in space as well as balance reactions.

visual association The process of relating concepts that have been presented visually.

visual discrimination The ability to differentiate between and among various shapes, sizes, colors, numbers, and letters.

visualization Imagery; the ability to retrieve a mental image or to produce a mental image.

voluntary muscles The muscles in the body over which there is conscious control of contraction.

"W" sitting position Sitting on the buttocks between the heels of the feet (the knees are bent, forming a *W*).

Women, Infants, and Children (WIC) program A federally funded program that provides pregnant women, new mothers, infants, and young children with food vouchers, nutrition counseling, and referrals to health care.

working memory The capacity to hold and manipulate information in our minds for a short period of time, for example, follow multistep directions.

zero project The principle that no child should be refused a free appropriate education if other children the same age are being served.

Source: Many definitions come from *The Early Intervention Dictionary*, by J. G. Coleman, 2006, Rockville, MD: Woodbine House.

References

Adams, E. J. (2011). Teaching children to name their feelings. *Young Children, 66*(3), 66–67.

Adams, M., Foorman, B., Lundberg, I., & Beeler, T. (1998). *Phonemic awareness in young children.* Baltimore: Brookes.

Administration for Children and Families. (2017, January). *Early childhood homelessness in the United States: 50-state profile.* Retrieved from https://www.acf.hhs.gov/sites/default/files/ecd/homelessness_profile_package_with_blanks_for_printing_508.pdf

Ahlgrim-Delzell, L., Browder, D. M., Wood, L., Stanger, C., Preston, A. I., & Kemp-Inman, A. (2016). Systematic instruction of phonic skills using an iPad for students with developmental disabilities who are AAC users. *Journal of Special Education, 50,* 86–97.

Aikens, N., Klein, A., Tarullo, L., & West, J. (2013). *Getting ready for kindergarten: Children's progress during Head Start.* FACES 2009 Report. OPRE Report 2013-21a. Washington, DC: Office of Planning, Research and Evaluation, Administration for Children and Families, U.S. Department of Health and Human Services. Retrieved from https://www.acf.hhs.gov/sites/default/files/opre/faces_2009_child_outcomes_brief_final

Ainsworth, M. D. (1973). The development of infant–mother attachment. In B. M. Caldwell & H. Riciutti (Eds.), *Review of child development research* (Vol. 3, pp. 1–94). Chicago: University of Chicago Press.

Ainsworth, M. D., Blehar, M. C., Waters, E., & Wall, S. (2015). *Patterns of attachment: A psychological study of the strange situation.* New York: Psychology Press.

Akhtar, N. & Gernsbacher, M. A. (2007). *Lang. Linguist. Compass., 1*(3), 195–207.

Albert, N. L., Sparks, R. W., & Helm, N. A. (1973). Melodic intonation therapy for aphasia. *Archives of Neurobiology, 29*(2), 130–131.

Alfonso, S. (2017). Implementing a project approach in an inclusive classroom: A teacher's first attempt at project-based learning. *Young Children, 72,* 57–65.

Allen, K. E. & Cowdery, G. E. (2015). *The exceptional child: Inclusion in early childhood* Education. Stamford, CT: Cengage Learning.

Allen, R. & Steed, E. A. (2016). Culturally responsive Pyramid Model practices: Program-wide positive behavior support for young children. *Topics in Early Childhood Special Education, 36,* 165–175.

Allen, S. F. (2007). Parents' perceptions of intervention practices in home visiting programs. *Infants & Young Children, 20*(3), 266–281.

American Music Therapy Association. (2010) *Statement of purpose: Special education music therapy research and evidence-based practice support.* Retrieved from http://www.musictherapy.org/assets/1/7/bib_Special_Education.pdf

American Occupational Therapy Association. (2014, November). *Establishing toileting routines for children.* Retrieved from https://www.aota.org/~/media/Corporate/Files/AboutOT/consumers/Youth/Establishing-Toileting-Routines-for-Children-Tip-Sheet.pdf

American Psychiatric Association. (2013). *Diagnostic and statistical manual of mental disorders* (5th ed.). Arlington, VA: American Psychiatric Publishing.

American Speech-Language-Hearing Association. (1991). *Report: Augmentative and alternative communication. American Speech-Language-Hearing Association, 33*(5), 9–12.

American Speech-Language-Hearing Association. (2010). *Roles and responsibilities of the school-based speech-language pathologist.* Retrieved from http://www.asha.org/policy/PI2010-00317/#AP1

Aparicio, T. S. & Balaña, J. M. (2009). A study of early fine motor intervention in Down's syndrome children. *Early Child Development and Care, 179,* 631–636.

Apgar, V. & James, L. S. (1962). Further observations on the Newborn Scoring System. *American Journal of Diseases of Children, 104,* 419–428.

Aron, L. Y. & Loprest, P. J. (2007). *Meeting the needs of children with disabilities.* Washington, DC: Urban Institute Press.

Auer, C. R. & Blumberg, S. L. (2006). *Parenting a child with sensory processing disorder.* Oakland, CA: New Harbinger.

Austin, K. (2014). Ten things every paraprofessional wishes you knew! *Innovations and perspectives.* Retrieved from http://www.ttacnews.vcu.edu/2014/02/ten-things-every-paraprofessional-wishes-you-knew/

Autism and Developmental Disabilities Monitoring Network, Surveillance Year 2010 Principal Investigators. (2014, March 28). Prevalence of autism spectrum disorder among children aged 8 years—Autism and Developmental Disabilities Monitoring Network, 11 sites, United States, 2010. *MMWR,63*(SS02),1–21. Retrieved from http://www.cdc.gov/mmwr/PDF/ss/ss6302.pdf

Averett, P., Hedge, A., & Smith, J. (2017). Lesbian and gay parents in early childhood settings: A systematic review of the research literature. *Journal of Early Childhood Research,15,* 34–46.

Ayres, A. J. (2005). *Sensory integration and the child: 25th anniversary edition.* Los Angeles: Western Psychological Services.

Bailey, A. L. & Osipova, A. V. (2016). *Children's multilingual development and education.* Cambridge: Cambridge University Press.

Bailey, J. & Penhune, V. B. (2012). A sensitive period for musical training: Contributions of age of onset and cognitive abilities. *Annuals of the New York Academy of Sciences, 1252,* 163–70.

Baker, B. & Ryan, C. (2014). *The PBIS team handbook: Setting expectations and building positive behavior.* Minneapolis, MN: Free Spirit.

Bang, Y. (2009). Helping all families participate in school life. *Young Children, 64*(6), 97–99.

Banks, J. B. (2002). Childhood discipline: Challenges for clinicians and parents. *American Family Physician, 66*(8), 1447–1452.

Barber, P. A., Turnbull, A. P., Behr, S. K., & Kerns, G. M. (1988). Family systems perspective on early childhood special education. In S. L. Odom & M. B. Karnes (Eds.), *Early intervention for infants and children with handicaps* (pp. 179–198). Baltimore: Brookes.

Barfoot, J., Meredith, P., Ziviani, J., & Whittingham, K. (2015). Relationship based parenting to support developmental outcomes for a young child with cerebral palsy: A practical. *British Journal of Occupational Therapy, 78*(10), 640–664.

Barnes, S. B. & Whinnery, K. W. (2002). Effects of functional mobility skills training for young students with physical disabilities. *Exceptional Children, 68,* 313–324.

Barnett, W. S. & Frede, E. (2010). The promise of preschool: Why we need early education for all. *American Educator, 1,* 21–30.

Barrio, B. L., Miller, D., Hsiao, Y. J., Dunn, M., Petersen, S., Hollingshead, A., & Banks, S. (2017). Designing culturally responsive and relevant individualized educational programs. *Intervention in School and Clinic, 53,* 114–119.

Barton, E. E. (2016). Critical issues and promising practices for teaching play to young children with disabilities. In B. Reichow, B. A. Boyd, E. E. Barton, & S. Odom (Eds.), *Handbook of early childhood special education* (pp. 267–288). Cham, Switzerland: Springer.

Bauer, L. & Schanzenbauh, D. W. (2016). *The long-term impact of the Head Start Program.* Washington, DC: Brookings Institute.

Baumrind, D. (1971). Current patterns of parental authority. *Developmental Psychology,4*(1, Pt. 2), 1–101.

Beach Center on Disability. (2014). *Family quality of life survey.* Lawrence: University of Kansas. Retrieved from http://www.beachcenter.org

Belsky, J. (2006). Determinants and consequences of infant–parent attachment. In L. Balter & C. S. Tamis-LeMonda (Eds.), *Child psychology: A handbook of contemporary issues* (pp. 53–77). New York: Psychology Press.

Berko Gleason, J. & Ratner, N. B. (2013). *The development of language* (8th ed.). Boston: Pearson.

Bernheimer, L. P. & Weisner, T. S. (2007). "Let me just tell you what I do all day . . ." The family story at the center of intervention research and practice. *Infants & Young Children, 20*(3), 192–201.

Berns, R. M. (2016). *Child, family, school community*. Boston: Cengage Learning.

Bernstein, D. K. & Levey, S. (2009). Language development: A review. In D. K. Bernstein & E. Tiegerman-Farber (Eds.), *Language and communication disorders in children*. Boston: Pearson.

Bernstein, V. J. (2002, Summer). Supporting the parent–child relationship through home visiting. *IDA News, 29*(2), 1–8.

Berson, I. R. & Baggerly, J. (2009). Building resilience to trauma. Creating a safe and supportive early childhood classroom. *Childhood Education, 85*, 375–379.

Best, S. J., Heller, K. W., & Bigge, J. L. (2005). *Teaching individuals with physical and multiple disabilities* (5th ed.). Upper Saddle River, NJ: Merrill/Prentice Hall.

Beukelman, D. R. & Mirenda, P. (2013). *Augmentative and alternative communication* (4th ed.). Baltimore: Brookes.

Bidell, R. R. & Fischer, W. W. (1989). Commentary. *Human Development, 32*, 363–368.

Bierman, K. L., Nix, R. L., Heinrichs, B. S., Domitrovich, C. E., Gest, S. D., Welsh, J. A., & Sukhdeep, G. (2014). Effects of Head Start REDO on children's outcomes one year later in different kindergarten contexts. *Child Development, 85*(1), 140–159.

Biermeir, M. A. (2015). Inspired by Reggio Emilia: Emergent curriculum in relationship driven environments. *Young Children, 20*(5), 72–79.

Bijou, W. W. (1977) Practical implications of an interactional model of child development. *Exceptional Children, 44*, 6–14.

Billingsley, B. S. & McLeskey, J. (2014). What are the roles of principals in inclusive schools? In J. McLeskey, N. L. Waldron, F. Spooner, & B. Algozzine (Eds.), *Handbook of effective inclusive schools: Research and Practice* (pp. 67–89). New York: Routledge.

Bird, E. K. R., Cleave, P., Trudeau, N., Thordardottir, E., Sutton, A., & Thorpe, A. (2005). The language abilities of bilingual children with Down syndrome. *American Journal of Speech-Language Pathology, 14*, 187–199.

Bjorklund, D. F. & Causey, K. B. (2018). *Children's thinking: Cognitive development and individual differences* (6th ed). Thousand Oaks, CA: SAGE.

Blacher, J., Begum, G. F., Marcoulides, G.A., & Baker, B. L. (2013). Longitudinal perspectives of child positive impact on families: Relationship to disability and culture. *American Journal of Intellectual and Developmental Disabilities, 118*(2), 141–155.

Blackwell, P. L. (2004). The idea of temperament: Does it help parents understand their babies? *Zero to Three, 24*(4), 37–41.

Blair, T. R., Rupley, W. H., & Nichols, W. D. (2007). The effective teacher of reading: Considering the "what" and "how" of instruction. *The Reading Teacher, 60*(5), 432–438.

Bloom, B. S. (1964). *Stability and change in human characteristics*. New York: John Wiley & Sons.

Bloom, L. & Lahey, M. (1978). *Language development and language disorders*. New York: John Wiley & Sons.

Bobath, K. & Bobath, B. (1984). The neurodevelopmental treatment. In D. Scurtton (Ed.), *Management of the motor disorders of children with cerebral palsy* (pp. 6–18). Philadelphia: Lippincott.

Bodison, S. C. & Parham, L. D. (2018). Specific sensory techniques and sensory environmental modifications for children and youth with sensory integration difficulties: A systematic review. *American Journal of Occupational Therapy, 72*, 1–11.

Boehm, A. E. (2001). *Boehm Test of Basic Concepts—3 Preschool*. New York: Psychological Corp.

Bondy, A. & Frost, L. (2001). The Picture Exchange Communication System. *Behavior Modification, 25*(5), 725–744.

Bondy, A. & Frost, L. (2011). *A picture's worth: PECs and other visual communication strategies for autism*. Bethesda, MD: Woodbine House.

Bower, E. (2009). *Finnie's handling the young child with cerebral palsy at home* (4th ed.). Oxford, UK: Elsevier.

Bowlby, J. (1982). *Attachment and loss: Vol. 1. Attachment*. New York: Basic Books. (Original work published 1969.)

Boyd, D. (1950). *The three stages*. New York: National Association for Retarded Children.

Brandt, K., Perry, B. D., Seligman, S., & Tronick, E. (Eds.). (2014). *Infant and early childhood mental health: Core concepts and clinical practice*. Arlington, VA: American Psychiatric Publishing.

Branson, D. & Bingham, A. (2017). Child care providers' competence and confidence in referring children at risk for developmental delays. *Infants and Young Children, 30*, 41–57.

Brazelton, T. & Nugent, J. K. (Eds.). (2001). *Neonatal Behavioral Assessment Scale* (3rd ed.). London: MacKeith Press.

Bricker, D. (Ed.). (2002, 2006). *Assessment, evaluation, and programming system for infants and children (AEPS®)* (2nd ed.). Baltimore: Brookes.

Bricker, D. D. (1988). Commentary: The future of early childhood special education. *Journal of the Division of Early Childhood, 12*, 276–278.

Bricker, W. A. & Bricker, D. D. (1974). An early language training strategy. In R. L. Schiefelbusch & L. L. Lloyd (Eds.), *Language perspectives—acquisition, retardation and intervention*. Baltimore: University Park Press.

Bridges, W. (2009). *Managing transitions: Making the most of change* (3rd ed.). Philadelphia: Da Capo Press.

Brillante, P. & Nemeth, K. N. (2017). Teaching emergent bilingual learners with disabilities and challenging behaviors in preschool. *Journal of Multilingual Education Research, 3*, 43–52.

Bronte-Tinkew, J., Carrano, J., Horowitz, A., & Kimukawa, A. (2008). Involvement among resident fathers and links to infant cognitive outcomes. *Journal of Family Issues, 29*, 1211–1244.

Brotherson, M. J., Summers, J. A., Naig, L. A., Kyzar, K., Friend, A., Epley, P., & Turnbull, A. P. (2010). Partnership patterns: Addressing emotional needs in early intervention. *Topics in Early Childhood Special Education, 30*(1), 32–45.

Browder, D. M., Gibbs, S., Ahlgrim-Delzell, L., Courtade, G., Mraz, M., & Flowers, C. (2009). Literacy for students with severe disabilities. *Remedial and Special Education, 30*(5), 269–281.

Browder, D. M., Wakeman, S. Y., Spooner, F., Ahlgrim-Delzell, L. & Algozzine, B. (2006). *Exceptional Children, 72*(4), 392–408.

Brown v. Board of Education, 347 U.S. 483 (1954).

Brown, D., Pryzwansky, W., & Schulte, A. (2006). *Psychological consultation: Introduction to theory and practice*. Boston: Allyn & Bacon

Brown, G. T. & Burns, S. A. (2001). The efficacy of neurodevelopmental treatment in pediatrics: A systematic review. *British Journal of Occupational Therapy, 64*(5), 235–244.

Brown, J. M. (2013). Recurrent grief in mothering a child with an intellectual disability to adulthood: Grieving is healing. *Child and Family Social Work, 21*(1), 113–122.

Brown, N. B., Howerter, C. S., & Morgan, J. J. (2013). Tools and strategies for making co-teaching work. *Intervention in School and Clinic, 49*, 84–91.

Brown, S. T. & Stanton-Chapman, T. L. (2017). Experiences of paraprofessionals in US preschool special education and general education classrooms. *Journal of Research in Special Educational Needs, 17*, 18–30.

Brown, T. L., Gatmaitan, M., & Harjusola-Webb, S. M. (2014). Using performance feedback to support paraprofessionals in inclusive preschool classrooms. *Young Exceptional Children, 17*(2), 21–31.

Bruder, M. B. (2000). Family-centered early intervention: Clarifying our values for the new millennium. *Topics in Early Childhood Special Education, 20*(2), 105–115.

Bruder, M. B. (2005). Service coordination and integration in a developmental systems approach to early intervention. In M. J. Guralnick (Ed.), *The developmental systems approach to early intervention* (pp. 29–58). Baltimore: Brookes.

Bruinsma, Y., Koegel, R. L., & Koegel, L. K. (2004). Joint attention and children with autism using behavior modification procedures. *Journal of Child Psychology and Psychiatry, 44*(3), 456–468.

Bruner, J. (1982). The organization of action and the nature of the adult–infant transaction. In E. Tronick (Ed.), *Social interchange in infancy: Affect, cognition and communication* (pp. 23–35). Baltimore: University Park Press.

Bruni, M. (2016). *Fine motor skills for children with Down syndrome: A guide for parents and professionals* (3rd ed.). Bethesda, MD: Woodbine House.

Bruns, D. A. & Thompson, S. D. (2012). *Feeding challenges in young children*. Baltimore: Brookes.

Butler, C. & Darrah, J. (2001). Effects of neurodevelopmental treatment (NDT) for cerebral palsy: An AACPDM evidence report. *Developmental Medicine and Child Neurology, 43*, 778–790.

Buysee, V. & Peisner-Feinberg, E. (2010). Recognition & response: Response to intervention for PreK. *Young Exceptional Children, 13*(4), 2–13.

Buysee, V. & Wesley, P. W. (2005). *Consultation in early childhood settings*. Baltimore: Brookes.

Buysee, V. & Wesley, P. W. (Eds.). (2006). *Evidence-based practice in the early childhood field*. Washington, DC: Zero to Three Press.

Buysee, V., Wesley, P. W., Snyder, P., & Winton, P. (2006). Evidence-based practice: What does it really mean for the early childhood field? *Young Exceptional Children, 9*(4), 2–11.

California Department of Education. (2009). *Preschool English learners: Principles and practices to promote language, literacy, and learning* (2nd ed.). Sacramento, CA: Author.

Campbell, A. & Namy, L. (2003). The role of social referential context and verbal and nonverbal symbol learning. *Child Development, 74*, 549–563.

Campbell, F. A., Conti, G., Heckman, J. J., Moon, S. H., Pinto, R., Pungello, E., & Pan, Y. (2014). Early childhood investments substantially boost adult health. *Science, 28*, 1478–1485.

Campbell, P. H., Milbourne, S., Dugan, L. M., & Wilcox, J. M. (2006). A review of evidence on practices for teaching young children to use assistive technology devices. *Topics in Early Childhood Special Education, 26*, 3–13.

Cannon, J. S., Kilburn, M. R., Karoly, L. A., Mattox, T., Muchow, A. N., & Buenaventura, M. (2017). *Investing early: Taking stock of outcomes and economic returns from early childhood programs*. Santa Monica, CA: RAND Corp. Retrieved from https://www.rand.org/pubs/research_reports/RR1993.html

Carroll, D. (2001). Considering paraeducator training, roles, and responsibilities. *Teaching Exceptional Children, 34*(2), 60–64.

Case, R. (1985). *Intellectual development: A systematic reinterpretation*. New York: Academic Press.

Caskey, M., Stephens, F., Tucker, R., & Vohr, B. (2014). Adult talk in the NICU with preterm infants and developmental outcomes. *Pediatrics, 133*(3), 578–584.

Catts, H. W. & Kamhi, A. G. (Eds.). (2012). *Language and reading disabilities* (3rd ed.). Boston: Pearson.

Causton-Theoharis, J. & Malmgren, K. (2005). Building bridges: Strategies to help paraprofessionals promote peer interaction. *Teaching Exceptional Children, 37*(6), 18–24.

Center for Applied Special Technology. (2014). *Universal Design for Learning*. Retrieved from http://www.cast.org/UDL/

Center for Parent Information and Resources. (2017, February). *Support, modifications, and accommodations for students*. Retrieved from http://www.parentcenterhub.org/accommodations/

Center on the Developing Child at Harvard University. (2017). *Three principles to improve outcomes for children and families*. Retrieved from http://www.developingchild.harvard.edu

Center on the Social and Emotional Foundations for Early Learning. (2009, April). *Fostering emotional literacy in young children: Labeling emotions*. What Works, Brief Training Kit #21. Retrieved from http://csefel.vanderbilt.edu/kits/wwbtk21.pdf

Center on the Social and Emotional Foundations for Early Learning. (n.d.). *How to choose a social emotional curriculum. How do I decide?* Series of Guidelines #2. Retrieved from http://csefel.vanderbilt.edu/documents/dmg_choose_se_curriculum.pdf

Centers for Disease Control and Prevention. (CDC). (2008). *Birth defects—Data & Statistics*. Retrieved from http://www.cdc.gov/ncbddd/birthdefects/index.html

Centers for Disease Control and Prevention. (CDC) (2016, April). *Adverse childhood experiences (ACEs)*. Retrieved from https://www.cdc.gov/violenceprevention/acestudy/

Chambers, C. R. (2006). High-probability request strategies: Practical guidelines. *Young Exceptional Children, 9*(2), 20–28.

Chan, S, & Chen, D. (2011). Families with Asian roots. In E. W. Lynch & M. J. Hanson (Eds.), *Developing cross-cultural competence: A guide for working with children and families* (4th ed., pp. 234–318). Baltimore: Brookes

Chandler, L. K., Cochran, D. C., Christensen, I. K. A., Dinnebeil, L. A., Gallagher, P. A., Lifter, K., . . . Spino, M. (2012). The alignment of CEC/DEC and NAEYC personnel preparation standards. *Topics in Early Childhood Special Education, 32*(11), 52–63.

Chao, R. & Tseng, V. (2002). Parenting of Asians. In M. H. Bornstein (Ed.), *Handbook of parenting: Social conditions and applied parenting* (pp. 59–93). Mahwah, NJ: Erlbaum.

Charlesworth, R. (2017). *Understanding child development*. Boston: Cengage Learning.

Chasnoff, I. J. (2001). *The nature of nurture: Biology, environment and the drug-exposed child*. Chicago: NTI Upstream.

Chasnoff, I. J. (2010). *The mystery of risk. Drugs, alcohol, pregnancy and the vulnerable child*. Chicago: NTI Upstream.

Cheatham, G. A., Hart, J. E., Malian, I., & McDonald, J. (2012). Six things to never say or hear during an IEP meeting: Educators as advocates for families. *TEACHING Exceptional Children, 44*(3), 50–57.

Cheatham, G. A., Jimenez-Silva, M., & Park, H. (2015). Teacher feedback to support oral language learning for young dual language learners. *Early Child Development and Care, 185*, 1452–1463.

Cheatham, G. A. & Ostrosky, M. M. (2011). Whose expertise? An analysis of advice giving in early childhood parent–teacher conferences. *Journal of Research in Childhood Education, 25*(1), 24–44.

Cheatham, G. A. & Santos, R. M. (2005). A-B-C's of bridging home and school expectations for children and families of diverse backgrounds. *Young Exceptional Children, 8*(3), 3–11.

Chen, D. (2014). Understanding hearing loss: Implications for early intervention. In D. Chen (Ed.), *Essential elements in early intervention: Visual impairments and multiple disabilities* (2nd ed., pp. 294–340). New York: AFB Press.

Chen, D. & Downing, J. E. (2006). *Tactile strategies for children who have visual impairments and multiple disabilities: Promoting communication and learning skills*. New York: AFB Press.

Chen, D. & Gutiérrez-Clellen, V. (2013). Early intervention and young dual language learners with special needs. In Governor's State Advisory Council on Early Learning and Care, *California's best practices for young dual language learners: Research overview papers* (Paper #6, pp. 209–230). Sacramento: California Department of Education. Retrieved from http://www.cde.ca.gov/sp/cd/ce/documents/dllresearchpapers.pdf

Chen, D. & Klein, M. D. (2008). Home-visit early intervention practices with families and their infants who have multiple disabilities. In C. A. Peterson, L. Fox, & P. Blasco (Eds.), *Early intervention for infants and toddlers and their families: Practices and outcomes* (pp. 60–74). Young Exceptional Children Monograph Series, No. 10. Longmont, CO: Sopris West.

Chen, D., Klein, M. D., & Haney, M. (2007). Promoting interactions with infants who have complex multiple disabilities: Development and field-testing of the PLAI curriculum. *Infants & Young Children, 20*, 149–162.

Chen, D., Klein, M. D., & Minor, L. (2008). Online professional development for early interventionists: Learning a systematic approach to promote caregiver interactions with infants who have multiple disabilities. *Infants & Young Children, 21*, 120–133.

Chen, D., Klein, M. D., & Osopova, A. V. (2012). Two is better than one. *In defense of home language maintenance and bilingualism for young children with disabilities* (pp. 133–147). Young Exceptional Children Monograph Series, No. 14.

Chen, D., Rowland, C., Stillman, R., & Mar, H. (2009). Authentic practices for assessing the communication skills of young children with sensory impairments and multiple disabilities. *Early Childhood Services: An Interdisciplinary Journal of Effectiveness, 3*, 323–338.

Chen, D. D., Calvello, C., & Friedman, C. T. (2015). *Parents and their infants with visual impairments* (2nd ed.). Louisville, KY: APH.

Chess, S. & Thomas, A. (2013). *Goodness of fit: Clinical applications from infancy through adult life.* New York: Routledge.

Child Trends. (2014). *Dual language learners: Indicators of child and youth well-being.* Retrieved from https://www.childtrends.org/wpcontent/uploads/2014/11/127_Dual_Language_Learners.pdf

Childress, D. C. (2004). Special instruction and natural environments: Best practices in early intervention. *Infants and Young Children, 17*(2), 162–170.

Christensen, D. L., Baio, J., Braun, K. V., Bilder, B., Charles, J., Constantino, J. N., & Yeargin-Allsopp, M. (2016). Prevalence and characteristics of autism spectrum disorder among children aged 8 years, Autism and Developmental Disabilities Monitoring Network, 11 states, 2012. *MMWR, 65* (SS3), 1-23. Retrieved from https://www.cdc.gov/mmwr/volumes/65/ss/ss6503a1.htm

Clark, C. & McDonnell, A. P. (2008). Teaching choice making to children with visual impairments and multiple disabilities in preschool and kindergarten classrooms. *Journal of Visual Impairment & Blindness, 102*(7), 397–409.

Clements, D. H. & Sarama, J. (2016). Math, science and technology in the early grades. *The Future of Children, 26,* 78–94.

Cohen, H., Amerine-Dickens, M., & Smith, T. (2006). Early intensive behavioral treatment: Replication of the UCLA model in a community setting. *Journal of Developmental and Behavioral Pediatrics, 27*(2), 145–155.

Cohen, J. & Stark, D. R. (2017). The basics of infant and early childhood mental health. *Zero to Three, 38*(2), 28–31.

Coleman, J. (2017). The use of music to promote purposeful movement in children with visual impairments. *Journal of Visual Impairments & Blindness, 11,* 73–77.

Coleman, M. R., Roth, F. P., & West, T. (2009). *Roadmap to pre-K RTI.* Retrieved from http://www.RTINetwork.org/PreKRTIRoadmap

Collins English Dictionary. (2017). *Empathy.* Retrieved from https://www.collinsdictionary.com/dictionary/english/empathy

Collings, C. (2008). That's not my child anymore! Parental grief after acquired brain injury (ABI): Incidence, nature and longevity. *British Journal of Social Work, 38,* 1499–1517.

Cologon, D. (2013). Debunking myths: Reading development in children with Down syndrome. *Australian Journal of Teacher Education, 38*(3), 130–151.

Cologon, D. & McNaught, M. (2013). Early intervention for literacy learning. In L. Ashton & B. Beecher (Eds.), *Diverse literacies and social justice: Implications for practice.* Melbourne: Australian Council for Educational Research.

Cologon, D. M., Wakeman, S. Y., Spooner, F., Ahlgrim-Delzell, L., & Algozzine, B. (2006). Research on reading instruction for individuals with significant cognitive disabilities. *Exceptional Children, 72,* 392–408.

Colombo-Dougovito, A. M. (2017). Exploring the effect of gender and disability on gross motor performance in kindergarten children. *Physical Educator, 74,* 183–197.

Comfort, M., Gordon, P. R., & Naples, D. (2011). KIPS: An evidence-based tool for assessing parenting strengths and needs in diverse families. *Infants and Young Children, 23*(1), 56–74.

Commission on Teacher Credentialing. (2015, December). *California school paraprofessional teacher training program. An annual report to the legislature as required by SD 1636 (Chap. 1333. Stats.1990).* Retrieved from https://files.eric.ed.gov/fulltext/ED579184.pdf

Committee on Obstetric Practice, American Academy of Pediatrics—Committee on Fetus and Newborn. (2015, October). *The Apgar score.* Committee Opinion, No. 644, pp. 1–4. Retrieved from https://www.acog.org/-/media/Committee-Opinions/Committee-on-Obstetric-Practice/co644.pdf?dmc=1&ts=20180111T0218002172

Council for Exceptional Children. (2018). *Homelessness and students with exceptionalities.* Retrieved from https://www.cec.sped.org/Special-Ed-Topics/Specialty-Areas/Poverty-and-Homelessness

Cook, B. G & Odom, S. L. (2013). Evidence-based practices and implementation science in special education. *Exceptional Children, 79,* 135–144.

Cook, R. E., Klein, M. D., & Chen, D. (2016). *Adapting early childhood curricula for children with special needs.* (9th ed.). Boston, MA: Pearson.

Cook, R. E., Richardson-Gibbs, A. M., & Dotson, L. N. (2018). *Strategies for including children with special needs in early childhood settings* (2nd ed.). Boston: Cengage Learning.

Cook, R. E. & Sparks, S. N. (2008). *The art and practice of home visiting.* Baltimore: Brookes.

Cook, R. E., Tessier, A., & Klein, M. D. (1996). *Adapting early childhood curricula for children in inclusive settings* (4th ed.). Upper Saddle River, NJ: Merrill/Prentice Hall.

Copple, C. & Bredekamp, S. (Eds.). (2009). *Developmentally appropriate practice in early childhood programs serving children from birth through age 8* (3rd ed.). Washington, DC: National Association for the Education of Young Children

Crais, E. R. & Woods, J. (2016). The role of speech-language pathologists in providing early childhood special education. In B. Reichow, B. A. Boyd, E. E. Barton, & S. Odom (Eds.), *Handbook of early childhood special education* (pp. 363–383). Cham, Switzerland: Springer.

Cross, T. (1984). Habilitating the language-impaired child: Ideas from studies of parent–child interaction. *Topics in Language Disorders, 4,* 1–14.

Cummins, J. & Swain, M. (1986). *Bilingualism in education.* New York: Longman.

Cummins, J. & Swain, M. (2014). *Bilingualism in education: Aspects of theory, research and practice.* New York: Routledge.

Curenton, S. M. (2010). Understanding the landscape of stories. *Early Childhood Development and Care, 18*(6), 791–808.

DaFonte, M. A., Boesch, M. C., Edwards-Bowyer, M. E., Restrepo, M. W., Bennett, B. P., & Diamond, G. P. (2016). A three-step reinforcer identification framework: A step-by-step process. *Education and Treatment of Children, 39,* 389–401.

Davenport, C. A. & Alber-Morgan, S. R. (2016). I have a child with a cochlear implant in my preschool classroom. Now what? *TEACHING Exceptional Children, 49*(1), 41–48.

Davys, D., Mitchell, D., & Martin, D. (2017). Fathers of people with intellectual disability: A review of the literature. *Journal of Intellectual Disabilities,21,* 175–196.

DeChurch, L. A., Mesmer-Magnus, J. R., & Doty, D. (2013). Moving beyond relationship and task conflict: Toward a process state perspective. *Journal of Applied Psychology, 98,* 559–578.

Deiner, P. L. (2013). *Inclusive early childhood education.* Boston: Cengage Learning.

Demetrious, A. & Raftaopoulous, A. (Eds). (2004). *Cognitive developmental change: Theories, models and measurement.* Cambridge, UK: Cambridge: University Press.

Demetrious, A., Shayer, M., & Efklides, A. (2017). *Neo-Piagetian theories of cognitive development.* New York: Routledge.

DeVore, S., Miolo, G., & Hader, J. (2011). Individualizing inclusion for preschool children using collaborative consultation. *Young Exceptional Children, 14*(4), 31–43.

Diachenko, O. M. (2011). On major developments in preschoolers' imagination. *International Journal of Early Years Education, 19*(1), 12–25.

Diamond, K. E. & Hong, S. Y. (2010). Young children's decisions to include peers with physical disabilities in play. *Journal of Early Intervention, 32*(3), 163–177.

Deming, D. (2009). Early childhood intervention and life-cycle skills development: Evidence from Head Start. *American Economic Journal: Applied Economics, 1*(3), 111–134.

Derman-Sparks, L. & Edwards, J. O. (2010). *Anti-bias education.* Washington, DC: National Association for the Education of Young Children.

DiCarlo, C. F., Baumgartner, J. I., & Caballero, J. O. (2016). Using least-to-most assistive prompt hierarchy to increase child compliance with teacher directives in preschool classrooms. *Early Childhood Education Journal, 45*(6), 745–754.

DiCarlo, C. F., Baumgartner, J. I. & Caballero, J. O., & Powers, C. (2016). Using least-to-most assistive prompt hierarchy to increase child compliance with teacher directives in preschool classrooms. *Early Childhood Education Journal, 45*(6), 745–754.

DiCarlo, C. F. & Vagianos, L. (2009). Using child preferences to increase play across interest centers in inclusive early childhood classrooms. *Young Exceptional Children, 12*(4), 31–39.

Dicker, S. & Gordon, E. (2006). Critical connections for children who are abused and neglected. *Infants and Young Children, 19*(3), 170–178.

Dickinson, D. K. & Newman, S. B. (2006). *Handbook of early literacy research* (Vol. 2). New York: Guilford Press.

Diliberto, J. A. & Brewer, D. (2012). Six tips for successful IEP meetings. *Teaching Exceptional Children, 44*(4), 30–37.

Dinnebeil, L. A. & McInerney, W. F. (2011). *A guide to itinerant early special education services.* Baltimore: Brookes.

Dinnebeil, L. A., McInerney, W., Roth, J., & Ramaswamy, V. (2001). Itinerant early childhood special education services: Service delivery in one state. *Journal of Early Intervention, 24,* 36–45.

Division for Early Childhood. (2002). *Position statement: Responsiveness of family culture, values, and language.* Retrieved from http://www.decsped.org/uploads/docs/about_dec/position_concept_papers/PositionPaper_Resp_FamCul.pdf

Division for Early Childhood. (2007). *Promoting positive outcomes for children with disabilities: Recommendations for curriculum, assessment, and program evaluation.* Retrieved from http://www.dec-sped.org/position-statements

Division for Early Childhood. (2014). *Recommended practices in early intervention/early childhood special education.* Retrieved from http://www.dec-sped.org

Division for Early Childhood & National Association for the Education of Young Children. (2009). *Early childhood inclusion: A joint position statement of the Division for Early Childhood (DEC) and National Association for Education of Young Children (NAEYC).* Chapel Hill: University of North Carolina, FPG Child Development Institute.

Division for Early Childhood of the Council for Exceptional Children, National Association for the Education of Young Children, & National Head Start Association. (2013). *Frameworks for response to intervention in early childhood: Description and implications.* Retrieved from http://www.dec-sped.org

Dodge, D. T., Berke, K. L., Bickart, T., Colker, L. J., & Heroman, C. (2016). *The Creative Curriculum for preschool* (6th ed.). Washington, DC: Teaching Strategies.

Dodge, D. T., Rudick, S., Berke, K. L., Heroman, C., Burts, D., & Bickart, T. (2015). *The Creative Curriculum for infants, toddlers and two.* Washington, DC: Teaching Strategies.

Dote-Kwan, J. (2014). Creating accessible preschool learning environments. In D. Chen (Ed.), *Essential elements in early intervention. Visual impairments and multiple disabilities.* New York: AFB Press.

Downing, J. E. (2010). *Academic instruction for including students with moderate and severe intellectual disabilities in inclusive classrooms:* Thousand Oaks, CA: Corwin.

Downs, A., Downs, R. C., Fossum, M., & Rau, K. (2008). Effectiveness of discrete trial teaching with preschool students with developmental disabilities. *Education and Training in Developmental Disabilities,43,* 443–453.

Drager, K. D., Light, J. C., & Finke, E. H. (2008). Using AAC technologies to build social interaction with young children with autism spectrum disorders. In P. Mirenda & T. Iacono (Eds.), *AAC for individuals with autism spectrum disorders* (pp. 247–278). Baltimore: Brookes.

Duncan, G. J. & Murnane, R. J. (Eds.). (2011). *Whither opportunity? Rising inequality, schools and children's life chances.* New York: Russell Sage.

Dunlap, G. & Fox, L. (2012). Function-based interventions for children with challenging behavior. *Journal of Early Intervention, 33*(4), 333–343.

Dunlap, G. & Powell, D. (2009). Promoting social behavior of young children in group settings: A summary of research. *Roadmap to Effective Intervention Practices #3.* Tampa: University of South Florida, Technical Assistance Center on Social Emotional Intervention for Young Children.

Dunlap, G., Wilson, K. J., Strain, P., & Lee, J. K. (2013). *Prevent-teach-reinforce for young children: The early childhood model of individualized positive behavior support.* Baltimore: Brookes.

Dunn, L. M. (1968). Special education of the mildly retarded—is much of it justifiable? *Exceptional Children, 35,* 5–22.

Dunst, C. J. & Bruder, M. B. (2006). Early intervention service coordination models and service coordinator practices. *Journal of Early Intervention, 28*(3), 155–165.

Dunst, C. J. & Gorman, E. (2009). Research informing the development of infant finger drawing. *CELLreviews, 2*(1), 1–6. Retrieved from http://www.earlyliteracylearning.org/cellreviews/cellreviews_v2_n1.pdf

Dunst, C. J., Gorman, E., & Hamby, D. W. (2010). Effectiveness of adult verbal and vocal contingent responsiveness on increases in infant vocalizations. *CELLreviews, 3*(1), 1–11. Retrieved from http://www.earlyliteracylearning.org/cellreviews/cellreviews_v3_nl.pdf

Dunst, C. J., Meter, D., & Hamby, D. W. (2011). Influences of sign and oral language interventions on the speech and oral language production of young children with disabilities. *CELLreviews, 4*(4), 1–20.

Dunst, C. J., Trivette, C. M., Masiello, T., Roper, N., & Robyak, A. (2006). Framework for developing evidence-based early literacy learning practices. *CELLpapers, 1*(1) 1–12.

Duran, L. J., Hartzheim, D., Lund, E. M., Simonsmeier, V., & Kohlmeier, T. (2016). Bilingual and home language interventions with young dual language learners: A research synthesis. *Language, Speech, and Hearing Services in Schools, 47,* 347–371.

Duschinsky, R. (2015). The emergence of the disorganized/disoriented (d) attachment classification. *History of Psychology, 18,* 32–46.

Dweck, C. S. (2016). *Mindset: The new psychology of success.* New York: Random House.

Dweck, C. S. (2017). *Summary of Mindset.* New York: FastReads.

Easterbrooks, S. R. & Trussell, J. W. (2015). Effects of morphographic instruction on morphographic analysis skills of deaf and hard-of-hearing students. *Journal of Deaf Studies and Deaf Education, 20*(3), 229–241.

Edelman, L. (2004). A relationship-based approach to early intervention. *Resources and Connections, 3*(2), 1–9.

Edmister, E., Staples, A., Huber, B., & Garrett, J. W. (2013). Creating writing opportunities for young children. *Young Exceptional Children, 16*(3), 24–35.

Edwards, C., Gandini, L., & Foreman, G. (Eds.). (2012). *The hundred languages of children* (3rd ed.). Santa Barbara, CA: Praeger.

Eicher, P. S. (2013). Feeding and its disorders. In M. L. Batshaw, N. J. Roizen, & G. R. Lotrecchiano (Eds.), *Children with disabilites* (7th ed., pp. 121–140). Baltimore: Brookes.

Elias, E. R. & Murphy, N. A. (2012). Home care of children and youth with complex health care needs and technology dependencies. *Pediatrics, 129,* 996–1005.

Eliasson, A. C., Krumlinde-Sundholm, L., Rosblad, B., Beclimg, E., Arner, M., Ohrvall, A. M., & Rosenbaum, P. (2006). The Manual Ability Classification Systems (MACS) for children with cerebral palsy: Scaled development and evidence of reliability and validity. *Developmental Medicine & Child Neurology, 48*(7), 549–554.

Ellis, D. G. & Fisher, B. A. (1994). *Small group decision making: Communication and the group process* (4th ed.). New York: McGraw-Hill.

Emck, C., Bosscher, R., Beek, P., & Doreleijers, T. (2009). Gross motor performance and self-perceived motor competence in children with emotional, behavioural, and pervasive developmental disorders: A review. *Developmental Medicine & Child Neurology, 51,* 501–517.

Eme, R. & Millard, E. (2012). Fetal alcohol spectrum disorders: A literature review with screening recommendations. *The School Psychologist, 66*(1), 13–20.

Ennis, R. P., Blanton, K., & Katsiyannis, A. (2017). Child find activities under the Individuals with Disabilities Education Act: Recent case law. *Teaching Exceptional Children, 49,* 301–308.

Epstein, A. S. (2007). Mathematics and scientific inquiry. In *The intentional teacher: Choosing the best strategies for young children's learning* (pp. 41–65). Washington, DC: NAYC.

Epstein, A. S. & Hohmann, M. (2012). *The HighScope preschool curriculum.* Ypsilanti, MI: HighScope Press.

Erikson, E. H. (1971). A healthy personality for every child. In R. H. Anderson & H. G. Shane (Eds.), *As the twig is bent.* Boston: Houghton Mifflin.

Erikson, E. H. (1993). *Childhood and society.* New York: Norton. (Original work published 1963.)

Erickson, K. A., Hatton, D., Roy, V., Fox, D., & Renne, D. (2007). Literacy in early intervention for children with visual impairments: Insights from individual cases. *Journal of Visual Impairment & Blindness, 101,* 80–95.

Espinosa, L. M. & Gutiérrez-Clellen, V. F. (2013). Assessment and young dual language learners in preschool. In Governor's State Advisory Council on Early Learning and Care, *California's best practices for young dual language learners: Research overview papers* (Paper #5, pp.172–208). Sacramento: California Department of Education. Retrieved from http://www.cde.ca.gov/sp/cd/ce/documents/dllresearchpapers.pdf

Fahey, K. R. & Hulit, L. (2018). *Born to talk: An introduction to speech and language development*. Boston: Pearson.

Fahey, K. R., Hulit, L. M., & Howard, M. R. (2019). *Born to talk: An introduction to speech and language* (7th ed.). Boston: Pearson.

Feltmate, K. & Bird, E. K. R. (2008). Language learning in four bilingual children with Down syndrome: A detailed analysis of vocabulary and morphosyntax. *Canadian Journal of Speech-Language Pathology and Audiology, 32*(1), 6–20.

Fenichel, E. (Ed.). (2002). Perinatal mental health: Supporting new families through vulnerability and change. *Zero to Three, 22*(6). (See entire issue.)

Ferguson, D. L. & Baumgart, D. (1991). Partial participation revisited. *Journal of the Association for Persons with Severe Handicaps* (JASH), *16*, 218–227.

Ferguson, P. M. (2002). A place in the family: An historical interpretation of research on parental reactions to having a child with a disability. *The Journal of Special Education, 36*(3), 124–130.

Fernald, A., Marchman, V. A., & Weisleder, A. (2013). SES differences in language processing skill and vocabulary are evident at 18 months. *Developmental Science, 16*(2), 234–248.

Ferretti, L. K. & Bub, K. L. (2017). Family routines and school readiness during the transition to kindergarten. *Early Education and Development, 28*, 59–77.

Feurstein, R., Rand, Y., Hoffman, M., & Miller, R. (1980). *Instrumental enrichment*. Baltimore: University Park Press.

Fialka, J. (2001). The dance of partnership: Why do my feet hurt? *Young Exceptional Children, 4*(2), 21–27.

Fialka, J. (2016). *What matters. Reflections on disability, community and love*. Toronto, Ontario, Canada: Inclusion Press.

Fialka, J. M., Feldman, A. K., & Mikus, K. C. (2012). *Parents and professionals partnering for children with disabilities: A dance that matters*. Thousand Oaks, CA: Corwin

Fialka, J. & Fialka-Feldman, E. (2017). IEP meetings: Building compassion and conversation. *Educational Leadership, 74*(7), 46–51.

Finn, C. D. (2003). Cultural models for early caregiving. *Zero to Three, 23*(5), 40–45.

Finnegan, E. G. (2012). Two approaches to phonics instruction: Comparison of effects with children with significant cognitive disabilities. *Reading and Writing, 31*, 173–183.

Finnie, N. (1997). *Handling the young child with cerebral palsy at home* (3rd ed.). Oxford, UK: Butterworth-Heinemann.

Fiore, S. M., Grasser, A., Greiff, S., Griffin, P., Gong, B., Kllonen, P., . . . von Davier, A. (2017, April). *Collaborative problem solving: Considerations for the national assessment of educational progress*. Retrieved from https://nces.ed.gov/nationsreportcard/pdf/researchcenter/collaborative_problem_solving.pdf

Floress, M. T., Beschta, S. L., Meyer, K. L., & Reinke, W. M. (2017). Praise research trends and future directions: Characteristics and teacher training. *Behavior Disorders, 43*, 227–243.

Fox, C., Dunlap, G., & Cushing, L. (2002). Early intervention, positive behavior support, and transition to school. *Berson, 10*(3), 149–158.

Fox, L. & Hemmeter, M. L. (2011). Coaching early educators to implement effective practices: Using the pyramid model to promote social-emotional development. *Zero to Three, 32*(2), 18–24.

Fraiberg, S. (1974). Blind infants and their mothers: An examination of the sign system. In M. Lewis & L. Rosenblum (Eds.), *The effect of the infant on its caregivers*. New York: John Wiley & Sons.

Freeman, N. K. (2007). Preschoolers' perceptions of gender appropriate toys and their parents' beliefs about genderized behaviors: Miscommunication, mixed messages, or hidden truths? *Early Childhood Education Journal, 34*, 357–366.

French, N. (2007). *Supervising paraeducators—What every teacher should know*. Retrieved from http://www.cec.sped.org/AM/Template.cfm?Section=Home&TEMPLATE=/CM/Content

Friend, M. (2016). Welcome to do-teaching 2.0. *Educational Leadership, 73*(4), 16–22.

Friend, M. & Cook, L. (2013, 2017). *Interactions: Collaboration skills for school professionals* (8th ed.). Boston: Pearson.

Frith, G. H. & Mims, A. (1985). Burnout among special education paraprofessionals. *Teaching Exceptional Children, 17*, 225–227.

Frost, L. & Bondy, A. (2002). *The Picture Exchange Communication System training manual.* (2nd ed.). New Castle, DE: Pyramid Education Consultants.

Fullerton, E. K., Conroy, M. A., & Correa, V. I. (2009). Early childhood teachers' use of specific praise statements with young children at risk for behavioral disorders. *Behavioral Disorders, 34*(3), 118–135.

Furth, H. (1970). *Piaget for teachers*. Upper Saddle River, NJ: Prentice-Hall.

Gaisford, K. L. & Malott, R. W. (2010). The acquisition of generalized matching in children with developmental delays. *The Behavior Analyst Today, 11*, 85–94.

Gallagher, P. A., Fialka, J., Rhodes, C., & Arceneaux, C. (2002). Working with families: Rethinking denial. *Young Exceptional Children, 5*(2), 11–17.

Gallagher, P. A., Kresak, K., & Rhodes, C. A. (2010). Perceived needs of grandmothers of children with disabilities. *Topics in Early Childhood Special Education, 30*(1), 56–64.

Gallaudet Research Institute. (2011, April). *Regional and national summary report of data from the 2009–2010 annual survey of deaf and hard of hearing children and youth*. Washington, DC: GRI, Gallaudet University. Retrieved from http://research.gallaudet.edu/Demographics/2010_National_Summary.pdf

Garcia, E. E. & Garcia, E. H. (2012). *Understanding the language development and early education of Hispanic children*. New York: Teacher's College Press.

Gargiulo, R. M. & Kilgo, J. L. (2014). *An introduction to young children with special needs*. Boston: Cengage Learning.

Gargiulo, R. M. & Metcalf, D. (2010). *Teaching in today's inclusive classrooms*. Belmont, CA: Cengage Learning.

Gately, S. E. & Gately, F. J. (2001). Understanding co-teaching components. *Teaching Exceptional Children, 33*(4), 4–7.

Gatmaitan, M. & Brown, T. (2016). Quality in individualized family service plans: Guidelines for practitioners, programs, and families. *Young Exceptional Children, 19*(2), 14–32.

Gelman, R. & Brenneman, K. (2004). Science learning pathways for young children. *Early Childhood Research Quarterly, 19*, 150–158.

Gelman, R., Brenneman, K., MacDonald, G., & Roman, M. (2010). *Preschool pathways to sciences: Ways of doing, thinking, communicating and knowing about science*. Baltimore: Brookes.

Genesse, F. (2004). *Dual language development and disorders*. Baltimore: Brookes.

Genesee, F. (2008). Early dual language learning. *Zero to Three, 29*, 17–23.

Genesee, F. (2016). Foreword. In A. L. Bailey & A. V. Osipova, *Children's multilingual development and education: Fostering linguistic resources in home and school contexts*. Cambridge, UK: Cambridge University Press.

Gestwicki, C. (2017). *Developmentally appropriate practice: Curriculum and development in early education*. Boston: Cengage Learning.

Giangreco, M. F. (2009). *Critical issues brief: Concerns about the proliferation of one-to-one paraprofessionals*. Arlington, VA: Council for Exceptional Children. Retrieved from: http://www.dddcec.org/positionpapers.htm

Giangreco, M. & Doyle, M. B. (2002). Students with disabilities and paraprofessional supports: Benefits, balance, and band-aids. *Focus on Exceptional Children, 34*(7), 1–12.

Giangreco, M. F., Edelman, S. W., Broer, S. M., & Doyle, M. B. (2001). Paraprofessional support for students with disabilities: Literature from the past decade. *Exceptional Children, 68*, 45–63.

Giangreco, M. F. & Suter, J. C. (2015). Precarious or purposeful? Proactively building inclusive special education service delivery on solid ground. *Inclusion, 3*, 112–131.

Giangreco, M. F., Suter, J. C., & Doyle, M. B. (2010). Paraprofessionals in inclusive schools: A review of recent research. *Journal of Educational and Psychological Consultation, 20*, 41–57.

Giangreco, M. F., Yuan, S., McKenzie, B., Cameron, P., & Fialka, J. (2005). "Be careful what you wish for . . .": Five reasons to be concerned about the assignment of individual paraprofessionals. *Teaching Exceptional Children, 37*(5), 28–34.

Gilkerson, L. & Taylor Ritzler, T. (2005). The role of reflective process in infusing relationship-based practice into early intervention systems. In K. M. Finello (Ed.), *The handbook of training and practice in infant and preschool mental health* (pp. 427–452). San Francisco: Jossey-Bass.

Gollnick, D. M. & Chinn, P. C. (2009). *Multicultural education in a pluralistic society* (8th ed.). Upper Saddle River, NJ: Merrill/Pearson.

Gongola, L. & Sweeney, J. (2013). Discrete trial teaching. *Intervention in School and Clinic, 47*, 183–190.

Gonzalez-Mena, J. (2008). *Diversity in early care and education: Honoring differences* (5th ed.). Boston: McGraw-Hill.

Goodman, K. & Goodman, Y. (1986). *What is whole about whole language.* Portsmouth, NH: Heinemann.

Goods, K. S. Ishijima, E., Chang Y. C., & Kasari, C. (2013). Preschool based JASPER Intervention with minimally verbal children with autism: Pilot RCT. *Journal of Autism Development and Disorders, 43*(5) 1050–1056.

Goodway, J. D., Robinson, L. E., & Crowe, H. (2010). Gender differences in fundamental motor skill development in disadvantaged preschoolers from two geographical regions. *Research Quarterly for Exercise & Sport, 81*, 17–24.

Goswami, U. (Ed.). (2011). *Cognitive development in early childhood* (2nd ed.). West Sussex, UK: John Wiley & Sons/Blackwell.

Gotts, E. E. (1973). Head Start research, development and evaluation. In J. L. Frost (Ed.), *Revisiting early childhood education.* New York: Holt, Rinehart & Winston.

Goudie, A., Havercamp, S., Jamieson, B., & Sahr, T. (2013). Assessing functional impairment in siblings living with children with disabilities. *Pediatrics,132*, e476–e443.

Gray, C. (2006). *The new social storybook: Illustrated edition.* Arlington, TX: Future Horizons.

Gray, C. (2010). *The new social story book, revised and expanded 10th anniversary edition: Over 150 social stories that teach every day social skills to children with autism or Asperger's syndrome and their peers.* Arlington, TX: Future Horizons.

Gray, C. & White, A. L. (2002). *My social stories book.* New York: Jessica Kingsley.

Gray, P. (2017). What exactly is play and why is it such a powerful vehicle for learning? *Topics in Language Disorders, 37*, 217–228.

Greenspan, S. I. & Greenspan, N. T. (1985). *First feelings: Milestones in the emotional development of your baby and child from birth to age four.* New York: Viking Penguin.

Greenspan, S. I. & Wieder, S. (2003). Infant and early childhood mental health: A comprehensive developmental approach to assessment and intervention. *Zero to Three, 24*(1), 6–13.

Greenspan, S. I. & Wieder, S. (2005). *Infant and early childhood mental health: A comprehensive developmental approach to assessment and intervention.* Arlington, VA: American Psychiatric Association.

Greenspan, S. I. & Wieder, S. (2006a). *Engaging autism: The Floortime approach to help children relate, communicate and think.* Reading, MA: Perseus Books.

Greenspan, S. J. & Wieder, S. (2006b). *Helping children relate, communicate and think with DIR Floortime approach.* Cambridge, MA: Da Capo Press.

Greer, C. W. & Erickson, K. A. (2018). A preliminary explanation of uppercase letter-name knowledge among students with significant cognitive disabilities. *Reading and Writing, 31*, 173–183.

Guardino, C. & Cannon, J. E. (2015). Theory, research and practice for students who are deaf and hard of hearing with disabilities: Addressing the challenges from birth to postsecondary education. *American Annals of the Deaf* (16094), 347–355.

Guitar, B. (2014). *Stuttering: An integrated approach to its nature and treatment* (4th ed.). New York: Lippincott, Williams and Wilkins.

Guralnick, M. J. (2000). An agenda for change in early childhood inclusion. *Journal of Early Intervention, 23*(4), 213–222.

Guralnick, M. J. (2005). Inclusion as a core principle in the early intervention system. In M. J. Guralnick (Ed.), *The developmental systems approach to early intervention* (pp. 59–69). Baltimore: Brookes.

Guralnick, M. J. & Bruder, M. B. (2016). Early childhood inclusion in the United States: Goals, current status and future directions. *Infants & Young Children, 29*, 166–177.

Guthrie, A. C. (2000). Fathers' involvement in programs for young children. *Young Children, 55*(4), 75–79.

Hage, C. & Leybaert, J. (2006). The effect of cued speech on the development of spoken language. In P. Spencer & M. Marschark (Eds.), *Advances in the spoken language development of deaf and hard-of-hearing children* (pp. 193–211). New York: Oxford University Press.

Hall, L. J. (2017). *Autism spectrum disorders: From theory to practice* (3rd ed.). New York: Pearson.

Halliday, M. A. K. (1975). Learning how to mean. In E. Lenneberg & E. Lenneberg (Eds.), *Foundations of language development* (Vol. 1, pp. 17–32). New York: Academic Press.

Hanft, B. E., & Pilkington, K. O. (2000). Therapy in natural environments: The means or end goal for early intervention? *Infants and Young Children, 12*(4), 1–13.

Hanft, B. E., Rush, D. D., & Shelden, M. L. (2004). *Coaching families and colleagues in early childhood.* Baltimore: Brookes.

Hanson, M. J. (2011). Diversity in service settings. In E.W. Lynch & M.J. Hanson (Eds.), *Developing cross-cultural competence: A guide for working with children and families* (4th ed., pp. 2–19). Baltimore: Brookes.

Hanson, M. J., Horn, E., Sandall, S., Beckman, P., Morgan, M., Marquart, J. & Chou H.Y. (2001). After preschool inclusion: Children's educational pathways over the early school years. *Exceptional Children, 68*(1), 65–83.

Hanson, M. J. & Lynch, E. W. (2004, 2013). *Understanding families—Supportive approaches to diversity, disability, and risk.* Baltimore: Brookes.

Hanson, M. J. & Zercher, C. (2001). The impact of cultural and linguistic diversity in inclusive preschool environments. In M. Guralnick (Ed.), *Early childhood inclusion: Focus on change* (pp. 413–431). Baltimore: Brookes.

Hanson, R. F. & Spratt, E. G. (2000). Reactive attachment disorder: What we know about the disorder and implications for treatment. *Child Maltreatment, 5*, 137–145.

Hardy, L. L., King, L., Farrell, L., Macniven, R., & Howlett, S. (2010). Fundamental movement skills among Australian preschool children. *Journal of Science and Medicine in Sport, 13*, 503–508.

Harris, K. C. & Klein, M. D. (2002). Itinerant consultation in ECSE: Issues and changes. *Journal of Educational and Psychological Consultation, 13*(3), 237–247.

Harry, B. (2010). *Melanie. A bird with a broken wing. A mother's story.* Baltimore: Brookes.

Hart, B. & Risley, T. R. (1999). *The social world of children learning to talk.* Baltimore: Brookes.

Harte, H. A. (2010). The project approach: A strategy for inclusive classrooms. *Young Exceptional Children, 13*(3), 15–27.

Hatton, D. (2001). Model registry of early childhood visual impairment: First year results. *Journal of Visual Impairment & Blindness, 95*, 418–433.

Hatton, D. D., Ivy, S. E., & Boyer, C. (2013). Severe visual impairments in infants and toddlers in the United States. *Journal of Visual Impairment & Blindness, 107*(5), 325–336.

Haven, E. L., Manangan, C. N., Sparrow, J. K., & Wilson, B. J. (2014). The relation of parent–child interaction qualities to social skills in children with and without autism spectrum disorders. *Autism, 18*, 292–300.

Haugaard, J. J. & Hazan, C. (2004). Recognizing and treating uncommon behavioral and emotional disorders in children and adolescents who have been severely maltreated: Reactive attachment disorder. *Child Maltreatment, 9*(2), 154–160.

Heath, S. B. (1983). *Ways with words: Language, life and work in communities and classrooms.* Cambridge, UK: Cambridge University Press.

Heath, S. B. (1986). Taking a cross-cultural look at narratives. *Topics in Language Disorders, 7*(1), 84–96.

Hebbeler, K. M., Smith, B. J., & Black, T. L. (1991). Federal early childhood special education policy: A model for the improvement of services for children with disabilities. *Exceptional Children, 58*, 104–111.

Heitin, R. (2014). *Writing IEP goals.* Retrieved from: www.wrightslaw.com/info/goals.lesson.heitin.htm#top

Heller, T. & Kaiser, A. (2017). *Research related to siblings of individuals with disabilities.* Retrieved from http://siblingleadership.org/research/research-related-to-siblings-of-individuals-with-disabilities

Helm, J. H. (2015). *Becoming young thinkers: Deep project work in the classroom.* New York: Teachers College Press.

Hemmeter, J. L., McCollum, J., & Hsieh, W. (2005). Practical strategies for supporting emergent literacy in the preschool classroom. In E. Horn & H. Jones (Eds.), *Supporting early literacy development in young children* (pp. 59–74) Young Exceptional Children Monograph Series, No. 7. Missoula, MT: Division for Early Childhood.

Hemmeter, M. L., Snyder, P. A., Fox, L., & James, A. (2016). Evaluating the implementation of the "Pyramid Model for promoting social-emotional competence" in early childhood classrooms. *Topics in Early Childhood Special Education, 36,* 133–146.

Hendrickson, W. & Gray, E. J. (2012). Legitimizing resistance to organizational change: A social work social justice perspective. *International Journal of Humanities and Social Science, 2,* 50–59.

Heron, T. E. & Harris, K. C. (2001). *The educational consultant: Helping professionals, parents and mainstreamed students* (4th ed.). Austin, TX: PRO-ED.

Hess, E. B. (2013). DIR/Floortime: Evidence based practice towards the treatment of autism and sensory processing disorders in children and adolescents. *International Journal of Child Health and Human Development, 6*(3), 267–274.

Hester, P. P., Hendrickson, J. M., & Gable, R. A. (2009). Forty years later—The value of praise, ignoring, and rules for preschoolers at risk for behavior disorders. *Education and Treatment of Children, 32,* 513–535.

Highbee, T. (2010, October). *Photographic activity schedules to promote independence in children with autism/related disabilities.* Paper presented at the 26th Annual International Conference on Young Children with Special Needs and Their Families, the Division for Early Childhood of the Council for Exceptional Children, Kansas City, MO.

Hodapp, R. M., DesJardin, J. L., & Ricci, L. A. (2003). Genetic syndromes of mental retardation: Should they matter for the early interventionist? *Infants & Young Children, 16,* 152–160.

Hoff, E. (2003). The specificity of environmental influences: Socioeconomic status affects early vocabulary development via maternal speech. *Child Development, 74*(5), 1368–1378.

Hohmann, M. & Weikart, D. P. (1995, 2002). *Educating young children: Active learning practices for preschool and child care.* Ypsilanti, MI: HighScope Press.

Hohmann, M., Weikart, D. P., & Epstein, A. S. (2008). *Educating young children: Active learning practices for preschool and child care programs* (3rd ed.). Ypsilanti, MI: HighScope Press.

Holcomb, T. K. (2013). *Introduction to American deaf culture.* New York, New York: Oxford University Press.

Hollingsworth, H. L (2005). Interventions to promote peer social interactions in preschool settings. *Young Exceptional Children, 9*(1), 2–11.

Holloway, E. (2008, 2009). Sensory processing in the context of early intervention, part 2. In D. Chen (Ed.), *Early intervention in action. Working across disciplines to support infants with multiple disabilities and their families* [CD-ROM]. Baltimore: Brookes.

Holzman, M. (2004). *Public education and black male students: A state report card.* Cambridge, MA: Schott Foundation for Public Education.

Homans, G. C. (1992). *The human group.* New York: Transaction.

Hoon, A. H. & Tolly, F. (2013). Cerebral palsy. In M. L. Batshaw, N. J. Roizen, & G. R. Lotrecchiano (Eds.). *Children with disabilities* (7th ed., pp. 423–450). Baltimore: Brookes.

Hooper, S. & Umansky, W. (2009). *Young children with special needs* (5th ed.). Upper Saddle River, NJ: Merrill/Pearson.

Horn, E. & Banerjee, R. (2009). Understanding curriculum modifications and embedded learning opportunities in the context of supporting all children's successes. *Language, Speech and Hearing in Schools, 40,* 406–415.

Hoskins, B. (1996). *Developing inclusive schools: A guide.* Port Chester, NY: National Professional Resources.

Howard, V. F., Williams, B. F., Miller, D., & Aiken, E. (2014). *Very young children with special needs* (5th ed.). Upper Saddle River, NJ: Pearson.

Howe, M. B., Brittain, L. A., & McCathren, R. B. (2004). Meeting the sensory needs of young children in classrooms. *Young Exceptional Children, 8*(1), 11–19.

Howle, J. M. (2007). *Neuro-development treatment approach. Theoretical foundations and principles of clinical practice* (3rd ed.). Laguna Beach, CA: NDTA.

Huffman, J. M. & Fortenberry, C. (2011). Developing fine motor skills. *Young Children, 66*(5), 100–103.

Hulit, L. (2004). *Straight talk on stuttering* (2nd ed.). Springfield, IL: Thomas.

Hunt, J. M. (1961). *Intelligence and experience.* New York: Ronald Press.

Hyndman, B., Benson, A., & Telford, A. (2016). Active play: Exploring the influences on children's school playground activities. *American Journal of Play, 8,* 325–344.

Hyter, Y. D., Rivers, K. O., & De Jarnette, G. (2015). Pragmatic language of African American children and adolescents: A systematic synthesis of the literature. *Topics in Language Disorders, 35,* 8–15.

Iruka, I. U., Durden, T., & Kennel, P. (2015). Changing faces: Parenting, culture, and child learning and development. *Zero to Three, 35*(4), 10–18.

Irvin, D. W., Ingram, P., Huffman, J., Mason, R., & Willis, H. (2018). Exploring paraprofessional and classroom factors affecting teacher supervision. *Research in Developmental Disabilities, 73,* 106–114.

Itard, J. M. G. (1962). *The wild boy of Aveyron.* New York: Appleton-Century-Crofts.

Jennett, H. K., Harris, S. L., & Delmonino, L. (2008). Discrete trial instruction vs. mand training for teaching children with autism to make requests. *Analysis of Verbal Behavior, 24,* 69–85. Retrieved from http://www.ncbi.nlm.nih.gov/pmc/articles/PMC2779923/

Jennings, D., Hanline, M. F., & Woods, J. (2012). Using routines-based interventions in early childhood special education. *Dimensions of Early Childhood, 40*(2), 13–22.

Jerugim, L. (2000). *A personal perspective on raising a child with developmental problems.* Unpublished manuscript.

Jimenez, M. E., Wade, J. R., Lin, Y., Morrow, L. M., & Reichman, N. E. (2016). Adverse experiences in early childhood and kindergarten outcomes. *Pediatrics, 137*(2), 1–9.

Johnson, C. P. & Kastner, T. A. (2005). Helping families raise children with special health care needs at home. *Pediatrics, 115*(2), 507–511.

Johnson, D. W., Nicholls, M. E. R., Shah, M., & Shields, M. A. (2010). Nature's experiment? Handedness and early childhood development. *Demography, 46,* 281–311.

Johnson, J., Rahn, N. L., & Bricker, D. (2015). *An activity-based approach to early intervention* (4th ed.). Baltimore: Brookes.

Johnson-Martin, N. M., Attermeier, S. M., & Hacker, B. (2004). *The Carolina Curriculum for infants and toddlers with special needs (CCITSN)* (3rd ed.). Baltimore: Brookes.

Johnston, J. M., Foxx, R. M., Jacobson, J. W., Green, G., & Mulick, J. A. (2006). Positive behavior support and applied behavior analysis. *The Behavior Analyst, 29,* 51–74.

Jones, E. (2012, March). The emergence of the emergent curriculum. *Young Children, 66–68.*

Jones, V. L., Higgins, K., Brandon R. R., Cote, D. L., & Dobbins, N. (2013). A focus on resiliency: Young children with disabilities. *Young Exceptional Children, 16*(4), 3–16.

Joseph, G. E. (2003). Enhancing emotional vocabulary in young children. *Young Exceptional Children, 6*(4), 18–26.

Judge, S., Floyd, K., & Woods-Fields, C. (2010). Creating a technology-rich environment for infants and toddlers with disabilities. *Infants & Young Children, 23,* 84–92.

Justice, L. M. & Kaderavek, J. N. (2009). Accelerating preschoolers' early literacy development through classroom-based teacher-child story book reading and explicit print referencing. *Language Speech and Hearing Services in the Schools, 40,* 67–85.

Kamhi, A. G. & Catts, H. W. (2012). *Language and reading disabilities,* (3rd ed.). Boston: Pearson.

Karaaslan, O. & Mahoney, G. (2015). Mediational analysis of the effects of responsive teaching on the developmental functioning of preschool children with disabilities. *Journal of Early Intervention, 37,* 286–299.

Kasari, C., Freeman, S., & Paparella, T. (2006). Joint attention and symbolic play in young children with autism. *Journal of Child Psychology and Psychiatry, 47*(6), 611–620.

Kasari, C., Gulsrud, A., Wong, C., Kwaon, S., & Locke, J. (2010). Randomized controlled caregiver mediated joint engagement intervention for toddlers with autism. *Journal of Autism and Developmental Disorders, 40*, 1045–1056.

Katims, D. S. (1991). Emergent literacy in early childhood special education: Curriculum and instruction. *Topics in Early Childhood Special Education, 11*(1), 69–84.

Katz, L., Chard, S. C., & Logan, Y. (2014). *Engaging children's minds: The project approach* (3rd ed.). Santa Barbara, CA: Praeger.

Keilty, B. (2010). *The early intervention guidebook for families and professionals*. New York: Teachers College Press.

Kennedy, E. T. & Effgen, S. K. (2016). Role of physical therapy within the context of early childhood special education. In B. Reichow, B. A. Boyd, E. E. Barton, & S. L. Odom (Eds.), *Handbook of early childhood special education* (pp. 403–417). Cham, Switzerland: Springer.

Keyes, A.W., Smyke, A. T., Middleton, M., & Black, C. (2015). Parenting African American children in the context of racism. *Zero to Three, 35*(4), 27–34.

Kincaid, D., Dunlap, G., Kern, L., Lane, K. L., Bambara, L. M., Brown, F., & Knoster, T. P. (2016). Positive behaviour support: A proposal for updating and refining the definition. *Journal of Positive Behavior Interventions, 18*, 19–73.

Kirk, S. (1958). *Early education of the mentally retarded*. Urbana: University of Illinois Press.

Klein, M. D. (2008). Early communication development and the role of caregiver–child interactions. In D. Chen (Ed.), *Early intervention in action. Working across disciplines to support infants with multiple disabilities and their families* [CD-ROM]. Baltimore: Brookes.

Klein, M. D. & Briggs, M. H. (1987). Facilitating mother–infant communicative interaction in mothers of high-risk infants. *Journal of Childhood Communication Disorders, 10*(2), 95–106.

Klein, M. D. & Chen, D. (2008). Home visiting practices in early intervention with infants with disabilities: An exploratory study. *Early Childhood Services, 2*(4), 207–223.

Klein, M. D., Chen, D., & Haney, M. (2000). *Promoting learning through active interaction: A guide to early communication with young children who have multiple disabilities*. Baltimore: Brookes.

Klein, M. D., Cook, R. E., & Richardson-Gibbs, A. M. (2001). *Strategies for including children with special needs in early childhood settings*. Albany, NY: Delmar/Thomson Learning.

Klein, M. D. & Harris, K. C. (2004). Consideration in the personnel preparation of itinerant early childhood special education consultants. *Journal of Educational and Psychological Consultation, 15*(2), 151–167.

Klein, M. D., Richardson-Gibbs, A. M., Kilpatrick, S., & Harris, K. (2001). *A practical guide for early childhood inclusion support specialists*. Los Angeles: Project Support, California State University Los Angeles, Division of Special Education.

Kling, A., Campbell, P. H., & Wilcox, J. (2010). Young children with physical disabilities: Caregiver perspectives about assistive technology. *Infants & Young Children, 23*, 169–183.

Kluth, P. & Chandler-Olcott, K. (2008). *A land we can share: Teaching literacy to students with autism*. Baltimore: Brookes.

Koegel, L. K., Vernon, T., Koegel, R. L., Koegel, B. L., & Paullin, A. W. (2012). Improving social engagement and initiations between children with autism spectrum disorder and their peers in inclusive settings. *Journal Positive Behavior Intervention, 14*(4), 220–227.

Koegel, R. L. & Koegel, L. K. (2012). *The PRT pocket guide: Pivotal response treatment for autism spectrum disorders*. Baltimore: Brookes.

Koegel, R. L., Bradshaw, J. L., Ashbaugh, K., & Koegel, L. K. (2014). Improving question-asking initiations in young children with autism using Pivotal Response Treatment. *Journal of Autism and Developmental Disorders, 44*, 816–827.

Kollins, S. H. & Greenhill, L. (2006). Evidence base for the use of stimulant medication in preschool children with ADHD. *Infants and Young Children, 19*(2), 132–141.

Kostelnik, M. J., Soderman, A. K., Whiren, A. P., Rupiper, M., & Gregory, K. M. (2015). *Guiding children's social development and learning*. Boston: Cengage Learning.

Kran, B. S. & Mayer, D. L. (2015). Assessment of visual function and functional vision: Clinical assessment and suggested methods for educators. In A. H. Lueck & G. N. Dutton (Eds.), *Vision and the brain: Understanding cerebral visual impairment in children* (pp. 277–342). New York: AFB Press.

Krashen, S. (2017). The case for comprehensible input. *Language Magazine*. Retrieved from http://www.languagemagazine.com/2017/07/case-for-comprehension/

Kübler-Ross, E. (1969). *On death and dying*. New York: Macmillan.

Kuhaneck, H. M., Spitzer, S. L., & Miller, E. (2010). *Activity analysis, creativity, and playfulness in pediatric occupational therapy*. Boston: Jones and Bartlett.

Kunjufu, J. (2005). *Keeping black boys out of special education*. Chicago: African American Images.

Kurpius, D. (1978). Consultation theory and process: An integrated model. *Personnel and Guidance Journal, 56*, 335–338.

Kurtz, L. A. (2008). *Understanding motor skills in children with dyspraxia, ADAD, autism, and other learning disabilities. A guide to improving coordination*. London: Jessica Kingsley.

Kuster, J. M. (2010). Making books and creating stories. *ASHA Leader, 15*, 732–733.

LaGasse, B. (2013). 2013 Early childhood research snapshot. *Imagine 4*(1), 30–33. Retrieved from http://www.imagine.musictherapy.biz

Ladd, P. (2003). *Understanding deaf culture: In search of Deafhood*. Toronto: Multilingual Matters.

Lally, J. R., Torres, Y. L., & Phelps, M. C. (2010, February). How to care for infants and toddlers in groups. *Zero to Three*, Parenting Resource. Retrieved from https://www.zerotothree.org/resources/77-how-to-care-for-infants-and-toddlers-in-groups

Lamorey, S. (2002). Evil eyes, prayer meetings and IEPs. *Teaching Exceptional Children, 34*(5), 67–71.

Lang, R., O'Reilly, M., Healy, L., Rispoli, M., Lydon, H., Streusand, W., & Giesbers, S. (2012). Sensory integration therapy for autism spectrum disorders: A systematic review. *Research in Autism Spectrum Disorders, 6*, 1004–1018.

Lasater, M. (2012). *Power teaming: Strategies to enhance teacher-paraeducator partnerships*. Retrieved from http://www.lasaterconsulting.com

Lavin, J. L. (2001). *Special kids need special parents*. New York: Berkeley.

Lawrence, S., Smith, S., & Banerjee, R. (2016, April). *Preschool inclusion: Key findings from research and implications for policy*. Child Care and Early Education Research Connections. Retrieved from http://nccp.org/publications/pdf/text_1154.pdf

Lazar, I. & Darlington, R. (1979). *Lasting effects after preschool* (OHDS 79-30179). Washington, DC: Office of Human Development Services Administration for Children, Youth and Families.

Lazar, I. & Darlington, R. B. (1982). Lasting effects of early education: A report from the Consortium for Longitudinal Studies. *Monographs of the Society for Research in Child Development 47* (Serial No. 195).

Lederer, S. H. & Battaglia, D. (2015). Using signs to facilitate vocabulary in children with language delays. *Infants & Young Children, 28*, 18–31.

Lehr, D. H. & Greene, J. (2002). Educating students with complex health care needs in public schools. The intersection of health care, education and the law. *Journal of Health Care, Law and Policy, 5*(1), 68–90.

Leon, K. & Spengler, L. (2005). *Helping children adjust to divorce: A guide for teachers*. Retrieved from http://www.extension.missouri.edu/explore/shop/

Leong, H. M., Carter, M., & Stephenson, J. R. (2015). Meta-analysis of research on sensory integration therapy for individuals with developmental and learning disabilities. *Journal of Developmental and Physical Disabilities, 27*, 183–206.

Lester, R, R., Allanson, P. B., Bolton, P. & Notar, E. C. (2017). Routines are the foundation of classroom management. *Education, 137*, 398–412.

Lieberman, A. F. & Osofsky, J. D. (2009). Poverty, trauma, and infant mental health. *Zero to Three, 30*(2), 54–58.

Lifter, K., Mason E. J., & Barton, E. E. (2011). Children's play: Where we have been and where we could go. *Journal of Early Intervention, 33*(4), 281–297.

Lillard, A. S. (2017). *Montessori: The science behind the genius*. New York: Oxford University Press.

Linder, T. (2008). *Transdisciplinary play-based assessment (TPBA2)* (2nd ed.). Baltimore: Brookes.

Lloyd, M., MacDonald, M., & Lord, C. (2013). Motor skills of toddlers with autism spectrum disorders. *Autism, 17*, 133–146.

Lo, L. (2012). Demystifying the IEP process for diverse parents of children with disabilities. *TEACHING Exceptional Children, 44*(3), 14–20.

Loeb, D. F. (2003). Diagnostic and descriptive assessment. In L. McCormick, D. F. Loeb, & R. L. Schiefelbusch (Eds.), *Supporting children with communication difficulties in inclusive settings* (2nd ed., pp. 189–234). Boston: Allyn & Bacon.

Loughlin-Presnal, J. E. & Bierman, K. L. (2017). Promoting parent academic expectations predicts improved school outcomes for low income children entering kindergarten. *Journal of School Psychology, 62*, 67–80.

Lovaas, O. I. (1987). Behavioral treatment and normal educational and intellectual functioning in young autistic children. *Journal of Consulting & Clinical Psychology, 55*, 3–9.

Lovaas, O. I. (2003). *Teaching individuals with developmental delays: Basic intervention techniques.* Austin, TX: Pro-Ed.

Lowman, D. K. (1998). Preschoolers with complex health care needs in preschool classrooms. *Young Exceptional Children, 4*, 2–6.

Lueck, A. H., Chen, D., Kekelis, L. S., & Hartmann, E. S. (2008). *Developmental guidelines for infants with visual impairments. A guidebook for early intervention* (2nd ed.). Louisville, KY: American Printing House for the Blind.

Luke, S., Vail, C. O., & Ayres, K. M. (2014). Using antecedent physical activity to increase on-task behavior in young children. *Exceptional Children, 80*(4), 489–503.

Lynch, E. (2011). Developing cross cultural competence. In E. W. Lynch & M. J. Hanson (Eds), *Developing cross-cultural competence: A guide for working with children and their families* (4th ed., pp. 41–77). Baltimore: Brookes.

Lynch, E. & Hanson, M. J. (2011a). (Eds). *Developing cross-cultural competence: A guide for working with children and their families* (4th ed.). Baltimore: Brookes.

Lynch, E. W. & Hanson, M. J. (2011b). Steps in the right direction. Implications for service providers. In E. W. Lynch & M. J. Hanson (Eds.), *Developing cross-cultural competence: A guide for working with children and families* (4th ed., pp. 472–489). Baltimore: Brookes.

MacDonald, J. (1989). *Becoming partners with children: From play to conversation.* San Antonio, TX: Special Press.

MacDonald, J. & Stoika, P. (2007). *Play to talk: A practical guide to help your late-talking child join the conversation.* Madison, WI: Kiddo.

MacDonald, J. D. (2004). *Communicating partners: 30 years of building responsive relationships with late-talking children including autism Asperger's syndrome (ASD), Down syndrome and typical development.* Philadelphia: Jessica Kingsley.

Macintyre, C. (2010). *Play for children with special need: Supporting children with learning differences, 3–9.* (2nd ed.). New York: Routledge.

MacNamara, J. (1972). Cognitive basis of language learning in infants. *Psychological Review, 79*, 1–13.

Mahoney, G. (2009). Relationship focused intervention (RFI): Enhancing the role of parents in children's developmental intervention. *International Journal of Early Childhood Special Education (INT-JECSE), 1*(1), 79–94. Retrieved from http://www.int-jecse.net/files/EPO-JH2EMMJ8GLCVE.pdf

Mahoney, G. & Perales, F. (2003). Using relationship-focused interventions to enhance the social-emotional functioning of young children with autism spectrum disorders. *Topics in Early Childhood Special Education, 23*(2), 77–89.

Mahoney, G. & Perales, F. (2005). Relationship-focused early intervention with children with pervasive developmental disorders and other disabilities: A comparative study. *Journal of Developmental and Behavioral Pediatrics, 26*(2), 77–85.

Mahoney, G. & MacDonald, J. (2007). *Autism and developmental delays in young children: The Responsive Teaching Curriculum for parents and professionals.* Austin, TX: PRO-ED.

Malekpour, M. (2007). Effects of attachment on early and later development. *The British Journal of Developmental Disabilities, 53*(105), 81–95.

Mancil, G. R. (2009). Milieu therapy as a communication intervention: A review of the literature related to children with autism spectrum disorder. *Education and Training in Developmental Disabilities, 44*, 105–117.

March of Dimes. (2004). *Facts you should know about teenage pregnancy.* White Plains, NY: Author.

Marogliano, M. L. & Russo, M. J. (2011). Moving bodies, building minds. *Young Children, 66*(5), 44–49.

Marotz, L. R. & Allen, K. E. (2016). *Developmental profiles: Pre-birth through adolescence.* Boston: Cengage Learning.

Maslow, A. H. (1998). *Toward a psychology of being.* New York: Van Nostrand Reinhold.

Matson, J. L., Mahan, S., Fodstad, J. C., Hess, J. A., & Neal, D. (2010). Motor skill abilities in toddlers with autistic disorder, /ervasive developmental disorder-not otherwise specified, and atypical development. *Research in Autism Spectrum Disorders, 4*, 444–449.

May, P. A., Baete, A., Russo, J., Elliott, A. J., Blankenship, J., Kalberg, W. O., & Hoyme, H. E. (2014). Prevalence and characteristics of fetal alcohol spectrum disorders. *Pediatrics, 134*, 855–866.

May, P. A., Chambers, C. D., Kalberg, W. O., et al. (2018). Prevalence of fetal alcohol spectrum disorders in 4 US communities. *Journal of the American Medical Association, 319*(5), 474–482.

Mayo Clinic Staff. (2017, June). *Nutrition for kids: Guidelines for a healthy diet.* Retrieved from http://www.mayoclinic.org/healthy-lifestyle/childrens-health/in-depth/nutrition-for-kids/art-20049335

McCathren, R. B. & Allor, J. H. (2005). Using storybooks with preschool children: Enhancing language and emergent literacy. In E. Horn & H. Jones (Eds.), *Supporting early literacy development in young children* (pp. 75–86). Young Exceptional Children Monograph Series No. 7. Missoula, MT: Division for Early Childhood.

McClure, R. (2017). *5 ways to get dad involved in early childcare programs.* Retrieved from https://www.verywell.com/involve-dad-in-early-child-care-programs-617222?print

McCormick, K. M., Jolivette, K., & Ridgley, R. (2003). Choice making as an intervention strategy for young children. *Young Exceptional Children, 6*(2), 3–10.

McCormick, L., Loeb, D. F., & Schiefelbusch, R. L. (2003). *Supporting children with communication difficulties in inclusive settings* (2nd ed.). Boston: Allyn & Bacon.

McCormick, M. C., Brooks-Gunn, J., Buka, S. L. Goldman, J., Yu, J., Salganik, M., . . . Casey, P. H. (2006). Early intervention in low birth weight premature infants: Results at 18 years of age. *Pediatrics, 117*, 771–780.

McDuffie, A. & Yoder, P. (2010). Types of parent verbal responsiveness that predict language in young children with autism spectrum disorder. *Journal of Speech, Language, and Hearing Research, 53*, 1026–1039.

McGee, G. & Daly, T. (2007). Incidental teaching of age appropriate phrases to children with autism. *Research and Practice for Persons with Severe Disabilities, 32*(2), 112–123.

McGrath, M. Z., Johns, B. H., & Mathur, S. R. (2010). Empowered or overpowered? Strategies for working effectively with paraprofessionals. *Beyond Behavior, 19* (2), 2–6.

McNally, S. A. & Slutsky, R. (2017). Key elements of the Reggio Emilia approach and how they are interconnected to create the highly regarded system of early childhood education. *Early Childhood Development and Care, 187*, 1925–1937.

McManus, B. M. (2015). Integration of the Newborn Behavioral Observations (NB) system into child care settings for high-risk newborns. *Zero to Three, 36*(1), 11–20.

McWilliam, R. A. (2007, October 11). *Early intervention in natural environments.* Retrieved from http://natural environments.blogspot.com

McWilliam, R.A. (2010). *Routines-based early intervention: Supporting young children and their families.* Baltimore: Brookes.

McWilliam, R. A. (2012). *Overview of Routines Based Interview and how it fits into overall schema of early intervention.* Retrieved from https://www.youtube.com/watch?v=yhcUotSkYAY

Meadows, D., Elias, G., & Bain, J. (2000). Mothers' ability to identify infants' communicative acts. *Journal of Child Language, 27*, 393–406.

Meltzer, M. (2015, July 2). *10 simple calm down strategies for young children.* Retrieved from https://nspt4kids.com/parenting/10-simple-calm-down-strategies-for-young-children/

Meisels, J. J. (1985). The efficacy of early intervention: Why are we still asking the question? *Topics in Early Childhood Special Education, 5*(2), 1–11.

Mesibov, G. B. & Shea, V. (2010). The TEACCH program in the era of evidence-based practice. *Journal of Autism and Developmental Disorders, 40*, 570–579.

Mihai, A., Friesen, A., Butera, G., Horn, E. Lieber, J., & Palmer, S. (2005). Teaching phonological awareness through story book reading. *Young Exceptional Children, 18*(4), 3–18.

Miller, D. F. (2016). *Positive child guidance*. Boston: Cengage Learning.

Miller, L., Cermak, S., Lane, S., Anzalone, M., & Koomar, J. (2004). Position statement on terminology related to sensory integration dysfunction. *SI Focus*. Retrieved from http://www.spdbayarea.org/SPD_why_the_name_sensory_processing_disorder.htm

Miller, L. J., Robinson, J., & Moulton, D. (2004). Sensory modulation dysfunction: Identification in early childhood. In R. DelCarmen-Wiggins & A. Carter (Eds.), *Handbook of infant, toddler, and preschool mental health assessment* (pp. 247–270). New York: Oxford University Press.

Minahan, J. & Rappaport, N. (2012). *The behavior code: A practical guide to understanding and teaching the most challenging students*. Cambridge, MA: Harvard University Press.

Mindes, G. (2011). *Assessing young children*. Upper Saddle River, NJ: Pearson.

Mirenda, P. & Beukelman, D. R. (2006). *Augmentative and alternative communication: Supporting children and adults with complex communication needs* (3rd ed.). Baltimore: Brookes.

Mitchell, S., Foulger, T. S., & Wetzel, K. (2009). Ten tips for involving families through Internet-based communication. *Young Children, 64*(5), 46–49.

Monk, T. H., Burk, L. R., Klein, M. H., Kupfer, D. J., Soehner, A. M., & Essex, M. J. (2010). Behavioral circadian regularity at age 1 month predicts anxiety levels during school years. *Psychiatric Research, 178*(2), 370–373.

Montgomery, J. W. (2002). Understanding the language difficulties of children with specific language impairment: Does verbal working memory matter? *American Journal of Speech-language Pathology, 11*, 77–91.

Moore, M. L., Howard, V. F., & McLaughlin, T. F. (2002). Siblings of children with disabilities: A review and analysis. *International Journal of Special Education, 17*(1), 49–64.

Mooney, C. G. (2013). *Theories of early childhood: An introduction to Dewey, Montessori, Erickson, Piaget, and Vygotsky* (2nd ed.). St. Paul, MN: Redleaf Press.

Morales, B. A. & Ledford, J. R. (2016). *Peer training. Evidence-based instructional practices for young children with autism and other disabilities*. Retrieved from http://vkc.mc.vanderbilt.edu/ebip/peer-training

More, C. M. & Hart, J. E. (2013). Maximizing the use of electronic individualized education program software. *TEACHING Exceptional Children, 46*(6), 24–29.

Morrison, J. & Lighter, L. (2017). Putting paraeducators on the path to teacher certification. *Phi Delta Kappan, 98*(8), 43–47.

Morrow, L. M., Roskos, K. A., & Gambrell, L. B. (2016). *Oral language and comprehension in Preschool*. New York: Guilford Press

Moss, J. (2006). *Child preference indicators*. Center for Learning and Leadership/UCEDD, College of Medicine, University of Oklahoma Health Sciences Center, Publication No. CA 298.jm. Retrieved from http://www.imdetermined.org/files_resources/547/child-preference-indicators.pdf

Mueller, M. M., Palkovic, C. M., & Maynard, C. S. (2007). Errorless learning: Review and practical application for teaching children with pervasive developmental disorders. *Psychology in the Schools, 44*, 691–700.

Mukherjee, R. A. S., Hollins, S., & Turk, J. (2006). Fetal alcohol spectrum disorder: An overview. *Journal of the Royal Society of Medicine, 99*, 298–302. doi:10.1258/jrsm.99.6.298

Mundy, P. C. (2016). *Autism and joint attention*. New York: Guilford Press.

Murata, N. M. & Tan, C. A. (2009). Collaborative teaching of motor skills for preschoolers with developmental delays. *Early Childhood Journal, 36*(6), 483–489.

Murawski, W. W. (2009). *Collaborative teaching in elementary schools: Making the coteaching marriage work*. Thousand Oaks, CA: Corwin Press.

Murawski, W. W. (2012). 10 tips for using co-planning time more efficiently. *Teaching Exceptional Children, 44*(4), 8–15.

Murawski, W. W. & Spencer, S. A. (2011). *Collaborate, communicate, and differentiate*. Thousand Oaks, CA: Corwin.

Murphy, J. (2017, May). Colin Farrell quotes parents of a child with a disability should hear. Retrieved from https://themighty.com/2017/05/colin-farrell-quotes-parents-of-a-child-with-a-disability-should-hear/

Myers, S. M. & Johnson, C. P. (2007). Management of children with autism spectrum disorders. *Pediatrics, 120*(5), 1162–1182.

National Academy of Sciences. (2009). *Mathematics learning in early childhood: Paths toward excellence and equity*. Washington, DC: Author.

National Association for the Education of Young Children. (2002a). *Executive summary: Early mathematics: Promoting good beginnings*. Joint position statement National Association of Education of Young Children (NAEYC) and National Council of Teachers of Mathematics (NCTM). Retrieved from http://www.naeyc.org/files/positions/mathematics

National Association for the Education of Young Children. (2002b). *Early learning standards: Creating the conditions for success*. Retrieved from http://www.naeyc.org/positions/pdfposition_statement.pdf

National Autism Center. (2010). *Evidence-based practice and autism in the schools: A guide to providing appropriate interventions to students with autism spectrum disorders*. Retrieved from http://www.national autismcenter.org/pdf/NAC%20Ed%20Manual_FINAL.pdf

National Autism Center. (2014). *The facts about autism spectrum disorder*. Retrieved from http://www.national autismcenter.org/pdf/nac_facts_about_autism.pdf

National Autism Center. (2015a). *Evidence-based practice and autism in the schools* (2nd ed.). Randolph, MA: Author. Retrieved from http://www.national autismcenter.org/pdf/national-standards-project/phase-2/

National Autism Center. (2015b). *Findings and conclusions: National standards project, phase 2*. Randolph, MA: Author.

National Center on Birth Defects and Developmental Disabilities. (2016). *Helping children live to the fullest by understanding developmental disabilities*. Annual report. Retrieved from https://www.cdc.gov/ncbddd/aboutus/report/documents/ar-2016-helping-children.pdf

National Center on Family Homelessness (2010). Retrieved from www.famlyhomelessness.org/Children

National Heart, Lung, and Blood Institute. (2013, May 23). *Students with chronic illness: Guidance for families, schools, and students*. Retrieved from http://www.nhlbi.nih.gov/health/public/lung/asthma/guidfam.pdf

National Institute for Literacy. (2008). *Developing early literacy*. Retrieved from http://www.nifl.gov

National Institute for Literacy (NIFL). (2008). *Developing early literacy*. Retrieved from: www.nifl.gov

National Joint Committee on Learning Disabilities. (2006). *Learning disabilities in young children: Identification and intervention*. Retrieved from http://www.ldonline.org/article/Learning_Disabilities_and_Young_Children%3A_Identification_and_Intervention

National Research Council. (2001). *Educating children with autism*. Committee on Educational Interventions for Children with Autism. C. Lord & P. McGee (Eds.), Division of Behavioral and Social Sciences and Education. Washington, DC: National Academy Press.

National Research Council. (2005). *Mathematical and scientific development in early childhood: A workshop summary*. Washington, DC: National Academy Press.

National Scientific Council on the Developing Child. (2004). *Young children develop in an environment of relationships*. Working Paper No. 1. Retrieved from http://www.developing child.net

NECTAC. (2012). *Response to intervention in early childhood*. Retrieved from http://nectac.org/topics/RTI/RTI.asp

NECTAC. (2013) *Outcomes for children served through IDEA's early childhood programs: 2011–2012*. Retrieved from http://ectacenter.org/eco/assets/pdfs/Outcomes for Children-FFY2011.pdf

Nelson Goff, B. S., Springer, N., Foote, L. C., Frantz, C., Peak, M., Tracy, C., . . . Taylor, V. (2013). Receiving the initial Down syndrome diagnosis: A comparison of prenatal and postnatal parent group experiences. *Intellectual and Developmental Disabilities, 51*, 446–457.

Nemeth, K. & Brillante, P. (2011). Dual language learners with challenging behaviors. *Young Children, 66*(4), 12–17.

Neuman, S. B., Copple, C., & Bredekamp, S. (2000). *Learning to read and write: Developmentally appropriate practices for young children.* Washington, DC: National Association for the Education of Young Children.

Neuman, S. B. & Dickinson, D. K. (Eds.). (2011). *Handbook of early literacy research.* New York: Guilford Press.

Neuro-Developmental Treatment Association. (2015, January). *Research article summaries.* Retrieved from https://www.ndta.org/downloads/NDTA%20Research%20Article%20Summaries%202007-2013.pdf

New America. (2016, January). *Multilingual paraprofessionals: An untapped resource for supporting American pluralism.* Retrieved from https://na-production.s3.amazonaws.com/documents/DLLWH_ParasBrief6.1.pdf

Nicholas, J. G. & Geers, A. (2006). The process and early outcomes of cochlear implantation by three years of age. In P. Spencer & M. Marschark (Eds.), *Advances in the spoken language development of deaf and hard-of-hearing children* (pp. 271–297). New York: Oxford University Press.

Nittrouer, S. (2009). *Early development of children with hearing loss.* San Diego, CA: Plural Publishing.

Noble, K. G., Houston, S. M., Brito, N. H, . . . et al. (2015). Family income, parental education and brain structure in children and adolescents. *Nature Neuroscience, 18*(5), 773–780.

Noonan, M. J. & McCormick, L. (2006, 2014). *Teaching young children with disabilities in natural environments.* Baltimore: Brookes.

Nugent, J. K. (2015). The Newborn Behavioral Observations (NBO) system: A form of intervention and support for new parents. *Zero to Three, 36*(1), 1–10.

Nwora, A. J. & Gee, B. M. (2009). A case study of a five-year-old child with pervasive developmental disorder—not otherwise specific using sound-based interventions. *Occupational Therapy International, 16*(1), 25–43.

O'Connor, R. E. & Bell, K. M. (2004). Teaching student with reading disability to read words. In C. A. Stone, E. R. Silliman, B. J. Ehren, & K. Apel (Eds.), *Handbook of language and literacy* (pp. 481–498). New York: Guilford Press.

Odom, S. L. (2016). The role of theory in early childhood special education and early intervention. In B. Reichow, B. A. Boyd, E. E. Barton, & S. Odom (Eds.), *Handbook of early childhood special education* (pp. 21–39). Cham, Switzerland: Springer.

Odom, S. L. (Ed.). (2002). *Widening the circle: Including children with disabilities in preschool programs.* New York: Teachers College Press.

Oelwein, P. (1995). *Teaching reading to children with Down syndrome: A guide for parents and teachers.* Bethesda, MD: Woodbine.

Office of Head Start. (n.d.). *Head Start services snapshot. National (2015–2016).* Retrieved from https://eclkc.ohs.acf.hhs.gov/sites/default/files/pdf/service-snapshot-EHS-2015-2016.pdf

Olds, D. L., Sadler, L., & Klitzman, H. (2007). Programs for parents of infants and toddlers: Recent evidence from randomized trials. *Journal of Child Psychology and Psychiatry, 48*, 355–391.

Orem, R. C. (1969). *Montessori for the special child.* New York: Putnam.

Owens, R. E. (2015). *Language development: An introduction* (9th ed.). Boston: Pearson.

Pacer Center. (2001). *Tips for parents from siblings' viewpoints.* Early Childhood Connection. Minneapolis: Author.

Pacer Center. (2013a). *Siblings forever. Brothers and sisters of children with disabilities share their stories.* Minneapolis: Author.

Pacer Center. (2013b). *Tips from Dads for raising children with disabilities.* Early Childhood Connection. Minneapolis: Author. Retrieved from https://www.pacer.org/newsletters/ec/summer13.pdf

Palisano, R., Rosenbaum, P., Bartlett, D., & Livingston, M. (2007). *Gross Motor Function Classification System—expanded and revised.* Hamilton, Ontario: CanChild Centre for Childhood Disability Research, McMaster University. Retrieved from https://canchild.ca/system/tenon/assets/attachments/000/000/058/original/GMFCS-ER_English.pdf

Palmer, H. (2001). The music, movement and learning connection. *Young Children, 56*(5), 13–17.

Paparella, T. & Kasari, C. (2004). Joint attention skills and language development in special needs populations: Translating research into practice. *Infants and Young Children, 17*, 269–280.

Paradis, J., Genesse, F., & Crago, M. B. (2011). *Dual language development and disorders. A handbook on bilingualism and second language learning* (2nd ed.) Baltimore: Brookes.

Parette, H. P. & Blum, C. (2014). Using flexible participation in technology-supported, universally designed preschool activities. *TEACHING Exceptional Children, 46*(3), 60–67.

Parish, S. L., Rose, R. A., & Andrews, M. E. (2010). TANF's impact on low-income mothers raising children with disabilities. *Exceptional Children, 76*(2), 234–253.

Park, J., Turnbull, A. P., & Turnbull, H. R. (2002). Impacts of poverty on quality of life in families of children with disabilities. *Exceptional Children, 68*(2), 151–170.

Parlakian, P. & Park, H. S. (2001). *Building strong foundations, practical guidance for promoting the social-emotional development of infants and toddlers.* Washington, DC: Zero to Three Press.

Parmar, P., Harkness, S., & Super, C. M. (2008). Teacher or playmate? Asian immigrant and Euro-American parents' participation in their young children's daily activities. *Social Behavior and Personality, 36*, 163–175.

Parten, M. B. (1932). Social participation among preschool children. *Journal of Abnormal and Social Psychology, 27*, 243–269.

Patti, A. L. (2016). Back to the basics: Practical tips for IEP writing. *Intervention in School and Clinic, 51*(3), 151–156.

Pears, K. C., Kim, H. K., Fisher, P. A., & Yoerger, K. (2016). Increasing pre-kindergarten early literacy skills in children with developmental disorders and delays. *Journal of School Psychology, 57*, 15–27.

Peckham-Hardin, K. D. (2014). Positive behavior supports: Preventing and managing difficult behavior. In A. M. Richardson-Gibbs & M. D. Klein (Eds.), *Making preschool inclusion work* (pp. 195–218). Baltimore: Brookes.

Peer, J. W. & Hillman, S. B. (2014). Stress and resilience for parents of children with intellectual and developmental disabilities: A review of key factors and recommendations for practitioners. *Journal of Policy and Practice in Intellectual Disabilities, 11*(2), 92–98.

Pelco, L. E. & Reed-Victor, E. (2003). Understanding and support differences in child temperament. *Young Exceptional Children, 6*(3), 2–11.

Pentimonti, J. M., Murphy, K. A., Justice, L. M., Logan, J. A., & Kaderavek, J. N. (2016). School readiness of children with language impairments predicting literacy skills from pre-literacy and social behavioral dimensions. *International Journal of Language & Communication Disorders, 51*(2), 148–161.

Phipps, S. & Roberts, P. (2012). Predicting the effects of cerebral palsy severity on self-care, mobility, and social function. *American Journal of Occupational Therapy, 66*, 422–429.

Piaget, J. (1954). *The construction of reality in the child.* New York: Basic Books.

Piaget, J. (1963). *Play, dreams, and imitations in childhood.* New York: Norton.

Piaget, J. (1977). *The development of thought: Equilibration of cognitive structure.* New York: Viking Press.

Piaget, J. & Inhelder, B. (1969). *The psychology of the child.* New York: Basic Books.

Piek, J. P. (2006). *Infant motor development.* Champaign, IL: Human Kinetics.

Pierce-Jordan, S. & Lifter, K. (2005). Interaction of social and play behaviors in preschoolers with and without pervasive developmental disorder. *Topics in Early Childhood Special Education, 25*(1), 34–47.

Poyadue, F. (1998). *Helping families travel an unchosen path.* Santa Clara, CA: Parents Helping Parents.

Pretti-Frontczak, K. & Bricker, D. (2000). Enhancing the quality of individualized education plan (IEP) goals and objectives. *Journal of Early Intervention, 23*(2), 92–105.

Prizant, B., Wetherby, A., Rubin, E. M., Laurent, A. C., & Rydell, P. J. (2006). *The SCERTS model: A comprehensive educational approach for children with autism spectrum disorders.* Baltimore: Brookes.

Prizant, B. M. (2015). *Uniquely human: A different way of seeing autism.* New York: Simon and Schuster.

Prizant, B. M., Wetherby, A. M., & Rydell, P. J. (2000). Communication intervention issues for young children with autism spectrum disorders. In A. M. Wetherby & B. M. Prizant (Eds.), *Autism spectrum disorders* (pp. 193–224). Baltimore: Brookes.

Prutting, C. (1979). Process the action of moving forward progressively from one point to another on the way to completion. *Journal of Speech & Hearing Disorders, 44,* 3–23.

Public Laws 85-926, 88-164, 90-538, 92-424, 93-380, 94-142, 95-568, 98-199, 99-457, 100-77, 101-336, 101-476, 102-119, 105-17, 107-110, 108-446, 110-134, 110-325, & 110-335. Washington, DC: U.S. Government Printing Office.

Public Laws PL 93-247 (Child Abuse Prevention and Treatment Act, CAPTA); PL 108-36 (Keeping Children and Families Safe Act of 2003); PL 108-446 (IDEA of 2004). Washington, DC U.S. Government Printing Office.

Puma, M., Bell, S., Cook, R., Heid, C., Broene, P., & Downer, J. (2012). *Third grade follow-up to the Head Start Impact Study.* Final OPRE Report #2012-45. Washington, DC: Office of Planning, Research and Evaluation, Administration for Children and Families, U.S. Department of Health and Human Services. Retrieved from https://www.acf.hhs.gov/sites/default/files/opre/head_start_report.pdf

Purcell, M. L., Turnbull, A., & Jackson, C. W. (2006). Linking early childhood inclusion and family quality of life. *Young Exceptional Children, 9*(3), 10–19.

Pyle, A. & Danniels, E. (2017). A continuum of play-based learning: The role of the teacher in play-based pedagogy and the fear of hijacking play. *Early Education and Development, 28,* 274–289.

Rajan, R. S. (2017). Preschool teachers use of music in the classroom: A survey of Park District preschool programs. *Journal of Music Education, 28,* 89–101.

Rappley, M. D. (2006). Actual psychotropic medication use in preschool children. *Infants and Young Children, 19*(2), 154–163.

Rathus, S. A. (2014). *Childhood: Voyages in development.* Boston: Cengage Learning.

Raver, S. A. & Childress, D. C. (2015). *Early education and intervention for children from birth to three.* Baltimore: Brookes.

Ray, J. A., Pewitt-Kinder, J., & George, S. (2009). Partnering with families of children. *Young Children, 64*(5), 16–22.

Rendon, T., Harjusola-Webb, S., & Gatmaitan, M. (2014). Standard policies to support young dual language learners. *Young Exceptional Children, 17*(1), 21–38

Reynolds, A. J. & Temple, J. A. (2005). Priorities for a new century of early childhood programs. *Infants & Young Children, 18*(2), 104–118.

Reynolds, A. J., Temple, J. A., Ou, S., Arteaga, I. A., & White, B. (2011). School-based early childhood education and age-28 well-being: Effects by timing, dosage, and subgroups. *Science, 333,* 360–364.

Reynolds, T., Zupanick, C. E., & Dombeck, M. (2013). *History of stigmatizing names for intellectual disabilities.* Retrieved from https://www.mentalhelp.net/articles/history-of-stigmatizing-names-for-intellectual-disabilities/

Reichow, B., Boyd, B. A., Barton, E. E., & Odom, S. L. (Eds.). (2016). *Handbook of early childhood special education.* Cham, Switzerland: Springer.

Reutzel, D. R. & Cooter, R. B. (2015). *The essentials of teaching children to read: The teacher makes the difference.* Boston: Pearson.

Richards, J. A., Gilkerson, J., Dongxin, X., & Topping, K. (2017). How much do parents think they talk to their child? *Journal of Early Intervention, 39*(3), 163–179.

Richardson-Gibbs, A. M. & Klein, M. D. (2014). *Making preschool inclusion work: Strategies for supporting children, teachers and programs.* Baltimore: Brookes.

Riski, M. C. (2008). *Abby gets a cochlear implant.* Ottsville, PA: Cassidy.

Roberts, J., Burchjinal, M. R., & Zeisel, S. A. (2002). Otitis media in early childhood in relation to children's school-age language and academic skills. *Pediatrics, 110*(4), 696–706.

Roberts, J. & Zeisel, S. (2004). Otitis media and speech and language: A meta-analysis of prospective studies. *Pediatics, 113,* 237–247.

Rogow, S. M. (2000). Communication and language: Issues and concerns. In B. Silverstone, M. A. Lang, B. P. Rosenthal, & E. Faye (Eds.), *The lighthouse handbook on vision impairment and vision rehabilitation: Vol. 1. Vision impairment* (pp. 395–408). New York: Oxford University Press.

Romski, M., Sevcik, R. A., Adamson, L. B., Cheslock, M., Smith, A., Barker, R. M., & Bakeman, R. (2010). Randomized comparison of augmented and non-augmented language interventions for toddlers with developmental delays and their parents. *Journal of Speech, Language, and Hearing Research, 53*(2), 350–364.

Rous, B., Myers, C. T., & Stricklin, S. B. (2007). Strategies for supporting transitions of young children with special needs and their families. *Journal of Early Intervention, 30,* 1–18.

Rowan, L. (2006). Tips on providing services to grandparent families. *News Exchange, 11*(2), 1–2, 7.

Rowland, C. (2004). *Communication matrix.* Portland, OR: Design to Learn.

Rubin, K., Coplan, R. J., & Bowker, J. C. (2009). Social withdrawal in childhood. *Annual Review of Psychology, 60*(1), 141–171.

Ruff, H. & Capozzoli, M. C. (2003). Development of attention and distractibility in the first 4 years of life. *Developmental Psychopathology, 39,* 877–890.

Rush, D. D. & Shelden, M. L. (2011). *The early childhood coaching handbook.* Baltimore: Brookes.

Rysstad, A. L. & Pederson, A. V. (2016). Brief report: Non-right-handedness within the autism spectrum disorder. *Journal of Autism and Developmental Disorders, 46,* 1110–1117.

Sachs, J. & Newman, R. (2013). Communication development in infancy. In J. B. Gleason (Ed.), *The development of language* (8th ed.). Boston: Pearson.

Sadao, K. C. & Robinson, N. B. (2010). *Assistive technology for young children: Creating inclusive learning environments.* Baltimore: Brookes.

Salcedo, P. & Chen, D. (2008). Vision development and visual impairment. In D. Chen (Ed.), *Early intervention in action. Working across disciplines to support infants with multiple disabilities and their families* [CD-ROM]. Baltimore: Brookes.

Salvia, J. & Ysseldyke, J. E. (2007). *Assessment in special and inclusive education* (10th ed.). Boston: Houghton Mifflin.

Sameroff, A. (Ed.). (2009). *The transactional model of development: How children and contexts shape each other.* Washington, DC: American Psychological Association.

Sameroff, A. J. & Mackenzie, M. J. (2003). A quarter-century of the transactional model. *Zero to Three, 24*(1), 14–22.

Sameroff, A. J., McDonough, S. C., & Rosenblum, K. L. (2005). *Treating parent–infant relationship problems. Strategies for intervention.* New York: Guilford Press.

Sandall, S., Hemmeter, M. L., Smith, B. J., & McLean, M. E. (2005). *DEC recommended practices: A comprehensive guide for practical application in early intervention/early childhood special education.* Longmont, CO: Sopris West.

Sandall, S. & Schwartz, I. S. (2012). *Building blocks for teaching preschoolers with special needs* (2nd ed.). Baltimore: Brookes.

Sandall, S. R., Schwartz, I. S., & Gauvreau, A. (2016). Using modifications and accommodations to enhance learning of young children with disabilities: Little changes that yield big impacts. In B. Reichow, B. A. Boyd, E. E. Barton, & S. L. Odom (Eds.), *Handbook of early childhood special education* (pp. 349–361). Cham, Switzerland: Springer.

Santelli, B., Poyadue, F., & Young, J. (2001). *The parent to parent handbook: Connecting families of children with special needs.* Baltimore: Brookes.

Sanz, M. T. & Menéndez, J. (2010). Parents' training: Effects of the self-help skills programme with Down's syndrome babies. *Early Child Development and Care, 180,* 735–742.

Scanlon, K. (2012). *My toddler talks: Strategies and activities to promote your child's language development.* North Charleston, SC: Createspace.

Schaaf, R. C., Dumont, R. L., Arbesman, M. L., & May-Benson, T. A. (2018). Efficacy of occupational therapy using Ayres Sensory

Integration: A systematic review. *American Journal of Occupational Therapy, 72*, 1–10.

Schweinhart, L. J., Montie, J., Xiang, Z., Barnett, W. S., Belfield, C. R. & Nores, M. (2005). *Lifetime effects: The High/Scope Perry Preschool Study through age 40.* Ypsilanti, MI: High Scope Press.

Schneider, M. (2002). *Do school facilities affect academic outcomes?* Washington, DC: National Clearinghouse for Educational Facilities.

Schwartz, E. (2008). *Music therapy and early childhood: A developmental approach.* Gilsum, NH: Barcelona Publishers.

Schwartz, E. (2012). *You and me make we: A growing together songbook.* Melrose, MA: The Center for Early Childhood Therapy.

Schweinhart, L. J. (2016). Use of early childhood longitudinal studies by policy makers. *International Journal of Child Care and Educational Policy,10*(6), 1–10. doi:10.1186/s40723-016-0023-5

Scruggs, T. E., Mastropieri, M. A., & McDuffie, K. A. (2007). Co-teaching in inclusive classrooms: A metasynthesis of qualitative research. *Exceptional Children, 73*, 392–416.

Seaver, J. L. & Bourret, J. C. (2014). An evaluation of response prompts for teaching behavior chains. *Journal of Applied Behavior Analysis, 47*, 777–792.

Segatti, L., Brown-DuPaul, J., & Keyes, T. L. (2003). Using everyday materials to promote problem solving in toddlers. *Young Children, 58*(3), 12–18.

Seiger-Gardner, L. & Almodovar, D. (2009). Preschool language impairment: Characteristics, assessment, and intervention. In D. K. Bernstein & E. Tiegerman-Farber (Eds.), *Language and communication disorders in children* (6th ed.). Boston: Allyn & Bacon.

Seligselner, M. & Leord, M. (2012). *Birth defects.* Retrieved from https://www.healthline.com/health/birth-defects

Semega, J. L., Fontenot, K. R., & Kollar, M. A. (2017, September). *Income and poverty in the United States: 2016.* United States Census Bureau Library. Retrieved fromhttps://www.census.gov/library/publications/2017/demo/p60-259.html

Sensory Processing Disorder Network. (2010). *About SPD.* Retrieved from http://www.spdnetwork.org/about-sensory-processing-disorder.html

Shea, T. & Bauer, A. (2003). *Parents and schools: Creating a successful partnership for students.* Upper Saddle River, NJ: Merrill/Prentice Hall.

Shea, T. M. & Bauer, A. M. (2002). *Parents and teachers of children with exceptionalities: A handbook for collaboration.* Boston: Allyn & Bacon.

Shelden, M. L. & Rush, D. D. (2014). IFSP outcome statements made simple. *Young Exceptional Children, 17*(4), 15–27.

Shonkoff, J. P. & Meisels, S. J. (Eds.). (2000, 2009). *Handbook of early childhood intervention.* Cambridge, UK: Cambridge University Press.

Shonkoff, J. P. & Phillips, D. A. (Eds.). (2000). *From neurons to neighborhoods: The science of early child development.* Washington, DC: National Academy Press.

Shuss, D. J. (2015). *Supporting play in early childhood. Environment, curriculum, assessment* (2nd ed.). Stamford, CT: Cengage Learning.

Sibling Leadership Network. (2013a). *Young siblings of individuals with intellectual and developmental disabilities.* Retrieved from http://siblingleadership.org/wp-content/uploads/2010/07/SLN-Young-Siblings-research-brief-final.pdf

Sibling Leadership Network. (2013b). *Adult siblings of individuals with intellectual and developmental disabilities.* Retrieved from http://siblingleadership.org/wp-content/uploads/2010/07/SLN-Adult-research-brief-final.pdf

Siebert, E. A., Hamm, J., & Yun, J. (2017). Parental influence on physical activity of children with disabilities. *International Journal of Disability, Development and Education, 45*, 855–865.

Sileo, J. M. (2011). Co-teaching: Getting to know your partner. *TEACHING Exceptional Children, 43* (4), 32–38.

Simpson, K. & Keen, D. (2011). Music intervention for children with autism: Narrative review of the literature. *Journal of Autism & Developmental Disorders, 41*, 1507–1514.

Skeels, H. (1942). A study of the effects of differential stimulation on mentally retarded children: A follow-up study. *American Journal of Mental Deficiency, 46*, 340–350.

Skeels, H. (1966). Adult status of children with contrasting early life experiences. *Monographs of the Society for Research in Child Development, 32*(2).

Skeels, H. & Dye, H. A. (1939). A study of the effects of differential stimulation on mentally retarded children. *Proceedings of the American Association on Mental Deficiency, 44*, 114–136.

Slaughter, V. & de Rosnay, M. (2017). *Theory of mind developmental context.* New York: Routledge.

Slavin, R. E. (2017). *Educational psychology: Theory and practices* (12th ed.). Boston: Pearson.

Sluss, D. J. (2015). *Supporting play in early childhood.* Boston: Cengage Learning.

Smith, J. M. & Smith, D. E. (1976). *Child management.* Champaign, IL: Research Press.

Smith, T. & Lovaas, O. I. (1998). Intensive and early behavioral intervention in autism: The UCLA Young Autism Project. *Infants and Young Children, 10*, 67–78.

Smith, T. E. C., Gartin, B. C., Murdick, N. L., & Hilton, A. (2006). *Families and children with special needs.* Upper Saddle River, NJ: Merrill/Prentice Hall.

Snell, R. (2008). Motor development and physical disabilities. In D. Chen (Ed.), *Early intervention in action. Working across disciplines to support infants with multiple disabilities and their families* [CD-ROM]. Baltimore: Brookes.

Snodgrass, M. R., Meadan, H., Ostrosky, M. M., & Cheung, W. C. (2017). One step at a time: Using task analysis to teach skills. *Early Childhood Education Journal, 45*, 855–865.

Snow, C. E., Barnes, W. S., Chandler, J., Goodman, I. F., & Hemphill, L. (1991). *Unfulfilled expectations: Home and school influences on literacy.* Cambridge, MA: Harvard University Press.

Snow, K. (2013). *Disability is natural: Revolutionary common sense for raising successful children with disabilities* (3rd ed.). San Antonio, TX: Braveheart Press.

Soto, C. J. (2016). The little six personality dimensions from early childhood to early adulthood: Mean-level age and gender differences in parents' reports. *Journal of Personality 84*(4), 409–422.

Souto-Manning, M. (2010). Family involvement: Challenges to consider, strengths to build on. *Young Children, 65*(2), 82–88.

Spencer, P. & Marschark, M. (Eds.). (2010). *Evidence-based practice in educating deaf and hard-of-hearing students.* New York: Oxford University Press.

Squires, J. & Bricker, D. (2006). *Activity-based approach to developing young children's social and emotional competence.* Baltimore: Brookes.

Stafford, A. M. (2005). Choice making: A strategy for students with severe disabilities. *Teaching Exceptional Children, 37*(6), 12–17.

Stalker, K. & McArthur, K. (2012). Child abuse, child protection and disabled children: A review of recent research. *Child Abuse Review, 21*(1), 24–40. Retrieved from https://strathprints.strath.ac.uk/27452/

Stanton-Chapman, T. L. & Schmidt, E. L. (2016a). Caregiver perceptions of inclusive playgrounds targeting toddlers and preschoolers with disabilities: Has recent international and national policy improved overall satisfaction? *Journal of Research in Special Educational Needs, 17*, 237–246.

Stanton-Chapman, T. L. & Schmidt, E. L. (2016b). Special education professionals' perceptions toward accessible playgrounds. *Research and Practice for Persons with Severe Disabilities, 41*, 90–100.

Stillman, R. & Mar, H. (2009). Authentic practices for assessing communication skills of young children with sensory impairments and multiple disabilities. *Early Childhood Services, 3*(4), 328–339.

Stockall, N. S. (2014). When an aide really becomes an aid: Providing professional development for special education paraprofessionals. *Teaching Exceptional Children, 46*(6), 197–205.

Stockall, N. S., Dennis, L., & Miller, M. (2012). Right from the start—Universal design for preschool. *Teaching Exceptional Children, 45*(1), 10–17.

Stokoe, W. C. (2001). *Language in hand.* Washington, DC: Gallaudet University Press.

Stoneman, Z. (2005). Siblings of children with disabilities: Research themes. *Mental Retardation, 43*(5), 339–350.

Storey, K. & Post, M. (2017). *Positive behavior supports in classrooms and schools: Effective and practical strategies for teachers and other service providers* (2nd ed.). Springfield, IL: Charles C. Thomas.

Streissguth, A. & O'Malley, K. (2000). Neuropsychiatric implications and long-term consequences of fetal alcohol spectrum disorders. *Seminars in Clinical Neuropsychiatry, 5,* 177–190.

Strickland, D. S. & Shanahan, T. (2004). What the research says about reading: Laying the groundwork for literacy. *Educational Leadership, 6*(16), 74–77.

Stromberg, J. (2013). *How growing up in poverty may affect a child's developing brain.* Retrieved from https://www.smithsonianmag.com/science-nature/how-growing-up-in-poverty-may-affect-a-childs-developing-brain-180947832/

Sturm, L. (2004). Temperament in early childhood: A primer for the perplexed. *Zero to Three, 24*(4), 4–11.

Subcommittee on Attention-Deficit/Hyperactivity Disorder, Steering Committee on Quality Improvement and Management. (2011). ADHD: Clinical practice guidelines for the diagnosis, evaluation, and treatment of attention-deficit/hyperactivity disorder in children and adolescents. *Pediatrics, 128*(5), 1–16.

Sue, D. W. & Sue, D. (2016). *Counseling the culturally diverse: Theory and practice* (7th ed.). New York: John Wiley & Sons.

Sulzer-Azaroff, B., Hoffman, A. O., Horton, C. B., Bondy, A., & Frost, L. (2009). The picture exchange communication systems (PECS): What do the data say? *Focus on Autism and other Developmental Disabilities, 24*(2), 889–103.

Swan, W. (1981). Programs for handicapped infants and their families supported by the office of special education. *The Communicator, 7*(2), 1–15.

Swinton, J. (2012). From inclusion to belonging: A practical theology of community disability and humanness. *Journal of Religion, Disability and Health, 16*(2), 172–190.

Tabors, P. O. (2008). *One child, two languages: A guide for early childhood educators of children learning English as a second language* (2nd ed.) Baltimore: Brookes.

Tager-Flusberg, H. (2000). Understanding the language and communicative impairments in autism. *International Review of Research in Mental Retardation, 23,* 185–205.

Talbot, M. E. (1964). *Edward Sequin: A study for an educational approach to the treatment of mentally defective children.* New York: Columbia University Teachers College.

Tambyraja, S., Schmitt, M. B., Fraquharson, K., & Justice, L. M. (2017). Home literacy environment profiles of children with language impairment: Associations with caregiver and child specific factors. *International Journal of Language and Communication Disorders, 52*(2), 238–249.

Tannock, R. Girolametto, L., & Siegel, L. (1992). Language intervention with children who have developmental delays: Effects of an interactive approach. *American Journal on Mental Retardation, 97,* 145–160.

Teaford, P., Wheat, J., & Baker, T. (2010). *HELP curriculum guide* (2nd ed.). Palo Alto, CA: VORT Corp.

Texas Tech University. (1984). *The special child: Student laboratory manual.* Lubbock, TX: Home Economics Curriculum Center.

Thant, M. H., Peterson, D. A., & McIntosh, G. C. (2005). Temporal entrainment of cognitive function: Music mnemonics induce brain plasticity and oscillatory synchrony in neural networks underlying memory. *Annals of New York Academy of Sciences, 1060,* 243–254.

Thomas, A., Chess, S., & Birch, H. G. (1968). *Temperamental and behavior disorders in children.* New York: New York University Press.

Thomas, A., Chess, S., & Birch, H. G. (1970). The origin of personality. *Scientific American, 223,* 102–109.

Thompson, S. D. & Rains, K. W. (2009). Learning about sensory integration dysfunction: Strategies to meet young children's sensory needs at home. *Young Exceptional Children, 12,* 16–26.

Tomchek, S. D. & Dunn, W. (2007). Sensory processing in children with and without autism: A comparative study using the Sensory Profile. *American Journal of Occupational Therapy, 61,* 190–200.

Tomlin, A. M. (2004). Thinking about challenging behaviors in toddlers: Temperament style or behavior disorder? *Zero to Three, 24*(4), 29–36.

Topor, I. (2014). Functional vision assessment and early intervention practices. In D. Chen (Ed.), *Essential elements in early intervention: Visual impairments and multiple disabilities* (2nd ed., pp. 214–293). New York: AFB Press.

Trawick-Smith, J., Wolff, U. J., Koschel, M., & Vallarelli, J. (2015). Effects of toys on play quality of preschool children. Influence of gender, ethnicity, and social economic status. *Early Childhood Education Journal, 43,* 249–256.

Trivette, C. M., Dunst, C. J., & Hamby, D. W. (2010a). Acceptability and importance of adaptations to early literacy learning practices for young children with disabilities. *CELL papers, 5*(4), 1–4. Retrieved from http://www.earlyliteracylearning.org/cellpapers/CELLpapers_v5n4_AcceptofAdap.pdf

Trivette, C. M., Dunst, C. J., & Hamby, D. W. (2010b). Influences of family-systems intervention practices on parent–child interactions and child development. *Topics in Early Childhood Special Education, 30*(1), 3–19.

Trivette, C. M., Dunst, C. J., & Hamby, D. W. (2013). Influences of different types of writing activities on the emergent writing abilities of toddlers and preschoolers. *CELLreviews, 6*(3), 1–8. Retrieved from http://www.earlyliteracylearning.org/cellreviews/cellreviews_v6_no3.pdf

Trivette, C. M., Hamby, D. W., Dunst, C. J., & Gorman, E. (2013). Emergent writing among young children from twelve to sixty months of age. *CELLreviews, 6*(2), 1–18. Retrieved from http://www.earlyliteracylearning.org/cellreviews/cellreviews_v6_n2.pdf

Trivette, C. M. & Keilty, B. (Eds.). (2017). *Families: Knowing families, tailoring practices, building capacity.* DEC Recommended Practices Monograph Series No. 3. Washington, DC: Division for Early Childhood.

Tsorlakis, N., Evaggelinou, C., Grouios, G., & Tsorbatzoudis, C. (2004). Effective of intensive neurodevelopmental treatment in gross motor function of children with cerebral palsy. *Developmental Medicine & Child Neurology, 46,* 740–745.

Tucci, S. L. & Easterbrooks, S. R. (2015). A syllable segmentation, letter-sound, and initial sound intervention with students who are deaf or hard of hearing and use sign language. *Journal of Special Education, 48,* 279–289.

Turbiville, V. P. & Marquis, J. G. (2001). Father participation in early education programs. *Topics in Early Childhood Special Education, 21*(4), 223–232.

Turnbull, A. P., Turnbull, H. R., Erwin, E., Soodak, L., & Shogren, K. A. (2011, 2014). *Family professionals and exceptionality: Positive outcomes through partnerships and trust.* Upper Saddle River, NJ: Pearson.

Turnbull, A. P. & Turnbull, H. R. (2014). *Families, professionals and exceptionality: A special partnership.* Upper Saddle River, NJ: Merrill/Prentice Hall.

U.S. Census Bureau. (2017, September). *Language Line Solutions Team. American Community Survey.* Retrieved from https://www.census.gov/programs-surveys/acs/

U.S. Department of Agriculture. (2016). *Healthy eating for pre-schoolers.* Retrieved from https://wicworks.fns.usda.gov/wicworks/Topics/Preschooler.pdf

U.S. Department of Agriculture, Economic Research Service. (2017, October). *Poverty demographics.* Retrieved from https://www.ers.usda.gov/topics/rural-economy-population/rural-poverty-well-being/poverty-demographics/

U.S. Department of Education. (2010, June). *Questions and answers on the individualized education programs (IEPs), evaluations and revaluations.* Retrieved from https://www2.ed.gov/policy/speced/guid/idea/iep-qa-2010.pdf

U.S. Department of Education. (2017, December 7). *Questions and answers (Q & A) on U.S. Supreme Court case decision* Endrew F. vs. Douglas County School District Re-1. Retrieved from https://www2.ed.gov/policy/sped/guid/idea/memosdeltrs/qa-endrew-case-12-07-2017 .pdf

U.S. Department of Education, Office for Civil Rights. (2016). *2013–2014 Civil rights data collection. A first look: Key data highlights on equity and opportunity gaps in our nation's public schools.* Retrieved from https://permanent.access.gpo.gov/gpo84346/2013-14-first-look.pdf

U.S. Department of Health and Human Services & Department of Education. (2015). *Policy statement on inclusion of children with disabilities in early childhood programs.* Retrieved from http://www2.ed.gov/policy/sped/guid/earlylearning/joint-statement-full-text.pdf

U.S. Department of Health and Human Services & U.S. Department of Education. (2016a). *Policy statement on family engagement from the early years to the early grades.* Retrieved from http://www2.ed.gov/about/inits/ed/earlylearning/files/policy-statement-on-family-engagement.pdf

U.S. Department of Health and Human Services & U.S. Department of Education. (2016b). Policy statement on inclusion of children with disabilities in early childhood programs. September 14, 2015. *Infants and Young Children, 29*, 3–24.

van Kleeck, A. (2004). On the road to reading fluently: Where is the science in helping us find the best balance between meaning-oriented and skills-oriented approaches? *American Journal of Psychology, 117*(2), 300–316.

Varias, L. (2005). Bridging the widest gap. *Education Update, 47*(8).

Venetsanou, F. & Kambas, A. (2010). Environmental factors affecting preschoolers' motor development. *Early Childhood Education Journal, 37*, 319–327.

Venkateswaran, S. & Shevell, M. I. (2008). Comorbidities and clinical determinants of outcome in children with spastic quadriplegic cerebral palsy. *Developmental Medicine & Child Neurology, 50*, 216–222.

Vincent, L. (1988, March). *Curriculum development. Inservice training for early childhood special education teachers.* Los Angeles: Unified School District.

Vygotsky, L. (1978). Mind in society: The development of higher order psychological processes. In M. Cole, J. Scribner, J. John-Steiner, & E. Souberman (Eds.), *Culture and thought: A psychological introduction.* Cambridge, MA: Harvard University Press.

Vygotsky, L. (1980). *Mind in society: The development of higher psychological processes.* Cambridge, MA: Harvard University Press.

Vygotsky, L. (1986). *Thought and language.* Cambridge, MA: MIT Press.

Wakeford, L. (2016). Occupational therapy in early intervention and early childhood special education. In B. Reichow, B. A. Boyd, E. E. Barton, & S. Odom (Eds.), *Handbook of early childhood special education* (pp. 385–401). Cham, Switzerland: Springer.

Waldman, D. & Roush, J. (2009). *Your child's hearing loss: A guide for parents* (2nd ed.). San Diego, CA: Plural Publishing.

Walker, J. E., Shea, T. M., & Bauer, A. (2006). *Behavior management: A practical approach for educators.* Upper Saddle River, NJ: Merrill/Prentice Hall.

Warren, S. R., Martinez, R. S., & Sortino, L. A. (2016). Exploring the quality indicators of a successful full inclusion preschool program. *Journal of Research in Childhood Education, 30*, 540–553.

Warshaw, S. P. (2013). *HELP Strands 0–3.* Menlo Park, CA: VORT Corp.

Wasik, B. A. & Jacobi-Vessels, J. L. (2017). Word play: Scaffolding language through child-directed play. *Early Childhood Education Journal, 45*, 769–776.

Weiner, B. (2005). Motivation from an attribution perspective and the social psychology of perceived competence. In A. J. Elliot & C. S. Dweck (Eds.), *Handbook of competence and motivation* (pp. 73–84). New York: Guilford Press.

Weider, S., Greenspan, S. & Kalmanson, B. (2008). The developmental individual-difference relationship-based DIR/Floortime model. *Zero-to-Three, 29*(4), 31–37.

Weiss, A. L. (2009). Planning language intervention for young children. In D. K. Bernstein & E. Tiegerman-Farber (Eds.), *Language disorders and communication disorders in children* (6th ed., pp. 436–496). Boston: Allyn & Bacon.

Weitzman, E. & Greenberg, J. (2002). *Learning language and loving it.* Toronto: Hanen Centre.

Wells, R. A. & Thompson, B. (2004). Strategies for supporting teenage mothers. *Young Exceptional Children, 7*(3), 20–27.

Wesley, P. (2002). Early intervention consultants in the classroom. *Young Children, 57*(4), 30–34.

Wesley, P. & Buysee, B. (2006). Ethics and evidence in consultation. *Topics in Early Childhood Special Education, 26*, 131–141.

Wesley, P., Buysse, V., & Skinner, D. (2001). Early interventionists' perspectives on professional comfort as consultants. *Journal of Early Intervention, 24*(2), 112–120.

Wetherby, A. M. & Prizant, B. M. (Eds.). (2000). *Autism spectrum disorders.* Baltimore: Brookes.

Whalen, C. & Schreibman, L. (2003). Joint attention training for children with autism using behavior modification procedures. *Journal of Child Psychology and Psychiatry, 44*(3), 456–468.

Whipple, J. (2004). Music in intervention for children and adolescents with autism: A meta-analysis. *Journal of Music Therapy, 41*(2), 90–106.

White, R. (1959). Motivation reconsidered: The concept of competence. *Psychology Review, 66*, 297–333.

Whitehurst, G. J. & Lonigan, C. J. (2001). Emergent literacy: Development from prereaders to readers. In S. Neuman & D. Dickinson (Eds.), *Handbook of early literacy research* (pp. 11–29). New York: Guilford Press.

Winders, P. C. (2014). *Gross motor skills for children with Down syndrome* (2nd ed.). Bethesda, MD: Woodbine House.

Williams, K. E., Berthelsen, D., Nicholson, J. M., Walker, S., & Abad, V. (2012). The effectiveness of a short-term music therapy intervention for parents who have a child with a disability. *Journal of Music Therapy, 49*(1), 23–44.

Williams, P. D., Piamjariyakul, U., Graff, J. C., Stanton, A., Guthrie, A. C., Hafeman, C., & William, A. R. (2010). Developmental disabilities: Effects on well siblings. *Issues in Comprehensive Pediatric Nursing, 33*(1), 39–55.

Wolfberg, P. J. (2015). Integrated play groups for children on the autism spectrum. In H. G. Kaduson & C. S. Schaefer (Eds.), *Short-term pay therapy for children* (3rd ed., pp. 353–370). New York: Guilford Press.

Wolraich, M. L. (2006). Attention-deficit/hyperactivity disorder: Can it be recognized and treated in children younger than 5 years? *Infants and Young Children, 19*(2), 86–93.

Wong, C., Odom, S. L., Hume, K. A., Cox, C. W., Fettig, A., Kurcharczyk, S., & Schultz, T. R. (2015). Evidence-based practices for children, youth, and young adults with autism spectrum disorder. A comprehensive review. *Journal of Autism and Developmental Disorders, 45*, 1951–1966.

Wynkoop, K. S. (2016). Watch this! A guide to implementing video modeling in the classroom. *Intervention in School and Clinic, 51*, 178–183.

Yell, M. L., Katsiyannis, A., Parks Ennis, R., Losinski, M., & Christle, C. A. (2016). Avoiding substantive errors in individualized education program development. *Teaching Exceptional Children, 49*(1), 31–40.

Yoshinaga-Itano, C. (2006). Early identification, communication modality, and the development of spoken language skills. In P. Spencer & M. Marschark (Eds.), *Advances in the spoken language development of deaf and hard-of-hearing children* (pp. 298–327). New York: Oxford University Press.

Zeanah, C. H. (2009). *Handbook of infant mental health* (3rd ed.). New York: Guilford Press.

Zeanah, C. H. & Zeanah, P. D. (2009). The scope of infant mental health. In C. H. Zeanah (Ed.), *Handbook for infant mental health* (3rd ed., pp. 5–21). New York: Guilford Press.

Zero to Three. (2005). *Diagnostic classification of mental health and developmental disorders of infancy and early childhood, revised* (DC: 0-3R). Washington, DC: Author.

Zero to Three. (2016, December). Parents face a discipline dilemma. Retrieved from https://www.zerotothree.org/resources/1668-parents-face-a-discipline-dilemma

Zero-to-Three (2016). *Infant-Early Childhood Mental Health.* Retrieved from https://www.zerotothree.org/resources/110-infant-early-childhood-mental-health

Zevenbergen, A. & Whitehurst, G. J. (2003). Dialogic reading: A shared picture book intervention for preschoolers. In A. van Kleeck, S. A. Stahl, & E. B. Bauer (Eds.), *On reading books to children* (pp. 177–183). Mahwah, NJ: Erlbaum.

Zhai, F., Brooks-Gunn, J., & Waldfogel, J. (2011). Head Start and urban children's school readiness: A birth cohort study in 18 cities. *Developmental Psychology, 47*, 134–152.

Zigler, E. (1978). The effectiveness of Head Start: Another look. *Educational Psychologist, 13*, 71–77.

Zimmer, K. (2017). Enhancing interactions with children with autism through storybook reading. *Young Exceptional Children, 20*(3), 133–144.

Zimmer, M. & Desch, L. (2012). Sensory integration therapies for children with developmental and behavioral disorders. *Pediatrics, 129*(6), 1186–1189.

Zuniga, M. E. (2011). Families with Latino roots. In E. W. Lynch & M. J. Hanson (Eds.), *Developing cross-cultural competence: A guide for working with children and families* (4th ed., pp. 190–233). Baltimore: Brookes.

Name Index

Note: Page numbers followed by e refer to exhibits, f refers to figures, and t refers to tables.

Subject Index

Note: Page numbers followed by e refer to exhibits, f refers to figures, and t refers to tables.